D1572480

IN THE INTERESTS OF PEACE

DOUGLAS A. ROSS

In the Interests of Peace:
Canada and Vietnam
1954–1973

UNIVERSITY OF TORONTO PRESS
Toronto Buffalo London

© University of Toronto Press 1984
Toronto Buffalo London
Printed in Canada

ISBN 0-8020-5632-6

Canadian Cataloguing in Publication Data

Ross, Douglas A. (Douglas Alan), 1948–
    In the interests of peace : Canada and Vietnam
    1954–1973
    Includes bibliographical references and index.
    ISBN 0-8020-5632-6
    1. Vietnamese Conflict, 1961–1975 – Canada.
    2. Canada – Foreign relations – 1945–   I. Title.
    DS558.6.C3R68 1984   959.704'31   C84-098817-6

This book has been published with the help of a grant from the Social
Science Federation of Canada using funds provided by the Social Sciences
and Humanities Research Council of Canada, and a grant from the Publications Fund of the University of Toronto Press.

Contents

1
Canada in Vietnam: a three-dimensional approach towards policy
explanation / 3

2
Indochina and the diplomacy of constraint 1950–4 / 35

3
The descent begins: from Geneva to the jungles / 67

4
The emergence of the refugee dilemma: August-November 1954 / 93

5
... the terrible things that are being done / 120

6
Coping with the electoral dilemma 1955–6 / 146

7
Perceptions of aggression 1954–6 / 203

Figures

Tables

Preface

This book would not have been possible without the generous support of the following people: Margaret Doxey of Trent University for her friendship, inspiration, and encouragement; Franklyn Griffiths of the University of Toronto for his helpful criticism of early drafts; John Holmes, for his encouragement, many thoughtful reflections, and access to his private papers; John English of the University of Waterloo, for constructive comments and sound counsel; and Mark Zacher of the University of British Columbia for his unstinting moral and material support as well as many humorous moments that lightened a taxing scholarly burden. The following individuals were very patient, helpful, and generous with their time in the course of interviews and conversations: Arthur Blanchette, and Paul Bridle, the late Marcel Cadieux, Georges Charpentiers, Ralph Collins, Thomas Delworth, J. Price Erichsen-Brown, Ross Francis, Michel Gauvin, Gilles Grondin, Mrs Sherwood Lett, Christopher Malone, Arthur Menzies, Escott Reid, Louis Rogers, Chester Ronning, Mitchell Sharp, Donald Smiley, and Bruce Williams.

Many thanks are due also to Jane Barrett of the CIIA library in Toronto; Gaston Blanchet of Historical Division of the Department of External Affairs, Ottawa; the staff of the Vancouver City Archives; and Mary Goldie for considerable assistance in completing final manuscript revisions. R.I.K. Davidson and Jean Wilson of University of Toronto Press deserve a special vote of thanks for persevering with the project in rather unusual and complicated circumstances. Joanne Heath and Nancy Wong performed heroically in typing different drafts of the book.

This work is gratefully dedicated to my wife Veronica Strong-Boag, our son Christopher, and our niece Miranda, all of whom shared the burden of the too-lengthy gestation period. To all of them my heartfelt thanks for their patience.

DAR

Abbreviations

CFA	Cease-Fire Agreement (Franco-Vietminh agreement of 20 July 1954)
CIA	Central Intelligence Agency, United States government
CPA	Continuing Political Authority
DEA	Department of External Affairs, Ottawa
DND	Department of National Defence, Ottawa
DRVN	Democratic Republic of Vietnam (Hanoi)
FD	Final Declaration of the Geneva Conference on Indochina (21 July 1954)
FEC	French Expeditionary Corps
FT	Fixed Team (of the ICSC)
FUF	French Union Forces
ICCS	International Commission of Control and Supervision in Vietnam (1973)
ICSC	International Commission for Supervision and Control in Vietnam (1954–73)
JCS	Joint Chiefs of Staff, United States government
KMT	Kuomintang (Guomindang in the Pinyin system)
MAAG	Military Assistance Advisory Group (US military mission to the RVN)
MACV	Military Assistance Command Vietnam (replaced MAAG in the 1960s)
MT	Mobile Team (of the ICSC)
PRC	People's Republic of China (Beijing)
RVN	Republic of Vietnam (Saigon)
SLA	Senior Legal Adviser (to an ICSC delegation)
TERM	Temporary Equipment Recovery Mission (US Army)
VNA/ARVN	Vietnamese National Army/Army of the Republic of Vietnam

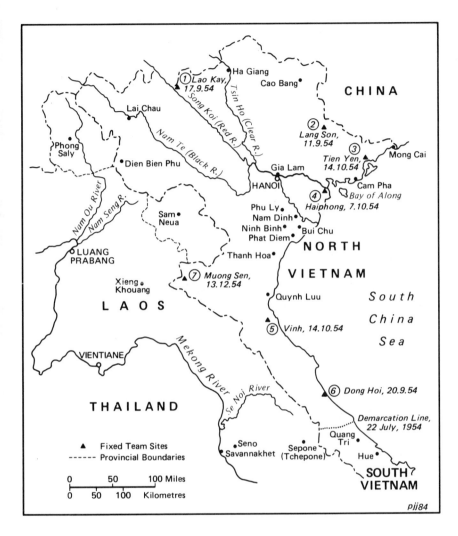

Fixed Team Sites in the Northern Zone

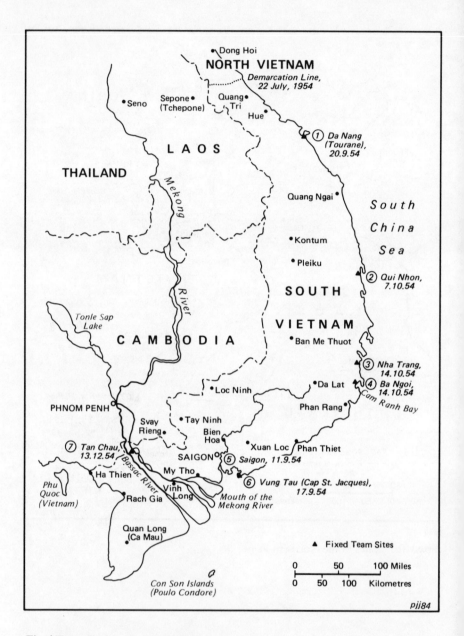

Fixed Team Sites in the Southern Zone

IN THE INTERESTS OF PEACE

For there is not a just man upon earth, that doeth good, and sinneth not.

Ecclesiastes 7:20

I

Canada in Vietnam:
a three-dimensional approach
towards policy explanation

the cybernetic nature of self and the world tends to be imperceptible to consciousness, insofar as the contents of the 'screen' of consciousness are determined by
considerations of purpose.

Gregory Bateson, *Steps to an Ecology of Mind* (1968)

Appropriately enough, the Vietnam war has come to symbolize American
defeat, frustration, and humiliation. For many Canadians it connotes shame
as well because of perceived Canadian complicity in American war crimes.[1]
The record of the Vietnam war and more generally of the Indochina conflict
poses profound and disturbing questions about the nature of American
society, the political and strategic doctrines which animate its élites, and the
character of the American relationship to the poor countries of Asia and the
Third world generally. For Canadians the record of the Indochina conflict
has raised alarming doubts about the nature of the Canadian-American relationship, especially the perceived lack of responsiveness to Canadian perceptions, analysis, and policy recommendations vis-à-vis western security.
   In Canada just as in the United States there is much fundamental confusion in debates concerning the meaning of the Indochina wars and the
lessons to be derived from them. For some observers the exodus of the boat
people after 1977 has validated the terrible violence inflicted upon the people
of Southeast Asia by American aircraft and artillery. For others this diaspora
of anti-communist or otherwise disaffected elements from Vietnam and
Cambodia constitutes one more chapter in a legacy of suffering and bitter-
ness bequeathed by America's frighteningly arrogant attempt at 'nation-
building.' Equally problematic, some see in present Vietnamese domination
of Laos and Cambodia the fulfilment of Eisenhower's 'domino theory,' while
others believe such thinking to be totally discredited in light of the Sino-

Vietnamese border war of February-March 1979 and the overall trend towards polycentrism in the communist world. In short, there is no established
consensus about even the most basic aspects of the conflict. The Indochina
wars involved a sufficiently ambiguous and complex set of events that no
single interpretive persepctive is likely to command widespread support for
the foreseeable future. Perhaps the rudiments of a comprehensively accurate
explanatory scheme already exist, most likely in the work of Franz Schurmann,[2] but it is all too probable that the definitive statement on the Vietnam
war may never be written. For the moment there is no single work that can
successfully bridge the gaps among the different ideologically rooted perspectives on the war. The Indochina conflict is in one sense utterly beyond
any diffusely objective comprehension, because any attempt at causal explanation must become coloured unavoidably by subjectively rooted doctrinal
judgments about the nature of communist and liberal-democratic political
systems, the relative malignance or benevolence of the Soviet and American
imperial systems, and the varying thrust towards domination, self-extension,
and control of these systems. Like the Spanish Civil War, the Indochina
problematic defies straightforward explanation and evaluation. Conservatives, liberals, and socialists cannot now and probably will never be able to
explain this conflict through mutually acceptable causal arguments. The end
of ideologies is nowhere in sight.

This book has been shaped by several interdependent premises or working
hypotheses, some of them being beyond empirical verification. The first
premise is a belief that the American intervention was unlikely to succeed
from the outset. American power could have destroyed Vietnam, but it was
highly improbable that it could ever have engendered a stable anti-communist regime in South Vietnam. The Vietnamese social and political revolution had proceeded too far to be reversed or contained, although it was
postponed at the price of enormous and ultimately unjustifiable suffering by
the Indochinese people. South Vietnamese society was rent by too many
cleavages – political, ethnic, regional, and class – to be susceptible to coherent reorganization imposed from Washington. The corollary to this premise
is that the American decision to intervene in Indochina was not merely
unwise, it was devoid of sound moral judgment. One cannot find absolution
for errors of this magnitude from repeated declarations of right intention. A
consequentialist ethic must be adhered to in evaluating matters of foreign
policy.

A second related premise of the book is based on the idea that American
policy-makers decided to pursue their interventionary project despite their
knowledge at each stage along the way that the probabilities for success were

poor. Readers who doubt this premise should consult the interpretive work of Leslie Gelb, Richard Betts, and Daniel Ellsberg.[3] The tragic errors in prosecuting the intervention were made by presidents and their advisers who knew that the odds were not in their favour. This is one of the central paradoxes of the war which must be dealt with by all those who would explain either American behaviour or Canadian diplomacy. To date, assessments of Canadian policy towards the Indochina conflict have failed to take this fact into account, just as they have failed more generally to situate the evolution of Canadian policy towards Indochina within the context of ongoing American policy debates and decisions.[4]

The third major premise of this book, the most important analytically and probably the least subject to conclusive empirical verification, entails the assumption that throughout the protracted evolution of the Vietnam struggle and throughout the period of direct Canadian involvement in the work of the Indochina truce supervisory commissions there was an ever-present risk of escalation of the conflict to tactical nuclear warfare. Thus World War III was always a contingent but distinct threat, especially in the years 1954–67. The Vietnam war, despite the deaths of over a million Vietnamese – ten times the number of Canadians killed in both world wars and Korea combined, almost twice the number of Americans who died in those conflicts – must be classified nevertheless as a limited war for this reason.

Daniel Ellsberg has ably documented his recent assertion that 'in the thirty-six years since Hiroshima, every president from Truman to Reagan, with the possible exception of Ford, has felt compelled to consider or direct serious preparations for possible imminent u.s. initiation of tactical or strategic nuclear warfare, in the midst of an ongoing, intense, non-nuclear conflict or crisis.'[5] Nuclear 'diplomacy' has been a hidden reality throughout the post-war period. Nuclear weapons have been invoked or their use seriously considered on many occasions for many lesser objectives than the deterrence of Soviet nuclear attacks on North America: Iran, 1946, to compel Soviet withdrawal from the northern provinces; Berlin, June 1948, when atomic-capable bombers were moved pointedly to foward bases in Europe; Korea, November 1950, over the encirclement of American troops at the Chosin Reservoir; Korea in the spring of 1953, to compel the communist forces to implement an armistice; the Formosa Strait in 1954–5 and again in 1958, when President Eisenhower ordered formulation of contingency plans for nuclear strikes in the event of mainland Chinese attempts at invasion of Quemoy; Berlin, 1961; Cuba, 1962; the Persian Gulf area, 1980 and 1981, when both President Carter and President Reagan indicated an explicit willingness to resort to nuclear strikes if American vital interests in the region were threatened by Soviet conventional attack.[6] One should also note parenthetically that the standing posture and doctrine of the NATO forces were based on a rapid and early use of nuclear weapons in the event that deterrence failed in Europe throughout this entire period.

With particular reference to Indochina there have been several instances of serious consideration of the use of nuclear weapons against communist military formations. In the spring of 1954 American Secretary of State John Foster Dulles apparently offered French Prime Minister Georges Bidault the use of tactical nuclear weapons on two separate occasions to help relieve the besieged French Union Forces at Dienbienphu. The US Army's G-3 planning division at one point proposed the use of one to six 31-kiloton atomic bombs to be dropped by carrier-based aircraft.[7] Both Dulles and Eisenhower went so far as to canvass Canadian and British opinion concerning possible American use of atomic weapons to relieve the garrison.[8] In 1961 senior Pentagon officials, among them Air Force General Curtis E. LeMay and Army Chief of Staff General Decker, recommended to President Kennedy and members of his cabinet that the United States should seriously consider heavy military intervention even though it might necessitate nuclear strikes in Laos, North Vietnam, and southern China. Some senior officials were at this time convinced of the inevitability of war with the People's Republic of China and accordingly argued for taking the initiative in selecting the time and circumstance for such a confrontation.[9] In 1968 President Johnson was advised by General William Westmoreland of the possible necessity of using nuclear weapons to defend besieged marines at Khe Sanh.[10] Finally, between 1969 and 1973 President Nixon made numerous veiled hints at possible escalation of American coercive diplomacy to the level of tactical nuclear strikes.[11] As destructive as the American intervention was for the people of Indochina, there is little doubt that it might have been much worse.

American nuclear diplomacy and contingency planning was facilitated from the late 1940s through the mid-1960s by an American strategic counterforce superiority that was, as Ellsberg notes, 'so overwhelming as to amount to monopoly.' As both American and Soviet leaders well knew, the United States possessed a very credible first-strike option until well into the 1960s when the first Soviet ballistic-missile–launching submarines became operational. As late as October 1962 during the Cuban missile crisis, the Soviet strategic rocket forces had only four 'non-alert, liquid-fuelled ICBMs at one site at Plesetsk that was vulnerable to a small attack with conventional weapons.'[12] The greatest risk of a nuclear war in the period of direct Canadian political and diplomatic involvement in Indochina stemmed from possible American first use of nuclear weapons. Canada's closest ally was the greatest single threat to the nuclear peace.

This fact, sensed strongly by some Canadian and Indian officials, was to shape both Canadian and Indian actions in their capacity as supervisors of the complex, ambiguous, and very fragile Geneva armistice for Indochina that was negotiated in the spring and summer of 1954. One commentator aptly summarized Prime Minister Jawaharlal Nehru's intuition in this regard: 'An apocalyptic vision of nuclear war propelled him into efforts toward peace-making as it had [Lester] Pearson.'[13] Both Canadian and Indian policy-making aimed prudentially at conciliation of critical disputes between the blocs. To be sure, different interests informed their respective policies towards the region, but the dominant aspect of the historical record was the common emphasis on first promoting a peaceful reconciliation of the local parties so long as this seemed politically realistic (1954 and 1955); second, sustaining a regional balance of power in so far as Indian and Canadian actions on the truce supervisory commissions could buttress this objective (1956 to 1962); and third, making every reasonable effort to facilitate serious negotiations between Hanoi and Washington from 1964 to 1973 following the DRVN's earlier commitment to political-military intervention in South Vietnam and the consequent US decision to intervene in force after 1960–2.

The fourth and final premise that underpins this book is the admittedly debatable notion that 'saving' South Vietnam was never strategically vital or even beneficial to American security. United States involvement in Vietnam, Laos, and Cambodia did not 'buy time' for the stabilization of Thailand, Malaysia, Indonesia, or the Philippines as some US observers now argue. Instead hundreds of thousands of lives were lost needlessly, scarce economic resources were squandered, the domain of Cold War political rivalry was extended to encompass the societies of all Southeast Asia, and the militarization of the region was virtually guaranteed. The Vietnamese communist movement initially had limited aspirations that were coterminous with the attainment of national reunification. They had few opportunities politically or militarily to extend their control in Southeast Asia. In fact, American intervention *helped* to pave the way for the subsequent extension of Vietnamese control into both Laos and Cambodia. Had the United States never intervened to try to 'save' South Vietnam from communist control, both Laos and Cambodia in all probability would today be the independent neutralist kingdoms called for in the Geneva armistice agreement of 1954.

The domino theory was a classic case of self-fulfilling prophecy. Domino thinking as applied to Indochina by various American officials was either unconscious delusion or, more probably, a conscious rationalization for broader policy objectives espoused by the most vigorously anti-communist elements in Washington's national security policy process. For the most extreme elements in Washington the hidden agenda of intervention in Vietnam included an early decisive confrontation with communist China, before China acquired nuclear weapons. It was precisely this policy current which most terrified officials in both Ottawa and New Delhi.

Because of the ongoing contingent threat of US-Asian security policy falling into the hands of right-wing anti-communist extremists, accommodation with more liberal policy elements in Washington was imperative, for both India and Canada. From early 1956 through 1966 this accommodation was carried through by the Canadian government. The Indian accommodation lasted only until 1962. For both governments the accommodative process aroused deep misgivings and frustration, undoubtedly more intensely felt by the Indians. For both governments Indochina decision-making consistently involved a policy of the lesser evil. It could not have been otherwise.

Most commentators have ignored the very real risk of nuclear warfare that existed throughout the period of Canada's involvement in Indochina. Consequently they have misperceived the inner dynamic of both Canadian and Indian policy-making towards this conflict, and underestimated the value of Indo-Canadian diplomacy from 1954 to 1962. Reduced to its essentials, the record of Canadian policy-making and diplomacy is not cause for shame. Successive Canadian governments accommodated the policy imperatives of various American administrations not because they believed in the wisdom or practicality of intervention but because they hoped to constrain the play of policy in Washington. Ottawa decision-makers consistently took positions on Indochina that were markedly more moderate than the consensus views in Washington.

When Washington pressed for the partition of Vietnam in 1954–5, Canadian policy effectively backed electoral reunification and communist control throughout all Vietnam. When the United States was moving towards unconstrained unilateral military support for the Diem regime between 1956 and 1961 Ottawa did its best to inhibit American denunciation of the Geneva armistice terms. In this effort it was successful. When President Johnson began the American air assault on North Vietnam in late 1964 and early 1965, Prime Minister Lester Pearson was the first NATO leader to criticize this approach to the war publicly, while Paul Martin was evidently among the first of the delegates to the Atlantic Council meetings who demanded a halt to grossly intimidatory methods. In 1973 the Trudeau government, to its credit, accepted a role on the international supervisory commission created by the Kissinger–Le Duc Tho cease-fire agreement of January 1973 and thereby facilitated American disengagement from the region. That military disengagement did more for the eventual attainment of peace in Vietnam than all the efforts of Canadian anti-war critics put together. Some observers who have turned a blind eye to political realities have criticized this decision by saying that it amounted to a supine accommodation of American attempts at winning 'peace with honour.' Such criticism is as grotesque as it is illogical and short-sighted. In 1972–3 the Canadian government stood for détente and compromise between the blocs and American disengagement from Southeast Asia – just as it had for over twenty years of involvement in Indochina's torment. By accepting a role on the 1973 commission Ottawa helped to promote those objectives in a concrete and expeditious manner. These salient elements of the policy record somehow have been overlooked by the rather obsessive and narrow-minded advocates of pure impartiality and utter objectivity in Canada's peacekeeping endeavours. It is time to cast off such self-imposed blinkers from discussions of Canadian foreign policy.

Canadian involvement in the various sub-conflicts in Indochina spanned a period of almost two decades, 1954–73. Four successive Canadian governments, despite variation in their effective policy philosophies, were animated by one overriding concern: how best the Canadian government might contribute to stabilizing or restoring peace in the troubled countries of Southeast Asia. In 1952 Prime Minister Louis St Laurent declared that Canada's Indochina policy was framed 'in the interests of peace.'[14] By this he meant that Canadian policy was not committed to any unswervingly military approach to the problems of containing communist expansion in Asia. If negotiated solutions were possible, Canada would favour negotiations. If economic instruments of policy seemed able to accomplish the objectives of Canadian policy then they would be used. Canadian governments consistently opposed the use of force by other western states, especially the United States, preferring peace agreements with the communist bloc which seemed able to contain the communist giants without challenging any of their vital interests. Even disadvantageous outcomes were seen as preferable to options which inevitably entailed a high risk of escalation towards nuclear war.

This commitment to peaceful coexistence and to a diplomacy of constraint was not, however, without limits. A prudential and realistic assessment of Canada's potential influence was an inescapable policy imperative given the limited military and economic instruments available to Ottawa, the complexities and ambiguities of the policy environment (in both Indochina and Washington), and finally, the very high stakes involved. The nuclear peace had to be sustained and buttressed; Canada's location astride the bomber and missile flight paths between the Soviet Union and the United States dictated that this objective had to be the highest priority of Canadian policy and diplomacy. Acting in support of this objective required regular access to senior decision-makers in Washington. And regular access depended on American perceptions of Canada as a sympathetic ally. Hence, the limits to Canadian dissent.

At the height of Canada's international influence between 1949 and 1957, Canadian policy-makers, most notably the then secretary of state for external affairs, Lester B. Pearson, were constantly alert to the possibility of any sudden shifts in American foreign policy. Major shifts in US policy inevitably required sudden problematic renegotiation of the various tangled compromises, both overt and implicit, which knitted together the global fabric of peace. Prudence, perseverance, moderation, and realism were in general the hallmarks of the Canadian approach to international politics during this period, commendable qualities in any country's foreign policy at any time, but particularly so with respect to the pattern of Canadian response to America's ill-considered, tragic course of intervention in Vietnam. This is not to say that Canadian policy was error-free, rather that the broad pattern of Ottawa's response in light of Canadian interests and environmental threats was both constructive and responsible.

VIETNAM AND THE CANADIAN POLICY PROCESS

The Canadian foreign policy decision-making élite was far from uniform in terms of the political preferences and associated perceptual frameworks of the various individuals who composed this group. Prime Minister John Diefenbaker's dismissal of DEA's staff as a group of 'Pearsonalities'[5] undoubtedly has done much to further the false impression of organizational conformity and continuity. It is the fundamental argument of this book that the uniformity of the public rhetoric of DEA's liberal-internationalist, or as it is here referred to 'liberal-moderate,' mainstream obscured the hidden but very real dimensions of the policy process which diverged markedly from the precepts and attitudes of the Pearsonian approach to foreign policy. It is towards a definition, elaboration, and analysis of these hidden currents or 'tendencies' of policy-making that much of this book is directed. For reasons sons that will become clear these alternative strains in the DEA policy process are denoted as 'conservative' and 'left-liberal' respectively.

With respect to Indochina decision-making a diversity of viewpoints was both an operational reality and a functional necessity for an effective, adaptive, and constructive foreign policy. Canadian policy-makers had to contend with strongly antithetical pressures for the duration of the Canadian involvement in Southeast Asia. [In 1954–5 American policy strongly opposed the Anglo-French willingness to accommodate communist political and military strength in Indochina. The Canadian government sided with the Europeans, accepting for the time being that peace could only be preserved in the region via implementation of the political settlement provisions of the Geneva Agreements. Following Diem's consolidation of power in 1955, the French military withdrawal from Vietnam in 1955–6, and the concomitant rise in the American commitment to 'Free Vietnam,' major alterations in approach were required. From late 1956 until 1966 a new conservative consensus in Ottawa decreed that the optimum approach towards peace promotion lay in preserving a shaky balance of military power between the fledgling RVN regime and its more disciplined, efficient, and experienced rival in Hanoi.] Liberal-moderate policy-making premises were supplanted in Ottawa by a 'conservative' doctrinal approach that was far more congenially received by Washington leaders. For a middle-power state with a moralizing penchant it was doubly imperative that perceptions and attitudes strongly underpin the tactical requirements of particular issues. [The story of Canada in Vietnam thus became a record of declining liberal-moderate influence in Indochina policy-making and ascending conservative fortunes. But conservative influence was not destined to monopolize Ottawa's approach. By 1966 the conservative hold on policy was relaxing. The old liberal-moderate norms were reasserted, and the quest for peaceful accommodation between the blocs once more provided the central thrust of Canadian policy. This would remain the case through the end of Canadian involvement in the second truce supervisory operation for Vietnam in July 1973.

[Canadian policy-making towards the Indochina conflict was a composite product of the interplay of three distinct policy tendencies. The liberal-moderate element aimed at promoting a peaceful resolution of the war, supported a responsible Canadian commitment to a role in the truce supervisory operations in Vietnam, Laos, and Cambodia, and generally favoured a close relationship with the United States so as to maximize opportunities for exerting Canadian influence on the pattern of US decision-making. No illusions were entertained that Ottawa alone could alter American decisions, but it was hoped, not unreasonably, by Pearson, John Holmes, and other articulators of this policy tendency that Canadian diplomacy could help to inhibit the more extreme elements in Washington's policy struggles.] As one analyst of Canadian policy rightly noted, liberal-moderates such as Pearson were disposed towards thinking that 'since Canada can take the American [security] guarantee, because it is based on American self interest, for granted, it is better situated to restrain the dominant partner than most junior members in unequal alliances.[216]

The liberal-moderate approach was based on a definition of western security interests that was decidedly Eurocentric. For liberal-moderates Canada had become involved in Korea solely in light of Canada's obligation to collective security pursuant to membership in the United Nations. Liberal-moderate articulators saw no vital strategic interests for the Western alliance in either Korea or Indochina. The first and most important line of defence lay along the so-called 'Iron Curtain' between Eastern and Western Europe. Until that perimeter was secure, military commitments elsewhere by NATO members were ill advised at best. While adherents to the liberal-moderate tendency shared many of the sentiments of the conservative anti-communist approach to foreign policy, they refused to admit that intervention in Asia was either wise or practical. They were, moreover, constantly on edge concerning the continuing American flirtation with the idea of full-blown confrontation with China.

In light of interview research and a systematic review of a considerable body of classified documentation,[17] the liberal-moderate approach to Vietnam decision-making from the mid-1950s to the early 1960s can be said to have rested on the following policy axioms:

(a) that Canada should support whatever opportunities that arose for aiding the establishment of an independent non-communist government in Vietnam, but that such support must respect, and not in any way infringe upon, the terms of 'political substance' of the Geneva Agreements, ambiguous though they may be, since maintaining peace, not an effective anti-communist resistance, was the proper basis for Canadian involvement;

(b) that the Catholic refugee movement of 1954–5 from North to South Vietnam while of some domestic political concern was not intrinsically significant in comparison with the prime Canadian objective of maintaining the fragile structure of peace that had been embodied in the cease-fire agreements;

(c) that the political and moral basis of the Diem government was very dubious and precarious, but support of it after 1956 was a calculated gamble that was probably worth the risk (if only for lack of better options);

(d) that the American presence in Vietnam was legitimate and did not contravene the Geneva Agreements; that American sponsorship of the Diem regime probably helped to deter overt attack from the North, and therefore enhance the prospects of peace, and that support for the US was appropriate given the inherently non-imperialistic, benevolent goals of Canada's chief ally;

(e) that the Vietnam conflict involved the risk of great-power military confrontation and that the basis of Canadian policy should be directed towards maintaining the armistice and dissuading the American leaders from overt intervention, thereby forestalling the possibility of another Korean-style Chinese-American war, or worse;

(f) that the Vietminh-DRVN forces had committed aggression in attempting to subvert the regime in the South;

(g) that repression in the South was largely the result of the policy and actions of the DRVN and its agents and allies in the South, and furthermore that reprisals were inevitable after such a bitter and prolonged war (ie, the seven years of the French-Vietminh conflict);

(h) that Canada should support containment where possible, but in a limited fashion that was consistent with Canada's limited capabilities and responsibilities – and most certainly not at the cost of involvement in a 'land war in Asia.'

Above all else the liberal-moderate tendency emphasized the maintenance of peace as the first objective of Canadian policy in the region. From that viewpoint the 1954 Geneva armistice was politically hard won and extremely unstable. Western countries' actions, especially American actions, had to be particularly closely monitored in terms of the probable impact on DRVN actions. The prospect of DRVN attack was deemed sufficiently grave to require constant intelligence monitoring of the operations of the PAVN (People's Army of Vietnam, sometimes translated as the Popular Army of Vietnam), and frequent assessment of the possibility of imminent invasion. At least until 1960–1 those who fastened on this posture thought that a Korean-style partition of Vietnam might possibly be feasible indefinitely (provided that no one publicly proclaimed the fact), and that peace and a 'free' Vietnam thus might be simultaneously obtainable. Only after 1961, when these goals became clearly contradictory, did the liberal-moderates choose to back the American policy of intervention, *faute de mieux*. At least until 1960–1 liberal-moderates were strongly inclined to challenge the condescending, too-easy American dismissal of the Geneva settlement as at best irrelevant window-dressing, at worst a cowardly 'sell-out' facilitating French withdrawal from the region. For Canadian liberal-moderates the Geneva Agreements were independently important and usefully ambiguous – so much so that a genuine political outcome might become achievable given the apparent Chinese and Soviet willingness to reach an accommodation with the Western powers. The informal partial acceptance of some of the armistice provisions of the Geneva Agreements by the Diem regime complicated matters all the more, but did not seem to create insuperable barriers to an eventual political settlement, a genuine compromise, and widening détente between the blocs.

The central difficulty faced by the liberal-moderate perspective was that once war had resumed in the South in earnest after 1959, there was no longer any room for either moderation or reasoned liberal compromise. At this point, tacit political negotiation had to give way to a test of strength, and once troops were committed, Canadian diplomacy was compelled to choose sides unreservedly. Escalation of the fighting guaranteed that External's policy-making would fall into the hands of those who championed the conservative posture. The voices of moderation were muted for lack of realistic or even plausible policy prescriptions.

Following the resumption of hostilities in South Vietnam and coeval American decisions to assist the South Vietnamese to whatever degree was required to break the insurrection against Diem's authority, Canadian liberal-moderates inevitably fell into line with the conservative point of view which advocated measured diplomatic and political support for u.s. intervention. For those who adhered to this perspective, whether as newly 'converted' conservatives or as liberal-moderates in retreat, adoption of the very limited tactic of using the ICSC to state the American-Western case as forcibly and as ably as possible seemed appropriate. By the early 1960s the distinction between the conservatives and liberal-moderates had temporarily collapsed, at least in so far as the two perspectives could be compared vis-à-vis support for American policy. Only when American assistance degenerated into the barbarism of carpet-bombing, napalm-phosphorus incendiary bombing, the extensive use of chemical defoliants, 'anti-personnel' devices, and the horrors of the u.s.-devised, South Vietnamese-administered counter-terror reprisal programs (ie, systematic torture and assassination) did the support of u.s. policy by the liberal-moderates once more grow attenuated – and then only incrementally, and as a result of public criticism.

During their tenure of power, 1963–8, both Prime Minister Pearson and his secretary of state for external affairs, Paul Martin, gradually shifted their publicly enunciated views from the conservative to the liberal-moderate perspective. The shift was necessitated by the growing public protest over Canadian support of American policy, protest which demanded vigorous public criticism by the Canadian government. The actual change in concrete policy substance of the government was, however, modest. For Pearson and Martin the tenets of 'quiet diplomacy' were deemed to be all-important.

Public criticism of Canada's most important ally was out of the question so long as the government expected or hoped to have Canadian advice listened to in Washington. Hence the only evidence of this shift was a move from strong to lukewarm support of the American intervention and an accentuation of the public rhetoric in support of early negotiations. To the end of his tenure of public office Pearson never openly condemned the American intervention. His Philadelphia speech of April 1965 recommended only a bombing pause and more flexibility in negotiations. In 1967 he chided and reprimanded his old friend and cabinet colleague Walter Gordon for the latter's outspoken call for American withdrawal. Furthermore, Pearson never ceased to castigate what he saw as the unjust war of conquest being waged by the DRVN government through its agents, saboteurs, guerrillas, and main force units in the South. Finally, both Pearson and Martin saw the American-RVN cause as just in its origins, though neither could remain comfortable as the bombing tonnage being dropped on the people of Vietnam mounted unceasingly. As Americans assumed total direction of the war in the South, and as the Pentagon attempted to substitute technological terror for the sacrifice of American infantry, the tragic dimensions of the American 'errors' were beyond remedy. The shift in Canadian policy emphasis away from unqualified support for U.S. actions proceeded in tandem with the growth in public revulsion at American tactics.

Several reasons may be adduced to explain the slowness of Pearson and Martin in distancing themselves from American policy: first, the weight – psychological and rhetorical – of preceding Canadian commitments to the right of the South Vietnamese to national self-determination (ie, to a non-communist government); second, Pearson's evident belief that Lyndon Johnson needed some psychological support and approval from other allied leaders if Johnson was going to be able to sustain his restraint of the Pentagon's most bellicose elements; third, the politically weak stance of government critics in Canada who were seen to be much too anti-American in their rhetoric; fourth, Pearson's continuing desire not to lose channels of communication to Washington, a development that would jeopardize any residual Canadian capacity – admittedly negligible – to limit the damage of escalatory crises in Southeast Asia. Private representations and informal criticism constituted the sole Canadian contribution to international political pressure on President Johnson to cease the bombing and to remove American forces. Not until 1967–8 did any Canadian governmental leaders publicly go on record criticizing the nature of the American intervention. And even then Walter Gordon's initiative in departing from Canada's Vietnam policy was not well or easily received by the government. Even with the accession to power of a new government, the first Trudeau ministry, and the arrival of the high tide of anti-war sentiment throughout North America, the combined forces of the liberal-moderate and left-liberal tendencies were in no position to reassert dominance over Canadian Vietnamese decision-making. In fact, policy between 1969 and 1973 seems to have involved a continued mixture of conservative and liberal-moderate features, with the latter predominating.

The essential thrust of the conservative tendency as it was forged in the 1950s and championed by conservatively inclined bureaucrats in the 1960s was defined by the following eight axiomatic principles:

(a) that Canada should support the Indochina armistice to the maximum, but it should support equally whatever possibilities existed for building an independent non-communist Vietnam; communist aggression must not be rewarded;

(b) that the Canadian government should establish as one of its highest priorities Canadian diplomatic and political assistance to the refugees who wished to move from the North to the South; and as a partial corollary

(c) that the massive size of the movement (roughly one million people made the trip to the South) proved the legitimacy of the Diemist government, and enhanced that of its successors to a very significant extent; the refugee movement proved that the anti-communist political tendency in Vietnamese society was vital and significant;

(d) that Canada should do its utmost to establish the international legal legitimacy of Western assistance to the RVN, and the limited American military presence in Vietnam (which had been instituted prior to the cease-fire of 20 July 1954), since substantial American military aid was apparently essential to the survival of any non-communist government in the South;

(e) that Canada (after 1961) should rhetorically support U.S. military intervention because American goals were worthy in themselves (ie, they conformed to broader Western, some said 'Free World,' security interests), because American leaders had committed themselves strongly to the defence of the possibility of a 'free' Vietnam, and last, because in the final analysis the defence of freedom and political liberty was worth even the grave risks entailed in intervention and escalation;

(f) that the Vietminh-DRVN forces were guilty of 'aggression' against the RVN because they had fomented and organized insurrection in the South against the duly constituted authority – contrary to the provisions of the armistice agreement of 1954, and contrary to the principles of the UN Charter;

(g) that political repression in the RVN, while deplorable in itself, was excusable given the 'extraordinary' nature of the indirect aggression from the North; furthermore, that the repression was certainly no worse in its social consequences than the regime of totalitarian institutional controls set up in the North following the Vietminh takeover of 1954, and, unlike the case of the DRVN, one might plausibly hope for an eventual liberalization of the RVN regime;

(h) that expansionist tendencies were at the root of both communist Chinese and Soviet foreign policy, and therefore American determination to contain the communist bloc – even at the cost of exercising extreme, sometimes deplorable, coercive methods – was on balance justifiable because war, especially modern war, is hell – and unavoidably so.

In short, the conservative perspective on the Vietnam conflict provided whole-hearted verbal-diplomatic support for the collective Western effort to establish non-communist rule in South Vietnam. Not surprisingly, the conservatives strongly supported Diem's struggle against the reunification of Vietnam through elections, the eventual political settlement mentioned in the Final Declaration of the Geneva Conference of 1954. At root, the conservative tendency of value and perception articulation within the department was founded upon undiluted anti-communism. The attitude formed the doctrinal bedrock on which all secondary premises were based. From 1957 to 1965, Canadian policy-makers adhered fairly closely to most premises of the conservative approach in their actions and rhetoric. The doctrine of containment in its liberal American manifestation was quite congenial to a large majority of the Canadian foreign policy élite, but it was departmental conservatives who most frequently invoked its logic in policy debates.

In addition to the conservative and liberal-moderate tendencies in the Department of External Affairs there was a third body of opinion, apparently always in a minority position, that held an altogether different image of the nature of the Indochina war. The key perceptual/prescriptive axioms of this 'left-liberal' approach were as follows:

(a) that while promoting peace was the prime objective of Canadian policy, the Geneva Agreements constituted a 'package deal' such that the armistice provisions could not be detached from the terms of the Final Declarations – that the elections and the cease-fire would stand or fall together, even though the holding of elections would mean, in all probability, the accession to power of Ho Chi Minh's communist government throughout all of Vietnam;

(b) that the refugee movement was in part the product of over-zealous and rather paranoid Catholic priests; that too many Canadian officials had been unduly impressed by the issue, and that the issue was not significant enough to affect one way or another the Canadian position regarding the political or moral legitimacy of the Diem regime;

(c) that the Vietminh-DRVN forces, however despicable in their methods, had substantial support from the Vietnamese people in both the North and the South because of the obvious justice of their struggle in the savage anti-colonial war against the French, and because they were far more credible proponents of the cause of Vietnamese reunification;

(d) that the West benefited from the Geneva Agreements by having 150,000 French Union troops saved from possible massacre, and by having the prospect of Laotian and Cambodian neutrality in the Cold War, and therefore that the American attempt to foster partition and an anti-communist regime in the South directly violated the substance of the Geneva settlement;

(e) that DRVN communism would in all likelihood achieve substantial independence from both Beijing and Moscow, that Tito's survival might prove to be the model for some Asian communist movements – and therefore that there was no logical reason to risk global conflagration by trying to impose a Western solution to the Indochina question;

(f) that the DRVN recourse to violence in the late 1950s was a natural and predictable (some left-liberals even said justifiable) response to American-RVN attempts to 'renegotiate' the Geneva arrangement unilaterally;

(g) that the need for widespread military repression in the South was evidence of lack of popular support and that large-scale American intervention to bolster the faltering RVN regime was doomed to failure by the difference of race which could only generate substantial support for the Vietminh-DRVN-NLF cause;

(h) that the warfare practised by the Americans was utterly obscene and inhuman, and was the result of the inappropriate application of the containment doctrine – inappropriate for Asia since it was based on a fundamental misunderstanding of social phenomena and social change in Asia; in short, that Asia was not composed of 'dominoes.'

Where people such as Lester Pearson, John Holmes, Arthur Menzies, and Canada's first commissioner to the ICSC for Vietnam, former BC Supreme Court Justice Sherwood Lett, were the chief proponents of the liberal-moderate approach, and others such as Marcel Cadieux, Arnold Heeney, and Jules Léger seemed the most vigorous supporters of conservative axioms, the left-liberal doctrinal perspective was put forward by people such as Escott Reid, Chester Ronning, and Herbert Norman. Of these last three men, Escott Reid seems to have commanded the most influence within the department.

The key differences between the left-liberals on the one hand, and the conservatives and liberal-moderates on the other, centred on the perceptions and opinions concerning the following issues: the degree of 'nationalist' credibility of the communist-led Vietminh organization; the degree of totalitarian conformity in the newly constituted DRVN; the political and emotional significance of the plight of the would-be refugees from North Vietnam; the degree of political influence of Moscow and Beijing in the determination of Hanoi's policies, domestic and external; and last, the meaning of the Geneva Agreements themselves.

For the left-liberals nationalism and communism most certainly could be fused 'legitimately.' This was especially the case in Asian societies that were still in the throes of transformation from primitive, landlord-dominated economies to modernizing, industrializing, urbanizing systems, in which the new urban propertied classes could only engender rural hostility as they began to disrupt traditional social forms. When the remnants of colonial rule and discrimination were added to this process, the mixture of social pressures naturally would give rise to a most volatile situation. Somewhat more sensitively attuned to the nuances of Asian culture and the strength of Asian anti-colonialist feeling, left-liberals were therefore more psychologically prepared to grant to the Vietminh-DRVN side the legitimacy of the nationalist label, since the rurally based communist-led insurgents could quite easily capture the conscious support of the disaffected peasantry. Left-liberals could more easily admit that communist/socialist doctrine had a great and quite rationally rooted appeal for many Asians, because such doctrine did hold much more promise for promoting immediate and genuine state autonomy and national independence given the particular economic conditions and geopolitical environments of these societies.

Left-liberals were by and large individuals who had spent a considerable amount of time in Asia, who usually appreciated Asian culture, and more important, were people who normally sympathized deeply with Asian determination to assert political and economic independence. By contrast, the conservatives in DEA and most of the liberal-moderates normally held no deep-rooted affection for Asian culture, and not infrequently found 'the mysterious East' to be dirty, noisy, disease-ridden, and unpleasant. Exceptions to this pattern did occur, but in general only those who had developed some capacity to identify with Asian life-styles seem to have been prepared to admit that Asian communism might eventually have some constructive role to play in Asia's long-term economic transformation.

The early imposition of autocratic methods in North Vietnam caused great distress among conservative and liberal-moderate ranks in External Affairs. This distress was focused on the refugee issue of late 1954 and early 1955. Under Article 14(d) of the Vietnam armistice the two Vietnamese parties (the DRVN and State of Vietnam authorities) were obliged to permit and assist all citizens to choose their zone of residence pending reunification of the country. Although some 900,000 or more residents of Tonkin managed to leave the north, many more families were forced to remain. The Canadians' inability to help these people escape communism (even if only temporarily) pained the conservative element deeply, and helped to provoke an equally deep distrust for the Hanoi leadership among Canadian conservatives.

To the extent that they were liberals this group abhorred the repression, uniformity, and conformity involved in the Stalinist regime that the DRVN leadership was said to have instituted, but they were nevertheless prepared to countenance the legitimate existence of this system. With respect to the refugees, the left-liberals tended to see them as unfortunate pawns in the Cold War struggle who had been incited to flee by Catholic leaders, who in turn had panicked prematurely and unnecessarily. For left-liberals the thesis that the extension of communist control to Vietnam necessarily involved the strengthening of the communist 'empire' seemed less than conclusive, given the strength of independentist sentiment in the ex-colonial countries, and given the precedent of Titoist-type 'heresy' in the communist bloc. Finally, the left-liberals were of the opinion that the electoral provisions of the Final Declaration ought to be respected and deserved Canadian support, since they represented a fundamental part of the Geneva great-power compromise. Where the left-liberals were at least quite sceptical about the supposed monolithic solidarity of the communist bloc, both the conservatives and liberal-moderates accepted the argument that the extension of communist rule constituted an addition to the strength of a reasonably coherent system with global aspirations, which therefore implied a genuine long-term threat to the security of the Western world.

So far as the Geneva Agreements were concerned the conservatives were convinced that the Geneva compromise was open to interpretation since the text of the agreements was extremely vague on many of the most crucial issues. As a result, articulators of the conservative approach argued that a politically ambiguous arrangement naturally permitted a continuing politico-diplomatic struggle in which it was both reasonable and fair for the Canadians to formulate a partisan interpretation of the legal implications of the Agreements that would favour the RVN regime. Proponents of the liberal-moderate tendency needed to be persuaded on this point.

Articulators of the left-liberal doctrinal perspective were consigned to a relatively peripheral role in the policy process by the onrush of events and by the dynamics of the tripartite commission structure. The minority of the department who might otherwise have expressed 'radical' dissent from the basic premises of both liberal-moderate and conservative doctrine were progressively inhibited by an ever larger chorus of junior and middle-ranking FSO, freshly returned from service in Indochina, who deplored 'the knavish tricks of the North Vietnamese, committed not only in Vietnam but in Laos as well.'[18] As John Holmes has pointed out (Holmes was a central figure in the Indochina policy debate of the Department of External Affairs between 1954 and 1960), 'virtually all Canadian veterans of Indochina have returned with more hawkish attitudes than prevail at home.'[19] In the face of the right-radicalization which occurred among those who actually went to Indochina, and perhaps fearing the charge of 'localitis' from having spent too many years in Asian milieux, left-liberal articulators were unable to make any headway in the flux of decision-making. One of the few trump cards available to the left-liberal wing of the department was the need to accommodate Indian perceptions of and policies towards the Indochina conflict. So long as the alleged special relationship between New Delhi and Ottawa existed it provided bureaucratic leverage for individuals such as Escott Reid (Canadian high commissioner to India from 1952 to 1957). When that relationship deteriorated in the early 1960s, so too did left-liberalism's already slender inputs into Canadian policy-making. According to Reid, Indochina policy became 'a major irritant' between Canada and India and was 'one of the principal causes of the erosion of the special relationship.'[20]

Because of the peripheral status of the left-liberal element, the basic differences betwen Canadian and American policies towards the Indochina wars may be ascribed to the perceptions and objectives framed by Ottawa's liberal-moderate elements that were divergent from American premises and goals. According to John Holmes:

Our role in Indochina was the classic case of middlepowermanship. There was not, before 1954, much theorizing about the role of a middle power. That came after the Suez crisis when this phase of Canadian policy had reached its crest. The Indochina experience of the fifties confirmed the view of many Canadians and of our friends that this was our special destiny and our best contribution to international order. It

22 In the interests of peace

satisfied our desire to do our own thing, complementary to that of the great powers
but by no means that of a handmaiden. It enabled us to differ from the United States
without opposing the interests of the United States as we saw them.[21]

Liberal-moderates such as Pearson and Holmes, like Falstaff, knew 'enough
to avoid getting killed when the fight was not worth it.'[22] For the Canadian
foreign policy élite the war in Vietnam was simply not worth any material
expenditures by the Canadian state. The heavy American intervention between 1964 and 1972 posed grave problems for Ottawa's policy-making élite.
What were the limits of dissent for Canada in this ambiguous situation?
Ultimately the American intervention exploded the assumption that had
hitherto been axiomatic in Ottawa, that Canada could never expect to stay
out of a major war in which the United States was involved. The liberal-
moderate rationale for non-involvement in American policy in the late 1960s
was concisely phrased by Holmes in 1967 (he was by then outside the Department of External Affairs):

To join in the fighting would please American opinion without contributing essential
military strength. On the other hand to denounce u.s. policy officially would only
stiffen their determination at the expense of incalculable damage to u.s.-Canadian
relations. The problem is difficult for Canadians who honestly believe that one or
other of those straightforward positions is our moral obligation, but the Government
knows that neither would carry the judgment of a majority. More important, the
abandonment of a position [on the ICSC truce supervisory body] which, if hardly
neutral, is at least disposed to impartial service, would deprive Canadians of the
chance to make use of their unique access to Hanoi and participate in any new
international commission. It is a classical example of the dilemma between satisfying
a moral compulsion (but which one?) and trying for a solution conceivable in an
admittedly wicked world.[23]

This middle-of-the-road policy which avoided direct support for American policy in the form of troop levies but which stopped short of severing
the defence production-sharing relationship, denouncing morally unacceptable methods of warfare, or publicly advocating early American withdrawal
was not received happily by the left-liberal tendency in the department. As
one former official summed up Canadian policy in the 1960s:

It was, as I think Pearson knew from the beginning, just an obscene exercise of a
wealthy, powerful – the wealthiest and the most powerful – state, that was trying to
impose its way on a small, remote, poverty-stricken people. It was just ignorant,

obscene and tragic. Staying on the Commission made Canadians too pro-American. It distorted the judgements of a whole generation of officials. It made us more hawkish than Americans – at least they had a George Ball who opposed the war. Canada could have and should have done something more to try to change the American course. I am doubtful that Paul Martin's efforts at the NATO meetings were serious ... The Indochina business was probably one of the main reasons for the decline in Canadian foreign policy influence abroad. We were too American on this issue.[24]

If good policy-making thrives on constant re-examination of the fundamental premises of policy, on meaningful dissent within bureaucratic organizations, then Canadian diplomats and policy-makers seem to have been relatively 'conscious' of the difficulty and ambiguity of the issues involved – certainly more conscious of the political and social ambiguities of the Vietnamese war than were their American counterparts. In the American foreign policy process there seems to have been a considerably greater tendency towards the 'group-think' uniformity (perceptual-cognitive homogenization) that undermines effective and sensitive decision-making. But despite the greater diversity of opinion within the Canadian policy-making élite, the consensus position of the Department of External Affairs never in fact repudiated the conservative line of policy that was implemented in the 1956–65 period – not even after a partial swing away from conservative doctrinal tenets in the 1966–73 period towards a more liberal-moderate approach. The dénouement of the American intervention did not cause any wholesale rejection of conservative perspectives within the department. After 1968 the alteration in policy style in Vietnam decision-making stemmed rather from the fact that policy was increasingly politicized and thus taken out of the hands of the bureaucratic élite to a much greater degree than previously.

The Canadian government was almost silent on Vietnam publicly after 1968 both because the issue area was judged to be too hot for rational debate, and because there was no pressing requirement that Ottawa take a stand on any aspect of the sordid mess in Indochina. The ICSC for Vietnam had been effectively dead since 1965, when all the truce supervisory teams had been withdrawn consequent to the onset of 'Rolling Thunder' bombardment. The peace-feeler diplomacy of the 1965–8 period in which Canada had played a role had drawn a complete blank and, by 1969, the parties were sitting around a table communicating with each other directly. Though the departmental consensus had shifted back once more towards the liberal-moderate perspective, there was literally nothing for External staff to do but wait for the call to armistice supervision. After 1969 there was little reason for active criticism of the left-liberal variety, since the American administration was clearly committed to eventual disengagement from Indochina. After 1968 the only issue for External Affairs' old Indochina hands was the terms of reference of any projected supervisory role Canada might be asked to play. Liberal-moderate tacticians went at this problem with quite immoderate enthusiasm in order to lay the groundwork for future withdrawal. Disillusioned conservatives would have preferred a blanket refusal to serve enunciated well in advance of any settlement. That was not to be. Liberal-moderate internationalism prevailed yet again and the Canadian government took on the unhappy task of attempting to separate the combatants so as to facilitate an American withdrawal.

By 1973 the basis of liberal-moderate logic had altered completely. In 1954 fear of American nuclear adventurism triggered a Canadian decision to become involved in a region where Canada had no vital interests. In late 1972 fear of political and economic retaliation by an American government enraged at possible Canadian 'obstructionism' helped to preclude any serious thought of turning down a role on the new International Commission of Control and Supervision (ICCS). Where the 1954 draft came from China via India and Canadian participation was assented to at the expense of Canadian-American relations, the 1972 invitation to a supervisory role came on Washington's initiative. Canadian acceptance was motivated by both a desire in some quarters to facilitate American disengagement and a wish to avoid giving offence to the unpredictable President Nixon.

By 1973 Vietnam decision-making was leaving a very bitter taste in the mouths of Canadian officials. Many believed that the RVN government was doomed and that Nixon and Kissinger were preparing an elaborately disguised betrayal of their Vietnamese allies. For some eight years Ottawa had been unable to convince the Indians to take a more active role in the ICSC for Vietnam, and the frustration experienced in that forum was only too likely to be repeated on the ICCS operation of 1973 with the Indonesians, Poles, and Hungarians. In this context it is not surprising that R.D. Jackson, the Canadian delegate to the last meeting of the old ICSC for Vietnam on 13 March 1973, read out the following indictment:

The International Commission for Supervision and Control has for much of its existence been an ineffectual and rather pathetic body. In recent years problems from without and within rendered it a veritable vegetable of an institution. It received all too little external support and boasted all too little internal cooperation in the performance of its appointed tasks. Its achievements fell pitifully short of what was expected of it. It squandered its time, it frittered away its energies, it consumed its own resources, while the smoke and flames of war engulfed it. A victim in part of the perversity of nations, *it also became a sad monument to poorly conceived and poorly employed international machinery*. The Canadian Delegation trusts that it at least provided all concerned with experience that can be usefully applied in the future.[25]

For many conservatives and disillusioned liberal-moderates the major lesson learned was sadly short-sighted: Canada should avoid peacekeeping duties that have little prospect for complete success. That conclusion to the Vietnam experience is lamentably simplistic and wholly inappropriate.

Despite the ultimate operational failures of the Indochina truce supervisory commissions, each of them made useful contributions to politically complex conflicts. Canadian involvement in the first Vietnam ICSC was especially significant. For some six to eight years that commission helped inhibit the outright resumption of hostilities in Vietnam. The Canadian effort, tedious and frustrating though it was, helped postpone the test of military strength that eventually occurred between 1964 and 1972. The hiatus in the conflict from 1954 to 1961–2 may have been especially critical in view of American reliance on nuclear weapons for virtually every significant military threat for the duration of this period. Only with the accession to power of President Kennedy did the Pentagon acquire a diversified conventional force capability with which it could respond to low-level military challenges. Prior to the Kennedy administration the Dullesian doctrine of massive retaliation and President Eisenhower's economically inspired reliance on tactical nuclear firepower had created a global political-military environment that was terribly risk-laden. From 1954 through 1962 the nuclear peace was very tenuously rooted. Canadian and Indian diplomacy helped carry the international system through a very precarious phase of international politics. That lesson is apparently still to be appreciated in present-day Ottawa – or, more accurately expressed perhaps, that lesson is something which needs periodic reaffirmation because it is constantly in jeopardy of being forgotten.

ATTITUDINAL TENDENCIES IN THE
CANADIAN FOREIGN POLICY PROCESS*

When referring to liberal-moderates, conservatives, and left-liberals in this book, I do not intend to suggest that there are in fact any formal or informal

---

* The remarks in this section are for specialists in the field of foreign policy analysis. Non-specialists may pass them by.

fraternities, factions, cabals, or so on within the Canadian government. Quite the contrary seems to be true: an ethos of élite collegiality pervaded the corridors of the foreign policy mandarinate during the years under review in this work. The 'tendency groupings' so far identified seem to represent, and here I am engaged to be sure in speculative hypothesizing, fundamental clusters of attitudes concerning the nature of Canadian foreign policy, the threats, problems, and challenges confronting it, and the dominant interests and values that must be served in actually formulating and executing policy. In any pluralist society, in fact in any modern complex polity, we may reasonably expect to find substantial diversity in basic political-doctrinal orientations throughout the state bureaucracies, if only because of the extraordinary variety of constituencies which different segments of government must either serve, cultivate, or neutralize.[26] Accordingly there is a substantial body of literature in western political science devoted to the theory of interest group behaviour and accommodation. The insights from this literature have been applied in the last fifteen years to communist societies as well, reflecting the realities of political and socio-economic stratification within communist-bloc decision-making structures. Most such studies employ a concept of interest group that is premised on the group as a coherent social aggregate with definable characteristics, consciously shared aspirations, or some mix of these qualities. That is not the approach of this book.

Theoretically the present work draws on insights and concepts formulated by Franklyn Griffiths, Robert Levine, and Franz Schurmann, writers whose principal research areas are Soviet studies, American armaments policy, and Asian politics respectively.[27] What they share in common is a perception of policy-making processes as the visible manifestation and in many cases the final expression of basic societal imperatives that animate the entire body politic. Griffiths, for example, talks of the 'system-dominant' characteristics of state behaviour. By using this phrase he would have us focus upon the 'regularities in the interactions of the [social] whole which represent parametric givens for intermediate participation and to which the latter must be accommodated if it is to have any effect.'[28] Intermediate participants such as political parties, institutionalized interest groups, and single-issue lobbying groups must adjust their demand and support articulations in light of the pre-existing structure of values and legitimized norms of the society. Bureaucratic behaviour, another form of intermediate participation, can also be assumed to reflect and embody, in microcosm, the overall value-norm imperatives of the society in which it is embedded. To adapt Griffiths directly to the present analysis 'it will be suggested that the formation and execution of policy' in Canada 'may be understood in terms of a system-dominant conflict of tendencies of articulation, through which specific values are allocated for' Canadian 'society.'[29]

In identifying the axiomatic doctrinal dimensions of conservatives, liberal-moderates, or left-liberals (see figure 1 for a summary) 'the object of inquiry is not an aggregate of individual policy makers but a pattern of interaction.'[30] In short, I am here engaged in an attempt to identify the system-dominant propensities of the Canadian polity as manifested in foreign policy decision-making. By so doing we may then hope to move to a higher order of explanation that at a minimum may help to clarify the logics that now animate Canadian foreign policy, and may ultimately provide us with higher confidence procedures in the comparatively uncharted waters of foreign policy prediction. Along the way I shall recapitulate the history of Canadian policy-making towards the International Commission for Supervision and Control in Vietnam, 1954–73 (ICSC), and towards the International Commission of Control and Supervision, January–July 1973 (ICCS).

The ICSC/ICCS case study is offered as a suitable domain for empirical investigation of the Canadian polity's system-dominant regularities because it cuts to the heart of all possible doctrinal perspectives concerning the ways in which the Canadian state should relate to the international political-military environment. It is an especially good vehicle for investigation because involvement in Indochina by Canada was consistently free of any direct material incentives or vested interests which might otherwise contaminate or obscure the interplay of pure doctrinal tendencies of articulation. Vital interests were at stake (viz, the risk of World War III, the health of Canadian-American relations) even if material interests were not (at least not until the late 1960s when Canada-US trade under the Defence Production Sharing Agreements rose dramatically as a result of the massive injection of US ground forces in Vietnam).[31]

Between 1953 and 1973 Canadian exports to all Indochina never reached an annual total of more than 0.027 per cent of total Canadian exports; Canadian Indochinese imports were never more than 0.004 per cent of total Canadian imports.[32] Canadian trade with all Southeast Asia (Burma, Malaysia, Singapore, Indonesia, Thailand, and the Philippines) never amounted to more than 0.72 per cent of total Canadian trade throughout the period 1953 to 1973.[33] There were no credibly significant, let alone vital, economic interests for Canada anywhere in Southeast Asia. In fact by 1965 Canadian trade with the PRC was considerably more important to Canada's trade position than trade with all of Southeast Asia. Matters have remained so since that time.[34]

Because domestic economic interests were not directly relevant to Canadian policy formulation in the 1950s and early 1960s – and in internal policy memoranda no one seems to have suggested anything to the contrary – we may proceed under the assumption that the broadest and most fundamental political and strategic attitudes were instrumental in shaping the pattern of Canadian response to the Indochina policy dilemma. Doctrinal assumptions about the nature of the communist threat to the West, the preferred limits of Western response to perceived aggression, and the character and fitness of American political leadership and national security planning were undoubtedly engaged.

After the US intervention expanded rapidly in 1964–5 the health of the Canadian economy was no doubt a factor of increasing consequence in policy-making calculations. The impact of the war on Canadian manufacturing exports was sizeable.[35] Nevertheless, publicly available evidence suggests that the broad lines of the internal policy debate were set less by economic considerations and more by political and strategic calculations about the desirability of facilitating an end to America's longest, most internally divisive, and most internationally debilitating war. The Canadian stake in an early renaissance of American strength, prestige, and confidence was appreciable. Many conservatives and liberal-moderates understood this fact. Among left-liberals this argument carried weight, but it was still more significant for the departmental left that the United States seemed highly unlikely to engage in a humiliating unilateral withdrawal. Given left-liberal preference for ending the war as soon as was practically achievable, thus to minimize the suffering of the Indochinese, they accepted the realistic proposition that another face-saving truce supervisory operation was probably inevitable, and that Canada had a moral duty to facilitate the whole process of US disengagement.

Figure 1 contains more information than the content of the various attitudinal axioms listed under each 'tendency of articulation.' It indicates implicitly the effective boundaries of politically tolerable discourse within the External Affairs policy community concerning the Vietnam war and the shape of Canadian and American participation. For a member of the policy-making élite to subscribe to views beyond the range of opinion listed here was simply an unthinkable event. As Schurmann has noted in the American context, bureaucrats often must think 'woodenly' not merely to demonstrate adherence to established doctrine for the sake of reinforcing collegiality, but more importantly to adapt and tailor their views to conform to the pre-existing political currents that dominate their particular policy milieux. As Schurmann put it: 'Every ideological current, however repulsive, has a mass basis in some segment of the population. Interest politics are always elitist – corporate and bureaucratic officials always like to do their jobs quietly without outside interference. Ideological politics, whether of the left, right or center, are always democratic in that they necessarily involve major segments of the general population. Ideology is the door through which the people enter the closed rooms of the realm of interests.'[36] For present purposes Schurmann's 'ideological current' and Griffiths' 'tendency of articulation' will be treated as interchangeably descriptive terms.

To the extent that system-dominant tendencies of articulation are in fact derived from mutually interpenetrating ideological forces percolating throughout the society at large we may also expect to see ideological/tendency amalgams in particular individuals. Few individuals are wholly consistent ideologically, because it requires an extreme degree of mental closure to eliminate all discrepant beliefs.[37] Mental closure is a very unhappy and disadvantageous state of mind for any policy-maker to develop, given the need for flexibility, adaptability, and skilful accommodation of the fluctuating pressures from the external environment. As numerous works of diplomatic history testify, a reputation for mental rigidity is something to be feared in Ottawa. For this reason it was with some reluctance that various individuals have been labelled as archetypically conservative, liberal-moderate, or left-liberal. The boundaries between the categories presented here were quite permeable, and particular individuals may have subscribed to axioms that fell under two or sometimes even all three of the categories simultaneously. For members of Ottawa's policy community the adoption of these 'tendencies of articulation' may have been a matter of conscious 'stylistic' preference. In interview sessions the three tendencies seem to have occurred with the following frequency: liberal-moderate articulations, some 45 per cent of the time; conservative, some 35 per cent of the time; left-liberal, some 20 per cent of the time. Given the unstructured character of the interviews these figures are no more than crude estimates – and little weight can be put on them for that reason. Nevertheless, it may be more than coincidental that these figures parallel the average post-war distribution of popular electoral support for Canada's three federal parties.

The three tendencies of articulation presented in this book are to be seen as emerging 'from the total system of interaction' of the Canadian polity and as forming 'effective alternate directions of policy' for any national government.[38] These tendencies should be viewed as being in a state of constant dynamic tension, and on given issues policy outputs can become internally contradictory because of the need for temporary compromises among mutually antagonistic policy imperatives. In these struggles there are no final victories for particular tendencies of articulation. Elimination of any of these macro-political programs would ipso facto reduce the inherent adaptability of the total system. Accommodative flexibility is a direct function of the number of 'alternate directions of policy' available. That premise flows naturally from the intellectual acceptance of the cybernetic character of governmental activity. The assumptions of the cybernetic 'paradigm' are a central part of this book.

Following John Steinbruner,[39] governmental decision-making may be said to conform to a cybernetic pattern to the extent that it embodies or reflects the following traits.

The prevalence of non-purposive adaptation over rational outcome calculation: In a cybernetic decision-making process, policy actors do not try to explore alternative options or their probable consequences. Neither do they engage in anything more than the most rudimentary cost-benefit calculations. Value-maximizing or 'optimizing' procedures are not used. Instead, behaviour is more accurately describable as being non-purposively adaptive. Decision-makers interpret goals as constraints that define minimally acceptable standards of performance for their organization. Goals define the acceptable ranges for important politically determined internal policy variables.

Uncertainty control through selective attention: In cybernetic process there is no serious effort to comprehend the external environment. New or discrepant data are usually ignored or repressed until external demands become highly threatening. By acting in this fashion the disturbing or debilitating effects of uncertainty are minimized. The wilful repression of information is 'an essential aspect of any sustained political action.' Furthermore, 'information screens or filters are ... essential for the functioning of a complex self-steering system.'[40]

Highly focused sensitivity: Information is perceived only if it arrives by highly focused 'feedback channels' or 'receptors' (ie, channels that are a formal or quasi-formal part of the decision-making unit). Organizational routine actively reduces and filters information flowing towards the apex of the decision-making unit in accordance with pre-established guidelines that are in turn formulated in light of the critical internal variables of the system.

Action occurs through highly programmed policy output responses: Governmental action almost invariably occurs through the activation of pre-programmed behaviour patterns already accumulated in the repertoire of the organization. These are often referred to as 'standing operational procedures' (sops for short). These responses are normally applied with a minimum of critical reflection. They are applied experimentally. Behaviour is essentially adaptive, not purposive.

Sequential attention to goals: Generally speaking, decision-makers arrive at decisions without first trying to 'integrate' goals that may be in a trade-off relationship. Neither do they attempt to incorporate information and recommendations from a great variety of sub-systems in the organization. Most decisions are made by the highest level of the organization within the context of the sub-unit that raised the issue.

Incrementalism is the normal mode of activity: 'Incremental' (per Lindblom)[41] or 'bit' (per Etzioni) changes in policy are the norm. As Allison noted[42] 'the best predictor of $t + 1$ is t.' Although it is theoretically conceivable that the cybernetic repertoire (another appropriate metaphor is that of a recipe cookbook) might include some policy responses that involve very large and dramatic changes in policy, such responses would be unusual. Normally only modest alterations in policy will be attempted in efforts to restore the critical internal variables to their desired range of tolerable values. 'Satisficing' behaviour (ie, acceptance of levels of goal accomplishment short of maximization)[43] is the standard approach of policy-makers.

Instrumental, not causal, learning: Cybernetically functioning organizations do not search through all or even many possible responses for the purpose of deliberation before action. Scanning of information through established channels is very limited. Learning occurs slowly as a result of the accumulation of a record of failures by given response patterns (ie, given SOPs). Chronically unsuccessful or unused patterns eventually drop out of the repertoire, while new ones are formulated on an ad hoc experimental basis. There is rarely if ever any searching examination of the repertoire's overall capabilities, or of its 'fit' to the environment.

For present purposes the system-dominant tendencies of articulation thus far identified may be seen as analytical relatives of the Standing Operational Procedure. They represent, in fact, SOP policy aggregates, and thus they might be referred to as 'Standing Operational Doctrines' (or SODs for short). As is the case for SOPs, in a cybernetically functioning organization any given SOD will remain in the doctrinal repertoire of an organization so long as its operational record remains – or appears to remain – failure-free. The study which follows will examine the decision-making record of policy towards the Indochina wars at least partly in an effort to map out the evidence for success or failure for each of the SODs in the Canadian foreign policy process. Perhaps the process of instrumental learning can thereby be accelerated modestly.

Although the study is presented within the framework of the cybernetic 'paradigm,' it is not meant to imply that the various policy actors were somehow intrinsically non-rational in their response to the problems of decision-making. In some quarters there is a reflexive resistance to the use of cybernetic 'modelling' or language – perhaps due to a mistaken belief that the approach somehow consigns human intellect to a mechanical subsidiary role. The anxieties that have given rise to such resistance are unfounded. The cybernetic approach is valid because it recognizes the inherent limitations of the human intellect in an infinite, uncertain, and ambiguously structured universe. The sheer size and breadth in both space and time of many if not most of the difficult problems confronting national societies dictate the use of an experimental, adaptive mode of policy-making. To assert this as fact in no way reflects badly upon past or present policy-making actors. Neither does it deny the possibility that truly exceptional human intellects might comprehend the workings of the external phenomenal world with far more power and explanatory precision than is now the case. Those analysts with reservations about the cybernetic approach must surely admit that while there may have been outstanding intellectual figures within the Ottawa policy community, the groups both in Cabinet and the House of Commons who have had the final say on our collective response to the international political realm together constitute – in conformity with the practical institutionalized wisdom of liberal-democratic process – something less than the intellectual aristocracy of Canadian society. Elected officials, like their professional underlings, are frequently if not usually overloaded with demands on their time and resources, especially those in Cabinet, and thus they are unable, by and large, to engage in the elaborate requirements of rational, analytic decision-making.[44]

Employing a method first developed by Robert Levine,[45] figure 1 provides a schematic representation of the various positions taken in Canada's Vietnam/Indochina debates. The horizontal line bisecting the diagram from top to bottom divides policy advocates into two groups: those who made incremental and conditionally qualified policy recommendations (for the most part, people within government bureaucracies, Cabinet, the caucus of the governing party in the Commons, as well as 'moderate' non-governmental policy analysts who adhered to parliamentary opposition parties, the media or academic institutions), and those who favoured policy recommendations involving large change and who made such recommendations unconditionally (usually people from opposition parties far from power and 'radical' critics in the media or academia). The first group will be referred to as policy 'marginalists,' the second group as policy 'systemists.' Based on interview material and on an extensive review of the classified record, it may be stated unequivocally that all policy actors within the Department of External Affairs were 'marginalists.' Only in Commons debates or in the pages of the

FIGURE 1
Five schools of thought on Canada's Vietnam involvement
Fundamental value commitment

Type of recom- mendations	Primarily favours international egalitarianism and strict respect for national self- determination	Primarily concerned with the promotion of peace	Primarily anti- communist, but for peace through appease- ment avoidance
Conditional, incremental policy recommendations / All staff in DEA and many public 'marginalists' ↑	marginalist left-liberal school	marginalist liberal-moderate pro-'Quiet Diplomacy' school	marginalist peace through containment school
Unconditional recommendations involving a large degree of change / public only 'systemists' ↓	systemist anti-American pro-Vietnamese 'nationalism' post-1962		systemist anti-communist, pro-Australian option school (post-1965)

press can one find vigorous recommendations seeking public denunciation of American imperial intervention (left-liberal systemism) or alternatively the dispatch of Canadian troops or financial assistance in aid of the Republic of Vietnam's valiant struggle for freedom (conservative systemism). Such is the analytical framework;* now to the evidentiary record itself.

---

* For those readers familiar with the recently published work by David B. Dewitt and John J. Kirton, *Canada as a Principal Power* (Toronto: Wiley 1983), I would note that their version of the policy trinity is rather different from mine. They collapse the currents of left liberalism and liberal moderation presented here into one single current labelled 'liberal internationalism.' For example, John Holmes and Escott Reid are placed in the same category. While Holmes and Reid shared many views and values, my research would indicate that they took quite distinct postures on the Indochina problem. Furthermore, from my reading of the location of the boundaries of tolerable policy discourse in External Affairs, the peripheral-dependence perspective as they depict it (being fairly heavily influenced by neo-Marxist premises) seems far too radical or 'systemist' to be part of serious policy debate in Ottawa. Perhaps it was not – until very recently, and I am just out of touch. But I need to be persuaded on this point. I would therefore place their peripheral-dependence advocates in the lower left corner of figure 1. There is, however, a substantial overlap between the axioms of their 'complex neo-realists' and my conservative marginalists. But I doubt that Ottawa's realists are all that 'neo,' and I dislike the use of the prefix 'complex,' which seems unnecessarily obfuscatory. Does it imply the other approaches are simplistic?

Indochina and the diplomacy of constraint 1950—4

In the Franco-Vietminh war of 1946–54 the French Union Forces (FUF) suffered some 230,000 casualties. Of these casualties 71,100 were inflicted on soldiers from metropolitan France, 21,000 fatal. The effective casualty and mortality rates experienced by French troops were nearly twice as high as the rates suffered by the American forces in the 1964–72 period.[1] *La guerre sale* was every bit as savage for French troops as the later conflict was for Americans. The French expenditure of blood and treasure was futile. Political leaders in Paris sought to maintain the *gloire et présence* of 'the French fact in Indochina.' They obstinately held to the view that France still had a *mission civilisatrice* in Southeast Asia. As that rationale grew hollow they became convinced that they were saving the people of Indochina from communist tyranny. French obstinacy and self-delusion would eventually lead directly to the slaughter of millions of Vietnamese. Some one million Vietnamese died in the famine immediately after World War II while the French tried to force their way back into Indochina. Another million or more would die either directly or indirectly from the ravages of the Franco-Vietminh war. And still another million or more would die in the course of the US intervention, which grew directly out of the collapse of the French campaign, and which would never have occurred without the original French effort to reconquer the region.

France's colonial administrators had indeed 'milked' Indochina for decades, as Franklin Roosevelt phrased it, when they were deposed by the Japanese on 9 March 1945.[2] Land rents for the peasant population rose steadily throughout the French occupation, as did rural indebtedness and foreign control of the economy. Per capita food consumption among Vietnamese was stagnant or in decline. French policy effectively created a small class of indigenous bureaucratic collaborators and their hangers-on who were allowed to staff a relatively powerless state apparatus that had no jurisdiction over French citizens. All significant avenues of social and economic mobility were blocked for the Indochinese. Violent military repression was the standard French response to Vietnamese demands for self-government. French methods of governance – economic exploitation and political subjugation – effectively precluded the evolution of a progressive liberal middle class in Vietnam and drove self-respecting patriotic Vietnamese towards conspiracy, intrigue, and terror.[3]

In 1940 Japanese forces had occupied all Indochina for the purpose of acquiring military bases and strategic position to support their war effort in the Pacific. Admiral Decoux's regime collaborated with the Vichy government until the fall of 1944. By March 1945 the Japanese had to depose Decoux because they feared the effects of increasing French governmental co-operation with the Gaullist resistance. In 1944–5 the war against the Japanese by Vietnamese forces gradually came under the control of the Indochinese Communist party (ICP) headed by Ho Chi Minh and Vo Nguyen Giap. With assistance from the Kuomintang's southernmost warlord, as well as modest help from American OSS personnel (Office of Strategic Services, the CIA's wartime forerunner), the ICP-directed Revolutionary League for the Independence of Vietnam (Viet-Nam Doc-Lap Dong Minh, or Vietminh as they came to be known) took charge of the fighting in the five northernmost provinces of Tonkin. When VJ Day arrived the Vietminh moved into Hanoi to take the Japanese surrender ahead of the Kuomintang (KMT) forces assigned to that role by the Potsdam Conference. They thus took effective control of Vietnam north of the 16th parallel. The Vietminh simultaneously attempted to consolidate power in the south, but the politically and militarily weaker southern branch of the Vietminh was quickly evicted from Saigon by the occupying force of British General Douglas Gracey, who did not hesitate to arm Japanese prisoners of war for the purpose of 'liberating' the south from local control. Gracey promptly handed over administration of the southern zone to interned and returning French forces.[4]

In the north, matters took a much different turn. Ho persuaded Emperor Bao Dai to abdicate on 29 August. On the same day the formation of the Provisional Government of the Democratic Republic of Vietnam was announced. Bao Dai, soon to become Supreme Counsellor Vinh Thuy and a diplomatic emissary for Ho's government, transferred the Great Seal to the new authorities. When the KMT occupying army finally arrived, it did not depose Ho's government. It declared itself to be neutral in the Franco-Vietnamese dispute over sovereignty – until the French were prepared to make economic concessions to the KMT. When the French finally gave in to this economic blackmail in the spring of 1946, the Chinese forces began to withdraw. From March through December in Paris Ho tried to negotiate a satisfactory equivalent of dominion status within the French Union for the new provisional government, despite strong opposition from ICP/Vietminh colleagues who advocated an alliance with the Chinese on whatever terms necessary. To such critics Ho declared that 'the white man is finished in Asia' but that the Chinese, if allowed to stay at this critical juncture, 'will never leave.' Personally, he said, 'I prefer to smell French shit for five years rather than Chinese shit for the rest of my life.'[5]

Ho's optimism was misplaced. The French refused meaningful concessions. War broke out in Tonkin, the northernmost of the three regions of Vietnam (the others being Annam in the centre and Cochinchina in the south), in December 1946.

Despite the massive famine in the north during 1945–6 (estimates of deaths range from 500,000 to 2 million)[6] when the French were apparently obstructing food imports to try to break the provisional government, the new leadership in Hanoi consolidated its power through shrewd political concessions to potential opposition groups to neutralize them temporarily until such time as they could be selectively liquidated by Vietminh assassination squads. Popular reforms of all kinds were promulgated by the new government (eg, abolition of all taxes), secure in the knowledge that it would not have to fulfil its promises.[7] In Cochinchina the Indochinese Communist party and its Vietminh front had much less popular support and therefore had a greater need for coercive methods. Scores of non-communist leaders were assassinated.[8]

From 1946 to 1949 the Vietminh fought a savage guerrilla struggle. They fought against a French Expeditionary Corps composed of Senegalese, Moroccans, and Germans in the Foreign Legion element of the corps, as well as an all-volunteer group from France. The FEC grew from some 40,000 strong in 1946 to over 150,000 by 1954. By the early 1950s the bulk of the French Union Forces, however, would be composed of native Vietnamese. From 1946 to 1949 the French spent 27 per cent of the defence budget on the war in Indochina.[9] After the communist victory on the Chinese mainland in the autumn of 1949 the Vietminh began to receive substantial military assistance from across the Tonkinese frontier with China, and Paris spent still more. The prospect of direct Chinese intervention in support of the Vietminh loomed ever larger in French eyes.

As early as 1947 the French leadership in Paris realized that the war in Indochina could be won only through gaining wide Vietnamese support, something which in turn depended upon an early devolution of power to a genuinely representative Vietnamese assembly. But the *colons* fought all concessions to the Vietnamese relentlessly, both in Indochina and in Paris through their informal lobby. Their victory in delaying the most important concessions until 1954 was a major setback to the cause of a non-communist Vietnam. The protracted devolution process began with the birth of the State of Vietnam regime under a recalled Bao Dai as a result of a vague and impossibly contradictory promise of 'independence ... within the French Union' made at the Baie d'Along in 1947. The much-maligned and altogether changeable Emperor Bao Dai had been retrieved from a self-imposed exile from his country following his disillusionment with the Provisional Government in 1946. But the 'night-club Emperor' soon returned to Hong Kong when no further action was taken by the French authorities towards devolution. The constitutional provisions of the French Union did not permit independent status for member states.[10]

The Elysée Agreements of March 1949 transferred some modest authority to the State of Vietnam, but foreign affairs, direction of the military, and most of the economy were still in French hands. Independence was still far off. At the Pau Conference from June to November 1950 powers over immigration, customs and foreign commerce, and domestic and foreign currency control were nominally transferred to the State of Vietnam government. Currency control was not in fact handed over until 1954. French citizens, moreover, continued to enjoy a special status before the courts in Indochina. Control of the Vietnamese armed forces was not fully relinquished until 1955.[11] Such was the atavistic and finally self-defeating tenacity with which the French clung to their foothold in Asia. The vision of a *mission civilisatrice* and of *la France de cent millions d'habitants* died very hard.

The Canadian government was quite ignorant of events and issues in Indochina until very late in the day. General Georges Vanier, Canadian ambassador to France, and the counsellor of the Paris Embassy, Charles Ritchie, both were inclined to believe French versions of the conflict. France, so it was said, was fighting for Western interests, liberal values, and ultimate self-determination of the Indochinese people, free from communist tyranny. The two Canadians were encouraged to believe that devolution of power to the Indochinese would soon be enacted. Vanier and Ritchie, according to James Eayrs, were too enamoured of French society to exert a critical and balanced judgment on such wishful thinking.[12] From Vanier and Ritchie came arguments in favour of early recognition of the sovereign capacity of the Bao Dai government: communist expansion was occurring in Asia not Europe and help was needed; France required moral support from its allies to help sustain domestic support for its sacrifices on behalf of the Western countries; respect for NATO solidarity demanded a sympathetic response; and delay in recognition, it was said, would undercut the psychological value of the act. Prime Minister Louis St Laurent and his secretary of state for external affairs, Lester B. Pearson, were unconvinced. Word had reached them by early 1950 that Indian Prime Minister Jawaharlal Nehru was increasingly impressed with Ho Chi Minh and with Ho's prospects for eventual success.[13]

Indian policy at this point had seen three years of deliberate indifference to Vietminh appeals for recognition and support from Nehru's government.[14] But in January 1950 Nehru had also refused to see an emissary from Bao Dai, saying, 'He does not represent anybody to us.'[15] For Nehru there was a 'civil war' in progress in Indochina in which the French were heavily committed on one side while the communist Chinese were only marginally involved on the other. Respect for the principle of non-intervention was given the highest priority by Nehru, despite much pro-Vietminh clamouring within his own Congress party.[16]

St Laurent and Pearson respected Nehru, appreciated the Indian prime minister's realism (he had helped to suppress or denounced communist insurrections in Burma, Malaya, Indonesia, and in India itself),[17] and were determined to accommodate his views because Nehru was the foremost spokesman for Asian Commonwealth attitudes. Accordingly, when the United States moved to recognize the independence of the State of Vietnam in the first week of February 1950 and was followed shortly thereafter by Britain, Ottawa moved much more cautiously, extending a form of recognition that did not meet full legal requirements and which therefore failed to satisfy the French government.[18] In May the Department of External Affairs produced a review memorandum which summed up the merits and costs of early full recognition. On balance, the arguments listed favoured continued non-recognition, although the implication of Indochinese recognition on the impending Canadian decision[19] to recognize the People's Republic of China was not included. As Eayrs rightly noted, the desire to apply consistently the principle of recognition of factually autonomous governments meant that the China recognition problem was an important factor militating against recognition of Bao Dai's regime.[20]

The onset of the Korean war in June 1950 made recognition of China unthinkable in the near future. But North Korean bellicosity and massive Chinese intervention in the conflict throughout 1951 no doubt had a corrosive effect on Prime Minister St Laurent's desire to hold firm against recognition. In December 1952 Canada at last moved towards recognition following a Cabinet decision in the first week of that month to allow Canadian Mutual Aid defence equipment to be shipped to Indochina from France 'in accordance with the [NATO] Standing Group's recommendations.'[21] Indochina was now seen as a key part of the 'Free World' struggle by decision-makers in Washington, and Canada could not afford to stay too far out of step. On 30 December 1952 Ambassador Vanier informed the Quai d'Orsay that Canada now recognized the sovereign status of the three member states of the French Union in Indochina.[22]

Recognition of the State of Vietnam's sovereignty did not match the political or military realities of Indochina. Not until June 1954 in the midst of the Geneva Conference on Indochina were authentic independence treaties involving a final complete cession of powers drawn up, and on this occasion the documents were initialled only. They were never formally signed or ratified by either the French or the State of Vietnam governments. In short, the State of Vietnam never did obtain formal independence from France. From June 1954 until the unilateral declaration of the Republic of Vietnam by Ngo Dinh Diem in October 1955 France was still, according to technical legal criteria, the sovereign power in Vietnam.[23]

By late 1953 and early 1954 the military forces of the Democratic Republic of Vietnam, the People's Army of Vietnam (PAVN), either controlled directly, or could deny control to the French, over four-fifths of the territory of Vietnam.[24] At this point the communist-led forces had an incomparably better basis for a claim to status as the de facto government of the country. By early 1954 the FUF with over 600,000 troops under its command in Indochina outnumbered the communist forces by a wide margin. But as the American forces would rediscover a decade later, even advantageous ratios of four or five to one were not sufficient to accomplish effective 'mopping up' of guerrilla forces given the more substantial disadvantages of mountainous jungle-covered terrain and a hostile or at best *attentiste* local population. By early 1954 the French effort to reconquer Indochina by force was at an end. French public opinion would no longer tolerate the war. More officers were being killed in Indochina annually than were graduating from the French officer training program.

Despite the clear decline in French popular support for the war, General Navarre, the newly appointed head of FUF, decided to go ahead with an aggressive campaign of intervention and disruption of Vietminh rear areas, both to protect Laos against imminent moves by PAVN forces in that direction and to draw enemy forces into large conventional confrontations where it was assumed superior firepower could be brought to bear by the French. The plan backfired. When seven of the best battalions were parachuted in to

Dienbienphu their camp on a valley floor was soon surrounded. Ho and Giap decided to gamble heavily that they could pull off a final politically decisive battle against FUF which would break French willingness to continue the war even though their own forces were close to total collapse.[25]

Some 49,500 Vietminh combat troops, about 50,000–55,000 logistical support personnel, several score heavy artillery pieces, and many hundreds of Chinese artillery gunners and 'advisers' were moved in to invest the French Union 'fortress.' Navarre reinforced the 5,000 troops already there. Altogether some 15,000 troops passed through Dienbienphu. When the camp surrendered on 7 May, the day before the Geneva Conference on Indochina opened, there were fewer than 10,000 FUF troops captured.[26] In taking the camp (the People's Army of Vietnam) expended somewhere in the order of 30,000 lives. But the gamble succeeded. French political will was irretrievably broken. The stakes of the Vietminh gamble were far higher than Ho and Giap then knew. The use of atomic bombs to relieve the French forces was at the time actively considered in Washington. The Canadian government was actually consulted in the matter. Nuclear war in Asia was a very real possibility in the spring of 1954. Since 1950 successive governments in Paris had argued that Indochina was, like Korea, an example of aggression by the communist bloc. Many important American policy-makers needed no convincing. They saw Dienbienphu as another opportunity to be seized and exploited as the first step in a projected campaign of nuclear counter-attack and anti-communist rollback.[27] Their hopes were the subject of Canadian, Indian, and European nightmares.

THE 'ASIA-FIRST' CURRENT IN US POLICY
AND THE CANADIAN AVOIDANCE OF SEATO

For Canadian decision-makers, Asian policy-making was the most difficult, intractable, and frustrating experience that faced Ottawa in the post-war era. With respect to Asia, Ottawa and Washington rarely saw eye to eye. On successive issues Canadians found themselves unable to agree with either American tactics or strategic priorities. In a chapter very appropriately entitled 'Containing America,' Denis Stairs portrayed the basic divergence in Canadian and American policies as follows: 'Ottawa placed a higher value upon the defence of the "free world" in Europe and in North America than in the Far East, and now that Canada was embroiled militarily [ie, in Korea] in such a remote quarter of the globe it had become very much a part of the national interest to limit as fully as possible the intensity, duration and territorial scope of the hostilities.'[28]

What was true for Korea was still more relevant to Indochina. Throughout Canada's involvement in Southeast Asia successive Canadian governments adhered to a principle of minimum involvement. Each sought to reduce political and military commitments to a level consistent with the requirements dictated by a desire to affirm and support the principles of collective security and international peacekeeping. The 'diplomacy of constraint' with respect to American actions in Korea was in fact a logical adjunct to a policy of minimum involvement.

There were undoubtedly a few sympathizers towards America's highly anti-communist line in the Canadian policy community,* but these articulators of the conservative perspective were in a weak position. Similarly, supporters of the left-liberal tendency had to refrain from pressing too vigorously their advocacy of Asian-Commonwealth perspectives. Until 1956 Canada's Asian policy was dominated by the liberal-moderate definition of a reasonable consensus. This consensus may be best interpreted as a floating policy mean which constantly sought the middle ground between the two policy extremes of alliance with the United States in its program of anti-communist containment on the one hand, and sympathy towards the progressive liberal elements of many new, left-wing, nationalist, anti-colonialist governments such as India's, on the other. In his role as secretary of state for external affairs Lester Pearson exemplified the liberal-moderate tendency at work in Canadian Korean decision-making when he said on 4 December 1950:

The Chinese Communists have now made it abundantly clear that they regard United Nations action in Korea as something that menaces their interests so greatly that they are willing to risk a general war in challenging it. Therefore as soon as circumstances make it possible, we must take up again the effort to reconcile on the one hand the determination of the United Nations to resist aggression, and on the other *whatever legitimate interests the Chinese may have in the future of Korea and the adjacent area.* I am not sure that we can reconcile these two – our interests in world peace with the purposes behind their intervention – but we must try.[29]

American leaders were quite unable to speak of the 'legitimate interests' of the communist Chinese because of a swelling chorus of anti-communist hysteria in the United States. By December 1950 the prospects for rational debate on the legitimate security concerns of the PRC had been eliminated by

---

* 'Policy community' is a useful term coined by James Eayrs. See his *In Defence of Canada*, IV *Growing Up Allied* (Toronto, Buffalo, London: University of Toronto Press 1980) 9n.

the cumulative effects of the Soviet detonation of an atomic bomb in the summer of 1949, the 'loss' of China to Mao's armies in the autumn of 1949, the North Korean invasion, the publicity accorded the spy trials, and Senator McCarthy's continuing allegations concerning 'communists in high places.'

Canada's American problem in Asia stemmed from the fact that the US government could not be relied upon to make sensible or prudent decisions about its security commitments to the Pacific 'rimlands.' The recently perceived absolute insecurity of the atomic age had precipitated a geopolitical perspective on the world in Washington that was naïve because it substituted 'bravery for thought' and 'action for reflection,' and ruthlessly calculating because this perspective held that only the most lethal responses would be acknowledged by adversaries who practised totalitarian brutality.[30]

While President Eisenhower was a vital moderating influence within his own administration, his strategic nuclear doctrine, involving as it did vague threats of 'massive retaliation,' unsettling ambiguity for friend and foe alike, and a belief in the value of Dullesian 'brinkmanship,' left much to be desired. The judgment of one of America's finest contemporary historians is apt: 'He [Eisenhower] achieved his goal of greater deterrence at less cost, but only through too casual a willingness to use nuclear weapons in limited war situations, an unnecessary confusion over what, in the Third World, he was trying to deter, a failure to follow through on his own commitment to negotiations, and it must be added, a fair amount of plain good luck.'[31] According to John Lewis Gaddis, Eisenhower also exhibited 'a persistent failure to follow through on his usually quite sound initial instincts a curious unwillingness to grasp the reins of power at all levels.'[32] This 'curious unwillingness' may have been a matter of lack of will and determination, but it may also have reflected a deliberate willingness by Eisenhower to allow low-level deviations in policy implementation from the broad strategic policy objectives of his administration. 'Flexibility' in policy implementation was in all likelihood an inescapable political necessity imposed on Eisenhower by the need to control very divergent political tendencies within his own government.

Following Franz Schurmann,[33] the post-war American debate on foreign policy may be effectively divided into two rival doctrinal approaches. The dominant current in Washington favoured George Kennan's 'containment' concept, which connoted a firm, patient, and inherently defensive response to possible communist-bloc expansion. To supporters of this viewpoint Europe was to be the fundamental concern of American policy-makers. Trade, investments, and shared political values dictated such an approach. Europe as a reviving industrial society had tremendous 'denial value' vis-à-vis Stalin's Soviet empire, which was still trying to recover from the material devastation and the twenty million Soviet deaths caused by World War II. Institutionally the containment approach found favour with a majority of both Congressional parties, but especially the Democratic party, with successive presidents, the State Department, the senior officers of the army, and the analysis section of the Central Intelligence Agency.

In accordance with the rhetoric of the early 1950s Schurmann labelled the second tendency at work in official Washington as the 'Asia-first' policy current. According to articulators of this tendency American objectives were to be based on securing and controlling the unstable but populous societies of Pacific Asia. America's 'natural' field of expansion was said to lie in further moves westward across the Pacific. Expansion of the American sphere of influence was seen as vital: the 'rollback' of the communist sphere of influence was a necessary corollary. Institutionally, articulators of the 'rollback' posture were most commonly found in the right wing of the Republican party, in senior positions of the navy and to a lesser extent the air force, and in the clandestine operations branch of the CIA. Notions of 'preventive war' against the communist bloc, and especially against the new regime in Beijing (referred to by the nationalist Chinese name 'Peiping' well into the 1960s to indicate that the civil war was still in progress), were viewed favourably. To advocates of this policy current the atomic bomb – and later the hydrogen bomb – was 'just another weapon.' The supporters of such 'forward strategies' reasoned that an early confrontation with the Soviet bloc would be a very good thing because the American monopoly in large numbers of deliverable atomic bombs assured the United States of either major communist concessions or an early military victory at relatively low cost.[34] In short, the 'rollback' of the communist bloc's sphere of influence was seen as a practical policy option. Schurmann argues persuasively that the supporters of this approach consistently manoeuvred to try to gain effective control of Washington's strategic decision-making in Pacific Asia. An early war with China was held to be particularly sensible and sentiments along this line intensified as the Chinese moved towards a nuclear capability in the early 1960s. For the nuclear extremist element in Washington politics 'rollback' was never seriously entertained concerning Eastern Europe, although that was the only region publicly named by John Foster Dulles when he spoke of liberating communist-held areas.[35] Asia, not Europe, was most dear to the most bellicose elements of the Washington élite.

Articulators of the Asia-first doctrine were often the most vigorous supporters of the 'domino theory' as applied to Indochina. In its extreme form the concept asserted that the loss of Indochina would inevitably lead to the loss of all Southeast Asia to the communist bloc, to be followed shortly thereafter by the collapse of the offshore island chain up to and including Japan, as well as the fall of Thailand, Burma, and eventually India.[36] Because of the McCarthyite purge of 'China hands' from the State Department during the early 1950s there was an absence of professional expertise (and bureaucratic will) in official circles which might have otherwise negated the empirically suspect premises of the domino theorists.

The steadily growing commitment to the French war effort in Indochina was made necessary by the 'loss' of China. Both the Europe-first containment supporters and the Asia-first advocates were agreed that a firm line had to be drawn against any further spread of communist doctrine. In addition to this the rollback element hoped to generate crises that could be used to catalyse wider political support for a policy of reactivating the Chinese civil war on the mainland. In the spring of 1954 the then chairman of the US Joint Chiefs of Staff, Admiral Arthur Radford, clearly hoped to use the 'crisis' of Dienbienphu to trigger an irrevocable American commitment to 'victory' over Asian communism. At that time Radford advocated massive conventional air strikes by American forces in an attempt to relieve what the Western press were calling 'the gallant defenders of Dienbienphu.' Subsequently, Radford noted that he was at that time quite prepared to recommend the use of atomic weapons if conventional bombing failed to retrieve the situation for the French[37] – a most probable outcome given the lateness of serious American analysis of the intervention option.[38]

The American government eventually decided not to intervene at Dienbienphu, but not before it had explored Radford's proposal thoroughly. Moderates like Eisenhower and Army Chief of Staff General Matthew B. Ridgway had to formulate grounds for rejecting intervention if they were to forestall a political backlash in Congress from allies of the pro-rollback bureaucratic planners. Part of the process of containing Washington's militants at one point (probably early April 1954) involved a direct query to Prime Minister St Laurent and his secretary of state for external affairs L.B. Pearson pursuant to the secret understandings reached under the so-called 'ABC Agreement' (America, Britain, Canada) concluded in Washington in November 1945.[39] President Eisenhower apparently asked on that occasion for Canadian reaction to a possible American atomic strike in Indochina. St Laurent and Pearson objected in the strongest terms. They tried to their utmost to discourage the idea. London apparently reacted in a similar fashion.[40] Accepting Townsend Hoopes's cogent analysis of John Foster

Dulles's objectives at this time, it is probable that both Dulles and Eisenhower may have been looking for external excuses for blocking the advocates of unilateral intervention and massive retaliation within their own government – most notably Admiral Arthur Radford.[41] Pearson and St Laurent could hardly look back on this episode with equanimity. So far as Canadian liberal-moderates were concerned, any talk of breaching the nuclear peace was fundamentally unacceptable.[42] Such ideas emanated from what former Canadian ambassador to Washington, Hume Wrong, politely called 'the unstable and irresponsible side of the United States.'[43] In the end Radford was not even able to secure air-naval strikes from US carriers to help relieve the garrison at Dienbienphu. Lack of allied co-operation, especially lack of British willingness to become involved, was decisive in the defeat of the Radford porposals. On this occasion 'quiet diplomacy' accomplished much.

In Ottawa the thought of initiating nuclear war over strategic stakes that were considerably less than those threatened by all-out Soviet assault on Europe was morally and politically unthinkable. On this point Canadian conservative doctrine was probably in agreement. Canadian attitudes towards nuclear weapons were thus directly antithetical to the objectives of the Asia-first tendency in the American policy debate, which constantly sought to 'normalize' the use of atomic, and later thermonuclear, devices so as to enhance the credibility of threats of massive retaliation which were then the chief instrument of American diplomacy vis-à-vis communist 'salami tactics.' Under Eisenhower's 'New Look' concept for the armed forces, the army and navy budgets at this time were being severely slashed, while the US Air Force had been ordered to drastically expand the mobility, flexibility, and size of its nuclear strike forces in the Strategic Air Command.[44] Economies were effected, but only by generating intolerable risks of a third world war.

In light of the implementation of this policy by Washington in early 1953, and in light of rumours (which were well founded) to the effect that the new administration had threatened the communist Chinese in the spring of 1953 with nuclear assault unless a stable armistice developed in Korea,[45] the query by Eisenhower to St Laurent and Pearson may have come as no surprise. It was surely exceptionally disquieting to the Canadian leaders, reflecting as it did the growing political strength in the United States of the proponents of 'preventive war' (ie, a premeditated, disarming, surprise attack on the PRC and/or the Soviet Union while the US still enjoyed massive nuclear superiority).[46] Canadian diplomats, and Lester Pearson in particular, had been exposed only too directly to the ultra-nationalist policy views held by Washington's atomic 'wild men.'[47]

The Dienbienphu crisis was significant for the framing of future policy because it undoubtedly left a strong impression in Pearson's mind of the fundamental instability of the American policy process. It did not create this impression in the minds of other senior policy-makers or diplomats in the Department of External Affairs: St Laurent and Pearson apparently did not discuss the incident formally within the department.[48] The pattern of American actions in the Korean conflict had generated, however, much the same type of disquiet and concern throughout all ranks in DEA.

When the Korean conflict broke out in June 1950 Canadian policy had attempted to limit the war to the Korean peninsula, to do everything possible to forestall PRC intervention in the dispute, and to block the extension of the conflict to the Taiwan coastal region. Canadian diplomacy did its utmost to restrain, and indeed 'contain,' American activists who wanted to drive to the Yalu or beyond. The Canadians, in conjunction with the other champions of restraint, succeeded in the first and third objectives, but failed of course to realize the second. When Chinese intervention did occur, Ottawa and the proponents of moderation then pressed for early armistice talks and compromises in areas where no vital interests on the United Nations side seemed likely to be prejudiced.[49]

Strategic priorities in Ottawa and Washington were very different. Canadian participation in the Korean 'police action' had not been undertaken because of the perceived strategic importance of the Korean peninsula. Involvement arose out of Canada's United Nations obligations. Disputes were not to be resolved by resort to aggressive force. Illegitimate force had to be met with collective resistance by the international community. But unlike the United States government, Canadian officials were not disposed to fight communism per se, only illicit acts of interstate aggression. Canadian thinking was determined to avoid the Munich syndrome if possible, but it was also alert to the growing risks of another Sarajevo because of the emerging adventurist tendency in US foreign policy in Asia. Much of the credit for such sensitivity must go to Pearson for, in addition to being a master tactician, he was a very capable strategic analyst as well. Pearson's ability to put events in long-term strategic perspective was demonstrated clearly in November 1949 just after proclamation of the People's Republic of China. When others were inclined to read the most dire consequences into the 'fall' of China, Pearson told the Commons' Standing Committee on External Affairs that 'China has usually been able to absorb its outside influences; but sometimes it has taken from fifty to one hundred years to do so.' Getting to the heart of the matter, he noted that 'we must all hope that whatever government is in power and recognized in China will be independent and national.'[50] Chinese independence from Soviet control, not the internal character of Chinese society, was the critical variable for western security planning. Unlike many an American Wall Street lawyer turned strategist, Pearson could impart historical perspective to the flux of current events. Soviet imperial power, not communism, was the chief threat to the West. It would take the American political élite another two decades to appreciate this fact.

Prime Minister St Laurent may indeed have been the strongest critic of even indirect association with the French effort in Indochina, but Pearson and his immediate circle of advisers were also less than eager to step up Canadian support. With staff such as Escott Reid, Chester Ronning, and others pressing for careful consideration of the views of independent Asians, the Ottawa foreign policy community was in no danger of rushing into headlong defence of the French campaign. Involvement militarily, such as it was,* had been pressed upon Canada by both French and American officials via the NATO forum. Alliances can on occasion be used to constrain imprudent hegemons, but the price for buying occasional restraint is often distasteful: in this case a reluctant contribution of weaponry to a neo-colonial war.

It is clear that the prime minister was not happy about any form of assistance to the French military because it 'would involve our assumption of some responsibility for the colonial or dependency burdens of the metropolitan members of NATO, and that is something we originally decided we would not do.' To accommodate the prime minister's declared reservations the cabinet defence committee decided on 26 August 1952 to send equipment requested by France to the NATO Standing Group authorities for them to allocate as they saw fit. The Canadian government would neither approve nor disapprove of the diversion of its mutual aid from France to the French Union Forces in Indochina. Modest practical support was thus given to the French, who were, after all, valued NATO allies fighting alongside the Canadian and American forces in Korea, but without establishing a precedent of formal involvement by Ottawa in the conflict. In March 1953 Foreign Minister Georges Bidault and French Premier René Mayer were turned down

---

* According to James Eayrs, 72 anti-tank guns, anti-aircraft guns, and 14,000 rounds of munitions arrived in Indochina from Canada via France (*In Defence of Canada*, v, *Indochina: Roots of Complicity* [Toronto, Buffalo, London: University of Toronto Press 1983] 26). The Vietminh used neither tanks nor aircraft; thus the shipment seems to have been of negligible military consequence for the French Union effort. Hereafter cited as Eayrs, *Indochina*).

once more by Ottawa when they sought formal authorization for arms transfers to Indochina.*

Pearson was willing enough to give modest rhetorical and material support to the French effort so long as Canada incurred no obligations by doing so. In April 1950 he told Canadian parliamentarians that 'the forces of Soviet communist imperialism' were doing well in Indochina. The rhetoric might have led to more direct measures of support, but for the fact that American behaviour in Korea had not inspired confidence in Pearson – quite the contrary. In April 1951 Pearson learned from British sources that Washington was thinking of supporting Kuomintang landings on the Chinese mainland. Had such assaults, or related aerial bombardment, occurred, Pearson was prepared 'to dissociate Canada from the decision taken.'[51] Such proposals, in addition to the foolhardy invasion of North Korea by General Douglas MacArthur in the autumn of 1950, seem to have convinced Pearson that Indochina policy needed the most circumspect approach. MacArthur's zeal for dramatic intervention and total victory over the forces of darkness represented in microcosm the most perilous aspects of the nationalist, Asia-first tendency in American policy. That approach risked nuclear war willingly, almost casually. Never was America in greater need of counsels of restraint.

In January 1952 Pearson clearly indicated that the Canadian government saw no security obligations for itself arising out of the Indochina conflict. Because there might not be a 'clear-cut breach of the peace' as in Korea, there might be 'no clear-cut basis for collective defence.'[52] In fact, Pearson seems to have meant 'no clear-cut basis for collective security' operations, as these terms are now commonly used (collective defence referring to group measures against third-party aggression; collective security referring to universalist schemes for 'police action' by the international community through its co-operative institutions). Pearson's comment hearkened back to a remark he made one year earlier to Max Freedman of the *Winnipeg Free Press* concerning Korea in which Pearson had indicated a preference for 'selective collective security' so that Ottawa could decide 'where and when and if we will do anything under the Charter.' As John Holmes describes Pearson's assessment of the problem it seems that Pearson was reluctant 'to abandon the

---

* The comment by St Laurent is recorded by James Eayrs in his 'A Blind Eye: The Canadian Position in Indo-China,' *Toronto Star*, 30 Jan. 1975, an article which argues that the decision was an example of 'deception,' not 'discretion,' in decision-making. It is hard to know who was being deceived. In the House of Commons the PC party would have supported formal authorization of shipments. By mid-1954, if not earlier, the trans-shipments of arms were a matter of public discussion. See Douglas Anglin, 'A Difficult First Contact,' *Winnipeg Free Press*, 13 Aug. 1954.

principle of universal collective security lest a failure to respond to any cry for help destroy the authority of the U.N. and the credibility of "the West,"' but he understood too that 'nothing would be more fatal to the organization than to make a desperate military effort and be defeated.'³ Hence, anxiety and tension ensued. Pearson fully appreciated that if and when the 'cry for help' came, the Western nation most inclined and able to respond significantly could do so only with the blunt and barbarous instrument of massive retaliation. In that event, as Pearson rightly noted in February 1954, 'if it becomes a question of the atomic bomb and all-out war, or nothing, it may be, too often, nothing.'⁴

As a recapitulation of Pearson's broad attitude towards collective security under the UN, Holmes's summary is persuasive.* With respect to Indochina in particular, selectivity would reach new heights – and more precise dimensions. Pearson and most other centrists in the policy community in Ottawa wanted no part of any Western collective defence operation that might be hatched by the American Secretary of State John Foster Dulles. To establish this policy St Laurent and Pearson carefully specified the conditions under which Canadian participation in Asian security management might be possible. In September 1952 the prime minister set the tone of the Canadian approach to relations with Asia.

Peace and trade, these are the foundations of our Far Eastern policy as they are of our entire foreign policy. In Korea by counter-force [sic] we are trying to hold back the flood of violence which threatens to engulf all of Asia. In Japan we are working for the restoration of normal diplomatic and trade relationships. And in Southeast Asia through the establishment of the Colombo Plan not only are we trying to provide wider commercial relations, but we are also fighting another Asiatic war against Communism *in the interests of peace, this time with economic rather than military weapons.* We Canadians know that in the struggle against Communism there are two

---

* James Eayrs confuses the paradoxical relation Holmes portrays between Pearson's wanting to sustain the universal collective security principle while fearing simultaneously that the principle in action would fail badly – with Pearson's unfortunate propensity for using the terms collective security and collective defence synonymously (Eayrs, *Indochina* 38n). In the process he appears to attribute to Holmes the same incapacity for distinguishing the now conventional usages of the two terms, a most curious and one hopes inadvertent result. For Holmes's exemplary clarification of the somewhat muddy issue under discussion see *The Shaping of Peace: Canada and the Search for World Order, 1943–1957* (Toronto, Buffalo, London: University of Toronto Press 1982) II, 161–3. In using the terms collective defence and collective security interchangeably, Pearson was not alone in 1952. See, for example, Eayrs's adoption of this procedure in his 'A Pacific Pact: "Step in the Right Direction"?' *International Journal* VII, 4 (Autumn 1952) esp. 293, 300.

useful weapons, the economic and the military. While *we much prefer to use the economic weapons, as we are in the Colombo Plan*, we know that we may have no choice but to use the military weapons as we have been forced to do in Korea.[55]

This speech hinted at what already was effective Canadian policy, a willingness to apply economic assistance to security problems in Asia, but a strong desire to avoid any sort of military involvement. The practical basis for the latter half of this approach had been articulated by Pearson in comments to the Commons' Standing Committee on External Affairs over four months earlier. On that occasion he explicitly rejected any possible role for Canada in defending Formosa. Canada, he said, had no 'special obligation' to protect Chiang Kai-shek's regime, and it would undertake none vis-à-vis possible communist Chinese attack: 'The only possible circumstances which would bring about any obligation on our part would be an attack on Formosa by some other power than the Peking regime.'[56] The only obligations Canada had for contribution to Asian security arose out of United Nations membership and such obligations would not be invoked by any assault by Mao's armies: 'an attack by the Chinese communist government would not be an attack by one state on another. It would be only an incident of the civil war which is going on in China at the present time.'[57]

This formula was of course very relevant for the situation in Indochina. There could be no UN obligations arising out of the Vietminh insurrection. As in the case of China, this was an example of rebellion and civil war, not interstate aggression. If the rule were adhered to strictly, there could be no Canadian obligations arising out of the French 'pacification' effort, a struggle that the French themselves had refused to bring before the United Nations, claiming that it was an internal matter.

While Ottawa's liberal-moderates were busy during 1949–53 framing the policy rationales for non-involvement in possible future conflicts in Asia, a good many influential Americans were working towards opposite objectives. After the retreat of the Kuomintang forces to Taiwan in late 1949, the American military – especially the navy led by Admiral Arthur Radford – had reversed itself and decided that the Nationalist Chinese government should be supported strongly. With the vocal Congressional support of Senators Robert Taft, William Knowland, and Styles Bridges, the American Joint Chiefs of Staff (JCS) increased military assistance to the Kuomintang. As Schurmann notes, until September 1949 the JCS had backed the Truman-Marshall strategic concept of a 'Europe-first' force deployment. By December, because of the psychological impact of the Soviet detonation of its first atomic bomb, the JCS opted to diversify and extend US security commitments to include various Asian 'strong-points.'[58] According to some Republican congressmen, Formosa-Taiwan was much more important than South Korea, since the former represented 'a point in the line of defenses which include Japan, the Philippines, and Okinawa, all essential and vital to the national defense of the United States.'[59]

In due course the navy's position was bolstered and its request to have Taiwan 'protected' was granted. In Schurmann's view, army and air force support had materialized in part because the navy's major weapons requests for 1949 (new aircraft carriers) had been denied flatly and the other joint chiefs were desirous of compensating the navy admirals. Indirect political pressure on the White House helped secure a favourable decision as well. The navy objective of securing Taiwan was partially attained when President Truman ordered the Seventh Fleet to patrol the Taiwan Strait and prevent aggressive moves 'in either direction,' and wholly won when Eisenhower and John Foster Dulles decided to 'unleash' Chiang Kai-shek as one of their first acts in office in 1953. At that time Eisenhower assured the world that 'this order implies no aggressive intent on our part.'[60] But in fact ever since 1950 the American Central Intelligence Agency's clandestine operations section had been actively assisting KMT forces in a campaign of coastal sabotage and blockade. For some three years prior to the formal 'unleashing' of the KMT the US government had covertly encouraged Nationalist Chinese attacks on the mainland. As Schurmann interprets Washington politics during this period, 'since Washington's dominant policies eschewed rollback, something had to be given to minority bureaucratic interests to compensate them for their policy losses. Covert war in East Asia was the "compromise" form that rollback took.'[61]

Covert war, according to Schurmann, involved 'far-reaching programs of dropping arms to insurgents in China, landing commandos on the China coast, and sending sabotage teams deep into Chinese territory.' Raids and sabotage against communist troop positions were conducted in Vietnam, Laos, and southern China. Bombing raids by American-supplied KMT aircraft on the mainland port cities within range of Taiwan kept the population of southern China in serious difficulties because these cities had traditionally relied on imported food.[62] Thus despite Truman's attempt to foster a nominal American neutrality in the Chinese civil war, the Beijing government could hardly find the stance credible when Chiang was being actively counselled by CIA operatives; by Admiral Charles M. Cooke, a former commander of the Seventh Fleet; and by Claire Chennault (of flying Tiger fame), who had proposed to friends in Washington the creation of another 'private' air armada to assist the KMT in the rollback of the PRC state.[63]

It is not clear to what extent leadership in Ottawa was aware of American covert operations along the Chinese coast, or in Southeast Asia. In oral interviews none alluded to the US 'presence' as possible grounds for avoiding the ICSC invitation. One senior official intimated that Ottawa and all other NATO capitals were kept in the dark concerning such operations, since there was no explicit obligation to inform other member states in the NATO organization. However, it is possible that Canadian diplomats might have had some suspicions of American activities, possibly through contacts in New Delhi who were confidants of the new Chinese regime. If Pearson was aware of the American campaign he evidently left no public indication of it, or any private communications on the subject. In any case, one can be confident that had Pearson and the senior DEA staff been made aware of the continuing American efforts to harass Mao's regime through covert means, their determination to avoid involvement in potential open warfare in East Asia would have been dramatically reinforced.

Globally Pearson sought stability and equilibrium, not confrontation. He was very unhappy with the French campaign in Indochina, 'a running sore' he termed it, because it meant that France could not 'build up forces for the defence of Western Europe as quickly and effectively as she would otherwise have been able to do.'[64] In this respect he reluctantly acknowledged that the NATO front and the Indochinese conflict were connected. The war in Indochina was blocking an active role by the French in NATO and thereby exacerbating popular French fears that in any European defence community (a scheme for integrated European collective defence to supplement NATO and provide for the rearmament of Germany) the German armed forces would predominate by default. In such a climate Pearson knew that the EDC legislation before the French Assembly stood a decreasing probability of approval. Neither would the French be willing to accommodate German rearmament outside EDC. This would leave the Germans terribly insecure, a result that would not be conducive to the stabilization of liberal-democratic government in Germany. Assisting Germany's transition to stable democratic government was one of Pearson's highest priorities in the early 1950s.[65]

On several occasions Pearson paid lip-service to the domino theory,[66] but though familiar with the lyrics he was not very conversant with the melody. To Pearson, working to preserve the independent non-communist character of Japan and the independence of China from Soviet control was a rational and feasible objective for Western policy in Asia.[67] Pearson was particularly distressed at the possible bellicosity of the incoming Eisenhower-Dulles team in the early 1950s and explicitly cautioned against the consideration of nuclear warfare in Korea in February of that year many weeks before the articulation of the threat to Beijing by Eisenhower and Dulles. On that occasion Pearson criticized American 'emotionalism' concerning China and noted that it carried with it the risk of short-sighted imprudent US action in Korea that might very well precipitate 'war on the mainland of China, which it is clear would not stop there.' He criticized Dulles's talk about hitting 'the aggressor in new places with new weapons' by observing dryly that 'it is wise to realize that in consequence he may hit us somewhere else with new weapons. There are for instance about two million people on the very small and rocky island of Hong Kong.'[68] Finally, Pearson was upset by the fact that the militant nuclear extremists in the US were contemplating use of atomic weapons once more against an Asian population.[69] Even if a third world war did not ensue, the United States and its allies would stand convicted before the people of non-aligned Asia as wicked, irremediably racist governments.

All of Pearson's concerns were justified. Although Eisenhower had not been enthusiastic about using nuclear weapons in Korea because Chinese troops were so well dug into their positions, he did see value for them against 'strategic targets in North Korea, Manchuria and off the Chinese coast.'[70] Eisenhower did not believe in widening and deepening the nuclear threshold. He was, in fact, an early advocate of counter-force nuclear targetting. In March 1955 he commented: 'Where these things [nuclear weapons] can be used on strictly military targets for strictly military purposes, I see no reason why they shouldn't be used just exactly as you would use a bullet or anything else.'[71] The general approach he would follow towards the communists, said the president to assembled congressmen from both parties in December 1954, was 'to blow hell out of them in a hurry if they start anything.' Early in 1955 Eisenhower formally authorized first-use resort to tactical nuclear warfare in limited war 'local situations,' 'if such use will bring the aggression to a swift and positive cessation.' By contrast, Pearson's philosophy was that 'use of the ultimate weapon should be kept ultimate.'[72]

The tension between Ottawa and Washington on nuclear weapons employment policy (a concise phrase now fashionable in strategic analysis) did not abate. In September 1953 Dulles explicitly linked the threat of massive retaliation to Indochina by declaring that if Chinese troops intervened directly in the fighting, 'a second aggression could not occur without grave consequences which might not be confined to Indochina.'[73] Pearson responded via an article in an American magazine, *World*, with the title 'Don't Let Asia Split the West.' In it he asserted:

We must not compromise with Communist aggression. *This does not mean, however, that we should assume that every anti-colonial, nationalist or revolutionary movement is Russian Communist in origin or direction*, any more than we should assume that with patience and sympathy *every Asian Communist leader can be turned into a Tito* ... We must *avoid taking up rigid and inflexible positions based on emotion rather than intelligence*, on short-term rather than long-term considerations ... Our policy in Asia must be more than a policy of mere opposition to Communism. It must be constructive; and *anti-communism should not be the only claim to our assistance.*[74]

This article constituted a minor landmark in Canadian Indochina policy. The publication of Pearson's views in December 1953 foreshadowed the stance St Laurent would take in New Delhi only weeks later. The views contained in this article can be seen as a declaration of independence: independence from American attempts to forge a tight anti-communist alliance in Asia firmly under the control of Washington's chief policy-makers.

On Asian policy Pearson and St Laurent were looking for diplomatic allies who might help their efforts to moderate American enthusiasm for 'victory' in whatever theatres the Cold War turned hot. Ultimately such allies would be found: in London, where Prime Minister Winston Churchill and his foreign minister Anthony Eden took an equally jaundiced view of American nuclear extremism; and in Paris, where political leadership was increasingly beleaguered by a hostile electorate who wanted an early end to 'the dirty war.'

In Canada the government's policy came under criticism from both right and left. The leaders of the Cooperative Commonwealth Federation party were mildly unhappy at what they saw as Canadian deference during the NATO Lisbon Conference of 1952 to Pentagon demands for allied support of the Indochina war. M.J. Coldwell was evidently worried that the indirect aid Canada was giving to France might somehow grow into formal participation. He constantly sought, and received, assurances that Canada had made no formal commitments to the Indochina conflict. Of the opposition parties in the House of Commons the CCF was the most satisfied with the government's line. The Progressive Conservative party under George Drew, and the Social Credit party under Solon Low, took a strongly pro-involvement stance. In January 1954, Drew denounced the 'mass murderers,' Chou En-lai and Mao Tse-tung, who he said headed a 'puppet government' that directed a system of 'ghastly slavery.' Drew opposed 'appeasement' of China in any way. Compromise and even negotiations with the communists were to be avoided: 'in Canada we want no bargain with the devil.'[75] Mr Low opposed 'appeasement' through negotiations in still stronger terms. He also indicated to the Commons in November 1953 that he felt that 'this evil thing, communism, could easily have been stopped by courageous and decisive action,' but because of 'perfidious men in high places in the free countries, and too many others who chose to remain blind to what was going on around them ... no really effective countermeasures have ever been taken.'[76] In these darker days of the Cold War such language was common. Although McCarthyite hysteria did not come to Canada, some of McCarthy's ideas and terminology did.

The parliamentary right in general stood for dogmatic inflexibility and uncritical support for collective defence against any form of 'communist aggression.' Politicians on the right were distinctly unhappy with Pearson's insistence on flexibility, accommodation of legitimate Chinese interests, and a willingness to support a negotiated end to the Franco-Vietminh war.

Pearson forged on despite the lingering spectre of McCarthyite criticism at home (Senator Joseph McCarthy was not cast into political decline until his televised performance in the 'army-McCarthy' hearings of May–June 1954 shocked the United States and provoked official Senate censure in December). Although Pearson and his advisers were largely ignorant of the details of the struggle in Indochina, his strategic calculations about Asian policy were sound. On the same day that Drew denounced 'bargaining with the devil,' Pearson warned the House against automatic approval of anti-communist intervention: 'as I see it, by associating counter-revolution which can develop indigenously as the whole history of China shows, with foreign intervention and foreign assistance we may strengthen rather than weaken communist regimes.' The correct road for Canada, he suggested, was constructive action through the Commonwealth.[77] For Pearson and his prime minister economic assistance was the preferred avenue for action.

Just as Canada was firming up its commitment to non-intervention, officials in Washington were moving in opposite directions. The US chief of naval operations, Admiral Robert Anderson, called for the deployment of 'combat forces in Indochina on the "reasonable assurance of strong indigenous support of our forces," whether or not the French government approved.'[78] Other naval personnel and army officers were upset at what they regarded as a fallacious assumption that American 'air-naval assistance' (ie, carrier-based air attacks) alone would turn the tide for the French. In the autumn of 1953 General Henri Navarre embarked on a new build-up of FUF troop levels. Washington defence planners believed that Navarre's concept, while sound on paper, was unlikely to succeed without genuine political independence for the three Associated States. A vigorous inter-agency debate ensued in the first months of 1954 as Navarre's forces headed for what would prove to be their final showdown with Vo Nguyen Giap's army at the 'fortress' at Dienbienphu (the so-called fortress was an unprepared valley floor that offered no protection from artillery fire from adjacent high ground). Supporters of intervention tended to believe that there was a 'monolithic communist expansionary bloc' which had to be stopped, that the loss of China to Soviet control 'could have been averted.' As one Pentagon analyst commented, 'a few' defence officials 'hoped [the loss] would still be reversed.'[79] These latter individuals constituted the dangerously 'emotional' minority in Washington whom Pearson feared.

Between January and the end of March 1954 a debate unfolded among the three services over the issue of possible US intervention. Eventually the army under General Matthew Ridgway dissented from the view that air and naval forces alone could be employed, and questioned the value of committing ground troops that were needed for NATO duty.[80] Faced with strong army objections the JCS backed off and recommended in effect that strong pressure be applied to the French to 'Vietnamize' the FUF effort. Part of the JCS reluctance to press its pro-intervention case can be attributed also to the lack of support from Dulles, who because of his concern for effecting governmental expenditure reductions was less than eager to embark so soon on a second land war in Asia.[81] Dulles was an altogether atypical militant. He espoused rollback where possible, and in Asia in particular, but he was also determined to 'draw the line' and undertake such counter-revolutionary probes at least cost to the US treasury. If the line in Indochina could be held at the Chinese border using only American Mutual Defense Assistance Program funds and Franco-Vietnamese troops so much the better. If FUF proved incapable of handling the task alone, and especially if Chinese troops intervened as 'volunteers' as they did in Korea, then Dulles's fallback position would be to press for some form of multilateral military action. Both Dulles and Eisenhower were quite determined that the United States would not bear the burden of containment in Indochina alone, particularly in a war that remained tainted with colonialist overtones.[82]

Between the autumn of 1953 and February 1954, the military situation had deteriorated badly for the French. By November 1953 it was obvious that the Laniel-Bidault government was willing to negotiate a peace in Indochina, if possible. General Navarre nevertheless went ahead with his ill-conceived plan to deploy troops at Dienbienphu. The French response to the mounting pressure on Dienbienphu was to send General Paul Ely to Washington to enlist further American support. Originally the Ely Mission was intended to extract an undertaking from Washington that it would offset (and deter if possible) use of Chinese MIG-15 jet fighters over Dienbienphu. By the time Ely arrived in Washington the battle had been transformed, but not with jet aircraft – only Chinese advisers and artillery. At this point Ely pressed for American air support and Admiral Radford responded favourably by promising more B-26 light bombers for FUF while implying that he certainly would personally favour American B-29 heavy bomber missions covered by carrier-based naval fighters to relieve Dienbienphu if the 'fortress' was in clear danger of collapse.[83] Radford's plans to get Operation Vulture (Vautour) into action, whereby some sixty B-29s from Clark Field would carpet-bomb the hills about Dienbienphu,[84] provoked consternation on Dulles's part because he feared that some French leaders might 'be preparing to place upon us responsibility if Dien Bien Phu should fall.'[85] Given Radford's uncompromising support for relief of the garrison and his announced willingness to go nuclear when necessary, the French were somewhat confused when both Eisenhower and Dulles spoke to Ely in terms of the a priori political conditions under which US intervention might be considered.

On 29 March 1954 Dulles gave a major speech to the Overseas Press Club in New York in which he declared that the communist great powers were clearly bent on overrunning all of Southeast Asia, a region with 'many raw materials,' 'tremendous economic values,' and 'great strategic value.' He therefore declared that the threat to the 'whole free community ... should be met by united action.'[86] On 31 March Pearson addressed the Commons and refused to accept the too vague principle of 'united action.' He supported the idea of collective action by Western governments, but only if such action was measured, restrained, and defensive; moreover, he did not indicate that the Canadian government was willing to consider participation in such action.[87]

The Canadian government was clearly worried about an attempted American draft of Canada for service in the collective defence of Southeast Asia. The Canadian Embassy was instructed to ascertain details of Dulles's thinking on 'united action.' On 6 April Douglas MacArthur II of the State Department told the Canadian ambassador, Arnold Heeney, that the French seemed to be on the verge of collapse in Indochina and that Dulles was hoping to forestall such collapse. MacArthur then 'expressed the hope that Canada would support steps to prevent Southeast Asia from falling into Communist hands.'[88] The following day Secretary of State Dulles was no doubt disappointed to learn, again in conversation with Heeney, that Pearson had recently publicly indicated that 'Canada's commitments in the Far East' were 'closely tied to the United Nations'.' In reply to what Dulles probably felt, and accurately so, was a preliminary evasive move by Ottawa, the secretary of state noted that he was trying to persuade the French to put Indochina before the UN. He also noted that any such move by France to internationalize their war effort by obtaining UN support would face 'a Soviet veto in the first instance, and it was at least uncertain that we could get quick and satisfactory action in the U.N.' That probability undoubtedly had long figured in Canadian policy calculations, aimed as they were at precluding Canadian involvement in the conflict. Pearson was probably less than enthusiastic when Ambassador Heeney reported that Dulles went on to say that he hoped to secure UN action, if the opportunity arose, through Article 51 of its charter and the invocation of the Uniting for Peace Resolution.[89]

Clearly Pearson was under pressure to affirm his government's general commitment to the containment principle and its specific application to Asia. Pearson may have believed that a Korean-style invasion in Indochina by Chinese troops would justify comparable collective action by the Western powers. However, it was also clear that there might not ever be any overt Chinese intervention or 'aggression.' Furthermore, the French were still attempting to maintain their precarious colonial control over the Associated States, while French tactics against the Vietminh guerrilla campaign seemed ineffectual to say the least. In this ambiguous situation, caution was the order of the day. Pearson had earlier indicated that the government would be 'sympathetic' to discussion concerning Canadian membership in the ANZUS Pact.[90] However, this essentially irrelevant offer was made to try to assuage the opposition critics who were then attacking the dilatory and evasive response to the call for 'united action.'

Pearson's Progressive Conservative parliamentary critics had already denounced the convening of the Geneva Conference as a victory for the Soviet Union,[91] called for Canadian participation in the ANZUS Pact as well as in some organizational equivalent of NATO for the South Pacific region,[92] proposed the dispatch of four Canadian divisions to Indochina to help the FUF effort,[93] reiterated Dulles's call only to 'negotiate from strength,'[94] and asserted that the Vietminh war effort would collapse immediately without Chinese support. Their rhetoric was so lurid that Pearson pointedly asked them to tone down the 'pretty violent language' being used given the little time left before the start of the Geneva Conference.[95]

The cause of these 'systemist' policy recommendations (most notably the four divisions proposal) was Pearson's refusal to budge from his 'no participation without UN umbrella' policy formula, which he had reaffirmed on 25 March,[96] in the course of an address which strongly criticized Dulles's 12 January policy statement on massive retaliation. In that same speech he had argued strongly for the value of negotiating with the Soviet and Communist Chinese leaders, refusing to accept Progressive Conservative and Social Credit charges that it would lead to Munich-style appeasement of aggression. He even went so far as to indicate governmental willingness to consider the extension of de facto recognition of the PRC prior to the convening of the Geneva Conference on 26 April.[97]

In all probability the Eisenhower-Dulles telephone query to St Laurent and Pearson concerning the possible use of atomic weapons occurred sometime just prior to the crucial 3 April meeting of Dulles, Radford, and eight leading congressional figures.[98] That meeting featured yet another Radford scheme for air-naval relief of Dienbienphu, this time attacks from 200 aircraft aboard the carriers *Essex* and *Boxer* that were already on station in the South China Sea. The carriers had atomic weapons on board, but their use was not considered except in the event of 'a massive Chinese troop intervention' which might then have led to retaliation 'with strategic nuclear weapons against targets in China.' The meeting ended with the five Democratic and three Republican congressmen refusing support unless US intervention included coalition partners, and unless the French accelerated the devolution process and promised to continue their involvement after independence.[99]

Churchill and Eden refused to go along with the 'united action' concept partly because they refused to accept the domino principle as the Americans were presenting it, second because they felt joint intervention was likely to precipitate the Chinese intervention that Dulles wished to deter, and third because they felt the Pentagon's military planning was ill conceived and quite impractical. They did, however, see some merit in a collective approach to security problems in Southeast Asia and they indicated a theoretical interest in the subject to Dulles. This proved to be a tactical error because it eventually gave rise to the most severe mutual recriminations. When Dulles demanded concrete action on a pact the British responded by saying that the talks were merely exploratory and that nothing was to be firmed up before the conference in any case. Dulles then charged the British with bad faith. The British saw themselves as victims of attempted manipulation.

The French rejected the scheme out of hand because they still wished to sustain strategic direction of the war and political control in Indochina. In addition they were virtually paralysed by the increasingly desperate situation of the garrison at Dienbienphu.[100] Despite rejections, Dulles persisted in his collective defence proposals through late April and May hoping to include Britain, France, the Associated States of Indochina, Australia, New Zealand, Thailand, and the Philippines in a new US-led treaty group. Canada was on no one's list,[101] probably because of the lukewarm reaction shown thus far by both St Laurent and Pearson, in particular the non-committal response provided by Heeney to Dulles on 7 April.

The day before the Dulles-Heeney conversation Pearson had once more appeared before the Standing Commitee. He came under constant pressure from Progressive Conservatives present to explain the government's policy in light of allegations on 5 April by Dulles of stepped-up communist Chinese involvement (Chinese manning of anti-aircraft artillery near Dienbienphu). When queried about the conditions under which US retaliation might occur – 'action which might not be confined to Indochina' – Pearson said there was 'a difference of degree if not kind between Chinese intervention as alleged yesterday [and] ... the movement across the border of a mass of Chinese forces ... formally taking part in the war.' Pearson went on to say that any possible US retaliation 'should require consultation before any action of that kind is taken.' He also reiterated Canada's highly circumscribed obligations: 'So far as our obligation in Indo-China is concerned it arises because of our membership in the United Nations and the pledges we have taken under the United Nations charter to cooperate in resistance to aggression. That was the basis of intervening in Korea and that basis does not exist at the present time in Indo-China.' After further questioning Pearson restated this latter point when CCF MP Stanley Knowles sought additional reassurance. To mollify anti-communist critics of his stand such as George Pearkes and Howard Green, who were attempting to underscore the government's lack of solidarity with the United States in the face of communist Chinese 'aggression,' he added that he was 'aware of the importance of what is going in Indo-China and what it means in the struggle between communist forces and the forces on our side.'[102] That statement could be interpreted in several ways.

One week later Pearson appeared before the committee once again. Given Dulles's trip to London in the interim to seek support for joint intervention, Stanley Knowles again sought reassurance that Canada was still not involved. Pearson accurately noted that there had been no change in Canada's 'formal and legal commitments,' that Dulles had briefed Ambassador Heeney but had made no 'suggestions for Canadian action' (which was quite true), and that Ottawa approved the formation of 'some sort of collective security system' for Indochina.[103] On this latter point Pearson may have really meant collective defence. It is also quite possible, and here Eayrs's account is too categorical, that he meant collective security as we now understand it. By mid-April London was thinking certainly of 'some sort of col-

lective security system' for Indochina – but not on NATO lines. Eden's theoretical model was the Locarno Pact* of 1925, which was decidedly less provocative in Eden's mind and therefore much more suitable as the basis for
mutual accommodation in Southeast Asia with China.

On 26 April St Laurent repeated Pearson's formula of 25 March (no participation without a UN framework) and ruled out any other role for the
country. According to the prime minister: 'the government has taken the
position that it was not directly participating in what was taking place in
Indochina, and, as a consequence, that it had no standing to participate in
decisions which might be made with respect to military action in Indochina.'[104] This was not quite true given the categorically negative Canadian
'vote' on atomic strikes, but St Laurent's partial deception is certainly excusable in retrospect. Nuclear weapons employment policy was surely part of a
much larger strategic issue area where Ottawa clearly did have a justifiable
role. St Laurent backed Pearson's independent stand on Asia policy to the
hilt. He too shared Pearson's belief that the Chinese communist regime
should be recognized and its interests accommodated.[105]

Though leaving the door open to involvement ever so slightly, both St
Laurent and Pearson had made their preference for non-intervention clear.
At a time when the Anglo-American alliance was close to rupture, the Canadian leaders were in nearly complete agreement with the British approach.
Pearson in particular had expressed extreme irritation with Dulles's methods
and had taken issue publicly with the US secretary's attempt to invoke the
'massive retaliation' doctrine with respect to the Indochina conflict. The

---

* The Locarno Pact confirmed the inviolability of the boundaries between Germany and
  Belgium and Germany and France, as well as the status of the demilitarized zone of the
  Rhineland. France, Germany, and Belgium signed the treaty. Britain and Italy guaranteed
  its terms. The treaty was respected until Hitler's occupation of the Rhineland in March
  1936. Eden attempted to sell the Locarno concept to Dulles in June 1954 by noting that
  under the Locarno system any of the signatories or guarantors could act unilaterally to
  redress violations. Eden indicated to Dulles both a British desire for a wider system of
  guarantees to include the Soviet Union and China, as well as a willingness to consider
  some arrangement for collective defence against possible communist aggression. Dulles
  refused US participation in the preferred British approach (Locarno) noting that it
  required 'Congress to guarantee, in effect, the communist domination of North Vietnam.' Anthony Eden, *The Memoirs of Sir Anthony Eden: Full Circle* (London: Cassel 1960)
  132. Eden may also have been attracted to Locarno because it helped to rehabilitate Germany's status after World War 1. He may have harboured fantasies about a similar
  'rehabilitation' for China. On that score Dulles was the realist. The limits of congressional tolerance were not sufficiently broad.

Canadian government sincerely hoped that the Geneva Conference would produce agreements of substance which the Western countries could accept. British assessments of Indochina had been very influential in Ottawa.[106] But despite the pragmatic and sensibly realistic character of the British perspective, neither Eden nor his senior officers were intimately acquainted with the political complexities of the Indochina situation. They did not foresee the one enormous obstacle to any 'rational' scheme based on partition: the violent opposition of the North Vietnamese to partition of their country. Notwithstanding that judgmental oversight, Eden was considerably more restrained and balanced in his evaluation of the 'threat' to the West posed by the Vietminh insurgency than any of the Americans involved. Where Dulles saw Indochina as akin to the Japanese invasion of Manchuria in 1931 or Hitler's reoccupation of the Rhineland in 1936, Eden saw the Malayan insurgency on a larger scale. Where Dulles feared another Munich, Eden sought a new Locarno, though the very mention of the latter by Eden and Churchill to leading Americans provoked anger and charges of 'sell-out.' Congressional leaders incorrectly considered the two agreements to be similar if not identical.

The Locarno concept was appealing to Ottawa, and so too was British emphasis on taking into consideration the views and policies of the Indian government. Eden for one felt that the Geneva Conference's outcome would depend 'to a considerable extent upon the position taken up by India and other Eastern nations with an interest in a settlement.' He believed that 'it was essential not to alienate India by our actions in a part of the world which concerned her closely.'[107] The Canadian government concurred. According to Escott Reid, 'the search for policies acceptable to India and satisfactory to the United States was one of the principal features of Canadian diplomacy under St. Laurent and Pearson. It was the essence of the special relationship which then existed between Canada and India.'[108] And for India the highest foreign policy priority of early 1954 was its effort to make the Geneva Conference a success. The Indo-Canadian 'special relationship' held up in the spring and summer of 1954. Both countries were highly active in the complex diplomacy of the conference, and both were duly awarded the dubious honour of attempting to implement and stabilize the armistice for Indochina that eventually was negotiated at Geneva. As Reid sadly noted,[109] the special relationship ultimately foundered, in large part because of tensions between the two governments over Indochina policy. Nevertheless, for nearly a decade the two countries mounted a responsible and internationally significant truce supervisory operation.

CONCLUSION

Canadian Indochina policy prior to the Geneva Conference was informed by a rational conception of the country's interests: minimization of the risk of escalation of the conflict to tactical nuclear warfare, given Canadian, British, and Indian fears that this would precipitate a third world war; termination of the Franco-Vietminh war at the earliest possible date by negotiated concessions to the communist side if necessary, so as to end the depletion of French military strength that was preventing an effective French contribution in NATO; encouragement of further international tension reduction, now that Korea was stabilized and now that Moscow and Beijing seemed inclined towards détente; and last, the prevention of direct Canadian military involvement in the conflict should the Geneva talks fail, but in such a way that Canada's NATO allies would not be offended.

Those who would search only for the roots of Canadian 'complicity' in America's later intervention err by applying a standard of evaluation that is both reductive and unhelpful. The logic of Canadian policy was coherent, its implementation measured, and the results constructive. A strategy of denunciation of the neo-colonial aspect of the war was not realistic. It would have alienated the French and seriously disrupted NATO's internal politics. Canadian interests lay in helping the French retreat from Indochina, not tallying up in public the injustices committed by France during its colonial occupation. By the early months of 1954 Ottawa was in league with the supporters of inter-bloc accommodation in London, Paris, and New Delhi. The Canadian foreign policy community saw that the Western states had few if any vital interests in Vietnam per se – only an interest in containing the further spread of communist influence by shoring up the perimeter of anti-communist resistance at plausibly defensible points. Unlike the 'emotional' fanatics in the US Congress or in some quarters of the American executive branch, the Canadian government could live with a spheres-of-influence partition of Indochina. In this respect Canadian policy was both realistic and prudent. The outstanding difficulty to be resolved as the May 1954 sessions on Indochina loomed was the concrete character of the Indochina compromise. Was partition of Indochina feasible? If so, along what boundaries? This, the hardest question, was yet to be faced.

From 1950 to 1954 the government's position on Indochina policy had gradually shifted leftward (see figure 2) from a marginalist conservative position, under conditions of comparative ignorance and no real threat of involvement, to a marginalist liberal-moderate stance, characterized by greater understanding of the problem and a rapidly increasing threat of

FIGURE 2
The first tendency shift in the governmental Indochina policy consensus, spring 1954
Fundamental value commitment

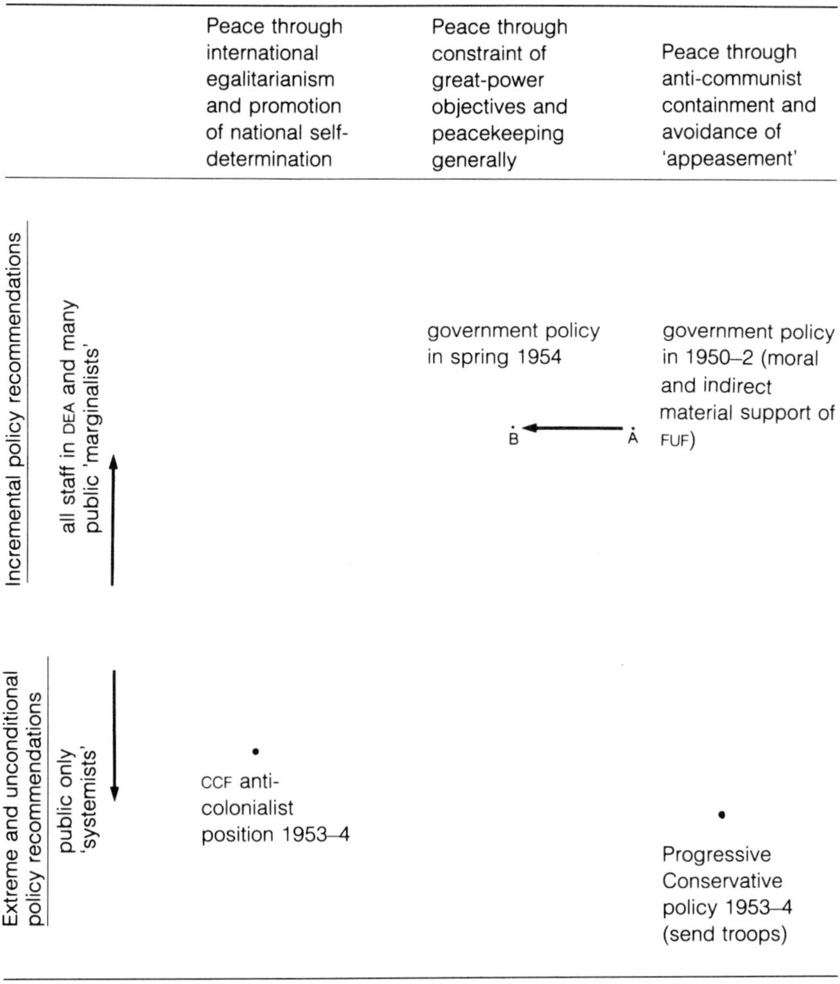

	Peace through international egalitarianism and promotion of national self-determination	Peace through constraint of great-power objectives and peacekeeping generally	Peace through anti-communist containment and avoidance of 'appeasement'

Incremental policy recommendations

all staff in DEA and many public 'marginalists'

government policy in spring 1954

government policy in 1950–2 (moral and indirect material support of FUF)

Ḃ ◄───── Ȧ

Extreme and unconditional policy recommendations

public only 'systemists'

•

CCF anti-colonialist position 1953–4

•

Progressive Conservative policy 1953–4 (send troops)

involvement. This was but the first of several swings in the Indochina policy pendulum. In the 1950–4 period the dominant factor causing this first tendency shift was almost certainly the growing perception in Ottawa of a trend towards nuclear adventurism in American foreign policy. A liberal-moderate strategy of damage limitation was thus wholly in order.

3

The descent begins:
from Geneva to the jungles

It must be recognized ... that fear of massive American retaliation must have played a powerful role in Communist willingness to seek a truce. If Dulles' policy had been calculated brinkmanship it would have made sense. There is every evidence, however, that he was quite serious about keeping up the fighting.

John W. Holmes[1]

THE KOREAN SECTION OF THE GENEVA NEGOTIATIONS

John Foster Dulles set the tone for the American role at Geneva by denouncing the Soviet Union and 'its satellites' as 'a vast monolithic system which, despite its power, believes that it cannot survive except as it succeeds in progressively destroying human freedom.'[2] These comments made during his first address to the plenary sessions indicated that so far as the American secretary of state was concerned, America would be no party to shameful compromise. Dulles understood clearly that the Asia-first elements in Congress would never accept an accommodation with the Chinese, although they might be persuaded to let other Western allies effect such compromises. Dulles himself seems to have given his blessing to the formula: containment in Europe, harassment and 'rollback' in Pacific Asia. It was for this reason that he spurned Chou En-lai's handshake at Geneva, for it would have symbolized a commitment to containment policies in Asia, rather than the more aggressive posture of rollback, and thus would have violated the essence of the bureaucratic compromise which lay at the heart of the Eisenhower administration.[3]

From 26 April to 15 June delegations from nineteen countries including Canada attended fourteen plenary sessions and one restricted session 'for the purpose of reaching a peaceful settlement of the Korean question.'[4] No agreement was reached. From 7 May until 21 July the governments of the United States, Britain, France, the Associated States of Indochina, the Democratic Republic of Vietnam, the Soviet Union, and the People's Republic of China held sessions on the status of Indochina, also in an effort to negotiate a peace settlement. A limited peace agreement would be negotiated, but not a settlement worthy of the name. The Indochina sessions were held interspersed among, and sometimes concurrently with, the Korean sessions until 15 June when the Korean talks were adjourned indefinitely. Canada, although not an invited party to the Indochina sessions, was nevertheless able to contribute informally to the progress of those talks until mid-June when its representatives departed. India was also a factor in the Indochina talks thanks to the energetic diplomacy of V.K. Krishna Menon, someone who, like the Canadians, felt that it was very much in the common interest that a settlement should emerge.

It was no secret that the Indochina sessions had begun with the Western powers in serious disarray. Just as Pearson had feared, Asia had 'split the West,' although the secretary of state for external affairs did his best to downplay the divisions in public. The British had gone to Geneva without making any firm commitment to a collective defence pact for Southeast Asia. Dulles felt betrayed and angry. Consultations on this proposed alliance continued haphazardly in tandem with the Geneva negotiations. The communist delegations were well aware of Dulles's efforts in this regard. These 'secret' talks would eventually bear fruit at Manila on 8 September 1954 with the signing of the Southeast Asia Collective Defence treaty by the United States, Britain, France, Thailand, the Philippines, Pakistan, Australia, and New Zealand. At no point was Canada asked to consider membership, nor did Ottawa inquire.

All governments were aware of the high stakes in the Indochina negotiations, and thus the Korean section was very much of a sideshow. Anglo-American differences in the Indochina talks apparently contributed significantly to difficulties between the British and the Americans in the Korean section of the negotiations. Despite pleas to the contrary by Canada and other lesser powers the American posture in both forums was characterized by dogmatic inflexibility and stern self-righteousness. The British were not prepared to dissent from Washington's line in both sections (recognizing full well where the priority effort had to be made), and thus they refused to criticize the American approach in the Korean section.

The only concession to flexibility made by the US and South Korean delegations to their UN allies was to drop their initial proposal for elections held only in North Korea, and substitute a very remotely feasible plan for a

UN-supervised census of the entire peninsula to be followed by a UN-supervised general election based on representation by population – in which the South thereby would have twice the number of representatives of the North.[5] The North Korean and Soviet delegates refused this scheme and proposed instead a plan featuring a veto system over candidate nominations which they clearly hoped would either work to their narrow advantage or halt the talks. A deadlock ensued. Chester Ronning as acting head of the Canadian delegation accurately noted that the nub of the electoral problem was the absence of real democratic freedom in the north, and the North Koreans' unwillingness to alter this condition.[6]

During the internal UN-side debate the Canadians and the New Zealanders strongly pressed for a non-communist but non-combatant supervisory body. Their tactical line angered the Americans greatly and was voted down thirteen to two. Public unity of the UN group was preserved, but the Canadian representatives privately 'reserved their freedom of action in the event of a future conference.'[7] The Korean portion of the conference adjourned sine die on 15 June for lack of any basis for agreement. The two remaining Canadian delegates, John Holmes and Chester Ronning, left shortly thereafter.

During the Korean talks Pearson modified the government's stand slightly concerning possible membership in a collective security pact for the Pacific Asian area. He noted on 28 May to the Commons that 'the international communist conspiracy ... has made progress in securing control of southeast Asia,' and that 'this was a danger which cannot be exorcised by comforting interpretations of Asian communism as merely agrarian reform or as nationalism painted red.'[8] This apparent swing to a more conservative perspective was actually no more than rhetorical sugar-coating on a bitter policy pill to be administered to the Progressive Conservative and Social Credit advocates of Cold War confrontation, non-appeasement, and Canadian accession to the proposed 'Pacific pact.' Involvement by Canada in Pacific collective security operations aimed at Indochina, said Pearson, now depended upon five conditions: any such multilateral action must conform to the UN Charter; it had to be divorced from all elements of colonialism; it had to be more than a military alliance; it had to meet with the will of the people directly concerned; and finally, other 'free Asian states' had to support it directly or in principle.[9] A sixth condition was also made explicit further on in Pearson's remarks: that France had to refer Indochina to the United Nations before Ottawa would look seriously at collective security involvement in Southeast Asia.[10] In sum, these conditions created, if adhered to strictly, an airtight basis for non-involvement in the Indochinese fighting. None of the major

Western powers was interested in concluding a collective defence treaty that was 'more than a military alliance.' France was not likely to agree willingly to the complete extinguishing of its colonial privileges in the region. And the 'free Asian states' such as India would never approve existing American schemes, premised as they were on participation by the former colonial powers. Given the past record of determination not to refer the conflict to the UN, it was also highly unlikely that France would change its approach in that regard at this late date. Pearson's defence of this strategy of evasion lay in his assertion that Canada had its capabilities stretched to the limits in attempting to meet its existing security commitments in North America and Western Europe. So far as alliances were concerned, NATO was enough. According to Pearson, 'Canada cannot be expected to accept special or regional defence commitments in every part of the world where collective agreements may be advisable.'[11]

The Progressive Conservatives were not happy with the government's plea of limited resources.* On the same day John Diefenbaker replied to Pearson's list of conditions by accusing the government of contributing to the disunity, confusion, and doubt in the 'allied camp' and by reiterating the now standard PC demand for Canadian membership 'in a pact in Asia designed to assure peace to the same degree as peace has been assured in Europe through ... the North Atlantic Treaty Organization.'[12] Diefenbaker was echoing the views of Howard Green, Gordon Churchill, and party leader George Drew. St Laurent and Pearson thus knew that they were exposing themselves to some political risk at home in diverging so markedly from the American approach to Asian security. By contrast the CCF party effectively approved Pearson's stand, declaring that it was much better not to get tangled up in a new round of 'obsolete colonialism.'[13]

---

* Neither was James Eayrs, it would seem. A little over eighteen months previous to Pearson's statement in the Commons, Eayrs, then a lecturer in international relations at the University of Toronto, had argued strongly for Western governments' participation in a Pacific-area defence pact. Said Eayrs: 'Granted that Chinese communism is likely to retain its aggressive character for many years, does it follow that economic aid is our only guarantee of security? To answer affirmatively is to overlook the fact that the communist creed is only one of the several weapons in the communist arsenal. Out-and-out aggression is definitely another, as Korea has shown. Distinct treatment is required for each: economic aid and skilful counter-propaganda for the former, and a military collective security pact for the latter. Both are urgently required. At the same time, practical policy dictates that priorities be assigned. Here it is useful to bear in mind that a policy of economic assistance is essentially a long-term policy, while that of a military defence pact is designed to combat an immediate threat.' See 'A Pacific Pact: "Step in the Right Direction"?' *International Journal* VII, 4 (Autumn 1952) 302.

Canadian behaviour at the Geneva talks on Korea irked the Americans greatly. The US delegates, General Walter Bedell Smith, Walter Robertson, and U. Alexis Johnson, were under strict instructions not to associate with the Chinese because of their government's still unyielding determination not to recognize the PRC in any way, shape, or form. But 'every day at the coffee breaks' Chester Ronning, the son of a Canadian missionary to China (Ronning had grown up there), would chat amiably in Chinese with an old diplomatic acquaintance, Chou En-lai, the head of the PRC's delegation. According to Ronning: 'It was at Geneva that Chou En-lai asked to talk to Pearson who was equally eager to talk. After I had introduced them they conversed for a very long time. Then Dulles came over because he was so upset and wanted to get Mike away from him. Chou put out his hand and at that point Dulles shook his fist at him.'[14]

Other interviewees have suggested that this might be a somewhat embellished portrayal of the event, but the account accurately captures the broad character of Canadian diplomacy during the negotiations: a stress on balance, flexibility, and a maximal exploration of the possibilities for agreement. It was less than coincidental that the Chinese eventually proposed Canada as the Western representative on the International Commission for Indochina, and that the Americans would have preferred Belgium.

HAMMERING OUT THE GENEVA COMPROMISE ON INDOCHINA

The Geneva Agreements on Indochina were the product of not one but two compromises: the first was Anglo-American, the second Sino-European. The British and French began the talks on Indochina expressing their desire to come to a concrete bargain with the communist powers, while Bedell Smith, the head of the US delegation, expressed only a willingness to discuss 'the problem of restoring peace in Indo-China.'[15] Less than three weeks earlier Secretary of State Dulles had put the American position more vigorously: 'We hope to find that the aggressors come here in a mood to purge themselves of their aggression, and that it will thus be possible to ... enable the peoples of Vietnam, Laos and Cambodia to enjoy and perfect the political freedom which is now theirs.'[16] Dulles was determined to do his best to sustain the flagging French will to fight on in Indochina (at the time the French government was collapsing), to persuade the British to agree to joint intervention there in support of the French, and to avoid according any sort of legitimacy or international political credibility to the communist Chinese via the Conference proceedings.

From May through July 1954 American policy was in constant flux. Bureaucratic rivalries were being played out in Washington. The Asia-first interventionists, led by Admiral Radford, Air Force Chief of Staff Nathan Twining, Vice-President Richard Nixon, Senators Knowland, McCarthy, and Bridges, and other members of the China Lobby, pressed strongly for a unilateral military commitment to the anti-communist struggle. Fortunately Eisenhower as an ex-army general of considerable political acumen preferred the advice he received from Army Chief of Staff, General Matthew Ridgway, and former General of the Army Walter Bedell Smith: avoid any unilateral commitment, and avoid a land war in Asia.[17] From 7 to 27 April Eisenhower and Dulles pushed the 'united action' approach only to see Churchill torpedo it in his statement to the House of Commons on 27 April. They immediately changed their direction of policy concern towards the formation of a regional collective security pact,[18] something Dulles may have intended all along. As early as 3 May Dulles publicly portrayed Dienbienphu as a military victory because of the enormous cost in casualties inflicted on the Vietminh.[19] By 11 May Dulles talked publicly of a new line of containment which might not include Vietnam, Laos, or Cambodia since the latter two countries were poor and had small populations.[20] By the end of May the US military apparatus as a whole concurred in the new approach.[21] The militants were no longer in a position to challenge for control of policy.

The British position was influenced no doubt by non-strategic factors: fear of strong left-wing criticism at home; a desire to economize on defence spending; a desire to develop détente with the communists and concomitant East-West trade prospects. A self-interested strategic calculation that Britain would profit from the neutralization of Indochina through the region's conversion into a buffer zone may also have been a factor.[22] Both Churchill[23] and Eden were pragmatists in strategic matters, and, as Eden said bluntly to Dulles in late April 1954: 'None of us in London believe that intervention in Indochina can do anything.'[24] The anti-French insurgency was too far developed to envision any allied retrieval of the situation. British argument as to the basic political as well as military weakness of the Western position was strengthened with the collapse of the French government in the wake of the capture of Dienbienphu by the Vietminh on 7 May, the day before the Indochina sessions began.

With the fall of the Laniel government in Paris and the accession to power of Pierre Mendès-France in mid-June, Washington leaders lost much of their leverage over French policy. The government of Mendès-France publicly set an arbitrary time limit of thirty days for achievement of an Indochina settlement. Failure would mean resignation. This was a tactically brilliant ploy.

American desire not to alienate French opinion in view of the upcoming EDC vote further inhibited resort to pressure tactics. Mendès-France could argue convincingly that his government could not possibly submit the EDC legislation for ratification prior to an Indochina settlement, because defeat of the EDC program (or any other scheme leading to partial German rearmament) was a high priority objective of Soviet policy, and the French desperately required strong Soviet pressure on the Vietminh leaders. In making such an argument the French may have been playing a double game (covertly guaranteeing an EDC defeat to the Russians in return for pressure on Ho Chi Minh), since the EDC ratification measure was finally defeated in August, but the argument as made in late June nevertheless put a severe crimp in Dulles's plans to eviscerate the Geneva negotiations. American policy softened quickly, but only privately. Publicly the policy of disassociation and discourtesy continued at Geneva. There were congressional elections to consider in the autumn and Eisenhower and Dulles could ill afford to do anything to alienate conservative sentiment.

In late June the position of the FUF was becoming increasingly precarious, facing 'defections on a mounting scale' that could have 'become very large if the Vietminh scored major victories or if the French were believed (and Vietnamese suspicions were rife on this score in Hanoi and Saigon) about to abandon Hanoi and portions of the [Red River] Delta.'[25] An Anglo-American rapprochement of sorts was worked out through the formulation of a seven-point program of principles to guide Western and especially French negotiators at Geneva. From the US administration's point of view the Seven Points were the minimally tolerable basis for 'settlement.' It was made clear to both the British and French that winning a diplomatic victory based on the Seven Points was still considered a strategic defeat by Washington leaders, who would have preferred that the Indochina conflict be brought before the United Nations (which the French still refused to consider) and that the fighting be expanded and 'internationalized' through immediate 'united action.'[26] By late June this preference had become irrelevant. The French and British, and more important still, the Soviets and communist Chinese, seemed determined to come to an agreement. Eisenhower and Dulles were resigned to trying to salvage what they could from Geneva without covering themselves in the mud of 'appeasement.'

The seven-point Anglo-American communiqué stipulated the minimum terms acceptable to Washington if the United States were to be able to 'respect' (but not approve) a peace settlement. Inter alia, any agreement had to: secure Vietminh withdrawal from Laos and Cambodia: concede territory to the DRVN only down to 17° 30' of latitude; create no conditions inimical to the maintenance of adequate internal security forces in 'retained Vietnam,' or to arms importation or to the resort by 'free Vietnam' to foreign military advisers; provide for the 'peaceful and humane transfer, under international supervision' of people in the North who wished to flee south to escape the communists; and lastly, provide 'effective machinery for international supervision' of the agreement.²⁷ In its final form the Geneva political package for Vietnam would bear a strong resemblance to the list of American demands.

In a narrow perspective, the Soviet Union was willing and perhaps eager to reach a political settlement over Geneva primarily because it hoped to benefit indirectly by having the French block passage of the upcoming EDC legislation. There may have been a secret quid pro quo arrangement with Mendès-France, but this seems unlikely. There is no hard evidence to back up such speculation. It is more likely that the Soviets were banking on a decreased perceived need by the French for EDC passage once their own security was directly augmented by the return to France of the troops of the French Expeditionary Corps.²⁸ In a wider perspective, the Soviet leadership was committed to exploring the possibilities for détente and peaceful coexistence. Malenkov's momentary ascendance in the Soviet regime may have helped promote this accommodative tendency in Soviet policy.

Certainly Moscow leaders perceived no direct geopolitical interests at stake in Indochina except for the generally shared interest in avoiding a major war in Asia. The Soviet leaders were very wary of what the authors of the Pentagon Papers study themselves termed 'American recklessness with nuclear weapons.'²⁹ They were also apparently quite aware that Washington had looked very closely at intervention during the Dienbienphu crisis.³⁰ There were also political benefits to be considered. An agreement in Indochina might help to drive a wedge between the US and European governments. The PRC's status as a major international power would be enhanced. The 'forces of peace' in the United States would be strengthened. A breathing space for domestic economic consolidation and internal political realignment would be created. And not the least significant, the external threat to the Soviet state would be significantly reduced pending the completion of development and deployment of Moscow's 'new weapons': heavy strategic bombers and new IRBM and ICBM rockets with atomic and thermonuclear warheads.

These new bombers (the TU-16 medium-range jet bomber, the TU-20 intercontinental turboprop bomber, and the Mya-4 intercontinental jet bomber) would not be deployed in significant numbers until mid-1956. There were never more than 200 intercontinental bombers deployed in any case. IRBM deployment to hold Europe hostage would come on line about the same time. But ICBM deployment was, in 1954, three years from the testing stage (the Sputnik launch was October 1957), and over eleven years from serious deployment. By contrast, the Soviet military then faced 1,082 American strategic bombers configured for bombing roles stationed at thirty American and eleven overseas bases. The American stockpile of atomic warheads in 'active storage' was estimated at between 2,000 and 3,000. In mid-1954 the Soviet Long Range Air Force had only a few TU-16 jets in service capable of reaching the United States on one-way missions only. Their stockpile of warheads was limited – only 300–400 altogether.[31] In 1954 the Soviet Union was extremely vulnerable to an American disarming counter-force strike on its nascent nuclear deterrent force. Moscow leaders were vulnerable to strategic intimidation. Any serious risk of Soviet-American confrontation had to be handled cautiously.

After the costs and frustration of the Korean campaign the PRC leadership was extremely anxious to avoid another confrontation with the American military. Economic stability and progress were essential for consolidating the revolution. The Chinese were worried about the radical elements in Washington's 'ruling circles' and they were especially concerned about continuing US support for KMT harassment of the mainland coast. Whether they knew that many American military leaders were advocating a complete naval blockade of China in the event of American intervention in Indochina is not clear,[32] but Beijing's leaders undoubtedly were gravely concerned over many other provocative rollback statements that had been made by various navy and air force spokesmen in the US. Nuclear weapons had not yet been dismissed as 'a paper tiger.'[33]

Politically the Chinese had much to gain in terms of international status from being seen as a peacemaker at Geneva. If the Chinese wanted to secure their southern border against provocative American actions, a partitioned Vietnam and a neutralized Laos would accomplish this result just as well as a communist victory throughout Indochina, and without running the risk of American nuclear intervention. War with the United States in 1954–5 would have meant great damage to the Chinese people, an opportunity for counter-revolutionary insurrection under KMT auspices, and continued extreme dependence on Soviet goodwill.[34] Negotiated neutralization of Indochina was a far better option. Cautionary warnings to the Chinese delegation from worried diplomats such as Eden, Krishna Menon, Pearson, and Ronning concerning the dangerous trend in policy-making in Washington could only have added to Chinese willingness to force a compromise.[35]

The Indochina talks were recessed between 20 June and 9 July. This was when the Anglo-American Seven Points were drawn up. It was also when

Chou En-lai went to Nanning China, near the Vietnamese border, to meet with Ho Chi Minh. Between 3 and 5 July Chou obtained Ho's concurrence in the central political and military provisions of the Geneva package: a military armistice, regroupment, and withdrawal long before the final political settlement; 'provisional' partition of Vietnam; a genuinely neutral supervisory body; and military neutralization of the whole Indochina region.[36]

The balance sheet for the Vietminh in early July following the great power accommodation at their expense was still positive, but there was little cause for joy. A capital city, fixed territory, and the formal cession of the Red River delta strengthened DRVN claims to sovereignty. The FUF, over 600,000 strong,[37] would not have to be defeated militarily. The risk of nuclear attack by Washington had receded. But Vietminh influence in Laos and Camboida was now threatened, and anti-communist forces in South Vietnam would be given an opportunity of two years to add to their strength before a final electoral confrontation. Some Vietminh leaders realistically feared that the elections might be blocked by 'American imperialist scheming.'[38]

Between 10 July, when negotiations resumed in earnest at Geneva, and 20 July, the day the three Cease-Fire Agreements (hereafter CFAs) were signed, the bargaining was intense and centred on the terms of regroupment, the positioning of the line of 'temporary demarcation' between the French Union and PAVN zones of influence (some line between the 13th and 18th parallels), the duration of time before electoral reunification, and the terms of neutralization which would necessarily impinge on the sovereignty of the Laotian, Cambodian, and the two de facto Vietnamese governments. Between 10 and 14 July the French and American governments overcame the differences remaining between the two delegations (caused primarily by Dulles's lack of faith in French determination to win a settlement acceptable to most of Washington), and Dulles authorized the return of a high-level American representative, the under secretary of state, Walter Bedell Smith, whose presence had been withheld up to this point.

Smith's return was symbolic in another sense, because he represented the forces of restraint within the US government. Like Eisenhower, this former general, former ambassador to Moscow (1946–8), and former CIA head (1950–3, but he scorned clandestine operations),[39] was determined to play a prudent game in the Cold War struggle. The Chinese delegation erroneously interpreted Smith's return as yet another attempt by Dulles to block the armistice.[40] Smith's return and preparations in public by Mendès-France for the dispatch to Indochina of France's first conscripted divisions in the event the conference failed seem to have strengthened the British and French position considerably during the last days of bargaining. Under the exceptionally generous posture taken by Molotov and the Chinese, the partition controversy (as a result of Molotov's enthusiasm for agreement) was resolved at the 17th parallel, the electoral settlement was not the period of one year sought by Ho's government but two years, and last, Laos and Cambodia were exempted from the important 'no foreign military bases' and arms-import ban provisions that were a major feature of the Vietnam armistice.[41]

Both the Indian and Canadian delegations contributed to the negotiations as they could. On the Canadian side, until 15 June, Pearson, Holmes, and Ronning did what was possible to facilitate agreement among the principal negotiating powers. Pearson and Holmes were congenial to the American and European allies, while Ronning's friendship with Chou En-lai provided vital initial personal contact between the East and West bloc delegations. St Laurent's misgivings aside,[42] there is no evidence that the Canadians contributed decisively to any of the concrete terms of the three armistice agreements, but they may have done much towards improving the 'atmospherics' – a not insignificant role in critical international gatherings. Certainly Pearson accorded the Indochina negotiations great weight. In his last comment to the Korean plenary sessions on 4 May, he warned the assembled delegates that any overt failure of the Indochina talks would lead to 'futher collective consideration' by the interested Western powers. Failure of the talks might, he said, 'harden and make more dangerous the great and tragic division in the world.' For Pearson 'the penalty of failure' was 'even greater in terms of increasing tensions and the risk of a war which would engulf and destroy us all.'[43] Three days later in a letter to his prime minister he declared in equally apocalyptic tones that 'if the Indo-China question goes very wrong, serious and widespread conflict might result from whose consequences we would not be able to escape.'[44]

On the Indian side, V.K. Krishna Menon apparently helped to facilitate the negotiations, especially during the last days of bargaining. D.R. Sar-Desai has noted, but does not necessarily agree with, Menon's claim that he helped to determine the location of the zonal demarcation line, the force regroupment and territorial transfer time limit of 300 days, and some aspects of the projected political settlement. The Indian leaders eagerly took on a role in supervising the armistice agreements. They shared at the time, so it was thought, a growing zone of common interest with the government of China, specifically support for the neutralization of Southeast Asia, the termination of great-power intervention in the region, and the foreclosure of any opportunities for nuclear adventurism by Washington. In these respects there was genuine overlap in Indian and Chinese foreign policy objectives. If Mr Nehru was not happy with the prospect of a new communist Vietnamese state, neither was he unhappy at the prospect of a tacit cession of Laos and Cambodia to India's political and diplomatic sphere of influence.[45] A British diplomat summed up India's 1954 position aptly when he said: 'Vietnam is on the other side of Mr. Nehru's Rubicon, whereas Cambodia and Laos are on his side.'[46]

For the Indians any coalition such as the proposed SEATO* pact was quite repugnant. Nehru sought a 'zone of peace' instead. If the Geneva Agreements were portrayed as another Munich in the United States, and as a 'second Dunkirk' in the United Kingdom,[47] in India they were regarded as a spectacular diplomatic triumph, 'an hour of moral triumph.'[48]

In sum, one can view the Geneva Agreements as the product of a very complex, interdependent set of relationships. The Indians and Chinese were anxious to assert their newly won status as sovereign actors in world affairs. This they did by taking a leading role in the Geneva negotiations, thereby stifling a war that threatened to embroil the two Cold War hegemons. For the French, domestic political unrest, the cost of the war, and simple fatigue guaranteed acceptance of what Mendès-France termed a 'cruel peace treaty based on cruel military realities.' Mendès-France exploited the American presence at Geneva, and Dulles's nuclear rhetoric for all it was worth. The Soviet leaders gained by fomenting divisions within the Western bloc and securing more time to build up their strategic deterrent. And for a short time America's Asia-first militants were inhibited. From London's perspective the peace settlement had been secured against long odds, and it seemed a realistic accommodation with the communists based on the hard fact of an indigenous, communist-led nationalist movement. More important, the British had forestalled a headlong plunge by the United States into another war in Asia which the British believed could only be far more debilitating than Korea. Ottawa too was pleased with these accomplishments. For Washington, Geneva was a setback, but not the major disaster many had feared. Only the Vietminh and State of Vietnam delegations came away from Geneva soured by the experience. But these were significant exceptions to the trend.

Despite the satisfaction resulting from the signing of the armistice, major problems remained. First, the new South Vietnamese government of Ngo Dinh Diem, appointed during the Indochina Conference itself, like its predecessor totally rejected any agreement which involved partition of the country. As head of the government of the State of Vietnam, Diem still con-

* The Southeast Asia Collective Defense Treaty of 8 Sept. 1954 came to be referred to by the inaccurate acronymn 'SEATO' (Southeast Asia Treaty Organization), because it was popularly assumed to be a close analogue of the NATO agreement.

sidered himself to be ruler of the whole country despite the French assent to factual partition. Second, the United States did not explicitly support the armistice agreements, although it expressed an intention not to use force, or the threat of force, to 'disturb' the armistice arrangements.[49] Dulles's tactics had been modestly successful in evading responsibility for the settlement. Additionally, the United States had not compromised its position of non-recognition of the PRC, but neither could it justifiably claim to have – in Dulles's words – 'called the Chinese to account before the bar of world opinion.' In their strategic assessment of the outcome of the Geneva Conference the Americans could take some small comfort from the fact that though part of Vietnam had been 'handed over to the communists,' part of it had been 'saved' and without fighting a costly war to do so, a development which in view of the deteriorating state of the FUF army was an accomplishment.

The unambiguous results of the conference were that the fighting was halted, that American (and NATO) intervention had been prevented, and that a reasonable prospect for the indefinite neutralization of Southeast Asia had been created. The ambiguous results were that the Geneva Agreements were not specific concerning the nature of the political commitments undertaken by the various parties to the conference. The situation was very muddy in this respect. However, the great powers, in the words of the American peace movement of the 1960s, did decide to 'give peace a chance.'

Appendix 1 reproduces in full the text of the six chapters and forty-seven articles of the Geneva Cease-Fire Agreement for Vietnam (the CFA) that was signed on 20 July, as well as the thirteen articles of the Final Declaration (FD) that was given a blessing of sorts on 21 July by five of the nine direct participants in the talks. By 11 August the armistice was to be in force throughout all Vietnam. Armistice agreements were also concluded between the French and Vietminh military authorities for Laos and Cambodia.[50]

Chapter 1 of the Vietnam armistice established two regroupment zones, a demilitarized zone (DMZ) and demarcation line (DL) between them, and a Joint Commission (JC) composed of the parties and an International Commission (IC) to oversee regroupment and demilitarization. Chapter 2 established the staged application of the armistice in various regions of the country; allotted the 'civil administration' of each zone to the 'party whose forces are to be regrouped there' until 'the general elections which will bring about the unification of Vietnam'; prohibited reprisals, established a right to choice of zone of residence for all Vietnamese (movement being permitted for the 300-day regroupment period); and laid out a schedule for transfer of territorial subdivisions. Chapter 3 banned 'troop reinforcements and additional military personnel' except as stipulated in designated rotation procedures for the French forces. United States advisers were not mentioned. Banned too were 'reinforcements' of arms, munitions, and other 'war material.' The creation of new military bases was forbidden. Both zones were forbidden 'to adhere to any alliance.' Chapter 4 set up procedures for 'repatriation of all prisoners of war and civilian internees.' Chapter 5 provided for punishment of armistice violators by the respective high commands, the allocation of costs of operation of the JC and IC and their various 'inspection teams,' and stipulated that the signatories to the treaty 'and their successors in their functions' would be obliged to observe the armistice terms. Chapter 6 defined the structures and procedures of the JC and IC. Majority vote could decide routine matters in the International Commission, but unanimity was stipulated for 'questions concerning violations or threats of violations, which might lead to a resumption of hostilities.' The International Commission was to be composed of three delegations from Canada, India, and Poland – the Indian delegation to preside over deliberations of the IC and its organs.

The armistice agreement was signed by Brigadier General Delteil for the FUF and the vice-minister of national defence of the Democratic Republic of Vietnam (DRVN), Ta-Quang-Buu. The agreement nowhere specified the timing or modalities of the elections mentioned casually in Article 14. The core of the armistice then involved an immediate cease-fire and separation of combatants, a de facto partition of Vietnam, and an effort to 'neutralize' both parts of the country. The armistice agreements for Laos and Cambodia also aimed at the demilitarization and effective neutralization of those countries. Some 5,000 French military personnel were allowed to stay in Laos. No numerical restriction was imposed on French forces concerning Vietnam.

The other major document produced by the conference, in addition to the three Cease-Fire Agreements, was the Final Declaration. No representative of any delegation signed this last document. Only four of the nine governments at the conference gave direct unambiguous verbal assent to the final text of this piece of politico-diplomatic legerdemain.[51] The head of the State of Vietnam delegation to the conference and Diem himself vigorously stated their government's refusal to be bound by the agreements which emerged from the negotiations.[52] They consistently refused to accept the so-called political settlement provisions. Bedell Smith refused to associate the US government in any way with the FD (the US government would 'take note' of the Indochina CFAs and Articles 1–12 of the FD only) and pledged only to 'refrain from the threat or the use of force to disturb them' in accordance with Article 2, section 4, of the UN Charter. Smith also declared that the US government supported the right of the people of the State of Vietnam 'to determine their own future.'[53]

The first five articles of the FD 'took note' of the provisions of the Vietnam CFA and the arrangements made under the separate Laotian and Cambodian Cease-Fire Agreements. Special attention was drawn to the provisions of Articles 16–19 of the Vietnam CFA. The important articles of the declaration were numbers 6 and 7, which 'recognized' that the demarcation line 'should not in any way be interpreted as ... a political or territorial boundary.' The two articles also contained a 'declaration' that 'fundamental freedoms' were to be observed in Vietnam, that 'general elections shall be held in July 1956 under the supervision of an international commission composed of representatives of the Member States of the International Supervisory Commission,' and that electoral consultations between zonal authorities should begin on 20 July 1955.

The overall thrust of the Final Declaration was by and large sympathetic to the objectives of the communist side in the Geneva negotiations. It reaffirmed pointedly the objective of the neutralization of Indochina, and its isolation from foreign forces. It called for an early electoral decision, which seemed to favour the DRVN regime. Essentially it was the locus of the real concessions made by the French and British to the communist bloc. Obviously if the political settlement terms of the FD had been carried out all of Vietnam would have been communist by 1957. But in view of Article 10 of the FD, which approved the unilateral French declaration of their intention to withdraw French forces 'at the request of the Governments concerned,' the French government, though it 'approved' the FD, was clearly given the option of withdrawing its forces from Vietnam should the South Vietnamese authorities so request.

The French would then be in the position of lacking any influence at all over the course of South Vietnamese politics. It would seem that DRVN-PRC eagerness to speed the exit of French forces, presumably in the hope of eliminating one of the few remaining pillars of Bao Dai's support, overshadowed their fears of American 'indirect' intervention through the propping up of Diem and the training of the Vietnamese National Army. The French still had several hundred thousand battle-hardened troops in Indochina. The nearest American combat forces were across 550 miles of water in the Philippines, and though nuclear-armed, they may have seemed to constitute a less tangible threat by comparison.

THE LEGAL IMPLICATIONS OF THE CEASE-FIRE AGREEMENT
AND FINAL DECLARATION

The Geneva package was shot through with legal and political contradictions. The textual ambiguities and imprecisions soon were exploited for political purposes. The government headed by Ngo Dinh Diem was not sovereign in July 1954, only partially independent and autonomous in the summer of 1955, and only gained complete de facto and de jure sovereign powers by the winter of 1955 or the spring of 1956. Various critics of Diem and the American intervention conclude on the basis of this situation that the SVN/RVN regime was legally bound by French undertakings at Geneva, in particular the political settlement provisions of Articles 6 and 7 of the declaration. Such argument is very unsound, if not wholly fallacious.

By mid-1955 a number of unsympathetic governments acknowledged the SVN's de facto sovereignty over the southern zone. Full juridical sovereignty had been acknowledged by sympathetic governments much earlier. The reality was confused and ambiguous.

Vietnam was an anomalous situation of divided sovereignty – or more properly of contending, mutually exclusive claims of sovereignty. According to much if not all of subsequent international legal opinion, the Vietnam legal problematic stemmed from the fact that neither side possessed wholly unassailable claims to factual or juridical sovereignty over the whole territory of Vietnam. By 1952 over thirty nations recognized the SVN as the sovereign government of Vietnam. In the same year the UN Security Council voted ten to one (the Soviet Union dissenting) to seat the SVN as the sole Vietnamese delegation.[54] The General Assembly also passed a resolution calling for the admission of the SVN. In short, 'by 1952 the State of Vietnam was considered by the majority of the world community to have fulfilled the requirements of statehood.'[55] Given the less than 'perfected' condition of SVN sovereignty and the reality of ongoing civil war in the southern zone, such estimates were based more on the hopes and aspirations of the non-communist states than on the functional realities of Franco-Vietnamese relations.

On the other hand, as early as 1950 some nine communist bloc countries recognized the DRVN as the sole legitimate government of Vietnam.[56] The DRVN regime had carved out its own substantial status. It had a government, a growing system of permanent administration, and a permanent population. What it lacked was a capital city and a well-defined territory, even though the Vietnamese communists could at this time deny the French free access to over three-quarters of Vietnam. The DRVN regime did not possess any remaining benefits from the qualified act of recognition which the

French had extended in 1946. The acts of devolution of 1948, 1949, and 1950 had superseded French recognition of the Vietminh-VNQDD regime in 1946.[57] The DRVN was an insurgent organization which by 1953–4 had gained belligerent status. After implementation of the Geneva armistice the DRVN acquired uncontested factual sovereignty north of the 17th parallel. However, Western governments that had recognized the State of Vietnam as the sole legitimate government of Vietnam prior to 20 July 1954 did not withdraw or suspend such recognition thereafter. Paris, for example, continued to recognize Bao Dai as the sole legitimate ruler of Vietnam.

The heart of the legal problems posed by the Geneva Agreements lay in the fact that Ngo Dinh Diem and his government in South Vietnam were *not* obligated to assume all the French undertakings at Geneva, simply because these obligations were of fundamental character – so fundamental that they jeopardized the very existence of the SVN-RVN. In international law the duties of successor governments do not include any inescapable obligation to honour treaty commitments which compromise the survival of a new regime.

According to Robert Randle's thorough and cogent analysis, the SVN-RVN government was in no way bound by the French undertakings at Geneva, regardless of when the Diem government attained fully sovereign status. South Vietnamese protests at Geneva were of material significance. The SVN delegate denounced the central terms of the armistice agreement, chastised the French for giving up the northern half of the country, protested the arrogation by Paris of the right to set a date for elections without the concurrence of the government in Saigon, and called for UN-supervised electoral procedures.[58] The SVN delegate publicly dissented from the terms of the French-Vietminh political 'settlement' on more than one occasion.[59] He announced that the SVN was not going to consider itself bound by all the terms of the agreements. Furthermore, the SVN authorities had gained assurances from Paris in March 1953 that the French government would make no treaty commitments involving Vietnam without explicit SVN approval.[60] Thus in no way were the French acting at Geneva with implied SVN consent.

Critics of the RVN-American position frequently point to Article 27 of the CFA, which states that the 'successors in function' of the signatories must observe and respect the terms of the CFA. But neither the French nor the Geneva powers collectively had a clear legal power to bind a third-party successor regime to their political decisions. The 'successors in function' clauses of the agreements were of no legal significance.

State succession is one of the most confused areas of post-World War II international legal practice. New states have frequently rejected out of hand the legal obligations contracted by former colonial authorities.[61] The governments of former colonies in Africa and Asia have argued that 'dispositive' treaty obligations (ie, those which pertain to boundaries, frontiers, or other 'basic' facts of international life – or in the words of D.P. O'Connell, obligations whose 'performance was territorial and not fundamentally dependent upon the continued jurisdiction in the territory of the contracting State')[62] of predecessor colonial regimes are not binding upon successor local regimes. Such governments assert that the most basic principle of the international legal system must be the concept of the sovereign equality of states, a principle which must supersede any traditional arguments on behalf of a principle of continuity in 'dispositive' obligations. Many newly independent Asian governments, in particular, have denounced the principle of continuity in obligations as a biased self-serving outgrowth of European legal interpretation, as well as a manifestation of continuing indirect colonial servitude.[63]

Even if one supports the improbable doctrine of continuity of obligations in state succession, it is not clear that the State of Vietnam was bound by the Geneva Agreements of 1954. One common line of argument is based upon Judge McNair's dissenting opinion delivered to the International Court of Justice in 1950 in the *Status of South West Africa* case. He then declared:

From time to time, it happens that a group of great Powers, or a large number of States both great and small, *assume a power to create by multipartite treaty* some new international regime or status, which soon acquires *a degree of acceptance or durability extending beyond the limits of the actual contracting parties*, and giving it an objective existence. This power is used when some public interest is involved, and its exercise often occurs in the course of the peace settlement *at the end of a great war*.[64]

Superficially this theory may seem relevant, but under close analysis the facts of the Geneva Conference on Indochina do not match the concept. As Randle notes, the CFA was a bilaterally, not a multilaterally, signed document. Only the signatures of the FUF and PAVN representatives were on the actual agreement. There were no great-power guarantees or 'sureties' given at all. No delegation signed the Final Declaration, and five of the nine governments at the conference either rejected the FD or refrained from giving explicit verbal approval when called upon to do so. The Geneva Conference was characterized then by a fundamental lack of consensus on the crucial aspects of the FD – a situation which, given the self-imposed deadline of 20 July of the Mendès-France government, meant that the conference participants had to sacrifice the institution of an unambiguously multilateral treaty commitment to the projected political settlement in favour of a watered-down series of essentially unilateral affirmations of 'hope' concerning the possible pattern of political evolution in Vietnam. Such declarations of hope by the delegates of the PRC, the Soviet Union, France, and Britain could hardly generate obligations for other members of the conference who withheld direct consent, or who categorically rejected the terms of the FD.

Finally, the actual language of the FD is legally deficient. As Randle observed:

> Because the final declaration (paragraphs 4 and 5) merely 'took note' of articles 16–19 of the cease-fire agreement, we find no positive, mandatory 'law making' language that unambiguously evinces the intent of the great powers or 'a large number of States both great and small' to create a new international regime or status for Vietnam. Given the absence of real consensus at Geneva, we cannot infer an intent to legislate on the part of the Geneva powers.[65]

Equally problematic, the wording of Aricles 6–9 may involve no more than a *specification of understanding* with regard to the manner of operation of the CFA and the long-term objectives it might attain if fully implemented.[66]

Geneva 1954 was a 'rush job.' The drafters of the declaration did not attempt to resolve the explicit contradiction in France's position. For the French, their approval of the undertakings in Articles 6 and 7 of the FD was simultaneously nullified by their undertakings pursuant to Articles 10 and 11 (respect for Vietnamese independence and military withdrawal on request of the Vietnamese authorities). The French thus approved a 'political settlement' which they knew they could not enforce. In fact some of the French negotiators may have sought this result throughout the Geneva talks.[67]

Given the wording of the CFA and FD, there was no available course of action in which the French government could avoid some 'violation' of its undertakings if the southern authorities asked the French to leave Vietnam. This major internal defect of the Geneva arrangements may have been the product of French legal cunning. The confusion and haste of the Geneva negotiations no doubt contributed to this state of affairs too. In any case the Geneva package provided the French government with an enormous tactical loophole through which they could easily slough off a burdensome, repugnant task.[68] Not surprisingly, they used it when the RVN authorities asked them to leave. Even the ratification procedures followed by the French vis-à-vis the CFA and FD were legally deficient.[69]

Through good fortune or cunning diplomacy the French were provided with a way of deflecting all charges of non-fulfilment of the Geneva bargain. There was no such loophole available to the new DRVN authorities in Hanoi.

The Hanoi regime consistently proclaimed that the FD was binding on all the Geneva powers, so presumably DRVN leaders accepted that it was binding on themselves. Nevertheless they consistently violated most of the key provisions of both the CFA and the FD. As we shall see, they failed to assist northern residents in moving south. They attempted to undermine the political authority of the southern government by assisting a communist-led rural opposition to Saigon. They violated the territorial and political integrity of Laos by materially supporting and guiding the Pathet Lao insurgency. They imported armaments illegally (though the ICSC for political reasons declined to charge them for such violations). They accepted Soviet and Chinese military advisers illegally. And finally, they systematically obstructed the International Commission in its efforts to monitor the armistice implementation in the northern zone. Even if we assume that the FD was not binding upon the DRVN authorities, the provisions of the CFA clearly were. Articles 10, 19, 24, and 27 involved a total proscription on the use of force, which the DRVN systematically and covertly violated. Because the CFA was the only authoritatively binding document that emerged from the conference concerning Vietnam, and because the CFA said nothing regarding electoral procedures, negotiations, or dates, the legal implications of the Geneva framework were highly prejudicial to the long-term political objectives of the Hanoi leadership.

In summary, the legal consequences of the Geneva Agreements on Vietnam were confusing, contradictory, and ambiguous because of the fundamental absence of consensus among the Geneva powers. The Geneva Conference did not create new multipartite 'dispositive' obligations to which the RVN had to defer. Given the absence of firm principles in the international law of state succession, Diem's government was free to choose its own level of co-operation with the Geneva peace structure, including a choice of total non–co-operation.

The facts of the Vietnam legal problematic are of considerable significance. The Geneva 'accords,' as they have been misnamed in English through the widespread adoption of the French word for agreements, were in no way the product of a broad international consensus about the eventual disposition of Vietnam. The CFAs for Laos, Cambodia, and Vietnam and the Final Declaration were meant to obscure as much as they were meant to clarify, to assist in postponing the resolution of the Vietnamese struggle rather than to establish a genuinely workable scheme for the peaceful settlement of the rival Vietnamese claims in the contest. The essential common objective of the 'contracting parties' at Geneva (to use the term very loosely) was to effect a cease-fire to help stabilize the international system at a time of grave interbloc tension. The Geneva Conference produced a peace of sorts, but it did not produce any basis for a workable political settlement.

Ironically enough, the ambiguities of the CFA and FD ultimately worked to the advantage of the DRVN. Diem's failure to enter into electoral talks was subsequently pointed to as a 'material breach' of the agreements by various American anti-war legal specialists, which in some sense justified a recourse to arms by the DRVN.[70] Though this argument is not persuasive (the UN Charter, for example, sanctions the use of force only in situations of self-defence), it appears to have had an enormous political impact upon the image of the Vietnam conflict held by many anti-interventionist critics in North America and Western Europe.*

THE RELUCTANT DECISION TO ACCEPT

Canada was nominated for a role on the International Commission on 18 July, much to the shock of the government. The composition of the supervisory body had been an item of some substantial difficulty for the Geneva negotiators. Chou En-lai certainly contributed to the naming of Canada. Krishna Menon and Chester Ronning may have had something to do with Chou's declared preference.[71] The task was tentatively accepted by Ottawa on 28 July.

There was no enthusiasm at the nomination. The absence of a United Nations framework for the operation was certainly troubling, and at odds with the tenor of government policy. Troubling too was the absence of an officially constituted structure to which the ICSC might turn in the event of major difficulty. Fears were voiced that supervision of a truce might somehow grow to include an enforcement function. A Toronto paper noted that the Geneva Agreements had been greeted in Saigon by mass demonstrations against them, and that the United States government had pointedly refrained from approving any agreement which 'peacefully handed over millions to the communist bloc.'[72] On 22 July the government gave a qualified acceptance of the role. The press reaction was generally favourable, although some fears were expressed that Canada would get pulled into an eventual program of US intervention because of acceptance of an ICSC role[73] – an ironic reversal of the ensuing course of events.

In July, Blair Fraser echoed the general opinion that Geneva was a major setback for the western allies, but he noted that 'Canadian delegates feel the

---

* James Eayrs, for example, appears to still hold the erroneous view that the Final Declaration was a binding legal document. See his *Indochina* 48n, where he cites comments by G.F. Hudson that support such an interpretation.

dark side ... has been rather over-emphasized.' Officials in the Department of
External Affairs had 'never counted on a French victory,' and thus they did
not 'regard an armistice along a line of partition as an unanticipated catas-
trophe.' Fraser went on to say that:

some Americans in disquietingly high places seem to want nothing less than the
overthrow of the communist regime in China. They look upon any negotiated settlement with the present Chinese government as undesirable and immoral and,
although they don't actually advocate war on the Chinese mainland they are not
particularly upset by the prospect.

DEA officials were said to be doing everything possible to encourage a collective defence treaty for the southern Pacific region in an effort to create
constraints on American 'hawks.' The government steadfastly refused to
consider Canadian participation. Quebec Liberals were thus emphasizing
Progressive Conservative sabre-rattling in their own constituencies.[74]
On 22 July 1954 Pearson sent Eden a telegram which stated in part:

We shall be replying to the invitation to accept membership on the International
Supervisory Commission as soon as we have had time to consider the terms of
reference ... There is no disposition here to evade this responsibility which may,
however, turn out to be as onerous as it was unsought.[75]

Responsibility was a key word. For the last six years Pearson and St Laurent
had argued the merits of international commitment and the sin of isolationism, denouncing those who would shirk their responsibility to help maintain
international order.[76] In accepting earlier peacekeeping roles in Kashmir
(UNMOGIP, 1949) and Palestine (UNTSO, 1950), the Canadian government
had established modest precedents for Canadian involvement in the Geneva
armistice agreements.[77] The principle of 'middle-power' mediatory commitments had already been born in fact, though not yet in name.
On 28 July, apparently after consultations with officials in London and
New Delhi to clarify the 'terms of reference,' DEA released a lengthy statement worthy of close analysis which explained the Canadian decision to
accept a supervisory role. The document began by declaring that Canadian
officials would arrive in New Delhi by 31 July to participate with the Indians
and Poles in the first meeting of the ICSC which would establish the initial
logistical and organizational base of the commission. The statement continued in vintage Pearsonian prose, reaffirming Canadian avoidance of security responsibilities in the region:

There are no illusions about the magnitude and complexity of the task ... Canada is geographically remote from Indochina and her collective security responsibilities in Southeast Asia *are limited to those that arise from membership in the United Nations.* We know from experience, however, that *just as local conflicts can become general war, so conditions of security and stability in any part of the world serve the cause of peace everywhere.* If, therefore, Canada can assist in establishing such security and stability in Southeast Asia, we will be serving our own country, as well as the cause of peace.[78]

The 'indivisibility of peace' may have been conventional wisdom, but to Pearson and St Laurent with the memory of Dienbienphu's atomic spectre still vivid, it was much more than a cliché. The risk of escalation to nuclear warfare was now an unpleasant aspect of every local confrontation on the Asian periphery.

The statement went on to express regret at the lack of UN supervision of the peace, to emphasize the 'judicial,' 'supervisory,' and 'mediatory' nature of the Canadian role, and to stress the probable effectiveness of the three ICS, in contradistinction to the near paralysis of the Neutral Nations Supervisory Commission in Korea. Noting that in most cases majority-vote procedures would effectively carry the IC's work, the authors of the statement observed that the Geneva Conference powers would incur responsibility for resolving problems that occasioned majority and minority reports to them. If obstruction and frustration became normal, withdrawal by Canada would ensue. The task of supervision would not be 'either easy or of short duration,' in Ottawa's view, but an active Canadian role would be 'honourable,' 'worthy,' and 'responsible,' and would contribute significantly to the strengthening of peace.

Within four months over 150 Canadian diplomats and senior officers of the Canadian armed forces would be on duty at ICSC posts throughout Indochina, helping to implement an armistice intended by its advocates to freeze the strategic status quo in the Southeast Asian region if at all possible. The journalists' response was one of resignation to a seemingly unavoidable task, not unlike the reaction of the government. In mid-August a lengthy *Maclean's* editorial tried to explain why the Indochina agreements were not comparable to Munich, 1938 – as many articles in the American press had suggested. Unlike Czechoslovakia, no country in Indochina ever received pledges of support, and thus no Western state was morally obligated to fight: 'The war there is a civil war in which one side has got help from Red China and the other from the United States. We all wish the US supported side had won. It didn't. That is a matter for regret not for shame. Our only obligation in Asia is to defend our own interests – in the broadest sense and the longest run, if you will, but still our own interests.'[79] And the writer might have added, in the broad view and the long run, Canadian interests in Asia were clearly coterminus with 'the interests of peace.'

CONCLUSION

In mid-1954 the three policy tendencies of the Canadian system were just beginning to evolve distinct and coherent approaches to Indochina policy. The policy of determined non-involvement in Asian security matters had been widely accepted for quite some time. In July 1954 liberal-moderate rhetoric and idealism began to be questioned for the first time by Ottawa's conservative element. There was little reason for conservative policy advocates in DEA to dissent from the decision by St Laurent and Pearson to respond to the Indochina invitation by issuing a qualified acceptance of the task. External's conservative element was at this time in wholehearted agreement with liberal-moderates who advocated strategic Eurocentrism. Nevertheless many conservatives clearly had reservations about a role which Washington refused to approve. Canadian interests were most broadly and deeply engaged in the field of Canadian-American relations, and thus conservatives (who are national interest maximizers at heart) were naturally apprehensive about anything which seemed to carry with it a risk of destabilization of this most critical area of Canada's international transactions. Many conservative articulators no doubt approved strongly of any action by Canada which helped to preclude a growing American strategic commitment in Pacific Asia. Conservative marginalists viewed American efforts in Asia as a misallocation of strategic capabilities, unlike public conservative systemists who were eager to jump on almost any anti-communist bandwagon that came along.

Left-liberal articulators probably concurred with the liberal-moderate thrust of the decision to accept with much less reluctance than the conservative element. Participation in the work of the ICSC seemed likely to contribute to the overall containment of the radical right in Washington, those well-known individuals who wished to reactivate the Chinese civil war, by affirming the principle of non-intervention. The Geneva Agreements also underlined the feasibility of compromises between the blocs. For left-liberals Vietnam was no place to take a stand against the expansion of communism, because, just as in China, the communists had captured the mantle of nationalist legitimacy and progressive political reform.

In sum, it may be said that there was a relatively high degree of concurrence among the three tendencies of the Canadian foreign policy community concerning the initial decision to accept participation on the Indochina supervisory commissions. Liberal-moderates like Lester Pearson also were worried about possible adverse effects of acceptance. Pearson knew that right-wing American Congressional opinion would be angered, and that even US State Department moderates had refused to endorse Canadian participation when conversing with so sympathetic a representative as Arnold Heeney.[80] Beyond this immediate lack of support, Pearson and Prime Minister St Laurent may very well have feared that involvement on the Indochina commissions might indeed somehow pave the way for involvement in some future instance of 'united action.' Propinquity to crises usually carries with it some risk of entanglement. Furthermore, if the Anglo-American tensions over Asian policy were to recur, the Canadian role on the supervisory bodies might force Ottawa to side openly with the British against the radical interventionists in the United States, with dire results for Canadian-American relations. Canada, moreover, had no economic interests in the region, and this surely militated against acceptance. So too did the reservations of DEA officials concerning the possible Polish veto, the practical feasibility of the agreements, and the lack of a UN umbrella over the armistice framework. There was certainly considerable anxiety in all corners of External that the truce supervisory role would entail an enormous drain on the department's already hard-pressed manpower resources, as well as on those of the Department of National Defence.[81] Finally, sheer ignorance of the complexities of Indochina's politics argued for rejection.

The case for acceptance was more compelling, however. At the head of the list of pro-involvement factors was the fear of American military intervention in Asia. There was a clear and present danger as evidenced by the Dienbienphu crisis that American decision-making in Asian policy might fall into the hands of extremist elements who advocated preventive war on the PRC. A Canadian refusal to participate could conceivably have led to the breakdown of the armistice (and thus reopened the door to US intervention), if a replacement could not have been found that was acceptable to both blocs.[82] Second, Ottawa's well-demonstrated strategic commitment to protecting Western Europe in preference to Asia argued for acceptance. Strategic resources should not be committed to a secondary theatre. Geneva was not a cause for celebration, but, as an act of constructive disengagement, neither did it seem like a serious crisis for the Free World's strategic interests. Third, the prospect of a neutralized buffer zone in Southeast Asia comprising Burma, Laos, Cambodia, and possibly southern Vietnam seemed both feasible and desirable. It appeared to be a sensible way to define the containment perimeter in Asia without risking any great power's vital interests.

Fourth, Indo-Canadian relations were extremely amicable. Given this happy state of affairs an Indo-Canadian majority might dominate the ICSC's operations. In the event of Polish obstructionism, withdrawal would be a feasible option. Finally, Ottawa's liberal-moderates were to a great extent already locked into a standing commitment to 'responsible internationalism.' Rejection would look hypocritical.

Refusal was a genuine option. The decision to proceed was made reluctantly. During the last week of July 1954 the debate of the foreign policy community was structured around one central trade-off relationship. On the one hand, there was a somewhat amorphous, conservatively inspired anxiety that Canadian-American relations would somehow be damaged by the long-term consequences of a decision to accept. On the other hand, Ottawa's Eurocentric security priorities, a desire to encourage prudent retreat from an untenable position by the French, and quite legitimate liberal-moderate fears of American nuclear adventurism argued for acceptance of a supervisory role. To the government's credit, it forged ahead with participation.

4

The emergence of the refugee dilemma: August–November 1954

Many Canadian diplomats shifted towards conservatism because of their experiences in Indochina. In Vietnam Canadian officials saw the extremely brutal consequences of revolution in a poverty-stricken country. The 'curtain of terror' was not a phrase used loosely. Vietnamese communism had depended to a significant degree upon savage if selective acts of terrorist reprisal to punish collaboration with the French during the anti-colonial war. The use of terror had a long tradition in Asia generally. Many targets of assassination were publicly executed in relatively conventional ways. But a few were buried alive – for example, a brother and a nephew of Ngo Dinh Diem. Others were tortured and mutilated. This was to be the special fate of the RVN's principal liaison officer to the ICSC, Colonel Hoang Thuy Nam, in 1960. Collective resistance to communist organizing in the rural areas of southern Vietnam sometimes provoked the execution of such opposition by tying these people up in 'bundles' back to back, then throwing them into rivers where the victims would drown slowly and agonizingly – a practice visited on the Vietminh themselves in pre-1954 Cochinchina. As one Canadian conservative subsequently commented: 'Vietnamese communism was most definitely not "socialism with a human face."'[1]

War has always been hell. But in Vietnam the hellish aspects of conflict were exaggerated beyond anything in Canadian experience. Vietminh and later Viet Cong* rationales for terrorism were not new. Terror, like guerrilla methods generally, is the inevitable policy of the tactically weaker side. Terror in conflicts which are fed by additional inputs of class hatred is correspond-

---

* The term 'Viet Cong' (literally, Vietnamese communist) came into use in the mid-to-late 1950s. Communist organizers rejected its appellation because it had been used as a term of opprobrium by the Saigon government in its propaganda.

ingly more brutal. It was not accidental that Tom Dooley, a US Navy doctor who became deeply involved in assisting the movement of would-be refugees from the northern to the southern zones, entitled his narrative description of the event *Deliver Us from Evil*. A Catholic himself, he saw the horrible effects of revolutionary 'praxis' as inflicted upon Vietnamese children, who were persecuted and sometimes assaulted and tortured because they were Roman Catholic (and hence tainted with collaborationism), or because they came from relatively well-to-do families in the *chrétientés* (the Catholic enclaves in the north).[2] If the Canadians did not see such barbarism at first hand, some of them soon heard about it from French and South Vietnamese officials or Canadian Catholic missionaries. Such tales, and still more important the human impact of a flood of refugees from the communist-held north, produced a new realism in the minds of many Canadian officials. This realism involved a strengthened conviction that communism was fundamentally abhorrent and pathological because of its utterly ruthless use of what some have termed 'moral terror.' To Canadian officials terror against children, women, and the aged was completely immoral – unjustifiable in any circumstances. Cultural and ideological predispositions barred the moral admissibility of such actions. No end justified these means – just as no political end could justify first use of nuclear weapons. Vietnam confronted Canadian officialdom with a dilemma. Two fundamentally immoral means seemed counterposed: the reality of 'conventional' revolutionary terror emanating from Hanoi, and the potential for 'unconventional' nuclear terror being threatened by Washington. Canadian diplomacy anxiously sought solutions that could preclude the operation of these repugnant policy instruments.

From 11 August 1954, the day when the International Commission for Supervision and Control convened its first formal meeting in Hanoi, until 20 July 1955, the first anniversary of the signing of the Geneva Agreements, Canadian policy-making was concerned with one overriding issue: how to approach the refugee problem that had been generated by Article 14 (d) – the so-called 'freedom of movement' clause. No other aspect of the Vietnam situation caused such serious anxiety for the Canadians or raised such disturbing, ambiguous, and finally insoluble moral difficulties. Because of the perceived risk of American intervention in a possible PRC-KMT confrontation in early 1955, Ottawa officials eventually had to make the very hard choice of avoiding systematic public pressure on the DRVN government to fulfil the latter's commitment to Article 14(d). They thus implicitly abetted the 'imprisonment' in the northern zone of some hundreds of thousands of Vietnamese who would have chosen to flee south, had they not been harassed, intimidated, and ultimately coerced into remaining in the north. In political, diplomatic, and strategic terms the refugee question was a secondary aspect of the whole Vietnam tangle. But because the refugee issue engaged the most elemental humanitarian and ideological values of Canadian representatives in Indochina, it had a profound impact on ensuing Canadian bureaucratic perceptions of the nature of the Vietnam conflict and the legitimacy of the eventual Amrican intervention.

The first year of the ICSC's life saw the crucial success of the military regroupment process, the successful transfer of administrative-political authority to the DRVN in the north, the departure of most of the French military, and the establishment of Ngo Dinh Diem's system of patriarchal rule south of the 'provisional' demarcation line following eight months of continuing political crisis in the semi-sovereign State of Vietnam. While these major structural aspects of the Vietnam policy problem were changing, the Canadian policy debate came to focus on one key problem: should Ottawa fight as hard as possible to extricate as many potential refugees from the north as possible? Battling on this issue risked overturning the armistice. Any refugees who were thus liberated from communist control then faced a very dubious future given the still real and very ominous prospect of 'reunification' under DRVN rule. Would not reunification lead to reprisals against the would-be deserters from the north?

In the first twelve months of the armistice great progress was made, but it was progress from which the Canadian could take little comfort. If they felt pride or satisfaction in being a party to the re-establishment of peace in Indochina it was sentiment tempered with anxiety and, for some, a sense of guilt. For the Canadians the first year brought very hard choices involving the most tragic personal consequences for thousands of people. That the 'logic of events' seemed to make the Canadian decisions ineluctable was of little consolation to many of the officials most directly involved. On a more pragmatically political level, those in Ottawa who had to oversee the direction of Canadian policy were plagued by a gnawing anxiety that Canadian governmental actions, while politically and diplomatically sound to all those privy to the full complexity of the Indochina crisis, might appear cowardly and morally indefensible to the Canadian (or American) public. Officials in Ottawa, especially Lester Pearson, were therefore most concerned about 'shaping' the official record, about demonstrating the sincerity and depth of Canadian concern for the plight of the refugees and the 'terrible things' that were being done by the northern regime. Finally, Ottawa officials wished to ensure that responsibility for a flawed outcome of the armistice agreement implementation should be properly placed with the Geneva powers as a group, and not with the commission alone.

The Canadian government decided that it was both prudent and politically wise to forsake the emotional, propagandistic tactics that would have been required in any serious attempt to force DRVN compliance with Article 14(d). Governmental thinking at that point seems to have been influenced by several factors. First, the North Vietnamese might very well choose to defy the ICSC and restart the fighting. Second, in the face of almost certain Indian opposition Ottawa might have to withdraw unilaterally from the commission, thus risking the collapse of the Geneva peace structure and a resumption of the war. Third, any such rupture in the 'fabric of peace' in Southeast Asia in the context of an ongoing crisis in PRC-Sino-American relations over the Formosa Strait problem might very well lead to an American nuclear assault on the Chinese mainland and a world war that no sane person could countenance.

The evolution of Canadian policy-making on the refugee issue may be divided into two periods: the first from August to early November 1954 saw the emergence of the issue within departmental debates, the second from mid-November 1954 through June 1955 was a time of action and hard decisions. The balance of this chapter traces the development of Canadian attitudes in the first phase.

THE FIRST DAYS

The work of the Neutral Nations Supervisory Commission in Korea was no cause for optimism. In Korea the communist delegations were composed of forensically skilled staff, who had rehearsed their approach in simulations beforehand. At NNSC meetings they had kept voluminous, well-organized, constantly analysed files on commission proceedings. Communist legal-bureaucratic skills in keeping track of, and exploiting, all possible procedural precedents apparently had been awesome. Ottawa feared that the Canadian delegations in Indochina would run into difficulty in the same manner as had the Swiss and the Swedes.[3]

Canadian apprehension was at least partially assuaged by the first ICSC meeting in New Delhi during the first week of August. The Poles were co-operative and seemed eager to play their role. The delegates to this first meeting on the Canadian side included Escott Reid, the then Canadian high commissioner to New Delhi, R.M. Macdonnell, who was to be the first Canadian representative to the ICSC for Vietnam (on an interim basis as acting commissioner), Air Commodore H.H.C. Rutledge, Brigadier R.E.A. Morton, and Bruce M. Williams, the then first secretary at the New Delhi High Commission office (later to be acting commissioner for Canada in Vietnam; later still, commissioner of the ICSC Vietnam). Minimum levels of representation to the three Indochina commissions, eleven per delegation per commission, were determined. It was agreed as well that the Vietnam commissioners should more or less be accorded an informal seniority by each of the three governments. High Commissioner Reid in his opening remarks praised Indian diplomacy warmly and the Indians responded in similar fashion. The Poles were veritable models of diplomatic restraint. Thus began the 'honeymoon period.'[4]

After the first representatives had arrived on the spot in Indochina the first month passed very quickly as the three delegations, but mainly the Indian, struggled with the problems of building a viable organizational structure for the commissions. Substantive commission proceedings focused on facilitating prisoner-of-war exchanges, deploying the first eight fixed teams (FT) at Control points in the three countries,* establishing a system of press accreditation, acquiring the necessary assurances and commitments of modern means of transport from the parties' liaison missions, and finally, attempting to acquire permanent lodging for the ICSC Vietnam HQ in Hanoi (the commissioners initially requested Bao Dai's palace, which the DRVN had reserved for Ho Chi Minh).[5]

By the last week in August tensions were already developing among the delegations. The Canadian acting commissioner, R.M. Macdonnell, became embroiled in debate with Polish Ambassador Przemyslaw Ogrodzinski over French-PAVN (People's Army of Vietnam) disputes concerning the release of prisoners of war. French officials wanted as rapid a schedule as possible. PAVN officials, apparently because of logistical problems, preferred a much slower release rate. Macdonnell supported French objectives and also pressed for commission approval of procedures that would permit prisoners held by the French Union Forces to exercise their choice of zone of residence (pursuant to Article 14[d]) prior to transfer to PAVN regroupment areas. The Indian acting chairman declined to take any significant action,[6] agreeing only to send a letter to the two high commands requesting them to publicize Article 14(d) as widely as possible.[7]

Real difficulties with 14-(d) had become apparent by the end of August. By then, petitions to the ICSC Vietnam were 'pouring in' to the Hanoi office requesting assistance in effecting exit to the south.[8] As the number of peti-

* See map of Vietnam, p xiii.

tions began to mount, Ambassador Ogrodzinski drew attention to the first DRVN allegation concerning 'people who were alleged to have been moved South against their will.'⁹ Further complicating the situation was a report from General de Beaufort of the French Liaison Mission that 500 to 4,000 PAVN prisoners at Hue had 'mutinied' against being handed back to the PAVN authorities.¹⁰ Fears that another Korean-type prisoner-of-war controversy would emerge suddenly seemed all too plausible.

The French Liaison Mission soon proposed major amendments to the CFA's prisoner-of-war exchange modalities, proposals which included the creation of ICSC-run intermediary camps. The Indian chairman rejected them, saying that the proposals seemed contrary to 'the principles on which the Geneva Agreement was based.'¹¹ The Canadian delegation, not wanting to prejudice the relationship with the Indians at this early date, declined to press the French proposals and acquiesced in the Indian line of action.

From the beginning the Canadians, like the Poles, were wary of offending Indian sensibilities. Initial Canadian assessments of Indian policy saw New Delhi as seeking: the restoration of peace in the Indochina area, the effective neutralization of the Indochinese states, the complete withdrawal of the FUF from Southeast Asia, the growth of stable governments based on the aspirations of the indigenous peoples of the region, the inflow of foreign aid provided it entailed no political or military commitments to any bloc alliance (such as SEATO), and the admission of the Indochinese states to the United Nations.¹²

Four years of Indo-Canadian co-operation in attempts to restrain and constrain the deployment and use of American military forces concerning Korea provided some grounds for optimism. So far as Ottawa could tell, the Indians and Canadians shared a desire to stabilize the peace in Indochina, to contain the further spread of communist influence, and to work for the admission of the Indochinese states to the UN as fully independent entities. Although Canada was supporting a collective defence pact in principle for Southeast Asia, its government had indicated that it would never be a party to such an agreement, and more important that it was willing to respond to Asian policy preferences. The only insuperable difference between the Indians and Canadians concerned attitudes towards France, and here it was hoped that the Canadians could reasonably and plausibly downplay their sympathies for their NATO allies.¹³

India's first ambassador to the ICSC for Vietnam, M.J. Desai,¹⁴ arrived in the first week of September. Canadians, although at times frustrated by his inability to delegate work and handle the Western corps effectively, felt that Desai was an outstanding diplomat, possessed of a shrewd intellect and great will-power. Being totally devoid of Krishna Menon's pretentious didacticism, he was quite congenial to Canadian officials. Under Desai the Indian government evolved a pattern of practice in the commission which the Indians referred to as a 'parallel approach in respect of similar problems.'[15] This meant that the Indians would refrain from unilateral criticism of either of the parties to the Geneva Agreements and would insist upon 'balanced' criticisms of both parties simultaneously in virtually every public and private statement of commission opinion. In Desai's view the ICSC should have been named a commission for supervision and conciliation – not control.[16] Desai was a vigorous and generally effective conciliator despite the adverse circumstances imposed by fragmented political control in the south. He strove valiantly, though in vain, to institutionalize the 'spirit of unanimity' in commission proceedings.[17]

By the end of September the ICSC had set up office in Hanoi and many of the FTs and some of the first mobile teams (MTs) had moved into position. In addition to the prisoner-of-war question, the ICSC had tried to come to terms with the problem of deserters or, as they were known in the commission proceedings, 'ralliés.' Little progress was made and though many thousands of prisoners were eventually transferred successfully between the parties, some hundreds of ralliés continued to bedevil the ICSC agenda for over a year.

By late August and early September the basic lines of Canadian policy had been established. The letters of instruction of the first Canadian commissioner, Sherwood Lett, a corporate lawyer from Vancouver,* clearly reflected liberal-moderate objectives. Lett was told that he had to function both as an independent, impartial jurist vis-à-vis the disputes and problems of the commission and as a representative of the Canadian government. No contradiction was foreseen between the requirements of judicial impartiality and ambassadorial representation. In this respect, thinking in the department had been unusually naïve and optimistic.

According to the letters of instruction of 27 August 1954 'the first objective of Canadian policy' was 'the maintenance of the peace in Indochina.' This was the central objective of the government's approach, and would be for the next two decades. Lett was told that the Geneva armistice had eliminated 'for the time being, at least, one of the most serious threats to the general

---

* Lett was fifty-nine when he arrived in Vietnam. He had served in both wars (was wounded twice, once at Dieppe; awarded the Military Cross and DSO). He had attended Oxford as a Rhodes Scholar, and had practised law since 1922. On his return he was appointed chief justice of the BC Supreme Court.

peace of the world.' As the authors of the instructions noted, 'there is no question in our minds that if the military and political situation, as it was three months ago had continued it would have resulted within a fairly short time either in a much more general and serious war or in the extension of Vietminh control over the whole of Indochina.'

Ottawa's second objective was 'to encourage the development of a Southeast Asia Defence Organization [to which Ottawa would not belong], as a safeguard against, and a deterrent to, overt Chinese aggression in southeast Asia, in a way that will cause the least possible offence to the neutralist countries' such as India. Third, the government sought through its Colombo Plan assistance to strengthen the social and economic life of the region. Last, Ottawa wished to foster 'strong, independent non-communist regimes on the Asian mainland,' but Canadian officials did not think that 'shoring up France's remaining foothold' was the way to attain this objective. Only the granting of 'full independence' provided any basis for hope that communist 'infiltration and subversion' might be successfully resisted.[18]

The last three objectives were certainly 'anti-communist,' but given the thrust of the government's foreign policy this was both logical and appropriate. And unlike American extremists Canadian officials adhered to a prudent doctrine of containment. They were not about to join a crusade. As John Holmes would later put matters, the government could hardly be 'neutral' in the struggle for Indochina, but it was disposed favourably towards a posture of judicial impartiality – to the extent that circumstances permitted it. Ultimately circumstances would guarantee that 'partisanship' would prevail over judicial impartiality. It was a development which should have been anticipated. Failure to do so paved the way for ambivalence, potential lack of direction in policy implementation – and an endless litany of misguided accusations of moral turpitude by anti-interventionist critics.

Lett was told to be careful in dealings with the British, so as not to appear to be seeking 'advice or guidance'; with the French, many of whom might look on him as their 'friend at court'; and with the Americans, because of an obvious need for 'friendly discretion ... particularly in your off-duty activities.'[19] An image of judicial objectivity and discretion had to be cultivated, if only to put Lett on a better footing in negotiations with the Indian delegation. The Ottawa policy community erred at this juncture in not taking a more overtly Western stance in its activities on the commission. The tripartite structure of the ICSC was not ill conceived. It provided a potentially powerful mechanism for joint political endeavours across what had hitherto been an unbridgeable political abyss. By cultivating the image of impartiality to the degree that it did, Ottawa would raise both Canadian and Indian hopes too high. The inevitable disillusionment from these unrealistic expectations did much to fuel the resentment and antipathy that led to the demise of the Indo-Canadian special relationship.

In practice, other Western governments did not try to pressure Canadian commissioners on the ICSC. By minimizing informal contacts with the French and Americans and by refraining from the temptation of 'coaching' the Franco-Vietnamese presentations to the commission, the Canadians avoided later difficulties, though the sense of self-righteous dignity thus acquired did appear, in some instances, to have subsequently impeded critical self-reflection concerning later Canadian policy.

The Canadians entered Indochina warily. Their trepidation was justified. At the very moment that Canadian officials and representatives in Indochina thought that they had come down squarely on their feet and were prepared to carry out a disagreeable though straightforward task, American officials in both Washington and Vietnam were taking steps that would immeasurably complicate Canadian policy-making.

AMERICAN POLICY AND THE REFUGEES 1954–5

Franco-American relations had not been improved by the outcome at Geneva, though by mid-July the American leaders were quite prepared privately to admit that Geneva had not been 'Municheering.' By late August, Washington leaders seemed prepared to try to squeeze the French out of their dominant position of influence in Indochina.[20] French failure to approve the EDC legislation in the last week of August evidently had confirmed the wisdom of eroding the French effort in Indochina. Respect for the French was extremely scarce in American policy-making circles.[21]

American policy-makers forged ahead with arrangements for the Southeast Asia Collective Defense Treaty, 'SEATO,'* and its associated protocol which brought Cambodia, Laos, 'and the free territory under the jurisdiction of the State of Vietnam' within the ambit of Articles 3 and 4 of the treaty proper (the key articles pertaining to economic assistance and measures of collective defence against aggression). The Manila Pact was signed on 8 September 1954, a little over one week after the collapse of the EDC scheme. Surprisingly, it was the US joint chiefs who insisted that the US not be irrevocably committed to specific lines of military action under the SEATO arrangements. American military leaders were determined to preserve 'freedom of action.'[22] The SEATO concept was seen by the communist bloc as a

---

* The familiar though inaccurate acronymn will be used henceforth.

direct challenge to the Geneva approach, despite the vagueness of the treaty commitments.[23] The thrust of US policy was clear: to secure the territory south of the 17th parallel indefinitely for the American-led bloc despite whatever understandings had been reached by the European and communist negotiators at Geneva. United States policy with respect to SEATO may have been poorly conceived and very ill advised, but it was neither illegal under prevailing international law and agreements, nor surprising given the American posture of ominous disassociation at Geneva. The United States had declared a willingness not to use force 'to disturb' the agreements. And it did not: military force was not required to assist Ngo Dinh Diem in defying the electoral provisions of the Final Declaration, only military and economic assistance.

The Americans used, in the first instance, political and economic assistance to Diem's government to try to 'stabilize' the situation in the south, combined with low-level covert operations to try to keep the new DRVN regime off balance through sabotage, while doing what was possible to accelerate the flow of refugees from the north via various 'black propaganda' measures. Stories were planted of communist Chinese troops raping Vietnamese women in Vietminh-controlled areas. CIA agents arranged for the distribution of fraudulent pamphlets, supposedly written for Vietminh cadres, in which communist stalwarts were guaranteed protection from 'imperialist air and submarine attacks.' CIA staff sabotaged the Hanoi public transport system. A CIA 'proprietary corporation,' Civil Air Transport, was actively involved in the refugee transport program. Finally, a paramilitary group of Vietnamese was trained in the Philippines and some eight and one-half tons of arms, ammunition, radios, and other equipment were cached in the north for use after the cease-fire. According to the Lansdale group report these operations had to be concealed both from the Vietminh and the ICSC 'with its suspicious French [sic] and Poles and Indians.'[24]

It is not clear what effect these operations had on the volume of the refugee flow. It may have been negligible. In light of the fact that the vast majority of the refugees were Roman Catholic and that most of them had to overcome terrible pressure, harassment, and obstruction, it is reasonable to infer that only those truly determined to go south actually made the trip. The major result of CIA covert operations in the north may have been the partial discrediting of the political significance of this massive exodus. Such are the ironies of history.

The difference between the Canadian and American responses to the refugees lay in the fact that the United States was willing to use unethical tactics to speed up the exodus from Tonkin. Rumours that 'Christ and the Virgin

Mary have gone south,' or that the north might be attacked with atomic bombs, could not be attributed solely to feverish, panic-stricken Catholic priests.[25]

American policy-makers were not sure during 1954–5 whom they would support in the internal political struggle for the State of Vietnam governmental apparatus. Dulles's support of Diem was lukewarm at best throughout 1954, but eventually Colonel Edward Lansdale* seems to have won over both John Foster Dulles and Eisenhower to Diem's cause through Allen Dulles, the new CIA director. As late as May 1955 John Foster Dulles nearly decided to liquidate US involvement in Vietnam because of continuing French opposition to the francophobe Diem regime.[26] After the joint US-UK-French consultations over Diem and the State of Vietnam in early May 1955, Dulles eventually decided to strike an independent course in Indochina, despite the fact that this would inevitably mean the liquidation of the French military presence there. The American decision came at the very time when Diem was surmounting his crisis with the Binh Xuyen gangster sect and was preparing his campaign against the Hoa Hao and Cao Dai politico-religious sects.† Diem's progress may have been the decisive element leading to the fateful American choice of going it alone in the Indochinese conflict.

In any case, the early steps taken by the State Department and CIA from September through December, in the campaign both to destabilize the northern sector of Vietnam and to promote Diem's struggle for power in the south, seem to have remained wholly unknown to the ICSC representatives and, indeed, to Ottawa decision-makers as well. The Canadians do not appear to have been kept informed of the shifting and still ambivalent character of American policy. Canadian officials may have suspected such operations, but they probably would not want to have been informed of their nature, which would of course immediately compromise Ottawa in its self-assigned and determined commitment to act in a 'scrupulously impartial' manner. Until mid-1955 at least, the Canadian adhered to the view that the Geneva Agreements including the 'political settlement' terms of the Final Declaration would be carried out. Reports from the Canadian delegations in all three Indochinese states indicated that the Poles were continuing to be 'all sweetness and light,' while the Pathet Lao and Vietminh commands were

---

* Colonel Edward G. Lansdale was a member of the US Military Assistance and Advisory Group in Saigon in 1954, and an 'adviser to the armed forces and government of the State of Vietnam on Internal Security matters.' FRUS, 1952–1954, XIII, part II, xx

† The Hoa Hao and Cao Dai sects had close to 2 million adherents each, and both had substantial armies. The Binh Xuyen racketeers had an army, but no mass following.

behaving in a reasonably co-operative manner. The communist side evidently was going to carry out its obligations to the letter.[27]

It was public knowledge in September that the United States government had committed extensive funding for the refugee movement program. Ships from the US Seventh Fleet were assigned to carry refugees (along with French ships) and the US 'provided a sum of $93 million for the overall relocation program.'[28] State of Vietnam statistics accepted by the ICSC as reasonably accurate indicated that between July 1954 and mid-May 1955, 888,127 persons left the northern zone for the south. Only 2,598 'civilians' went south to north in the same period.[29] Of the total of over 890,000 who eventually went to the south, some 250,000 belonged to the SVN army or administration (or were dependents of same), and about 650,000 were Catholics not connected to the VNA or the SVN bureaucracy. The enormous movement of Catholics to the south (some 85 per cent of the 900,000 who went south were Catholic) tripled the south's Catholic population, according to most estimates, raising the Catholic proportion from just over 2 to almost 7 per cent.[30] Though only some 4,269 'civilians' went from south to north through French-SVN procedures by 20 July 1955,[31] some 150,000 Vietminh troops and dependents are estimated to have made the trip to the north on Polish and Russian ships as part of the 300-day regroupment process.[32]

The composition of the refugee movement in terms of employment and religious affiliation was known at the time, but it was not appreciated that this exodus might sow the seeds of future social and political strife in the south. At the time the emotional reaction of many Westerners was relief that the Catholic refugees would still be able to practise their faith free from Stalinist oppression, coupled with pride that this massive act of 'voting with the feet' somehow validated all Western efforts to save 'free Vietnam.' But it should also be noted that in the year following the Geneva Agreements, the area north of the 17th parallel suffered the worst famine since the calamity of 1945–6, when 10 per cent of the population in Red River delta had died. Millions were on the edge of starvation in the north once more in the winter of 1954–5. Neither the Soviet nor Chinese governments showed any serious concern for the situation. In most Western observers' minds the famine and the refugee exodus were only marginally associated though there may have been a significant link between the two developments, as one Polish writer (and former ICSC commissioner) has argued.[33]

In any case American policy and actions materially affected the volume of the refugee movement. And while American officials scrambled frantically to put together a program of political, economic, and military support for the

Diem government, the Canadians became ever more enmeshed in the murky, oppressive difficulties which confronted the ICSC.

INITIAL CANADIAN ATTITUDES TO THE ARMISTICE
IMPLEMENTATION AND THE OPERATION OF ARTICLE 14(d)

On 27 September 1954, Sherwood left, the first Canadian commissioner on the ICSC for Vietnam, was interviewed on the CBC radio network concerning Canada's role in Indochina just prior to his departure for Hanoi. During the interview he noted that the terms of the agreement were imprecise because they were drawn up in such haste. He feared that each side would doubt the good faith of the other, and that both sides would be especially vexed by the consequences of Article 14(d). He expressed the hope that Indian and Canadian policies would work in a complementary fashion since their 'ultimate objectives' were 'similar.' He noted finally that:

when these tasks [the armistice implementation measures] have been successfully carried out, *the stage will be set for the next operation which will be the holding of general elections in 1956 for the establishment of an All-Vietnamese Government.* I expect that the making of agreements for these elections, the holding of the elections and *the establishment of an All-Vietnam Government will be a more difficult task than the execution of the cease-fire itself.* The prerequisites for a political settlement, if such a settlement is attainable, are the maintenance of the truce which has been attained ... the Canadian view is that the *successful implementation of the three cease-fire agreements* in Indo-China *is a first step* towards the achievement of conditions of stability and security throughout Southeast Asia ... Indications so far are that the two parties are carrying out the terms of the agreement in good faith and without serious difficulties. So long as this attitude persists, the possibility of carrying out the military phase of the settlement would appear fairly bright. *It is too early to say anything about the political phase which will come later.*[34]

Already, in late September 1954, the Canadian side had grave doubts about the feasibility, perhaps even the desirability, of attempted unification through elections. Lett's lengthy interview contained, in fact, the conceptual germ of the future Canadian position, which argued that the armistice measures and the political settlement provisions of the Geneva Agreements were entirely distinct and not necessarily interdependent aspects of the Geneva 'settlement.' In years to come this distinction would become an accepted axiom of the Canadian posture vis-à-vis Indochina. In September 1954, however, the idea though 'in the wind' was by no means firmly held. In any case, with respect to the implementation of Article 14(d) Commissioner-designate Lett clearly anticipated the difficulties to come, and knew full well which aspects of the Geneva Agreements were going to prove most troublesome.

Lett did not arrive in Hanoi to join the commission proceedings until the last week of October. While in London, on his way to Vietnam, he was briefed by the British chief of the imperial general staff, who told him essentially that there was virtually no hope that the supervisory commissions could slow down a communist take-over of all Indochina.[35] From this depressing conversation Lett journeyed to Hanoi, where he found that numerous complaints had been lodged by both French and State of Vietnam authorities – letters from the latter being an occasion for great surprise on the part of the ICSC delegates, who had been well briefed on Diem's repudiation of the Accords. Chairman Desai hoped that this 'first official gesture' by the State of Vietnam, which acknowledged the existence and mandate of the ICSC for Vietnam, might be an omen of growing co-operation.[36]

By the time Lett arrived over 50 per cent of the eventual Canadian Indochina contingent had been transported in – the Canadians being the only group to meet the New Delhi arrival timetable.[37] The Canadian delegations to each of the three ICS were smaller than either the Polish or Indian contingents. By Christmas the Indians serving on the Vietnam ICSC numbered 580, being charged with all the administrative and communications task in the commission secretariat, the Poles about 132 including numerous additional interpreter staff, and the Canadians but 85.[38] Despite the fact that the military officers comprised about three-quarters of Canadian personnel deployed in the three Indochinese states, the Department of National Defence wanted no part in overall direction or formulation of Canadian policy vis-à-vis Indochina. This was to be entirely a DEA operation. Their attitude was described well by John Holmes in an August letter to R.M. Macdonnell in Hanoi:

National Defence have been insistent that External Affairs accept the direction of the enterprise. They will not produce a single body or do anything at all unless they receive written instructions from us. They get quite annoyed in fact if we leave any choice to them at all ... The army paymasters will of course look after pay and allowances and the army will attend to the personal needs of the soldiers. All their requirements, however, as members of the Commission must go through our financial channels. The Minister has accepted these proposals ... in his talks with Mr. Campney because he thinks it is very important for us to maintain the direction of the enterprise.

In the same letter, Holmes, then head of Far Eastern Division, noted that 'the Indochina octopus' had 'pretty well strangled every division in the Department.'[39] The calibre of officer staff was high, but clerical staff who were willing to go were extremely scarce.

In years to come the 'octopus' would diminish slightly in size as DEA grew larger, but the whole scale of operations remained large enough to constitute, if not an octopus, then a very large albatross. At the New Delhi Conference of the commission powers it had been decided to establish six-person teams at each of the fixed team locations. Each FT would be composed of both fixed and mobile 'elements.' Though this decision was hardly binding, in practice precedent dominated subsequent activity, and thus the six-person format was the norm forever after. By mid-October all but two of the FTs were deployed.[40]

By mid-October the Vietnam ICSC's operations were well under way. Thousands of prisoners of war and civilian internees had been exchanged. By 9 September 1954 some 65,470 prisoners had been handed back to the PAVN by FUF, while the French received back some 11,740.[41] On 9 October the transfer of Hanoi from FUF to PAVN authority was successfully completed, despite great tension and minor difficulties over the quantity of equipment, machinery, and so forth which the French were required to leave behind in the public institutions (the waterworks, hydroelectric facilities, telegraph communications, post office, etc.) so as to permit effectively continuous administration of the city. The commission did valuable work in this period in smoothing out the problems which the French and PAVN high commands could not resolve by themselves.

By mid-October the Canadian delegation, perhaps somewhat less anxious since the prisoners-of-war exchange and the early regroupment operations had fared so well, decided to begin to push for more ICSC vigilance concerning effective implementation of 14(d). Several mobile team 'investigations' had already been carried out with respect to the regroupment and transfer operations. Macdonnell and Cadieux suggested that mid-October was an appropriate time to monitor the progress of evacuation from the northern zone.

By early October so many requests for such action had been lodged with the commission that Chairman Desai reluctantly agreed. In Desai's view: the operation was to be 'fact-finding, not fault-finding.' The chairman wanted all ICSC investigations to proceed in this manner.[42]

Desai somewhat grudgingly assented to the dispatch of a mobile team to both Nam Dinh and Phat Diem, two northern regions predominantly Catholic in character, to ascertain whether there was any 'floating population on the move' seeking exit to the south. Ambassador Ogrodzinski, seeing that the Indian chairman was determined to carry out this operation to placate the Canadians (as well as the French), expressed concern that the ICSC was not conducting a parallel investigation in the south. To balance the day's decisional record Desai compensated the Poles by agreeing to send MT investigators to look into conditions at the Xuan The prison camp in the south.[43]

The same meeting also witnessed the formation of the Freedoms Committee, which was charged with the task of coping with the thousands of individual petitions from the North. The committee was empowered to act as a mobile team, and it was to work directly with the liaison missions of the parties in attempting to foster more effective implementation of Article 14(d). The establishment of the Freedoms Committee did not lead to any early action by the commission. From this point onward the Canadian delegation began to chaff at Indian reluctance to risk offending the DRVN authorities.

With the assumption of the role of acting commissioner by Marcel Cadieux on 14 October the Canadian stand on 14(d) stiffened markedly. In connection with the case of one Le Tan Ly, a resident of the north who claimed he had been arrested by the DRVN authorities when he sought permission to go south, Cadieux argued impassionedly for IC protection for this would-be refugee. Asylum should be available, he declared, through the ICSC. The action of Fixed Team Hanoi in handing back Le to the DRVN authorities was 'against humanity.'[44] Ogrodzinski then noted that the 'juridical aspects' of the matter of asylum were quite complex and that the IC would be well advised 'to avoid any diplomatic embarrassments.' Desai again flatly overruled the asylum camp proposal. He did, however, agree to Cadieux's fallback suggestion that the local authorities must inform the commission regarding the place of detention where particular would-be refugees were to be taken, so that they could be made available as the commission required.[45]

At the 42nd meeting the Canadian moves to obtain 14(d) MT investigations in the north met with strong opposition from Colonel Ha Van Lau, chief liaison officer of the PAVN High Command, who appeared before the ICSC in Hanoi. The colonel stated that 'propaganda' by 'certain parties' claimed that the DRVN was blocking would-be refugees. The reverse was true, he said. 'As a matter of fact if the Democratic Republic appealed to the people in the South to evacuate to the North millions would come.'[46]

After this ludicrous assertion, Ha Van Lau went on to argue that responsibility for ensuring the carrying out of Article 14(d) was a matter solely for the parties themselves and the Joint Commission. The ICSC had no business interfering, and would be overloaded with work if it did. Desai immediately dissented from Lau's line of argument and firmly asserted the IC's right and obligation to monitor 14(d) progress. Colonel de Beaufort from the French Liaison Mission agreed with the IC's actions, naturally enough, and strongly approved the creation of the Freedoms Committee. To Desai's credit, in both this the 42nd meeting and the 43rd as well, he forcefully but persuasively won acknowledgment of the need for, and legitimacy of, this ICSC subcommittee. As a concession to Polish and DRVN pressures, Desai agreed that MT investigations of the 14(d) question should also be charged with looking into 'the problem of forced evacuation' to the south – an allegation made by the North Vietnamese and championed by the Poles which amounted to an oblique and finally not very effective allusion to American-French-Catholic propaganda efforts to induce North Vietnamese Catholics to flee south.

By 19 October the Committee on Freedom of Movement draft proposal, drawn up primarily because of the urging of Marcel Cadieux, was approved. The Canadian refugee 'offensive' had begun.

Part of the difficulties facing the Canadians, which kept the delegation off balance during its first two months of ICSC duty, stemmed from the inescapable heat and problems with food and water purity. Keeping Canadian digestive tracts healthy became a major preoccupation. Said one early assignee: 'We weren't at all prepared in External. I found out after living there for awhile that the military detachment was all taking Paludrine and other pills to combat the local parasites and bacteria in the food and water. I didn't even know what the mosquito netting was for. We were totally green.' The Canadians faced other 'environmental' difficulties as well:

The Indians were very friendly. So friendly that things were rarely quiet at the Canadian headquarters. At night it was very amusing to hear the Indians sing 'Alouette' while drinking vodka until 2 a.m. ... Our image of the Far East is that it is mysterious – and, I always thought, quietly mysterious. But it wasn't. Occasionally the Indians would put on some of their music that would sound awful – that sort of wailing that sounds like someone's put the singer's balls in a meat grinder and is turning the handle slowly. And then there were other noises all night long. A man selling noodles would come around clicking shears, then someone else knocking sticks together, another ringing bells ... So far as food was concerned the fare was quite austere. Since they knew Westerners were meat eaters they insisted on providing us with quantities of buffalo steak – and steamed cauliflower, called ironically enough 'misère.' Every night more misère ... One delicious meal of small fish, cooked intact, was greeted with horror by most of the others as 'a plate of fish eyes.' The standard trick played by the Indians on all Canadian newcomers was to consume whole pimentos with great gusto – fresh, bright red and green pimentos – and then invite these unsuspecting novices to try some. They would of course, and then nearly choke to death. The Indians enjoyed all this immensely and never got tired of this routine.[47]

Green, indeed. However, once adjusted to these novel and disturbing conditions, the Canadians became rather more disposed to a stiffer line in ICSC proceedings. The line was not easily or confidently formulated, however. Said one Canadian ICSC representative who was a Catholic:

Personally the ICSC was traumatic primarily because of the situation of the Catholic refugees. It was really a moral dilemma for us. What should we do? We entered with the expectation that the agreement would work. The presence of the Indians gave us hope, and the fact that the Russians had accepted indicated to us that they might want to play ball. We expected at least two years duty plus. *We all assumed Ho Chi Minh would win the elections when they were held.* Desai, for example, thought that Ho Chi Minh was the embodiment of Vietnamese nationalism. Clearly we were there on the ICSC to help get these people out of the north – *but if the elections still to come went the wrong way then the refugees we had helped would be much worse off than if they had never moved, since their disloyalty to the new government would be a matter of record.* It was a moral problem. But then *Diem took it out of our hands.* He was a man that impressed me very much with his great courage. *His position and actions on the refugee problem cleared up any doubts we had.*

The same 'conservative' interviewee declared later:

One of the problems we faced was that the reporting in *the Western media used our criteria,* or standards, *to measure the policies of Diem.* And they did *not judge the North in the same way.* The Diem government was worth defending. Certainly it had repressive controls, the regime taxed heavily, the war went on and on, and millions were slaughtered. But the measure of their worth is that hundreds of thousands of people in the North insisted on moving south. And *it was a humanitarian act of the South to accept them* – to put them in the tents of the camps, to take on all the associated problems of resettlement in the South. *That government was worthy of our support.* The Diem government was not composed of democrats or liberals, by any stretch of the imagination. They could not be concerned with such goals. The problems were intractable. And of course, *once people become committed to opposition to the Communists we could not deny them support. We had to back them since the stakes were so high. Life or death.*[48]

Canadian conservatives adhered to essentially humanitarian criteria in making their arguments and advancing their proposed line of response to various situations. In reply to a query whether he thought the CIA might have been one of the main causes of the refugee exodus, this same Catholic conservative most emphatically dissented:

The Catholics [Vietnamese] were purely motivated, sincerely motivated by fear of religious persecution and a desire to be free. It was not just a case of one-sided propaganda manipulation. After all, the DRVN could and did engage in that kind of thing too. Giap and others even had the nerve to say: 'Your Catholics are attacking my soldiers.' And the only thing I could do was burst out laughing. When Giap and Ho were being realistic they would indicate that they were very worried about people 'voting with their feet,' since if another million moved south the balance in the 1956 election would be shifted against the Vietminh.[49]

In concluding his comments on the refugee issue, this conservative referred explicitly to the Tra Ly affair, which was a protracted incident at a village near the coast of North Vietnam, where several thousand Catholics apparently were congregated in a river estuary, standing in the water for some days, awaiting rescue by French or American ships. The DRVN successfully blocked entry of any ships, and through procedural delays in the commission proper, a mobile team investigation of the situation was prevented until the local authorities had been given sufficient time to disperse this 'floating population on the move.' Thus,

Tra Ly kept me very much awake at night. I would ask myself: Is there some trick or procedure or method that I've missed that will alter the ICSC's position to the advantage of the refugees? Have I been out-maneuvered? Could I have done better? And so on. Giap and Pham Van Dong were very forthcoming, pragmatic and unemotional on this subject. One could talk seriously about it with them. They would note that the Catholic population in the north was very much in the control of the local priests. And this was unfair in a way. They argued in private that they too should be given at least a chance. Fear rules all under the priests, they said. To some extent they had a point.[50]

In the 14(d) debates that followed, the newly arrived Ambassador Lett stressed the 'mandatory' character of the wording of Article 37, which stipulated that the ICSC had to carry out 'necessary investigations.' He also resisted Polish demands for parallelism in investigations. Chairman Desai noted that all the petitions simply could not be investigated; it was beyond the physical capacity of the commission.[51] Ogrodzinski, heartened by this implied rebuke to Lett, argued that it was not clear that the Freedoms Committee could exist without a parallel body in the Joint Commission. Desai dissented. Still obviously unhappy with Lett's zestful introduction to the IC, he then asked Lett to comport himself more 'in the spirit of the Geneva Agreement.' The business of the IC was to avoid 'lengthy judicial debates,' to find 'practical solutions,' and to 'build up an atmosphere of effective cooperation by the Parties.'[52] Lett's concept of the commission as a judicial body charged with the task of interpreting the 'law' of Geneva needed revision. The commission would clearly be engaged in 'judicial policy-making' and mediation, not just legal analysis.

In *The War of the Vanquished*, Mieczyslaw Maneli badly misrepresents the position of the Canadian delegation, claiming that it opted for a narrow interpretation of the freedom of movement of the fixed and mobile teams.[53] In fact, the Canadians, primarily because of the refugee issue, were champions of *maximum* freedom of movement for the IC teams, realizing that the only leverage they had on securing effective implementation of 14(d) was to get IC teams on the spot quickly, whenever 'concentrations' or 'floating populations' were alleged to have materialized. The Poles and the DRVN Liaison Mission objected. According to the IC minutes:

The Canadian Ambassador stated that it was evident from the letter from the Democratic Republic Liaison Mission that *it wished to restrict the movement of the fixed teams. In his view, it would be impossible for the fixed and mobile teams to carry out their duties of inspection and observation* as visualized under Article 36, and to be 'the eyes and ears of the Commission' if *any restrictions or limitations were placed on their movement*. Article 37 of the Geneva Agreement clearly showed that the International Commission could utilize 'inspection teams' for conducting any enquiry. These 'inspection teams' included both fixed and mobile teams and *the Article made it quite clear that such enquiries could on occasion be conducted on the Commission's own initiative*. He further stated that if the Commission's supervision and control was to be effective, *a fixed team should be able at a moment's notice to convert itself into a mobile team*.[54]

No stronger statement of the principle of maximal investigatory powers is to be found anywhere in the ICSC minutes. Desai firmly supported Lett's position, rejected Ogrodzinski's appeal to 'operational precedents,' and called for the creation of fourteen zones for the fourteen FTs which would encompass the whole of Vietnam. His strong position was based on a belief that 'it would be impossible to enforce the provisions of the Agreement throughout the whole country unless the teams had freedom to move in any part of the whole area as and when necessary.' Desai rejected Polish attempts to rebut this argument saying that a restrictive interpretation of Articles 35 to 37 would lead to 'action after the event and this could hardly be supervision.'[55]

On this occasion, Desai and Lett carried the day, as well they should have. Unconstrained movement was essential for the execution of the manifold tasks conferred on the IC such as: supervising the demilitarized zone; supervising prisoner exchanges throughout the country; monitoring the borders of the country, and its airports, to ensure compliance with the no-reinforcement provisions of Articles 16 and 17; and making sure that no new military bases were being built anywhere in the country. But Desai and Lett would lose this struggle.

The DRVN was determined to block 'freedom of movement' for IC teams, and they succeeded from the outset of supervisory operations. Hamstringing IC mobility was important for two reasons. First, according to Maneli, the DRVN was importing heavy weaponry (including tanks) by the end of 1954.[56] Second, they were worried about the growing refugee exodus. Quite understandably.

By the end of October some 400,000 had left. The 900,000 in total who went raised the south's population to well over 12 million. The northern zone's population was diminished to a figure of about 14 million. If there had been a truly open frontier, somewhere between 500,000 and 1 million more Catholics and petit-bourgeois 'rich peasants' would probably have emigrated to the south, thereby throwing into doubt the guaranteed majority of the 'captive electorate' in the north. By early November the dimensions of the refugee movement were unmistakably evident, and this no doubt was an extremely important factor in continuing DRVN-Polish resistance to Indo-Canadian attempts at establishing the FT-MT free movement principle. Under steady and intense pressure Desai suggested a compromise which unfortunately would in the end undermine the effective operation of the IC teams and render most of the IC's operations useless. Desai proposed: that FT's activities as fixed teams be restricted to fairly narrow zones; that a secondary, much wider area be designated for each FT as its zone of operations as a mobile team; that the DRVN and FUF-SVN authorities be asked for 'general permission' to operate in the secondary zone; that an FT when moving into its 'area of mobility' had to contact local liaison officers to acquire the 'necessary logistical support'; and that the fourteen FT 'zones of mobility' had to cover the entire country.[57] The DRVN authorities were pleased. Desai's decision provided them with just enough operational leeway to ensure a sufficient number of selective acts of obstruction on issues they deemed most important (specific arms imports and refugee dispersal operations) to warrant agreement.

If one believes that it was in the interests of all concerned to keep the Geneva structure intact for the time being, Desai's compromise was an example of brilliant tactical ingenuity. Neither side was so upset that it was driven to consideration of withdrawal from the armistice arrangements as a whole. The net result of the compromise was that a marginal improvement in the implementation of 14(d) did occur. The compromise also paved the way for significant and ongoing violations of Articles 16 and 17.

In the First Interim Report of the ICSC for the period 11 August to 10 December 1954, the commission unanimously agreed with regard to the refugee issue that

the High Command of the People's Army of Vietnam, while they did cooperate with the Commission and took measures to secure freedom of movement in the case of about 8,000 Phat Diem refugees, have so far done little to develop adequate administrative arrangements, with the result that complaints continue to pour in. Restrictions on internal movements from province to province and a cumbersome system of permits can hardly assist in the effective exercise of the right of freedom of movement under Article 14(d).[58]

By Christmas of 1954 numerous MT investigations had taken place but the obstruction, delays, and procedural wrangles engendered by the 'local authorities' in the north were by then so pervasive and skilful as to block most of these limited IC interventions on behalf of the would-be refugees. The Canadian delegation was at an impasse. How hard should it press for fulfilment of 14(d)?

ADDITIONAL COMPLEXITIES: THE SAINTENY MISSION AND
AMERICAN UNPREDICTABILITY

To complicate the difficulty of the Canadian position still more, the growing rift in Franco-American relations cast into doubt the ability of the Western 'alliance' to contribute effectively to the growth of a stable SVN regime. During the pre-Geneva diplomatic crisis the Canadians had been able to support the British-French lead in seeking a negotiated settlement to the Indochina conflict in a fairly straightforward fashion, in opposition to Washington militants who wanted the war prosecuted to victory. The outcome of the Geneva talks seemed to create hope for a neutral, but truly independent Laos and Cambodia. The provisions of the Laotian Cease-Fire Agreement, which permitted the French to maintain up to 1,500 officers and NCOs in Laos for training the Laotian National Army, as well as 3,500 men at two bases, seemed adequate to ensure continuing Western influence, in fact predominance, in the western Indochinese states. Neutralist autonomy, at the very least, seemed to be a reliable prospect for both Laos and Cambodia. But what of the State of Vietnam? How far would the Americans go in supporting Diem's regime financially?

The French were at best very reluctant supporters of the francophobe Diem government. For the first ten to twelve months after Geneva, they did intend to live up to the electoral provisions of the Final Declaration. Presumably in recognition of the probable DRVN victory in the unification ballot, the Quai d'Orsay sent Jean Sainteny in the autumn of 1954 on yet another special diplomatic assignment, to negotiate with Ho and the DRVN leadership. Some Canadian observers thought this new mission had quite a few similarities to Sainteny's 1946 mission when he had been sent to Hanoi to explore the prospects for an early negotiated settlement to the first Indochina war.* The Sainteny Mission seems to have represented one weak factional position in French policy advocating accommodation and co-operation with the DRVN in the hope of thereby minimizing Soviet and Chinese influence on Hanoi. French economic assistance was to be the bribe which it was hoped would wean Ho and Giap away from a tight communist orbit. Briefly, the Sainteny Mission sought to foster 'Asian Titoism.' The reappearance of this accommodationist tendency in French policy placed Canadian decision-makers in somewhat of a quandary. They were required to evaluate the objective merits of Sainteny's tactics, and to estimate whether this policy posture would in fact be accepted by the French government.

In mid-September the Canadian delegation feared an inevitable asymmetry in the application of the armistice provisions. Fragmentation of authority in the south and growing unity and 'monolithic solidarity' in the north guaranteed that prisoner-of-war exchange modalities, the operation of the freedom-of-movement clause of the armistice agreement, and the implementation of the 'democratic rights – no reprisals' clause would all favour the northern regime. Canadian conservatives in Vietnam feared, rightly enough, that few people in the north would be able to get to the ICSC team sites to lodge protests or petitions. Hence, it appeared to the Canadians that they might have to take part in a long series of investigations aimed only at

* For details see Jean Sainteny, *Histoire d'une paix manquée* (Paris: Amiot-Dumont 1953). Of the Canadians, Marcel Cadieux, at least, was familiar with the book.

blackening the reputation of the Franco-SVN side. The regime in the south was weak and inexperienced. In any elections it would be totally out of its depth against the DRVN 'machine.' By mid-October some hope was expressed from the Canadian delegation in Hanoi that Desai was beginning to see through the ruses and trickery of the DRVN, but the political outlook in Saigon was by then so chaotic that there were no grounds for optimism. To compound matters for the Canadians, the French Liaison Mission was now sending in poorly drafted, careless, and generally ineffective submissions.[59]

As members of the Canadian delegation interpreted it, the approach espoused by Jean Sainteny's group in Hanoi began with the premise that the DRVN was going to gain control of all Vietnam. If exerting control required force, force would be used and that in turn would lead to more Stalinism, more anti-colonialism, and more dependence on Moscow. Why not seek to reduce that dependence by a policy of positive incentives? Hanoi was vulnerable to seduction given its prostrate economic condition. Therefore, why not turn this to Western advantage? Why not, indeed? Some liberal-moderate elements in Ottawa had their interest pricked by reports of the Sainteny group. But conservative argument soon put an end to any such speculative endeavours in this direction.

According to Canadian conservative thinking it was indeed true that the DRVN leadership would eagerly seek independence from both Moscow and Beijing, the latter in particular. Yes, Hanoi would be war-weary. But what could the French hope to accomplish alone? American concurrence in a 'Tito-ization' program was a sine qua non for its success. And in the autumn of 1954, a number of Americans were busily looking for their 'honest patriot.' Would Diem be that figure? And had not Washington an accumulated investment of well over a billion dollars in the fight to stop Vietnam from going communist? The conclusion of SEATO was surely additional evidence that the Sainteny line was doomed. Ottawa's liberal-moderates got the message.[60]

Because of American economic intervention to sustain the Diem regime as well as Diem's astounding victories over the three sects in 1955, Sainteny's mission was a total failure. He failed to convince the French government that his goals were realizable. Sainteny eventually left Hanoi on 'temporary leave' in 1957 and never returned. French efforts to maintain *la présence française* were a total failure and French economic interests went largely uncompensated except for a partial, though apparently far from satisfactory, indemnity to the owners of the Hon Gay-Cam Pha coal extraction-exporting complex.[61] In late 1954, however, it was not at all clear that the Sainteny 'line' was doomed to an early demise.

At approximately the same time as the Canadian delegation was sending home its negative appreciation of the Sainteny Mission, Ottawa decision-makers had arrived at a similar position, though it was expressed in less categorical language. On 19 October 1954 John Holmes wrote Chester Ronning an appreciation of the then current complexities posed by the lack of unity in French policy:

The Americans seem to have got over some of their original doubts as to whether South Vietnam could be saved and are talking about large programmes of economic aid and 'information.' There is still a good deal of suspicion in the United States that the French are playing a double game, that while they are ostensibly supporting the government in Saigon they are preparing to do business with the Viet Minh. The French have denied this to the Americans, but I suspect that they are not themselves firm and united in their policy. Their man Sainteny, whom they sent to Hanoi as Liaison Officer with the Viet Minh, has certainly been on record as strongly favouring an accommodation with Ho Chi Minh. Perhaps in the not very hopeful situation in which they find themselves, there is a good deal to be said for such a policy.[62]

In Ottawa, remote from the immediate crisis of the Catholic petitioners, perspective on events in northern Vietnam was more readily achieved. The main objective of the liberal-moderates like Holmes was maintaining the armistice. If that goal could be obtained by a Sainteny-style approach, then it deserved consideration at least. However, in Ottawa just as in Hanoi, the signs of a deepening American commitment were growing numerous, and an American 'strategic commitment' to the Vietnam struggle would most certainly preclude any attempts by lesser Western powers to carry through on an operation regarded as a diplomatic 'sell-out' in Washington. Neither had the fear of nuclear war been completely expunged. The unpredictability of American policy argued for extreme caution in relations with American leaders.

In June, contingency plan estimates had been drawn up by the CIA to forecast probable Soviet and PRC reactions to American intervention in the Indochina war with air and naval forces. Nuclear weapons were assumed to be required in various connected scenarios, which began with their use in Indochina and ended with their extensive use against military targets in China (but avoiding the civilian population as far as possible). The final phase of this five-part forecast of Soviet-PRC probable reactions to American intervention and escalation concluded that the communist governments probably would retreat in the face of extensive nuclear attack, the destruction of all Vietminh-PRC forces in Indochina, the imposition of a naval blockade all along the Chinese coast, 'seizure or neutralization of Hainan,' and the commencement of KMT operations against the mainland. These CIA planners believed that Soviet-communist Chinese forces, if confronted with such a multidimensional threat, would inevitably withdraw and sue for peace 'under any U.S. terms which preserved the integrity of China under the Chinese Communist regime.'[63] In short, in the event of a shoot-out in Indochina, Washington could look forward to victory if only American leaders would climb the escalatory ladder to the level of 'limited strategic warfare.'

Pressure from the adventurist, rollback element in Washington's policy debates did not cease with the signing of the Geneva Agreements. Thus a prudent Anglo-Canadian concern regarding the risk of precipitate American military commitments in Indochina was still justified.

It had not troubled the Canadians when US authorities had rushed to inflate the personnel of the Military Assistance Advisory Group in Vietnam to beat the 11 August deadline.[64] That move had indicated a measure of respect for the Geneva armistice terms. They were also aware of the great variation in US assessments of the SVN's capacity to survive, ranging from Senator Mansfield's negativism in recommending that Vietnam be 'written off,' to Colonel Lansdale's hubris in engaging in palace coup planning.[66] But being aware of these contradictory trends did not make the environment any more predictable. In late September a Franco-American conference in Washington agreed that as of 1 January 1955 all US aid would go directly to the SVN forces and administration.[67] On 23 October Eisenhower wrote directly to Diem promising him US support. On 8 November, the President's personal emissary, General J. Lawton Collins, arrived in Saigon to co-ordinate all US operations. As it turned out, 'Lightnin' Joe' Collins would be one of Diem's sternest critics. But paradoxically it was Collins who, with the joint effort of General Paul Ely, the new French commissioner general, effectively solidified Diem's position – this despite efforts by lower-level officials of both the American and French groups to interfere with each other's activities.[68] Without active French support Diem could not have survived as head of his government.[69] In the autumn of 1954 it was the French who still had many thousands of troops at their disposal in Indochina, not the United States.

Under General Ely the provisional grant of sovereignty to the SVN of 4 June 1954 was carried through by a complete transfer of all administrative functions. The *colons* protested this surrender of French control and their often violent acts of sabotage account for misleading American tales of French attempts at subversion of Diem.[70]

CONCLUSION

The period from August through early November was a time for familiarization with the real political environment of Vietnam. The first weeks of operations, the first successes in separating the combatants and conciliating minor disputes, all gave hope that the armistice could be made to stick. But SEATO portended serious problems for the future. So too did the apparently contradictory policy practised by the French. These were, however, problems of grave political import over which Canadians were unlikely to exert substantial influence. The French, Americans, and British were going to make their decisions regardless of what Ottawa's position was. Countries of the middle rank would either find ways and means of accommodating or reconciling the diverse demands made by the great powers, or they would be required to help clean up the still larger mess when massive collisions occurred. A high level of anxiety was an inevitable concomitant of an ICSC role.

The emerging problem of the refugees substantially added to the already chronic state of concern and worry experienced by Canadians. No one had imagined having to deal with an enormous mass movement of hundreds of thousands of Vietnamese 'fleeing from Communist tyranny.' What were the Canadians now to do? If Vietnam was truly going to be won by the communists in the elections of 1956, as everyone expected at that time, what was the point of fighting relentlessly to try to force communist respect for 14(d)? But on the other hand, once the potential scale of the migration had become undeniable, a Canadian failure to win maximum possible observance of the terms of 14(d) might very well spell the difference between potential northern or southern dominance of any projected national assembly consequent to the political settlement. In November 1954 these questions were on the verge of clear articulation. The full measure of the psychological and moral burden of ICSC participation would not become clear until the last weeks of the 300-day period for military regroupment and civilian zonal migration. The more the Canadians learned about the Vietnam problematic, the more tense and doubt-ridden they became.

5

... The terrible things that are being done

According to Thomas Delworth and Christopher Dagg, respectively current and former members of the Department of External Affairs, the refugee crisis of 1954–5 'helped shape for the first time the perception in Canada of, and a sympathy for, an anti-communist, nationalistic Vietnamese community that was not a French creation.' Furthermore, 'witnessing on a daily basis the ruthlessness of the North Vietnamese government in its treatment of its citizens ... engendered a profound antipathy to the North Vietnamese approach to government.' In the opinion of these two old Indochina hands, 'Hanoi's tactics in preventing people from leaving the North were not the aberrations of a new, insecure government; they were the stock-in-trade of a system of government to which Canadians reacted with disbelief and with extreme distaste.'[1] Their comments are well founded.

The effect of the receipt of many thousands of petitions from northerners wishing to escape south was immediate and profound. Many members of the Canadian policy community, in both Hanoi and Ottawa, felt that they had a deep moral obligation to help these victims of religious persecution. But how? Reunification loomed, and the risk of renewed fighting had not disappeared. The French were in retreat from Indochina, and it was not clear that the Americans were either willing or able to replace their influence in the area. Article 14(d) did have the advantage of being quite unambiguous in its wording, although there was some doubt in Canadian minds whether the framers of the armistice had really expected that the provision would be respected.[2] The Canadian government did not have a clearly thought out policy on this issue. Perhaps, given the uncertainty of the situation, that was an impossibility. In lieu of such, they reacted to events, rather than actively attempting to shape them. If the provisions of 14(d) were not going to be met, Canadian officials were determined that Canada would not bear the brunt for the blame of such an outcome. The Geneva powers and the parties themselves had the chief responsibility for the execution of the armistice, and the Canadians wished to keep that primary line of responsibility crystal clear. Accordingly Ottawa devoted much time and effort to 'shaping the record' and to forcing the Indian delegation to act promptly – and in plenty of time for adequate response – in conveying warnings of non-compliance on 14(d) to the Geneva co-chairmen.

Shaping the record was not an easy task. The Poles were equally deter-mined not to sacrifice the interests of the SRVN in the latter's efforts to slow or halt the haemorrhage of its population to the south. Polish tactics con-sisted of demanding 'reciprocity' for each and every investigation that was conducted in the north regarding 'freedom of movement.' The Poles de-manded equal attention to alleged violations of Article 14(c), which enjoined the parties not to commit 'reprisals or discrimination against persons or organizations on account of their activities during the hostilities' and also to 'guarantee their democratic liberties.' There was no shortage of reports of alleged violations: the SVN authorities did not hesitate to crush opposition to their efforts at consolidating rule in the south throughout the first two years of the armistice. The network of some 6,000–10,000 Vietminh 'stay-behind' agents in the south responded by calling 14(c) infractions whenever possible. The upshot of this process was a competition between the Canadians and Poles for the scarce personnel resources of the ICSC for Vietnam.

The Indian delegation considered the 14(d) affair to be an irritating and comparatively minor matter. If reunification was in the cards, why make more unnecessary trouble? To sustain their self-respect and to give effect to their policy of careful avoidance of blame for the breakdown of key provi-sions of the armistice, the Canadians were driven therefore to mildly partisan tactics. Of necessity the Canadians downplayed or ignored the significance of the incidents in the south. Their rationale was twofold: first, there was a time limit of 300 days on civilian freedom of movement, but not on the operation of 14(c); second, it was doubtful that 14(c) would ever prove enforceable – not in the north because the police effectively stifled political dissent, and not in the south because the Saigon government did not con-sider itself bound by this provision of the armistice.

The evidence of violence and brutality in the south was unmistakable. According to Lett 'the investigations ... by mobile teams provide an ugly picture of beatings, torture and murders of former members of the resis-tance' that occurred in the autumn of 1954. All in all, he said, there existed in the south 'what can only be described as a shocking state of law and order in many areas.'[3] But the violence witnessed in the north was in many respects still more appalling. Not only was the commission in receipt of thousands of petitions from civilians who had been harassed, intimidated, or physically prevented from leaving the north, there were also disturbing reports of a quite oppressive 'agrarian reform' program being conducted in the spring of 1955.[4] Thousands of relatively well-to-do peasants were 'tried' for 'crimes against the people' and then imprisoned, or in many cases executed. President Ho and General Giap were eventually required to intervene to replace the left-wing zealot, Truong Chinh, in 1956 and to initiate a well-publicized 'self-criticism' for the unnecessary destruction wrought by the party's radicals. Bernard Fall has estimated that some 50,000 were killed and 100,000 were sent to forced labour camps.[5] A more recent assessment sets the figures at 'only' 3,000 to 15,000 killed with an unspecified number imprisoned.[6] The Canadian perception of such events in the 1950s was impressionistic. No numbers were involved. But the arbitrary and merciless character of the land reform process was clear, as were its pervasive effects on the whole population. The net result was a stiffening of anti-communist attitudes within the Department of External Affairs, a growth in sympathy for the plight of the non-communist Catholic Vietnamese, and increasing tolerance for the obstinacy of the Diem government. The 14(d) affair and northern land reform began a process of 'right-radicalization' which changed the thrust of Canadian Indochina policy by the late 1950s. Of the two factors, 14(d) was more consequential.

The DRVN did its utmost to block ICSC investigation of the petitions to go south. They refused French and American ships the right to enter DRVN waters to pick up would-be emigrants.[7] They did everything possible to slow down the rate of investigation: for example, suggesting that previous surveys and interviews had to be repeated.[8] They refused to allow the ICSC personnel to use non-DRVN transportation in their zone when they were 'unable' to procure their own.[9] The DRVN instituted a permit system for would-be refugees that was not well publicized and was very arbitrarily applied. In fact its sole function was to complicate exit procedures, thus slowing or blocking departures. In this whole sordid affair the Poles played a steady collaborative role, working closely with the DRVN authorities. Once the scale of the exodus became visible the North Vietnamese did not hesitate to apply a noose to their dissidents. The election positions of the two zones might have been influenced had the flow continued unabated.

Economic deprivation, fear of religious persecution, and fears of atomic attack were commonly cited reasons for departing from the north when queries were made by ICSC personnel.[10] The Indians were quick to seize upon any explanation (such as CIA-incited fears of atomic war) which might justify inaction (and indeed one might say this of Indian authors who have written accounts of this period).[11] The result of this too-easy accommodation of DRVN obstruction was rapidly growing Canadian frustration. By the end of November with the Phat Diem affair behind them (several thousand Catholics at a cathedral had been blocked and then forcibly dispersed by the 'local authorities' before ICSC personnel could achieve any remedies).[12] Ambassador Lett had had enough. By 20 November Lett had been given authorization to prepare a 'showdown' on the issue from Pearson himself, who had been kept well informed of the simmering controversy.[13] On 24 November Lett responded by charging the DRVN's central authorities with systematic obstruction.[14] Chairman Desai would not support the charge, or the interpretation – yet.

On 29 November the Poles pleaded that they were suddenly unable to furnish adequate numbers of staff to keep the mobile teams functioning at full strength.[15] On 30 November Ambassador Ogrodzinski dutifully parroted the DRVN line on mass 'forced evacuation' from the northern zone (the communists never specified precisely who was doing the 'forcing').[16] As the Canadians sought to carry out more patrols in the north to help effect evacuation, the Poles responded by a frantic demand for 'reciprocity' of investigations in the south, no matter how trivial the issue.[17] The Poles might as well have been DRVN liaison representatives.

The Poles defended DRVN obstructionism on matters of frontier control as well. On 8 November Anthony Eden told the British Commons that the PAVN forces were undergoing a massive expansion program. 'By the end of this year this will probably mean that the Vietminh will have twice as many regular field formations as at the time of the Geneva settlements.'[18] The arms for this build-up were all being imported illicitly. Border control on the Sino-Vietnamese frontier was effectively nil at this point.[19] The Canadians thus supported French requests for new FTs to be stationed at Lai Chau and Cao Bang. Desai and Ogrodzinski refused.[20] In frustration Lett suggested on 3 December that it was time to tell the Geneva powers that ICSC supervision of Articles 16 and 17 had broken down. Again Desai demurred.

The conditions the refugees were facing at this point were horrific, much worse according to a US expert, 'than anything he [had] ... ever experienced, including Germany at [the] end [of the] war.' The French authorities within the Haiphong perimeter gave priority in evacuation to 'French soldiers, dependents and equipment, paying little attention to refugees.' No one supervised the refugee camps, which had no sanitation. In addition the

medical staff had all quit, 'not having been paid.' According to US Ambassador to Saigon Donald Heath, these 'desperate circumstances ... could not
have been better planned by Viet Minh themselves for Communist propaganda purposes.'[21] And that of course is precisely what the DRVN authorities
thought in claiming that there had been 'forced evacuations.' They clearly
hoped many of the refugees would change their minds and return to the
north if queried by ICSC personnel about their new conditions. In an attempt
to initiate this process the DRVN authorities even sent 'fake refugees' to the
Haiphong perimeter from Phat Diem who attempted to claim that they had
been 'forced to evacuate.'

Under 14(d)'s provisions the zonal authorities were required to 'assist'
those who wished to change zones of residence. Lett argued for provision of
food, medicine, and transport. The Poles and Indians said 'no.'[22] People in
the north were told by DRVN police that they could not approach ICSC
personnel 'without first reporting to D.R. authorities.' Would-be escapees
were physically removed from ICSC vehicles, under IC protests.[23] On a number of occasions soldiers were 'billetted' with any families expressing a desire
to leave.[24] In many cases, children were detained by the 'local authorities.'
When roving mobile teams were finally dispatched by the ICSC to look for
'floating populations on the move,' the Polish members of the teams would
do their utmost to slow team movement by tardiness, by sickness (which
may not have been feigned), or most deviously, by demanding lengthy
entries under the 'nothing to report' sections of team report memoranda,
whenever designated sites were found to be empty. Vehicles supplied by the
DRVN would frequently break down. DRVN liaison officers that had to
accompany teams were frequently 'sick' or enjoying 'local holidays.' Govern-
ment-inspired and -directed mass demonstrations would intimidate and
'manhandle' petitioners, crowds would obstruct investigations, 'spontaneous' demonstrators would drag people away who were trying to reach IC
team members. At one point some 'local officials' even went so far as to seize
petitions from the hands of an Indian member of an ICSC team.[25] That was a
major tactical error, for it evidently upset Chairman Desai greatly.

Pearson and his senior staff were clearly getting anxious over the situation
as the autumn of 1954 progressed. In late November the minister told Lett in
effect that various interest groups in Canada and the United States might be
on the verge of strong public protest. According to James Eayrs the US
government also put 'pressure' on Ottawa 'to adopt a hard line within ICSC
Vietnam' by urging formal ICSC condemnation of the DRVN. This is an
unwarranted distortion of the facts. While he documents 'concern,' Eayrs
provides no evidence at all of 'pressure' from Washington.[26] This is because

there was none.* The Americans wished to score propaganda gains on 14(d), and they evinced an interest in this objective to Ottawa in the autumn of 1954. External Affairs staff did not like the idea at all and said so to the State Department (fearing that propaganda would only reduce the numbers of people who might get out of the north).

A major part of the misunderstanding between Desai and Lett on the subject of 14(d) derived from the fact that Desai apparently believed that there were only some 500,000 Catholics in Tonkin.† Canadian Redemptorist priests privately opined to Canadians that up to two million Roman Catholics would leave the north if 14(d) were fully implemented.[27] The Vatican's Apostolic delegate supported such assertions. Vietnam, after all, was the most Christianized country in Asia on a percentage basis.

By 1 January 1955 some 539,000 people had been evacuated including 246,000 military personnel and dependents.[28] For Desai this was no doubt interpreted to mean that well over half the Catholic population had been able to emigrate. For the Canadians it was only one-eighth of the hypothetical maximum.

On 5 December General Giap sent a formal letter of complaint to the ICSC alleging that Article 14(c) had been massively violated through the killing of 619 'former members of the resistance' and the imprisonment of 6,112 others. Giap wanted nine incidents in particular investigated. Torture was alleged in various instances, almost certainly with justification. The Canadian delegates were in a bind. Many felt that the South Vietnamese authorities were guilty of violent repression, but that they were not in violation of 14(c). They accepted the SVN argument that former Vietminh were being arrested or killed, not for reprisals for acts committed *prior* to the armistice (the only valid reason for invoking 14[c]) but for continuing in the period

---

* In mid-April 1955 in justifying the dispatch of quite prosaic weekly summaries of ICSC activities to friendly Western governments (UK, France, the US, Australia, and New Zealand), A.R. Menzies rightly noted that the governments had in fact been 'more sympathetic' to problems facing Canada in the Commission. 'The fact that *none of the five governments concerned had exerted pressure on us* to take *any particular stand in the Commission* or has otherwise shown any misunderstanding of our problems would seem to indicate that the belief is well-founded.' Menzies to the High Commissioner, London, 13 Apr. 1955, DEA files: 50052-A-40 vol. 10. Emphasis added.

† Confidential source. Ten years after the event Indian estimates had risen to a figure of 1.2 million. See B.S.N. Murti, *Vietnam Divided: The Unfinished Struggle* (New York: Asia Publishing, 1964) 72 n3. Murti's oft-cited account is selective and tendentious on the refugee affair. In the relevant chapter, for example, he nowhere cites the aggregate figures on population movement accepted by the ICSC as reasonably accurate (892,876 North to South; 4,269 South to North).

post-armistice in overt defiance of Saigon's authority. In response to many 14(c) allegations by the DRVN, the French Liaison Mission usually responded with counter-allegations that attempted subversion was taking place. After watching the sorry performance of the ICSC in the north, the southern authorities had a solid excuse, so they thought, for progressively reducing co-operation with the ICSC on all 14(c) investigations, co-operation that the French High Command extended while it was in control. The South Vietnamese were also determined to underline the fact that they had never accepted all the terms of the CFA, and that they were at liberty to reject particular provisions. Summary convictions of the SVN were thus inevitable at some point and there was nothing the Canadians could do to ensure a fuller measure of justice. It should be noted that the ICSC found in its investigations of fifteen incidents from September 1954 to August 1955 a total of 319 cases of 'injury to life' (presumably death in the convoluted prose of the IC) and 203 cases of 'loss of liberty.'[29] With literally hundreds of thousands of people being made to suffer by the DRVN's harassment and its refusal to meet its binding legal obligations under 14(d)'s mandatory injunction to 'assist' would-be evacuees, it is no wonder that Canadian perceptions of the balance of virtue in Vietnam fell increasingly in favour of the SVN. To argue, as some have, that 14(c) violations somehow offset or excused the 14(d) violations reflects a moral sensibility that is deeply confused to say the least.

Polish progress in eroding the mobility of the fourteen fixed teams was substantial during the first months of the armistice. The Indian delegation clearly was prepared to trade practical effectiveness of team operations for the DRVN's public acceptance of a theoretical IC right to investigate anywhere in the country.[30] By early December, under protest to Desai, Lett accepted but did not approve an Indian 'compromise' on team mobility. In a ten-kilometre strip around the perimeter of both zones, FTs would be given a 'blanket authorization' by zonal authorities to conduct 'control' missions. Each FT would then have a 'sphere of action' covering main transport routes in their vicinity beyond the ten-kilometre zone where FT personnel would 'be free to move and would also observe and record [sic], but would not conduct any investigations.'[31] On 21 December Lett attempted to have Desai include 'examination and inspection' in team 'spheres of action.' The chairman declined, and for fear of alienating the Indians, Lett at last gave way to Desai's debilitating proposal.[32] In deploying two additional border control teams to Cao Bang in the north and Loc Ninh in the south (mobile teams deployed semi-permanently), Lett fought the ten-kilometre battle again, and lost once more.[33]

By February, Lett began to win concessions from the Indians on 14(d). Evidently Desai had been given new instructions on the subject during his mid-January trip to New Delhi.

An Indo-Canadian majority did eventually order on 1 February 1955, fourteen major changes in the parties' exit procedures. The changes were aimed totally at DRVN abuses and comprised recommendations to speed up the exit process once individuals had made declarations of intent to depart, to decentralize and publicize the location of exit-permit granting offices, to provide specific reasons for failure to grant permits, to allow children to go with their parents, to accept simple declarations of desire to exit as sufficient basis for departure, to help in the transport of would-be emigrants' movable property, and to allow groups of 'intending evacuees' to congregate 'in an orderly manner.'[34]

Few if any of the recommendations were actually implemented. Fewer than 10,000 of the approximately one million people who went south actually obtained DRVN exit permits. Most refugees had to leave all their possessions behind to have any hope of escape. To reiterate, children were often detained by 'local authorities' for the sole purpose of blocking family departures. The Canadians could not force DRVN compliance single-handedly, and the Indians refused to take the issue seriously.

By March 1955 the Canadians did score one coup in the battle over 14(d) by suffering the ludicrous and lengthy Polish-DR allegations of 'forced evacuation' patiently, and co-operating in the dispatch of MT survey groups to the refugee camps in the south.[35] When the first survey was undertaken in a camp with some 985 refugees, not one of the 500 people interviewed by the team indicated a desire to return to the north. The Polish delegates on the MT evidently became quite upset and insisted that the team interview all 985 persons. The Indian and Canadian members thought 500 was more than enough.[36] When queried about this bizarre affair, Marcel Cadieux, who had been a member of the Canadian delegation, responded:

There's a good story there. The North was caught out at their own game. Their thinking was, *a priori*, that colonial or neo-colonial control and administration was so unattractive that substantial numbers of those who went South would subsequently regret it and would want to go back to the North. The North thought these refugees were the victims of propaganda, that they had been dragged south under many illusions. Thus they were willing to take the gamble that if they promoted these 'forced evacuations' many people would step forward to verify them. But of course when the Commission checked out these allegations, the reverse was true. No one wanted to go back to the North. The reaction was so one-sided in the refugee camps that at first the Indians thought that the refugees' response was organized by the South Vietnamese government. They later thought it was beyond the capacity of the South Vietnam government to do such a thing. So ultimately the whole affair backfired on them.[37]

Backfired, indeed. The investigation of the 500 people in the Truoi refugee camp was only the first of many. As the minority note by the Canadian delegation summarized the affair:

On the strength of about 320,000 petitions from third parties alleging that friends and relations had been forced to move South under pressure from the FUF High Command, two mobile teams carried out investigations in refugee camps in the State of Vietnam. In spite of demonstrations hostile to the PAVN Liaison Officers attached to these teams, the task was completed. Some 25,000 out of a total of 121,000 in these camps were contacted by the teams, which reported that *there was no evidence of forced evacuation and none of the persons interviewed wished to return to the North*. Throughout the 300 day period the Commission considered numerous allegations of forced evacuation, but in *no instance was evidence discovered to substantiate these complaints*.[38]

This clear example of manipulation and deceit of the allegedly 'spontaneous' protest from the north by the DRVN authorities unequivocally demonstrates the involvement of the DRVN central authorities. Contrary to Eayrs,* it was not insubordinate 'local officials' who sabotaged the operation of Article 14(d).[39]

The outcome of the 'forced evacuation' controversy gave heart to the Canadians, especially the conservative element, but it could do little to mitigate the fact that Canadian efforts on 14(d) had largely come to nothing. The refugees who escaped from the north did so by their own efforts. The extension period for 14(d) which was eventually granted from 18 May to 20 July saw only 4,749 more people leave the north. The Indian government earnestly wished the 14(d) problem would disappear as soon as possible. The Indians eventually got their way. A prudent regard for international circumstances prevented the Canadians from sustaining their pressure on 14(d).

---

* The mythical divisions in the DRVN power structure to which Eayrs alludes (per Maneli) are not credible. Maneli was blatantly wrong in characterizing stands on the control issue, and he is most certainly wrong here too. Eayrs obviously did not consult the ICSC minutes, or he would have realized his error. See *Indochina* 138.

Canadian ability and willingness to pressure the Indians was limited by the fact that it was an overriding objective in Ottawa to sustain amicable relations with India over Indochina. No single dispute was to be allowed to jeopardize the achievement of a wider entente between the two countries with respect to the overall approach to Indochina policy-making. Still another more basic reason for not pressing maximally on 14(d) was a fear of alienating the DRVN and causing the abrogation of its commitment to the CFA. It was undoubtedly this fear which had produced India's extreme reluctance to press hard on 14(d). As Lett noted in early February 1955, in classically liberal-moderate prose:

The issue should not be pressed [ie, 14(d)] to the point where the precarious military balance established by the Agreement may be upset ... the Commission has a fair chance of being able to keep the record clear and to show that if Article 14(d) has not been carried out fully the fault lies with the parties themselves. The weakness in this situation and the possible risks for Canada stem from the danger that public opinion in friendly Western countries may not appreciate that even if the outcome of the Commission's efforts in this field are not as satisfactory as might be desired, failure to achieve full success was not worth risking a resumption of hostilities. We can protect our position to some extent through private discussions with the friendly Geneva Powers and through formal reports to the co-Chairmen but there is no doubt that it will be easier for most people to yield to emotional reactions than to exercise political judgment which is needed to accept the situation.[40]

Lett was a thoroughgoing liberal-moderate. He put the value of peace ahead of other important concerns,* much to Pearson's satisfaction no

---

* Eayrs interprets the quote above as evidence of Lett's 'conversion to a realist position' (*Indochina* 148). The evidence does not support the argument. Lett had acknowledged maintenance of the armistice as the priority objective of Canadian policy ever since he first accepted the role as commissioner. See, for example, his comment to the CBC made on 27 Sept. 1954: 'I trust – and I'm sure the Canadian Government hopes – that the commission will not become a new cockpit for the struggle between East and West. The Commission has been set up to do a specific job, and it is the view of the Canadian government that everything possible should be done to be sure that the Commission sticks to this job, and does not become involved in side issues.' The 14(d) affair was one such 'side issue.' Maintaining the armistice, not just between the Vietminh and the French, but between East and West, had always been Lett's highest priority objective. See 'The Work of the International Supervisory Commissions in Indo-China,' *External Affairs*, Oct. 1954, 301. Lett's dispatches from November through January reflected this priority concern for maintenance of the armistice.

doubt. According to Lett, Canada was performing 'a limited but useful task here' and so far Canada's international standing had not been hurt.[41]

Halting progress was made in March on 14(d), after promises of action by Desai in January and February were not implemented. Mid-March, contrary to Eayrs, was not a time of 'major setback,'[42] but rather a time of modest achievements in winning Desai over to the Canadian activist approach on 14(d).

For the Canadian delegation in Hanoi, mid-March 1955 was the height of the crisis. On 12 March the Canadians pressed for five remedial measures: complete and early notification to the Geneva powers of the DRVN's systematic violation of Article 14(d); the immediate dispatch of three 'roving' mobile teams throughout the northern zone to ascertain the degree of compliance of the DRVN with the ICSC's mandatory recommendations of 1 February; the dispatch of additional MTs to locales where problems were detected; the preparation of a thorough report to the Geneva co-chairmen to be submitted by 1 April detailing 14(d) violations by the DRVN government, not the local authorities; and finally, the submission of a formal request to the Geneva powers to take necessary action to remedy the situation if no real progress was detected by 1 April.[43]

The Canadian pressure finally was having some effect on Desai. But even more important was the effect of a now overt campaign of obstruction by the DRVN. On the very same morning of 12 March, Desai had delivered a strong, indignant denunciation of DRVN security procedures after DRVN guards had forcibly removed a large stack of 14(d) petitions from the Indian driver of an ICSC vehicle into which the petitions had been thrown by desperate would-be refugees.[44] When the afternoon session of 12 March began, Desai was still bristling with righteous indignation. When Ambassador Ogrodzinski attempted in a vague and general way to press for 'reciprocity' in mobile team investigations, Desai would have none of it. The chairman demanded a specific reply from the Pole concerning Lett's proposals. When Ogrodzinski then asked for an equal number of MT investigations in the south, Desai crushed him by saying that the French had always responded immediately and satisfactorily to any IC directives concerning 14(d). There were many exit-permit offices in the south, 14(d) was well-publicized, and most damningly, 'there had not been a single case of complaint from the South that an individual wanted to move to [the] North, but for want of facilities he could not do so.'[45]

Chairman Desai then agreed to the Canadian request to send special mobile teams, with 'high-powered Liaison Officers' if possible. But he refused as yet to consider sending any special report on a single sub-article of the CFA which, he said, might appear to be catering to propaganda manoeuvers by one side. He offered ICSC press releases concerning 14(d) on a fortnightly basis as a substitute measure for special detailed reports informing both the Geneva powers and the world press.[46] When Lett then pressed for a secret telegraphic dispatch to the Geneva powers, Desai refused. As a matter of policy the Indian delegation would only allow reports to go forward to the co-chairmen which involved a review of both parties' behaviour under all articles of the CFA.

On 14 March Desai reiterated his general position on 'parallelism' in reporting, and noted further that though it was quite clear to the Indians that the DRVN was guilty as charged, there was still insufficient evidence according to rigorous legal criteria to prove intentionally systematic violations of Article 14(d). The ICSC had to be able to quote 'chapter and verse' against the offenders.[47] If there was insufficient evidence this was only because the Indians had refused to accept Canadian investigatory proposals for four months running.

On 15 March Desai joined Commissioner Lett in denouncing DRVN attempts to block access to ICSC teams by people without 'adequate' identification papers.[48] The Canadians were mildly encouraged by this further act of support. But they could hardly be optimistic about real progress with 18 May so close. Desai's firmness in representations to General Giap in a conversation held the same day[49] concerning the need for effective remedial action was no doubt a product in part of Desai's injured dignity. DRVN affronts to the ICSC now seem to have been taken as an indirect affront to the government of India. On 18 March, Desai bluntly warned the DRVN that any further failures to comply with ICSC recommendations by 'local authorities' would henceforth be treated as defiance on the part of the DRVN High Command.[50] Lett followed up this major tactical victory with a proposal that all MT investigations could proceed in their operations by majority vote.[51] Desai balked at this. In an apparently idealistic fashion,* he argued that a 'spirit of unanimity' had to be encouraged at the team level.[52]

Any further progress was halted by yet another development: movement towards a full-scale civil war in the south. In December 1954, Ngo Dinh Diem had barely escaped a coup by General Nguyen Van Hinh. In January he was strengthened by the commencement of direct US funding, in February by the rallying to his cause of a leading Cao Dai general. But this general defected in March and between 21 and 26 March the three sects delivered an

---

* Desai, of course, may not have wanted that much 'progress,' because of the difficulties it would have caused for the DRVN.

ultimatum to Diem that he had to share power with them. In early April, with the sects' coalition in a shaky state, the Binh Xuyen gangsters attacked Diem's forces because Diem had moved to shut down the gambling and prostitution operations.[53] At precisely this point General Collins recommended to Washington that all support to Diem be withdrawn.[54] Through diplomatic contacts with other Commonwealth governments the Canadians were privy to the internal differences among the Americans.*

In sum, the emergent anarchy in the south chilled Canadian enthusiasm for fulfilment of 14(d). So too did a threatening international crisis.

THE FORMOSA STRAIT CRISIS AND THE REFUGEE AFFAIR

On 7 April Pearson approved instructions for the Canadian acting commissioner in Hanoi, Saul Rae, a young but experienced and shrewd career diplomat. The instructions called for a sustained but now carefully circumscribed commitment to progress on 14(d). No longer was there any talk of a 'showdown.'

In approaching this problem I believe we should keep in mind that the primary objective is to enable as many people as possible who wish to do so to go from one zone to the other, and that the secondary objectives are (a) to ensure that the public record of the Commission – and of Canada – shows that everything possible has been done to achieve the primary objective and (b) to ensure that the Commission's handling of this question will not leave the Viet Minh with an apparently clean bill of health and will not involve some compromise on principles, thus creating an unfortunate precedent for the political phase of the settlement.

Pearson wanted continuing criticism and 'firm measures,' because 'fear of public criticism is the best stick with which to goad the Viet Minh into action,' and also, he thought, the best way 'to draw the Indians into agreeing to a fairly strong line.' Acting Commissioner Rae was instructed to 'reluctantly agree' not to call a formal violation on the DRVN under 14(d), and not to demand a formal extension of the 14(d) time limit. In return for such concessions he was to press once more for as many specific measures as Desai would agree to, and in particular for a telegraphed dispatch to the Geneva co-chairmen asking them to consult with all the Geneva powers pursuant to paragraph 13 of the Final Declaration so that they might study measures for ensuring implementation of 14(d).[55] Pearson did not expect 'any useful practical results' from referral to the Geneva powers, rather:

* The provision of 'intelligence' is a two-way street, although some analysts, like Eayrs, tend to ignore one-half of the flow.

We do not, however, wish a situation to come about in which responsibility for not ensuring full performance on this article will rest wholly on the Commission. This responsibility should in our view be shared with the Geneva Conference Powers, particularly as the requirement for freedom of movement is specifically mentioned in paragraph 8 of the Final Declaration.

It was left to Rae as to whether he should approach Desai indirectly or 'bomb the IC directly.' An appended comment noted that Lett counselled the indirect approach.[56]

Rae accepted Lett's advice and found that Desai seemed amenable to some sort of reference to the Geneva co-chairmen, but it would not be on 14(d) alone. The status of 14(c) would be alluded to as well. In the end, all such efforts came to nothing. There was no unanimously supported telegraphed dispatch, only a minority Canadian note dated 25 April 1955 to the co-chairmen noting imminent non-fulfilment of 14(d).[57]

Rae was carefully instructed to do nothing that might jeopardize the armistice or alienate Desai badly. Caution was imperative. An emerging crisis in the Formosa Strait had now precluded Canadian statements that might exacerbate the policy debate in Washington and thus play into the hands of nuclear extremists. The timing of the Formosa Strait crisis and of Diem's showdown with the sects could not have been better for frustrating Canadian attempts to win better observance of 14(d).

Eisenhower and Dulles had approved greatly increased military assistance to the Kuomintang regime since they had taken office.[58] Chiang Kai-shek had called 1954 'a year of decision' when the KMT would begin the re-conquest of the mainland.[59] In August 1954 Chou En-lai warned the United States to stay clear of internal Chinese matters following a series of KMT bomber raids on Amoy and other cities.[60] On 3 September communist Chinese artillery began firing at the KMT-held islands of Quemoy and Matsu, just a few miles offshore from the port cities of Amoy and Foochow. The shelling was probably defensive, intended to forestall KMT operations against the mainland,[61] but once under way it effectively sealed off the islands from resupply. In November the Congressional 'China Lobby' pressed for a full-scale naval blockade of the Chinese coast. To reaffirm the containment aspects of their policy, containment being essentially an exercise in line drawing, Eisenhower and Dulles responded by concluding a US–Republic of China mutual security treaty. In January 1955 the passage of the Formosa resolution empowered the American president to intervene militarily in any conflict over the offshore islands should such action appear to be but a prelude to attack on Formosa itself. Some 30,000 KMT troops were evacuated from the Tachen Islands, the US Navy (the most militant of the three military branches) dissenting from approval of such a move.[62] On 14 February Mao declared that any Sino-American war would lead to the early demise of imperialism.[63] Dulles intentionally left the American commitment to Quemoy and Matsu ambiguous. Eisenhower let it be known that the US was considering a tactical nuclear response in the event that communist shelling did not cease. He was never more in earnest.* Fortunately the Chinese eventually halted the artillery barrage, but not before the US had edged precariously close to an atomic first-strike.

Pearson reacted to these developments very negatively. As acting secretary of state for external affairs, Paul Martin expressed an explicit Canadian preference for the neutralization of Formosa rather than Western involvement in any conflict. In late March the crisis came to a head with a number of extremely provocative statements by various American admirals. After Admiral Carney's statement of 23 March,[64] Pearson officially disassociated Canada from American China policy.[65] The basis for disassociation was, not coincidentally, identical with the formula rationalizing non-participation in the SEATO Pact: no involvement without a UN umbrella over the operation.[66] Compromise was the only acceptable alternative to the Canadian government. So too for the Indian government. Krishna Menon spent ten days in Beijing in May attempting to secure a cease-fire in the strait.[67]

During the last two weeks of March, Sherwood Lett was preparing to return to Canada via London for consultations with his government. On 18 March Lett wrote, in preparation for these talks, a long assessment of the current situation and of the prospects for elections. In view of the continuing crisis in Asia, the continuing intervention by the great powers in Indochina, and the still tenuous and ambiguous legal obligations of the Geneva armistice, Lett came to the conclusion that the present ICSC structure and mandate were hopelessly inadequate to the tasks seemingly set by the Final Declaration. His solution? Reconvene the Geneva Conference 'well before the political consultations envisaged for next July.' Lett noted that Canada was involved 'as a contribution to the maintenance of peace and security in an area which, though far from our traditional interests, is of great significance to the maintenance of peace on a global basis.' That objective, he thought, could best be served not by participating in the forthcoming electo-

---

* From the most detailed and comprehensive look at the US classified record yet conducted, John Lewis Gaddis concluded: 'The administration appears to have come closest to using nuclear weapons in the situation which, in the eyes of its critics, least called for them: the two crises over Quemoy and Matsu in 1954–55 and 1958.' Domino logic decreed an atomic 'defence.' Gaddis, *Strategies of Containment* (New York, Oxford: Oxford University Press 1982) 169–70

ral process, which at most, he said, would be a 'continuing "political Pan-munjon,"' but rather by pressing for a new, less obscure Geneva contract. Here Lett's preference for legal clarity overcame his fast-maturing political sensibilities. In light of what Lett saw as the practical impossibility of secur-ing full implementation of either 14(c) or 14(d), he adhered to his earlier recommendation that priority concern be given to efforts towards strength-ening the basis of the cease-fire, the core objective of Canadian policy.[68]

Over the next few weeks Canadian diplomats solicited the opinions of other Western governments. Neither the French nor the British found favour with a serious campaign of pressure on Hanoi, given the tension over the Formosa Strait. Neither government wanted to jeopardize the movement towards détente which had developed since the Geneva Conference. Fur-thermore, both governments were of the view that the Geneva Conference should most certainly *not* be reconvened. Peace was far too tenuously rooted in Asia to risk public demonstrations of the lines of cleavage both in the international system and among the Western powers. The French and the British preferred that the ICSC states cope with problems as best they could.[69]

On 24 March Pearson addressed the Commons on problems in Asia. In explaining the work of the three international supervisory bodies in Indo-china, he tactfully avoided a categorical denunciation of the faltering control system, saying only that 'if one of the parties to the agreement is determined to circumvent these provisions of the agreement the international commis-sion is not likely to be able to prevent it, though the inspection activities which are possible, and which are being undertaken, will certainly make, and indeed are making, violations more difficult.'[70] He went on to note that Article 14(d) had been of 'great concern' to the government but that in view of the limitations inherent to the CFA 'all the commission can do is mediate, supervise and conciliate; it cannot enforce.' The northern government had followed 'obstructive tactics' but implementation of the CFA depended en-tirely on the 'good faith' of the parties.[71] Canadians would continue to serve on the ICSC 'as long, but only as long, as they can make a useful contribution to the implementation of the armistice agreement reached at Geneva, and therefore to peace in that part of the world.'[72] These comments were merely prefatory to the key portion of Pearson's address.

Formosa and the coastal islands, not Vietnamese refugee movement, was the critical issue of the moment. Canada, said Pearson, 'cannot subscribe to all aspects of United States policy in this Asian area, especially in regard to the coastal islands.' Quemoy and Matsu were 'part of the Chinese mainland' and their strategic role was 'more important in the defence of that mainland against attack than in offensive action against Formosa and the Pescadores.'

Not for the last time, Pearson lauded the US president as a man 'with a passion for peace.'[73] Through such praise he counselled restraint, a standard Pearsonian tactic. Canada rejected commitments 'to share in the defence of either Formosa or the coastal islands.' Canada could become involved only through its 'responsibilities as a member of the United Nations.' Pearson went on to say that 'it would be impossible in my view, for either the United States or Canada to be neutral if the people of the other country were engaged in a major war in which their very existence as a people was at stake, and ... in working out our foreign and defence policies we can never forget this fact.' But he then added, 'It is inconceivable to Canadians, *it is inconceivable certainly to me, that the United States would ever initiate an aggressive war. It is also inconceivable that Canada would ever take part in such a war.*'[74]

Pearson was giving a not-so-veiled ultimatum to Eisenhower, Dulles, and the American Congress to the effect that Ottawa would openly and publicly denounce any attempts by Washington to build an Atlantic Alliance war psychology preparatory to the 'final showdown' with the communist Chinese regime. So far as Ottawa was concerned Washington would go it alone until such time as Soviet bombers began to fly towards North America.

Pearson concluded this explicit warning to American militants with the observation that in the Cold War struggle, neutrality really was impossible – as Dulles had long argued – but the very impossibility of neutrality

underlines our obligation to concern ourselves with, and make our view known on, the policies of others, especially of the United States, when questions of peace and war are involved. Its possession of the greatest power in the world gives us, I think, the right to be especially pre-occupied with the policies of the United States. It makes consultation and a continuous exchange of views imperative. *It emphasizes our obligations to do everything possible to avoid every kind of war big or small.*[75]

Pearson declared that his greatest fear was 'limited intervention,' defensive in character, by the US, which 'might have a chain reaction with unforeseen consequences.'[76] Appropriately enough, Pearson concluded his address with a plea for nuclear arms control, praise for Premier Nehru's articulated concerns on the same subject 'a few weeks ago in London,' and a categorical rejection of nuclear weapons as an effective deterrent to limited war.[77] Clearly anxiety about the risk of nuclear war provided much of the psychological underpinning of the Indo-Canadian 'special relationship.'

In Pearson's mind the situations in Indochina and the Formosa Strait were inextricably linked. Doing 'everything possible to avoid every kind of war' meant among other things stifling a campaign of public pressure against the

DRVN's failure to comply with Article 14(d). As a good liberal-moderate Pearson knew that this was the time to 'cool it.' Krishna Menon's recent visit to Washington could only have confirmed Pearson in this judgment. Menon, who came away very upset over American determination to pursue their policy of confrontation in the Formosa Strait, told the Canadian representative to the United Nations, David Johnson* (who would be Lett's successor on the ICSC for Vietnam), that the 'honeymoon period' of the ICSC was over.[78] American bellicosity was poisoning some Indian assessments of Canadian policy.

DEA conservatives were particularly upset about Indian perceptions of Canadians as 'Western Poles.' The Canadians had not indulged in the deceit and trickery perpetrated by the Poles and DRVN officials over 14(d) and border control. The Canadians had never obstructed or delayed reprisals investigations in the south, or investigations into SVN prisons, detention camps, or refugee centres. Nevertheless, Menon seemed to equate Canadian behaviour with Polish practices. Many Indians seemed also to believe that objectivity on their part as delegates of the chairing state simply meant finding a 'mathematical mean' between the two sides, on the assumption that each of the bloc nominees on the ICSC would follow a partisan approach.[79] In point of fact, Indian negativism and scepticism in this regard may have set in motion a process of self-fulfilling prophecy.

Léger's reaction to the Menon comment was revealing as an indication of conservative sentiment that, if anything, Ottawa had been too impartial in its duties. In pointing to the 'mathematical' approach, Léger had underlined the core problem that obstructed Indo-Canadian amity: where the Indians as a matter of tactical expediency (in, at times, impossible situations) chose to split the difference between Canadian and Polish positions, the Canadians initially did their best to meet what they saw as probable Indian objectives in any particular situation. The end result was mutual recrimination with the Canadians often feeling cheated and the Indians unreasonably put upon.

Back in Hanoi when Saul Rae finally issued his threat of a minority Canadian reference to the Geneva powers regarding 14(d), Desai was quite disturbed by it. But in the end, all that the Indian government was prepared to consider was action in securing a limited extension of the 300-day period for civilian transfers. A telegraphed message of Canadian concern was appa-

* Menon did not address his 'end of honeymoon' remarks to Léger, as Eayrs reports (*Indochina* 205–6). Léger wrote a memorandum analysing the meaning and implications of Menon's comments to Johnson. The Menon-Johnson conversation took place on or about 18 March. Léger's memorandum was written on 28 March.

rently sent to the Geneva co-chairmen, but Desai refused to concur in the Canadian call for deliberations by the Geneva powers,[80] although he had led Rae to believe that his position might be altered shortly. But events in Hanoi had now been superseded by conversations in Ottawa on 14 April among the senior staff of the department and Norman Robertson, who had come back to Ottawa for consultations.

As Jules Léger reported these talks to Pearson, Robertson emphatically stated that the British in his opinion wanted no reconvening of the Geneva Conference 'during the present sensitive state of East-West relations.' As Robertson interpreted London's position, the Geneva Conference was not 'a court of appeal,' it had no 'formal continuing existence,' and there was no reason to expect that the conference powers could solve the problems of Indochina any more readily than the ICSC member states. When pressed concerning the reasonable desire of the ICSC powers to diffuse responsibility among the Geneva powers, Robertson replied that Indochina ought to 'be seen in the broader context of east-west relations' and that Canadian policy should be framed in light of this, 'particularly with a view to the effect of the action on the Formosa Straight situation.' Finally, Robertson cited Krishna Menon's view that 'the Geneva settlement for Indochina was a thin fabric or skin graft which covered a kind of local co-existence between the Communist and free worlds, and that it was undesirable that the Commission powers should do anything which might tear that fabric unnecessarily.'[81] Menon's metaphor seems to have carried the day in the ensuing discussion. Henceforth, there was no doubt that Canadian protests on 14(d) would be limited to prudent efforts at placing the blame for non-implementation where it belonged: with Hanoi in the first instance, and the Geneva powers in the second.

Robertson's views should be seen as adding further support to what Pearson had already decided were the most appropriate tactics to follow, tactics that were implicit in his remarks to the Commons of 24 March concerning Asian security.

Conservative elements in External Affairs at about this time (April–May 1955) began to see some potential merit in the failure to win effective compliance by the north under Article 14(d). Conservative policy advocates were becoming appalled by the prospect of elections in which the southerners would be terribly divided among themselves. Failure on 14(d) might somehow help in creating the conditions necessary for sidestepping the political provisions (Articles 6 and 7) of the Final Declaration. The looming electoral tangle, not the immediate Formosa problem (the liberal-moderates' bête noire), led to conservative acquiescence in a relatively mild and obviously ineffectual posture by the Canadian government on 14(d). Finally, many liberal-moderates and conservatives were increasingly alert to the limits to Saigon's capacity to absorb refugees. By July the SVN authorities were expressing a desire not to encourage more activity on 14(d), not only because of an inability to look after the refugees, but also out of fear of the arrival of hundreds or even thousands of DRVN agents among the ranks of the refugees.[82]

In light of these trends in the policy community, it is certain that much consternation was provoked by *Newsweek* magazine's mid-April report that frustrated Canadians in Hanoi were 'getting ready to blow the lid off the Indo-China truce.'[83]

On 3 May 1955 Pearson gave a major address on 14(d) to the Commons. In it he declared:

This is not a situation, I suggest, which will be solved merely by letting off steam. We are convinced that in order to ensure that the provisions of the agreement are carried out to the greatest degree possible in the circumstances, we must continue to work through our representative on the Commission in the same manner as we have done over the last eight months, pressing for better performance in every way possible and exposing violations when they can be detected. That still seems to us to be the *most likely method of ensuring that the greatest possible number of people who wish to do so can leave North Vietnam for the south.*[84]

He explicitly rejected withdrawal, noting that:

Such a move would, however, prejudice also *the fulfillment of the main military provisions of the agreement, thus creating new tensions and possibly jeopardizing the maintenance of peace, not only in Vietnam but also in the neighbouring countries of Laos and Cambodia.* Nor would our withdrawal be of any assistance whatsoever to those in North Vietnam who want to leave. Indeed it might eliminate any remaining hope that their lot might be alleviated. We must therefore *keep our sense of perspective in this matter, but without condoning or forgetting some of the terrible things that are being done.*[85]

The statement honestly reflected the Canadian determination to maintain peace in Indochina if at all possible. It also reflected honestly Canadian frustration over an inability to secure real progress on 14(d). But it failed to indicate accurately, first, that the refugee exodus had already been completely strangled by Hanoi and, second, that there was in fact a direct trade-off between promoting the fulfilment of 14(d) and assuring a high probability of maintaining the armistice. Absolute honesty by Pearson would not have increased the outflow of refugees, and it might have played into the hands of American adventurists who wished to heighten the climate of confrontation in the strait crisis. This was a risk Pearson quite sensibly refused to take. It was precisely the kind of ethical dilemma which would arise repeatedly in Canadian Indochina decision-making.

The 14(d) story for Canada ended with communications from Ottawa to the governments in London and Paris seeking diplomatic support for the extension proposal. In late May the DRVN and Soviet authorities indicated they were agreeable to a one-month extension. Eventually, by early June, after a series of mainly bilateral consultations between the co-chairmen and other governments, a two-month extension was agreed to. Canadian 'face' was saved to some extent and Canadian consciences were slightly eased by the new informal agreement to amend the Geneva Agreement on a de facto basis. Lett and the Canadians in Hanoi doubted that the extension was going to have any real effect. DRVN techniques seemed by then to be 'airtight' in application, and the southern zone was at this point in a steadily increasing state of disorder.

Sherwood Lett, on his return to Hanoi, came to focus intently upon the possibilities for subversion by the DRVN if the 'freedom of movement' migration continued indefinitely. This too may have been an act of rationalization, but it was a not unreasonable hypothesis. Lett had the outlook of a dedicated liberal-moderate. He willingly accepted Pearson's peace-oriented policy imperatives. By mid-June Lett believed that the Canadians had to tread warily so as not to jeopardize the increasingly slender prospects for electoral negotiations. But on this last point, Lett was increasingly out of step with the evolving policy consensus in Ottawa, which was moving rapidly away from a belief in the inevitability of an electoral resolution of the Vietnam problem.

In June and July Lett was told to pursue 14(d), but in an essentially perfunctory manner.[86] Pearson and his senior advisers had given up on 14(d) despite having achieved the minor victory of the two-month extension of the article from 18 May to 20 July. The victory was a hollow one.

Officials in Ottawa were relieved to be able to tell Sherwood Lett in early July that the 14(d) affair had evoked very little comment in Canada. They instructed Lett to give away nothing so far gained on 14(d), to secure as many press releases and commission notes as possible on the subject, and to ensure that the Canadian opinion on the clear breach of 14(d) by the DRVN was firmly lodged in the ICSC documentary record.[87] Lett followed his instructions carefully, but without achieving any further concessions from the

Indian delegation. The dispatch of additional MT probes was curtailed, the refugee outflow subsided to a trickle, and the Canadian protest on 14(d) was limited to a lengthy minority note in the *Fourth Interim Report* (written by Lett's successor as commissioner, David Johnson), which graphically demonstrated how the provision had been subverted by the DRVN authorities.[88] This same minority note did not call for any extension of the operation of the article. By the summer of 1955 the 14(d) affair was a closed chapter. Nevertheless, Canadian officials would not soon forget the DRVN's acts of harassment, intimidation, and obstruction which had effectively violated this important provision of the armistice. For many in Ottawa's foreign policy community recollections of the 14(d) affair would colour all subsequent assessments of DRVN policy and 'moral worth.'

CONCLUSION: THE REFUGEES AND THE
ONSET OF TENDENCY DIVERGENCE

The first tumultuous year on the ICSC opened many Canadian eyes to the incredible violence and brutality of revolutionary methods. Canadian officials had had no direct experience of the colonial repression which had driven the Vietnamese to adoption of such means, only repression's aftermath. A Cold War ideological perspective was the basic frame of reference for virtually all Canadians involved in Indochina decision-making. It could not have been otherwise. Léon Mayrand summed up the attitude of many in the department when he noted in January 1955 that the DRVN leaders were now applying their extraordinary discipline, forged in a war in which they had fought against immense odds, but 'without any sense of morality, as if the ends justified the means.' After visiting the DRVN, he declared: 'When I came to Indo-China, three months and a half ago [sic], I wondered from the books I read if North Viet-Nam was not more nationalist than anything else. Three days in Hanoi have convinced me that they are not less Communist than in Moscow or Peking. They have learned fast.[89] John Holmes's comment of July 1955 that Hanoi's 'Muscovite atmosphere' was reminiscent of Moscow in the 1920s or 1930s was serious despite its somewhat humorous presentation.[90] The totalitarian character of the DRVN regime was all too plainly evident. Subsequent behaviour of the DRVN leaders has done nothing to cast doubt on the accuracy of these characterizations.

Conservative articulators were most affected by the inhumanity of DRVN-style socialism, with its active encouragement of class hatred and its reliance upon omnipresent mutual surveillance techniques. Disillusionment over

14(d) led many of these officials to think the first Canadian thoughts about unilateral withdrawal from the Indochina commissions. Liberal-moderate centrists, while appalled at DRVN duplicity and callousness, were much more inclined to look at the Vietnam problem in its international context. Maintaining the armistice and precluding Sino-American intervention and confrontation had to remain the focus of Canadian Indochina policy. For liberal-moderate articulators the DRVN's failure to comply with 14(d) was significant, but it was still more significant that evasion had not precipitated a total rejection of the ICSC and the Geneva package by Diem when he repudiated electoral consultations on 16 July 1955. Apparently de facto partial co-operation by the SVN with the ICSC was going to be possible on a continuing basis. Given the anarchy in the south, Diem certainly could use the Geneva structure as a partial shield to deter a massive attack on the south by Giap's army. Paradoxically, the politically determined failure of the ICSC to publicly convict the DRVN government for its clear breach of 14(d) probably had strengthened the conviction among Hanoi's leaders that the Geneva Agreements were still a potentially useful political instrument. Because they sensed Hanoi's continuing interest, Canadian liberal-moderates saw a practical basis for continuing ICSC involvement in Vietnam, distasteful though it was, and they perceived as well a continuing need to do what they could to lessen the risk of Sino-American collision.

Canadian left-liberals were sympathetic to liberal-moderate perceptions and logic, but they could not identify at all with the growing, emotionally rooted antagonism of departmental conservatives towards the DRVN, the ICSC, and especially towards the Indian propensity to 'sacrifice basic principle in dealing with communists.' Canadian left-liberals concurred with the Indians in hoping that the brutal methods and iron discipline of the DRVN regime would eventually soften after 'the trials of nation-building' had been surmounted. Escott Reid, in Ottawa on home leave from New Delhi in the summer of 1955, made a strong case for a left-liberal approach to Indochina policy. In view of British and French beliefs that the line of containment could only be drawn between Laos and Cambodia on one side, and Vietnam on the other, Reid felt that the establishment of the electoral process was an appropriate priority objective of Canadian policy. Reid bluntly stated that he agreed with the Indian view that Paris and London had 'implicitly acquiesced at Geneva in Ho Chi Minh taking over the whole of Vietnam as the result of elections.' Then according to Reid: 'The roof fell in on top of me. Officer after officer ... attacked me for my callous, immoral proposal which would betray millions of anti-communist people in South Vietnam into the clutches of the communists.'[91]* Gone was the air of pre-1954 theoretical detachment from Ottawa's policy debates. The emotions engendered by the 14(d) affair now threatened the diplomatic objectivity and political judgment of Canadian decision-making. Reid accurately noted in his account of these events that the softening of Canadian enthusiasm for elections would be interpreted by Nehru and his advisers as evidence that Canadians 'were giving in to United States pressure to sabotage the arrangements for elections.'[92] This interpretation no doubt found support in India, especially among friends of Krishna Menon. But the perception was wrong. North Vietnamese treachery, not US pressure, had shifted the policy consensus in Ottawa.

Another left-liberal said upon reflection

Canadian policy changed in the first year or so and it had a lot to do with the refugees. X and Y [certain 'conservatives'] had substantial influence on policy, but they never shed any tears over the ten million refugees in India-Pakistan in 1948 ... The Indians were very doubtful about encouraging refugees since it would clearly be held against these people when Ho's government was brought in. You must remember that the Indians were quite conditioned to refugee problems on a scale of millions not hundreds of thousands. So why should they get upset? It was such a sad story from start to finish.[93]

The left-liberal element offered perspective of a different kind on events in Asia. But their views would soon become quite tangential to the main thrust of Canadian policy. As American policy diverged more and more from toleration of the Anglo-French consensus of July 1954, the left-liberal posture (like the perspective proferred by the Sainteny faction in France) became increasingly irrelevant to the practical political options available to the government.

In the summer of 1954 there had been but one fairly uniformly held set of perceptions in DEA vis-à-vis the Indochina problematic. In mid-1954 there were no overtly detectable traces of a distinctly conservative or left-liberal approach towards Indochina decision-making. Conservative and left-liberal tendencies of articulation were then more a matter of latent potential rather than manifestly expressed policy alternatives. By the summer of 1955 the

---

* Not without an element of quite justifiable but bittersweet self-righteousness, Reid added in parentheses: 'Twenty years and millions of deaths later not only they but also the Laotians and Cambodians would be "betrayed" into the hands of the communists.' Escott Reid, *Envoy to Nehru* (Delhi, Toronto, Oxford: Oxford University Press 1981) 83. Having been 'right' in a tragedy of this magnitude is of little if any consolation.

FIGURE 3
The shift from latent to manifest tendency differentiation,
October 1954 to summer and autumn 1955
Fundamental value commitment

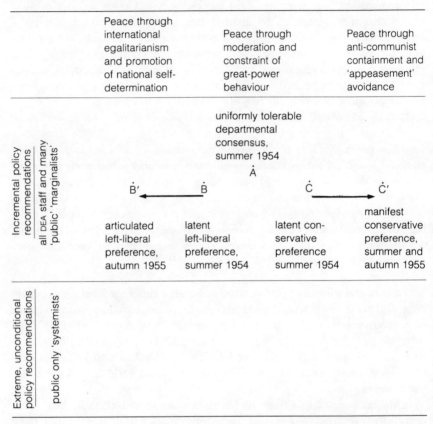

basis for three distinct approaches had emerged (see figure 3). A conservative tendency of policy articulation vis-á-vis Indochina had now congealed. A left-liberal tendency alternative was not long in forming thereafter. Once the attitudinal uniformity of the liberal moderate approach had been challenged by the 'insurgent' conservative school of thought, the way was cleared for articulation of a coherent 'left-wing' marginalist position. But of the two marginalist wings in DEA, the conservative element was clearly responsible for the *initial* breach in the liberal-moderate line of policy logic. Reflecting societal attitudes in general, the conservative element was subsequently far stronger than the left-liberal tendency in Vietnam decision-making for the duration of Canadian involvement in Indochina.

The refugee affair had set in motion a process of 'right radicalization.' Soon even confirmed liberal-moderates would not be immune to it. On 14(d) liberal-moderate discretion had prevailed over an ethical concern to try to help the northern Roman Catholics. In light of the now well-documented American flirtation with nuclear adventurism and notions of preventive war the decision of the spring of 1954 was unquestionably a wise one. At the time, many conservative articulators conceded the necessity of this approach, but the price for them was a sense of guilt. Irrational sympathy for the devout Catholic Ngo Dinh Diem and his family *may* have been one by-product of this guilt among many Canadian officials – but that is pure speculation. Diem was highly autocratic, a would-be mandarin. This is indisputable. But he was also moderately forceful, and well-schooled in French mores and intellectual traditions, however much he detested French influence in his country. Moreover, he knew the Americans well, having spent a good many years in the United States prior to his return to Vietnam in 1954. Diem and his family were autocrats to be sure, but, asked Canadian conservatives, was not Salazar's Portugal a member of the NATO community? Diem's intellectual posturing was abstract and disconnected, his regime repressive and quasi-fascist, but Canadians could always suspend their criticism of such naïveté and political barbarity more easily in the congenial surroundings of Saigon than they could in Stalinist Hanoi. The memories of the Catholic exodus and communist perfidy lived on in the minds of Ottawa's policy community long after the Canadian public had forgotten the hectic events of the 300 days.

6

Coping with the electoral dilemma
1955–6

From April 1955 through December 1956, the Indochina issue as a whole began to recede in international political importance, but not without some anxious moments for the Canadians directly involved. Many officials hoped that resolution of the problem of the Final Declaration's electoral provisions could be postponed indefinitely. In the context of a widening international agreement on the need for 'peaceful coexistence,' as well as the progressive consolidation of Ngo Dinh Diem's power in South Vietnam, this was not unreasonable. Henceforth the Canadian government would act in Indochina under a principle enunciated by Pearson himself in April 1956: 'we are willing to continue our work on the commission in Vietnam as long as there is any possibility of that work being useful in the maintenance of peace there and the establishment of conditions of stability.'[1] After the autumn of 1955, acting 'in the interests of peace' was interpreted to mean supporting the military armistice and the indefinite partition of the Vietnamese nation, while hoping that the American presence in Vietnam would successfully deter any attack upon the southern regime. The division of both Korea and Germany seemed ample international precedent to justify such a policy, although Canadian officials recognized that the political and military realities of Vietnam were very different from the situations in these earlier examples of partition.

After expressing unqualified support for elections and unification in 1954, Canadian policy began to retreat steadily from this position in March and April 1955, when, for the first time, Ottawa declared that any electoral supervision had to occur under the aegis of a new electoral commission, not some subcommittee of the existing ICSC. Further, Ottawa would only support truly free elections that would be acceptable to Western public opinion generally. There would be no compromise on principles the way there had been on 14(d).

During 1955 France withdrew most of its military forces from South Vietnam despite US pressure to stay involved. In the late spring and summer of 1955 Diem made impressive gains in subduing the sects militarily, but his army was certainly no match for the 300,000 or more DRVN regulars now armed and equipped with Soviet supplies, most of which had been brought in through the totally porous system of border 'control' exercised by the ICSC. In North Vietnam the imposition of Stalinist controls (ie, the spread of mutual and self-criticism procedures, the establishment of institutionalized political surveillance mechanisms, and the deployment of the most strident propaganda apparatus imaginable) guaranteed a near 100 per cent pro-DRVN vote were the elections to be held. With a slight majority of Vietnam's population in the north, Ho's government therefore needed to pull only a small fraction of the vote in the south to prevail. Ho's charismatic appeal and the political heterogeneity of the southern zone (typified by the large and diverse appeal of the sects) guaranteed that. As one left-liberal put it: 'I could never get over the feeling that large numbers of people in the South slept with pictures of Ho under their pillow.' Ho's cheerful demeanour, personal magnetism, and linguistic virtuosity were so impressive that he 'could have won an election as mayor of New York.'[2]

United States policy during 1955–6 publicly backed electoral negotiations. The State Department was consistent in this regard. But other elements of the American government were not in agreement. Officials with the CIA or the US armed services almost certainly pointed out to Diem that he could count on US support if he continued to defy the terms of the Final Declaration. From February 1955 onward the government of India feared the effects of such activities and grew more and more distressed at what was seen as the subversion of the original Geneva settlement. At various points India sought to reconvene the Geneva Conference to resolve the electoral ambiguity of the Geneva 'contract.' As the French progressively disengaged, the Indians grew increasingly upset. Who would succeed the French High Command as signatory to the armistice? Who or what would assume the role of the French Liaison Mission? Who would pay the bills of the ICSC in Vietnam? Ottawa worked hard to try to patch together a compromise that was acceptable to both India and Diem's government. Possibly availing themselves of US pressure on Diem, Ottawa helped to extract a commitment from Saigon to set up the Commission chargé des Relations avec la Commission Internationale de Contrôle, to replace the French Liaison Mission. Diem was induced to make a statement expressing a willingness to co-operate with the ICSC. The Indian government then had to be content with the uncomfortably hypocritical rationalization that Saigon was gradually being led to complete accession to the Geneva program.

Engaged in the rituals of a succession struggle, Soviet leaders were remarkably quiescent on Indochina throughout this period. Moscow, like Washington, seemed to think that partition was feasible and tolerable. In 1957 the Soviets would go so far as to propose the simultaneous admission of the two Vietnamese governments to the UN.[3] Only the Chinese protested Saigon's anti-electoral stance in vigorous terms. But given Chinese preoccupation with problems of their own in the Formosa Strait, the seriousness of their protests was doubted.

In light of this spectrum of responses and the opportunities they afforded for the Western alliance, to do less than support Diem where possible seemed pointlessly generous to the communist bloc. Détente, while spoken of, was far from a reality, and if the Soviet leadership was willing to acquiesce in a German-style approach to Vietnam at the expense of their Vietnamese colleagues, how could the Canadians seriously counsel any other route but partition in Western diplomatic circles? In its most fundamental aspect, the Vietnam problem, as seen from Ottawa, amounted to a search for an approach which would minimize the threat of military invasion or 'indirect aggression' from the north, and thus would win still more time for the fledgling RVN state. Almost imperceptibly the liberal-moderates' control of the DEA policy consensus about Indochina weakened and the conservative rationales and recommendations for Canadian policy went into a period of ascendancy which was to last some ten years. The March 1956 Canadian initiative against South Vietnamese avoidance of legal encumbrances was one of the last instances of liberal-moderate predominance within the policy process. During the next decade Canadian decision-makers would look increasingly on the Vietnam struggle through the prism of conservative policy axioms.

After mid-1955 Ottawa adhered to a restrictive, legalistic reading of the ICSC's mandate, and it sought reductions in the operational strength of the Indochina ICs wherever possible. The value of the commissions now was measured in two dimensions: their symbolic importance reflecting the capacity of the blocs to effect compromise over difficult collisions of interest; and their deterrent capacity vis-à-vis the renewal of armed violence by the DRVN. The Vietnam ICSC had no explicit procedural mandate for involvement in electoral negotiations. Its chief mandate concerned the arms control provisions of the Vietnam armistice, the monitoring of personnel and arms imports under Articles 16–19. By late 1955 the commission came to be seen by almost all Canadian officials as a device that was useful in shielding the RVN from DRVN-recourse to conventional armed attack, both because of the capacity of the ICSC to generate adverse publicity in the event of an armed attack, and because the commission could inhibit to some extent the overt import of arms – or so the theory of the day argued.

During this tense transition period the most critical problems for the Canadian liberal-moderate element were, first, preventing conservative policy rationales from effecting a withdrawal from the three ICSCs and, second, persuading the Indians to tacitly co-operate in maintaining a new transformed inter-bloc compromise on the status of Vietnam. To effect the necessary change in Indian policy, L.B. Pearson may have consciously advocated maximal economic assistance to the government of India. The aid relationship, if conceived of in those terms by Pearson (and the proposition so advanced is speculative), was more akin to seduction than bribery, and may be denoted more precisely as contextuating persuasiveness. To be sure, India's status as the world's most populous liberal democracy, one of its poorest countries, and a vital member of the Commonwealth, all argued for high donations of aid. But so too did geopolitical calculations that listed India as a critical asset for the West even if the Indians could be brought only to a position where they knew 'whom to be neutral against.' Canada's nuclear assistance program may have figured prominently in such an approach.

SHERWOOD LETT'S AMBIVALENT SUPPORT FOR ELECTIONS 1954–5

From the very beginning of their involvement Canadian officials had, conceptually, tended to split the tasks of armistice supervision and 'political settlement' implementation.[4] From August 1954 through the end of March 1955, the Canadians postponed close evaluation of the political settlement provisions, but by April 1955 the External Affairs policy machinery had to focus upon this difficult issue. Indo-Canadian relations had become increasingly strained because of conflict over 14(d), attitudes towards SEATO, and now anxieties about the holding of elections. Indo-Canadian differences on the elections reflected a divergence in fundamental interests between the two countries. Both sought peace in the region as a primary policy objective, but at the secondary level Ottawa sought to further anti-communist containment while Indians acted out of an interest-maximizing balance-of-power calculus.

South Vietnamese officials repeatedly told Canadians that the Indians and Chinese had concluded a spheres-of-influence understanding prior to the Geneva armistice of 1954. The historic line of division in the cultural influence of China and India in Indochina (roughly down the Annamite Cordillera) was to be the basis of the political settlement hammered out at the Geneva Conference. All Vietnam would fall into China's sphere of influence, after the 1956 elections had 'unified' the Vietnamese people, while neutralized Laos and Cambodia would drift into Nehru's non-aligned 'zone of peace.'[5] But the scheme was ruined when Diem and the US did not concur.

If the Americans were going to connive at blocking communist control of southern Vietnam, the Vietnamese communists were most certainly not going to relinquish their existing control of Sam Neua and Phong Saly provinces, which were adjacent to the northern half of Vietnam. The two Laotian provinces would be held hostage to try to bring persistent, indirect political pressure to bear on Diem, in hopes that this might force him to fulfil the terms of the original Geneva bargain. Assistance to the Pathet Lao by the DRVN would ensure continuing great-power involvement in the region. No genuine political settlement would be permitted for Laos alone. The strategic value of easy access to eastern Laos implicit in Pathet Lao control of that territory would never be surrendered by the DRVN without genuine prospects for unification through elections or other non-violent means. The elections issue in Vietnam thus became the litmus test of whether Canadian and Indian policies could ultimately be reconciled.

Lett and the Canadian delegation were initially concerned about the electoral provisions of the Final Declaration because of their potential impact upon the civilian refugees who moved south. The 14(d) affair had brought home to Canadians the fact that if people moved south in sufficient numbers the assured majority of the north might be called into question.[6] The events of the spring of 1955 destroyed this slender prospect. Partly because of the interconnection between 14(d) and the eventual outcome of the political settlement, the Canadian delegation began to grope towards some detailed assessment of the probable shape of the future electoral settlement.

Article 14(c) played a central role in these preliminary assessments. This article enjoined the parties to 'guarantee' the 'democratic liberties' of former 'partisans' or 'resistance workers,' and thus carried with it, by implication, a presumption that there should be a regime of 'democratic liberties' (nowhere defined) throughout the country. If there were to be elections then a definition seemingly had to be formulated and applied. But how? Because of the intricate analysis that was thought to be required to arrive at a satisfactory interpretation of this section of the CFA, the commissioners referred the matter to the ICSC's Legal Committee. On 10 May 1955 the Legal Committee submitted its report to the commission proper, which read in part:

As regards Article 14(c), we are of the opinion that the effect of its express provisions is to guarantee democratic liberties *only to persons who may have carried on political activities during the hostilities* and who may not, on that account, be discriminated against. In addition to the express provision as above, there is *an implication in the sub-article that there must be a regime of democratic liberties for the whole population in the two zones.*[7]

Chairman Desai quickly elaborated the Indian interpretation which would be placed on the phrase 'a regime of democratic liberties for the whole population.' According to Desai, if there was a 'common standard' then it had to be 'relative to the laws, regulations and practices prevailing in the area':

there was *no conception of democratic liberty which could be imported from outside* and followed in the areas as a standard, and *the standard had to be actually evolved from the conditions prevailing in the area, viz., local laws, regulations and customs and the extent of democratic liberties that people were enjoying* ... the democratic liberties had to be evolved from the current local laws and regulations prevailing in the area.[8]

Here the Indians erred badly, if they had hoped sincerely to promote an electoral resolution of the conflict.

Lett voiced what the Canadian delegation saw as the most critical aspect of the problem when he asked whether there was not an implicit need for a clear definition of 'democratic liberties.' Desai refused to permit such theoretical exercises saying:

democratic liberties were not absolute but relative ... If Articles 14(c) and 14(d) were examined together, it would be quite clear that *the intention of the Geneva Powers was that both regimes will have their own practices and laws for the people in their areas, but those persons who did not like the laws and practices in one zone could migrate* and live in the other zone. During the continuance of the regroupment arrangements in the two zones, the standard of democratic liberties would be the standard prevailing under the laws and regulations of the zone concerned. He stressed that *there was no implication in the Agreement that the same standard should be maintained both in the North and in the South.* Once the standard was established according to current laws and regulations, that standard should be applicable to all persons and there should be no discrimination against *previous resistance workers* and they should not be deprived of what rights were available to others.[9]

Thus Desai arbitrarily precluded the possibility of forging some common standard which might conceivably have lessened South Vietnamese fears concerning a possible political settlement. Lett was left with the unappetizing prospect of having to investigate 'specific cases' of violations of Article 14(c).

Lett returned to this issue on 17 May 1955 by proposing that it might be a sound idea for the IC to 'attempt to define the standards prevailing in either zone in relation to democratic freedoms ... in connection with the question of getting the parties together for election purposes.'[10] Lett noted that the Laotian Commission had already discussed the issue in some detail and that a co-ordination in the definition of the term 'democratic freedoms' might be a very salutary exercise for all three ICs. Commissioner Ogrodzinski dissented, bluntly denying that a common standard was needed for countries with different political, social, and economic systems. Desai again declined to embark on such debate. Ironically enough he foreshadowed the eventual position the Canadian government would take on the elections, when he declared: 'With regard to the question of elections and a common standard for the purpose ... this would be the subject of negotiations between the parties and *there would naturally be uniform standards accepted by both zones.* This was, however, *not relevant at this stage of the Commission's work.*'[11]

Desai's decision was yet another minor watershed in the history of the commission. Lett decided not to pursue the matter. Ogrodzinski concurred as well in the Indian position, though he had exhibited some ambivilance on the question because of a genuine desire to start the electoral process moving forward. Within a matter of months the Canadians would fall back on the argument that it was solely up to the parties themselves to negotiate a mutually acceptable electoral law. Unfortunately, a clear-cut opportunity to enunciate a comprehensive list of democratic liberties and electoral guidelines was neglected. Turning away from this task at this specific moment (less than two months from the projected date for the commencement of pre-electoral negotiations) meant foregoing potential leverage against the South Vietnamese government in the attempt to persuade it to accede to the political provisions of the Final Declaration.

On the last day of the 300-day regroupment period, 18 May 1955, Desai again refused a Canadian suggestion to discuss electoral methods and standards, saying:

The Geneva Agreement which we have been asked to administer does not want the Commission to do something which is based on absolute standards. What the Agreement requires us to do is to produce formulae, modalities and methods of action which satisfy the two parties, and that is why the experience of the people and their social and political institutions is of very great importance in the interpretation of the Agreement and its application. Naturally all of us wish that the social and political order should conform to an ideal pattern. But the ideal pattern is the ideal pattern of the people in the area and not that of *all* of us, or *any* of us. [Desai's emphasis][12]

It is of course quite probable that Indian officials wished to avoid discussion of 'democratic freedoms,' sensing, quite rightly, that it could lead to a very unfortunate confrontation which would polarize the issue in the commission proceedings and force the Indians to make some hard choices about basic electoral procedures long before the parties themselves had begun to consider the subject. Then, too, Desai might have feared having to commit India to a definite position from which retreat or amendment might prove exceedingly difficult. Desai's decision to take the prudent course, to stall on this issue and play the game step by step to maximize Indian freedom of manoeuver, was clever and quite consistent with the overall Indian tactical approach. But with hindsight it was the wrong line to take. The Indian stance helped to prepare the way for RVN intransigence on the electoral negotiations question.

Lett's proposal was probably as much an exploratory foray as it was a genuine effort to start the ball rolling towards elections. It might have been an attempt to put the issue squarely on familiar ground where the Canadians could then indulge in their own line of stalling and delay should the electoral negotiations process take a turn for the worse after June 1955. But it is also true that Lett himself was ambivalent on the subject and was far from sure how to counsel his superiors in Ottawa, who were having their own difficulties in formulating policy on this thorny issue.

Lett was quite rightly pessimistic about the prospects for Diem or any other politician in the south building an effective alternative to the Vietminh-DRVN political-military machine. Lett fretted over subversion constantly. Indirect aggression was not likely to be halted by anything the ICSC might do. Lett knew that the French were opposing US efforts to use the SEATO meetings to try to build political support for South Vietnamese avoidance of the 1956 elections.[13] The French seemed disposed to try to carry through on their electoral commitments. But Lett also was aware that the sovereignty of the State of Vietnam was becoming more substantial all the time. It was much more than the fictional sovereignty of the 'phantom state' of pre-July 1954.[14] Diem would have a real say in whether elections actually took place. DRVN leaders understood this fact and voiced their fears to Lett.[15]

To complicate matters still further, Lett was convinced that infiltration of agents from the north, and subversion of the state apparatus in the south, had already begun by January 1955.[16] The assassination of so many leading local leaders – both governmental officials and non-communist opposition figures – convinced him that the DRVN campaign against the State of Vietnam was already well launched.[17] Front organizations such as the Movement for the Defence of Peace (hereafter MDOP) seemed part of an overall strategy to weaken the governmental structure in the south and to cut off external sympathy for Diem. Lett's very pessimism about Diem's prospects led to his support for the elections process. But Lett's efforts became increasingly out of step with the drift of policy in Ottawa, which was steadily more inclined to avoid electoral responsibilities.

In early 1955, St Laurent and Pearson had been in London at the Commonwealth Conference of Prime Ministers. Discussion with Nehru, Menon, and Eden apparently had focused mainly upon Formosa and the 'delicate situation' in the Far East generally, though the talks were ostensibly only about the commissions in Indochina. When talk finally shifted to the Vietnam problem the Canadians asserted that Ottawa would not allow the Indochina Commissions 'to be used as a cloak for elections which were not completely free.' When the Canadian leaders went on to assert that the existing ICSC had no responsibility for supervising the elections, the Indians demurred. Nor was the vigorous Canadian assertion of a desire to wind up the Cambodian IC as soon as possible happily received.[18]

While at the Commonwealth Conference, Canadian officials delivered a message on or about 7 February to the Indian delegation, which contained four specific aspects of the Canadian position on electoral procedures: the drafting of an electoral law should precede the writing of the terms of reference of any possible electoral commission; the Canadians hoped that an electoral law would emerge from the pre-electoral negotiations scheduled to start in July; but any assistance from the ICSC in establishing or conducting these negotiations would, in the Canadian view, require an initiative from the parties themselves or the Geneva conference powers; and finally, the existing responsibilities of the ICSC would extend only to the provisions of the CFA – not the Final Declaration – and the responsibilities of the ICSC in providing assistance to the electoral talks should be formulated by the two Vietnamese governments themselves and approved by the Geneva Conference member governments.[19] The four principles effectively precluded an activist Canadian stand on elections.

Near the end of February, Escott Reid, the Canadian high commissioner in New Delhi, met with a number of senior officials in the Indian Ministry for External Affairs. They seem to have indicated that there was a growing feeling within their government that the Formosa situation and the positions taken by the SEATO powers at the Bangkok meeting pointed towards an imminent breakdown in the Indochina settlement. In February Diem categorically declared to Indian diplomats that there would be no elections in 1956. The Indians told Diem that the elections were an integral part of the

Geneva settlement. To Ottawa, the Indians argued that the co-chairmen had the authority to request assistance to the parties from the existing Canadian, Indian, and Polish delegations. Some Indian officials told Reid, however, that New Delhi thought that Ottawa was under no explicit obligation to serve on any proposed electoral commission. Canada could legitimately refuse the invitation. Reid, at this point somewhere between the liberal-moderate and left-liberal positions but leaning towards the latter, was apparently quite dismayed by the dreadful vagueness of the 'obligations' embodied in the Final Declaration.[20]

By early March the Canadians were to learn that the Australian government had changed its position on the elections and had decided that the western side of the containment line of division in Indochina should now include South Vietnam because it seemed plausibly defendable. The Australians were inclined to take a progressively harder line depending on their practical assessment of the survivability of Diem's regime.[21]

By the end of March, DEA's conservatives in Ottawa were certain that Canadian involvement in the electoral situation was very ill advised. As one opponent of electoral activism, Jules Léger, noted, even the act of offering the 'good offices' or 'technical advice' from the ICSC might conceivably damage the competence of the ICSC to carry out its existing role, since this competence depended greatly upon maintaining a judicial posture while the very nature of good offices role demanded intimacy, flexibility, and informality.[22] Léger was right: the role contradictions were real.

Commissioner Lett recommended an evasion of electoral duties unless all the ambiguities were cleared up by the Geneva powers. Extracting electoral terms acceptable to Western public opinion might prove to be immensely difficult.[23] The Canadian ambassador was quite scornful of initial British thinking on electoral modalities, which Lett thought was far too simplistic and optimisitc. Vietnam had been devastated by eight years of civilization and continued overt and covert great-power intervention. Expecting that peaceful reunification could be achieved so straightforwardly was to him utterly fantastic.[24]

So far as Lett could assess prevailing attitudes of the parties, any attempt to bring in the electoral issue through the ICSC or an electoral commission would lead to interminable haggling. When accepting the ICSC role on 28 July 1954 the Canadian government had made no firm commitment to supervise the elections and therefore Lett saw no reason to assume such a commitment after matters had become even muddier.[25] The terrible record of the parties under both 14(c) and 14(d) did not bode well for elections. The limited powers of the existing commission would probably preclude the imposition of a priori standards of democratic freedoms. To date (mid-March 1955) only the Poles had wanted to discuss the electoral issue in the ICSC and Desai and Lett had kept the question off the agenda. In view of the imminence of elections Lett suggested that Ottawa might privately sound out other countries regarding the need to reconvene the Geneva Conference well before the political consultations phase was to start in July.[26]

Lett's early reluctance was well received by departmental conservatives, but the ambassador was not wedded to an aloof or passive posture. The sooner the elections were held, the sooner the Canadians could leave Indochina.* In early April during a trip back to Canada to consult with the department, Lett stopped in London and, with Norman Robertson, talked at length with Krishna Menon at Robertson's private residence. Menon argued strongly that the Final Declaration was indeed a major part of the original settlement, though he understood why the Canadians dissented from this view. Ho Chi Minh would win the 1956 elections, but, Menon argued (naïvely or perhaps disingenuously), this would not result in hardline communism, only a nationalist neutralism. The DRVN government under Ho and Pham would try to preserve its relations with France and certainly would work very hard to keep the country out of the Chinese sphere of influence. In his report of the conversation, Lett for the first time indicated that the Canadian delegation probably would not be able to reconcile its twin goals of preserving good relations with New Delhi and Washington over Indochina.[27]

LETT DEPARTS: THE CONSERVATIVES PREVAIL

Lett's suggestion that Ottawa look into the possibility of seeking a reconvened Geneva Conference had been quickly stymied by European reaction to any such talk. The Formosa offshore islands dispute militated against any airing of other contentious issues in the Far East. Many Canadian officials had been converted to the 'skin graft'–'thin fabric of peace' theory about the ICSC role in Indochina. This led them to recommend extreme caution concerning both 14(d) matters and the electoral issue. Conservatives in DEA thought this to be an especially important consideration. If the electoral

---

* On 19 March 1955, Lett observed: 'the continuing duties of the present Commission will last presumably until Vietnam is politically unified through the medium of the general elections ... to take place in 1956, and if unification is then achieved, our obligations here would terminate ... if elections are not held, or do not result in unification, the Agreement could theoretically exist forever.' Lett to Ottawa, DEA files, 50052-A-40, vol. 10

negotiations failed the blame should rest clearly on the parties – not the ICSC.

As the debate progressed inside DEA, the policy confrontation resolved into a struggle between the liberal-moderates and the conservatives. The numerically weak left-liberal forces were scattered about the periphery of the debate – both geographically and in terms of substantive policy recommendations. Herbert Norman, the most intellectually sophisticated member of the left-liberal tendency in DEA,* apparently made only one inconsequential contribution to the debate from his posting in Wellington, New Zealand, that included the comment that Ottawa ought to avoid doing or saying anything that might impede the holding of elections. Norman, like other left liberals, was quite convinced that Canada had a moral obligation to do what it could to assist in the holding of the elections. To foster delay would probably play into the hands of communist propagandists.[28] According to Norman, the government of New Zealand was on record favouring the entire Geneva 'settlement'; nevertheless, it was daily warming to the Australian conviction that a 'Korean solution' for Vietnam was possible, wobbly though Diem's government was. Officials in Wellington shared the Australian desire to strengthen the 'buffer zone' to the north, the Pacific rim *cordon sanitaire* about the Chinese mainland.[29]

Another left-liberal writing from New Delhi (but not Reid) informed Ottawa at the end of April that, according to Krishna Menon, many people at Bandung had expressed the opinion that Ottawa was less than enthusiastic on the elections issue. This official then replied that Ottawa's policy was not one of delay, but merely one of caution. The Canadians would not allow themselves to be forced into a role which was impossible to fulfil. The mechanics of the proposed electoral commission were of decisive importance, and the Canadian government was going to make certain that the arrangements were satisfactory.[30]

New Delhi, Wellington, and Oslo (Chester Ronning's posting) were, to say the least, inopportune locations for influencing policy in Ottawa on a crucial decision. Anxiety that the conservative element was correct, that Canada would be allowing itself to be drawn into a hornet's nest of contro-

---

* Norman's most impressive scholarly work was on the economic and socio-political origins of the Meiji Restoration phase of Japanese history, an analysis which synthesized and embellished much Marxist and neo-Marxist Japanese history. Norman was also a valued adviser to General Douglas MacArthur during the latter's post-war reorganization of Japanese society. For a useful sample of Norman's writing see John W. Dower, *Origins of the Modern Japanese State: Selected Writings of E.H. Norman* (New York: Pantheon-Random House 1975).

versy from which retreat or exit would be very difficult, seems to have inhibited stronger protest from the left wing of the department. No left-liberal dissent was forthcoming when Ottawa decided to press for the 14(d) extension period within the ICSC on 10 May 1955, despite French fears that a DRVN refusal of the request might supply the State of Vietnam with a ready-made excuse for bowing out of the 1956 elections.[31] The conservative element continued to demand tactical precision: there would be no participation in elections without clarification.

Lett meanwhile was facing a new dilemma back in Hanoi. In response to Desai's formal proposal of the extension of the 14(d) period to 20 July, 'by which time the parties were expected to discuss the settlement of the political problem,'[32] Ambassador Ogrodzinski replied that the 4 February declaration by the government of the DRVN (which called for a completely open frontier through the DMZ), coupled with recent State of Vietnam statements which extended more co-operation to the ICSC, constituted grounds for hoping that an extension on 14(d) might be arranged, but he added:

The essential part of the problem should be seen from the political angle and must be connected with the political problems preceding the elections and the unification of the country. If progress could be made in the direction of settlement of political problems, freedom of movement after 18 May 1955, and the opening of the demarcation line seemed quite logical. If however no progress was made or was delayed, it was very difficult to count on success in the direction of freedom of movement, because without unification this seemed to be a paradoxical situation.[33]

This unusually candid statement of communist thinking failed to elicit the desired response. Desai was not going to assent to a quid pro quo proposal involving such critically important measures.

When the three commissioners visited General Paul Ely at the end of the month of May, Lett's previous proposal to begin discussion of electoral matters in the ICSC had already been deferred indefinitely. It would not be revived. Ely actually pressed the commissioners to take an *active* role in the electoral negotiations, especially in bringing the parties together. Desai and the Indian delegation were still determined to proceed with matters on a 'step-by-step' basis. The net result was that the Indian approach prevailed and Desai merely reaffirmed the need for the Geneva Conference powers to call on the IC to actually do something concerning the political settlement.[34] In part, Indian restraint at this time may have been due to Desai's own 'left-liberal' caution, in contradistinction to Menon's more radically 'socialist' enthusiasm for electoral activism. During the above-mentioned ICSC visit to

Saigon, the three commissioners talked with the foreign minister of the State of Vietnam, Vu Van Mau, who reiterated the State of Vietnam's refusal to accept any obligations to either the armistice or the Final Declaration.[35]

In early June the DEA conservative element made its bid for an irreversible Canadian commitment to passive obstruction of the electoral provisions of the Final Declaration. A memorandum to Pearson, submitted in connection with the forthcoming visit of Krishna Menon to Ottawa, recommended that he articulate strong reservations by Canada concerning any electoral negotiations involvement by the existing ICSC. Pearson was advised to tell Menon: that the ICSC should not take initiatives in the electoral talks except on instructions from the co-chairmen and with the concurrence of both Vietnamese governments; that only 'good offices' and 'technical advice' should be provided by any electoral commission; that a new supervisory organization would be required to establish any new electoral commission – the present ICSC staff could not take on further duties; and that any electoral commission could not be formed until the parties themselves were quite close to agreement on electoral procedures.[36] This four-part program, apparently agreed to by Pearson without much comment, was a firmed-up version of the February communication to the Indian government. The difference was that the June statement expressed policy, not just opinion. The memorandum concluded with the affirmation that Canadian policy should avoid even acquiescence in any ICSC electoral activism.[37]

Thus, less than three weeks after the suggestion by Lett to the ICSC that it ought to consider definitions of 'fundamental freedoms' and democratic procedures prior to the elections, the left-liberal/liberal-moderate hope for exploration of the limited prospects for electoral implementation was effectively foreclosed in Ottawa. However, this did not mark the end of policy vacillation by the Canadians. Because of civil disorders in the South, Lett recommended on 9 June that the electoral consultations *should* be encouraged, because failure to hold pre-electoral talks might simply cause an immediate increase in infiltration and subversion in the south.* In Lett's view Canada's concerns over 14(d) should be shelved indefinitely, since the Canadian's central tasks in the commission were to assist in the continued maintenance of peace in Indochina and to prepare ground for a possible settlement.[38]

---

* Lett wrote on 9 June that it was important not to 'castigate' the DRVN on 14(d) because it would create 'a bad climate for the pre-elections talks.' He argued that 'if consultations are not held, the effect upon the maintenance of peace in Indochina might be extremely serious, since the DR[VN] are unlikely to sit idly by ... This does not necessarily mean a renewal of hostilities in the ordinary sense, it may simply mean an increase of infiltration and subversion in the South.' Eayrs, *Indochina* 158

Lett's cautionary warning was unnecessary. Ottawa was already committed to avoiding electoral entanglement if at all possible. The only effect Lett's
message had on DEA was a mild strengthening of the liberal-moderates'
position in making sure that the evasion of electoral activism did not evolve
into a policy of overt opposition to the elections. Ottawa officials subsequently commented that Lett was dead on the mark in emphasizing that DEA
should not do anything to lay the Canadians open to the charge that they
'were deliberately exacerbating relations between the parties at a time when a
conciliatory atmosphere for political consultations was required.'³⁹ Although
Lett was unconvinced that elections could actually be free, as Westerners
understood the word, because of police intimidation and the omnipresent
techniques of mutual criticism and 'autocriticism' in the DRVN's 'can-bo
regime,'* he still asserted that the possibilities for adequate electoral arrangements at least should be fully explored.

In one of his last dispatches to Ottawa, Lett argued on 4 July that Canadian policy should not jeopardize the possibility that the two sides might yet
come together to negotiate. From the point of view of the anti-communist
dimension of Canadian policy, the continued existence of the ICSC was still
important to Canada, since the IC did act as a buffer between the forces, and
as a modest obstacle to infiltration and subversion. Lett had no doubts that
the DRVN was directing the campaign of subversion in the south, but he also
thought that the ICSC could not *prove* such a relationship given its inherent
political and logistical limitations. Lett minimized the possibility of a renewal of open warfare but he foresaw a relentless campaign by the DRVN on
the elections question. Any decision about resorting to open warfare once
more would not be taken by Ho or Giap but by Moscow or Beijing.

Keeping the parties talking loudly at each other was far better than
fighting. With American backing of Diem, the State of Vietnam representatives were likely to talk very loud indeed. According to Lett, Ottawa deci-

* Of the can-bo regime, Lett wrote: 'This little game ... amounts in practice to nothing
more than the reciprocal denunciation by the members of a group of all actions done and
all opinions expressed which might possibly be unfavourable to the Government ... it
greatly reduces the number of people who would dare do, or say, anything against the
regime, lest one might be denounced ... it permits the governmental authorities to be
constantly aware of the activities and opinions of practically everybody ... it cannot be
doubted that it is a factor of importance in preventing the possible expression of any sort
of political opposition to the present regime and that it greatly reduces the free exercise
of civil liberties in North Vietnam. The implications of such procedures in the North for
free elections' required by the Final Declaration will be abundantly clear.' Lett to Ottawa,
'The Can-Bo Regime in North Vietnam,' 25 June 1955: DEA files, 50052-A-40, vol. 13

sion-makers had to exercise their 'calmest and best judgment.' The risk was very high that Canada would become involved in legitimizing elections which the United States might then feel impelled to repudiate and denounce. The Canadian government was in a very difficult and politically complex situation. Diem's government was becoming stronger. However, it was showing no more inclination towards assuming successor-duty obligations than it had in 1954. The very basis of the ICSC hung on Diem's decision to accept successor obligations.[40]

THE REVISION OF CANADA'S APPROACH TOWARDS ELECTIONS AND THE BEGINNING OF THE WITHDRAWAL DEBATE

Lett of course had not been alone in the Canadian delegation in Hanoi in espousing the liberal-moderate position. In March, Saul Rae, then Lett's senior political adviser, wrote a long letter to John Holmes which dealt in part with the forthcoming elections controversy. Among Western diplomats and journalists in Vietnam, there seemed to be two views. According to Rae:

The Neanderthal view was that no action should be taken on elections at all; the more enlightened view, however ... [which he personally shared] was that South Vietnam should not leave the initiative to the North in the matter of elections, and that both free elections and unification on acceptable terms should be advanced with vigour and determination by the Saigon government, at the same time spelling out clearly the preconditions of free elections and unity.[41]

Holmes made a lengthy visit to Vietnam in June 1955, and met with Diem and many of his senior officials, as well as Indian, French, American, Australian, and British diplomats. Holmes's visit apparently was aimed at sounding out both Canadian and foreign opinion on the spot, assessing Canadian morale, and providing a first-hand review of the situation by a senior Canadian official preparatory to the next phase of the armistice agreements. Holmes found Diem surrounded by some brilliant but violently francophobe personnel who felt that the French were bent on betraying the State of Vietnam and that the Sainteny Mission most accurately represented the Quai's basic inclinations. The Canadian assistant deputy minister did not agree: 'My impression in Hanoi, on the contrary, was that the Sainteny staff considered their mission to be washed up and were bitterly unhappy about the lack of any support or direction from Paris.'[42] So far as Holmes could ascertain, the contest for control of South Vietnam was still far from decided and much would depend on Diem's capacity to move beyond pacification of the remaining Hoa Hao and Cao Dai opposition elements towards building a viable governmental system.

On 11 July 1955 Holmes submitted his major review of the Canadian role in Indochina to Pearson. He began by reviewing the work of the ICSC to date and discounting various public charges by American and European leaders that the DRVN grossly violated Articles 16 and 17:

My impression after talking to a good many Canadian officers who had served on the Northern border, is that although there may be *a certain amount of traffic in small arms or vital parts there is probably no serious violation of the Agreement by the Chinese* ... As you are aware, in spite of the frequent public charges from Washington of violation on the Northern border on a large scale, *the Americans have never been able to produce for us through regular or through intelligence channels any valid evidence of such traffic since the time the Commission's teams were established on the frontier* last autumn.[43]

On the question of 'democratic liberties,' Holmes reiterated the now standard assumption that the provisions of Article 14 should be interpreted only according to conventional Western understanding of the term.

Holmes was certainly aware of the difficulties facing any attempts at implementing truly 'free elections.' With respect to specific cases of violation of 14(c), he noted: 'Whereas in the North there is a calculated and organized repudiation of democratic liberties, these violations in the South are undoubtedly the result of an anarchical situation, the inevitable passions resulting from years of civil war, the activities of the Sects, and probably also the authoritarian tendency of Diem's government.' Holmes was quite prepared to suspend or reserve judgment as to the 'real' nature of Diem's rule. Holmes and other Canadian officials thought that the French were overreacting to Diem's francophobia in labelling him a dictator, while the Americans were probably too optimistic in calling Diem 'a strong man doing what is necessary in a turbulent situation.'[44] In any case, one could be sure that henceforth Article 14(c) would work only on behalf of the DRVN.

Canadian officials were most concerned about the possibility of increased American pressure to withdraw from the ICSCs and thus force their dissolution. It was believed that replacement of the Canadians would require a reconvening of the Geneva Conference. This in turn would probably lead to failing attempts to renegotiate the entire basis of the agreements – as some Americans seemed to have hoped. If US pressure was applied (so far it had not materialized), the Canadian government would have to look very carefully at the broader consequences of withdrawal. Holmes then laid out what was to become the classic rationale for remaining on the Indochina commissions:

> In reaching any such decision we must keep our eyes steadily fixed on the fact that our real contribution in Indochina cannot be judged primarily by our success on any specific item of the agenda. The real contribution is in our being there. There could be no replacement for us on the Commission, and without us, therefore, there could be no Commission. Without a Commission there could be no Geneva Agreement. *To break up this framework of peace, however distasteful some of its aspects, would be an extremely serious step.* We might, therefore, have to stand firm against serious internal and external pressures.[45]

Possibly Holmes exaggerated the difficulty with which Canada could be replaced and the speed with which the CFA might collapse, but it is difficult to think of other politically acceptable countries who might have been willing to fill the gap on short notice. In any event, a mild exaggeration of the calculus of risk certainly did not hurt Holmes's plea for extreme caution in Pearson's consideration of the withdrawal option and for avoidance of precipitate action in response to any wilful, ill-conceived American 'advice.' Precisely because Pearson had never been happy with a Geneva peace framework lying outside of United Nations jurisdiction, and because Pearson's ambivalence about the Indochina commissions in July 1954 had only been increased by the frustrating events of the first year, Holmes had to tread carefully.

As Holmes portrayed the situation in a basic decision was needed about the value of the Geneva Agreements themselves. Were they making a real contribution to peace in the region or not? Or was US support of Diem's government the crucial factor on the Western side of the deterrence equation? In Holmes's view, Pearson could rely on the fact that a Canadian withdrawal probably would lead to the early demise of the ICSC, and with the death of that body any remaining hope for a peaceful political resolution of the Vietnam conflict would probably be at an end. For Holmes, the South Vietnamese and American attitude of dismissing the possibility of there ever being free elections in Vietnam was a very 'dangerous tendency.' The French had virtually no power over the Diem government, especially with regard to the latter's forced participation in electoral talks. Of the two sides, the DRVN was providing, by mid-1955, better facilities and co-operation because 'the Commission is an instrument for securing free elections which they will win.' Given this complex set of pressures, was it sensible for the Canadians to continue to support the Geneva plan?

Holmes summed up the essential aspects of the problem as follows:

There is a basic paradox in the present situation about which we ought not to kid ourselves any longer. The paradox is this: *It is of the greatest importance that peace be maintained in Indochina by maintaining the structure established at Geneva. This structure can be maintained only if the provisions concerning free elections are carried out. However there cannot be free elections next year which reasonably could be called free by Asian, European or by any other standards than those of the Soviet Union.* It is not a question of the modalities. The North might provide absolutely secret balloting and the other customs of democratic polling booths. They might even allow opposition parties to campaign. However, *you cannot have free elections in an unfree atmosphere.* Balloting might be secret but *campaigning must be open. It is not conceivable that many people in the North, even if they were encouraged by the government to do so and offered guarantees against persecution, would come out into the open and take a stand.*[46]

Holmes's assessment of the sympathies of the population in the North was yet another ambiguous and troubling factor in the political balance being calculated. The climate in Hanoi and Haiphong was undeniably 'Muscovite.' The atmosphere

was, in fact, much closer to the Moscow of the Twenties or middle Forties than to the more 'liberal' Moscow of today. I am not at all sure either that the 50,000 people who assembled at the race-track to shout for Ho on his 60th birthday would want to vote against him even if they were perfectly free to do so; *they seemed to be having the time of their lives.*[47]

To grant, as Holmes did, that free elections which would be acceptable to Western public opinion were a priori impossible was to place the analysis of the problem on a track which led in only one direction: eventual abandonment of support for the electoral provisions and acquiescence in Diem's intransigent defiance of the Geneva package. Conservatives in DEA favoured a policy of tacit collusion in Diem's opposition to the political settlement provisions, not merely liberal-moderate acquiescence. The implicit message of the memorandum, reduced to essentials, was simply: Canadian policy is facing a great dilemma; the options facing Ottawa are all bad; the most dangerous route of all would be withdrawal.

Holmes had carefully noted that the Americans were putting up a false front with respect to the Geneva Agreements, that they claimed to be urging Diem into electoral consultations with the DRVN, but 'the Americans unfor-

tunately talk too much to make their position convincing.' American officials
had told Indian diplomats that they were urging the consultations on Diem
confident that other obstructions would crop up and that the electoral law or
protocol would never be drawn up:

If one recognizes that the suspicions, not only of the Communists but also of the
Indians and other Asians, of the American role in Indochina arise out of *the equivocal
and fundamentally irresponsible position the us had adopted towards the Geneva Agreement*, it is not surprising that American intentions concerning elections are not
generally trusted.[48]

In Holmes's view the American stance was not technically inconsistent
with the agreements themselves because the Americans had never committed
themselves to supporting the Final Declaration. Nevertheless, the situation
in Indochina was not likely to remain peaceful if the then-current trends
persisted. Holmes was convinced that the DRVN leaders were 'maintaining
the Pathet Lao stake in Northern Laos as a hostage pending agreements on
elections in Vietnam,' and thus 'the unity of the Geneva Agreements is
becoming more and more clear.'[49] Could the Canadians really expect Chou
En-lai and the other Chinese leaders to abide by their commitment to respect
the neutrality of Cambodia and Laos if the provisions of the Vietnam agreement, as they understood them, were not fulfilled? Could Ottawa expect
peace to prevail in Indochina if the State of Vietnam became little more than
an American-backed satellite? Or were French and Indian ruminations about
some possible federal solution to the electoral problem worth exploring?
Whatever the answers were to these questions, Holmes was convinced that
Canadian policy could not back a do-nothing, hands-off posture: 'Diem
could not at this stage face a show-down with the Vietminh, given the
infinite possibility of infiltration and the ability of the D.R. to exploit the
problems with the Sects.'[50] With the American military presence in Vietnam
at fewer than 400 advisory personnel, the accelerating run-down of the
French Expeditionary Corps meant that South Vietnam was effectively defenceless.

Holmes's review was submitted to Lester Pearson only nine days before
the riots of 20 July 1955. The Polish and Indian quarters in Saigon and other
FT and MT locations in the southern zone were thoroughly ransacked, and
the Poles and Indians themselves were roughed up, intimidated, and denounced by angry mobs. The Canadian representatives on the ICSC by and
large went unharassed. Without doubt these demonstrations against the
Geneva Agreements were organized by Diem's officials.

Holmes also noted in his July 1955 memorandum that the Indians were still adamant on the subject of elections. Their position of complete and unqualified backing for adhering to the 1956 electoral timetable was unchanged.* Relations between Saigon and New Delhi were abysmal because of this continuing pressure from India, and because of the very short shrift Nehru and Menon gave to Diem's representatives at Bandung.[51] As Diem went from strength to strength inside Vietnam in the latter half of 1955, Indo-Canadian relations grew proportionately more tense.

By the end of July 1955 the liberal-moderates were in an untenable position. Given the structure of Canada's alliance commitments – specifically its growing military involvement with the United States – and given a growing American determination to subvert the electoral provisions of the Final Declaration, continued opposition by Ottawa to the American Cold War strategy in Vietnam might possibly lead to much higher levels of tension in Canadian-American relations. Conservatives in the DEA favoured tacit support of Diem and fairly explicit support for the application of containment in Vietnam along the 17th parallel.[52] Centrist observers like Holmes kept their eyes not on the opportunities for drawing the tightest possible ring about the communist zone of territorial control, but rather on the necessity of minimizing the probability of a worst-case outcome in Vietnam – ie, the breakdown of the armistice in Vietnam, Sino-American intervention, and finally, American nuclear strikes on Chinese territory.

By the end of the July 1955 east-west summit, the perceived probability of this worst-cast scenario had no doubt diminished in Pearson's eyes. United States leaders now seemed willing to take concrete steps towards lessening tensions. This permitted increased attentiveness and responsiveness by Pearson to conservative anti-communist articulations. Support for the US position, or Diem, no longer carried with it an implied support for the US policy of nuclear intimidation in Asia.

A shift in Canadian policy did occur in late 1955. The key to the shift was a subtle change in perspective of moderates like Holmes, who up to this point had shared more in common with Indian, not American, logic in Indochina policy-making. Hereafter, they were gradually forced towards a reluctant accommodation of conservative premises. Liberal-moderate 'diplomacy' did have the very constructive effect of blocking any sudden Canadian with-

---

*   On 10 April 1955 during Pham Van Dong's visit to New Delhi, Dong and Nehru issued a communiqué emphasizing 'the importance of free elections and the achievement of the unity of Viet Nam as provided for by the Geneva Agreements.' In June 1955 Nehru toured Eastern Europe and the Soviet Union, and reaffirmed the Indian determination to see the elections carried out. See D.R. SarDesai, *Indian Foreign Policy in Cambodia, Laos and Vietnam, 1947–64* (Berkeley and Los Angeles: University of California Press 1968) 88.

elements might conceivably have recommended had not the initial Holmes memorandum, as well as subsequent briefs by other liberal-moderates in DEA, skilfully precluded such a line. The terms of the debate over Canada's Vietnam policy were thus limited after July–August 1955 to considering ways of mitigating Canada's offence to New Delhi, now that Ottawa was set on a course which would see the eventual splitting apart of the military armistice and the political settlement provisions of the Geneva Agreements. It was implicitly understood by all concerned that despite the adjustment on the policy margin with respect to American – South Vietnamese views on the elections, the Canadian government still was firm in avoiding any and all military-security commitments to the region. The Canadians would not meddle with the policies of the western anti-communist 'front' in Indochina, which would be given its chance to 'win the peace,' but neither would they assist in the struggle on any serious scale. Without doubt there were many conservatives in DEA who found this particular compromise unpalatably faint-hearted.

HEADING OFF WITHDRAWAL: JULY–AUGUST 1955

On 16 July 1955 Premier Ngo Dinh Diem again repudiated the Geneva Agreements, reiterating the State of Vietnam's refusal to assume any legal obligation whatsoever for their implementation, recalling the State of Vietnam's categorical denunciation of the original agreements and the ensuing 'provisional,' de facto partition of Vietnam, saying that it was utterly out of the question for his government 'to consider any proposal from the Vietminh, if proof is not given us that they put the superior interests of the national community above those of communism; if they do not *cease violating their obligations, as they have done by preventing our countrymen of the North from going South ... the Free World is with us, of this we are certain.*[33]

The United States government condemned the 20 July incidents of assault on the ICSC. So did the British and French, who also were on record favouring the holding of elections. On 26 July, UK, US, and French diplomatic representatives delivered a *démarche* to Diem urging him to enter into the electoral consultations called for in the FD. Diem refused. On 17 August 1955 the DRVN formally protested to the ICSC the failure of the SVN to nominate representatives for the electoral talks. On Indian urging, the co-chairmen met in New York during the last week in September but could not agree on a course of action. On 23 October a referendum took place pitting Diem against an absent Emperor Bao Dai. The rigged results produced a landslide for Diem, who then proclaimed the Republic of Vietnam, with himself as president, on 26 October. Elections for a national constitutional assembly were to be held on 4 March 1956. By year end, the US, UK, France, Australia, New Zealand, and thirty-one other Western countries including Canada had recognized the RVN.[54]

Despite the fact that publicly the Canadian government seemed to have fallen into line with American determination to 'save free Vietnam,' such was not the case. When Ottawa learned in early July that various officials in the US State Department wanted to back Diem's proposal to refer the Indochina problem to the UN Holmes wrote a sharply worded message to the Canadian Embassy in Washington reminding the staff that such actions would destroy the ICSC because of an inevitably strong outcry from the communist powers. Such action by Washington would cause considerable bad feeling in Paris, London, and New Delhi. Did Washington want that? The message Holmes wanted communicated to State suggested that though the Canadians would be very happy to see the ICSCs fold and the Indochina problem transferred to the UN Canadian frustration would not be permitted to dictate Canadian policy. If the interests of peace required an eventual electoral settlement, Canada would support that objective. Holmes hoped that Canada and the United States were not about to relive the previous dispute the two countries had experienced over the Korean elections controversy.[55]

In what can only be construed as an attempt to rebuild support among DEA personnel, Holmes launched a miniature counter-offensive on behalf of the forces of liberal moderation shortly after submitting his 11 July policy review memorandum to Pearson. In this latest communication Holmes also noted that in his conversations with the South Vietnamese themselves, no desire was ever indicated that they wanted the ICSC to stay: 'When asked if they wanted the Commission to remain, they usually said politely they would like the Canadians to stay.' Holmes disavowed any desire to prolong the IC's life unnecessarily but, he noted, frustration by itself could not justify withdrawal. The very presence of the ICSCs was a barrier or deterrent to any intensification of the conflict between the two Vietnamese governments.[56] The note concluded with the observation that if DRVN co-operation with the ICSC fell away completely, Ottawa would probably have no reasonably alternative except withdrawal.

By the latter part of July these memoranda had produced the desired effect and a message was sent to Lett (then nearing the end of his tour of service) instructing him to side with the Poles and Indians in opposing any move by the RVN government to force the ICSC to move its Saigon headquarters to Dalat[57] – a move which could be expected to lower still further the IC's already much diminished prestige and effectiveness. At the same time a communication was received from Washington, apparently the direct consequence of Holmes's message, which declared that the State Department believed that the ICSC was serving a useful function in helping to prevent the resumption of hostilities, in deterring Vietminh subversion in the South, and enabling the refugees to reach 'Free Vietnam.'[58] Whether the communication was 'sincere' is a matter of speculation, primarily because of the extremely artificial tone of this anonymously written message. It is not inconceivable that some State Department officials dispatched the message in direct response to the request by Holmes or another liberal-moderate for a helpful and timely enunciation of 'Washington views' from State personnel known to be sympathetic to Canadian liberal-moderate thinking. This is completely speculative, but it is plausible given the crisis facing the liberal-moderates in their internal struggle with the conservative inclination to terminate Canadian involvement in Indochina as soon as possible.

By the end of July the debate in DEA on withdrawal had become serious enough to warrant the request of an opinion from Legal Division as to possible procedures and their probable associated consequences. The memorandum of inquiry apparently noted that there was no clear modality for ending the IC's activities or the participation of any of the members of the commission. So far as the desk personnel could tell, although the communist powers all claimed a veto over termination of any one of the three ICs, there was no record of French or British agreement to the principle that termination was the responsibility of the Geneva powers as a group.[59] In early August the position of the liberal-moderates was strengthened by receipt of a major review memorandum from Saigon which declared: that the main hope for promoting liberal-democratic process in Vietnam lay with the attempt of the South Vietnamese government to reform itself and widen its base of popular support; that the southerners had to declare a willingness to enter into elections at some point – not necessarily according to the Geneva timetable – to win time for strengthening the non-communist alternatives; that demands for partition were very ill advised and that acceptance of the 'genuinely free elections' called for in the Final Declaration were the only way to stall renewed communist attacks in the South.[60]

The author of this latter communication supported the recommendation for backing electoral talks by emphasizing that only France, of all the Western states, had any credible capability to influence the situation should the armistice break down. But the French were committed to leaving Vietnam and were already a negligible factor in any military calculations. For the Western countries to support any other line of action than carrying through with the 'spirit' of the original agreements seemed foolish at the least. Backing Diem in his bid to revise the Geneva settlement at a time when the

Western capacity to deter renewed hostilities in Vietnam was diminishing seemed a virtual invitation to a resumption of the war by Vietminh-DRVN forces.

By mid-August the internal debate in DEA had been resolved through a compromise. Another major review memorandum apparently assessed the policies towards elections in Vietnam of all the key powers involved. The nature of the compromise was that Canada should maintain its commitment to the ICSC but that it should take henceforth a very restrictive reading of the competence of the commissions with regard to involvement in the electoral talks. Of the DRVN, the report noted that it obviously stood the most to gain from the holding of elections. Diem and his advisers were seen to be profoundly ignorant of their need for international sympathy and political support. Diem could be counted on to pursue a policy of 'stalling' and obstruction on elections. Diem's fears were said to be understandable and the State of Vietnam's legal obligations to the Final Declaration were seen to be non-existent. But Diem's stand probably would not be generally understood in Western countries, where the aversion to anything which might disturb the Geneva armistice was apparently quite strong. The Canadian government therefore would not help in pressuring Diem to assume FD obligations for the moment, but neither would it publicly concur in the legality of the complete repudiation of these obligations.[61]

The United States government from May through August continued to give lukewarm support to Diem. Some American officials had spoken of free elections being held under United Nations supervision. State Department personnel had participated in, or been associated with, several Anglo-French representations to Diem regarding the electoral talks. Sentiment in State was inclined to oppose any active ICSC role since State officials wanted the responsibility for the expected breakdown in such discussions to rest squarely with the Vietminh and not to be diffused through the ICSC's assumption of responsibilities. Diem would not co-operate in this strategy. Nevertheless, US officials were fairly optimistic.[62]

The British were still basically pessimistic about Indochina. Partition was not a realistic option. Without elections the fighting would soon resume. The French were no more optimistic. After February 1955 French officials disclaimed any responsibility for carrying out the political clauses of the Geneva Agreements. Thereafter the French denied DRVN assertions that they had a legal responsibility to force implementation of Articles 6 and 7 of the FD, and said it was a matter for the Saigon government alone. The Geneva settlement was still popular in France and the SVN could in no way look to Paris for help should hostilities resume. By the autumn of 1955 the FEC was preparing contingency plans for the evacuation of French nationals and other Europeans in the event war broke out before the last French battalions had departed.[63]

While the British and French were reluctant supporters of an electoral strategy, the Indians were outright enthusiasts. New Delhi was determined to implement the Geneva 'package deal,' and Indian officials forecast war if it were not carried out. Behind Indian pleasure at the end of the French reign in Indochina and their avowed desire to see an extension of the non-aligned zone, Canadian diplomats had found evidence of a 'sphere of influence' arrangement with the PRC which revealed a rather darker, more self-interested side to Indian foreign policy. The Indians apparently hoped that both Chinese and DRVN influence in Laos and Cambodia would be inhibited by Indian diplomatic and moral pressure, but this could not be accomplished without elections. Indian officials, Menon in particular, saw Ho's DRVN as both highly nationalistic and thoroughly independent. Diem was little better than Bao Dai in their eyes.[64]

Canadian suspicions about the self-professed, disinterested character of Indian policy apparently originated in South Vietnamese accusations that India and China had agreed on their own version of partition in Indochina at the Bandung Conference in April. Whether this allegation was entirely justified is not clear from the available evidence, but the subsequent realignment of Indian policy in favour of Saigon, following the change in the regional balance of power after 1955, might support such an interpretation.

In any event Ottawa backed a restrictive definition of the ICSC's mandate that precluded electoral entanglement. Aware that this stand might be construed as the beginning of overt partisanship, the liberal-moderate element nevertheless deferred to conservative logic. All three tendencies were unhappy with the high cost of the ICSCs in terms of personnel resources. A legalistic approach to the agreements took hold.[65]

Despite Canadian reluctance in electoral matters, Donald Smiley* was soon sent to Indochina as an elections specialist. Few thought that he would ever be able to demonstrate his competence. Holmes wrote Saul Rae, the acting commissioner, suggesting that in the event of electoral obstacles Smiley might be used on other matters, such as the question of democratic liberties.[66] Rae, like Holmes, was very much inclined to postpone withdrawal from the ICSC, to press for a public declaration by Diem stating a

---

* Smiley subsequently enjoyed a distinguished career as an academic specialist on the institutional and political aspects of Canadian federalism. See his best-known work, *Canada in Question: Federalism in the Seventies*, 3rd ed. (Toronto: McGraw-Hill Ryerson 1976).

willingness to enter into negotiations that might lead to elections, and finally to look to the United Nations to supervise these elections at some point after 1956 (presumably after some solution to the problem of communist Chinese seating in the UN).[67]

Relations with Diem's government were beset with other problems as well. By mid-August 1955 Saigon was refusing to permit ICSC team patrols except on twenty-four or even forty-eight hours' notice 'on grounds of security,' instead of conforming to the two hours' notice procedure agreed to in 1954.[68] So far as the Canadians were concerned, this blatant attempt by the southern regime to reduce the effectiveness of the ICSC's mandate meant only that it would draw increasing criticism from the DRVN, which had already done much to restrict the IC movement as well, but in considerably more skilful ways.* The breakdown of the ICSC's capacity to monitor arms and personnel import regulations under Articles 16 and 17 caused much apprehension among Ottawa's liberal-moderates.[69] New Delhi then informed Ottawa that it was reconsidering its role on the ICSCs in light of the marked deterioration in SVN compliance.[70]

By September, after provoking the American State Department's revived interest in the ICSC, the liberal-moderates, especially Holmes, apparently had successfully headed off a precipitate Canadian withdrawal. As Holmes then viewed the rapidly shifting play of events:

It seems to me that the policies to be adopted by the major powers are important to us. A policy of bringing things quickly to a head or of abandoning the Geneva Agreements might serve our narrow interests best as it would probably lead quickly to the withdrawal of the Commission. A policy of stalling, however, of maintaining the peace but achieving little success in reaching a settlement could be for us very arduous. It might keep us involved in Indochina for a very long time and it would certainly engage our representatives in frustrating labours. It might, however, be the best chance of *keeping the peace and holding the line* in Asia.[71]

This analysis and program, which might be termed 'peace plus anti-communist bonus,' constituted the underlying politico-diplomatic rationale of Canadian policy for the next five years. The liberal-moderates like Holmes were nudged away from their tentative support for the elections by a combination of factors: the exit of the French; the indifference of the British;

---

* Delays were attributed to mechanical breakdowns, bad weather, local holidays, unavailability of transport, liaison officer sickness – carefully distributed to minimize the vulnerability of the government to charges of obstruction.

Diem's increased strength in South Vietnam and his continuing denunciation of elections; American willingness to underwrite Diem's regime; and internal conservative arguments that the non-communist alternative deserved a chance. The ambiguity of the agreements and American determination to back Diem swung the Canadian Vietnam policy debate to the right, but not so far right as to result in withdrawal. Holmes had been very relieved to discover that American State Department thinking on Vietnam and the ICSC was not that different from Canadian policy.* At least a few in the State Department were more susceptible to Holmesian persuasion and logic than were the conservatives within DEA itself, men who were much more emotionally involved than Washington's grand strategists. Ironically enough it may have been American assistance to the Canadian liberal-moderates which was decisive in helping the latter to limit the growth in influence of the embittered conservatives in DEA, and thus enabled the liberal-moderates to protect the Geneva structure from what would probably have been a 'fatal loss of pressure' incident to Canadian withdrawal. The episode was clearly an example of transnational political action: a bi-national coalition of moderate forces aiming to inhibit conservative approaches in both societies.

The pro-participation line prevailed as the departmental consensus because it seemed to offer the best prospects for sustaining peace and contributing to containment. Writing one year later, Holmes caught the essence of the compromise in the following remarks:

It is an interesting and significant fact to note that 1955 was the first year in over twenty when for twelve months there was no war in the Far East ... an uneasy peace it is true, but *in these perilous and revolutionary times, we should not count on anything like a permanent settlement*. We are taking part in an experiment on the result of which may depend the peace and stability of Asia. It is an effort to hold an armistice *in the hope that a settlement will be possible after peace has struck roots*. We have always tended to think of peace and a lasting settlement as the fruits of victory. Now we are forced to recognize that the unconditional surrender of the forces of communism in Asia is not something to be achieved by *conventional means. It certainly cannot be gained by military means*. We can, however, hope to *hold the communists behind their present lines*.[72]

---

* According to Holmes the American officials he conversed with about Indochina exhibited a 'cold but not hostile' attitude to the ICSC. Said Holmes: 'I was pleased to find that the State Department's thinking when dealing with the immediate future was along lines generally similar to our own.' John W. Holmes to the author

INDIAN DISCONTENT, SEPTEMBER–DECEMBER 1955

Nehru and Krishna Menon wanted peace in Indochina, but not peace based on a Cold War military stand-off between proxy armies of the two bloc leaders. This would defeat the central Indian objective of extending the 'zone of peace' concept throughout Asia. On several occasions they indicated to Canadian officials that India would not remain on the ICSCs merely to protect Diem's regime. When such threats made to Ottawa and elsewhere failed to elicit action, the second response was a careful look at the merits of withdrawal. Where the bureaucratic right wing in Canada had sought an exit to promote militarily based containment of Vietnamese communism, the Indian centre and left sought to use the threat of an exit (and the implied threat of the collapse of the Geneva Agreements) to force Saigon's accession to the full Geneva bargain. The threat was a bluff and Diem called it. New Delhi officials eventually concurred in the Canadian liberal-moderates' approach. They thereby concurred in a policy logic which they had been instrumental in formulating over the 14(d)–Formosa Strait crisis: the peace in Indochina was too fragile, and the possible worst-case consequences of its destruction too great, to warrant taking a stand on narrow legal principles.

The calculus of risk dictated extreme caution. Washington's militants were very close to the levers of power. The doctrine of massive retaliation was at its operational zenith. The strength of American Strategic Air Command bases in the Far East was increasing steadily. America's bellicose allies in Asia (Rhee in South Korea, Chiang on Formosa, and even some officials around Diem who spoke of a 'march to the north') advocated quite unrealistic but nevertheless dangerous thoughts of irredentist assault on the communist-held portions of their respective national domains.

Indian resignation from the ICSC structures, even more than Canadian resignation, would surely have produced an immediate collapse of the Geneva peace structure. Those Indians who argued for an exit undoubtedly did so in the hope that the Geneva armistice would indeed disintegrate, thus necessitating a reconvening of the Geneva Conference and the imposition of a new more workable peace agreement on the Vietnamese. But would the Americans go to Geneva a second time? Ottawa officials did not believe so. And suppose Washington used the collapse of the armistice commissions to initiate an arms build-up in Vietnam, perhaps to include the deployment of tactical nuclear weapons in the southern zone? New Delhi and Ottawa shared the same policy dilemma in this respect.

On 10 September 1955, the Indian delegation informed the new Canadian ambassador, David M. Johnson, that New Delhi was already engaged in an 'informal approach' to the Geneva co-chairmen concerning the failure of the Diem government to accept any obligations under the agreements. Indian officials were determined to make a formal approach to the co-chairmen, no later than the end of September, and they wanted to know whether the Canadians or Poles wished to associate themselves with this inquiry. Johnson believed that this initiative, in view of Desai's vigour in producing the ICSC's *Fourth Interim Report*, was part of the Indian chairman's 'swan song.'[73] Would it be part of India's 'swan song' too?

Pearson nevertheless resisted the informal approach and suggested that Johnson propose some interim arrangement of limited co-operation from Diem's government. He also stressed the inopportune timing of the Indian initiative in seeking a meeting of the co-chairmen when the French and South Vietnamese were in the midst of acrimonious negotiations that would create the legal framework for the final departure of the FEC. Pearson did not want to see the tactical initiative pass into Indian hands.[74] Canadian embassies were therefore told to emphasize that Ottawa wanted early progress in Laos and viewed Indian stalling there with misgivings. Ottawa also sought early reductions in the size of ICSC Cambodia now that the September elections had been held successfully.[75]

At this juncture, External Affairs learned that the US State Department believed that the US administration would almost certainly oppose any talk of a reconvened Geneva Conference.[76] Canadians in Saigon were reporting that it was unlikely that any South Vietnamese politician could survive by backing a pro-elections, pro-Geneva settlement stand. At the same time, quite favourable reports were arriving from Saigon concerning Diem's great strength of character. The conservative element was well represented in the Saigon component of the Canadian delegation. Diem's new strength now seemed to support Canadian diplomacy. In mid-September, London reacted coldly to the Indian initiative and explicitly supported Canadian legal interpretation that had claimed that the present ICSC was not mandated to function as an electoral commission.[77] This repeated an earlier rebuff administered by British minister of state for foreign affairs, Anthony Nutting, the previous June. On that occasion Nutting had declined to support an Indian approach to Diem on elections, declaring that 'we cannot order the government of South Vietnam about.'[78] Both British responses had surprised US State Department officials, and encouraged them in refusing allied requests to threaten Diem with a complete aid cut-off.[79]

On 15 September Pearson approved a new posture for Ambassador Johnson. Desai was to be told that if the Indians and Poles went ahead with an attempt to reconvene the Geneva Conference, the Canadians would feel free to communicate their views to the co-chairmen and to the other Geneva powers on any matters touched on by an Indo-Polish majority note.[80] The Canadians would not be unsympathetic to the Indians' overall objectives, but they had great reservations regarding Indian tactics. Ottawa counselled caution and discretion. Diem had given verbal assurances of more co-operation, so why not see how far he could be coaxed before causing any crisis? So far as officials in Ottawa were concerned, the Indians were now being 'more priestly than the bishops' over the electoral timetable, an accusation Menon had made against the Canadians in the spring of 1955.[81]

Indian counter-arguments were so strongly put that by early October the Canadian 'centrists' feared an irrevocable break between Ottawa and New Delhi if the Canadians persisted in trying to block the Indian effort to reconvene the Geneva Conference and get the electoral talks started. Accordingly, David Johnson was instructed to change tactics slightly and to indicate that the Canadian delegation would not actively protest the Indian dispatch of formal messages to the co-chairmen. Furthermore, Johnson was told to advise G. Frederick Reinhart, US ambassador in Saigon, that the US government should tell Diem in no uncertain terms that SVN assurances of MT and FT 'security' were not adequate to guarantee the continuation of the Geneva armistice arrangements. Something more was needed to save the Geneva structure.[82] The Americans were not easily convinced of the wisdom of Canadian 'concessions' to Indian pressure, feeling as they did that New Delhi cared nothing for the survival of an independent, non-communist southern regime (which was true) and that Indian officials would complain even if Diem agreed completely to the original Geneva Agreements (which was not). Officials in State did agree, however, to try to persuade Diem to be more accommodating over the elections, ICSC team security, and other aspects of co-operation.[83]

During his October 1955 visit to the Soviet Union, Pearson reiterated Canadian willingness to carry on in its unwanted burden of helping to maintain peace in that region, and the Russians expressed the opinion that the 1954 Geneva Agreements had done much to relieve tension and thus should be strengthened in any way possible. According to Molotov, the Canadians had shown realism over the China situation and he hoped implicitly that they might help where they could with respect to the 1956 elections, which were of special significance. Soviet officials did not apparently dwell on this subject at any length, reflecting perhaps a relatively low opinion on their part of the gravity of the situation, or alternatively of Canadian influence on the issue.[84]

On 18 October 1955 Pearson told the SVN's foreign minister, Vu Van Mau, that Ottawa would never support elections unless they were completely free, and that no communist regime had ever been willing to face genuinely free elections. By implication, political discussions with Hanoi on elections would be desirable, and entail little risk.[85]

Throughout October the Canadian delegation co-operated with the Indian delegation in ICSC proceedings despite Canadian perceptions of bias in Indian treatment of the Franco – South Vietnamese side over 14(c) cases of reprisals against 'former members of the resistance.' Letters would be sent to the southern authorities inquiring after any individuals said to have been unjustly arrested according to the DRVN authorities in violation of Article 14(c) of the CFA. So far as the Canadians were concerned 14(c) was a procedural device which acted as a legal shield to all acts of sabotage, subversion, and assassination by Vietminh 'stay-behinds.' In view of Indian anger over the electoral obstruction controversy, the Canadians did not press their interpretation of events very firmly. The Canadian representatives were not helped in their case by the blanket refusal of the South Vietnamese government to answer any of the queries put to it by the ICSC Secretariat.

In a further effort to placate Indian sentiment, some Canadian officials in Vietnam recommended that Ottawa not extend recognition to the new Republic of Vietnam, which Diem proclaimed on 23 October 1955, saying that such recognition could only affect Indo-Canadian relations adversely while threatening to increase Canada's involvement in the region should open warfare resume.[86] This liberal-moderate approach was defeated, however, as a result of a plea for recognition from Ambassador Johnson, who thought that the South Vietnamese needed some confidence that Canada was sympathetic, or else Diem might reduce the limited co-operation already extended. Recognition was extended in November,[87] but with no publicity at all in an effort to avoid upsetting New Delhi.*

---

* Eayrs makes the unpersuasive and unsupported argument that anxiety over the Canadian image as an ICSC member led to the recognition being extended 'furtively, even deviously' (Eayrs, *Indochina* 181). At this time Ottawa had to satisfy New Delhi that it was interested in sustaining the settlement in a form tolerable to India, while simultaneously assuring Saigon that Canada respected South Vietnamese rights. This act of 'quiet diplomacy' neatly fitted the contradictory pressures of the situation. Johnson strongly sympathized with the SVN's attempt to, in his words, 'exterminate communism.' His interventions were invariably conservative in character and aimed to strengthen anti-communist premises.

Canadian persuasion was being deployed in another policy arena at this time. In mid-September the Canadian and Indian governments jointly announced the existence of ongoing negotiations between them, which followed Indian acceptance in principle of an April 1955 offer by Canada to supply to India the design, and 54 per cent of the cost, for construction of an NRX-type nuclear research reactor under Colombo Plan auspices. The negotiations were not completed until the signing ceremony by Escott Reid and Mr Nehru on 28 April 1956.[88] Canadian nuclear assistance funding was to be over and above funds already committed under the Colombo Plan – an aspect of the program not announced until mid-October 1955, just prior to a Pearson-Nehru meeting in New Delhi.[89] During these talks Pearson suggested that the Indochina cease-fire lines of July 1954 might eventually prove to be as durable as the cease-fire lines in Germany and Korea. He also said that the future might see *five* Indochinese states, including both a partitioned Vietnam and a partitioned Laos. Nehru agreed that the Vietnamese and Laotian problems were inextricably linked, and that the Geneva powers should be reminded of that fact in any joint ICSC reference to the co-chairmen. He also agreed with Pearson's assertion that the ICSCs could not carry on indefinitely. The Indians too regarded duty in Indochina as very onerous – as well they might with some nine times the number of Canadian personnel directly involved. Nehru could not agree, however, with Pearson's statement that it seemed only fair to condemn the southern regime under 14(c) only as severely (or laxly) as was the northern government condemned with respect to 14(d). The Indian prime minister was of the opinion that the breaches in the south were more fundamental in character than were the breaches committed in the northern zone. Nehru apparently did not comment on Pearson's assertions that Canada would only be a party to elections that met Canadian standards.[90]

In sum, the Canadian diplomatic approaches to Nehru moderated the Indian stand somewhat, at least to the point where the overall state of Indo-Canadian relations was placed on a footing quite independent of whatever irritation was generated by relations incident to the Indochina commissions. For Pearson and DEA's liberal-moderates the timing of the ongoing nuclear reactor negotiations was, at the very least, fortuitous. D.R. SarDesai has said that Nehru 'bowed to expediency' in early 1956 by not confronting Diem on the elections.[91] More than expediency may have been involved in the Indian decision not to withdraw over Diem's non-accession to the Geneva package. After the Nehru-Pearson talks of October 1955 there were occasional comments from various left-wing Indian officials about imminent withdrawal, but they carried little weight.[92]

Prior to the Nehru-Pearson talks, the Canadian secretary of state for external affairs had conducted a major review of Indochina policy among Canadian officials gathered together at Singapore for the Colombo Plan meetings. Pearson expressed satisfaction with the outcome of the Cambodian elections held on 11 September 1955, in particular the unanimous ICSC opinion that 'the settlement foreseen under Article 6 of' the Cambodian armistice was now 'completed.'[93] Staff reductions were now possible. Within six months the new Canadian commissioner to Cambodia, Arnold Smith, would propose (unsuccessfully) the dissolution of the Cambodian ICSC.[94] Pearson went on to state that Laos seemed headed for partition. He approved the strong stand on behalf of the Royal Laotian Government but advised officials in Laos to take care not to complicate Ottawa's problems in Vietnam.[95] The Laotian elections of December 1955 were still to come and there was some possibility that the Pathet Lao could be induced to participate and to accept RLG authority in Phong Saly and Sam Neua. This proved to be a forlorn hope.

On Vietnam, Pearson informed the Singapore group that both the British and American* governments had expressed a clear desire to keep the Geneva structure intact.[96] Pearson was agreeable to contributing to Western security interests for the time being, but he expressed a desire to take unilateral action towards withdrawal, probably sometime in the spring of 1956. Canadian military assessments of PAVN strength may have helped to confirm Pearson's preference for leaving. The DRVN forces were said to hold a decisive military edge over the south and would prevail easily if Diem did not receive help.†

---

* In September US State Department officials had pressed Diem hard to extend more formalized co-operation, but State evidently could not persuade the White House or Pentagon that Diem should be threatened with a military aid cut-off if he failed to comply (A.D.P. Heeney, to Ottawa, 13 Sept. 1955: DEA files, 50052-A-40, vol. 16). State officials lamented to Heeney on more than one occasion that Diem simply did not believe US threats of an aid cut-off (ibid.; also Heeney to Ottawa, 7 Oct. 1955: DEA files, 50052-A-40, vol. 17). The fatal US problem of lack of 'leverage' over Saigon was already manifest. On this chronic difficulty see Leslie Gelb with Richard K. Betts, *The Irony of Vietnam: The System Worked* (Washington: Brookings Institution 1979).

† After noting the weaponry included in a PAVN independence day parade, Ambassador Johnson wrote on 5 September 1955: 'The mass demonstration is one of the most sobering achievements of totalitarian regimes. The spectacle of thousands of sheep-like marchers, smiling vacuously at the appropriate moments, shouting slogans on cue from the cheerleaders, and waving doves, party ikons and banners, has become a trademark of Communist regimes everywhere, and anyone with any doubts about the nature of Ho's regime certainly had them removed during the parade. It was frightening in its political implications, for here was a "demonstration of the masses" which was as well-organized as any held in the capitals of well-established Communist countries – and this after little

The head of the US MAAG had expressed the hope that his training group would have at least one more year to bring the Vietnamese National Army up to effective fighting strength. The ICSC would be able to buy time for this operation.[97] Presumably Pearson was looking to withdrawal as soon as the South Vietnamese were strong enough to stand on their own. At this point, 'peace' plus 'containment' was Pearson's dominant objective.

Diem's consolidation of power in the south had changed Canadian calculations.* So too had Washington's surprising willingness to support Diem. Within a few years Diem would be heralded in the American press as 'the saviour of free Vietnam.' In five years' time Vice-President Lyndon Johnson would refer to him as 'the Winston Churchill of Asia.'[98]

THE MODUS VIVENDI ACHIEVED: DECEMBER 1955–JUNE 1956

Though Holmes and other liberal-moderates had staved off Canadian withdrawal during and immediately following the 14(d) fiasco and the July 1955 crisis of frustration, the government was far from being committed to remaining in Vietnam past the original projected cut-off date of July 1956. That decision now had to be made, since the Canadians found themselves in the position by early 1956 of counselling restraint, prudence, and perseverance to New Delhi while privately complaining about the grinding and costly monotony of work on the ICSCs. If an exit from Indochina could be found that did not jeopardize the peace, Ottawa would take it.

As year-end approached, three major memoranda were written by senior officials of the department: John Holmes, assistant under secretary of state for external affairs, Jules Léger, the under secretary, and Arnold Heeney, the Canadian ambassador to Washington.

more than a year of ordered civic control by the Party. The techniques of regimentation obviously have reached the stage of development where they can be applied very quickly.' Johnson noted that many of the 'overworked doves of peace' did not fly and were trampled. 'How do they rehearse a pigeon?' Johnson to Ottawa, 5 Sept. 1955: DEA files, 50052-A-40, vol. 16

* In late March 1955, the Binh Xuyen sect was defeated by Diem's forces after they resisted forced closure of their gambling establishments. The 'united front' of the sect leaders disintegrated at the same time. Their military leaders could not agree on a common strategy. By mid-May 1955 Cao Dai generals 'rallied' to Diem. By late May and June only Hoa Hao generals were actively resisting Diem's army. By the end of June all organized resistance to Diem had ended in the Hoa Hao territories. In early October, Diem moved on the Cao Dai Holy See in Tay Ninh province. The head of the Cao Dai movement fled into exile, dying soon after. The key Cao Dai general who had 'rallied' to Diem in April was soon neutralized through arrest on a civil charge.

Holmes submitted the first of these important documents on 30 November 1955, and his was entitled 'Canadian Objectives in Indochina.' He began by noting that 'Communist strategy' was presently bent on 'yielding nothing but avoiding provocation.' The policy of the bloc 'in Asia will be more dynamic than in Europe.' The boundaries of coexistence were 'not very satisfactory,' and Korea, Formosa, Vietnam, and Laos were all 'dangerously unsettled.' Western 'offensive' initiatives had to be limited to 'economic and ideological' dimensions, because the West was in the weaker position militarily in Asia, 'leaving aside the last resort of nuclear weapons.' Because of such weakness it was important not 'to provoke or frighten the Communists into military advance.' The Eastern block military offensive had been 'dormant' since July 1954. The Formosa crisis, Holmes said, was not 'expansionist aggression' by China but 'irredentism.'* The truce supervisory commissions in both Korea and Indochina were seen as 'basic instruments of the detente which exists at the moment and which it is in our interests to preserve.' Bilateral compromises had produced these armistices. The commissions had to be supported by the Western powers or grave suspicion and 'dangerous reactions' might occur. The role of the ICSCs in Indochina was important in sustaining 'this delicate structure of co-existence,' and this role 'could well be extended if we are to achieve a state of co-existence throughout the world' – Formosa, for example. The 'principle of supervisory commissions' was now important, in and of itself. As 'symbols of international responsibility' the ICSCs provided 'an important deterrent,' and they embodied a concrete bargain with the Eastern bloc.

In Korea, Holmes pointed out, the US wished to see the NNSC dismantled. In Indochina the Indians were unhappy. *'The Americans (after some persuasion on our part) have become strong advocates of the retention of the Commission,* however unsatisfactory its performance on the details of the armistice.'† It was not possible to treat the four supervisory operations in Indochina and Korea separately, as some Americans wished to do, because the communist side viewed them in close relation to each other. Holmes thought Canada should too. The commissions were an integral part of 'the delicate fabric of peace in Asia.' The Geneva Agreements, including the Final Declaration, were seen by the communists, and by India, as a 'package deal.' For Holmes, Geneva had produced 'a nasty bargain accepted by all parties as the only way to avoid a dangerous conflagration.' The essence of the bargain was the

---

* This point was not included in Eayrs's summary. Eayrs, *Indochina* 253
† Sentences not included by Eayrs in his summary. J.W. Holmes, 'Canadian Objectives in Indochina,' 30 Nov. 1955: DEA files, 50052-A-40, vol. 19 (emphasis added)

Chou En-lai – Anthony Eden agreement 'to allow Laos and Cambodia to join the neutral bloc if Vietnam could be allowed to proceed in due course by the most respectable methods into the Communist camp.' Canada was 'not obliged to recognize this bargain to the extent of considering that South Vietnam should now be pushed into the arms of Ho Chi Minh, but we should constantly remember that the Communists see the Geneva Agreements in these terms and can be negotiated with further only on these terms.'

As to the Laotian situation, Holmes recommended protest but not pressure: 'We can proclaim, as we undoubtedly should *for the record*, that it is entirely wrong for the Viet Minh to use the Pathet Lao as a means of securing their aims in Vietnam, but *we must not expect to achieve anything thereby*.'* United States efforts to secure a 'violation' in Laos were misdirected. The Pathet Lao – controlled provinces could not be 'delivered up' by the co-chairmen. Any action on the Laotian provinces would surely see an Indo-Polish finding of a major violation of 14(c) in Vietnam, and a major discussion on elections which would only underscore Indo-Canadian differences. Any 'majority reference from Vientiane which condemned the Pathet Lao' would probably lead to retaliation by the communists over the Vietnam elections: 'We should thereby be forcing the Communists to raise a dangerous question which they have for some time now been prepared not to agitate.'*

For Holmes, a whole new series of compromises was likely to lead from the original Geneva compromise. For Canada, 'scoring points against the Communists' was *not* the essence of the game.* Canada was 'balancing on the Indochina tightrope' and it would be wise to 'lie low and accept the best bargains possible,' to 'hang tight,' and to 'avoid controversies.'* 'We may have to accept the *de facto* separation of Indochina into five rather than three states never admitting that the condition is permanent, but accepting the reality. (It may be that Laos will be healthier with the Communists confined to two minor provinces divorced from the body politic.)'* For Canada, the chief difficulty with this approach was, as Holmes observed, 'that the Commissions may last a long time.' There were 'abundant reasons for our seeking to get the Commissions out of Indochina as soon as possible,' but 'it would be a terrible responsibility to break the delicate structure on which the peace of Asia might depend.'[99]

The themes Holmes stressed were decisively important: the need for a continuing series of compromises between the blocs; the symbolic significance of the ICSC; the interdependent relationship of the various theatres of

* Quotations not reproduced in Eayrs summary

conflict in Asia; the need for prudent realism and for avoiding a point-scoring mentality; and finally, the extreme fragility of peace in Asia. These were all critical elements of the liberal-moderate tactical program. Promoting coexistence and détente were at the core of liberal-moderate objectives in Indochina. Assisting in the containment of communist expansion was a secondary objective, a mere instrument for the achievement of détente. If supporting containment was 'criminal,' then Canadians were clearly guilty of 'complicity.' But no reasonable argument can be made that Ottawa's version of containment was in any way 'criminal.' The liberal-moderate program as defined by Holmes was a sensibly restrained and realistic effort to help secure and stabilize an inherently unstable regional balance of power.

The prognosis for Holmes's recommendations looked good in December 1955. The approach had already produced results in terms of changing American policy, by encouraging US officials to adopt the view that the ICSCs had authentic deterrent value. There were also hopeful signs that Diem might be brought towards some more meaningful acknowledgment of the ICSC. The difficult question was whether he could be persuaded to go far enough to satisfy the Indians.

The mainstream conservative response to Holmes's memorandum seized on the deterrent concept of the commissions as a quite acceptable rationale for remaining in Indochina. In passing on the Holmes evaluation to Pearson on 23 December,* the under secretary of state for external affairs, Jules Léger, remarked that Geneva had been a 'bad' bargain, but it was clearly in Western interests to support the status quo which had evolved from it. The key problem would be 'selling' the agreement to India. Léger hoped that Indian moderates such as M.J. Desai were open to persuasion.

According to Léger, France, Britain, and the United States now shared the same long-term objective: 'the establishment of a strong non-communist government with a broad national basis.' The Poles, North Vietnamese, Soviets, and Chinese 'do not appear to wish to disturb unduly the status quo.'[100] New Delhi was worried about an image of 'apparent collusion' with the West. Léger therefore argued that the Indians were probably bluffing in articulating the withdrawal threat, because they knew withdrawal 'would immeasurably increase the threat of renewed hostilities.' Of the Indians Léger concluded: 'They want a marriage ceremony to legitimize the change-ling settlement which has replaced the settlement originally conceived at Geneva, so that they will not be accused of condoning illegitimacy.' The

---

* J. Léger to L.B. Pearson, 'The Next Move in Vietnam,' 23 Dec. 1955: DEA files, 50052-A-40, vol. 19. Eayrs gives other excerpts in *Indochina* 272–4.

entire Indian approach was a ploy to try to force Diem into accession to the agreements. But Indian demands that the Final Declaration be renegotiated 'under the threat of Indian withdrawal' were not going to be met. The French, British, and Americans all opposed the reconvening of the Geneva Conference. Renegotiation would mean, in present circumstances, that a 'realistic' political settlement – as compared with the present 'unrealistic,' 'high-sounding' phrases of the existing Final Declaration – would have to be framed. The DRVN would resist 'to the uttermost.' Renegotiation would be 'tantamount to asking the Viet Minh to surrender their birthright for a mess of pottage.' The existing situation was in fact a 'half settlement,' but it deserved support. 'The problem therefore reduces itself to finding some "obscure formula" ... which can be accepted for the time being by all the Geneva Conference Powers – as well as the Commission powers – in such a manner as to give the Commission the necessary sanction to carry out such residual tasks as may remain after 1956 "pending the general elections which will bring about the unification of Vietnam."'

Pearson unhappily noted in the margin of the document that this would entail a commitment 'to stay in Indochina indefinitely.' In response to Léger's recommendation that the IC should report to the Geneva powers that the commission operations would continue in place 'in the absence of fresh directives' and 'subject to such reductions ... as may be agreed on under Article 46,' Pearson wrote, 'How long?'

Léger argued that Escott Reid should be employed in efforts to persuade Indian moderates like Desai that perseverance was the best approach. Reid was to stress: the threat of SEATO intervention if the war resumed; the legal obligation to continue which the ICSC powers had incurred by accepting the supervisory role (Pearson rightly balked at this argument when Léger applied it to Canada earlier in the memorandum);* the diplomatic impracticality of negotiating new terms of reference for the ICSCs; the much greater degree of co-operation offered by Diem to the ICSC than that by Syngman Rhee to the NNSC; and the risk of war in Laos. Staying on now seemed 'inescapable' in light of 'the long-term objectives of our own policy.'[101]

Winning Léger's support was critical for the liberal-moderate element. The under secretary's perspective can be said to have been conservative, but he was no systemist zealot. The critical difference between Léger's view and Holmes's was that Léger believed that the settlement had become a 'change-

* There may have been some substance to Léger's claim that there was a legal encumbrance on New Delhi, because India's acceptance of the ICSC role had not been qualified – as Canada's had been.

ling,' whereas Holmes doubted that the DRVN leadership had changed its view of the Geneva 'settlement' at all, and that Hanoi could only be dealt with in light of its enduring commitment to the terms of the original 'bargain.' Léger was a marginalist conservative who responded to liberal-moderate arguments. Being at the apex of the External Affairs professional hierarchy, he had to exhibit that flexibility in policy that John Steinbruner rightly labelled 'uncommitted thinking.' Léger's adaptation of the Holmesian program reconciled the liberal-moderate and conservative lines on Indochina: peace would be supported henceforth through containment. The Léger memorandum effectively set Canadian Indochina policy for the next decade.

The only substantive critique of the new position came from Arnold Heeney, Canadian ambassador to the United States. Heeney said at the outset of his brief that he would take the role of 'devil's advocate' – undoubtedly because he appreciated that the Léger approach would gain wide acceptance within the department. Heeney pointedly rejected Holmes's analysis and prescriptions. He said that Léger's memorandum provided more 'balanced analysis' and should be the basis for policy discussion with other governments. Holmes's approach was to be avoided. At most the ICSCS could be said to be 'desirable' – they were not 'essential,' as the liberal-moderates claimed. An international supervisory presence had not stopped the North Koreans in 1950, why should it stop Hanoi now? The British and French were 'embarrassed' by their obligations, the Soviets and the Americans passive, while 'perhaps the most concerned party, South Vietnam [sic], openly opposes the Geneva settlement and has been cool towards the Commission.' 'Are the supervisory powers wise to be more interested in continuing their onerous duties than those powers on whose behalf they were invited to serve? Would it not be better to let the present commissions wither as fast as natural political forces allow, avoiding provocative action but leaving it to the powers who must assume responsibilities if the peace is threatened to make the peace?'*

Heeney's review was a skilful summation of the pure conservative marginalist perspective. What made it conservative was the paramount respect for Canadian national interests (as manifest in immediate economic and human costs) rather than concern for contributing 'responsibly' to an area where peace might be endangered. Absent also was any overt concern for the risk of nuclear war (cf Holmes's reference to a 'dangerous conflagration'). Holmes had clearly and accurately emphasized the risk of atomic warfare

---

* Heeney to Ottawa, 6 Jan. 1956: DEA files, 50052-A-40, vol. 19. Also Eayrs, *Indochina* 256–7

because of Western conventional force weakness in Asia. Finally, Heeney had ignored probable reactions in Hanoi. Where Holmes had implied, and Léger had dramatically underscored, the DRVN's deep commitment to the elections as an integral part of the armistice 'package deal,' Heeney simply dismissed the relevance of the DRVN. The implicit rationale for doing so was quintessentially conservative: 'We know from experience that Communist regimes cannot be trusted to carry out their pledged agreement, even to a bargain, and further that Communists generally tend to regard concessions by the other side as evidence of weakness to be exploited.'[102]

What were the costs of continuing involvement that worried Heeney? First, relations with *both* India and the United States would suffer.* Second, Canada's reputation as 'an objective middle-power' would probably be hurt. Third, there was a risk of being forced to accept new responsibilities if the Geneva package were to be renegotiated at some future date. The days of an impartial commission were over, so why stay on?

Heeney advocated withdrawal, but he did not advocate it out of any commitment to Western disengagement. Heeney, like other conservatives, was an early apostle of the doctrine now known as 'linkage.' According to Heeney, the concept of theatre interdependence stressed by Holmes in his memorandum could be applied quite differently: 'firm not provocative action by the non-communist powers concerned in one section of the chain would have beneficial effects elsewhere; if, for example, some balancing action is taken in Korea to offset obvious Communist violations of the armistice, there may be less inclination on the part of the Communists in Vietnam to follow these same practices.' Furthermore, Heeney bluntly recommended co-ordinating Canadian Indochina policy with American: 'Whenever we have adopted this practice we have had a measure of success in gaining for our positions the support of the State Department and its not inconsiderable influence on the matter under consideration.' Despite his enthusiasm for a close relationship with US policy, Heeney did not think that the spectre of US intervention should be raised in talks with India as Léger had recommended.[103]

Heeney, much more than Léger, disagreed with the 'package deal' concept of the Geneva Agreements. He was therefore upset by the idea that Ottawa might end up playing a role that seemed to legitimize the communist view of the 'settlement.' Heeney was worried that the Holmesian approach of 'lying low, hanging tight, and avoiding controversy' might help Hanoi by implic-

---

* James Eayrs elides the reference to India in the relevant passage in his summary. Eayrs, *Indochina* 257

itly supporting their definition of the Geneva bargain.[104] Heeney was, of course, quite right. The line advocated by Holmes unavoidably helped the DRVN in its political campaign to strengthen the status of Final Declaration.

Ultimately Heeney's critique had no effect. The cost of his conservative alternative was judged to be intolerably high in terms of risking Hanoi's early resumption of war. If Heeney's approach had prevailed, it would have shown that Ottawa had learned nothing from the US nuclear threats in Korea, the atomic consultations over Dienbienphu, and the crisis over the Formosa Strait. Turning away from the Indochina role in the fashion recommended by Heeney would have meant turning away from doing what was possible to minimize the risk of tactical nuclear warfare. It *also* would have meant opening Canada up to future pressures from the United States for contributions to collective defence in Asia. What other results could one expect from 'co-ordinating' national policies as Heeney had recommended? If the Heeney option had been taken, Ottawa might still have avoided direct participation in the war in the 1960s, but the probability of 'getting sucked in,' as some officials graphically put it, would have been much higher.

Heeney's views are analytically significant because they were a reflection of enduring conservative concerns that Canadian policy might drift too far from US objectives over an issue of little direct consequence to Canada. Anxiety concerning escalation to nuclear warfare played little or no role in conservative policy calculations. Moreover, many conservatives were vehemently opposed to liberal-moderate sympathies for a neutralist solution to the Vietnam problem.[105]

In any case the liberal-moderate argument for protecting the status quo remained the essential rationale for Canadian policy towards Vietnam for the remainder of the July 1955–July 1956 period. Liberal-moderate convictions were well summed up by Saul Rae in a letter to Holmes written from New Delhi, dated 16 January 1956:

The important thing is that we cannot leave this assignment in Indochina precipitately or unilaterally, since *to do so would be to abandon the important purposes for which we originally took on this assignment.* We can only seek to reduce and to clarify our commitments, and *eventually transfer them* when some alternative machinery for control and supervision in Vietnam has been put in its place. *Communism abhors a vacuum,* and I am of the view that *a withdrawal of the present Commission from Vietnam could only serve to increase the difficulties in this area and widen the prospect of increased tension and possibly even renewed hostilities should the general international climate deteriorate. The presence of the Commission is a deterrent* in the sense that Western and Communist governments as well as those who guide the destinies of India, follow the

188 In the interests of peace

still tense situation here, with responsibility, and with organized machinery and procedures for settling fundamental differences. *This machinery should not be hastily dispensed with until something comparable or better can be put in its place*; at the same time we should do all we can to find substitute methods both for maintaining the cease-fire and *considering the problem of political settlement* which would allow us to reduce our own national commitment in this area.[106]

While DEA officials were resolving doubts about tactics and strategy, Indian officials were undoubtedly experiencing considerable turmoil themselves. Above all else, New Delhi wanted the original pact honoured. The extent of the surprise and shock among Indian Ministry officials which resulted from Diem's success is indicated by the fact that one fairly senior diplomat suggested, and not in jest, that perhaps East Germany could be 'traded' for South Vietnam through separate elections. Indian reactions were evidently becoming erratic, if not unbalanced.

At this point, Pearson refused to ratify the Holmes-Léger program until Nehru's reactions had been very thoroughly sounded out. He was determined to preserve, if at all possible, Indo-Canadian harmony, the one dimension of Canadian external relations which was indisputably threatened by the type of solution emerging vis-à-vis Indochina. Revealing his unmistakably liberal-moderate leanings, he instructed Escott Reid to discuss the Vietnam situation in detail with Nehru, to stress that above all else Ottawa was interested in preserving peace in the area, and that the collapse of the existing armistice arrangements would inevitably generate pressure inside both the DRVN and RVN governments to seek additional outside assistance – much of which would be military.[107] Believing that the Indians greatly wished to avoid blame for the failure of the original settlement, Pearson suggested that ICSC states might simply refer the whole problem to the Geneva co-chairmen to obtain their *formal acquiescence* in the continuation of the status quo. Acquiescence would absolve the ICSC states from any responsibility for the 'amendment' of the original Geneva settlement. Both governments were eager to divest themselves of their burden, but Pearson wanted it clearly understood in New Delhi that the Canadians were concerned that they themselves did not contribute to the development of new tensions in Indochina by the very act of leaving.[108]

The Indian response to the Canadian proposal was clear and prompt. Failure to carry out the FD relieved the northern government of its legal obligations under the CFA. Politically speaking it was unrealistic to expect the north to make the greater sacrifice. Continuing with the status quo was acceptable, but consultations had to start before July 1956. The 17th parallel frontier had to be 'unsealed' as well. Diem's effort to turn the DMZ into an international border had to be blocked immediately. Perhaps because an Indian moderate delivered this statement of Indian opinion and policy, Reid interpreted this set of comments as but the opening gambit in negotiations between Ottawa and New Delhi on the final shape of an eventual reference to the co-chairmen from the ICSC. The statement seemed to be a list of maximally favourable terms for Indian continuation on the ICSC. The Indians were open to persuasion, and their withdrawal seemed less imminent.

In later meetings reasons were given for rejection, among them the probability of DRVN resort to subversion. Nehru expressed a desire for a series of concrete practical concession from Diem: the opening of north-south trade, mail services, population movement, and so on, which would build towards electoral negotiations. In fact, Nehru's private opinions were not clear – except that he was not impressed by the Canadian approach and seemed to the Canadians to be preoccupied with domestic problems.[109] Conceivably this was a façade by Nehru to permit him to acquiesce to Canadian policy in the end, but with the record 'well-shaped' to combat Indian critics on the left.

By late January 1956 the diplomatic cable traffic was becoming furious. Heeney reported from Washington that he thought State was coming under great pressure from the Pentagon to agree to back the expansion of MAAG operations in the south.[110] The office of the Canadian high commissioner, London, reported that the British seemed now to be completely behind American policy, and were not prepared to back any diplomatic initiatives through their role as co-chairman of the Geneva Conference which contradicted the American objective of containing the communists as far north as possible.[111] London hoped the 17th parallel would become a normal international frontier, because the Americans seemed prepared to give the South Vietnamese all the assistance needed to deter the Chinese-assisted North Vietnamese. At least some British officials had been won over to the attractiveness of partition, and a belief that it was attainable.

In Hanoi, Polish Ambassador Michalowski was extremely worried that, with French forces down to 15,000 troops, Paris would soon be totally without influence. He therefore proposed a one- or two-year electoral postponement in return for 'unsealing' the DMZ. Michalowski's concern was justified. The RVN regime (Diem's State of Vietnam became a republic by decree in October 1955) had requested the French government on 19 January to enter into negotiations to effect a complete French military withdrawal from Vietnam.[112] Michalowski's proposal was timed to follow up the PRC's public call of 25 January 1956 for a reconvening of the Geneva Conference.[113] By early February the ICSC was embroiled in tense argument.

For the next few weeks the 'stall' proposed by the Canadian liberal-moderates was put into effect, although probably more out of a lack of dynamic alternatives for the Western side than because of any comprehensive plan for obstructive lobbying by Canadian diplomats. Partly as a result of Canadian persuasion the Americans came to favour it. For the US government, especially the State Department, the stall was a very useful approach since it purchased invaluable time for Diem's security forces in their efforts to round up some 10,000 estimated Vietminh operatives.

Throughout February and March the cables and memoranda streamed back and forth among the capitals of the Geneva powers and the supervisory states. Not surprisingly, nothing was agreed upon and the French meanwhile continued to run down the FEC units in Indochina. As the date for the elections in the south neared (4 March) communist disquiet mounted. An angry formal protest from the DRVN to the ICSC was lodged by General Giap on 17 February. Prior to Giap's communication, Colonel Ha Van Lau of the PAVN Liaison Office forwarded a copy of Pham Van Dong's letter to the co-chairmen to Ambassador Parthasarathi. The letter accused the RVN regime of instituting a de facto alliance with a foreign power, of creating 'concentration camps' contrary to 14(c), of permitting the construction of foreign military bases on Vietnamese territory, and of preparing to launch a 'campaign to the North.'[114] Parthasarathi did not respond.

Pearson was determined to show to New Delhi that the Canadian commitment to peace was the dominant factor shaping Ottawa's Indochina policy. He went so far as to suggest to London that the British and Canadians might be well advised to recommend to Paris that some French personnel should stay behind to take care of the logistical tasks, in which American personnel were about to become engaged through the dispatch of the American Temporary Equipment Recovery Mission (TERM).* Alternatively Pearson wanted the US to send only civilian technical personnel to look into the recovery and export from Indochina of all the excess, unused MDAP equipment that otherwise was going to be abandoned by the departing French forces. This initiative made no visible headway in practical terms, but it may have helped to convince New Delhi of Canadian sincerity. And sincere the Canadians were on this issue, because they saw the Western position in Southeast Asia being directly threatened by the crudity of Pentagon policymakers. So far as the Canadians could tell, the State Department backed Ottawa's approach strongly: the chief problem was how to cope with the timetables of the Washington generals.[115]

* More will be said of TERM in Chapter 8.

In mid-February the Soviet government sent a message to London suggesting that it was time for the co-chairmen to convene a new conference to discuss the difficulties in Indochina.[116] The British government refused, saying that it was 'premature' to convene a conference, and that it would be much preferable to 'seek further clarification of the views of the other countries concerned.'[117] On 30 March 1956 Moscow repeated its suggestion for reconvening the Geneva Conference.[118] At that point the British offered 'early discussions' between the co-chairmen states to commence on 11 April. By the time the Gromyko-Lloyd talks got under way in mid-April there was only a handful of French military personnel left in Vietnam.

The month of March was especially crucial for Canadian policy. The Canadians, especially the liberal-moderates, although favouring a program of stalling to help lengthen the 'breathing space' of the RVN regime, did not think it could be realized without a clear-cut assumption of some successor responsibilities by the Diem government. Nothing else was likely to induce the communist side, particularly Hanoi, to postpone an assault on the southern government, which now lay virtually defenceless against a major assault by the northerners and their sympathizers in the south itself. John Holmes, for one, had received several pessimistic reports from Canadian officials in Indochina. One very lengthy analysis from Saigon written in December asserted that the Vietminh were ready, or close to being ready, to launch a major and probably successful assault on the Diem government, a regime which had failed to strike roots among the southern population and which probably was incapable of winning widespread popular support. According to this writer, Guy Beaudry,[119] Diem was the only chance for Western interests in Vietnam, but supporting him amounted to an increasingly desperate gamble. The West was headed for 'a political Dien-Bien-Phu' in South Vietnam. The anti-communist ranks were badly divided. The Americans had two or three separate approaches, depending on whether one talked with State, Pentagon, USIS, or OSS [sic] personnel. 'OSS' people (ie, the CIA) drew criticism because of their 'post-war anti-colonialist psychosis.' The US military was particularly troublesome because 'they operate on the basis of "heavy fire cover" – without ever giving thought to taking stock of the problem, or making an objective appreciation of the situation.' Furthermore Beaudry thought the French assessment of Diem was correct, the American assessment, naïve and self-deluding:

The French notwithstanding all their grave errors and in spite of their being greatly responsible for the general situation in South Vietnam held important trump cards, and they could have been persuaded by the U.S., the U.K. and who knows ourselves, in playing them in a sequence which could possibly have saved the situation. Now they are being squeezed out completely, creating a vacuum which no one can properly fill promptly when time is the all important factor.

As Beaudry saw the trend of events, the Western side needed several 'finesses' to make its contract. Laying out the 'high cards,' weak as they were, all at once was going to doom the South Vietnamese to defeat in their struggle to preserve independence from the North.

Diem appeared, to Beaudry, to be possessed by 'a despotic inclination.' He was actively driving out all French commercial interests in the south, while devaluing the Vietnamese currency continuously to make it impossible for the French financial interests to liquidate their holdings and get their investment out of the country. To date, Diem's campaign against communist infiltration of major religious groups and labour organizations had featured brutal methods taken directly out of the Vietminh-DRVN tactical repertoire. Beaudry stated that he was putting this information on paper 'not as a complete condemnation of the lesser of two evils but as a forewarning of what is to take place.' His pessimistically prescient, remarkably lucid conclusion gave everyone in DEA who read the message pause for thought:

I should like to say that the Diem clan, that is his family which consists of about twelve people, is day-by-day exerting a dictatorial hold over the country. It is the old mandarin system which they are applying. However this group (mandarin) never had close contact with the people except in the role of master and servant. Furthermore these modern mandarins are westernized by reason of the many years that they all have lived in the United States, in France and in Europe generally. They are not true Asians. They do not feel like Asians. They have been brought up in a Christian way and not in a Buddhist or Confucianist faith and do not understand the all-importance to the Asians of this fraternity which is found throughout Vietnamese history, and which links the mandarin and the people. They have not understood the moral law which made the Buddhist mandarins feel absolutely secure because they know that the religion commands the people to protect them. The important error of this present-day group of mandarins has been to try to establish in an oriental country an occidental set-up, assisted and advised by an occidental power knowing little if anything of the Asian mind and Asian problems. It is not that they have not learned of these problems in theory, but because they have never lived in this part of the world, in Vietnam particularly where it is all important that one rubs elbows with the people in order to understand them. It is more important even than logic, particularly Western logic which is definitely not applicable anywhere in this part of the world.

All in all whatever effort Diem has made to combat Communism, whatever successes he may seem to have to his credit, his psychological mistakes are overriding, and will more than possibly end in complete failure unless a radical change takes place in a very short time.[120]

More than the liberal-moderate group about Holmes was affected by this message and other cautionary warnings from Canadian military personnel serving in Vietnam. One conservative reacted by saying that Beaudry was 'a Cassandra preaching impending doom,' and that the situation had improved greatly over recent months.[121] The label was a particularly ironic choice: the gift of prophecy conferred upon the original Cassandra was blighted by Apollo's simultaneous removal of her capacity to persuade. Beaudry would fit the mythic name all too well.

The Beaudry letter nevertheless did have an effect. If many of the American hard-line cold warriors in CIA and the Pentagon were guilty of an arrogant presumption that the United States could have its way in Southeast Asia relatively easily, the Canadian conservatives were rather more calculating and considerably more aware of the risks involved in Vietnam. They had concurred, after all, in the implicit prime objective of Pearson and the liberal-moderates, which was to head off any potential outbreak of violence involving American forces which might lead to a third world war. They admitted the possibility of a 'blow-up' over Diem's failure to accede fully to the Geneva Agreements. They saw clearly as well that while Diem's government had made enormous progress it probably could not stand on its feet if hostilities resumed. Nearly all diplomatic observers concurred in this view in December 1955, and military-intelligence appreciations available to Ottawa in January and February 1956 confirmed this assessment.[122] Thus, if the Indochina war resumed at the DRVN's initiative, the Americans would be faced with the decision of whether to intervene 'massively' or not in order to save Diem. The potential for escalation incident to such a scenario could not easily be discounted. Consequently the conservatives deferred to a most remarkable if temporary *reversal* in the trend of Canadian policy: Ottawa began to urge on the British and the French governments in late February and March 1956 that the Republic of Vietnam *not* be ceded unqualified sovereignty through the formalized departure of the last French troops, until Diem undertook in writing all the legal obligations incurred by the French at Geneva.

The Indians were most concerned about extracting an electoral commitment, but in Pearson's view this was still impractical: 'An attempt to revise nothing more than the date for the elections might at this point push the South Vietnamese into adopting positions which would prejudice the possibility of their assuming obligations for the maintenance of the cease-fire.' The idea of a reconvened conference was just as bad, if not worse. The best line of advance was pressure on Diem to accede completely to the Cease-Fire Agreement, 'which should greatly reduce the difficulties now facing the Commission and provide the basis for a more stable armistice.' Once the armistice was secure, it might then be possible to consider 'modifications of the settlement and a redefinition of the Commission's responsibilities.'* The critical standard to be applied to all proposals was the probable effect on the maintenance of the armistice.

This sincere show of fidelity to the Geneva Agreement by Ottawa extended into mid-March. It may have affected Indian views. India at this time was asking for a unilateral verbal affirmation of the RVN government's successor status vis-à-vis the agreements. The Canadians in contrast wanted this change in status in black and white, embodied in the FEC force withdrawal agreement then still under negotiation between the French and South Vietnamese in Paris. Perhaps in part because of the sudden revived enthusiasm by Ottawa for the Geneva Agreements, the Indians did not put up the extremely stiff fight against the introduction of US TERM personnel,† which US State Department officials had anticipated.[123]

New Delhi was pleased at this shift in Canadian policy. The US State Department expressed shock.[124] Diem's government finally made a limited commitment to the armistice on 3 April 1956. The statement affirmed the RVN's 'desire for peace,' declared respect for 'the demarcation line and demilitarized zone,' and then went on to say:

As it has declared on many occasions, the Government of the Republic of Viet-Nam *will seek unification of the country on which it has set its heart by all peaceful means, in particular by means of truly free and democratic elections when conditions of freedom have been really established* ... The Government of the Republic of Viet-Nam considers the International Control Commission to be an organisation working for peace. Because of their common peaceful objectives the Government of Viet-Nam *will continue to extend effective cooperation to the Commission, will ensure security of its members and will,*

---

* L.B. Pearson to Canadian High Commissioner, New Delhi, 20 Feb. 1956: DEA files, 50052-A-40, vol. 20

† Eayrs attributes Indian tolerance to ignorance, or to their belief in the accuracy of the mission's full title (ie, Temporary Equipment Recovery Mission); Eayrs, *Indochina* 231. This is almost certainly wrong. Canadians on the spot have said that TERM's 'illicit' activities were 'an open secret.' See below, Chapter 8.

to the fullest extent possible, facilitate the accomplishment of its mission of peace, although the Government of Viet-Nam still considers the Geneva Agreements as *res inter alios acta*.[125]

The text did not quicken the hearts of any in External Affairs. This statement amounted to no more than a public declaration of the de facto policy of minimal co-operation extended by the SVN-RVN authorities throughout the preceding fifteen months. However, Diem would go no further.

RVN confidence in American support may have been strengthened by Pentagon execution in February 1956 of a major amphibious military exercise at Iwo Jima involving 41,000 troops 'under simulated conditions of full atomic warfare,' and of major SEATO manoeuvres in Thailand a few days later (in which Bangkok airport was 'taken' through the use of atomic-capable Honest John rockets) on *less than one week's notice to the United States'* SEATO partners.[126] This could only have been construed by Diem as a vote of confidence and support in his policy of firm opposition to the Geneva Agreements.

By 10 April, Pearson, Léger, and Holmes were resigned to the fact that nothing more could be extracted from Diem. At this time Pearson evidently sent a message to Canada House, London, which was to be communicated to the British government before the commencement of the Anglo-Soviet talks. The message essentially capitulated before Diem's stand and indicated that Ottawa would be prepared to continue its participation on the ICSC after the FUF High Command had been dissolved – merely on the basis of Diem's declaration. The Canadians would not be the proximate cause for the dissolution of the ICSC armistice structure.[127] Ottawa was now back to the policy of December 1955, seeking more 'practical co-operation' from the RVN.

Unsure of the duration of its ICSC mandate, Ottawa officials now began to consider ways of reducing the 'onerous burden.' As John Holmes saw matters:

During this period of wrangling, in which the teams might become pretty well ineffective, would it be legitimate for us to reduce our military strength in Vietnam? Hitherto, we have been inclined to think that some time this spring great decisions would be taken by the Geneva Powers or the French or the South Vietnamese which would suddenly make our future role clear. Given [a lack of violent issues] ... *the only decisive event which could take place in the near future would be the complete withdrawal of the French.* I have a feeling, however, that *even this will be confused in some temporizing formula, and in a few months' time the situation with regard to the work of the Commission will remain pretty much the same* as it is now. It may be that we are now in a period when *the future of the Commission is in the balance.* Tempting as it is to turn this situation to advantage by taking drastic action now to rationalize the work of the Commission, I think *we will have to hold our hand for the moment in the interests of not rocking the boat in the midst of a difficult passage.* On the other hand we will have to beware of getting into the dreary situation of complete frustration such as has overtaken our friends the Swiss and Swedes in Korea.[128]

Because no one wished to be responsible for 'rocking the boat' the Indians and Canadians agreed to implement personnel and cost reductions privately. Here Ottawa and New Delhi saw eye-to-eye.

While these reductions were being carried out, planning was occurring on another front. In April, officials were finalizing the terms of the Canada-India Atomic Reactor agreement, whereby the Cirus generating facility at Trombay was to be built, ostensibly to provide 'lasting benefits for agriculture, industry and medicine.'[129] The agreement was signed on 28 April 1956, the reactor shell completed by 1957, and the reactor started up by 1958. Numerous Indian technical personnel received training at the NRX (Chalk River, Ontario) plant and many others received relevant engineering skills in Canada at Canadian expense. The gift reactor was also one of the most efficient plutonium-producing units in the world,[130] a characteristic which of course was instrumental in permitting the eventual construction of India's 'peaceful' fission device in 1974. With the benefit of hindsight, we may reasonably assume that obtaining the Canadian reactor was a major attraction for the government of India.

During a meeting with Pearson in Ottawa on 29 March 1956, Krishna Menon criticized the nuclear safeguards policy of the major Western states. According to Menon, 'although the insistence on control was ostensibly for reasons of security it was really intended to prevent the economic development of countries like India.' At the same meeting Indochina was discussed and Pearson did his best to reassure Menon that Eisenhower and Dulles were not tending to rely more on a 'SEATO solution.' Menon reiterated the Indian position that Diem had to agree to face elections soon – regardless of what commitment he made to the armistice – in one to two years at the latest. Pearson stuck to the Canadian line on accession to the armistice if possible, and said he was 'sure that the Americans and British were putting steady pressure on Diem to accept some sensible provision.' Menon indicated that he thought Diem might not survive too long, and that 'the Northern region was more widely accepted than the Southern.' Holmes or Pearson then expressed 'with some vehemence' the Canadian view of the 'state of freedom in the North.'[131]

Canadian officials were no doubt relieved. If the Indians were going to attempt something dramatic, they would have let Pearson know at this meeting. Now it was unlikely that a crisis would result because of an Indian withdrawal. The modus vivendi was 'negotiated' between the co-chairmen, the Vietnamese parties, and the ICSC states in April and early May. After some minor skirmishing by the Indian and Polish delegations, the deed was accomplished by letters from the co-chairmen to the ICSC expressing the assumption 'that the Commission will remain in being and continue its normal activities' after the formal departure of the French High Command.[132] On 8 May 1956 the co-chairmen sent more letters: one to the parties calling on them to maintain the armistice 'and to ensure the implementation of the political provisions and principles embodied in the Final Declaration'; [133] a second letter to the ICSC noting 'the difficulties' caused by the French departure but expressing confidence 'that the authorities in both parts of Vietnam will show effective cooperation and that these difficulties will in practice be removed';[134] and a third letter to the French government asking it to provide 'good offices to facilitate the work of the ICSC.'[135] On 22 May 1956 RVN Foreign Minister Vu Van Mau reaffirmed his government's refusal to accept legal obligations, but promised stronger 'effective cooperation.'[136] The elections crisis was over.

CONCLUSION: OTTAWA'S POLICY CONSENSUS BEGINS TO SHIFT

Of this period James Eayrs has written: 'Canada concurred in Diem's decision to refuse to enter into consultation with North Vietnam on holding all-Vietnam elections as prescribed by the Geneva Accords, joining the United States in support of Diem's regime. The United States, in turn, looked more and more to Canada to defend Diem's government within ICSC Vietnam and, when Canada responded as desired, came to regard the Commission not as an obstacle but as an instrument.'[137] In light of the documentary evidence, this statement is little more than a caricature of the pattern of Canadian policy and diplomacy. The available evidence warrants a much more favourable interpretation.

Canadian diplomacy was applied thoughtfully and effectively throughout the elections crisis. As a result of Canadian persuasion the US State Department was won over to the view that the ICSCs were a useful adjunct to American containment objectives. Washington initially supported pressures on Diem to accept successor obligations in a quite cynically irresponsible way,[138] but many American moderates were inclined by early 1956 to explore the potential for a political resolution of the Vietnam problem. Movement *towards* that posture helped to diminish the influence of the advocates of bellicose unilateralism in Washington debates. Surely that was a notable achievement. Canadian diplomacy helped persuade the Eisenhower administration to pay more attention to its coalition partners on Indochina rather than giving freedom of sway to the Pentagon planners. The us State Department *was* struggling with the Pentagon throughout the 1950s and well into the 1960s.[139] Canadian policy materially assisted the forces of moderation in the us executive branch in their efforts to inhibit Admiral Radford and the other 'massive retaliation' militants in the armed services.

Significant American movement towards acceptance of the Geneva armistice, and the equally significant modus vivendi achieved through RVN extension of 'effective co-operation' in May 1956, were probably the minimally acceptable terms needed to induce India to remain on the ICSC. (They were probably also the irreducible minimum that was needed to preclude an early recourse to war by Hanoi.) Without India the formal basis of the armistice would have publicly collapsed. With the de facto lapse of the armistice it is highly probable that a full-scale insurgency in the south would have received support and direction from the North much sooner than it ultimately did in 1959. The results of that line of development would probably have been catastrophic. By 1956, forward bases had already been established for the Strategic Air Command in the western Pacific from Japan to the Philippines (at Guam). Intermediate-range nuclear-armed missiles were deployed on Taiwan under us Navy control in the autumn of 1957. Furthermore, the 'missile gap' exploded on the international political scene in 1958 after the launch of Sputnik in October 1957. Given these developments it is not unreasonable to infer that there would have been a very high probability that Hanoi might well have gambled on Moscow's strategic backing, despite Soviet counsels of caution and restraint.* If war had erupted in Vietnam between 1956 and 1960, us decision-makers would have had no other options but 'surrender' (as they saw it) or an extensive and inevitably murderous tactical nuclear assault on the 'communist aggressors.' In light of recent analysis† it is highly probable that war would have ensued.

Liberal-moderate logic in arguing for a careful stabilization of the armistice was fitting, timely, and historically justified. Pearson, despite his obvious

---

*   It was less than coincidental that Khrushchev and Bulganin emphasized imminent Soviet ICBM advances during their April 1956 visit to Britain, just as Anglo-Soviet talks on Vietnam were to begin. See David J. Dallin, *Soviet Foreign Policy after Stalin* (Philadelphia, Chicago, New York: Lippincott 1961) 235–6.
†   See John Lewis Gaddis, *Strategies of Containment* (New York, Oxford: Oxford University Press 1982) esp. chs 5, 6.

frustration and his evident desire to withdraw at the earliest possible date, responded rationally to a very complex and dangerous situation. Under the influence of John Holmes and Jules Léger his priorities were clear: do what was necessary to stabilize the armistice and inhibit a DRVN recourse to arms; second, do what was necessary to persuade the Indians to stay on the commissions. Sustaining the peace, even a temporary one, without realistic hope of an eventual political settlement, was infinitely preferable to letting American militants loose to wreak havoc on much of Pacific Asia. Down that road lay World War III.

Eayrs is quite incorrect in his summary judgment that Canada 'concurred' in Diem's evasion of elections. Ottawa supported both the armistice and the elections unreservedly until the spring of 1955. After examining the details of the 'Geneva package' and reviewing the State of Vietnam's consistent record of refusal to become engaged (dating from June 1954), the legal specialists in both Ottawa and London came to the retrospectively sound conclusion* that Diem was not legally bound to respect the Geneva Agreements. But legalities alone did not determine Canadian policy (notwithstanding Holmes's implicit criticism of the overly legalistic bent of some of his colleagues). Practical political considerations, and a clear definition of abiding Canadian interests, shaped the Canadian response. Ottawa coped well with major structural changes in the policy environment, most notably: the exit of the French Expeditionary Corps, and the concomitant refusal of Paris to accept any responsibility for either the armistice or the political settlement; the collapse of Eden's original Indochina policy that had been based on cession of the southern zone to the communist bloc, and the unmistakable move by London in the autumn of 1955 towards complete support of Washington's commitment to containment at the 17th parallel; and finally, the changed circumstances within South Vietnam, where Diem's regime had grown dramatically stronger to everyone's surprise, including the Indians'.†

The Canadian decision of February 1956 to split the armistice and Final Declaration and press hard towards full accession by Diem to the armistice (with its *undated* commitment to elections in Article 14) was both tactically ingenious and politically sensitive. It was tragic that the US State Department could not prevail in Washington debates to the point where Diem

---

* See Chapter 3, 'The Descent Begins: From Geneva to the Jungles.'

† See Escott Reid's comment to Krishna Menon (a pro-DRVN zealot in most circumstances) of May 1956 to the effect that Indian officials in Vietnam 'now credited Diem with much more popular strength than they had previously thought he had, and certainly did not consider him a mere puppet of the Americans.' *Envoy to Nehru* 85

could have been persuaded to move farther towards acceptance of the proposal. Whatever chance existed for avoiding the subsequent war was lost through failure to keep the hope of a political settlement alive among the Western governments. Nevertheless, the true measure of the value of Canadian policy in supporting both the 'armistice-accession line' and, as a fallback, the 'increased effective co-operation line' lay in the very success it produced. The DRVN regime did not resume the war at an early date. India did not withdraw from the commissions. No one publicly proclaimed the death of the Geneva Agreements. These were major achievements that helped to sustain 'the delicate fabric of peace.'

The period of the electoral crisis was a turning-point in Canadian policy in more ways than one. Just as the balance of forces had altered in Indochina, so too did the balance of tendency opinion with the Ottawa foreign policy community. The 14(d) affair had given many in External Affairs a highly negative assessment of the DRVN's worth. Witnessing the complete dismantling of civil liberties in the north throughout the electoral crisis phase of the ICSC's life was equally impressive and alarming, and what is more, frightening. Many Canadian officials subsequently became obsessed with what they saw as the terrible unfairness of the DRVN's propagandistically successful claim to democratic virtue, when they had systematically eliminated any prospect of free elections in the northern zone through the establishment of totalitarian social and political institutions.* The third and final dimension of alienation was ripening: the perception of DRVN subversive intent aimed at Diem's struggling republic. Together these three elements would shortly generate a groundswell of support for the RVN within the Department of External Affairs that would prevail for a decade.

In mid-1955 the liberal-moderate image of Vietnam was the dominant perceptual tendency among Canadian officials. It had been liberal-moderates such as Lett, Holmes, Arthur Menzies, Saul Rae, and J.R. Maybee who had constructed the original departmental 'consensus' on Vietnam policy which prevailed from April 1954 through September 1955. From September 1955 through July 1956 liberal-moderate dominance of both policy outputs and perceptual inputs waned. The conservative commitment to strong support for Ngo Dinh Diem was winning many converts in the foreign policy community – not the least of whom would be the secretary of state for

---

* The record of General Vo Nguyen Giap's conversation with Sherwood Lett on the need for elections and of Giap's personal willingness to support any conceivable standard of liberal-democratic excellence is pathetically touching because it was probably sincere. See Eayrs, *Indochina* 168. Giap's views were irrelevant to the facts of the situation, which included the DRVN's effective homogenization of opinion in the northern zone.

health and welfare, Paul Martin.* Ideological predispositions and tactical objectives shifted substantially over the course of 1956. Heeney's articulation of the 'devil's advocate' position at the beginning of the year – withdraw and let the Americans make the hard strategic decisions alone – was significant as an indication that conservative perceptions and policies were now part of the legitimate 'domain of policy discourse' within the department. Heeney's advocacy of withdrawal was not the most significant aspect of his dissenting memorandum; rather it was his advocacy of a firmer Canadian commitment to containment through non-recognition of any aspect of the Final Declaration. That view would spread in years to come under the vicissitudes of partisan combat on the new-model Indochina commissions – the new buttresses to 'deterrence' in Southeast Asia.

Figure 4 provides a schematic illustration of the shifts in Canadian policy that occurred from the spring of 1955 through the summer of 1956. In April 1955 the effective consensus in External Affairs still believed that elections would be held which would unify all Vietnam under communist control. By July 1955, however, as Diem gained in strength and as the French were in the process of departing, the Canadian commitment to the electoral timetable weakened. Canadian policy at this point backed the RVN's accession to the armistice through more 'practical co-operation.' Under the threat of Indian withdrawal Pearson moved Canadian policy back to the left in February and March 1956 by supporting written RVN acceptance of the French armistice commitment. By the summer of 1956, after the modus vivendi was in place, Canadian policy drifted back to the right under the pressure of accumulating conservative articulations about RVN worthiness and DRVN repression and brutality.

As officials became more and more emotionally engaged in Vietnam policy-making, their recommendations became increasingly 'unconditional.' For this reason, the operational consensus drifted 'downward' on the chart. By the end of 1956 Canadian policy was still framed primarily in the interests of peace, but it would now be expressed by a quest for peace through a careful manipulation of the balance of political and military forces in Vietnam. Peace through containment was the new formula that would guide Canadian policy-making until 1966.

---

* After a Nov. 1956 meeting with Diem, Martin overflowed with support for the RVN. His views were not yet representative of departmental opinion, however, although they would be within a few years. See Eayrs, ibid. 184–5. Pearson's reactions to Martin's proposals for assistance to the RVN unfortunately were not recorded in the files.

FIGURE 4
The policy oscillation of 1955–6

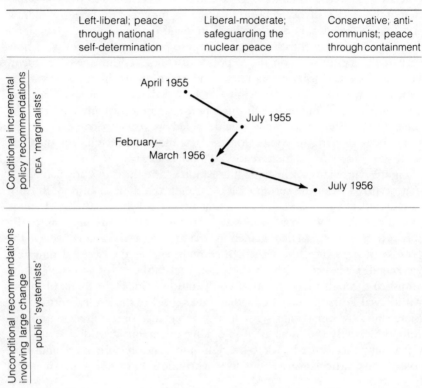

7

Perceptions of aggression 1954–6

... this country of confusion where the forces of good seem to lack a clear conviction, while the forces of evil press on with furious intensity.

Canadian military staff adviser, August 1955

CIVIL DISORDER IN THE SOUTH

Diem's subjugation of the sects took place from April to November 1955. Thereafter, only small bands remained from the once powerful sect armies. By January 1956 Diem's security forces were able to turn on the communist infrastructure, especially in the northern provinces of South Vietnam, where French forces had never been established. The business of conquest and pacification was extremely brutal. Few if any restraints were in effect on Diem's forces. Suspected communist organizers were tortured routinely.* Critics of Diem have alleged that whole villages in dissident areas were 'executed by artillery fire.'¹ The ICSC received many complaints, but it was never able to investigate very many of them satisfactorily because of Saigon's refusal to co-operate. The ICSC's mandate did not include oversight of the civilian population at large. It was only charged with preventing discriminatory mistreatment of *former combatants* of the two sides for actions that were committed prior to the cease-fire. Not surprisingly, most if not all Canadians tended to give the Saigon authorities the benefit of the doubt when the latter declared that the thousands of communists, communist sympathizers, and

---

* Various forms of 'water treatment' were used to extract information, as well as the insertion of pepper into the eyes and nose of victims. Gasoline-soaked rags were put on individuals' heads in efforts to loosen tongues. The threat to light them often produced results. Confidential Interview Material

non-communist opponents of Diem's rule were being arrested, detained or executed for infractions of the common law committed after July 1954. The fact that the DRVN tried to use Article 14(c) to help rebels and dissidents in the south was seen by Canadians as proof that the Hanoi regime was actively directing the rural violence in South Vietnam. Anti-communist violence and repression was morally repugnant, but it did not contravene the 'law' of Geneva – only its 'spirit.' The toothless ICSC did nothing to inhibit the campaign. It could not.

The relatively low numbers of governmental officials assassinated or kidnapped in the RVN in 1956–7 compared to the early 1960s[2] presumably indicates that the communist opposition was not ready to resort to a trial of arms at that time. Evidence that has recently been made available indicates that both Hanoi and the southern communist leaders were hoping that the years immediately after 1956 would be a time of predominantly political rather than military struggle. Time was sought to consolidate the revolution in the north and to organize the politico-military struggle in the south.[3]

The conservative element in the Canadian policy process was very much inclined to excuse Saigon for such atrocities that came to light. A war of subversion, fomented and directed by the DRVN, was already in progress. Canadian conservatives agreed with the Americans that Diem was 'merely a strong man doing what is necessary in a turbulent situation.'* Canadians like Marcel Cadieux were prepared to excuse much because of DRVN treachery and inhumanity in the 14(d) affair. Conservatives like David Johnson saw Diem's regime as a lesser evil than North Vietnamese totalitarianism.

For many Canadians, not merely the conservative element, experiencing and observing the style of life under Hanoi's repressive, stern, and unforgiving brand of socialist construction did much to raise new Canadian doubts about the Vietnamese communist cause. Comparative observation of the 'psychologies' of the people in the two zones weighed heavily in favour of the Saigon authorities for Canadian personnel. As one Canadian military observer noted: 'Generally speaking I found the people in the South much happier. Very few people in the North ever smiled. They were serious as hell. And every morning there were the loudspeakers and propaganda with party officials out haranguing everyone about the day's duties and slogans.'[4] A

---

* On 11 July 1955 Holmes wrote: 'Whether Diem is something approaching a fascist dictator, as some of the French allege, or whether he is merely a strong man doing what is necessary in a turbulent situation, as the Americans think, is a matter of dispute.'
Holmes, 'Memorandum for the Minister'; DEA files, 50052-A-40, vol. 14. Eayrs elides the reference to the French. See Eayrs, *Indochina* 164.

liberal-moderate in External Affairs declared: 'The effects of communism on a society are almost mystical. A pall of gloom is cast over all spectra of life. In Vietnam one could almost feel the pall descending.'[5] While very authoritarian in its own way, Saigon's nationalist (vis-à-vis the French), petit-bourgeois, landlord-dominated capitalism seemed nevertheless to hold some potential for progressive political evolution towards liberal-democratic process. Hanoi's more efficient tyranny produced only a grave foreboding in the minds of Canadian diplomats. An Asian Portugal might eventually progress to democracy: a North Korea could not.

From mid-1955 onwards, Ngo Dinh Diem's security forces began a major effort to root out the remnants of the Vietminh organizational apparatus. Under Ordinance Number 6 of January 1956 the security chiefs were given extraordinary powers of arrest and detention.[6] This grant of powers was later widened further by Law 10/59 of May 1959, which suspended the last vestiges of due process in the Republic of Vietnam and established a system of military tribunals for dealing out summary punishment (usually incarceration without trial but often execution) to suspected communists.[7] For the Canadians on the ICSC, witnessing these developments was troubling enough without being called upon to defend such activities. By 1959–60 the Canadian delegation was required to do just that.

During the 300-day period some 90,000 Vietminh troops were regrouped to the north (with approximately 50,000 dependents). By 1958 these regroupees were being infiltrated back to the southern zone.[8] The actual date of the commencement of systematic attacks on RVN forces apparently occurred some time in early 1959.[9] These attacks began after three years (1956–8) of heavy losses to the insurgent side caused by Diem's Denunciation of Communists campaign. In January 1960 Giap declared that 'the North has become a large rear echelon of our army. The North is the revolutionary base for the whole country.'[10] In September 1960 Le Duan called for the liberation of the southern zone during the Third Congress of the Lao Dong party. In December 1960 the National Liberation Front was proclaimed within the RVN's own boundaries.[11] But long before 1958 the Canadians were convinced of the aggressive intent of the North Vietnamese communists.

As DRVN operations in the south moved forward, the Diem regime began its inexorable slide into incompetence, alienation from the population, and finally self-destruction. Electing to take another route than that of Vientiane, the Saigon government suspended the age-old Indochinese tradition of the election of village chiefs. Almost immediately communist forces began an accelerated program of assassination and abduction.

As the political struggle intensified, Saigon compounded its errors in almost all areas of civil administration and economic planning. Living standards for the peasants and urban poor dropped as expectations climbed. Only the new stratum of government and military employees benefited from US largesse under counterpart spending. From 1956 to 1961 only 2 per cent of US aid to the RVN was spent on social or economic development.[12] Between 1955 and 1959 47 per cent of Saigon's total budget went for military or quasi-military programs. Thereafter the percentage climbed.[13] By 1959 US counterpart funding under the Commercial Import Program (CIP) accounted for some two-thirds of RVN national revenue.[14] All moneys accumulated through the counterpart fund had to be spent under joint US-RVN approval.

The RVN was able to pay only 10 per cent of the costs of its military spending despite allocating half its revenue to that end, and from 1955 onwards the US government paid the salaries of the ARVN soldiers.[15] They were very well paid – twice the rate of pay of their Thai opposites.[16] It was the flow of cash to this burgeoning military stratum of RVN society which had to be soaked up through the luxury goods of the CIP. With total exports of the RVN at approximately $50–60 million per annum, RVN imports were consistently over $200 million per annum. Since this enormous bonanza was all state-controlled through import licensing procedures, the opportunities for graft and corruption were immense. As in Laos, the opportunities were subsequently exploited. And as in Laos the CIP corrupted nearly everyone who came in contact with it.[17]

Diem's land reform efforts were an even greater disaster. In all the newly pacified territories, the 'reformed' rent structure decreed by Saigon involved the payment of rent by peasants for the first time in over eight years. The Saigon military often was called in to collect rent at the point of a gun. United States economic assistance to the rural economy was virtually non-existent because of congressionally imposed strictures which blocked all agricultural development assistance for any commodities declared to be 'in world surplus' (ie, major American agricultural exports such as rice, cotton, and citrus fruits).[18]

Riddled with corrupt practice, top-heavy with military and security personnel, overloaded with northerners and Catholics at all levels of the civil and military bureaucracies, and increasingly alienated from the rural population,[19] Diem's government lacked any solid basis of legitimacy among the South Vietnamese population by 1961–2. When the regime proved to be ineffective as well, domestic discontent was not long in appearing, and such discontent was all too susceptible to exploitation by the resurgent communist apparatus in the RVN.

Many of these problems became visible only in hindsight, but many others were appreciated right from the outset. Ottawa was never under any illusion about Saigon's political or military strength. There was a solid streak of pessimism in the reports from Vietnam on the prospects for RVN survival. Still, the hand had to be played out – in the interests of peace.

INITIAL APPREHENSIONS 1954–5

By early 1955 it was clear that SEATO was going to be utterly irrelevant to the real security needs of the Saigon government. Of the member states only the Philippines had expressed any interest in assisting Diem's forces in counter-guerrilla methods, and that interest ceased with President Ramon Magsaysay's* death in 1955.[20]

Ottawa received an intermittent flow of information from Canadians in the field concerning changes in the military balance in Vietnam, based on direct observations of equipment and personnel, surveys of the SVN and DRVN press, and reports of conversations with French, South Vietnamese, American, British, and Australian observers. In 1955–6 the Canadians redoubled efforts to extend their contacts to the informal intelligence-sharing 'pool' which had grown up in Saigon, Hanoi, Vientiane, and Phnom Penh among Western diplomats and military personnel. All Canadians were instructed to exhibit great care in not compromising publicly in any way their self-declared status as impartial, objective observers in Indochina. They evidently carried out this task with reasonable efficiency. No reproving comments about illegitimate espionage activities by Canadians were ever directed at Ottawa from abroad. Unlike the South Vietnamese vis-à-vis the Poles, the DRVN never objected to Canadian activities. There was no reason to. It was understood by all concerned that the Poles and Canadians would be making appreciations of zonal military capabilities. That was part of their assigned arms control tasks. And none of the Geneva powers were naïve enough to believe otherwise. Nor is it credible to think that the Vietnamese parties were under any illusions about the ICSC personnel functioning purely as 'international civil servants.' That was a myth peculiar to Canadian journalists and left-liberal systemist academics. The Poles and the Canadians were bloc representatives. 'Sharing the intelligence product' with their respective allies was an implicit function they had in common, a function that was central to the 'troika concept' of the commissions, and also was a stabil-

---

* Magsaysay had been brought to power largely through the efforts and advice of Colonel Edward Lansdale – if US sources are to be believed. Lansdale had directed much of the campaign against the Hukbalahap insurgents quite successfully.

izing factor that contributed to maintenance of the armistice.* Like strategic satellite reconnaissance capabilities today, the gathering of intelligence can be used to calm anxieties and to contribute to peace. Zealots tend to ignore this fact.

The military and political intelligence gathered by Canadians was rarely cause for relief. The outlook was usually bleak. In late April 1955, the French Liaison Mission submitted the first charges against the DRVN regarding infiltration and deployment of agents, and the commencement of a campaign of subversion against the southern government. The ICSC investigation of these complaints proceeded slowly under the direction of the Legal Committee.

Commissioner Sherwood Lett was quite convinced that a failure to carry through on elections would precipitate an accelerated onslaught of DRVN-directed subversion.[21] He was also quite convinced that protests directed to him from 'peace groups' in Canada, specifically a letter from Dr James G. Endicott of the Canadian Peace Congress, demonstrated 'the co-ordination of communist propaganda in places as geographically separate as Toronto and Hanoi.'[22] Officials in Ottawa, especially the conservative element, tended to agree.

Lett noted in mid-1955 that the procedures and powers available to the ICSC were simply not adequate for ferreting out the truth in cases of attempted subversion. He concluded that this shortcoming would give the DRVN all the more incentive to press ahead.[23] Not everyone in the Canadian delegation agreed with Lett's perceptions, however. A few military and political analysts felt that Diemist repression had as much if not more to do

---

* It should be noted that the intelligence-gathering operations of Canadian personnel apparently did not include any activities of an illicit or covert character forbidden to diplomatic representatives. Canadian actions were marginally significant for producing useful data on DRVN troop deployments and weapons capability, because of the dispatch of Canadian personnel on the MT and FT investigations. Considering the obstruction and deception such investigations always encountered, it is doubtful if information of particular significance was ever obtained. The DRVN 'guided tours' were invariably unproductive. Much more could be learned from May Day parades and laudatory articles in the DRVN press about the 'vigilant,' capable units of the PAVN. It would have been an act of political stupidity as well as an abdication of governmental responsibility not to process publicly available information for its military intelligence content – and to exchange such information on an informal quid pro quo basis with other Western governments. Early reports on the PAVN apparently included detailed studies of life in the jungle for the typical guerrilla fighter, PAVN 'aid to the civil power' in systematically blocking petitions to the ICSC outposts, new weapons additions to the PAVN regular divisions, traffic movement on rural roads, and so forth. Sources: CIM

with the onset of violence in the south than did Vietminh agents. These same dissenters also tended to dismiss the discovery of arms 'caches' as being little more than the weapons of a retreating army. Some 130 'caches' were discovered up to December 1955. Many of the weapons were badly corroded and quite dangerous to use.[24]

In September 1955 Canadian legal analysts with External Affairs decided, after a careful review of the text of the Cease-Fire Agreement, that subversion could probably be said to be in contravention of the agreement. Certainly a good case could be made. In due course, it was.[25]

Aggressive intentions were perceived by Canadians in the founding of the Fatherland Front in Hanoi in early September 1955. Reports were sent immediately from Hanoi. Notwithstanding the implied military threat of an extensive front organization extending into the southern zone, Ambassador Johnson correctly saw the front's main threat to Saigon as essentially political in character.[26] Calls for scrupulous respect for the Geneva Agreements, for rent reductions and land reform in the southern zone, and for the expulsion of all foreign – especially American – influences seemed a likely recipe for a major propaganda victory over Diem. Diem's army had scored victories over the sects and the Vietminh remnant force, but his government was not implementing rural reforms quickly enough to win the support of the peasantry. Without peasant support there was no long-term political basis for Diem's regime in the outlying provinces. Southern Vietnam might very well prove to be so much dry tinder waiting for a revolutionary spark. According to some senior Canadian military analysts the real danger to Diem might indeed come from the people themselves, who for so long had been victims of intimidation, harassment, and insecurity.[27] Despite the arrest, imprisonment, or execution of hundreds, perhaps thousands, of DRVN-Vietminh agents and sympathizers, the northern-controlled network was still strong enough to be able to pass on detailed and complete information of RVN attacks on southern communists so that Hanoi could then specify 14(c) violations to the ICSC. The ceaseless flow of 14(c) allegations was a clear measure of the continuing strength of the communist underground.

By the end of November 1955, just after Diem had successfully beheaded the Cao Dai threat, Guy Beaudry filed his report on the socio-political failures of the Diem regime.* Many in the department concurred in Beaudry's pessimism. According to some sources, the South Vietnamese coastal navy was utterly incapable of stopping north-to-south infiltration by sea. Secret Vietminh radio transmitters were known to be operating continu-

* See Chapter 6.

ously in the mountain regions. Communications between Hanoi and communist groups in the south were known to take only a few hours. The Vietminh stay-behinds were already making some limited headway in the 'mobilization of silence' campaign. The Fatherland Front was trying to recruit or co-opt Hoa Hao, Cao Dai, and even old, ultra-reactionary Dai Viet and VNQDD personnel. Minority groups in the mountain regions were being successfully infiltrated. Infiltrated too were legal societies, political parties, unions, newspapers, and, some said, even the office of the presidency of the RVN itself. Rumour also had it that Diem was putting so much pressure on the Chinese community of Saigon-Cholon that they were responding to communist appeals with cash contributions.[28] Increasingly influenced by conservative perceptual axioms, few Canadians responded to the apparent ease of DRVN penetration with the conclusion that Ho's government and its unification program might have much appeal in the south.

The Canadian delegation pressed hard for investigation of French charges of subversion. The Indians insisted on leaving examination of the allegations with the ICSC Legal Committee. New Delhi would not allow Diem to score propaganda points through the commission when he would not agree formally to accept successor-state obligations to the CFA and FD. The stage was now set for a lengthy juridical struggle on the issue.

The three commissioners formally discussed the allegations of subversion for the first time at the 218th meeting on 26 August 1955. The Legal Committee submitted its first report to the commissioners on 30 January 1956. But the Canadian delegation could not get this report onto the commission agenda until November 1956. The report, which declared in effect that the ICSC was indeed competent to look into such matters as subversion, was then referred back to committee, and removed from the IC agenda until the three commissioners had time to consult their respective governments. Throughout 1957 there was much informal discussion of the issue but no action was taken. Finally, in mid-1958 the three commissioners ordered the Legal Committee to draw up a report as quickly as possible on the substance of some of the cases which had accumulated under this category.[29]

In April 1959, it was agreed that all new cases of alleged 14(c) abuse/ subversion would be routed to the Legal Committee for evaluation. The Legal Committee then decided 'that instead of any hypothetical discussion of jurisdiction each case should be considered separately on its merits.'[30] At this point successive Polish delegates to the Legal Committee concocted a lengthy series of excuses for being absent for scheduled consideration of the cases, thus blocking their resolution. Canadian pressure on the Indians to curb Polish delinquency failed to produce results. In February 1962, after nearly two years of forced postponements, the Canadians finally induced the Indians to move ahead in processing and evaluating the cases without Polish participation. One can only infer that the timing of the Indian decision to go forward was the product of: the impending crisis within southern Vietnam (by early 1961 Diem had already survived one coup attempt, the economy was in chaos, and the Viet Cong assassination toll was reaching new heights, while American arms and 'advisers' were beginning to arrive on an unprecedented scale); the deterioration of Sino-Indian relations; the deterioration of the armistice in Laos; and, perhaps, pressure on New Delhi from Washington to be more helpful and 'equitable' in conducting the ICSC's business.

It is reasonable to infer also that the Indian decision to support the Canadian anti-subversion initiatives was premised upon the capacity and perceived willingness of the United States to reinforce Diem's government militarily. Three years of relative stability (1956–8) had convinced the Indians that Diem did have a genuine prospect of succeeding in his open defiance both of the terms of the Geneva Agreements and northern attempts to subvert his government, and therefore that it would be wise for New Delhi to try to shape the ICSC's course of action so as to support the implicit balance of military force in Indochina.

The Indo-Canadian Legal Committee majority report of January 1956 paved the way for the 1962 *Special Report* condemnation of the DRVN. The 1956 report declared that:

No member of the Armed Forces of either Party may violate the territory of the other zone and commit therein any act against the other Party. This prohibition is explicit in Article 24.

Neither Party may organize espionage, sabotage or any hostile activity in the other zone by sending persons to that zone or by giving aid to indigenous elements for that purpose. This prohibition is implicit in Article 24 taken with Article 10 and the Geneva Agreement taken as a whole.

Neither Party may organize activity having as its aim the *subversion of the administrative authority* in the other zone by violent means either by sending persons to that zone *or by giving aid to indigenous elements for that purpose.* This prohibition is implicit in Article 10 and the Geneva Agreement taken as a whole.

The International Commission is both competent and *under an obligation to entertain and settle complaints* of the above nature.[31]

Despite collaborating in Canadian efforts to unmask subversion, it was the Indians' consistent view that 'subversion as such is not cognizable under the terms of the Geneva Agreement,' although the receipt of complaints that 'fall

under Articles 10, 19, and 24 read with 27' did create 'a right and an obligation to enquire and investigate such complaints.'[32]

In the public record hitherto available, the first cursory mention of the
ICSC deliberations over these matters is made in the *Tenth Interim Report* of 6
April 1960.[33] The *Eleventh Interim Report* of 18 September 1961 contained an
equally cursory statement indicating that the cases involving allegations of
'sabotage, subversion and espionage' were 'under consideration' by the IC's
Legal Committee, though 'no progress has been made.'[34] In the *Special Report*
of 2 June 1962, the issue of subversion emerged full-blown and almost without warning through the pronouncement of DRVN wrong-doing by the
Indo-Canadian majority: specifically, that there was indisputable evidence
that the DRVN had violated Articles 10, 19, 24, and 27 by sending 'armed and
unarmed personnel, arms, munitions and other supplies with the object of
supporting, organizing and carrying out hostile activities, including armed
attacks, against the Armed Forces and Administration of the Zone in the
South,' for the purpose of 'inciting, encouraging and supporting hostile
activities ... aimed at the overthrow of the Administration in the South.'[35]
However, although this controversy became a prominent public issue so late
in the IC's life (nearly eight years after the original Geneva Agreements were
signed), the controversy itself had roots which went back to the very beginnings of the IC's activity in Vietnam, and which extended throughout the
entire period 1955–65, conditioning and moulding the perceptions and policies of the member states of the ICSC, especially those of Canada.

For Ottawa's liberal-moderates, who ironically enough had a hand in
initiating the subversion dispute within the ICSC, the controversy by itself
was of limited significance. For conservatives in External Affairs it was a
weapon of great perceived tactical value initially, and would ultimately become an important instrument for the attempted moral vindication of their
perspective on the whole Vietnam conflict. Indian stalling in acting on the
subversion was the cause of much resentment among Canadian conservatives.

Indian hesitation to act is quite understandable and defensible. In 1955 and
for most of 1956 the fundamental objective of Indian policy was preservation
of peace through assisting the execution of the original political 'settlement'
concocted at Geneva by the British, French, Chinese, and Russians. From
1957 through 1962, the goal was the preservation of peace through the promotion of an effective deterrent balance of military force between the two
political tendencies vying for control of Vietnam. In both cases playing the
subversion card unilaterally was simply too risky to contemplate. It might

have driven either Saigon or Hanoi (or both) to renounce the Geneva armistice altogether. Subversion investigations and findings were an instrument of last resort. But such policy logic, however realistic and pragmatically inclined towards keeping the peace through a balancer role, could hardly convince Canadian conservatives who were now increasingly inclined towards a self-righteously legalistic posture.

THE DEMISE OF ARMS CONTROL
AND PERCEPTIONS OF AGGRESSION

By early 1956 London was strongly supportive of Washington's attempt to hold the line in Indochina at the 17th parallel. Americans, not for the first time, hoped that both Moscow and Beijing would pressure Hanoi into accepting the new status quo.[36] Ottawa was prepared to support 'containment' as well as 'peace,' and to stay on the ICSCs provided they had some meaningful contribution to those objectives. But by 1956 it was clear that the Fixed Team and Mobile Team supervisory capability was totally inadequate to the ICSC's mandate under Articles 16–19.

In mid-January 1956 Acting Commissioner Saul Rae wrote John Holmes as follows:

the principal objective of the Diem Administration is to preserve South Vietnam from Communism. This presupposes, for one thing, an effective control of the demarcation line and demilitarized zones. The French authorities are virtually powerless in this area and the Joint Commission has been ineffective for many months. The International Commission has a vital task to assume here, but *with South Vietnam unwilling to assume successor responsibilities or to share in a clear-cut redefinition of the remaining tasks, the consequence is that the position in the zone is becoming increasingly precarious, with increased opportunities for infiltration and subversive tactics by the Communists.* Similarly, in the field of the control of war materials, while on balance the record of the French and South Vietnamese is fairly good, *the South can benefit from an effective system of control.* There are other provisions such as 14(c) which the South finds strongly objectionable, but here again the answer lies not in their policy of 'innocence by disassociation,' but in providing the Commission with the necessary documentary evidence to counter the continuing flood of PAVN complaints, which the Viet Minh have exploited in typical fashion for their propaganda purposes.[37]

Rae, like other frustrated Canadian assignees to the ICSC, had grown weary of RVN incompetence, and wary of DRVN duplicity. If there were gaps in the control system, he presumed the DRVN authorities would exploit them according to their military objectives. For over nine months the DRVN had blatantly denied the ICSC teams the right to survey the Haiphong port complex, pleading an inability to procure a boat – this despite recreational boating excursions for the ICSC given by the government, and the sighting of modern Soviet-built naval launches, as well as new Soviet ocean-going tugboats. In the south, water transport was willingly provided to the ICSC. In the north, ICSC teams were denied the right to inspect lighters, and access to coastal islands was denied.[38]

Canadian military analysts were sure that new heavy military equipment for the DRVN forces had been brought in via the rail line through Lang Son – *after* the ICSC's team had been stationed there.[39]

As 'cheating' accelerated on Articles 16 and 17 – substantially in the north and much more modestly in the south – the notion of judicial impartiality, that malconceived product of Léger's conservative thinking, was in the process of being discarded. John Holmes was unconvinced by British and American reports of massive illicit imports by Hanoi. He nevertheless admitted to David Johnson in March 1956 that

the provisions the Commission has been able to establish to prevent arms shipments across the northern border and along the northern coast *would not be adequate to prevent importations on a considerable scale at any time the Communists wished*. Perhaps, given the terrain and length of coastline, this kind of control is *inherently impossible* without the use of enormous manpower.

Deterioration in control would lead in one probable direction:

We may be faced shortly with the determination on the part of the Americans and the South Vietnamese to defy the Geneva Agreement in respect to arms importation. If they do so *they are almost certain to point out that the Commission has been unable to control importation in North Vietnam and therefore it cannot expect the South to accept these limitations*.[40]

Canadian policy towards the ICSCs at this point amounted to seeking a 'rump commission' of reduced staff charged with overseeing fulfilment of the arms control articles and the security and integrity of the Demilitarized Zone.[41] Any reduction in the effectiveness of ICSC operations under Articles 16 and 17 necessarily involved a greatly heightened risk of subversion in the southern zone. Unless the IC could effectively seal the DMZ and the RVN's western frontier, agents from the north would be able to maintain links to dissident pro-Vietminh groups in the south with few problems. By early

1956 no one had any illusions that the IC teams were going to help significantly in this regard.

Conservatives in the Canadian delegation were distressed by what they perceived to be an Indian double standard:

In all the numerous investigations that confirmed arms smuggling and the provocation of incidents in the South by Northerners – agents provocateurs, *if the Southern forces did not react to these incidents then the Indians said it only showed that the State of Vietnam Government had no real authority – and if, in fact, they fired on demonstrators who disrupted things then they were accused of being brutal*. To their credit though, the Indians always emphasized that reconciliation would be difficult after so many years of conflict. So far as the PAVN was concerned they kept telling us that they'd just dropped out of the trees yesterday and that you aren't going to get guerrillas to turn into refined diplomats overnight.[42]

In February and March, military intelligence estimates placed the number of insurgents in the south at between 6,000 and 40,000. The Canadian estimate leaned towards the lower figure. Communist 'base areas' were said to constitute some 5–10 per cent of the RVN's territory. In addition, 'communist-controlled' areas constituted another 20–25 per cent. Canadian military analysts credited Hanoi with little or no independent initiative, deferring in a wholesale way to US intelligence appreciations.[43] Reports of active espionage (as opposed to 'passive' intelligence-gathering) by the Poles and DRVN liaison officers hurt liberal-moderate pleas for continued involvement with the ICSCs.[44]

In April 1956 the British government formally and publicly drew attention to the 200-per cent increase in DRVN divisional strength since July 1954 in a letter to the Soviet government. The British contrasted this increase with the exit of 100,000 French troops, and the decrease of the Vietnamese National Army (VNA) from 250,000 to 230,000, to refute categorically the DRVN-PRC allegations that Diem's forces were being trained and equipped preparatory to an attack on the north.[45] The British letter was somewhat less than balanced, although its central argument was valid. The VNA, though declining in absolute numbers, was being steadily improved in quality under the guiding hand of the US MAAG operation. In due course its weaponry inventory would be substantially increased through the activities of the Temporary Equipment Recovery Mission (TERM), which was covertly refurbishing and restoring for the use of the RVN army a portion of the arms and military support vehicles left in Vietnam by the departing French forces. TERM was engaged as well in its declared mission of shipping out of South Vietnam

several hundred thousand tons of military equipment.* The arms left behind
with the RVN forces were clearly not sufficient to permit offensive operations
against the north. In this sense, US efforts were 'defensive.'

In July 1956 the French Liaison Mission forwarded an RVN note alleging
the attempted landing of agents by the DRVN via coastal drops. Chairman
Parthasarathi refused to investigate the charge.[46]

The RVN's campaign to 'exterminate communists,' as Ambassador Johnson
phrased it, began with the promulgation of Ordinance Number 6 in January
1956. Seven months later, following a formal DRVN complaint against the
ordinance, Canadian Acting Commissioner Bruce Williams argued that, as
in the case of civil repression in the DRVN, the ICSC had no competence to
comment on the internal legislative acts of the governmental authorities in
the southern zone. Chairman Parthasarathi agreed, noting that it could not
be said that the decree was a discriminatory act infringing on the terms of
14(c), since it would have to be shown that those suffering under Ordinance
6 through relocation to 'civic re-education camps' were being penalized
because of their membership in the Communist party during 'the hostilities'
(ie, 1946–54). According to the chairman, Ordinance 6, however repugnant
in its retrospective aspect, was nevertheless an act of 'common law,' and thus
was beyond the jurisdiction of the International Commission.[47]

The promulgation of Ordinance 6 and the dispatch of the FLM July letter
were part of the opening phase of a serious campaign of counter-subversion
and counter-insurgency terror. From this point onwards the Canadian delegation was continuously under pressure to support the RVN as far as it could
within the terms and methods of operation of the commission. After the
early months of 1956, impartiality was utterly impossible – if indeed it had
ever been a real option for Ottawa's Indochina brigade. With mounting
evidence of communist preparations for a campaign of subversion in the
RVN, with the realization that the 'control' provisions of Articles 16 and 17
were of the most marginal value in restraining the growth of DRVN military
strength, and with the apparent commencement of a program by the Ameri-
can-assisted Diemist security forces to pre-empt the communists in applying
'order' through systematic terror in rural South Vietnam, Ottawa policy-
makers were confronted with some very difficult decisions.

CONCLUSION: THE SUBVERSION ISSUE AS A POLICY CATALYST

Throughout 1956, senior staff in Ottawa were clearly thinking about an early
end to Canadian participation on the commissions. The liberal-moder-

* See Chapter 8.

ate element emphasized the continuing symbolic value of staying on, but liberal-moderates were also aware of the costs of remaining involved in the changed circumstances: 'To carry on in futility would do Canada's reputation no good, it would do the reputation of the Commission no good, and would be a disservice to the idea of international supervision. Furthermore, we can ill afford to continue fielding so large and expensive a team if it can accomplish so little.' So said a memorandum from External's senior staff in March 1956. Without a doubt, the argument in support of staying on the ICSC because of its contribution to arms control was wearing thin: 'We have doubts as to the usefulness of the teams in this connection [ie, supervision of the DMZ and monitoring of Articles 16 and 17], and wonder whether the value of the teams as deterrents to the import of war materials is not outweighed by the false sense of security which their existence gives.'[48] According to Pearson's appended comment to a memorandum from Jules Léger in August: 'We should wind up the Commission – if we can – the moment we think its usefulness has ended, and not be kept there merely because India and Poland want to stay on for reasons which may be valid for them but *not* for *us*.'[49] If the immediate rationales for staying on the commissions were evaporating, why did Canada stay on? Two reasons may be put forward.

The first reason, but arguably *not* the most important, was the growing influence of conservative opinion in the department, and the conservatives' declared preference for contributing where Canada could to South Vietnamese independence from communist tyranny. This trend was manifest in two communications sent to Ottawa by the Canadian commissioner to the ICSC, Bruce Williams, in the late spring of 1956.

Williams expressed the broad rationale of Canadian policy well on 16 May 1956, after witnessing the departure of the French from Hanoi: 'It is on occasions like these that one remembers the importance and the usefulness of Canada's mission in this remote part of the world ... [as well as] the general purpose and end result of the Commission's work – maintenance of peace in Vietnam and hope for those in the South who are still free from communist rule.'[50] The hope, conservative to the core in its effect on policy, would be unfulfilled. The peace would be only temporary. This communication noted Canadian priorities accurately.

Less than one month later, Williams, recently promoted from acting commissioner to commissioner, took it upon himself to review the basis of Canadian policy as embodied in the letter of instructions to Canadian commissioners. These instructions had been unamended since given to Sherwood Lett in August 1954. According to Williams, 'the common denominator of the four policy objectives outlined in the letter of instructions seems to be holding the line against Communism. Canada wishes to maintain peace in

Indochina to provide "the time for a fresh effort to encourage the development of stronger, independent and non-communist states on the Mainland of Asia" ... Canada's main concern in Vietnam is not the fulfilment of the Geneva Agreements *per se*, but the maintenance of peace in Southeast Asia as a method of thwarting Communist ascendancy in the area.' Canada had ceased being impartial in the commission, because now it was necessarily softening criticism of the RVN on 14(c) while emphasizing DRVN 'misdemeanours.' Pressing for more and better arms control monitoring helped sustain a common understanding with the Indians, but there was now a chronic problem of having to 'buy' Indian support at a price that might be more damaging to the South than the North. On the question of successor obligations the Indians wanted full de jure obligations by the RVN; Canada was interested in de facto co-operation.[51]

In evaluating this memorandum James Eayrs declared: 'By June 1956 the third Commissioner for ICSC Vietnam had concluded that Canada's policy had changed. Thwarting communist expansion had become the Commissioner's primary responsibility. Impartiality had yielded to partisanship.'[52] The first and third statements are reasonable assessments, but the second requires careful qualification. Williams's memorandum was not an expression of settled policy. It was as much a query by Williams to his superiors about the broad pattern that he should adhere to, as it was a statement of his views. Unfortunately, officials in Ottawa, under the pressure of incipient crises elsewhere, did not find time to send a detailed reply. And, it must be acknowledged, there was no need to: Williams had *almost* 'got it right.' Tactically, in the work of the commission, partisan methods had been and would continue to be on the rise. This did *not* mean that the quest for peace had been subordinated to the anti-communist struggle, nor did it mean that there was now a 'full convergence' between Canadian and American policies, as Eayrs has argued. The differences between Ottawa and Washington were still real, and the common ground between Ottawa and New Delhi still substantial.

Just as he passed over the 16 May communication, Eayrs ignored a portion of Williams's communication that has more than a little significance. With respect to the critical question of successor obligations, Williams noted: 'Our conditions are different from those of the Indians in only one major respect. We are willing to modify our position in order to promote our long-range objective of halting communism at the seventeenth parallel. The Indians do not seem to be motivated by this goal and therefore are less than willing than we are to compromise in their demands.'[53] Implicit in the passage is the notion that the 'conditions' were intimately shaped by the 'objectives' of each country's broader foreign policy. Conversely, for some conditions to be similar, some objectives had to be shared in common. In fact, as of June 1956 the Indian and Canadian governments shared at least three objectives: the maintenance of peace in Indochina, which was the real 'primary responsibility' of the ICSC commissioners ('thwarting communist expansion' was actually a *means* to promoting the end of peace for Ottawa – not the other way around as Williams had suggested); second, restoring the effectiveness of the ICSCs in their arms control role, an objective Williams had explicitly acknowledged; and third, doing what was possible to deny the extension of DRVN influence into Laos and Cambodia. As recently as March and April one could have added a fourth common objective: pressing for full formal accession of the RVN to the Cease-Fire Agreement. That had been an extremely significant difference between Ottawa and Washington – indeed between Ottawa and London.* By the end of May this had been dropped as an objective by Ottawa, following achievement of the modus vivendi on the replacement of the French Liaison Mission.

Williams was correct to stress the increasingly anti-communist underpinning of Canadian policy. The 14(d) affair, perceptions of DRVN totalitarianism, and the heightened perception of DRVN-directed subversion in the south had changed the balance of opinion in the Canadian policy community. It was this dimension of change in Canadian policy that clearly brought Eayrs to the charge of 'complicity' in America's anti-communist crusade. But Williams was wrong in arguing that anti-communism was the key objective of Canadian long-range policy, and that the preservation of peace was now merely a means to that end. As recently as 16 May Williams had got the priorities right: peace first, containment second. What had changed since mid-1955 was the perception among Canadians of what was politically possible in this ambiguous situation. Prior to the Geneva summit of 1955 the crisis atmosphere in international politics had meant that 'peace' had to be served almost exclusively. The flowering of East-West détente in late 1955 now

---

* On 25 March 1956 Under Secretary Jules Léger had opposed both British and American protests that Canada should not be associated with the Indian appeal to the co-chairmen for pressure on Diem to assume obligations, lest it lend legitimacy to the status of the Final Declaration. Said Léger: 'We do not agree with this view and believe that if we were to omit any reference to the political settlement we might give rise to speculations that we had reservations about it. The fact that we are not responsible for the political settlement does not mean that we have to ignore the existence of the problem or that we cannot express the hope that those who have responsibility will give attention to it.' Léger to Pearson, 'Letter to the Co-Chairman,' 23 Mar. 1956: DEA files, 50052-A-40, vol. 22

meant that containment objectives could be served in addition to the primary objective of peace preservation.

What had confused Williams (and Eayrs) was the alteration of the Canadian tactical rationales for persevering with the ICSC. This altered rationale was in fact the decisive reason why Canada opted to continue with the 'thankless, onerous, unwanted burden' of participation. From the late summer of 1955 the government had been operating under the assumption that the commission was functioning as a genuine (albeit marginal) deterrent to DRVN armed attack on the southern regime. From this point onward, the ICSC was seen implicitly as a factor in the regional balance of power. Awareness of this situation – inchoate in 1956 – would grow in both New Delhi and Ottawa and shape the pattern of ICSC activities in a profound way over the next six years.

Pearson, to reiterate, clearly wanted out. Unlike Paul Martin or Marcel Cadieux or other conservative articulators in the department, neither his anti-communism nor his emotions had been deeply engaged. It was less than coincidental that Martin's conversion to the RVN cause occurred after a visit to South Vietnam and a long interview with Diem. Canadian conservatives decided 'independently' to back Diem and the southern cause – not out of some geopolitical calculus, or even of a philosophical abhorrence of communism, but out of a personal sense of human obligation to the South Vietnamese. Pearson was not so engaged. Why then did he not opt for withdrawal? Most probably, it was because he was locked into a situation where there were no clear guidelines. Specifically, there was no clear indication when the ICSC was *not* contributing to the maintenance of peace in Indochina. Deterrence is in the mind of the target. It is therefore subject to great ambiguity in interpretation. The ICSC clearly had some potential for inhibiting direct armed assault on the south. Might it not also have a role to play in the deterrence or inhibition of indirect assault? The perception that a campaign of subversion was under way was, in all probability, the catalyst that led to Canadian perseverance in 1956 – and forestalled an exit decreed by Pearson.

In historical perspective, if Ottawa had indeed backed Diem and the possibility of an independent South Vietnam as an act of 'humane concern,' it would still have been a tragically bad decision – however commendable the intentions. It is clearly not sufficient to have the best of intentions in international politics: a consequentialist ethic must be followed. But humane concern was not the only factor that bore on the situation. If personal concern (or for that matter anti-communist zeal) had been the decisive factor, it would surely have led to material assistance to the RVN (which never flowed to any meaningful degree), not to continued participation on the ICSC. Many in the department, Pearson included, appreciated that the peace of Asia – especially the nuclear peace – was still fragile. Liberal-moderate axioms had not been invalidated. Moreover, an assault on the south was perceived to be under way, and the ICSC was seen to have a potential role in ameliorating this problem. The logic which had led to acceptance of a role in July 1954, to the muting of criticism on 14(d), and to the accommodation of the DRVN's image of the Geneva 'package' was still at work. American over-reliance on nuclear weapons had not decreased – in fact, it was increasing steadily throughout this period. The risk of adventurists like Admiral Radford triggering the unthinkable was still tangible and intolerably high. So long as the RVN was weak, the ICSC had a role to play as a balance mechanism. Paradoxically, if the RVN had been strong, Ottawa would probably have left the ICSC immediately (the many disparaging comments about the sorry state of the NNSC support that assertion). RVN weakness and a Canadian concern to do what was possible to shore up a fragile peace were the critical factors at this juncture. From mid-1956 through 1965 Ottawa would adhere to this balance-of-power approach to the ICSC, using it as a device for helping Saigon and hindering the DRVN in the latter's campaign of subversion. Ironically but wisely, India, despite its constant non-aligned rhetoric, would reluctantly concur in this latest manifestation of middle-power efforts to shape the peace of Asia.

8

The partisan commission in operation
1956–62

We have always considered it desirable to treat the Cease-Fire Agreement as a flexible document designed to maintain peace and stability in Indochina.

Commissioner J. Price Erichsen-Brown to the ICSC, 13 April 1960

Two of the common myths surrounding the ICSC for Vietnam are that it actively favoured the DRVN during the critical years 1956–61 and that this pattern of alleged support reflected a marked deterioration in Indo-Canadian relations. James Eayrs has written, for example: 'The divergence in voting patterns within the ICSC Vietnam became pronounced after 1956. As the divergence developed, the early rapport between Canada and India was lost, to be replaced by sour mistrust. The relationship was more like a marriage on the rocks than the ending of a honeymoon.'[1] And again in support of his theme of 'complicity': 'As Canada and the United States drew close, Canada and India drew distant.'[2] Ramesh Thakur, on whose work Eayrs uncritically relies, has written in the same vein: 'In the 1954–1959 period, then, not only did non-alignment pit India against the West in Indochina, but even the specifics of its bilateral relations favoured the communists as against the Americans. In the ICC the Indian delegation generally found itself opposed to the South Vietnamese efforts to resist the Geneva settlement ... the Indian delegation chaired the ICC into favouring the North Vietnamese case in 72% of its decisions.'[3] In a later article Thakur also wrote: 'For the 1956–59 period, when South Vietnam was seen to have jeopardized the whole Geneva structure by its refusal to agree to unifying elections, India's votes were overwhelmingly in favour of North Vietnam. In India's view, jettisoning the political settlement was imperilling the entire Geneva framework for peace in Vietnam, increasing the risks of a wider conflagration, and therefore pursuing a course of action which militated against India's foreign policy.'[4]

If numbers could tell the whole story, then the interpretation offered by Eayrs and Thakur would make sense. But the numbers mask the truth of the situation. The voting record was not reflective of the degree of support accorded by India to Hanoi. The voting pattern masked the true thrust of Indian policy and concealed a prolonged period of Indo-Canadian collaboration at DRVN expense.

In terms of declared violations of the Geneva Cease-Fire Agreement from 12 December 1955 to 28 February 1961, the record is even more nominally biased than Thakur suggests. India apportioned (in a conservative estimate) more than 180 'citations' or 'violations' of the CFA to the Republic of Vietnam. The DRVN was found guilty of violations of only six occasions. In sum, over 95 per cent of the declared violations in this period were at RVN expense.[5] Nevertheless, from early 1956 onward the ICSC and Indian policy, as expressed through the ICSC, demonstrably and tangibly favoured the Saigon government. The Indo-Canadian entente lived on. Indeed, Indo-Canadian favouritism at DRVN expense rose steadily throughout the period.* Such favouritism was expressed not through recorded violations, or even Thakur's more inclusive definition of 'decisions.' It was manifest through *deliberate inaction*. As Bachrach and Baratz have noted, 'non-decisions' are frequently far more important than actions.[6] The ICSC record between 1956 and 1961 is a classic illustration of this phenomenon. Commission inaction with regard to the build-up in RVN military strength, and with regard also to RVN suppression of communists and dissidents, materially assisted Saigon in its efforts to build a stable structure of government. The RVN had clearly failed to attain this objective by 1960, but not for lack of Indian or Canadian assistance.

THE ICSC AND AMERICAN MILITARY ADVISERS 1956–61

Indo-Canadian partisanship was strongly manifest even before the modus vivendi on liaison representation was negotiated. Sometime prior to May 1956 Pentagon officials 'learned informally that the Indian government would instruct its representative to the I.C.C. to interpose no objection' to the dispatch to Vietnam of the Temporary Equipment Recovery Mission

---

* Thakur has noted some of this favouritism, dating, he thought, from 1959 through 1964 – the result of Sino-Indian conflict in the Himalayas. Sino-Indian rivalry was a factor, but not the most important one. 'Indian's Vietnam Policy, 1946–79,' *Asian Survey* XIX, 10 (Oct. 1979) 962–4. Eayrs ignores this argument by Thakur. It undermines one of the central themes of his book.

(TERM).[7] This advisory and logistics group, comprising 350 personnel (slightly larger than the existing Military Assistance Advisory Group, MAAG, in Saigon) was then sent to Vietnam with no prior clearance from the ICSC, nor with any advance notice to the commission. It did not respect ICSC control access point procedures as they had been established in the autumn of 1955. Both the Poles and North Vietnamese were stunned and distressed. Ottawa was shocked, not by the dispatch of this task force, which they had known about since 25 February (and which Pearson had tried to stop),[8] but rather by Indian passivity in the face of what seemed to be a prima facie violation of Article 16 (the prohibition of 'reinforcements' of foreign troops and advisers beyond the level that existed when the cease-fire went into effect in South Vietnam on 11 August 1954). Ottawa learned from Commissioner Bruce Williams in early June that TERM's activities were not going to be limited to shipping out several hundred million dollars worth of US Mutual Defense Assistance Plan equipment and weaponry left behind by the French. A significant portion of this equipment would be restored to working order and handed over to the RVN. Only 'the surplus that the South Vietnamese cannot use' would be shipped out.[9] Officials in Ottawa knew that State had been under pressure from the Pentagon to support a sizeable increase in MAAG's staff.[10] They also knew that the ICSC had been in receipt of a protest from General Giap since February, concerning an alleged threefold increase in MAAG.[11]

Canada had been told that the business of TERM would be focused upon the restoration of trucks, jeeps, artillery, and so forth, which were sitting in 'open storage' (ie, abandoned in fields). Left unserviced, the equipment would soon rust into unusability. The Pentagon generals were not going to allow this to occur to three-quarters of a billion dollars worth of war material. DRVN authorities had never accepted the legitimacy of the existence of MAAG after the cease-fire took effect, and they certainly were going to react badly to the arrival of TERM. MAAG staff had never been especially co-operative with the ICSC, and hence Ottawa feared the worst.[12]

American officials had already informed Ottawa that the bulk of the recovered equipment would be shipped out of Vietnam: the RVN could not make use of more than a small fraction of it. Furthermore, since the armistice the US had shipped out over 25,000 tons of equipment, importing but 3,500 tons – all of it spare parts. Ottawa therefore had no reason to suspect that massive 'violations' of Articles 16 or 17 would occur, and indeed they did . not – in light of a carefully favourable but legally permissible reading of the ambiguous Geneva text. It was certainly an option for the RVN to hire privately all the technicians required to put *all* of the abandoned MDAP equipment back in working order. (Pentagon officials had originally wished to hire and dispatch an additional 1,000 Philippino and Japanese technicians to expedite the recovery operation.) In this sense, TERM did effect a net reduction in the military potential of the RVN. It was for this reason that Ottawa saw nothing 'sinister' in the MAAG-TERM operations. Pearson accordingly suggested to Washington that the US should resort to French technicians – anything but the unilateral dispatch of US personnel.[13] This proposal was turned down flatly. The Pentagon at this time was seeking the early elimination of all French influence in Vietnam, while the South Vietnamese were busily expropriating French interests and thereby gravely alienating Paris.[14]

By the end of April, the US decision to dispatch TERM was confirmed. By mid-May, TERM personnel had left Oakland. In the last week of May, TERM elements began to arrive.

At this juncture, the ICSC's Legal Committee (LC) produced a report on the meaning of Article 17. Until then, most observers had argued that the intent of Articles 16 and 17 had been to freeze the military status quo in Vietnam. The LC Report overturned this interpretation by declaring that though the intention of Article 17 was clearly to ban the *importation* of new weapons and material beyond imports on a 'piece-for-piece' replacement basis, the article did *not* imply, however, that *internal* production of weaponry and equipment was illicit. In other words the build-up of the armed forces of the two Vietnamese regimes was not illegitimate within the terms of the CFA so long as it was accomplished with internally manufactured resources.[15] Nothing could have been more helpful to the RVN's interests at this time than such a statement. At the same time, Ottawa also learned that the LC had begun to examine the question of 'credits' which might be given to the RVN in recognition of the large quantity of military equipment shipped out of the southern zone by the departing French Expeditionary Corps during 1955–56. Worse was still to come for the DRVN.

On 30 May 1956 the ICSC decided to formally allow entry of TERM provided 'that the sole object of the Mission was to arrange for export.'[16] Were the Indians fooled, as Eayrs has suggested? It seems highly unlikely.

In retrospect, it is possible that Indian permission was a tactic which aimed to reduce the quantity of material handed over to the VNA by applying some pressure on the US government, while covering New Delhi against communist charges that it had deserted the letter of the CFA. It is possible that Chairman Parthasarathi was following a consciously two-faced policy, because Washington had been in contact with New Delhi for some two months prior to the decision.* It is very doubtful that American officials tried to hide any of TERM's projected duties from the Indian government. In this situation Parthasarathi really had little choice but to pretend publicly that the Americans were doing other than what he privately admitted they were probably engaged in (ie, refurbishing and handing over arms to the VNA). According to one former member of the Canadian delegation, TERM's covert mandate to help equip the Vietnamese National Army was 'an open secret,' and Parthasarathi's role was to 'paper over' the ambiguities of the task force's status.[17] This is one plausible construction of events – a better one than positing Indian ignorance.

A still better explanation looks to the subsequent Indian response to TERM monitoring operations by the ICSC. In permitting TERM's entry, the Indians sought details on personnel tasks, including names and duration of posting. The ICSC also requested 'fortnightly progress reports,' notifications for the entry and exit of personnel, and a right to conduct 'spot checks.'[18] But no progress reports were ever made on a fortnightly basis. United States personnel never permitted the ICSC to monitor the entry and exit of TERM personnel. The 'spot checks' were conducted so infrequently and with such long time notice (two days or longer), that they were virtually meaningless as an effective check on potential violations. TERM carried on operations for well over a year before the first check was executed.[19] Despite strong Polish and DRVN protests, the Indians refused to prod either the RVN Liaison Mission or the Americans. There was never the slightest implication that the Indians might threaten 'violations' over TERM. Indian behaviour suggests implicit collusion, not ignorance.

While frustrating Hanoi on TERM, the Indians also refused to pursue DRVN complaints about the expansion of MAAG via the addition of a 'Training Reorganization Inspection Mission' (actually the Training Relations and

---

* See Edwin Bickford Hooper, Dean C. Allard, and Oscar P. Fitzgerald, *The United States Navy and the Vietnam Conflict*, I, *The Setting of the Stage to 1959* (Washington: Naval History Division, Department of the Navy – US Government Printing Office 1976) 332–5. According to this study American approaches to the Canadian, Indian, and Polish governments concerning TERM began in earnest after the RVN requested France on 26 Feb. 1956 to withdraw all its military forces from Vietnam, including the logistical and maintenance personnel needed to care for the MDAP weaponry and other equipment. This account misrepresents the Indian position by claiming that New Delhi changed its policy 'at the last minute,' and withheld approval. The authors do not mention that the US naval authorities who headed up TERM refused categorically to accept entry and exit procedures whereby ICSC personnel could monitor the movement of TERM staff. New Delhi's initial approval of TERM was undoubtedly quite explicitly conditional upon American acceptance of ICSC supervision of all personnel movement.

Instruction Mission) and Combat Arms Training Organization (TRIM and CATO respectively). According to Hanoi, the four US missions together, plus regular contacts between RVN military personnel and SEATO opposites, had generated a 'factual materialisation of a military alliance between the Government of the Republic of Vietnam and the member countries of "SEATO."'[20] In response to what were clearly grave charges, the commission under Indian direction merely asked for 'comments' from the RVN authorities.

On 26 October 1956 foreign military personnel and 'warships and jet planes' from SEATO states took part in the RVN's National Day celebrations. Hanoi claimed it proved the existence of a de facto alliance. No violation was declared by the commission. The ambiguous wording of the passage describing the event in the relevant interim report contained no reprimand – only an expression of 'concern.' 'The Commission also concluded that the participation of foreign military personnel and war material in public celebrations ... did not necessarily prove the existence of a military alliance. The Commission has closed the case.'[21]

In September 1957, five months after the above finding, the Indian chairman succinctly summed up his delegation's new approach:

I would like all three delegations to remember that this [pointing at the Geneva Agreement] is our charter. *Our powers are limited. The implementation of the Geneva Agreement is a duty of the parties. We have merely to supervise such implementation.* We have made every effort possible to secure that implementation. This is an admission of failure. I admit that but *I think we should be realistic and objective and not create false hopes* in the minds of people or ourselves that by taking any further action we will achieve any better results.[22]

Under this new regime Saigon was not prodded or coerced. Its regular violations, as recorded in the pages of interim reports of the commission, were also masked under a smokescreen of legalistic verbosity. TERM operations were subjected to no serious scrutiny; MAAG was allowed to continue operations totally unhindered.[23]

RVN Liaison Mission declarations were accepted at face value concerning TERM. After being able to extract only three spot checks from the Indians in 1957, the Poles pressed for an end to TERM in November, asking for a set time limit. The Canadian delegation opposed setting any time limit at all because 'the function of this mission is to ship out war material out of South Vietnam ... [and] diminish the war potential of South Vietnam.'[24] At this late date it was common knowledge that TERM had freed up MAAG personnel from logistics tasks for the deployment of advisory personnel throughout the RVN forces. Nevertheless, the Indian chairman concurred in the Canadian position.[25] Furthermore, he refused to reduce the time notice prior to spot checks below two full days. The Polish ambassador had sought two hours. Chairman T.N. Kaul insisted on taking 'the party at its word until anything is proved to the contrary.'[26] This after the 'temporary' mission had already been at work for eighteen months and had given no indication as to when it might finish its tasks. Reporting from TERM was sporadic throughout 1957 and 1958 and the mission made little effort to meet even the lax two-day time notice requirement. India did not act.

In March 1958 the IC's pre-eminent concentration on the operations of TERM and MAAG yielded temporarily to a major debate over the nature of Article 17 and the status of serviceable military equipment which had been exported out of Vietnam when the French Expeditionary Corps (FEC) departed. According to the Canadian delegation, Article 17 was intended to stabilize the military balance in Vietnam as it existed at the time of the cease-fire. The FEC withdrawal of weapons and material endangered that balance. Hence 'credits' should be given to the RVN by the ICSC so that it might legitimately offset these exported arms with 'replacement' material. According to Canadian Ambassador T. LeM. Carter:

We feel that *it was indeed the intention and spirit of the Agreement to maintain the level of war material and potential in each zone as it existed at the Cease-Fire.* Since the Cease-Fire, a large amount of equipment, much of which was serviceable, has been exported out of South Vietnam. *Hence the balance of equipment as it existed at the Cease-Fire was disturbed by this export. The prohibition of Article 17(a) is a prohibition on the introduction of reinforcement* (sic). As I understand the construction of treaties, unnecessary words are not put in. If it was intended to be a prohibition on introduction of arms, munitions, and war materials, then the word reinforcement would not appear in the text. Hence, we assume that the word 'reinforcement' is central to this Article. Hence we assume that Article 17 permits a certain type of reinforcement, exceptionally replacement of a damaged or destroyed piece by a good piece. Replacement of a damaged or destroyed piece by a good piece is a reinforcement. This is permitted exceptionally under Article 17(b).[27]

The Canadian rationale for allowing the FEC export credit was an ingenious exploitation of the ambiguity of the wording of Article 17. It also reflected perfectly the new Canadian approach to the Indochina commissions: peace through 'containment' and a preservation of an equilibrium of force in Vietnam. On 14 May 1958, after two years of calculated inaction on the TERM and MAAG controversies, the Indian delegation furthered Saigon's interests fundamentally by enacting, through Indo-Canadian majority, Decision 470. Under this decision (which was deemed to be of such gravity that it required a separate report to the co-chairmen from the ICSC), the very wording of Article 17(b) was distorted. War material shipped out of Vietnam by the FEC in 1955–6 would now be considered as 'destroyed' by the ICSC. Only the submission to the commission of French ship manifests was required to establish export 'credits' with the commission. Polish Ambassador Goralski protested in vain that the preceding two years had witnessed a blatant build-up of forces in the RVN and that Decision 470 was another terrible error. The Canadian ambassador then replied:

The view of the Canadian Delegation is that this decision being in consonance with the letter and spirit of the Agreement merely serves to maintain *the equality in the strength of the armed forces established in this country before the cease-fire Agreement* and it is perfectly consonant with the disarmament proposals in other parts of the world *based on the equality of armed forces.*[28]

The Canadian commissioner's rationale summed up the change in Canadian attitudes and policy well. It also reflected the new foundation of Indian policy, which through its concurrence in Canadian arguments was no less partisan than Canada's in its service to the RVN's military-security needs.

Hanoi leaders were extremely upset. For the first time, they appealed directly to the co-chairmen of the Geneva Conference for remedial action against a decision that was 'contrary to the spirit and letter of the Geneva Agreement.' In addressing the appeal to the co-chairmen, Hanoi asserted that the ICSC had to withhold implementation of Decision 470 until word was received from the co-chairmen. Under Indo-Canadian majority vote the decision was reaffirmed and the presumed right of appeal to the co-chairmen was totally rejected.[29]

Publicly, the ICSC continued to score violations regularly against the RVN. It constantly lamented the failure of the parties to accept ICSC interpretations as authoritative. The commission also lamented the lack of progress towards the political settlement called for in the Final Declaration. But under Indian direction the ICSC did nothing to prod the RVN into greater co-operation. If anything it rewarded Saigon for its sheer ability to survive, while penalizing Hanoi for its very strength.

During 1957–8 the Demilitarized Zone was sealed shut because of RVN intransigence. Saigon totally rejected any representation on the original Central Joint Commission. Without an operating CJC there could be no valid issuance of permits for entry into the DMZ. Saigon authorities deepened partition in another way through the expulsion of the PAVN Liaison Mission to South Vietnam in 1958. The commission took no initiatives to forestall this move and merely issued pro forma expressions of 'concern.' The two Vietnams were now a political and military reality. Indian and Canadian policy clearly assisted in the reification of partition by their joint approach of benign indifference to the unilateral revision of the original Geneva principles by the RVN regime.

It is not coincidental that Indian tolerance, per Decision 470, was made manifest within six months of Ngo Dinh Diem's triumphant official visit to New Delhi in November 1957. Diem's brother, Ngo Dinh Nhu, had prepared the way for Diem's visit through private talks in New Delhi with Nehru and Menon in April 1957. According to D.R. SarDesai, eight Indian airforce jets escorted Diem's plane to New Delhi, and Diem himself was 'accorded full civil and military honours appropriate to a visiting head of state of an important friendly country.'[30] He received a twenty-one gun salute, a traditional guard of honour, a state processional drive, and other tributes normally bestowed on visiting heads of state. As a result of RVN diplomacy and Diem's own charm, Indian attitudes towards the RVN turned around completely in 1957. SarDesai commented: 'Diem impressed most Indians as an independent-minded Asian nationalist, contrary to the general image of a puppet dictator tied to Western apron strings which had prevailed before his visit.'[31]

Ho Chi Minh attempted to stem the tide of Diem's diplomatic success through a visit of his own to New Delhi in 1958. He too was accorded a glowing reception. Nehru paid tribute to Ho as 'one of the most remarkable men of our times, a man of peace, friendly, likeable, self-effacing, humble, a man of the masses ... a great revolutionary and an almost legendary hero.'[32] Ho succeeded in getting a public reaffirmation of the Indian commitment to Vietnamese unification through elections, but he failed to win a condemnation by Nehru of Diem's obstinate refusal to enter into pre-electoral talks.

By mid-1959 the Canadian ambassador, J. Price Erichsen-Brown, a vigorous, articulate, and shrewd conservative, was openly defending the right of the US to assist the RVN militarily because 'neither the United States nor South Vietnam signed the Geneva Agreement or its declarations.'[33] Erichsen-Brown also fired the first salvo within the ICSC in defence of the forthcoming US-RVN request to double the size of MAAG. He did so by strongly defending MAAG's right to exist when the group came under sustained DRVN-Polish attack. After a lengthy debate on US advisory staff, an Indo-Canadian majority found that: MAAG was legitimate, and consistent with the armistice legally; the Pentalateral Agreement of 1950 establishing MAAG did not constitute a formal military alliance in violation of Article 19; and, finally, MAAG personnel could not exceed 342 people, and could not import their own military equipment. To keep up some pretence of impartiality, the majority declared that the ICSC needed more information in order to pass judgment on the allegation of the creation of a 'factual alliance.'[34]

In May 1958, the RVN informed the ICSC that 43,000 tons of material remained to be processed by TERM. In April 1959, after being told by the ICSC that TERM should depart by June, the RVN reported that 'a new body of material' had been discovered. An Indo-Canadian majority decision then allowed the date for departure to be pushed back to 31 December 1960.[35] The Polish ambassador complained that at its demonstrated rate of progress the 'temporary mission' was likely to go on for one or two decades. No Indian or Canadian disagreed with this assessment.

In January 1961 the RVN Liaison Mission informed the ICSC that TERM had been dissolved on 31 December 1960, that of its 350 personnel total, some 261 had left South Vietnam during 1960, while the remaining 89 were transferred to MAAG 'on account of their technical ability' – though it was carefully pointed out that the transfer was effected within MAAG's personnel ceiling.[36] Allegations were received in the same month from the DRVN to the effect that the whole TERM operation was now incorporated into MAAG 'under the assumed name of the Logistics Section of the Military Assistance Advisory Group.'[37] To make matters even murkier, the ICSC was in deliberation throughout this period concerning a request from the RVN foreign minister Vu Van Mau, lodged on 23 February 1960, to increase the size of MAAG from 342 to 685 staff.

Ambassador Erichsen-Brown had promptly defended the MAAG increase request in April 1960, citing DRVN direction of the campaign of subversion in the south.[38] He also had argued for the right to 'rotate in' other foreign troops, in addition to French forces pursuant to Article 16.[39] On 19 April 1960 another Indo-Canadian majority approved the MAAG increase. The Indian chairman noted that the doubling of MAAG would leave the total number of foreign military advisers below the 888 present at the time of the cease-fire (ie, French and US advisers in total).[40] Hanoi did not find this observation consoling. For the second time, the DRVN launched an appeal against the ICSC to the Geneva co-chairmen.[41] In addition, the North Vietnamese commenced a 'large-scale propaganda campaign' throughout the north 'through the Commission's petition facilities.'[42] An Indo-Canadian majority once more chastised the DRVN for its abuse of the petition process.

In sum, the years 1956–61 saw decision after critical decision go against the DRVN: TERM was allowed entry in May 1956 and then was never scrutinized seriously; MAAG personnel were allowed to operate without any supervision at all; TERM was blatantly allowed to increase the military strength of the

RVN armed forces (even if the 'total military potential' of the southern zone declined); in March 1958, French military equipment exports were retro-actively allowed to count as 'destroyed' war material eligible for replace-ment; after postponing a decision on MAAG for some three years, the task force was eventually pronounced wholly consistent with the Geneva Agree-ment in November 1959; and, finally, in April 1960 the ICSC allowed MAAG to be doubled in size. Hanoi's sharp protests over these decisions, in several cases protests directly to the co-chairmen, testify to their gravely partisan character. Whatever the DRVN gained on the violations scoreboard was vastly out-weighed by the deliberate decision of the Indian government to refrain from hindering or obstructing the US military aid relationship to the RVN.

To cap this period of serious material reverses for the DRVN in the com-mission, even the little gained on the violations tally-sheet was called into question in the ICSC's *Eleventh Interim Report* of 18 September 1961. An Indo-Canadian majority declared that it was reasonable to condemn *both* parties *equally* for non-compliance with the Cease-Fire Agreement because 'the number of formal citations in itself is no fair measure of the degree of co-operation received from either Party.'[43] In this instance of artificially even-handed criticism of the parties, and in many others, an Indo-Canadian majority secured a decision where, as the Polish commissioner rightly phrased matters, there was 'an attempt to get a balance where there is no balance at all.'[44] The only balancing being done was by India and Canada, and all at North Vietnamese expense.

DEVELOPING THE SUBVERSION CHARGE INSTRUMENT 1956–62

While the military assistance issues were being thrashed out, the subversion allegations controversy proceeded on a broadly parallel course that was also very damaging to DRVN interests. In effect, the stage was set for a commis-sion conviction of the DRVN on the charge of 'indirect aggression.' The gravity of this instrument was sufficiently great that it had to be kept in reserve as a weapon of last resort in the Indo-Canadian campaign to hinder and obstruct politically and propagandistically the DRVN's resort to revolu-tionary guerrilla warfare in South Vietnam. It was a policy instrument that could only be used once, as a last desperate act of pressure.

Canadian officials were convinced almost from the outset of involvement that subversion was not merely a threat, but an ongoing aspect of the politi-cal struggle between the Vietnamese parties. Ottawa officials and successive Canadian commissioners were convinced that reports of some 6,000 to 10,000 Vietminh 'stay-behind' agents in the South were accurate. As Sher-wood Lett noted on 26 November 1954 in connection with the 14(c) incidents in the south: 'We are attempting to frame the instructions [to investigatory teams] to bring out what we think to be the facts, namely, that the Vietminh have agents in the South who are stirring up the people and inciting them to disorder.'[45] On 4 July 1955 Ambassador Lett rejected the possibility of open DRVN assault on the south, but forecast an intensification of subversion: 'There are, on the other hand, measures short of war, and the Communists are expert at them. We can look to a continuation of infiltration and subversion against "the American interventionists and their puppet Diem."'[46] Frustration at their inability to use the ICSC to help the beleaguered Saigon regime was typical for Canadians. Ambassador Bruce Williams wrote on 7 November 1956:

The South, in its efforts to weed out Communist agents, and thus to ensure the security of the State, arrests and harasses 'former resistance workers.' The standards of evidence are so low that a high proportion of the arrests made by the South turn into 14(c) cases; the South by not replying to the Commission letters lends credence to these charges. Over a period of time the situation is painted on paper which leads the casual on-looker to believe that the South possesses one of the most oppressive regimes ever created. Through inaction, the Commission has made it impossible for the South to balance the record by making charges about PAVN subversion and sabotage.[47]

Conservatives with the Canadian delegation responded to this frustration by demanding to Ottawa that they be allowed to pressure the Indians to refuse to accept 14(c) allegations altogether. Ottawa's liberal-moderate element, fearing for the good health of the Indo-Canadian entente, declined, not wishing to explore the limits of Indian tolerance.[48]

Canadian conservatives saw the DRVN regime in completely negative terms, a perception that was strongly complementary to the perception of 'aggression from the north.' According to one interviewee,

The communism of the DRVN was not that of Italy, or of 'human face' socialism. It was extremely brutal using torture, assassination, mutilation and so on – the most violent and cruel methods imaginable. They were determined to run the whole country by force. And with five per cent of the population actively supporting them they could do it. The problem for the Vietnamese was that you either accepted the communists and their programme totally or you were out. It's that aspect which I do not like at all. Fascists order you to follow their rules. Communists force you to believe in them too.*

* Confidential interview material (emphasis added)

The conservative element regularly complained about liberal-moderate accommodation of what they saw as a repugnant inhuman political system. Partly in reaction to this perceived overemphasis on peace preservation, conservative articulators were prone to exaggerate Diem's and the RVN's strengths in their reporting. But few of Diem's strongest sympathizers held out much hope for an eventual RVN victory in the south. Canadian conservatives were the first to embrace the combative role aspects of the new model 'balancer' commission. After mid-1956, conservative elements in the Canadian policy community were prepared to do everything practical to further RVN interests in the ICSC. This did not include stooping to Polish tactics and dissenting on every 'violation' committed by the RVN. According to Thakur's analysis of the Canadian voting record, overt partisanship was not manifest until early 1959, over two years after the resort by the Poles to plainly partisan practices.[49]

From 1956 onward, Canadian behaviour in the ICSC slid away from the role of jurist to legal advocate. Ottawa pressed for closing supervisory control gaps on the northern frontier, defended MAAG, TERM, and the RVN-US aid relationship, and denounced Hanoi's various attempts to pressure the ICSC into changing tactics. The ICSC was forced to move away from legal interpretations of the 'law' of Geneva into an area of hard political choices. The pretence of impartiality was increasingly hollow, especially with regard to decisions affecting the North Vietnamese.

Canadian policy was undoubtedly affected by Ngo Dinh Diem's capacity to impress Western visitors. Diem obviously had a deep effect on Paul Martin in late 1956,[50] just as he generated a very favourable impression in New Delhi one year later.[51] One of Diem's chief defenders in External Affairs remains convinced to this day that the disintegration of Diem's republic had less to do with his errors and values (or the failings of his family) than with the inappropriate character of American support. Diem was said to possess courage, passion, vision, and empathy. Many of his American allies lacked precisely these qualities.[52]

On the subversion problem, India and Canada saw eye to eye. Indian officials had regularly invoked the subversion risk in the RVN as grounds for pressuring Diem into accession to the full Geneva package: he would not survive long, so why cause needless bloodshed?[53] From mid-1956, once India had resigned itself to the inevitability of the partition experiment, it became a priority of Indian policy to do what was possible on the ICSC to inhibit the onset of a revolutionary war in the south. Indian and Canadian thinking thus converged when it came to subversion. It was appropriate for Nehru to stress the commonality of approach to Indochina during a visit to Ottawa in late December 1956:

We have found that Canada has shown a greater appreciation of the reality of today in Asia and that I think is one reason why we have got on so well with Canada. Although we have differed in regard to many matters there has been this basis, coming closer to each other and understanding each other more ... We have no problems between India and Canada. We are interested, all of us, in problems of the world, so the problems of the world were discussed between two friends without any conflict. I suppose it was more a question of emphasis.[54]

The Indo-Canadian relationship was most certainly not a 'marriage on the rocks.'

In public utterances about the ICSC's role, Indian officials soon began to preach the line of conciliation, 'good offices,' and the promotion of increased 'effective co-operation' vis-à-vis the steadfastly aloof posture of the RVN. Despite this move towards rhetorical as well as substantive convergence of policy in New Delhi and Ottawa, Canadian officials still worried about loss of Indian support – particularly in view of the shoddy level of co-operation extended to the ICSC by US officials, as well as their abysmal political ignorance of anything concerning the Geneva Agreements or the ICSC role. Canadian anxiety was a direct function of RVN-American deviation from the original 'spirit of Geneva.' Their fears proved groundless: India was committed to persevering partisanship.

During the summer of 1957, the RVN acted to eliminate the DRVN presence in the south altogether. DRVN liaison officers were eventually denied access to the southern part of the DMZ and Hanoi's Liaison Mission in Saigon was closed. Privately, Saigon officials had claimed that DRVN personnel had been contacting agents in the south.[55] When the RVN refused to entertain any further requests for investigations on 14(c), the British government supported Diem and noted the RVN assertion that there had been no reprisals for acts committed during the pre-July 1954 hostilities, only arrest and punishment for post-cease-fire activities. Furthermore, London officials claimed that the DRVN was probably just making charges to distract international attention 'from the bloody reprisals carried out against the civil population of North Viet-Nam in connection with the land reform programme and the inhuman repression of the recent risings at Thanh-Hoa and Nghe-An.'[56]

After a half-hearted Soviet initiative on behalf of Hanoi failed, Pham Van Dong sent a note of protest to the co-chairmen. The note apparently criticized the Diem government for reneging on the Geneva commitments, condemned Diem for partitioning Vietnam, and accused the RVN of preparing for a new war by collaborating in American imperial policies towards the region.[57] The note was almost a declaration of war. It was not such a declaration because of trouble at home in the north, where land reform was proceeding disastrously. Moscow certainly was not going to give its blessing to 'the revolution' during this still precarious period of international political and strategic manoeuvring.

The Canadian delegation pressed hard for subversion investigations in 1957, but the Indian delegation was determined to keep this issue buried in the Legal Committee's proceedings.[58] The Canadians therefore busied themselves with the task of blocking ICSC consideration of 14(c) violations incident to the launching of the Denunciation of Communists Campaign in the RVN, arguing that this operation by the southern regime was beyond the jurisdiction of the ICSC.[59] Their efforts were made irrelevant by the RVN's decision of November 1956 to return all ICSC queries on 14(c) unanswered. The RVN claimed that there was more freedom in the southern zone than in the totalitarian north and that, given this condition, the DRVN was merely attempting to exploit it through Article 14(c). The Indian delegation reaffirmed its long-held precedent that the ICSC could not attempt to define or impose a common standard of democratic liberties in each zone.[60]

During 1957, discussion of RVN subversion allegations was limited mainly to informal talks. In December 1957 the informal approach resulted in a directive from the IC proper to the Legal Committee to determine 'if any of the complaints in the letters [from the DRVN] attract any Article or Articles of the Geneva Agreement and to recommend what action, if any, should be taken thereon.'[61] Despite the appearance of action, this proposal amounted to yet another stalling tactic.[62]

By early 1959, commission debates were quite polarized. The insurgency was well under way. The Canadians had no doubt Hanoi was directing it. The battle for control of all Vietnam had been rejoined. So far as Canadian conservatives were concerned the evidence of systematic assassination of RVN officials could mean only one thing: aggression from the north. In this context, the key questions for Canadian conservative policy-makers were: how could Canada contribute most effectively to the security of the RVN? and how could the Canadians obstruct the plan of attack of the northern-directed forces? Certainly Canada could use its role in the ICSC to deflect or mute DRVN allegations against the RVN. The propaganda role of the ICSC was increasingly salient.

Indian handling of the TERM-MAAG issues was cause for Canadian optimism about the ICSC's future role. Canadians were optimistic too because by the end of 1957 the US had provided as much equipment to the RVN as the Pentagon deemed necessary to repel a Korean-style invasion.[63] The VNA, about 150,000 strong, was well-armed and increasingly capable of defending the RVN against a major onslaught, especially if it could count on American air and naval support. And such support seemed only too credible to the northern authorities who lamented in early 1958 that the Americans were preparing for 'atomic war' in Southeast Asia.[64]

Reports from the RVN leaders themselves were invariably optimistic. According to Diem's staff, the Denunciation of Communists Campaign had netted between 20,000 and 30,000 former Vietminh cadres. Foreign commentators such as Fall, P.G. Honey, and Buttinger – none of whom can be described as sympathetic to the DRVN cause – estimated the number of those detained in prison camps in much higher figures.[65] Land reform and other redistributive economic programs were almost totally ignored in this massive effort to root out opposition to the southern government. In an effort to mimic the methods of the DRVN, anti-communist 're-education centres' were set up in the south. The majority of those interned were neither communist nor communist sympathizers.[66] More often than not the lower echelon officials in Diem's security apparatus were quite corrupt, and used their arbitrary power of arrest and imprisonment to extort money and goods from the hapless peasantry. As Fall pointed out, it is 'little wonder, then, that the countryside largely went communist in 1958–60.'[67] Guy Beaudry's scenario was about to materialize.

In 1957 communist terror methods began in earnest, according to RVN officials, with the assassination of some 700 government personnel.[68] Many Western writers have questioned setting the date of the beginning of the insurgency so early. During 1958–9 there was no doubt, however, that the RVN was under systematic attack. Isolated acts of terror in the south in 1957, begun in response to the Diemist forces' own crackdown on any visible opposition to the regime and their vain attempts to extend government control to the countryside, gave way to a stepped-up campaign of subversion of the Diemist state apparatus. Although the National Liberation Front of South Vietnam (hereafter the NLF) was not formally constituted until 20 December 1960, there is much evidence that the organizational linkages to the DRVN from the NLF leadership were forged in the mid-1959 period, if not earlier.[69]

The new Progressive Conservative government was not enamoured of the Canadian role in Indochina.[70] But Paul Martin, now the Liberal party's foreign affairs critic, spoke out against any thoughts of withdrawal in November 1957, because of 'the role which the commission can play apart from its precise terms of reference.'[71] By this, Martin presumably was referring to the ICSC's contribution to South Vietnamese security. In July 1958 Martin referred to President Diem as a 'great liberal-minded statesman.'[72] Under the Progressive Conservatives, South Vietnam received no significant economic assistance. Generally speaking, the new PC Cabinet expressed interest only in reducing the financial cost of the ICSCs by effecting personnel cuts, or in withdrawing altogether. Professional opinion in External Affairs usually managed to head off such thoughts before they became insistent.

Beginning in early 1959, Canadian Ambassador J.P. Erichsen-Brown unilaterally removed all inhibitions against blunt discourse in commission debates. He regularly denounced DRVN charges as 'fantastic,' 'absurd,' or propagandistic, unstintingly praised American economic assistance to the RVN, and defended the legality of RVN military staff attending SEATO conferences in an 'observer' capacity.[73] His most critical language was applied to DRVN 'abuse' of the commission's petition facilities in connection with 'spontaneous' northern protest over alleged mass food-poisoning in the Phu Loi 'concentration camp.'[74] The rhetoric was unnecessary. The Indian delegation was not inclined to let either party use the ICSC for propaganda purposes.

Even though Erichsen-Brown was determined to push a hard line inside the ICSC, and despite his firm belief that the RVN was already under a DRVN-initiated and directed attack, he was not of the opinion that full-scale warfare was imminent between the north and south. On 20 March 1959 he wrote John Holmes as follows:

Both Ketcheson and I [his senior military adviser] as a result of our tour of Northern teamsites last December, and the negative team reports over a long period of time, have been disposed to the view that *the extent of the military build-up in North Vietnam is frequently exaggerated, that intelligence reports are not too good.*

Under the circumstances, *we have also been disposed to question the necessity for strengthening of the South Vietnamese military potential.* Any assumption that we favoured doing away with the Commission to achieve such an objective would be quite wrong. Our fear was rather that the withdrawal of the Commission might be forced under circumstances embarrassing to the West because of the pursuit of the objective despite the Commission.[75]

Erichsen-Brown was clearly apologetic for taking such a strong position that it risked New Delhi's goodwill. Perhaps to mollify Holmes and other liberal-moderates in Far Eastern Division, he asked for advice as to deportment vis-à-vis the representatives of other friendly governments in Saigon. Holmes replied that 'any too obvious effort to stand apart from them socially would look silly, and yet one had to maintain always in the eyes of the Indians and the Poles the figure of an entirely independent agent.' Although everyone knew the Poles worked 'hand in glove with the North Vietnamese on Commission matters,' Holmes noted that there never had been any attempt to agree on a permissible degree of association with the parties and their allies.* It was important, Holmes said, that Canadians not give the communists 'any real grounds for contending that we were acting as 'tools' of the Americans or anyone else.' It was established Canadian policy 'to avoid rocking the boat in Indochina.'[76] He then re-emphasized the basic thrust of the liberal-moderate approach:

The Geneva Agreements, however unsatisfactory they may seem to the American Military, represented a surprisingly good bargain for the West after Dien Bien Phu. The detente achieved is admittedly precarious, but as the Communists hold so many advantages in the area, it is a major Western interest to hold on to even a precarious detente … The 'tough-minded realists' maintain, of course, that you can't hold back the Communists with a paper understanding as they only respect force. *If these 'realists' were a little more realistic, however, they would realize that the kind of force they could ever deploy in this area is hardly calculated to make the Communists shudder and that there is, therefore, no easy alternative to relying on the Geneva Agreement* as an instrument for perpetuation of a mutual desire to avoid conflict.[77]

The real question for Holmes was how to moderate the inflow of American conventional weaponry so that it would not imperil the basis of the armistice. Maintaining the truce was still the prime objective of Canadian policy. Termination of the Canadian role on the ICSC was very much a secondary goal. The modality of termination had to be such that it did not incite the DRVN to extreme action. This was the problem as Holmes saw it, and as most other liberal-moderates defined the Indochina policy problematic. The essence of the liberal-moderates' approach was to 'avoid acrimony' in the ICSC. Holmes and other liberal-moderates believed that there was sentiment in the communist bloc for avoiding war in Southeast Asia. It was a rather different matter, however, when it came to assessing the intentions of the Hanoi leaders, as Canadian conservatives readily appreciated. Liberal-moderates could not deny the validity of conservative perceptions of an aggressive and repressive style of government in the DRVN, which had embarked on industrialization in the north through a form of 'corvée labour.'[78]

In any event, Erichsen-Brown and other conservatives in External Affairs still accepted the wisdom of liberal-moderate logic: maintaining the armis-

---

* A point of some significance in the debate over the alleged need for pure impartiality in peacekeeping-supervisory operations.

tice was still to be the basic objective of Canadian policy. When the Phu Loi propaganda campaign eventually collapsed after the Indians refused to intervene in the matter, thus eliminating a major source of conservative frustration, continued conservative approval for 'holding the line in Asia through keeping the peace' was assured.

On 23 July 1959 Ambassador Erichsen-Brown read out a strong statement rejecting the competence of the ICSC to comment upon 'domestic laws' of the RVN, such as the recently approved Law 10/59, another statute aimed at the elimination of the communists and 'communist thought' in the south. Law 10/59 was a supplementary statute to Ordinance Number 6 of January 1956, which had provided the legal basis for the Denunciation of Communists Campaign in 1956–7. Ordinance 6 had been challenged by Hanoi as intrinsically contradictory to the objective of Article 14(c). An Indo-Canadian majority rejected the challenge on 5 March 1956.[79] Under Law 10/59, military courts were set up with still greater arbitrary powers from which no appeal was possible. The operation of this law was to supersede all other laws of the RVN.[80] The Canadian ambassador declared that the law was simply a necessary response to 'the policy of murder, terror, and intimidation pursued by subversive elements.'[81]

The Canadian ambassador blocked Polish attempts to have the ICSC criticize RVN acquisition of a research reactor for the University of Dalat.[82] He also denounced all DRVN charges of repression in the south and blamed Hanoi for trying to use the ICSC to protect assassins.[83]

Despite Indo-Canadian efforts to facilitate US-RVN military assistance, the insurgency in the south spread quickly. The Diemist forces were not popularly rooted at all. Canadian officials began to urge that the subversion instrument should be brought forward in the ICSC proper. The Indians were not quite ready.

In April 1960 the ICSC finally considered formally the Legal Committee's long-stalled report on the compatibility of Law 10/59 with the Geneva Agreements. An Indo-Canadian majority on the committee found that: 'The law does not contain any provision designed to discriminate against or subject to reprisals persons or organizations on account of their activities during the hostilities'; and 'Law 10 as such does not attract Article 14(c) or any other Article of the Geneva Agreement.' Polish Ambassador Wisniewski dissented from the report, denounced it as a mere 'political decision' rather than constituting a proper 'legal report,' and declared that it should be sent back to the Legal Committee to be rewritten so as to demonstrate the 'long ... interesting,' and 'voluminous' discussions over the legal ambiguities and doubts inherent to the problem.[84] Erichsen-Brown immediately denounced the Polish delegation for its behaviour in the Legal Committee where, he alleged, 'every conceivable tactic was adopted to avoid bringing in any report.'[85]

The Indian chairman finally proposed a somewhat watered-down draft of the original Legal Committee findings, to which the Canadian ambassador then gave his approval. The final draft reiterated the substance of the committee report but added a reservation that the ICSC could still investigate prosecutions under 10/59 if it felt there were specific infringements of Article 14(c) involved.[86] With a victory on Law 10/59, Erichsen-Brown departed. His conservative bent lingered on among the members of the Canadian delegation.

The new Canadian ambassador, Mr C.J. Woodsworth,* immediately pressed for further action in the Legal Committee. Some twenty-one additional complaints of DRVN intervention were received concerning DRVN-directed acts of sabotage and murder. The prospect for Indian movement on the subversion front seemed excellent.†

On 24 June 1960 Woodsworth delivered a stinging criticism of DRVN attempts to use the ICSC to serve its own ends:

Propaganda campaigns of monumental size, ferocity and hypocrisy have been mounted with the aim of involving the Commission in their presentation. Every petition that reaches our teams is an authorized 'setpiece,' carefully rehearsed and mounted to serve the propaganda claims of the government. In this way the real aims of the petition procedure have been completely frustrated in the North. Not only is the Hanoi government using this procedure to forward its own aims, it is equally and evidently using every means in its power, including reprisals, to frustrate any genuine approach to the teams.[87]

By June 1960 the gloves were off. Regardless of any alleged pressure on the Diefenbaker government by the Kennedy administration to back Western interests more strongly in Indochina,[88] there is no doubt that the Canadians

---

* He was the son of James Shaver Woodsworth, one of the founders of the Co-operative Commonwealth Federation party.

† According to D.R. SarDesai, Indian policy on the RVN's subversion allegations turned decisively in favour of investigation in April 1960, though SarDesai does not know whether the Indian government was responding to new information about DRVN incitement and direction of the insurrection or simply to Canadian persuasion. See his *Indian Foreign Policy in Cambodia, Laos and Vietnam, 1947–1964* (Berkeley, Los Angeles: University of California Press 1968) 198–9.

were already fully 'partisan' in their criticism of the DRVN, and in their implicit defence of RVN interests through highly selective attention to items on the ICSC agenda.

By mid-September 1960 a draft agreement between Ottawa and New Delhi was hammered out concerning procedures and terminology to be employed in processing subversion complaints.[89] Despite Indian fears of an adverse DRVN reaction suggested by General Giap's heavy-handed letter to the Indian ambassador over the matter, New Delhi agreed to go forward. When Diem's forces began to reoccupy the provinces of Kontum and Pleiku in February 1961, after attacks of the previous October on RVN-held outposts and villages by Viet Cong units of sizeable strength, the Canadians responded by redoubling their efforts to get the Legal Committee's report on DRVN intervention in the south expedited.

Woodsworth pressed the Polish ambassador for a specific date when the Poles could assure the presence of a delegate for the Legal Committee's deliberations on the subversion report. The Polish ambassador 'hoped' that a legal adviser would arrive from Poland within three weeks, but he could not be sure. The Canadian ambassador then declared:

To us it is clear that the record of the Legal Committee is well known and that every effort has been made on the part of the Polish Delegation to evade coming to grips with this question. *Representatives of the Polish Delegation appointed to the Legal Committee time and again find it convenient to be absent.* We feel that the latest suggestion of the Polish Delegation is only one more attempt to delay the setting up of the Legal Committee to deal with the complaints ... *this matter has been postponed for two years.* We do not consider that it would be unreasonable if some time limit be set for action on this.[90]

The Indians would not agree to action immediately, however. At this point, as the war in Laos was 'widening' and the guerrilla warfare in the southern zone was intensifying, the Indian chairman operated under the maxim that 'citations are a measure of a failure of this Commission to be effective.'[91] The Indians still hoped to accomplish their objectives through the threat of a citation, not its issuance.

The Indians at this point had few courses of action still open to them, save stern criticism of the parties, unilateral withdrawal from the ICSC coupled perhaps with an appeal to the United Nations, withdrawal in silence, or finally, persisting in the 'good offices' role which they had tried so unsuccessfully to promote thus far. They continued to adhere to the last option.

Canadian attempts to convict the DRVN for border 'control' interference, and for permitting forty to fifty Soviet flights per day into Giam Lam airport without ICSC monitoring, got nowhere. Neither did Ambassador Wisniewski's attempts to pin arms import violations on the RVN, or win citations for American-RVN infractions of the MAAG personnel ceiling of 685 authorized staff. In mid-April 1961, the Poles strongly seconded Hanoi's charge of a 'factual military alliance' between the RVN and the United States. The Canadians replied with the charge of 'aggression from the north.' Clearly the armistice was on the verge of unravelling.

The spring of 1961 was a precarious time for the incoming Kennedy administration. In late April, Kennedy had to accept responsibility for the failure of the Bay of Pigs invasion which the CIA's Allen Dulles and Richard Bissell had thrown together with former Vice-President Richard Nixon's political backing. Towards the end of that month important decisions had to be made concerning the Laotian situation. On 29 April General George H. Decker, army chief of staff (as well as a veteran of the war in the Philippines and a former commander of US forces in Korea, 1957–9) told a meeting of the president and his national security advisers that the United States could not 'win a conventional war in Southeast Asia.' According to Decker, 'if we go in, we should go in to win, and that means bombing Hanoi, China, and maybe even using nuclear bombs.' Air Force Chief-of-Staff General Curtis E. LeMay concurred with Decker and argued for dispatch of troops to Laos with unlimited air support and for going 'to work on China itself,' while letting 'Chiang take Hainan island.' He observed further that 'the worst that could happen would be that the Chinese communists would come in.' LeMay agreed with Chester Bowles that the US was 'going to have to fight the Chinese anyway in 2, 3, 5, or 10 years and ... it was just a question of where, when, and how.' In this classic statement of the rollback program, LeMay argued that this forthcoming 'major war' with the Chinese should be fought very soon because 'the Chinese would have nuclear weapons within one or two years.'[92] Rumours of such bellicose proposals would eventually have a significant impact on Lester Pearson's appreciation of the dangers of the Indochina crisis. Diefenbaker's government, however, appears to have been preoccupied with other matters, or, more probably, had not heard of this dangerous development.

Fortunately, Kennedy rejected the Decker-Bowles-LeMay approach, but part of the package of decisions he made vis-à-vis Laos and Vietnam at this time[93] involved compensating the hawkish elements by virtually eliminating Brigadier General Edward G. Lansdale's role in the Vietnam situation.[94] The

State Department was allowed to insert conditions for American involvement limiting it to intervention within or under the SEATO legal-political umbrella. This was not happily received by Pentagon militants, who wanted a free hand for unrestrained use of American airpower in East Asia.[95] But with Lansdale out, Diem's position was now more shaky than ever because the American counter-insurgency specialist was the Vietnamese president's chief bureaucratic ally in the American government, and the only American patron standing between him and Pentagon-CIA attempts to have him ousted from power.

At this time, US officials also decided to ignore the Geneva armistice provisions. This decision was very warmly received by the Pentagon, which had long been lobbying for explicit repudiation of the armistice control measures. Press reports in Vietnam and North America had prompted Canadian fears that the United States was about to denounce the agreement outright. A meeting at the State Department on 15 May 1961 confirmed these fears. The Americans told assembled British, French, and Canadian representatives that MAAG was going to be expanded unilaterally well beyond any possible ICSC ceiling. Citing the armed attack at Kontum of October 1960 by several hundred DRVN-trained soldiers as an example of the northerners' violation of Article 24 (which prohibited aggressive acts of any kind), the State Department declared that action had to be taken to assist the Saigon government in meeting the new threat. Failure of the ICSC to execute its mandate had contributed to the problem. Hence American officials urged their allies that the ICSC for Laos be 'made effective.'

This was ominous. The Canadians knew full well that the ICSC's perceived 'deficiencies' could not be remedied at this late date without a reconvening of the Geneva Conference. And that was not feasible on short notice, if at all. Accordingly, on 20 June 1961 the Canadian ambassador to the ICSC for Vietnam privately urged the American ambassador in Saigon, Frederick E. Nolting, to take any action possible to avoid explicit repudiation of Articles 16 and 17. Officially, Woodsworth noted that Ottawa fully approved of American support for the RVN in principle. Unofficially, he and his senior military adviser, Brigadier J.B. Allan, recommended systematic evasion of ICSC control procedures through sending in military training staff dressed as civilians, and shipping in war material via 'river ports on [the] Mekong' or 'uncontrolled coastal areas.' Items too bulky to ship in by covert methods could be brought in, they noted, for credit against the 'French outshipment' of material in 1954–5. Both Canadians apparently stressed the still relevant deterrent effect of the armistice structure, claiming that the Kontum-style attacks had ceased precisely because the Indians had sided with the Canadians in backing investigation in such matters in principle, if not in actual fact.[97]

In October the Canadian delegation, Saigon, reiterated its advice to Ambassador Nolting and pointedly emphasized that Ottawa could not and would not try to defend an increase in the formally authorized MAAG ceiling of 685. Noting the distinction that the Indian government had not actually 'approved' the doubling of MAAG to 685 personnel in 1960, but only refrained from condemning the increase as beyond the letter of the armistice (an accurate characterization of the Indian decision), Woodsworth and Brigadier Allan expressed their concern that any substantial overt increase beyond the level of 685 MAAG personnel might very well provoke the Indians into ordering MAAG out altogether.[98] The destruction of the Geneva structure would then be inevitable and complete. Nolting accepted the Canadian advice and wrote Washington accordingly. His superiors did not, and Nolting was soon recalled.

The turning-point for the Canadians in the subversion debate came on 13 June 1961. On this day the ICSC discussed an RVN letter of 24 April 1960 which charged the DRVN with violations of Articles 1, 10, and 24 of the CFA. The letter drew attention to the 170 previous letters from the RVN which referred to over 700 specific charges of communist acts of subversion committed between 1955 and 1961. The charges of 'subversion,' according to the Canadian ambassador, were based on a campaign of attack against the RVN of 'such proportions that it has become nothing less than a subversive war conducted openly against the Republic of Vietnam.'[99] Woodsworth read out excerpts from Radio Hanoi broadcasts urging a more vigorous approach to the campaign of assassination in the south. He then read out the four main points of the Legal Committee Report of January 1956, which established the IC's competence in dealing with allegations of espionage, sabotage, and subversion. Woodsworth at last proposed, and Indian Chairman Gopala Menon added his support to, Decision 610 of the ICSC. This decision reaffirmed the Legal Committee findings of January 1956, noted the 'increasing number of complaints concerning acts alleged to be abetted by one Party against the other which may be detrimental to the peace and security of Vietnam,' and directed the secretariat to dispatch copies of the statement to the parties.[100]

Events leading up to the *Special Report* were rather tangled, but may be simplified to the following essentials. The Indian delegation continued to refer subversion allegations to the Legal Committee. The insurrection continued to expand in the RVN. American assistance to the RVN also continued to expand. By November 1961, a crisis was clearly at hand. The ICSC could no longer pretend that peace and order prevailed in Vietnam.* The number of American military advisers approached 1,100. On 11 December two US helicopter companies with 400 additional unauthorized personnel arrived. By the end of 1961 the final cards had to be played.

Mr Parthasarathi had the misfortune to chair the most acrimonious of all the ICSC meetings on 2 February 1962. This was the moment of truth for the new Canadian ambassador, Frank G. Hooton, who had recently arrived from his post as counsellor at the Canadian Embassy, Bonn. The Legal Committee had not been able to finish its work on the subversion allegations because the Polish delegation had continued its tactics of delay and obstruction. When the ICSC considered DRVN allegations that the RVN was being transformed into a 'military base' for the United States, the Polish commissioner made the mistake of declaring that the ICSC should move to support the DRVN allegation immediately, that there was 'no reason for delay.' Hooton seized on the phrase to recite a quite incredible list of Polish evasions of attendance of Legal Committee proceedings. From here, discussion degenerated into open recriminations.

Throughout March and April 1962 the ICSC discussed the reports of the massive inflow of American armaments into the RVN. The Polish delegation concentrated heavily on the constant increase in American personnel in the southern zone as well. The Canadian ambassador unceasingly argued that the introduction of American troops had to be seen in the context of the continuing DRVN effort to subvert the RVN.[101] While the IC proper was accumulating the data necessary for a 'final citation' against the RVN under Articles 16 and 17 for participating in a 'factual military alliance' with the United States, the Legal Committee was just as busy drawing up the majority report indictment (the Polish delegate continuing to absent himself from the discussions) of DRVN intervention in the southern zone. By 2 June 1962, the *Special Report* to the Geneva co-chairmen was ready.

Unlike the Poles, the Canadians agreed with the entire Indian draft of the report, with only one minor exception. Hooton registered Canadian disagreement with paragraph 20 which labelled the then-obtaining state of US-RVN relations as a 'factual military alliance,' but his objection was limited

---

*   Bernard Fall demonstrated in 1958 that there was a very high correlation between the timing and location of complaints to the ICSC for Vietnam by the DRVN authorities and the incidence of anti-governmental rebel activity in the southern zone as recorded in the RVN press and non-secret government reports. He declared: 'The conclusion is inescapable that there must be some coordination between the rebels and the North Vietnamese government.' See Bernard B. Fall, 'South Viet-Nam's Internal Problems,' *Pacific Affairs* XXXII, 3 (Sept. 1958) 241–60, esp. 255–6.

to the confines of the ICSC itself. Said Hooton: 'we do not consider that military assistance which is limited both in scope (advice and materials) and in time (duration of the North Vietnamese aggression) constitutes a military alliance in the normally understood sense of this term.'[102] The expanded American involvement, now fully acknowledged by the Canadians, was due entirely to DRVN aggression against the South Vietnamese government. The American violation of the MAAG ceiling of 685 began only in late 1961, in response to an enormously expanded campaign of subversion in the RVN.[103] In short, the Canadian declaration in the ICSC contained, in summary form, the essential argument of the Canadian minority statement which would be incorporated in the 1965 *Special Report* to the co-chairmen.[104] A new consensus image of the Vietnam conflict based on conservative perceptions and principles had fully congealed by mid-1962.

THE PARTISAN COMMISSION AND THE ERA OF CONSERVATIVE ASCENDANCE

On 8 April 1960 Commissioner Erichsen-Brown addressed the ICSC concerning the RVN's proposal to move ahead with a doubling of MAAG. His remarks carried a wider significance.

The Commission has a delicate task to perform to ensure that the balance of forces in Indo-China, either established in 1954 under the Cease-Fire Agreement or contemplated by the Geneva Agreements at that time, is not upset. Since 1954 there has only been one occasion when the balance of forces was in fact seriously upset. This occurred in 1956 on the occasion of the withdrawal of approximately 150,000 troops of the French Union Forces. Those of us who have reviewed the history of our Commission will appreciate with what anxiety the whole problem created by the withdrawal of such a large number of troops in 1956 was faced, particularly as the withdrawal took place prior to the reunification of Viet-Nam.

According to Erichsen-Brown, the sole purpose of the Geneva Agreement was to achieve a 'lasting peace in Indo-China.' French withdrawal in 1956 had threatened the 'delicate balance of military strength.' It had created 'a vacuum in the South' and 'anxiety, if not actual fear.'[105] The purpose of the commission was to try to secure an equilibrium of force in Indochina, not merely interpret the law of Geneva. 'My general view also would be that the Commission must in pursuit of the objectives of the Cease-Fire Agreement, pursue a flexible and intelligible position from time to time in reference to the facts as they exist. The Cease-Fire Agreement must always be applied to the facts as they exist."[106] For this reason the Canadian ambassador strongly supported the expansion of MAAG. Assassination, sabotage, and intimidation were rampant in the south. This had to be taken into account:

The most important single fact in any political appraisal of the proposal which is before us, is that there is no comparable situation in North Viet-Nam. It is not necessary, nor perhaps desirable, to compare the efficiency of the two regimes in North and South Vietnam, which to my way of thinking have many similarities. However, there does not appear to be any organized subversive activity in North Viet-Nam directed against the Government in Hanoi by the Government in Saigon. This single [fact] speaks volumes, so to speak, in favour of the basically defensive, and non-aggressive character of the South Vietnamese proposal ... our initial reaction to this situation is one of regret that it has arisen, and regret also over the policies of the DRVN which have, in our view, caused it to arise.[107]

In opposing this interpretation of the Geneva armistice, the Polish ambassador stressed that 'Geneva 1954' had involved more than the restoration of peace in Indochina. It had been an 'expression of victory over colonialism' and had opened up 'possibilities for the reunification of Viet-Nam.' Legitimizing MAAG's increase was bad, because it was contrary 'to the growing trends toward the easing of international tension.' Legitimizing the increase according to Erichsen-Brown's line of argument* would be disastrous. It would open the door to the replacement of the entire French Expeditionary Corps by the US forces.[108]

The Indian delegation formally refused to accept Canadian logic on the relevance of the subversion problem in coming to a decision. Subsequent Indian actions implicitly acknowledged it. Chairman S.S. Ansari's 'compromise' declared that the proposed increase was not prohibited by Article 16. The withdrawal of 546 French training instructors was said to be a factor that could not be ignored. According to Ansari, the purpose of Chapter 3 of the Geneva Agreement was 'to freeze the military potential of the two zones of Viet-Nam at the level existing at the time of the Cease-Fire.' Because the proposed increase left the number of foreign military instructors 'below the total ... present in South Viet-Nam as of the date of the Cease-Fire, it cannot

---

* Erichsen-Brown had argued that US troops were eligible for 'rotation' under Article 16 because once the French were no longer a party to the CFA by virtue of withdrawal, French troops ceased to be 'domestic' and became 'foreign.' Article 16 could therefore not be applied literally, and the provisions of the article should be extended to cover all foreign troops in Vietnam at the armistice. ICSC Vietnam, *Minutes*, 571st Meeting, 8 Apr. 1960, pp 27–8: DEA files, 50052-A-40, vol. 40

be argued that the action ... will constitute a violation of the spirit or letter of the Geneva Agreement.'[109] Polish fears that the Indo-Canadian decision might open the gate to wholesale replacement of the FEC were, he said, 'somewhat academic.' Within three years there would be some 15,000 US 'advisers' in South Vietnam. In seven years, over 500,000 troops.

The Indians always claimed to be merely interpreting and applying the 'law of Geneva.' The interpretation and application were clearly biased in favour of the south between 1956 and 1962. Such bias was partly concealed by the imprecise and contradictory provisions of the 'law' they were interpreting. But it is patently clear that New Delhi, had it so wished, could just as easily have read the ambiguous text to favour Hanoi. Polish-DRVN interpretations of the armistice text were, in many instances, equally if not more persuasive than the Indo-Canadian 'compromises' that were rammed through the commission.

Indian judicial policy-making favoured Erichsen-Brown's conservative logic in 1960: an equilibrium of force was seen to be important. But New Delhi could not afford to be seen to be visibly aligned with Western interests in Indochina; hence the careful avoidance of anti-communist rhetoric (Indians never used the word 'subversion,' for example), and the highly skewed record of 'citations' against Saigon. The *appearance* of non-alignment in Indochina had to be sustained, although its substance had been cast aside in the spring of 1956 with Indian acceptance of Diem's defiance of elections. The advantage of this admittedly duplicitous but politically defensible approach was that Indian options were kept open in the event that the balancing operation failed. By 1964 it was clear to most Indians that the South Vietnamese experiment was not going to succeed, and a reversal in policy orientation was now appropriate. Because they had not visibly compromised themselves by providing for 'legitimate' military assistance to the RVN between 1956 and 1961, the shift in Indian policy in favour of Hanoi remained feasible. Thus, Canadian irritation and frustration with the Indians grew, not as a result of events in the 1956 to 1962 period, but rather in response to India's foreign policy reorientation after 1964. Many Canadian officials, especially conservative articulators, felt betrayed.

Partaking in the balancer phase of the ICSC's operations markedly contributed to the ascendance of conservative policy axioms in the Canadian policy community. Table 1 presents eight aspects of attitudinal differentiation within the policy community and depicts how the effective policy consensus shifted between 1956 and 1962. The most critical shift concerned the redefinition of departmental understanding vis-à-vis the Geneva Agreements. The

TABLE 1
The shift in fundamental attitudinal premises of the operational consensus in External Affairs concerning Vietnam policy-making 1954–62

Issue in controversy	Left-liberal premises	Liberal-moderate premises	Conservative premises
Highest priority objective	Peace preservation through the implementation of the original settlement	Emphasis on peace before anti-communism, especially where West was vulnerable; sustain the armistice by doing what is politically necessary	Peace through containment and non-appeasement of aggression; peace through the maintenance of a balance of force in Indochina
Perception of the Geneva Agreements	A 'package deal' that should be respected both to secure peace in Vietnam and to keep Laos and Cambodia non-communist	The FD may be 'separated' from the armistice to serve containment objectives, but only if such separation carries with it no serious risk to the nuclear peace	The FD is a non-binding expression of hope; the armistice's 'loopholes' should be exploited to assist the RVN in maintaining an equilibrium of force in Vietnam
Legitimacy of the RVN government	The refugee issue was blown out of proportion and Diem reneged on the electoral commitment while benefiting directly from the CFA	The refugee exodus helped Diem politically but his government was not very popular and seemed unable to prevent communist penetration and subversion	Diem's aid to the refugees showed him to be worthy of support as did his success in putting down the dissident sects
Legitimacy of US-Canadian military and economic aid for Diem's government	Economic assistance is legitimate but ill advised; military assistance still more so, though MAAG might be technically legitimate	Token aid is a politically appropriate move, especially after mid-1956, but of doubtful status vis-à-vis the Geneva Agreements, particularly for an ICSC member state	Maximal assistance is morally, politically, and strategically warranted; a partisan aid policy by Canada would still be consistent with its Geneva undertakings

DRVN activities in the southern zone 1955–62	Morally understandable given US-RVN actions in overturning the electoral settlement called for in the FD –o–o–o–o–	Amounted to 'aggression' which was prohibited expressly by the CFA but should not be denounced if denunciation risks Indo-Canadian collaboration –*–*–*–	Totally illegitimate; constituted breaches of the CFA; denunciation appropriate regardless of costs for Indo-Canadian relations
RVN persecution of communists	The scale of the campaign demonstrated how widespread was the opposition to Diem's rule in the countryside –o–o–o–o–	Inevitable, but repugnant in its excesses and no guarantee that peace would be restored in the RVN –*–*–*–	Totally justified by DRVN-instigated acts of sabotage murder and intimidation
Probability of successful American intervention	Little prospect for success since the DRVN leaders seemed to command the support of most nationalists; intervention brought with it a grave risk of nuclear conflict –o–o–o–o–	Might succeed but 'adventurers' in the US government had to be restrained to minimize the risk of nuclear war –*–*–*–	Necessary and correct response though risky; but 'appeasement' would invite further 'salami tactics' by the communists
Legitimacy of a partisan defence of RVN interests in the ICSC	Withdrawal preferable to opposition to the DRVN and the Geneva Agreements –o–o–o–o–	A tactic of last resort; better to cultivate Indo-Canadian harmony; after 1956 the only way to help 'keep the peace' through 'holding the line' – the 'balancer' rationale –*–*–*–	Justified by Polish-DRVN collaboration and Indian opportunism

Departmental operational consensus: 1954–5: –o–o–o–o–; 1961–2: –*–*–*–

252 In the interests of peace

marginalist left-liberal view ceased to be relevant at all. Peace through containment as the prime imperative of Canadian policy meant that the conservatives' legally persuasive interpretation of the essentially hortatory character of the Final Declaration gained ground. The view that the Geneva armistice attempted to stabilize a balance of force between the two zones also gained ground. This latter policy belief had originated as the implicit, logical underpinning of the Indo-Canadian entente between 1956 and 1962. Five to six years of central operational relevance had legitimized the 'equilibrium of force' premise.* When the Indians realigned after 1964, their move probably was seen even by many Canadian liberal-moderate articulators as a 'betrayal of the Geneva essence,' because now the Indians seemed to favour the victory of one side, not the quest for peace as embodied in the late 1950s balancer entente. Only departmental left-liberals such as Escott Reid and Chester Ronning were able to put Indian policy into perspective. They saw it correctly as a reversion by New Delhi back to India's *original* policy of accommodation of Hanoi's legitimately nationalist ambitions.

The Indo-Canadian 'special relationship' did not founder because of the 'Americanization' of Canada's Indochina policy, as some would argue. It foundered because Diem and Diem's successors failed to build a politically viable regime. The RVN's failure ruptured the rationale for a balancer approach, and set Indian and Canadian policy objectives in antagonistic relation. Many Canadian conservatives, embittered by the DRVN's duplicity and inhumanity on 14(d), and repulsed by what they saw as expansionist, totalitarian tyranny in the north, were unable to forgive their Indian opposites for New Delhi's new 'bargain with the devil.' Canadian left-liberals knew that their conservative colleagues were expecting too much of Indian leaders. India, as Michael Brecher has emphasized,† must share a continent with both of the communist giants. The need for accommodation is therefore an ever-present fact of life that no responsible government in New Delhi can ignore.

The principal policy concern animating both Canadian and Indian thinking throughout the partisan phase of ICSC operations was securing and stabilizing the peace in Vietnam. Their balancing approach had facilitated RVN military improvements, but without provoking a formal break with the Geneva structure by Hanoi. In this respect their approach was a significant

---

* See figure 5 for a schematic representation of the shift 'rightward' and 'downward' by the operational consensus within DEA concerning Indochina policy.

† Michael Brecher, *Nehru: A Political Biography* (London, New York, Bombay, Toronto: Oxford University Press 1961) 212–13

FIGURE 5
Schematic diagram of the two-stage tendency shift in the
Department of External Affairs operational consensus 1954–6 and 1956–62

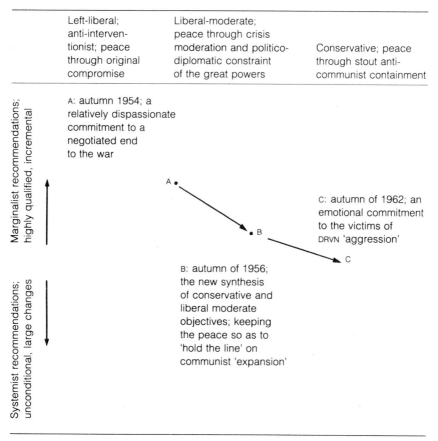

Fundamental value commitment

| Left-liberal; anti-interventionist; peace through original compromise | Liberal-moderate; peace through crisis moderation and politico-diplomatic constraint of the great powers | Conservative; peace through stout anti-communist containment |

Marginalist recommendations; highly qualified, incremental

A: autumn 1954; a relatively dispassionate commitment to a negotiated end to the war

A

C: autumn of 1962; an emotional commitment to the victims of DRVN 'aggression'

B

C

B: autumn of 1956; the new synthesis of conservative and liberal moderate objectives; keeping the peace so as to 'hold the line' on communist 'expansion'

Systemist recommendations; unconditional, large changes

political and diplomatic success. It was significant because by helping to strengthen Saigon a military stalemate was preserved in the south until 1959–60. The Geneva peace structure as applied by Indo-Canadian diplomacy materially contributed to the *postponement* of the resumption of the conflict between the communist and anti-communist elements of Vietnamese society and, still more important, the postponement of direct conflict between Hanoi and Washington. In view of the fact that Washington policy-makers seemed ever more determined after 1955–6 not to risk the loss of 'free Vietnam' to communism, this was a notable achievement. United States intervention prior to 1962–3 could have been 'massive' in only one way: the application of tactical nuclear firepower. American willingness to cross the nuclear threshold, even at the risk of war with China, was only too evident (as the Decker-Bowles-LeMay position in early 1961 makes clear). There were, to reiterate, no marine or army divisions to send into combat in Vietnam prior to the Kennedy administration build-up of conventional force strength in 1962–3.* For this reason, Indian and Canadian policy towards the ICSC during 1956–62 must not be considered to be a lengthy example of 'complicity' in American anti-communist interventionisn. In fact, it was a politically sensible response to a complex, dangerous, and ongoing crisis. The peace of Indochina was not secured by Indian and Canadian actions, which to be sure helped to pave the way for 'Lyndon Johnson's war.' But the *nuclear peace* of Asia may have been saved by the balancer entente. And because concern about sustaining the nuclear peace had long been both an Indian and Canadian priority, the Indochina policy of these two middle powers must be judged as a significant, if only partial, success.

---

* Arthur Schlesinger asserted that when Kennedy assumed office in 1961, he 'was appalled to discover ... that if he sent 10,000 men to Southeast Asia, he would deplete the strategic reserve and have virtually nothing left for emergencies elsewhere.' At that time there were only eleven combat-ready army divisions in total, most of them committed to duty in Europe, South Korea, and the mainland US. See Schlesinger, *A Thousand Days* (Greenwich CT: Fawcett 1965) 295.

9

Constraining Lyndon Johnson 1963–6

the root dilemma of our time is that if the quest for peace turns into the sole objective of policy, the fear of war becomes a weapon in the hands of the most ruthless; it produces moral disarmament.

Henry Kissinger, *White House Years*, 1979

THE CONSERVATIVE CONSENSUS AND THE PHILADELPHIA SPEECH

To date, the logic of the Canadian contribution to the so-called peace-feeler diplomacy between 1964 and 1968 has nowhere been adequately recounted. The approach followed by Pearson and Paul Martin during the two Pearson ministries has drawn the most searing criticism.[1] There was a logic behind the government's policy, but was it entirely or even primarily self-serving?

Canadian policy entered this period with a distinctly conservative cast to it. Publicly, both in speeches and in the two ICSC interim reports issued in 1962 and 1965, the Canadian line on the Vietnam war reflected a deep conviction that South Vietnam was the victim of 'aggression from the north.' Furthermore, there was a uniform assumption in most Canadian articulations on the war that the United States intervention was derived from the most high-minded principles. In many forums, Pearson claimed that the US was engaged in 'peacemaking' or 'peacekeeping.' Canadian governmental co-operation in furthering the image of the war preferred by the Washington policy élite was unreserved during this period. Gone was any sense of ambiguity or ambivalence concerning the origins of the conflict or the feasibility of partition. Was Canadian policy as unidimensional as it seemed? The answer, quite simply, is 'no.' Other logics were at work in the shaping of policy. Public uniformity in opinion masked private diversity.

Pearson's role in the framing of policy during this period was central. Foreign policy generally was not something that the prime minister discussed widely in Cabinet. He preferred very much to keep foreign affairs under the direction of himself and his secretary of state for external affairs. Pearson's views thus carried even more weight than they did in 1954–7 as a factor in the formation of policy.

Pearson had little confidence in Lyndon B. Johnson. His memoirs contain numerous explicit and veiled references to concern that Johnson would not be able to cope responsibly with the North Vietnamese challenge to American power.[2] Johnson, Pearson knew, was a foreign affairs neophyte: he had been thrust into the most critical political office in the Western world with precious little experience in international politics. From various conversations (which included one personal assault by Johnson on the prime minister), Pearson concluded that Johnson was earthy to the point of crudity, emotional to the point of irrationality, and needful of respect and affection to the point where its perceived absence generated moodiness and histrionics. In view of Johnson's personal instability, and the wider instability of the entire Washington arms community, Pearson judged that it was essential that Johnson be given sympathetic understanding for American problems as Johnson saw them, and that US determination to prevail in Indochina be accurately communicated to the government in Hanoi. Pearson therefore chose to underline Canadian credibility as a sympathetic ally and to employ the ICSC link in any way possible to facilitate a negotiated stand-off between the North Vietnamese and the Americans. His concessions to obtain these objectives involved serious damage to Canadian national honour, according to left-liberal systemist critics. These same critics claim that in return for the sacrifice of national integrity nothing was achieved. Such categorical judgments may involve an unwarranted overstatement of the costs, and a refusal to acknowledge genuine benefits that *may* have flowed from this policy.

The fabric of peace in Asia was still quite delicate in Asia, at least until 1966–7. Although the concept of preventive war vis-à-vis the Soviet Union had gone into steep decline, there were still elements in the Pentagon and the Congress who believed in the inevitability of war with China. On the theory that such a conflict was inevitable, they argued that it should be faced sooner rather than when China would have obtained nuclear weapons. The liturgically bellicose term 'rollback'* had disappeared altogether with the passing of John Foster

* An apt phrase used by Henry Kissinger in *White House Years* (Boston, Toronto: Little Brown 1979)

Dulles. The enthusiasm for scoring tangible victories over the communists did not disappear because it found a new focus: China's nascent nuclear capability. Similarly, although the use of domino rhetoric declined, the invocation of domino policy logic in the guise of the doctrine of 'alliance credibility maintenance' remained typical in American strategic debates. Concessions were not to be made anywhere along the communist periphery for fear that it would start a crumbling process by eroding all allies' morale and their will to resist – thus fuelling communist expansionary ambitions all the more.

Throughout the 1960s, Canadians held to their traditional Eurocentric emphasis in setting strategic priorities. Ottawa still favoured accommodation of Chinese interests and consistently argued against any provocative or destabilizing challenges to vital Chinese interests by US national security planners. This is not to say that Canadian advice actually influenced US policy: it is probably impossible to know with any confidence to what extent, if any, Ottawa's opinions shaped the attitudes and policy recommendations of critical actors in Washington. Nevertheless, it can be said that the character of Canadian counsel was responsibly prudent and moderate, supporting containment and eschewing confrontation. Canadian liberal-moderates, as always, had two broad options vis-à-vis Washington: the conventional tactic of quiet persuasion and constructively moderating influence, or the more feared method of confrontation and attempted manipulation of American public and élite opinion.

The first avenue, referred to by advocates and critics alike as 'quiet diplomacy,' held the promise of an ongoing stream of information concerning American intentions and probable action in major crises. For Pearson it meant inter alia the possibility of forewarning of any major American moves which might lead to nuclear confrontation. On the basis of this factor alone Pearson seems to have been willing to compromise the moral and political image of Canadian policy to a fairly substantial extent. He was certainly willing to risk criticism for collaborating in American imperial scheming to secure some 'early-warning capability.' Personal contact was important. The Canadian prime minister was determined to be seen always as an ally by the American president. Without a fundamental element of trust in Canadian-American relations, Ottawa would be left in the dark if and when the most significant decisions about war and peace were being made. The tactical rationale of such an approach has been succinctly summarized by the conservative Marcel Cadieux, who said of Canadian diplomacy: 'Our chances of influencing the policies of the great powers depend not alone upon our relationship with them, but upon the soundness of the commentaries we can put forward; and our influence can increase precisely to the extent that we can, on occasion, bring to light a policy corresponding not only to our peculiar interests but also to the interests of other powers.' Similiar advice is implicit in John Holmes's comment concerning the trade-off between ethics and influence: 'There are bound to be situations in which a country, either in its national interest or out of moral conviction, must refuse to go along. The world, however, will proceed on its course regardless. Jumping off a ship can be a grand gesture, but one is apt either to drown or end up permanently on an atoll.'[3]

PEARSON'S PHILADELPHIA SPEECH

Pearson followed this approach by arguing for 'caution and moderation' in US policy in Indochina.[4] He publicly declared that American objectives in 'saving' the Republic of Vietnam were 'honourable' and 'neither mean nor imperialistic.'[5] He believed that American Vietnam policy was made by 'men of goodwill' who were 'as peace-loving as we [Canadians] are.'[6] These remarks were neither naïve nor sycophantic. They were, in fact, rhetorical advice to a harried, insecure president who was daily confronted by advice for unlimited aerial warfare against North Vietnam.

At Temple University on 2 April 1965, Pearson became the first head of government among the NATO allies to publicly call for restraint in American bombing practices in Vietnam. But in the same speech he also referred to American actions in Vietnam as an exercise in 'peacekeeping and peacemaking.'[7] He accused North Vietnam of committing aggression against the RVN through subversion tactics.[8] He then asserted:

I am not, of course – I would not dare [sic] – propose any compromise on points of principle, nor any weakening of resistance to aggression in South Vietnam. Indeed resistance may require increased military strength to be used against the armed and attacking communists. I merely suggest that a measured and announced pause in one field of military action *at the right time* [emphasis in original] might facilitate the development of diplomatic resources which cannot easily be applied to the problem under existing circumstances. It could at least expose the intransigence of the North Vietnam government if they remained intransigent ... Both sides should examine the substance of a possible, rather than a perfect, settlement.[9]

Finally, having made the case for the now fused liberal-moderate and conservative tendencies in Canadian policy, Pearson ended on a strongly left-liberal note by heaping praise on the American offer to help in the post-war reconstruction of Indochina. With 'spectacular' international development assistance to both sides of the conflict (as in the discontinued UN-directed Mekong River Basin Project), both parties might be happily diverted to developmental competition: 'With that kind of great international development project, with a cease-fire followed by political negotiations, with the countries in the area given an international guarantee of neutrality [no talk of Locarno here] and an assurance of continued aid for peaceful development, then the danger, destruction and distress of the present hour might be replaced by peace, hope and progress.'[10]

It was not coincidental that this major policy speech by Pearson should embody policy elements emanating from each of the three policy tendencies in the department. As a whole, the Temple University address affirmed strong conservative support for American policy in Vietnam with but two liberal-moderate qualifications: an injunction against any acts which might lead to 'uncontrollable escalation,' and a warning to avoid policies or actions which could not encompass a 'face-saving' retreat by Hanoi from its campaign of subversion.[11]

Lyndon Johnson's adverse and grossly impolite reaction to Pearson's speech has been treated at length elsewhere.[12] But after the physical assault and the 'sulphurous language,' there was much substantive discussion at the Camp David meeting of 3 April 1965. When Johnson's anger had subsided, he proceeded to tell the prime minister 'with great vehemence' and 'many short and vigorous vulgarities at the expense of his opponents' that there were three approaches to Vietnam policy under consideration. The first and most 'hawkish' approach, strongly advocated by General Curtis E. LeMay (the former head of Strategic Air Command, and by then the air force chief of staff), was still a genuine option. Supporters of this approach wanted to 'wipe out Hanoi, Haiphong, even Peking [Beijing], and other Asian communist centres by using the Strategic Air Force: in short, all-out war.' Johnson told Pearson that he had 'been resisting this policy for 18 months and would continue to do so, come what may.' As Johnson described it to Pearson, the second option amounted to precipitate withdrawal from commitments in Asia, a virtual reversion to the 'Fortress America' concept of the early 1950s. The third was the president's preferred choice, a heavier commitment to the South Vietnamese at the existing scale of hostilities. The sheer intellectual poverty of these options has been noted before, but most recently by Henry Kissinger.[13]

Under the third option heavier conventional bombing was to be part of the American response, but constraints were still going to be placed on the bombing. No targets would be assigned 'within a 50 mile radius of Hanoi.'

Civilians would be avoided and so too would legitimate military targets situated close to the Sino-Vietnamese frontier.

Pearson indicated that he was greatly 'relieved' to hear about the constraints which he had not been aware of before.[14] He had earlier indicated to the president that he was convinced that a bombing strategy was intrinsically politically suspect. Canadian public opinion had already started a shift away from support for American action.[15] His diary account for the meeting concluded with the observation that Johnson was 'tired, under great and continuing pressure, and ... beginning to show it.' The president's very emotion seemed to be a sign of deep insecurity about his chosen line of action. Pearson also detected an emerging 'martyr complex.' Thus, he concluded: 'The crisis over Vietnam is going to be a great test for LBJ. I'm not now certain that he is going to be successful in meeting it.'[16] Pearson's perception of Johnson's emotional instability undoubtedly strongly conditioned his response to American policies. Influence with Johnson was critical if the Canadian prime minister was going to have even the possibility of moderating American behaviour. Pearson and other liberal-moderates could hardly stake everything on public pressure on the American government to halt the conventional bombing of the DRVN. The fundamental objective of Canadian policy had to remain the strengthening of sentiment in the US government which sought to avoid actions that were likely to lead to a direct confrontation with communist Chinese forces, or to the unilateral use of nuclear weapons by the United States.

For this reason, despite the severe dressing-down which he had received at Johnson's hands at Camp David on 3 April, Pearson wrote a long letter to the president shortly after his return to Ottawa. Contrary to Peter Stursberg's assessment, the letter was not 'apologetic.'[17] Rather it was a detailed recapitulation of the main arguments contained in the Temple speech. Johnson's reaction at Camp David had convinced Pearson that the president had not read the text of the speech. The letter reiterated Pearson's declaration of support for the 'unselfish' motives behind the American intervention. It broke new ground in noting that Pearson as head of a minority government had to respond politically to growing humanitarian criticism of American policy. If we may believe Escott Reid's coment to Stursberg, this humanitarian sentiment was something Pearson himself supported, though he refrained from making this clear to Johnson at the time. Reid's characterization of the motivation behind the speech is difficult to sustain. In 1965, with only a few months of bombing carried out, the logic behind Pearson's stance was liberal-moderate and political in origin. He did not believe that the bombing was likely to be militarily efficacious. More important, he probably suspected that a prolonged bombing campaign might lend itself to exploitation by hard-line elements in the American government.[18] It would take several more months of very intensive bombing before Pearson and his secretary of state for external affairs were moved to acknowledge tacitly that the bombing was inherently unethical. And this tacit acknowledgment may have been politically rooted to some extent – a recognition that even discriminate, controlled bombing was not politically feasible in North America, even though it might be an effective tool in the battle to contain the 'communist aggressors.'

Charles Taylor described Pearson's Philadelphia speech as 'obsequious in its deference to American war aims,' 'pathetic' in its reference to American peacekeeping and peacemaking, and pointlessly diffident in its suggestion merely of a well-timed bombing pause.[19] Peter Stursberg criticized the speech as a gratuitous and ultimately counterproductive insult to a harried president.[20] Both interpretations are seriously deficient and misleading.

To some extent Pearson had been responding politically (as he indicated in his memoirs) to growing left-liberal sentiment among the Canadian public. He was probably responding to pressure from the left-liberal wing of the Department of External Affairs as well. In the early drafts of the speech there was apparently a considerably stronger criticism of American military policy but this was subsequently toned down or eliminated in the course of extensive redrafting,[21] which had to be done to accommodate the conservative wing of the department and Paul Martin in particular. Because of Pearson's initial acceptance of the early drafts of the speech, Escott Reid saw the speech as being motivated by a basic moral revulsion at American savagery.[22] This is a very doubtful inference to make because Pearson at that time still accepted most of the conservative tendency's perceptions of the origins of the Vietnam conflict. Pragmatically, he also had to accommodate the views of his still conservative secretary of state for external affairs, the lingering conservative attitudes of his cabinet, and the still dominant influence of conservative opinion within DEA. Paul Martin had actually threatened to resign if Pearson gave the 'bombing pause' recommendation. Personal loyalty to Pearson was, he said, the only thing that stopped him.[23]

Pearson's accommodation of the conservative point of view was very large. In criticizing Johnson's means but not his ends, and in reaffirming the charges of subversion and aggression against the DRVN, he was explicitly validating the anti-communist thrust of the conservative perspective. Certainly he articulated the 'peace through international development' formula preferred by left-liberal egalitarians. But that program was envisaged as possible only *after* the North Vietnamese had desisted from their aggression in the south. At heart most liberal-moderates, including Pearson, could not concur completely in the 'aggression from the north' thesis – Pearson's remarks in the Temple address notwithstanding. One of the marks of a true liberal-moderate was the perception of the Vietnam conflict as a civil war. Liberal-moderates could not help but admit that the Americans were at best misguided, incompetent, and at times savagely brutal interventionists. But these same liberal-moderates were far more animated by the fact that the Americans were still the ultimate arbiters of questions of war and peace in the international system. Hence the overriding imperative for a credible alliance relationship with them.

In responding to the humanitarian impulse of departmental left-liberals, Pearson was articulating only a subsidiary element of the left-liberal tendency's 'program.' For the duration of Pearson's tenure of office as prime minister, the dominant thrust of Canadian Vietnam policy supported the containment aspect of American policy. This was necessary if Pearson was going to keep his secretary of state for external affairs and, more important, if he was going to maintain his credibility in Washington as a sympathetic ally in the struggle to defend the 'Free World.'

To charge that Pearson's speech was counter productive because it may have delayed for a few days the bombing pause of the spring of 1965 (it finally occurred from 13 to 18 May) simply misses the whole intention of Pearson's address and sidesteps the ongoing complexity of the war and American policy-making. The US government was not going to be easily diverted from the air war concept and Pearson seems to have understood this fact clearly, however much he may have been upset by the idea. The Temple speech was in part meant to 'shape the public record' of the Canadian government, to demonstrate its concern for the civilian population of Vietnam. That is why Pearson told Martin that the speech was 'a political act.' But it was also meant to convey serious tactical advice to a president with very little experience in diplomacy and foreign policy. Pearson may have understood even at this early date that a prolonged air war against the north would ultimately drive the people of all the NATO countries away from support of the American intervention. Air war was extremely susceptible to propagandistic distortion. If it continued for a lengthy period, the political basis for the North Atlantic alliance itself might become threatened.

Far more significantly, the prosecution of the air war could be exploited by the 'wild men' of the Johnson administration – the advocates of 'option (1).' 'Preventive war' *was* still a possibility since many American officials, civilian and military, were convinced of the inevitability of a showdown with the communist Chinese. The PRC had detonated an atomic bomb in October

1964. They would have a modest operational force within a very few years. A number of senior American officials privately advocated a punitive attack on the PRC (using conventional or nuclear weapons if necessary) to break communist Chinese capability for supporting insurrections abroad (specifically in Vietnam) and to destroy its nascent nuclear arms industry. In the early and middle 1960s, American officials were convinced that China was the chief cause of North Vietnamese 'aggression.'[24] President Kennedy apparently had ordered a feasibility study for a pre-emptive strike on all nuclear weapons and nuclear production facilities in the PRC.[25] President Johnson even entertained the idea of joint Soviet-American 'preventive military action' against Chinese nuclear weapons production facilities in 1964.* Some of Johnson's advisers like General LeMay would have been happy to commit the 'nuclear castration' of China unilaterally – and the sooner, the better.

Because of Pearson's experience in foreign affairs, he clearly understood that 'crises' were always dangerous because they were the moments when the adventurist element in Washington might gain control of the policy process and 'run with the ball,' just as General MacArthur had done in his drive to the Yalu, and just as the Navy admirals had wished to do in the spring of 1955. The precise timing of Pearson's speech in Philadelphia was probably a sudden decision. The prime minister presumably could have delivered another standard address on the theme of world peace. But three days prior to the Temple speech Pearson had apparently been warned by a very reputable non-governmental contact from Washington that the administration was in the midst of a serious policy debate concerning the tactics to be followed in its campaign of 'coercive diplomacy' in Vietnam. According to this source, one of the options under consideration might very well lead to eventual confrontation with the Soviet Union and the PRC. The maximum objective of the hawk element in Pentagon planning circles appeared to be air war against the PRC's nuclear installations. In view of the recent Soviet move to declare support for Hanoi, the new intensity of air strikes in Vietnam (Rolling Thunder attacks had commenced on 2 March), and given the bombing of the US Embassy in Saigon on 29 March, Pearson's source was not exaggerating at all in deeming the end of March a 'crucial' juncture.[26] The classified documentation of the Pentagon Papers bears out this characterization. Some background on the American policy crises is in order if one is to understand the possible constructive consequences of Pearson's liberal-moderate act of intervention in giving his speech on 2 April.

---

* See 'Bundy Memorandum of Johnson Conversation ...' in John Lewis Gaddis, *Strategies of Containment* (New York, Oxford: Oxford University Press 1982) 210.

Johnson and his advisers were at that very time debating the desirability of, and the policy rationale for, direct American intervention with ground combat forces. On 6 April, four days after Pearson's speech, such intervention was indeed authorized. An alternative 'maximum air war/no ground troops' package sought by navy and air force elements, especially Admiral U.S. Grant Sharp (commander in chief Pacific, 30 June 1964–31 July 1968), was turned down. Part of the 6 April package embodied in National Security Action Memorandum (NSAM) 328 sought to explore the feasibility of obtaining immediate participation of friendly governments (Australia, New Zealand, and Korea) to assist in combat duties in the Republic of Vietnam.[27] The extremely heavy bombing of northern military bases and airfields (especially Phuc Yen field near Hanoi) sought by CINCPAC (ie, Admiral Sharp) was deferred. So too was the mining of the DRVN's port facilities. Both Admiral Sharp and CIA Director John A. McCone argued strongly for maximum air strikes on the DRVN while US forces still had the advantage of surprise, and while northern military installations were still undefended by surface to air missiles (SAMs). On 5 April the first aerial reconnaissance evidence of SAM launch-site construction near Hanoi was forwarded to Honolulu and Washington.[28]

Through Pearson's American source named Secretary of Defense Robert McNamara as the chief militarist in need of restraint through possible Canadian public pressure,[29] McNamara was at this time working hard for President Johnson in an attempt to restrain the dangerously militant ambitions of Washington's air war zealots. McNamara argued for priority attention to the ground war in South Vietnam and a very secondary role to retaliatory attacks on the northern zone. As Franz Schurmann has so ably demonstrated, the decision by Johnson and McNamara to commit American ground troops to the conflict was, paradoxical though it may appear, a commitment to a *less* provocatively bellicose line of policy in Vietnam.[30] Dispatching the Marines to DaNang on 8 March 1965 to protect American bases and personnel led to the subsequent decision of 1 April to employ the marines in actual battle against the National Liberation Front's armed forces 'under conditions to be established and approved by the Secretary of Defense in consultation with the Secretary of State.'[31] McNamara and Dean Rusk were Johnson's bureaucratic allies in the struggle to rein in Sharp, CIA Director McCone, and Generals LeMay (air force), Wheeler (chairman of the JCS), and Taylor (US ambassador to the RVN). General Maxwell Taylor, the sometime ally of Walt Whitman Rostow in preaching graduated escalation and counter-insurgency pacification methods, had switched in 1964–5 to the logic of massive air war as embodied in the original air force/navy rationale for Rolling Thunder. McNamara, who had already fought within his bureaucratic domain to bring the air force and navy under proper civilian control by attacking the growth of Strategic Air Command (he had favoured missiles) and the construction of new heavy aircraft carriers (he favoured missile-launching submarines), was not a sudden convert to the comparatively dovish pro-containment camp within the administration.*

On the same day that Pearson gave his speech, McCone strongly attacked the basis of NSAM 328. He said that it was doubtful that US ground troops would be effective in overcoming the Viet Cong forces and that an attenuated commitment to the air war in the form of a graduated instead of sudden massive escalation of strikes on the north would accomplish little or nothing.[32] McCone rejected the incremental escalation proposed by advocates of measured coercive diplomacy. Such a campaign would merely provoke 'increasing pressure to stop the bombing ... from various elements of the American public, from the press, the United Nations, and world opinion.' Thus, he declared, 'time will run against us in this operation and I think the North Vietnamese are counting on this.'[33] Pearson's speech at Philadelphia after a mere four weeks of Rolling Thunder sorties was immediate proof of this thesis.

Thus Johnson was angry with Pearson because he was at that very moment under great strain in trying to find an acceptable policy compromise between the containment and rollback elements within his own government. Johnson's decisions of 1 and 6 April in approving NSAM 328 pointedly involved the acceptance of McGeorge Bundy's 'sustained reprisal' rationale for air strikes, rather than the Sharp-McCone preference for a rationale premised upon overwhelming pressure on Hanoi to capitulate. The air war now would be limited and carefully controlled. This was a major victory for the moderates in Johnson's administration. It reaffirmed the containment orientation of the US government, protected the administration from any subsequent charges that it had not done enough to save Vietnam (the loss of China syndrome),[34] and limited the opportunities for crisis creation and manipulation at lower levels through tight presidential control of reprisal air strikes.

Johnson was unsure about the ultimate wisdom or feasibility of a limited air war coupled with ground troop intervention (the RVN was again in political chaos). Thus, Pearson's political-diplomatic intervention may have

---

* McNamara's liberal proclivities would be clearly manifest as head of the World Bank in the 1970s. In 1982 he wrote, along with McGeorge Bundy, George Kennan, and Gerard Smith, a plea for the adoption of a nuclear 'no-first-use' pledge by NATO. His strategic thinking always reflected a minimum deterrence preference.

helped to tip the scales in Johnson's understanding of the policy problem in favour of a more restrained prosecution of the war. It should be noted that hard-liners like Sharp retrospectively see Johnson's decisions at this point as inflicting a fatal blow to the cause of victory through air war – the only feasible path for the US to victory in Vietnam.[35] Admiral Sharp may be correct in his ex post facto analysis. But his analytical narrative is incomplete. Massive air war against North Vietnam could very well have triggered Chinese intervention to a degree where victory could only have been purchased through use of nuclear weapons (possibly against the major passes on the Sino-Vietnamese frontier, against the lines of supply and communication extending into southern China, and against the military bases and staging areas in China as well). Both Sharp and LeMay were willing to risk this. General LeMay had stated on many occasions that the atomic bomb was 'just another weapon.'[36]

It should be clearly understood that the Rolling Thunder bombing program, destructive though it was, was nevertheless an extremely *light* response compared to what might have occurred if Sharp, McCone, and LeMay had had their way. These three men were the bureaucratic defenders of the rollback policy current which had been championed by Barry Goldwater in the 1964 presidential elections, and by virtually the entire Republican leadership in the two years leading up to the elections. These were the same bureaucratic elements (mainly air force, navy, and the CIA's clandestine wing) which had already managed to launch the 'secret' air war in Laos in mid-May 1964, and had supported a complementary CIA-administered operation, OPLAN-34A. This latter program was a massive covert war operation that commenced in February 1964.

OPLAN-34A was not limited to coastal harassment, as a quick reading of the Pentagon Papers might suggest. In its original conception it involved the training of 50,000 'elite South Vietnamese special forces troops ... to take the offensive in over-the-border strikes at Communist supply centres and communications routes ... to stop the southward flow of weapons and trained Viet Cong troops along the routes in Laos and Cambodia as well as inside North Vietnam.'[37] For rollback devotees, OPLAN-34A and the 'armed reconnaissance' and 'protective reaction' air strikes in Laos were but steps on the road to the virtual obliteration of North Vietnam through conventional air power. The 'light' bombing of Laos after May 1964 involving T-28 aircraft with allegedly Laotian pilots (many were CIA-introduced Thai) quickly gave way by June to US Air Force F-100 and Navy AD-6 jet fighter-bomber strikes launched from American aircraft carriers in the South China Sea and from Clark Field in the Philippines. The destruction of the Laotian rural peoples by B-52 carpet-bombing was not far off. As Schurmann noted: 'From May 17, 1964 until February 1973, Laos was bombed in one of the most brutal, repulsive campaigns in the history of warfare – "milk runs" over Laos were safe, unlike the more dangerous targets in North Vietnam.'[38] Only the Nixon-Kissinger bombing of Cambodia in the first seven months of 1973 would exceed the Laotian bombing campaign in sheer ferocity.[39]

Pending the public availability of the Department of External Affairs's main decision file for Vietnam for this period, it is impossible to say whether Pearson and the department knew of American covert war activities in Laos. It is doubtful. In any case it is not essential to know the answer to this question, since other publicly available sources indicate that Pearson was gravely concerned about the possibly calamitous instability of Washington's Asian policy. The Canadian government was not in a position to offer detailed military criticism of American policy options. The only avenue available for the exercise of constructively moderating influence was through high-level prsonal contact with the president or senior moderate elements in the American State Department. For this very reason it made sense for Pearson to try to persuade Johnson of the logic behind policies of caution and restraint in his Vietnam decision-making.

The tone of the letter that Pearson sent to Johnson in mid-April as a follow-up to the Camp David meeting was not at all apologetic – nor needlessly deferential (since he had 'sinned' politically by giving the speech on American soil). It was, in fact, a carefully calculated attempt to reinforce desirably moderate behaviour in Johnson and to reassure the president that at least one foreign leader really did understand and sympathize with his predicament. Pearson wrote:

I want you to know that I appreciate, as much as any person could the crushing nature of the problem[s], domestic and international, that you are facing with such courage and wisdom; that Vietnam is only one of these, though the one I suppose, of most immediate danger and stress. I am anxious to help you in this and other matters as the Leader of the Government of your closest neighbour and friend. But Canada is a political democracy too, with an active and often divided public opinion; sensitive that its leaders do not appear to be merely echoes of the United States but anxious I believe, to back up their neighbours when required to do so, as an independent friend should ... May I add that your exposition of the American case for *planned* and *limited air retaliation*, designed to do the job intended, *with a minimum of loss of life and without provocation to China or Russia was reassuring and impressive*. I am grateful to you for it, as I am for your kindness, and for your consideration in speaking to me so frankly last Saturday.[40]

He closed the letter by praising Johnson's Baltimore speech of 7 April, saying that it was 'magnificent,' in particular the president's declared willingness to engage in unconditional discussions and to assist generously in the post-war economic development of Southeast Asia.[41]

According to his memoirs, Pearson did not condemn the bombing of the north as a matter of principle at any point in his discussions with President Johnson. This is significant. He may very well have been directly informed of the American intention to bomb the DRVN when he met with Johnson and McGeorge Bundy in New York on 28 May 1964. And he may very well have responded by indicating 'great reservations about the use of nuclear weaponry,' but also that he 'personally understood' the need to resort to 'the punitive striking of discriminate targets by careful iron bomb [ie, conventional] attacks' should the North Vietnamese refuse to desist in their campaign of subversion in the RVN.[42] Charles Taylor was somewhat chary of accepting these quotations at face value from the diplomatic section of the Pentagon Papers,[43] but then he did not have the advantage of access to the third volume of Pearson's memoirs.

Pearson made the Temple speech out of anxiety that the US government was on the verge of actions which might lead to uncontrollable escalation. He had noted more than once that in Korea the world had missed World War III 'by a hair's breadth,' and that Vietnam seemed likely to involve much the same risk. Rigid moral standards in foreign policy was not a luxury that would stand Canada well in a world where nuclear war always loomed on the horizon. Pearson could not denounce conventional bombing per se and maintain his credibility as a 'realist' ally in Washington debates – whatever he thought privately on the subject of conventional air war. He criticized implicitly the notion of massive conventional bombing by arguing that it could quite possibly trigger Chinese or Soviet involvement. He was reduced to instrumental arguments as the price for an entrée to the range of 'legitimate' policy discourse in Washington. Pearson tried to follow a line of action which, though expedient, was nevertheless politically responsible.

Pearson was no less convinced than Martin that the DRVN authorities were waging an aggressive campaign of subversion in the south. No less than Martin he felt that the southern people were becoming victims in part because of their own political weakness, poverty, and illiteracy, and in part because of the venality, corruption, and sheer incompetence of their American-appointed leaders. Did the southerners deserve to be deprived of real political choice? Not at all. Were the Americans wholly to blame for the dilemma? Not entirely, though they had freely, if unwisely, elected to 'shoulder the burden' of containment in Indochina alone. Were the Americans likely to be forced by the size of their past investment or resources and prestige in the RVN cause to press the struggle to the point of victory? Yes, since American credibility as alliance guarantor and 'Leader of the Free World' was now on the line in an important and probably irrevocable way. Was there any alternative to 'victory' for either side in the conflict? Probably not, since the fundamental objectives of the two sides were mutually exclusive. There was some remote possibility that a return to the original Geneva formula of self-determination through free elections might offer some prospect for a negotiated end (read surrender) to the war. Could the United States hope to achieve its objectives through tactics short of 'massive retaliation' – whether conventional or nuclear? Probably not, given DRVN intransigence.

Just as in the 1950s, Pearson in the 1960s was still quite alert to the paradoxes and ambiguities of the Vietnam conflict. For Pearson, Vietnam was a dilemma for which there was no immediate answer. In this most difficult situation he reverted to traditional style, emphasizing his characteristic proclivity towards restraint, caution, prudence, and patience. The guilty party in the conflict was clearly Hanoi. Here he agreed with Martin's conservative inclinations. But he believed that the consequences of successful 'aggression' were not likely to be as serious as those that could issue from the actions of American adventurists, precisely because he also recognized the truth of the left-liberal claim that the Vietnam conflict was a civil war. The best approach to civil wars was non-involvement. Pearson's China policy had been founded on this principle. However, the US was committed irreversibly by 1965 to the war in the south, and American policy was in the hands of a foreign policy amateur who presided over an executive staffed in part with reckless fanatics. To cope with this problem, Pearson dusted off another old rule of thumb: if the path to peace is not immediately visible, stall for time. The bombing 'pause' was thus his tactic for the moment. Though a very weak response, the proposal, coupled with Pearson's associated message of sympathy and shared values, was precisely appropriate in terms of promoting this highly insecure[44] President's commitment to a series of discrete bombing reprisals rather than an undifferentiated response of 'massive retaliation.'

When viewed in light of the full complexities of the highly unstable policy debate in Washington in this period,[45] Pearson's move appears to have been yet another example of his exceptionally prescient tactical ingenuity. John Holmes's assessment of Pearson as a 'tactical and strategic genius'[46] is borne out by Pearson's subtle approach to Lyndon Johnson's war.

Paul Martin was not the only conservative in the cabinet or the Department of External Affairs to have serious reservations about Pearson's bombing pause recommendation. He was, however, the most visible. Many senior, conservatively inclined officials in the department were undoubtedly just as upset as Martin by the Temple speech. The conservative element had been surprised and overjoyed at the success of American policy in the 1956–60 period in shoring up Diem's RVN. In the conservative view, Diem's very success prompted the covert war launched by Hanoi when it took over direction of the 'liberation struggle' in the south. According to one conservative:

Many people said it did not matter whether communist governments came to power in Indochina, that the domino theory was simply wrong or irrelevant. But that always struck me as very much like people in North America who in the early stages of World War II, asserted that even if the Nazis came to power in London it was no real threat. But that was crazy. And neither was Indochina a matter of indifference to us. Millions of people were preferring to live in conditions of freedom and were not able to do so ... We were there to show when the North Vietnamese did not live up to the terms of the Geneva Agreement. And they didn't of course. They cheated – and that's on the record.[47]

Such proponents of the conservative perspective saw Pearson's speech as an unwarranted sapping of American resolve. They argued like Martin that the speech was foolish and only likely to antagonize the irascible Johnson, that the advice was gratuitous (since Canada had little knowledge of the military complexities of the war and was therefore going to be ignored), and finally that American anger at Canadian criticism might seriously impede Canadian-American relations in other policy areas.[48]

While substantive, these criticisms were in fact rationalizations formulated in liberal-moderate language which masked the real thrust of a solid anti-communist commitment by these same conservatives. Pure conservative opinion argued that the Americans had to be supported in their distasteful task, however inefficiently they executed it. In retrospect one conservative declared: 'The error of the Americans was that they did not intervene in force soon enough. They left it much too late. Intervention and occupation in force would have succeeded and they would have had to put up with two to three years of international opprobrium at most. How long did it take for world public opinion to "forget" Czechoslovakia [1968]?'[49]

Perhaps the best statement of the conservative tendency's perspective under the Pearson ministries is contained in Paul Martin's address to the Commons' Standing Committee on External Affairs of 10 June 1965. This speech, given only some two months after Pearson's Temple address, amounted to a virtual rebuttal of the prime minister's tactical approach as articulated in Philadelphia. Its liberal-moderate phrasing should not be allowed to obscure the basically conservative message Martin was communicating. The affirmations of liberal-moderate concern for promoting channels of communication between the principal disputants, for offering good offices, for working through 'quiet soundings of opinion to see whether there is any common ground on which we can build or help others to build,'[50] and for working 'in the interests of world peace' were sincere. But all these these statements were in a sense liberal-moderate window-dressing for the fundamentally conservative theses of the speech. The concessions to liberal-moderate norms may have been personally rooted since Martin must have had his eye upon the prime ministership at that point. With his shrewd political judgment he must have sensed that one could run for such office only under liberal-moderate colours.

Martin listed Hanoi's Four Points (enunciated on 8 April in the course of a categorical rejection of Johnson's Johns Hopkins initiative) and stressed, quite rightly, the 'uncompromising' character of these demands.[51] He then rejected any sort of pressure tactics aimed only at Washington by saying:

To apply pressure only to those who are susceptible to our concerns is, in my judgement, naive. It is definitely dangerous, and I say dangerous advisedly because the consequences of a refusal to base policy on facts and on a realistic assessment of objectives can only lead to a worse disaster than the one which it seeks to avert. In 1930 this was branded appeasement. We all know only too well where it led us.[52]

True conservatives invariably invoked 'the Munich syndrome.'

Martin went on to accuse Hanoi of 'clandestine but crucially important support from outside' for the NLF in the south. Hanoi was committing 'indirect aggression.' Labelling the internal conflict in the RVN 'a domestic rebellion' to justify a policy of inaction would repeat the errors of the interwar years: 'Aggression is aggression whether it takes place in Europe, in Ethiopia, or in Viet Nam.'[53] The basis of Martin's rapprochement with Pearson was then laid out succinctly:

on the one hand, surrender to Communist aggression only postpones the day when a firmer stand must be taken: on the other, *resistance in exclusively military terms raises the spectre of a wider conflict extending beyond the perimeters of Viet Nam. Both alternatives are unacceptable* and, because they are unacceptable, it is imperative that our best and most determined efforts should be directed toward finding a solution by some other means ... the only acceptable alternative is to negotiate. Our objective is to get negotiations started. We have lost no time and spared no effort in pursuit of this objective.[54]

Martin finally agreed, even if only implicitly, that the American government and its 'peacekeeping' policies in Indochina were at root very dangerous to Canadian and world interests. Washington had the option of transforming the conflict into a mini-Armageddon: Hanoi did not. Therefore, Washington's behaviour had to be carefully monitored, and then restrained if it seemed on the verge of erratic, escalatory drift. But Martin could not accept at all the argument of liberal-moderates with a residual left-liberal tinge which asserted that precisely because Washington was so dangerous it would be better to try to persuade Washington's moderates to withdraw unilaterally. Hence Martin's vigorously explicit condemnation of the 'civil war,' 'domestic rebellion' line of argument justifying non-intervention. Martin wanted the RVN to be 'saved.' He desperately hoped American leaders could achieve this objective without triggering a wider war.

Like DEA's conservative element he strongly supported containment, but abhorred the dangers of a forward strategy. But, like Pearson, he too faced a dilemma since he could hardly ignore the evidence from his contacts in Washington, from Pearson himself, or from the department's liberal-moderate element, that the chief advocates of a stout resistance to 'indirect aggression' in Vietnam were the direct bureaucratic descendants of the 'preventive war-rollback' policy current of the mid-1950s. Though he was coming to this position of highly conditioned and qualified 'support' for American intervention from the opposite direction of the prime minister, Martin's transnational political strategy, like Pearson's, inexorably came to focus upon efforts to strengthen the containment tendency in American foreign policy. Pearson, against his basic opinion of the situation, had to publicly acknowledge that American intervention in a civil war without benefit of any sort of United Nations legitimacy was somehow politically sound. Martin, on the other hand, because of his strong conservative commitment to the principle of collective defence against aggression (an attitude shared in common with most liberal-moderates), found it very difficult to bring himself to the point of tolerating public criticism of how the Americans chose to make their 'sacrifice' in Indochina. Collective defence operations are invariably politically complex and frustrating endeavours.

Martin's fundamental inclination was to give the Americans unqualified support for their intervention on behalf of the RVN regime, while making only the most modest tactical recommendations privately. Pearson was probably prepared to back consciously those lines of military action in Indochina which were doomed to ineffectiveness and which compromised the prospects for the long-term survival of the RVN. Martin was not. In short, Pearson was more deeply animated by apprehensive concern for the risks to Canada of American bellicosity in Asia. He was prepared to sacrifice Asian interests in 'freedom' to Canadian interests in survival, if American incompetence or risk-taking propensity was going to structure the situation so as to put these two objectives in a trade-off relationship. Martin only very reluctantly admitted that the trade-off existed at all. Because of his affective involvement, specifically his sympathy for the plight of the Vietnamese Catholics in the south and his earlier commitment to Ngo Dinh Diem, Martin could not seriously admit that the RVN regime was by 1965 intrinsically illegitimate and unpopular in the eyes of most southern peasants and Buddhists.

Martin agreed with other conservatives that the political support for the National Liberation Front in the south was illegitimate because it was founded upon terror and intimidation. Martin would probably have agreed with the departmental conservative who declared in 1977:

There are two peoples there [in Vietnam]. The Cochinchinese and Tonkinese are quite different. The Provisional Revolutionary Government was never a real political force. They were puppets of the DRVN and the irrefutable proof of that is their quick absorption into the DRVN after April 1975. There are physical and temperamental differences between northerners and southerners. The situation was complex. But we know that Communism was and is bad for the people. The evidence for that is their resort to torture and assassination ... Hanoi did not have the willing allegiance of the people in the south ... They were going to run the country by force. The co-operation of only five per cent of the population would do it. You either accepted them totally or you were out. It's that which I do not like. Fascists order you to follow their rules. Communists force you to believe in them too.[55]

Martin even went so far as to attempt to give an eight-page summary of Vietnamese history from 939 AD to 1962, in an effort to prove that 'the division of Viet Nam is not something created by the West in its own interests, but is something which represents the polarization of Vietnamese political forces in to Communist and non-Communist sectors.'[56] His version of history prior to 1954 was at best dubious. For the period 1954–62 he was on much more solid ground.

The conservative articles of faith which he enumerated included the following propositions: (a) the SVN-RVN was never legally bound to observe the Geneva Agreements, either in whole or in part; (b) the essence of the Geneva 'settlement' of 1954 was a tacit agreement to partition Vietnam by the French and communist Chinese; (c) Diem was legally and politically justified in refusing to consider the 'free elections' proposals when the North was ruled by totalitarian autocrats; (d) the one million refugees from the north in 1954–5 validated Diem's refusal to engage in political talks with Hanoi's leaders and showed that Vietnamese communism had no claim to 'the wholehearted support of the Vietnamese people'; (e) after the 1954 cease-fire and military regroupment the DRVN left behind 'secret caches of armaments and military personnel who shed their military identification and melted inconspicuously into the countryside, ready to organize political action or resume hostilities if necessary'; (f) terror, not the urge for reform, was the source of the appeal of the Vietminh stay-behinds, and the ICSC had accumulated fully documented proof of the murder of 'hundreds of trained and responsible administrators'; (g) and, finally, the political support given to the Viet Cong by southerners was a co-operation based on expediency, not on sincere political conviction.[57]

Martin's address to the Standing Committee was subsequently cited regularly by members of the Department of External Affairs's conservative wing whenever justification or explanation was sought for those aspects of Canadian policy which were supportive of the American intervention. The seven points of the conservative faith were a mixture of proven fact (especially points a, c, d, and e) and ambiguous, highly debatable, and finally unverifiable assumptions (points b, f, and g). Articulators of the conservative point of view such as Martin needed no persuasion that there was aggression from the north. To their way of thinking the ICSC had already established beyond any doubt that there were weapons and personnel being infiltrated into the southern zone. However marginal was the actual volume of material assistance from the DRVN to its NLF 'client,' it was clearly in contravention of key articles of the Geneva CFA (especially Article 24). The memories of DRVN duplicity over Articles 14(d), 16, and 17, and all North Vietnamese policy statements between 1956 and 1964 concerning the need for ongoing 'struggle' in the south left little doubt in conservative minds that Hanoi had fomented and was now directing the insurgency against the hapless, incompetent, and internally divided military clique in Saigon, which was clearly losing its battle for survival.

Pearson and other liberal-moderates could not accept these articles of faith (especially points b, f, and g). As one liberal-moderate put the problem: 'The northerners were the aggressors but aggression is not really the right word.'[58] Pearson appreciated that in one sense Vietnam was 'one country' and that the conflict was truly a 'civil war' in a very real sense.[59] Few conservatives could agree to that. Partly because many hostile questions were already being asked about this politically complex aspect of the conflict, primarily by New Democratic Party spokespeople,[60] the conservative wing knew that it had to work hard to maintain public support for its definition of the situation in Vietnam. All Canadian conservatives like Martin agreed with Pearson that 'it would be insanity to have a nuclear war break out as a result of anything happening in Indo-China.'[61] But for them it would also be a very serious and damaging blow at the structure of peace if communist aggression from Beijing via Hanoi[62] were allowed to go forward unchecked.

It was evidence of the strength of the challenge to the conservative image of the conflict that the secretary of state for external affairs felt impelled to put such a detailed summary of the conservative viewpoint in the public record in mid-1965. He would soon have need of it. By 10 June 1965 Blair Seaborn had already completed his five visits to Hanoi as an 'interlocutor in the interests of peace' – an interlocutor who had conveyed to Hanoi's leadership an implicit threat of air attacks upon the DRVN proper, some six months before Johnson's sustained Rolling Thunder bombing operations actually commenced.

THE SEABORN MISSIONS, JUNE 1964–JUNE 1965: 'DON'T SHOOT THE MESSENGER'

Both Charles Taylor and Peter Stursberg evince concern (and in Taylor's case also indignation) over whether J. Blair Seaborn functioned as an 'agent' of the US government, and whether he truly carried a 'threat' to Hanoi.[63] Their concern is misdirected. Despite Paul Martin's disingenuous (and probably self-deluding) assertions to the contrary,[64] Seaborn was indeed acting as 'the eyes, ears and mouth' of the American government, as Taylor phrased it. And he did indeed convey a reasonably explicit warning to Hanoi's leaders that unless the insurgency in the south was halted, the United States would 'carry the war to the north.'[65] American patience, he told them, was 'not limitless.' This clear-cut threat to the communist leaders could only imply either stepped-up cross-frontier commando raids (already occurring under OPLAN-34A by American and South Vietnamese Special Forces), or a substantial air war campaign against the north – or both.

Martin was correct in saying that Seaborn had not transmitted the entire contents of the American messages to Hanoi, but the deletions seem to have been of marginal significance. In his first meeting Seaborn had not undertaken, for example, to review to Pham Van Dong the dimensions of military superiority potentially available to American and South Vietnamese forces in any overt war with DRVN and Chinese communist armies, nor did he explicitly declare to the DRVN prime minister that 'the decision as to the future course of events in Southeast Asia rests squarely with Hanoi.'[66] In view of the meaty but quite unpalatable content of the rest of the communication these deletions were inconsequential. He did say, however, that the Canadian government did not see military escalation as being 'in anyone's interest,' though if it did occur 'the greatest devastation would of course result for the DRVN.'[67] The word 'bombing' was never used but in light of the regular bombing of communist-held positions in Laos after 17 May 1964, the nature of the threat could hardly have been mistaken by the DRVN prime minister.

Pham Van Dong did not show any significant apprehension about the prospects for his country. His reply was, from a North Vietnamese point of view, relentlessly optimistic and therefore fundamentally uncompromising. Peace could only come to South Vietnam through neutrality 'in the Cambodian pattern in accordance with the programme of the National Liberation Front.'[68] Defeat for the American interventionists was inevitable along any other course. The South Vietnamese 'mercenaries' and the US troops lacked conviction. Urban support for the NLF was growing. Informed American journalists such as Walter Lippmann were now pessimistic.[69] A major war, Dong implied, would trigger assistance from the PRC and the Soviet Union.[70] The closest he came to a negative statement was when he declared that the 'DRVN was very worried by the step-up of the USA military activities in Laos' and upset over 'USA overflights of DRVN territory and of commando raids across the border.'[71] But on the whole, the Hanoi leaders were confident, united, and optimistic. Said Pham: 'We want peaceful reunification, without military pressure. We want negotiation round a table. There must be sincere satisfaction with the arrangement for it to be viable. We are in no hurry. We are willing to talk; but we shall wait till SVN is ready.'[72]

The Americans ignored this part of the message. They did not want to consider any type of coalition government in the RVN in which the NLF would have a role using 'the Laos pattern of 1962 ... as a guide.'[73] American officials had already rejected that option in the summer of 1963 through their withdrawal of support for Diem and his brother. The Ngo brothers at that time had been busily negotiating with Hanoi regarding a possible coalition in which Diem would remain the titular head of government.[74]

In retrospect, if there are grounds for criticism of Pearson and Martin it lies in their failure to press harder on a possible coalition government formula. But it must be admitted that given the state of American policy at this time and the concomitant process of deterioration in the stability of the Saigon government,[75] the prospects for a constructive impact in this regard were virtually nil. In any case the Canadian government still operated under a pro-containment consensus which hoped to preclude an eventual communist victory in the south. Rightly or wrongly, Pearson, Martin, and the still generally conservative majority in DEA thought, as Seaborn told Pham, that any 'coalition would soon be taken over by the Front as had happened in other countries and that other representative elements would suffer or be ousted.'[76] The Czech coup of 1948 still seemed a compelling justification for avoidance of coalitions. Thus former US Assistant Secretary of State William Bundy was not wrong in characterizing Canadian attitudes towards American 'peacemaking' efforts in Vietnam as essentially 'benevolent.'[77]

To begin his second visit with Pham Van Dong on 13 August Seaborn said: 'Mr. Prime Minister can I use the old saying about not shooting the messenger.'[78] The North Vietnamese prime minister was so angry at the recent American 'reprisal' strikes following the Gulf of Tonkin incidents that Seaborn thought he was going to be summarily dismissed after a vitriolic denunciation of American policy. Pham explained to Seaborn that the Tonkin Gulf incidents were in fact part of a vain American effort to win the war, which was being lost in the south by extending it to the north. He said the Americans had made a miscalculation: 'If the USA is thinking of a new Korean war it should realize that conditions are not the same ... If the war comes to North Vietnam, it will come to the whole of Southeast Asia, with unforeseeable consequences ... We do not hide the fact that the people will have to make many sacrifices, but we are in a state of legitimate defence because the war is imposed on us.'[79]

The subsequent investigation of the events surrounding the passage of the Tonkin Gulf resolution would seem to bear out Pham's interpretation. Robert McNamara's version of the incidents was presented on national television shortly after American retaliatory strikes had been ordered. It was both misleading and erroneous. The North Vietnamese had every reason to suspect that the destroyers *Maddox* and *Turner Joy* were part of the commando raids which had commenced along the DRVN's coastline on 30–31 July. The two ships were loaded with electronic equipment capable of interfering with DRVN communications. They were not merely passive listening posts. They regularly intruded on the claimed twelve-mile limit of the DRVN even though the same ships never ventured closer than fifteen miles to the PRC coast. They may have opened fire on DRVN patrol boats without giving any warning shots. American naval authorities knew that the ships would 'be treated as belligerents from first detection' and wired the ships' commanders accordingly. There is evidence that the 'attack' on the destroyers may have been entirely fictitious. Without definite confirmation of an attack President Johnson ordered 'retaliatory' strikes.[80] There were very strong grounds for supposing that the US Navy was intentionally executing manoeuvers so as to provoke a North Vietnamese response. Either the president himself or important minority elements within the government were attempting to manufacture 'incidents' to trigger a wider involvement in the war and direct attacks on the DRVN itself. Johnson turned the incidents to good political effect through passage of the congressional resolution, but the hawkish elements considered this achievement quite an inadequate reward for the enormity of the opportunity.

Officials in the Canadian government were apparently ignorant of what had transpired in the Gulf of Tonkin.[81] It is very possible that the president and other containment-oriented officials in Washington were ignorant of the true facts of the 'unprovoked attack' as well. Accordingly, the Canadians saw no reason to doubt the McNamara-Rusk versions of the 'crisis.' Pearson and Martin naturally enough saw no reason to decline the American requests for any intelligence-relevant data which Seaborn might gather in the regular course of his duties in Hanoi. The information pertaining to population morale, war preparations in the capital, political attitudes of the DRVN leadership, and the like was passed on to the US government. Such information had been regularly transmitted to Washington for many years. There was no reason to break precedent, especially if Seaborn's reports of the steadfast determination of Hanoi's leaders might induce the Americans to reconsider the wisdom of joining battle. Surprisingly, just as in the first visit, Pham indicated that he still welcomed the Canadian interlocutory role – a fact that Martin rightly has emphasized in his subsequent defence of the Seaborn missions.

The last three visits by Seaborn (early in the second week of December 1964, on 4 March 1965, and in the first week of June 1965) were quite unproductive. The 4 March visit may have actually strengthened the position of hardliners in Washington because Seaborn reported that:

primary impression is that Hanoi thus far not seriously concerned by strikes ... which have not seriously hurt it and as USG is not urgently seeking conference it is to Hanoi's advantage to continue to hold back on agreeing to any conference which at this time could only as in 1954 result in depriving DRV of that full victory which it sees in sight as turmoil in SVN continues and pressures on US for withdrawal continue to mount.[82]

This would have been readily useful material for Admiral Sharp and Director McCone. But this is the paradox of functioning as an interlocutor for peace between warring parties: until such time as there is a genuine basis for compromise on both sides, the communications between parties conveyed by such interlocutors are inevitably going to involve implicit or explicit threats, and the passing of politico-military intelligence.

It is probable that such information flowed in two directions. Surely there was a 'price' for access to Hanoi? Martin was quite correct in stressing that Pham wanted the channel kept open. He does not suggest that it was for any other reason than the Hanoi leaders' desire to be able to communicate secretly with Washington. But is it not naïve to suppose that Blair Seaborn and Chester Ronning did not pass on their 'personal' impressions of the state of the policy debate in Washington, information which was as much political intelligence as Seaborn's August 1964 assessment of the internal politics and civilian morale of the DRVN? Ottawa officials were truly alarmed by the continuing high degree of influence held by Pentagon hawks. Is it not likely and reasonable that they passed such private assessments on to Hanoi?[83]

Even if they did not, the Canadian channel would have been valuable to Hanoi as a diplomatic early warning system in the event that the pro-roll-back (and the pro–nuclear-strike) tendency began to gain control of Vietnam policy in Washington. And to those who would think seriously about this subject, it must be clear that it would be impolitic (if not politically impossible) for Canadian officials and politicians to talk openly about this aspect of their diplomacy. However composed and self-confident they appeared to be in their dealings with the Canadian diplomats, DRVN officials could not fail to have been concerned by the prospect of possible atomic strikes on military targets in the DRVN and the PRC. The risk was all too real. At the very least, nuclearization of the war would have triggered direct, massive Chinese involvement in the conflict and that would undoubtedly have led in turn to Chinese domination of the DRVN for many years to come – provided North Vietnam still existed as a 'viable' society.

THE END OF AN ERA

Lester Pearson faced a serious policy dilemma as the end of 1965 approached. The conservative operational consensus to which he had given his blessing over the preceding two and one-half years was now being called into question by substantial numbers of departmental left-liberals. The overt political costs of publicly supporting the American intervention were rising and bound to increase much further. The prime minister's Philadelphia formula of publicly supporting American 'ends' while privately criticizing American 'means' was no longer a stable satisfactory policy compromise for his domestic audience. Pearson knew that if the bombing went on for any extended period it would inevitably provoke a strongly antagonistic public reaction.

He knew also that he would have to accommodate that reaction once it reached a certain critical size. In his Camp David talks and in his correspondence with Johnson thereafter, Pearson's comments in this regard were clearly anticipating the coming storm of criticism in Canada and the United States. In late 1965, Canadian protests against the American intervention were still limited to academics and the clergy. But the opposition ranks were growing. Street demonstrations were in the preparatory stage. Pearson seems to have sensed this.

The prime minister also knew that the war was not going to be ended soon. The military situation for the Americans and their various clients was still precarious. The appearance of DRVN regular troops in the south in 1964–5 did not bode well. The succession of coups in Saigon was undermining what little international credibility the RVN state apparatus still possessed. But the Pentagon's war planners were not likely to give up easily. They would certainly opt for further escalation of the conflict if the only alternative was defeat and dishonourable disengagement. Here was the crux of the policy problem. How long could Johnson be counted on to restrain his military commanders if the situation did not improve? And how long could Pearson's own government continue to support what was bound to become an increasingly unpopular war?

Pearson's conversation at Camp David with President Johnson was of considerable significance in the partial resolution of this dilemma. If Pearson could count on Johnson's declaration of restraint, it would no longer be necessary for the Canadian government to be seen as a wholly sympathetic ally in Washington. There was no longer the same need to monitor Washington's nuclear decision-making process so closely.

The end of the era of the massive retaliation doctrine and its replacement with the doctrine of 'second-strike assured destruction' (which may be dated from the coming to power of the Kennedy-McNamara team) had drastically lowered the risk of nuclear warfare. So too had the creation of much larger conventional forces pursuant to the Kennedy administration doctrine of 'flexible response.' It was no longer necessary to fight 'brush-fire wars' on an all-or-nothing basis. Johnson had shown no signs of breaking with this new doctrinal orthodoxy. After April 1965, it seemed clear to Pearson that Johnson would do everything in his power to avoid use of nuclear weapons, and to avoid the creation of situations where the unilateral use of such weapons might become a military necessity.

After April 1965, the risk of escalation of the war to a level which might trigger communist Chinese involvement or the unilateral application of nuclear weapons to the conflict was still real, but it apparently seemed lower to Pearson. Moreover, the Seaborn missions had established a new role precedent for Ottawa. This new role of 'interlocutor for peace' was quite consistent with the existing ICSC commitment. Pearson and Martin possessed all the requisite elements for a more distanced posture vis-à-vis the American crusade in Vietnam. It ony required some rhetorical and doctrinal renovations to set the government on its 'new,' but in fact quite traditional, policy heading.

Liberal moderation reasserted 1966–8

My hands are of your colour, but I shame to wear a heart so white.

Lady Macbeth, *Macbeth*, II, ii

THE RONNING MISSIONS: CATALYST FOR POLICY CHANGE

At the end of Chester Ronning's first visit to Hanoi from 7 to 11 March 1966, Premier Pham Van Dong told him that 'the Canadians were "men of good will" and while "good will" doesn't matter much, one should use it when one can.'[1] The premier's observation is a fitting epitaph for Canadian 'peace-feeler' diplomacy under the Pearson government.

Ronning's efforts were doomed to failure before they commenced, primarily because neither the Americans nor the North Vietnamese were ready to move towards a political settlement of the conflict. Neither side was ever seriously interested in a genuine compromise which might end the fighting and shift the struggle to the political plane – though this may be said with more confidence about Hanoi than about Washington. There was no plausibly feasible basis for compromise. With 'just war' proponents of a war of national liberation on one side and equally righteous champions of 'no appeasement of aggression' on the other, the room for negotiation was virtually non-existent.[2] Thus one should not view the Paris Agreement of 1973 as a genuine peace treaty: it was in essence a tacit agreement to de-escalate the war through the removal of American ground troops as active participants. Failure to grasp these basic facts precludes an accurate understanding of Canadian policy-making in the years 1966–73.

Hanoi's Four Points of April 1965 and all subsequent negotiating pronouncements by northern officials hearkened back to only part of the Geneva Agreements of 1954: the injunctions against foreign troops in Vietnam, and against alliances by the authorities in either zone with foreign powers (legally binding on the French and Vietnamese communist governments), as well as the non-binding terms of the original political settlement. Never did the northern communists admit that they had aided and directed the insurgency in the south or that this aggressive policy, which was in clear contravention of Articles 10, 14a, 19, and 24, might in some way be ended on a quid pro quo basis.

The US government, on the other hand, *was* prepared to enter into substantive talks provided there was at least an acknowledgment by Hanoi of its military involvement in the south and a concomitant willingness to begin reciprocal cuts in military activities by both sides. Hanoi never would talk on this basis because they were hoping to extract a major political victory (an unconditional bombing halt by the Americans) before sitting down to the negotiating table. It was equally important to Hanoi's leaders that they win substantial recognition from the US and world opinion for the National Liberation Front for South Vietnam (NLF) as an autonomous belligerent in the struggle, and in the maximum program, as the sole legitimate political authority in the south. Hanoi leaders were always determined to rely primarily upon the military instrument in their struggle to unify the country under their control. This policy was the result of one of the 'lessons' the northern communists had learned in 1954: negotiate only from a position of strength, and never rely in such negotiations on great-power allies whose interests will inevitably diverge markedly from one's own. For this obstinate and uncompromising attitude they deserve a significant share of the blame for the repeated failures of international mediatory efforts between 1965 and 1968. It is probable that Henry Kissinger, not revisionist historian Gareth Porter, provides the more accurate portrayal of the North Vietnamese negotiating stance.[3]

The North Vietnamese constantly attempted to resurrect the terms of the Geneva Final Declaration of 1954. In the most dogmatic language, their propaganda unceasingly reiterated the theme that peace could only come through fulfilment of the original 'agreement.' Not coincidentally, as soon as it became clear to the Hanoi leaders that the United States was going to intervene in a large-scale fashion (a perception that dates from the Tonkin Gulf incidents), their immediate response was an attempt to shore up the political status of the Final Declaration through a vigorous effort by the Polish delegation to the ICSC. The campaign collapsed in the face of Indian tradition.[4] Because of the deep ethno-linguistic and class cleavages of South Vietnamese society, any general elections leading to unification would inevitably have meant, just as in 1956, that power would have fallen to those who controlled the largest cohesive power bloc in the country: the leaders of the Vietnamese Workers' party. Thus, Hanoi favoured revival of the original political 'settlement' as contained in the Final Declaration of 1954. The Americans were willing to use the original armistice agreement as a basis for a new cease-fire in Indochina, but they were most certainly never going to agree to reviving the old political settlement concept. An impasse was thus inevitable. Chester Ronning's effort to define some common ground between Hanoi and Washington was destined to fail.

The failure of the Ronning missions was no doubt a contributing factor to Paul Martin's eventual conversion to the liberal-moderate camp within the Canadian policy process. So too was Martin's increasingly direct involvement in the frenzied diplomatic activity surrounding the Indochina crisis. Pearson, being perhaps more realistic vis-à-vis the prospects of the missions and having far less of a personal political stake in their outcome, had no reason for disillusionment when they came to naught. As secretary of state for external affairs, Martin made every effort possible to accomplish his newly adopted liberal-moderate objective: the resumption of talks on an 'unconditional' basis. His manner was irritating to his parliamentary colleagues, who had to endure his masterfully tedious circumlocutions, but Martin was truthful: there almost always *was* some mediatory effort under way of which the Canadian government had knowledge and which possessed marginally better prospects of success if it remained secret. It is also fair to say, however, that Martin was not at all averse to using privileged governmental access to such information in an attempt to silence parliamentary criticism of his government's approach to the Vietnam problem. The preferred strategy of the government was calculated inaction on the security aspects of the Vietnam problem coupled with simultaneous expressions of sympathy for the ultimate objectives of American policy, while executing a low-cost, self-appointed mission of 'honest broker' to the disputants. Like all liberal-moderate responses it was intended to lower the temperature of angry personalities, both at home and abroad – but in this case especially at home.

Pearson, Martin, and senior officials in the Department of External Affairs wanted the fighting stopped in the first instance because it was a major threat to world peace. They also wished to avoid the dilemma of having to choose between active support of the war and overt repudiation of America's interventionary mission. It was unlikely that Canadians would close ranks over Vietnam if it came to a hard choice. Massive internal political division was only too likely.

From mid-1966 through the end of 1967 the Canadian government repeatedly explored the possibilities for creating international support for the concept of a revived Geneva Conference to try to handle the crisis multilaterally. The Indians, Poles, British, and Russians were consulted on many occasions, but an acceptable formula was simply unobtainable.[5] There was in fact much time and much sincere effort devoted to the 'quiet diplomacy' of the Pearson ministry. Such activity also had the very desirable trait of sustaining a degree of Canadian credibility with the American administration as a sympathetic ally. Most conservatives and all liberal-moderates seem to have understood this fact clearly. All of the parliamentary, and a few of the bureaucratic, left-liberals did not care, hoping rather to influence the American Congress through promoting an overwhelming shift in both world and domestic American opinion against American policy.

If the Canadian government generally commanded a modicum of credibility in Washington, Chester Ronning in particular did not. His role at Geneva in 1954 had been highly irritating. At the Laos Conference of 1962 he had pointedly lectured the American delegation on the concrete benefits that the ICSC had conferred on the RVN-American side.[6] His rhetorical style, not dissimilar to John Diefenbaker's sermonizing, was regarded at best as eccentric by US State Department officials. His undisguised sympathy for the revolutionary achievements of the Asian peasant masses left many Americans aghast. So too did his respect for Ho Chi Minh and his contempt for South Vietnamese leaders.[7] Some American officials thought he was a communist.[8] Ronning did little to disabuse them of the notion. He certainly was convinced that the cause of justice lay with Hanoi's leaders.[9] Ronning's attitudes upset more than a few Canadian officials as well. In the process of accepting the briefing instructions for his first mission to Hanoi, Ronning became embroiled in a 'shouting match' with one of the most ardent conservatives in the Department of External Affairs, who had inserted a number of 'stiffly anti-communist' provisions in the text.[10] As a retired official, Ronning obviously possessed more latitude in the execution of these instructions than a regular foreign service officer would have.

The Americans were utterly 'naïve' in Ronning's view because they could not understand Ho Chi Minh's popular appeal in Vietnam. Ronning was also convinced that American China policy was 'the most dangerous point of view ever conceived by any of the great powers towards China.'[11] He had long argued for firm Canadian support for early admission of communist China to the United Nations. He later wrote in 1967 in this regard: 'Peking's membership ... is essential if the objective of the United Nations is to be realized – to settle all international disputes through the United Nations through peaceful means. The longer this is delayed *the greater is the temptation for great powers to make unilateral decisions involving the use of force.* International questions involving peace and war must be referred to the United Nations if chaos is to be averted."[12] Anxiety over the unilateral use of force by the American military was a priority concern for Ronning, as it was for Pearson. But Ronning was left-liberal to the core.

Despite his left-liberal predilections, Ronning managed to attract a sizeable public following among both liberal-moderates and conservatives. John Diefenbaker, for example, seems to have had much respect for Ronning.[13] Indeed, Diefenbaker's own views on the China question may have been strongly influenced by conversations with Ronning when the latter was high commissioner to New Delhi.[14] It was a rare American, however, who could appreciate Ronning's policy logic. To American officialdom Canadians like Ronning were only useful as diplomatic tools. They were not credible sources of advice for the actual framing of policy.

Detailed examination of the classified American record suggests that from late 1965 to the end of 1967 President Johnson was acutely aware of the American military dilemma in Vietnam: the troop levels necessary to contain and ultimately defeat the insurgency were too high to be sustainable politically, while the alternative option of massively expanded air war proferred by Pentagon militants carried with it an intolerably high risk of direct Chinese or Soviet intervention. Unable to devise a low-risk 'winning strategy,' Johnson was also driven to play for time by sending in only enough ground troops to block the collapse of Saigon, while applying only enough bombing pressure on Hanoi to 'signal' American determination to prevail. This approach was undertaken on the theory that 'killing the hostage' through massive air attacks on the north's population and economy (all industry and perhaps the dike system as well, which would have caused hundreds of thousands of fatalities) would destroy communist incentives to de-escalate and negotiate.[15] In short, the containment-oriented policy majority within the American government opted for a campaign of attrition. The choice was ill-starred, however, given the determination of the North Vietnamese to persevere indefinitely until victory was attained. It is also clear in retrospect that the president and his advisers knew that the prospects for success along the chosen path of policy compromise were very bleak.[16]

Given the inherent weakness of the American/RVN military position, and given yet another period of extreme political instability in Saigon military politics during the first six months of 1966, due in large measure to a growing opposition to the regime from Buddhist leaders, students, and disaffected tribal minorities (as well as heightened feuding among military leaders), the US government was in no position to go to the negotiating table with Hanoi unless it detected real willingness on the other side to engage in substantial compromise.[17]

Ronning's missions merely provided further evidence of Hanoi's steadfast determination. The communist leaders did not at any time suggest clearly to Ronning that the Four Points formula might be taken as the maximum and not the minimum terms of Hanoi's tentative negotiating stance. Pham Van Dong may indeed have been personally willing to countenance the opening of direct informal bilateral talks in return for a cessation of the bombing of the north, but he did not indicate any willingness to go beyond the position to talk about any hypothetical political compromises of substance.

It may well be true that the Washington leaders who defined the effective policy consensus on the American side were themselves only very vaguely attached to the idea that real negotiations were possible in 1965–7, as many accounts of the period have argued.[18] But it is definitely true that the communist side was committed to a decisive victory in the field before sitting down to any bargaining with the enemy.[19] At no time, for example, did Pham Van Dong or Ha Van Lau ever indicate to any foreign intermediaries that there might be a settlement based upon impartially supervised free elections in the south, prior to which the incumbent regime in Saigon could remain in power in the zones which they still controlled. Neither did they ever admit to their increasingly heavy material contributions to the struggle in the south being waged by their political 'ally,' the NLF. Hanoi's cause did not lend itself to compromise: any outcome short of unification on their terms would have constituted defeat.

Ronning's March visit yielded very little. He did bring back word that Hanoi would enter into talks provided there was an unconditional and final cessation of bombing of the north. Martin and other Canadian officials (Klaus Goldschlag was then head of Far Eastern Division and the Vietnam desk officer was W. Thomas Delworth) appear to have regarded this as a *potential* major breakthrough. For convinced liberal-moderates, it seemed very worthwhile to recommend to the United States government that the proposal should be looked at seriously. From a liberal-moderate perspective the theory was to get the two sides talking in the hope that the forces for moderation and compromise on each side might be given an opportunity to take charge of the dispute and move towards a peaceful resolution of the crisis. But there were no real 'moderates' in Hanoi on the negotiations issue.

The American government could hardly respond enthusiastically to Ronning's news from Ottawa. The 'talks-for-bombing-halt' proposal from

Hanoi did not seem likely to lead to some eventual compromise which would be even remotely tolerable to either élite or mass opinion in the United States. Furthermore, relinquishing the air war instrument entirely meant discarding much if not most of Washington's coercive leverage against Hanoi. It is speculative but none the less important to observe that had the North Vietnamese been more forthcoming at this time there might have been a possibility of achieving a negotiated end to the conflict, because Johnson himself earnestly sought to end 'that bitch of a war.' Hanoi's hands were not tied by its allies in 1966–7. The reverse is more true. Both the Chinese and Soviet governments were by then bidding for Vietnamese support given the progressively widening rift between Moscow and Beijing.

The significance of Ronning's mission lay more in its effect upon Canadian governmental perceptions. Ronning, in retrospect, agreed with Paul Martin that President Johnson seemed to go back on his promise to enter into talks provided there was 'some movement' in Hanoi's position. Ronning did extract 'some slight movement'[20] – as Martin himself phrased it. But the Americans would not respond to Canadian pleas for a more detailed and conciliatory reply to Pham's proposal. Here the inherent ambiguity of Johnson's verbal undertaking to Ottawa, coupled with increasing pressure from hawkish elements in the Pentagon, produced frustration and misunderstanding in both the White House and the East Block. Officials in Ottawa could not understand why Johnson could not try to be a bit more accommodating. Johnson thought he already was moving dangerously far from the existing political and bureaucratic consensus in Washington, which was becoming increasingly hostile to the dispatch of the many 'interlocutors on behalf of peace,' lest it be seen in Hanoi as weakness.[21]

Martin responded to the distinct lack of enthusiasm in Washington with a 'veiled form of pressure'[22] on his State Department contacts in an attempt to force the Americans to keep the channel open and to make it productive. Johnson, Rusk, and William Bundy finally agreed to a second trip to Hanoi but they would not agree to respond to the alleged softening in the North Vietnamese position. To the Americans the 'talks for bombing halt' formula was an implicit invitation to eventual negotiated surrender.

According to the American narrative of events, the Canadians had some difficulty in persuading the North Vietnamese leaders to accept another visit because of Pearson's speech of 1 May 1966, which had called for a reciprocal de-escalation in the fighting, a cease-fire in place, and phased reciprocal withdrawals by the DRVN and the 'forces of other governments' under international supervision.[23] Hanoi saw any such notions of reciprocity as implicit legitimation of American aggression. Ronning eventually saw the North

Vietnamese foreign minister, Nguyen Duy Trinh, during his visit to Hanoi from 14 to 17 June. The foreign minister declared that the Canadians were helping the Americans by contributing to a diplomatic 'peace offensive' when there were no new offers to be discussed and when the US was 'escalating' the bombing.[24] However, he indicated that Hanoi still valued the Canadian link.

Pentagon officials had wanted to initiate an intensified bombing campaign in the north in June. From 21 January through the end of May, the resumption of bombing following the thirty-seven-day pause had been subject to the same set of constraints in effect throughout 1965. But in the spring of 1966 pressures were building within the administration for approval of attacks on the petroleum-oil-lubricants facilities in and about Hanoi and Haiphong. These so-called 'POL strikes' were not actually conducted until late June (the initial date for such strikes was 24 June but weather and a press leak delayed execution until 29 June).[25] Ronning's second mission forced the postponement of these raids for some three weeks.

American officials had not requested or promoted the Ronning missions in any way. They were a wholly Canadian initiative. In retrospect, the former assistant secretary of state, William Bundy, reflected: 'the timing was just plain not propitious.'[26] Ronning, Martin, and other Canadian officials did not agree at the time. They subsequently felt that the Americans had been less than forthcoming. Ronning felt that Ottawa had been double-crossed by the State Department. The Canadians believed that the North Vietnamese had softened their stance in offering informal talks for an unconditional bombing halt. By not insisting that the Americans accept the Four Points before the two sides sat down to bilateral talks, Hanoi had seemed to open the door to the beginning of constructive talks – if only Washington would agree to the arrangement. By withdrawing the Four Points demand Hanoi had given the 'slight movement' which Washington officials had asked for as the price for responding concretely with new proposals.[27]

Ronning personally felt that there was a very good chance that peace negotiations at this time would have been productive. As he said: 'Hanoi was willing to negotiate peace if the United States would stop the bombing.'[28] But the Americans would not budge. They insisted that the infiltration of men and supplies to the south had to be the quid pro quo for an unconditional bombing halt. This early alleged opportunity for peace talks was thus lost. Ronning was inclined to rest the blame for American intransigence upon the Pentagon's most bellicose elements, many of whom appear to have been excited by thoughts of further gains, if not 'total victory,' following Hanoi's 'concession' of March 1966.[29]

There are a number of indications in the documentary record suggesting that Pearson was far less inclined to press the Ronning initiative than was Martin. This was not because he was at this time more of a doctrinal conservative than his secretary of state for external affairs – quite the contrary. He simply had a more realistic appreciation of the practical difficulties involved. According to the then US ambassador to Canada, Walton Butterworth, Pearson said in late January that the 'Ronning mission was Martin's idea' and, further, that he had 'scared the hell out of' Martin over the political risks involved. Pearson allegedly told Martin that controversy would lead him 'to disavow any involvement in the Ronning mission.'[30] The onus for the initiative then presumably would have rested entirely on Martin's shoulders. It was Martin who made the 'veiled threat' to release special information at American expense if Washington officials continued to stall before approving Ronning's second visit.[31] It was Pearson who seems to have lost heart in the wake of the collapse of the Ronning initiative, saying: 'I think no government has pressed harder for an end to hostilities in Viet Nam by negotiation than his government, and we will *perhaps* continue so to press.'[32]

Furthermore, it was only Martin who would repeatedly claim for many months subsequent to Ronning's last visit that the 'Ronning channel' was still open 'with the concurrence of all sides.'[33] There is no doubt that Martin was personally convinced that negotiations were feasible in early 1966 and that the Americans had failed to deliver on their informal undertaking to the Canadians to respond constructively to any movement in Hanoi's position. They had also violated an undertaking not to abuse the good offices role of the Canadians by escalating the bombing prior to, during, or just after Ronning's mission. Years later Martin still adhered to this view.[34] But was this attitude, one shared by both Martin and Ronning, wholly justified?

Charles Taylor certainly thought so, because he explicitly accused the Americans of sophistic evasion and unwarranted stalling.[35] But Taylor's narrative of the missions omitted the centrally relevant fact that in the 26 April memorandum to Ottawa (which approved a second Ronning visit), American officials wrote: 'As the Canadian Government is aware *a direct channel* between the United States Government and Hanoi *was opened in Rangoon* during the period of the recent bombing suspension [24 December 1965–31 January 1966] ... the record stands that a direct channel has been opened, but that *Hanoi chooses for the time being not to employ it*.'[36] American lack of enthusiasm for exploring Ronning's 'new' bombing halt-for-talks proposal is thus more understandable. The Americans had already seen the North Vietnamese face to face relatively recently, and they had seen no hint of 'give' whatsoever. Moreover, this secret channel for direct talks was still available to Hanoi leaders whenever they might wish to begin to negotiate a genuine

compromise. Thus, why give up the bombing instrument merely to dupli-
cate a negotiating mode already in existence?

American officials had strong grounds for being sceptical of any alleged
North Vietnamese willingness to compromise. In Hanoi's communication
to Ottawa, which finally agreed to Ronning's second visit, Colonel Ha Van
Lau implicitly repudiated Premier Pham Van Dong's earlier indication that a
halt to the bombing might lead to serious direct talks aiming at an eventual
political compromise. Lau's aide mémoire read in part: 'The Government of
the DRVN once again affirms that if the USA Government really desires a
peaceful settlement it must recognize the four point stand of the DRVN
Government, and prove this by actual deeds; it must announce a definitive
and unconditional end to its air raids and all other actions of war against the
Democratic Republic of Vietnam. Only then will it be possible to envisage a
political solution to the Vietnam problem.'[37]

Contrary to Charles Taylor's presentation of this response,[38] the North
Vietnamese leaders were not being either flexible or forthcoming. They were
in fact 'reverting' to their traditionally hard line in which there would be no
talks without some degree of implied American acceptance of the Four
Points. The third of these points stipulated the acceptance of the NLF's Five
Points which inter alia required virtual American co-operation in the dismantling of the existing government in Saigon and its replacement by a
coalition government in which the NLF would have a leading role.[39] Nor are
there any grounds for arguing that the colonel's inclusion of the hard-line
terms in the aide mémoire was accidentally or erroneously carried out. Lau
had voiced these same conditions in several prior discussions with Canadian
ICSC representative Victor Moore.[40]

This is not to say, however, that the Americans were entirely blameless for
the prolongation of this exceptionally savage war. To usefully criticize
Washington's behaviour one must look not at the minutiae of the disengagement process, where if anything the balance of political short-sightedness
and diplomatic inflexibility lies with Hanoi. Rather, one should examine
critically the overarching evolution and interplay of the political and strategic objectives of various elements of the American government which
supported American intervention in Indochina in the first place and then
sustained this intervention even after it had become apparent that such objectives could not be achieved at a tolerable human cost.

It is interesting none the less to reflect upon Martin's conversion to the view
that the Americans were fundamentally disinterested in a negotiated end to
the war.[41] It is not unreasonable to infer that Martin himself was experiencing some unconscious cognitive realignments in his central assumptions
about the war and the Americans' role in it. Martin's comment to Stursberg

that the North Vietnamese could not respond to Ronning's second visit to Hanoi because 'Hanoi was being pounded'[42] is a revealing example of psycho-logic at work: the tailoring of evidence to suit the preferred interpretive framework of the perceiver.[43]

Ronning was in Hanoi from 14 to 17 June. The bombing of the Hanoi and Haiphong POL facilities did not start until 29 June – almost two weeks after Ronning's departure.

The reason for Martin's retrospective (and apparently near contemporary) mental falsification of the record had much to do with the increasing political pressure Martin was facing over Canadian Vietnam policy, as well as the increasing ambiguity of Washington's ultimate intentions vis-à-vis the war in Southeast Asia. Martin was increasingly pressured by force of circumstance into adopting the operational norms and eventually the perceptual premises of the liberal-moderate school of thought on the war. Martin could not help but be influenced in a major way by the fact that Pearson by early 1966 was already moving quickly back to the doctrinal centre of the department from his temporary if rather lengthy sojourn on the incrementalist right wing of Canadian Vietnam policy-making.

It was Pearson who decisively resuscitated the liberal-moderate policy current in Ottawa's approach by arguing in a speech to a veterans' group on 1 May 1966:

There seems to be one overriding consideration here; not who is responsible for what, but how can the fighting and the slaughter and the suffering be ended and the people of that distressed land be allowed to live their lives in peace and freedom in a political society of their own choice without outside interference in making that choice and outside pressures after the choice has been made.[44]

This statement by Pearson publicly ratified the shift which Martin had foreshadowed in his lengthy statement to the Commons' Standing Committee on External Affairs of 4 April 1966, a statement which may be seen as a testing of the water for the ultimate political feasibility of a shift back towards a predominantly liberal-moderate approach to Indochinese policy-making. On 4 April Martin had indicated that the government had strongly regretted the resumption of bombing in early February and had favoured a continuation of the pause 'until all reasonable possibilities of eliciting some response from the other side has been exhausted.'[45] He indicated that he favoured UN Security Council involvement as well.[46] But the most critical part of the statement was Martin's declaration of a major new tactical and doctrinal emphasis in its policy:

on June 10 of 1965 I gave a detailed account and ... said I thought it was difficult to form a judgement of that situation without examining in its proper historical perspective the problem in Viet Nam. I believe the situation is no less true today than it was a little less than a year ago. I know there are interpretations other than that which the Canadian government has placed on the course of events in Viet Nam ... *I think, however, that no useful purpose would be served by going again over the ground which we covered last year*, but in that context I wish to make two comments. First I would like to remind the committee that while there are differences over the antecedents of the present conflict in Viet Nam, the assessment which the government has formed on this subject is an independent assessment resting on a long record of first hand Canadian experience ... Secondly, *if our foreign policy is to have any impact on the present situation, I believe we must now cast our thinking forward rather than backward*. I also believe we are unlikely to achieve anything useful by *a policy of denunciation which is sometimes being urged on the government by those who take issue with our position*. What we must do is to map out a course which we regard as *right and realistic*, which takes account of the facts as we know them and which has *some prospect of contribution to a peaceful settlement*. And this is what we have been trying to do.[47]

In this time of severe international political tension, a time also when the governing Liberal party did not possess a working majority in the Commons, Pearson and Martin began to make unmistakable overtures to the New Democratic Party rather than to the Progressive Conservatives. Just as Pierre Trudeau and Mitchell Sharp would bid for the support of the NDP in 1972–3, Pearson and Martin seem to have felt that there were more realistic possibilities of a policy accommodation with the left-liberal 'systemists' of the NDP caucus than with the anti-communist 'systemists' who seemed to be the chief architects of PC Vietnam policy. In both instances the Liberals' political judgment proved accurate. In both instances the key decision-makers in both Cabinet and External Affairs seem to have concurred in the view that Canadian interests lay more in calculated attempts to promote an armistice and to inhibit American bellicose propensities than in any effort to promote an image of political solidarity with the American war effort.

Not coincidentally, Paul Martin reaffirmed the shift in government policy shortly after the commencement of the American POL strikes. On 8 July 1966 he declared to the House:

We are all aware of the dangers that flow from the conflict that has raged in that area. We are dealing with the situation as it is now; we are not dealing with its genesis. We have sought not to emphasize the history of this situation, but to try and see if we could not make our position as a mediator more effective by taking the most objective position possible.[48]

Martin went still further by asserting explicitly that membership on the ICSC precluded 'any intention of dispatching Canadian armed forces' to Indochina. Henceforth Ottawa would devote all its efforts towards bringing about 'the beginnings of peace in Vietnam.'[49] There would henceforth be no more ringing declarations of support for American resistance to 'naked armed aggression'; neither would there be any more talk from the government benches of shameless NDP support for appeasement of communist imperialism.

Canadian foreign policy had at last shifted back to the doctrinal centre of the policy-making spectrum. The liberal-moderate tendency was back in the policy saddle. The tendency shift of 1966 was now complete.

The Ronning missions marked a watershed in Canadian Vietnam policy. Prior to February 1966 the Canadian government was a sympathetic middle power ally supportive of the American intervention, though not to the point of actively participating in the war. The ostensible reason for such qualified support was Canada's limited capabilities. The real reason, although this was never spelled out to the Americans, was because the Canadian government had never seen any impelling strategic reasons to draw the line of containment tight to the borders of China.

By the end of 1965 it was clear to Pearson and Martin that Ottawa would have to prepare for the 'long haul' on Vietnam. One part of these preparations was mediatory diplomacy to promote meaningful bilateral negotiations; a second was to work towards the reapplication of the terms of the 1954 Geneva bargain. In the original conception of the new reaffirmation of the liberal-moderate approach, there clearly was to have been a third element in the design. This was to be an attempted opening towards China.

In late 1965 a vote in the United Nations General Assembly had produced a tie on the question of communist Chinese representation at the UN. For many years the Canadian government had been trying to persuade the Americans to soften their line on Beijing's non-admission.[50] Liberal-moderate thinking of the time (and even much conservative opinion in Canada) was very much typified by John Holmes's assertion of August 1963 that communist China, 'a rogue elephant of enormous strength and savage will,' had to be brought into the United Nations so as to moderate and constrain its behaviour as soon as was humanly possible.[51] Martin certainly seems to have concurred in this view, and both Martin and Pearson shared Holmes's further opinion that the Sino-Soviet rift had caused the deterioration of conditions in Indochina in the first place. The Sino-Soviet bidding war for Hanoi's allegiance had given the North Vietnamese new freedom to press home their claims for national unification.

In the American account of the Ronning missions there is a curious reference to a projected trip by Ronning to Beijing to visit an old friend, Chen Yi. According to the American reading of events, the Chinese turned Ronning's visit down at the last minute because they did not want to encourage the peace-feeler diplomacy at all, preferring that Hanoi fight on to victory. The reference is curious because Ronning subsequently indicated that there were no plans for him to visit China that he knew of, and that he had never telephoned Chou En-lai when he was in Hong Kong.[52] Martin explicitly contradicts Ronning's version of events. He has indicated that though Pearson had some reservations about the China detour, Martin had been allowed to approve it, and that Ronning had carried out instructions to try to arrange the visit through Chou.[53]

It is possible that some memories have become partially confused. But it is still more probable that both versions are essentially accurate. The contact to Beijing may have been advertised to the Americans – but not executed (or excuted independently of Ronning's knowledge) – simply to test the intensity of the American reaction. Martin may also have wished to accustom the Americans to the idea that China would soon be a member of the United Nations, or at least not let them forget that PRC admission was imminent. According to William P. Bundy, the then secretary of state for far eastern affairs, they did not need too much prompting. In May 1966 they advised Ottawa that any Canadian efforts to get Beijing seated on a 'two-China' basis would have American support.[54] The Great Proletarian Cultural Revolution intervened, however, before the Canadians could get their initiative moving. The moment passed. By the end of the summer the State Department's attitude had changed once more. George Ignatieff was left with a proposal that attracted no support at all among the English-speaking governments.

The Ronning missions eased Canadian policy-making through a difficult transition. They effectively decoupled Canadian policy from the American strategic commitment to Southeast Asia, without necessitating any obvious public dispute with Washington's actions. The 'special relationship' was thus preserved in spirit, although not in the hard currency of security commitments. In military security terms, Canada was no longer even a faint-hearted ally. Ottawa was now a determined wallflower.

THE LIBERAL MODERATE LINE REFURBISHED:
JULY 1966–APRIL 1968

For the duration of the second Pearson ministry, Canadian Vietnam policy was prudent, restrained, and carefully modulated. Both the prime minister

296 In the interests of peace

and his secretary of state for external affairs were henceforth determined to avoid any divisive and potentially politically damaging confrontations in this issue-area. By the summer of 1966 the Vietnam problem was an extremely sensitive area of policy-making. Several hundred university professors and scores of Protestant and Roman Catholic clergy and concerned church laity had been actively lobbying the government for many months. The New Democratic Party parliamentary caucus had already been engaged in vitriolic denunciations of alleged American barbarism in Indochina for over two years. Moreover, although the Progressive Conservative party had toned down it advocacy of support for American and Commonwealth containment of aggression (the examples of Australia and New Zealand were regularly invoked as grounds for more material aid to the war), there was no hint at all that the Liberal government could move significantly to the left without coming under heavy fire from the parliamentary right. With respect to the way in which his government handled the question of unilateral Canadian recognition of the communist Chinese regime, Pearson later declared:

Normally unless there is some question of immediate principle or policy involved of immediate urgency in which the government feels very strongly on questions of principle, you do not take action on a foreign affairs matter where public opinion, in your view at least, is so evenly divided. In a situation like that, the attitude, the reaction to your decision by a neighbour like the United States becomes very important indeed. If you are not sure in your own country what you ought to do and you know that in doing it you would arouse a very strong and hostile reaction in the United States that is an additional factor which had to be taken into account ... At least that is the way we looked at it.[55]

His political rule of thumb for the China question was clearly invoked vis-à-vis Vietnam as well.

Many academic analysts of Canadian policy in this period found the government's approach to be sadly lacking in efficiency, imagination, leadership, and respect for fundamental human values. Paul Martin's ritualized pleading on behalf of restraint in public commentary on the American role in Vietnam became so commonplace that the term 'quiet diplomacy,' sedulously avoided by Pearson, inspired lengthy critiques by concerned individuals from both ends of the political spectrum.[56] The upshot of the extreme criticism from all quarters was a marked diminution in public respect for the norms and objectives of liberal-moderate doctrine. In effect, the distaste aroused in the public mind for these years of apparent indecision and, many said, outright moral cowardice and opportunism eventually prepared the way for the Trudeau years of comparative diplomatic disengagement from the international community.

The public debate on Vietnam in this period was revealing of the variation in passionately held, ideologically determined sentiments in the country and thus was destructive of national unity to a substantial extent. These facts appear to have impressed the first Trudeau ministry.

The physical savagery of the conflict, especially as it was waged by the American military (in full view of television cameras), and the increasingly dubious character of the 'communist threat to the Free World' elicited intensely rooted policy recommendations from all participants in the great Canadian Vietnam debate carried on from the spring of 1965 through the spring of 1968. The mechanically contrived and, at times, intentionally sterile public policy outputs of the government satisfied few members of the large and growing attentive public on this issue, but they accomplished several central objectives of the government: Canada was kept out of the conflict completely; Canadian-American relations were not seriously damaged by Canadian non-participation in the American crusade; and, finally, a coherent, plausible, and politically 'satisficing' role was created for Canada which did not threaten to alienate irrevocably from the Liberal party any major segment of the Canadian polity. The liberal-moderate quest for peace, however hypocritical and opportunistic it appeared to some, nevertheless functioned as an effective 'lowest common policy denominator' on which political decision-makers might base their approach to the Vietnam war.

Under the new liberal-moderate policy regime which grew up coeval with the Ronning missions, Canadian diplomats were to function as 'honest brokers' to the disputants. The first objective of Canadian Vietnam policy was to try to get the two sides together through Canadian 'good offices' for 'preliminary talks.' The ICSC as the only ongoing source of contact between Saigon and Hanoi was declared to be institutionally vital to the success of this operation.[57] These direct bilateral discussions were to lead to an ultimate political compromise which would then be ratified by some form of reconvened Geneva Conference – or so the liberal-moderate scenarios went. The mechanics of the eventual negotiations were accurately forecast: their political substance was not. Neither Pearson, Martin, nor any of the liberal-moderates in External Affairs seem to have suspected that American policy was ultimately doomed. For Canadians, that was probably an inconceivable outcome. In any case the particular fate of the Vietnamese nation was no longer a high priority concern of Canadian policy-makers, as it had been when the conservative tendency had prevailed. An end to the fighting per se was the prime objective of the Canadian policy process.

It was now made explicitly clear that Vietnam was once more beyond the pale of basic Canadian security concerns. The Eurocentric slant of Canadian policy was again dominant. Not coincidentally, one of the first key manifestations of liberal-moderate doctrinal ascendancy was the resurrection by Pearson and Martin of the traditional formula (employed in 1953–5) for fending off potential requests by Americans in search of willing allies in Asia. On 4 February 1966 Martin told the Commons: 'The United States is a party to the conflict in Viet Nam. Canada is not; and we have made it clear that *Canada could not contemplate military involvement in Viet Nam except as a part of a United Nations peace keeping operation*.'[58]

Even though the Canadian role on the ICSC seemed to offer a useful shield for deflecting the importunate demands of American anti-communist crusaders, Ottawa had some eight years of conservative rhetorical support for the 'ends' of American policy vis-à-vis Indochina on record – a not insignificant potential weapon available to right-wing critics. Ottawa might in due course require more than the ICSC 'chastity belt' (a phrase used frequently by some frustrated conservatives). A careful delimitation of the basic geopolitical concerns of Canada as a middle power seemed only prudent.

The Ronning visits to Hanoi were prompted by Martin's conviction in February 1966 that the Indian and Polish governments, although favourably disposed in theory towards a mediatory role for the commission powers, might nevertheless prove to be incapable of concurrence in Canadian definitions of this role.[59] Certainly Canadian inability to persuade commission colleagues about the desirability of maintaining an activist role in Laos and the border regions of South Vietnam seemed to justify this suspicion.

At a more practical level the new government line, this 'policy without history,' was expressed in terms of a series of mechanically contrived compromises. Canadians were not to be allowed to actively recruit in Canada for the American armed forces, but Canadians as private individuals could enlist south of the border without penalty.[60] The government would take no action either to halt or to encourage the immigration from the United States of draft resisters.[61] Medical, technical, and food aid would rise constantly in volume over time to the RVN,[62] but the Canadian government would also declare its willingness to consider without political bias any and all requests for medical aid to the civilian population of the DRVN,[63] while indicating further that private groups (such as the Canadian Society of Friends) would be entirely free to arrange shipments of this type without obstruction.[64]

Pearson's government was forced to proceed in a manner not dissimilar to the balancing act practised by the Indian government concerning ICSC fault-finding in the 1950s: for every public movement in one direction there had to be some compensatory counter-move in the opposite direction. An appearance of even-handedness and impartiality had to be fostered even if the substance of the decisions tended to favour one side in the conflict.

Martin's circumlocutory defence of such compromises was a source of unending frustration for his parliamentary critics. As Gordon Churchill of the Progressive Conservatives phrased it, attempting to pin down the thrust of Martin's policy statements was like trying 'to nail jelly to the wall.'[65] Martin's pleas for unanimous support for the government's quest for peace, for becoming agents for the 'wider international community,'[66] for using Canadian 'national influence in promoting the cause of peace in Vietnam,'[67] for committing Canada to a role on any new supervisory body 'within the limits of our capacity,'[68] all fell on as yet deaf ears. While the anti-communist conservative element saw a 'dangerous drift towards neutrality'[69] in such preaching, the anti-war left-liberals were angered by what they termed 'a series of platitudinous bromides calculated to put the house asleep and to lull the fears of the Canadian people.'[70]

As part of the general approach of trying to split the difference between the policy extremes, Pearson and Martin tried to finesse questions concerning two other very difficult issues: the Defence Production Sharing Agreements (of 1959 and 1963) with the United States and the official Canadian response to the American bombing of North Vietnam. These two issues cut to the heart of the Canadian Vietnam debate in the mid-1960s and thus require extended comment.

THE DEFENCE PRODUCTION-SHARING RELATIONSHIP

By 1966, Canadian arms exports to the United States were growing quickly. Between 1959 and 1966 Canada had sold $1.3 billion in war material to the American Department of Defense.[71] But of this amount some $260 million was sold in 1965 and $300 million in 1966 alone.[72] Martin's March 1966 attempt at enunciating a satisfactory compensatory policy compromise was limited solely to declaring that the government would not permit any exports of military commodities to either of the two Vietnams.[73] Pressure on the government to revise its policy continued unabated. In late August 1966, Industry Minister C.M. Drury noted that there were no bombs being exported to the United States.[74] This was true, but he did not mention Canadian shipments of napalm and other chemical explosives in bulk to the United States from plants at Sarnia and Valleyfield. In October, Drury reaffirmed that 'it is government policy not to grant export permits for shipment of military equipment to Vietnam.'[75] Criticism continued, for it was clear that substantial quantities of arms, munitions, and components thereof were being processed for eventual use in Vietnam.

Throughout 1966 and 1967, Pearson and Martin received a barrage of criticism on this issue. They remained firm, however. Constraints would not be applied on Defence Production Sharing (DPS) exports to the United States. Neither would the agreements be abrogated. Said Pearson on 18 January 1967: 'it is not our policy to stop the export of defence equipment to the United States or the other NATO allies in accordance with the agreements we have made with them' – notwithstanding the views to the contrary of 360 University of Toronto professors.[76] On 7 February 1967 Martin's parliamentary secretary, Donald S. Macdonald, again invoked the overriding significance of Canada's NATO commitments, saying: 'The alliance was formulated many years before the present involvement of the United States in Viet Nam. It is the hope of this government ... that this alliance will continue unimpaired after the present hostilities in Vietnam have been brought to a peaceful conclusion.'[77] For Macdonald, maintaining 'the principle of the open border with respect to export controls between our two countries' was of paramount importance. The government, he declared, would do nothing to 'risk throwing over the efficacy of the NATO alliance.'[78] The opposition did not relent.

On 13 February 1967 Martin admitted that there were 'illogicalities' in the government's posture.[79] He nevertheless asserted that the DPS relationship took precedence over role considerations in Vietnam, simply because it was 'very important to the economy of this country.'[80] Once more, his argument failed to mollify left-wing critics. T.C. Douglas of the NDP denounced the American role in the war as a 'bloody and barbaric incident that has no equal in our time.'[81] Trying to force an end to the American 'war of aggression' was, he said, 'the greatest moral issue of our time.'[82] He went on to say: 'I am not prepared to get $300 million of trade, if it is to be at the cost of seeing villages annihilated and defenceless people killed.'[83] Canada had a clear moral obligation to do its utmost to stop 'this barbarous bombing of a small undefended people in an undeclared war.' Liberal Vietnam policy was, he said, equivalent to the moral cowardice shown by Mackenzie King's government in the 1930s vis-à-vis Canadian metal and mineral exports to Japan while that state was committing aggression in Manchuria.[84]

Bryce Mackasey replied for the government with a bitterly sarcastic speech which accused Douglas and the NDP of fomenting 'socialism in its worst form ... anti-Americanism.'[85] This would be a standard charge by conservatives against left-liberal dissenters, and it was a politically effective weapon, false and calculated though the allegation was.

Pearson and Martin held firm on the DPS arrangement. There would be no retreat on this issue which seemed to strike too close to the heart of liberal-moderate doctrine. For most liberal-moderates it was axiomatic that the Canadian government could only maximize its influence internationally within the framework of the American alliance system. An optimal level of influence depended upon the maintenance of sound Canadian-American relations.

On 10 March 1967 Pearson tackled the issue head on. In his Victoria College speech (at the University of Toronto), the prime minister began by reiterating the now well-established premises of the refurbished liberal-moderate approach: Canadian policy must be pragmatic and realistic in its quest for peace; debate should not focus on the historical origins and 'rights and wrongs' of the conflict but rather on the 'search for common ground' between the two sides; efforts should be directed at promoting a confidential dialogue between the parties through 'calm and deliberate diplomacy,' not at criticizing publicly the actions of one of the parties.

He then went on at length to note that the DPS agreements of 1959 and 1963 were vital to the effectiveness of Canadian contributions to collective defence and to the continued health of the Canadian economy. He noted further that: the defence production-sharing arrangements dated back to the Hyde Park Declaration of 1941; the arrangements that evolved permitted Canada access to significant economies of scale in both production and purchasing which otherwise would not be possible; the Canadian government could, because of the DPS arrangement, acquire essential, technologically sophisticated equipment 'at the lowest possible cost, while at the same time permitting us to offset the resulting drain on the economy by the reciprocal sales' through exemption from the 'Buy American' Act in the United States; most Canadian exports were not weaponry per se, but rather 'electronic equipment, transport aircraft, and various kinds of components'; civilian production in Canada was significantly assisted by spin-off benefits from technologies developed for military purposes; and the 'open border' principle was of great value to Canada and would probably be destroyed in any vain attempt to place conditions on the ultimate use of Canadian DPS exports.

Most important, Pearson concluded by saying that any embargo by Canada on the export of military equipment was likely to have 'far-reaching consequences which no Canadian government could contemplate with equanimity.' Worst of all, he declared: 'it would be interpreted as a notice of withdrawal on our part from continental defence and even from the collective defence arrangements of the Atlantic Alliance.'[86]

In April, Martin hammered away in the same vein to the Commons Standing Committee, though with less dramatic emphasis. According to Martin, any attempt to force the Americans to refrain from sending Canadian-made equipment to Vietnam would challenge the basis of Canadian-American relations and was, moreover, doomed to fail. Furthermore, he argued, 'if we were to ask this of the United States Government officially, there would be no agreement [ie, no DPS arrangement] between the two countries.'[87] Martin, like Pearson before him, declared that the effective termination of the production-sharing relationship would inevitably compromise Canadian ability to contribute effectively to NATO security. This was, he said, because the United States supplied advanced weaponry to Canada 'at a very good price.'[88]

The government's critics did not find the arguments put forward very conclusive. Why not purchase somewhat more expensive, slightly less effective European equipment? Why not withdraw from NATO and NORAD? The issue was not quite so simple as some critics pretended. In years to come the relationship would be maintained because the agreements did help to foster high-technology industry in Canada and, still more importantly, because they contributed very significantly to the country's balance-of-payments position.[89] Finally, the symbolic value of the DPS relationship reflecting a basic common interest and sympathetic goodwill between the two countries should not be underestimated. In fact, precisely because of its symbolic significance, many anti-war critics argued for its termination. Only through such strong actions would the 'eyes and ears' of the American people be opened – even while diplomatic doors were being simultaneously slammed in Canadian faces.[90]

The logic of liberal moderation held firm, however. On this issue the governing party could count on the support of the Progressive Conservatives. The DPS relationship would survive the American intervention in Vietnam intact.

Like so many other aspects of Canadian foreign policy, the important wider questions concerning the DPS Agreements were not fully debated. The government merely announced its position. The opposition parties merely declared their support or rejection of the government line. It would be left to the academics to debate the implied significance of the government's declaration of economic dependence upon the United States in these matters.

It must be acknowledged that the DPS arrangements were not really susceptible to any sort of effective compromise. Ottawa had to decide on the overall merit of the arrangement without being able to insert hedges or qualifications. Martin and Pearson were undoubtedly quite correct in asserting that Washington would opt for abrogation rather than permit revision. After all, it was clear from the beginning that without some compensating device Canadian spending in the United States would, over time, far outstrip American spending in Canada, especially if Ottawa continued to adhere to a meaningful role in NORAD. It was not coincidental that the first DPS Agreement was signed shortly after the termination of the Canadian-built, CF-105 interceptor program. In effect, the DPS relationship forced the Americans to buy far more in Canada than otherwise would have been the case, thus permitting the Canadian government to purchase far more in the United States without exacerbating any further the country's already precarious balance-of-payments position. Pearson and the pro-American liberal-moderate 'internationalists' in Cabinet certainly appreciated this fact. To a government beset by chronic balance-of-payments difficulties caused by the high and growing level of American corporate ownership in Canada, cancellation of the DPS arrangement would have precipitated a major foreign policy crisis. The government would then have been faced with several unappealing options: cutting all foreign arms purchases abroad and attempting to build up military industries to produce for Canadian needs, but at much higher costs because Canadian production runs would be so short; negotiating some DPS equivalent with a European government (or governments), probably Britain; redefining the Canadian role to suit the country's reduced economic circumstances by pulling back to Canada all troops stationed in Europe, and limiting the Canadian contribution to NORAD to whatever high-technology products Canadian industry could provide; or slashing foreign aid. To a convinced supporter of both collective defence and international development assistance such as Pearson, none of these options seemed even remotely desirable or politically feasible.

THE BOMBING OF NORTH VIETNAM, ITS CRITICS, AND THEIR PRESSURE ON THE GOVERNMENT

More than any other single aspect of the war, the bombing of the north decisively alienated Canadian mass opinion from support for American interventionary objectives.[91] Attitudes within the political and bureaucratic élite seem to have been similarly affected. As with most intensely emotional issues, perceptive, reasoned discourse was rare.

From the beginning of the bombing in early 1965, Pearson apparently opposed it privately. Both Pearson and Martin publicly declared Canada's 'regret' at American decisions to resume bombing after the various bombing pauses (or bombing limitations) which had been instituted by President Johnson.[92] Whether they did so on ethical or purely instrumental grounds is not clear. It is likely that Pearson initially opposed the bombing out of the conviction that it would ultimately be domestically and internationally counterproductive for Johnson, militarily marginal to the American war effort, and strategically provocative to the communist Chinese. Both the prime minister and his secretary of state for external affairs were greatly reluctant to declare such opinions publicly, believing, quite reasonably, that official American attitudes would not be altered but American willingness to speak frankly to Canadian officials would. They thus limited their criticism to what Martin had mellifluously termed 'the rich opportunity of private diplomacy.'[93] Publicly, Pearson and Martin advocated a three-point program: the cessation of bombing of the north; an end of northern infiltration of men and supplies to the southern zone; and the commencement of 'unconditional talks.'[94] The political formula for coping with requests for denunciation of American bombing was soon ritualized: 'The bombing is a key factor, but it is not the only factor.'[95]

On 1 May 1966 Pearson issued his proposal for a halt to all military activity, including the bombing of the north, to be followed by reciprocal phased withdrawals of American and DRVN forces from South Vietnam under international supervision. Issuance of this proposal complicated the difficulties of arranging Ronning's second Hanoi trip without relieving the government from the pressure from the left-liberal elements inside Parliament and out.

In early July the government reaffirmed the three-point program as well as its previous commitment to the concept of eventual neutralization of all Southeast Asia.[96] At the same time, Martin did his best to deflect opposition demands for Canadian calls for a reconvening of the Geneva Conference. As he noted quite realistically, 'a conference lies at the end of the road not the beginning.'[97]

Left-liberal systemist criticism of the government's policy did not relent. Academics continued to sign lengthy petitions supporting an unconditional bombing halt and official Canadian condemnation of the American intervention. In January 1967 some 30 per cent of the 1,100 faculty of the University of Toronto signed a petition calling for Canadian advocacy of a US withdrawal from Vietnam. Signatories included Victoria College's Northrop Frye, Donald Creighton, a leading conservative historian, and Gregory Baum, the director of St Michael's College Centre for Ecumenical Studies.[98] All across the country clergy began to organize protests to the government over the moral inadequacy of its Vietnam policy. By mid-1966 Vietnam had become a major political issue. Whereas in 1963–4 heated dissent from American policy had been limited to left-wing magazines like Cy Gonick's *Canadian Dimension*, by 1965–6 the war was inspiring increasingly critical commentary on Canadian 'complicity' in alleged American atrocities in the pages of *Canadian Forum*, the principal literary vehicle of the Canadian left-liberal intelligentsia.[99] Universities across the country were becoming host to 'teach-ins' or other forms of educational moral uplift which invariably focused on Vietnam and Canadian non-recognition of communist China.

Leading figures within the United Church of Canada, most notably Reverend J.R. 'Ray' Hord of Toronto,* were working very hard by mid-1966 to build widespread opposition to the US role in the war by Canada's 'politically informed' (read left-liberal humanitarian) middle class. Hord, and other clergy like him of all faiths, together with the university community seemed to be targeting one of the principal constituencies of Liberal party support. Hord's efforts and his perspective on the conflict are worth examining briefly as an example of the left-liberal systemist approach to policy in action.

In the spring of 1965 Hord began a sustained lobbying effort by helping to organize various anti-war committees (eg, the interdenominational 'Toronto Committee of Clergymen for Vietnam'), by promoting the spread of the teach-in movement, and by helping to co-ordinate the efforts of other anti-war activists in the Voice of Women and the Student Union for Peace Action. He appeared on radio shows, wrote newspaper articles, and did his best to convert United Church ministers across the country to his perspective on the war.

As a left-liberal systemist he argued that: the Americans were 'aggressors' in the war; the conflict was predominantly a civil war; American prosecution of the war was barbaric and obscene (akin to Italian savagery in Abyssinia or Nazi depredations on the population of occupied Europe); the DRVN and NFL had captured the nationalist cause irrevocably; American policy would inevitably foment racial hatred of whites by Asians; and, lastly, the Western world should provide massive economic aid to the poor countries regardless of their choice of political systems. In a statement of August 1965 he declared: 'As Christians, we should remember with sorrow the crusades of the Middle Ages, launched by Christian nations against the Moslems ... If we could learn the lessons of history, we should not build a wall of intransigence and holy pride between the Christian and communist world, which would not be broken down for a thousand years.'[101]

Hord's fight to win official United Church sanction for his views was only partly successful. Many ministers were strongly anti-communist. However, a significant number of clergy in all parts of the country (save Quebec) were receptive to his arguments. One minister responded to Hord's plea for sup-

---

* Hord was secretary to the Church's Board of Evangelism and Social Service from 1963 until his death in 1968.

port by saying that he was 'thinking, as an old soldier, of raising a regiment of volunteers to assist the Viet Cong in what, from a military point of view, is [an] amazing struggle against the u.s. overwhelming power.'[102] Far more typical of replies were comments to the effect that the American military action was 'the crucifixion of a people who are unable to fight back' or that the American intervention 'could spell ruin for all mankind.'[103] Another correspondent noted that the idea of participating in a mass demonstration in the spring of 1966 scared him 'half to death' but 'if my Church asked me to in the name of Christ I would' so long as the rally was 'well-controlled ... and the whole effort responsibly led.'[104]

Under Hord's prompting, the church's Committee on International Affairs passed a resolution on 26 November 1965 calling for an official Canadian statement which supported a unilateral halt of the bombing in the north, phased withdrawal of DRVN and US troops, and peace negotiations involving the NLF as a principle party.[105] The resolution was sent promptly to the prime minister. In February 1966 Hord dispatched copies of this resolution together with a long letter to all ministers 'in the pastorate' which argued that Ho's regime was 'a popular revolutionary movement which is not going to be wiped out by force of arms.' He called for 'more forthright' criticism of the parties (both sides) by Ottawa, and noted the absence of Canadian neutrality in the war given Canadian military exports to the United States.[106] Later that month he circulated copies of the resolution of the World Council of Churches of 16 February 1966 which was implicitly critical of American policy.

Following Pearson's 1 May speech to the World Veterans Federation, Hord praised the prime minister. Shortly thereafter he noted to a friend: 'I am certain that an aroused public opinion has led to the Prime Minister taking a stronger stand on this issue.'[107] This may very well have been true. For the remainder of 1966 Hord's public speeches concentrated on the theme 'The American Rape of Vietnam.' In 1967 he made numerous speeches at teach-ins and anti-war rallies across the country, pressing for, among other things, medical assistance by Ottawa to both North and South Vietnam. The audiences grew larger.

In August 1967 the general synod of the Anglican Church of Canada publicly urged that the United States should halt the bombing. This statement also urged the North Vietnamese to move towards negotiations in response to such de-escalation, and that the RVN authorities should agree to negotiate with the Viet Cong. In October 1967 Hord persuaded the United Church's Board of Evangelism and Social Service to support American 'draft-dodgers' financially. But shortly after he secured approval of this measure from the board, the church's general council revoked the grant, saying the board had exceeded its authority.[108]

That same month saw 5,000 people demonstrate in Toronto (some were pro-American), 400 anti-war marchers converge on the Parliament Buildings, while still larger anti-war gatherings occurred in Vancouver, Edmonton, and Winnipeg. Smaller protests were held in Montreal and Halifax.

While the demonstrations and rallies proceeded outside Parliament, the NDP caucus echoed the charges inside the House of Commons. NDP MPs were especially worried about the risk of American military adventurism. The party also pointed to the race factor in the war, the increasingly 'farcical' nature of the ICSC role, and the mounting risk of Chinese intervention in the face of American provocation.[109] According to the NDP, the American intervention involved a massive violation of legal, democratic, and especially Christian ideals.[110]

Martin and Pearson began to show some signs of wilting under this sustained pressure. On 17 November 1966 the secretary of state for external affairs declared that a Canadian call for a unilateral cessation of bombing without a simultaneous demand for reciprocal de-escalation of fighting on the communist side was 'not realistic quite apart from the view one might hold as to the merits of the case.'[111] Presumably Martin himself now wholly favoured such a move privately. One week later Pearson reiterated his belief that the first steps towards negotiations would have to be reciprocal.[112]

On 11 January 1967 Martin returned to the theme that a bombing halt was just 'one of the necessary steps' towards the beginning of negotiations.[113] In mid-February to the Commons, and in mid-April to its Standing Committee on External Affairs, he gave extensive statements in defence of the government's position on the war. Both statements argued that it was Ottawa's first obligation to do everything possible to get the parties together and that this would not be assisted by highly critical statements aimed at Washington: 'We will neither bludgeon nor shame the parties into accepting a course of policy which they regard as contrary to their national interest.'[114] Canadian diplomacy was working tirelessly 'in promoting the cause of peace in Vietnam.' He virtually implored his critics to accept the government's definition of a role for Canadians 'as citizens of the wider international community.'[115]

In his major policy statement of 13 February, Martin added some important concessions to left-liberal attitudes: Ottawa would look towards finding 'an accommodation of interests of those primarily concerned' – presumably an indication that the government would try to treat DRVN and NLF claims as reasonably and fairly as possible; Ottawa would recognize 'the unity of the people of Viet Nam' even though the government believed that a continuing de facto division of the country was inevitable for the foreseeable future and reflected 'the political realities of the situation'; the government would back effective and genuine self-determination for the population of the two zones – even if this risked an NLF victory; the government 'would be prepared to cooperate fully in the constitution of a new supervisory force'; and the government looked with favour on American statements to the effect that NLF representation in peace negotiations was not an 'insurmountable problem.'[116]

These concessions together with Martin's vigour in proclaiming the government's serious interest in working for an armistice evidently helped to moderate left-liberal criticism of the government. Thus when Martin presented the government's four-point peace 'concept' (to be distinguished, Martin said, from a 'proposal') on 11 April 1967, the reception was far less hostile than it had been for previous policy statements. The essence of this program was a progressive reinstitution of the original Cease-Fire Agreement beginning first with a halt in the bombing against the north and a physical disengagement of the two sides at (and a withdrawal of all combatants from) the demilitarized zone close to the 17th parallel. This provision would reinstitute most of the measures contained in Chapter 1 of the CFA. Second, there was to be avoidance of any escalation in fighting in the rest of the country and no reinforcement of either side (the original Articles 16 and 17). Third, there would be a complete cessation of all hostilities; fourth, a complete return to the entire set of stipulations in the original CFA which would entail massive troop withdrawals by both the Americans and North Vietnamese.[117] When he introduced this scheme Martin immediately discounted any possibility of its early adoption, saying that the two sides were 'as far apart as ever' on the crucial question of the terms of NLF participation within the post-hostilities political life of South Vietnam.[118] Martin explicitly stated at this time that the Americans would have to negotiate with the Viet Cong. It was necessary, he said, 'to bring all the belligerents to the conference table.'[119] Although he did not state categorically that the NLF should be treated by the Americans and the RVN as an autonomous political entity, the overall thrust of the proposal/concept reflected a move to the left by the government.

In early April 1967 the prime minister spoke out again on behalf of extended bombing pauses, and again the speech was delivered in the United States, this time at the University of California at Santa Barbara.[120] On 10 May Pearson spoke in the Commons about the need to 'bring our worries and anxieties' and 'advice and counsel' to the attention of Washington policy-makers, given the then receding prospects for an early negotiated end to the war. Walter Gordon, long-time friend and confidant of Pearson, the then president of the Privy Council (and former minister of finance), privately praised Pearson for his outspokenness and then proceeded to deliver a speech in Toronto on 13 May which radically diverged from the careful line which the prime minister and his secretary of state for external affairs had been treading. The substance of the speech was left-liberal systemist – more radical, in effect, than some of the more measured criticisms put forward by the NDP of late.

Gordon's views had been strongly shaped by Professors James Steele (Department of English, Carleton University) and Abraham Rotstein (Department of Political Economy, University of Toronto), both of whom had long been active in the teach-in movement.[121] Steele was author of at least two strongly anti-war essays, which although factually inaccurate were nevertheless plausible, and more important, passionately humanitarian in tone. Gordon was also in regular contact at this time with Professor M.H. Watkins (also of the Department of Political Economy, University of Toronto), who shared most of the anti-war views of Steele and Rotstein.

In precisely the same way that NDP critics had regularly invoked American senators, generals, professors, and nationally syndicated columnists who were critical of the war, Gordon pieced together an extended series of quotations from many of the same sources. In essence, he argued that the United States had made a terrible and tragic error in intervening in a civil war. The American government was not about to 'confess its errors or change policies' and seemed only too likely to pursue its misguided course to some ultimate disaster. The risks to Canada and the Western world were fourfold. Asian 'distrust' of whites would be accentuated. The Sino-Soviet right might be forcibly healed. Communist Chinese forces might intervene. Worst of all, there was the 'gravest danger' that a Soviet-American nuclear confrontation would occur should Washington decide to employ nuclear weapons in an attempt to overcome a basically irretrievable situation.[122]

Paul Martin then tried to have Gordon removed from the Cabinet for breaking ranks on Vietnam and for articulating equally deviant positions on NATO and NORAD in another speech he had given on 12 May. Pearson 'criticized and disciplined' Gordon before the full Cabinet and caucus shortly thereafter. Gordon did not feel obliged to resign because Pearson had stated, evidently for the first time in Cabinet, that he hoped the Americans would simply cease the bombing of the North and demand talks for an armistice and settlement.[123] Pearson's criticisms were limited to the issue of Cabinet solidarity, not the explicit challenge to government policy premises raised by the speech. According to Gordon, Pearson had privately 'stated that he agreed with ninety-eight per cent' of the speech.[124]

Gordon's speech and the very substantial positive comment it elicited in the press and through mail[125] undoubtedly accelerated the shift by the government across the policy spectrum to the left-liberal incrementalist position. Perhaps in part to try to make amends for his initially violent reaction to Gordon's speech, Martin invited Gordon to accompany him to the NATO Council meetings at Luxembourg in June. There Martin organized 'a special private session on Vietnam, and alone among the foreign ministers spoke critically of United States policy in the war.'[126] According to Gordon's account of the meeting, Dean Rusk 'proceeded to slap Paul down' while 'no one else said anything.'[127]

The government did not finally come out publicly in favour of a unilateral bombing halt until 27 September 1966. The final obstacle to such action seems to have been Pearson's last liberal-moderate reservations. Only eleven days after Gordon's speech (and only one day before Lyndon Johnson's whirlwind tour of Expo '67 and his visit to Harrington Lake), the prime minister made a short speech in the Commons the like of which had not been heard from the government ranks in over fifteen months. To remind his audience that the Liberals had not adopted NDP policy wholesale, Pearson declared that the US role was being undertaken at the legitimate request of the RVN (ie, assistance in self-defence), and was therefore legal. Washington backed real national self-determination for the Vietnamese people, while on the other side the NLF was merely a front for a 'totalitarian communist regime in North Vietnam which has not allowed and does not intend to allow its own people any choice as to their social, economic or political system.'[128] The Americans were basically 'men of good will and as peace-loving as we are.' The bombing was a matter of 'regret' but nothing constructive would emerge from unilateral condemnation of American behaviour; moreover, the Americans had been far more serious about peace talks than had the North Vietnamese. Finally he declared:

I myself would not attach excessive expectations to peace and a negotiated settlement if the bombing should end tomorrow. We might as in the past – by 'we' I mean the western countries, the friends of the United States – well run up against what has been encountered before, namely, escalation of demand on the other side. So I think it might be desirable to find out what the reaction in Hanoi would be to an immediate and unconditional end to the bombing of the north. Would they stop fighting and begin talking and, *if they refused or attached a new condition, would the danger of massive escalation be increased? This is another factor we must have to take into consideration.*[129]

In the context of progressive increases in American troop strength in Vietnam and the already steadily escalating air war over North Vietnam, Pearson's use of the phrase 'massive escalation' could have referred to only two things: either Sino-American conventional warfare as in Korea, or unilateral American use of tactical nuclear weapons with all the potential for triggering World War III entailed therein. Some eight months later as the great Tet offensive of 1968 was being launched, Pearson specifically discounted rumours to the effect that the United States was actively considering use of nuclear weapons (rumours fed by Harold Wilson's distressed public musings on that subject). Said Pearson at that time: 'I do not believe the United States government would go in for that kind of madness.'[130] Some other kinds of madness perhaps, but not that kind. Pearson's fears thus probably centred on another conventionally fought Sino-American war.

Pearson's cumulative assessment of Johnson's character led him to believe that the president had meant precisely what he had said on several occasions about the strategically limited objectives of American Vietnam policy. The president's statement of his carefully limited objectives at Camp David in April 1965,[131] and the other declarations to that effect since that time,[132] had apparently convinced Pearson that Johnson would never issue carte blanche to the air war hawks who would willingly risk a nuclear shooting war with China to secure victory in Vietnam – provided the president remained firmly in control of himself and of his subordinates.

It was perhaps partly because of Johnson's agitated, somewhat illogical, and therefore rather disturbing performance during his visit to Harrington Lake on 25 May 1967,[133] and partly too because of the undeniably increasing pressure in Washington for an acceleration in the air war resulting from the Stennis Subcommittee Hearing in August,[134] that Pearson authorized Martin to give his United Nations speech of 27 September 1967 in which the secretary of state for external affairs unequivocally recommended a unilateral and unconditional cessation of the bombing of the DRVN. When one has few levers for exercising influence one must use them judiciously. Pearson had withheld the public 'stop the bombing' plea for as long as possible. He now played his last card, weak though it was.

Martin's UN speech was given at a time when both he and Pearson had come to despair that private diplomatic channels would ever effect a negotiated solution to the conflict. The various Canadian attempts to foster a revival of the original Geneva framework had all reached a dead end. In July the US government had rejected any thought of trading a bombing halt for the re-demilitarization of the original DMZ.[135] On 22 September American Ambassador to the UN Arthur Goldberg had reiterated the position that there would be no bombing halt without genuine reciprocal military concessions from the other side. A recent call by the Yugoslavian head of the World Federation of UN Associations for a Geneva meeting of the co-chairman states and the ICSC states had failed to produce results (only the Canadians and British ever responded favourably). The Soviets, Poles, and evidently Indians were unwilling to attend so long as the bombs continued to rain down on the north.[136]

Martin's actual recommendation for a bombing halt was carefully hedged in with qualifications. It was by no means a ringing denunciation of American military barbarism. Said Martin:

let us not for a moment pretend that a halt in the bombing would, in itself, bring the war to an end. There are no magic formulas; there are no simple prescriptions for the settlement of problems as complex as the issues behind the hostilities in Vietnam ... If, therefore, we are to recognize a halt to the bombing for what it is, namely the key to a solution, the starting point in the process of solving the Vietnam problem, let us be very clear in our minds that it is only one side of a military equation and that we cannot proceed, if we are to have any hope of success, as if the other side did not exist.[137]

Pearson and Martin harboured no illusions about the possibilities of an early move by the parties to adopt this plan. On 16 April *Nhan Dan*, the DRVN's official newspaper, had condemned Martin's four-point 'concept' for the progressive reapplication of the terms of the Geneva cease-fire as 'a crafty scheme of the u.s. imperialists on mutual de-escalation or reciprocity, which does not make a clear-cut distinction between the aggressor and those who oppose aggression.'[138] And Martin had made his UN bombing halt recommendation as part of his four-point plan. Hanoi's attitude did not change, nor did its generally unfriendly attitude to the Canadian government. The North Vietnamese had been annoyed at Canadian policy-makers for some time.[139] They were certainly not about to surrender their claims for a return to the original Geneva package, albeit broadly conceived, in exchange for an end to the bombing. A return to the terms of the original Final Declaration was at the heart of their political strategy. Pearson and Martin knew this. Martin's UN speech must therefore be interpreted as yet another attempt to constrain and moderate American behaviour, Martin's remarks about a two-sided equation nothwithstanding.

The decision to finally go public on the bombing issue was not made lightly. Even years later Pearson had doubts about the wisdom of doing so. The most probable cause for the decision was the Canadian government's perception that the war was escalating dangerously once more. As soon as the Stennis subcommittee hearings had commenced, American aircraft began bombing new targets close to the centre of Hanoi, and ever closer to the Chinese border. Pearson was certainly worried about the president's capacity to control the situation. Following the Harrington Lake meeting Pearson described the president as 'an older and more impatient and irascible enigma ... feverish in his insistence on activity.'[140] According to Pearson, Johnson in his 'laudable' effort to minimize civilian casualties through tight presidential control of the air war was attempting the militarily impossible: 'humane bombing.' Thus American policy was getting 'the worst of both worlds' because international criticism was no less condemnatory for all of the president's 'restraint.' Pearson's deep ambivalence on the bombing question is suggested by his description of the 1967 talks with Johnson on that subject:

In any event, ending the bombing would not stop the war, the ground combat would go on, I agreed that might well be true. *It was a worrying thought that perhaps we Canadians were wrong in attaching so much significance to ending the bombing as an element in ending the war.* Even if it was halted the Communists could readily find some excuse or other to refuse negotiations and continue fighting. Nevertheless, I said, such a move might have diplomatic results which would more than compensate for any military disadvantages if it failed.[141]

Pearson clearly understood the intimate linkage between the political and military dimensions of war. But Johnson would not, or could not (because of the political pressures he faced in Washington), respond to the prime minister's recommendation that he take a far more 'political' approach to the war. Pearson's reflection in this regard is revealing: 'I wonder *whether he really has control over these matters or whether – to keep the military from "going full speed ahead and damn the torpedoes" from China or anywhere else –* he has decided not to interfere in any of their existing military tactics, including bombing, in the hope of achieving good, political results.[142]

It is unfortunate that Pearson did not expand on the phrase 'good political results.' He may have been referring either to the president's own political prospects or, alternatively, to the political environment in Washington concerning relations among the Pentagon, State Department, CIA, and the Congress – or perhaps both. It is quite clear from this statement, however, that Pearson viewed policy outcomes in Washington vis-à-vis Vietnam as very much a contingent, highly politicized, and dangerously unpredictable process. His concern that American policy-making should not fall into the hands of adventurist elements in Washington should also be recognized.

It was not coincidental then that Pearson agreed to 'go public' on the bombing issue in late September. This becomes clear if events are examined in detail for the crucial weeks preceding the announcement. The Preparedness Subcommittee of the Senate Armed Services Committee, chaired by Senator John C. Stennis, held hearings from 9 to 25 August in which Admiral Sharp (the then CINCPAC) and most of the senior military officials directing the air war against North Vietnam were brought to Washington to discuss war policy. The final witness, the only one to support tight limits on the air war, was the secretary of defense himself, Robert McNamara. The subcommittee's intention from the beginning was to discredit McNamara's views. On 31 August the report from the subcommittee declared:

the plain facts as they unfolded in the testimony, demonstrated clearly that civilian authority consistently overruled the unanimous recommendations of the military commander and the Joint Chiefs of Staff for a systematic, timely, and hard-hitting integrated air campaign against the vital North Vietnam targets. Instead, for policy reasons, we have employed military aviation in a carefully controlled, restricted and graduated build-up of bombing pressure which discounted the professional judgement of our best military experts and substituted civilian judgement in the details of target selection and the timing of strikes. We shackled the true potential of air power and permitted the build-up of what has become the world's most formidable anti-aircraft defenses.

It is not our intention to point a finger or to second guess those who determined this policy [sic], but the cold fact is that this policy has not done the job and it has been contrary to the best military judgement. What is needed now is *a hard decision to do whatever is necessary, take the risks that have to be taken, and apply the force that is required to see the job through.*[143]

On 1 September, in response to the public furor caused by the Stennis hearings, Johnson 'called an unscheduled news conference ... to deny differences among his advisors and to generally overrule his Secretary of Defense on the bombing.'[144] On 10 September, Cam Pha, the third largest port in the DRVN, was bombed for the first time. Sharp pressed hard for the bombing of

Phuc Yen air field near Hanoi, the source of MIG aircraft attacks on American bombers. McNamara fought him off for another month. The take-out of Phuc Yen would mean that DRVN aircraft would all be moved to bases in southern China, opening new 'interacting possibilities.'[145] for escalation through hot-pursuit responses by American fighters. Without a doubt the supporters of 'rollback' were on the move in the autumn of 1967. McNamara would be squeezed out of the Cabinet by the end of the year as a direct result of their pressure.

For what it was worth, this was the time for Pearson the liberal-moderate to play the last Canadian card: the need to go public was now urgent. On 27 September 1967 Ottawa finally went on public record against any victory through unlimited conventional airpower. From this point on, until the end of Lester Pearson's tenure of office, Ottawa would preach restraint, prudence, and caution to the Americans. The government would never condemn the bombing as immoral, however, nor would it ever advocate a precipitate American withdrawal from Vietnam.

THE MID-1960S TENDENCY SHIFT IN REVIEW

Table 2 provides a summary of the key policy assumptions and recommendations of the five main positions in the Canadian Vietnam debate, from 1963 to 1968. Of the seven factors listed in the table for the liberal-moderates and conservatives, it is noteworthy that points 3–7 were frequently affirmed in the House. Points 1 and 2 (attitude towards the containment doctrine, and attitude towards Washington's élite vis-à-vis Vietnam specifically), however, must be inferred from related comments. Such coyness concerning the truly crucial geopolitical aspects of the war is reminiscent of the same reluctance to discuss fundamental elements of the western world's 'grand strategy' in Asia which characterized the earlier 'debates' on Indochina of 1953–4.

Inspiring this prudential rhetorical restraint (what journalistic and academic criticism would usually term timidity) was the reasonable apprehension that clear articulation of Canadian disinterest in the strategic value of Indochina would be received as a gratuitous political insult by the American government, then feverishly engaged in trying to sustain flagging public support for the war. Both liberal-moderates and conservatives deemed harmonious Canadian-American relations to be vitally important. Canadian Indochina policy had to be shaped accordingly. For liberal-moderates, it was important to maintain sympathetic credibility and diplomatic access to Washington's corridors of power simply because they wished to be forewarned of any crucial decisions involving possible major escalation of the

TABLE 2
PART A: Marginalist/incrementalist policy positions 1963–8

Left-liberal	Liberal-moderate	Conservative
1 Containment must be subordinate to the principle of national self-determination	1 Containment in Europe but not in Asia, especially Southeast Asia	1 Containment is needed everywhere; there must be no Munichs; but no troops from Canada
2 Encourage liberal wing of US political élite that the war is unjust and unwinnable	2 Strengthen liberal pro-containment wing in US to ensure that nuclear adventurist element is restrained	2 Vigorous support for US role of 'global policeman'; material support for the US/RVN side
3 Use diplomacy to inhibit US escalation of the war and if private arguments fail to constrain American behaviour, use public criticism	3 Seek political formula for the initiation of real talks; risk of escalation to Sino-American, nuclearized conflict is a priority concern	3 Regional neutralization on the Cambodian model is adequate and reasonable objective for Canadian diplomacy
4 Press strongly for a unilateral bombing halt; press for measures to delay escalation to give anti-war opponents in the US time to sway public opinion against the war; use the ICSC only so long as it can inhibit the American war effort	4 Recommend a unilateral American bombing halt privately; say nothing publicly to diminish Canadian credibility in Washington as a sympathetic ally	4 No criticism of US methods is permissible unless Canada has troops in the war
5 Early seating of the PRC at the UN deemed to be crucial and unilateral recognition by the Canadian government is a sensible idea	5 Early seating of PRC at the UN is a major concern; unilateral recognition of the PRC is out of the question	5 Early seating of the PRC at the UN is important but Taiwan's independence must not be sacrificed
6 Favours recognition of NLF autonomy	6 NLF representation within the DRVN delegation to eventual talks is adequate	6 Ottawa has no right to comment on the status of the NLF, and should avoid it in any case, since the front is 'a puppet of the DRVN'

7 Favours unilateral American disengagement, and a Canadian peacekeeping role if needed

7 Favours Canadian peacekeeping role; unilateral US disengagement is 'unrealistic'

7 Peacekeeping should be avoided in future and the existing ICSC role should be discarded; cost is a factor

PART B: Systemist policy positions 1963–8

Left-liberal	Conservative
1 'Containment' is merely a device to cloak great-power interventionism with a veneer of legality; as practised in Asia it is a violation of national self-determination	1 Containment everywhere is essential; Canadian participation on a limited basis is a good idea
2 Change US public opinion by official Canadian denunciation of this 'immoral and barbarous' war; support dissenting Americans wherever possible	2 Preach 'Free World' solidarity; no criticism of the Americans in their thankless but vital sacrifice
3 Diplomacy is irrelevant when many Pentagon hawks are scheming for war with communist China	3 Diplomacy is irrelevant; support balance-of-power logic wherever possible; 'aggression' is always easier to stop early on (cf. Hitler's course of expansion); domino theory is valid
4 The US bombing campaign is wicked, un-Christian, and can never be condoned	4 No criticism of US methods since communist atrocities are as bad if not worse
5 Canadians should do everything possible to force the UN into the picture and to make its role effective; working for the PRC's early admission and extending unilateral recognition of the PRC would be steps in the right direction	5 Communist China is the source of the aggression; everything must be done to force it to relinquish its aggressive designs on Southeast Asia
6 The NLF is a legitimate government, fully independent of Hanoi	6 The NLF is a puppet front with no serious political support in the south except what it can command through terror
7 Unilateral and precipitate disengagement of American forces is the only moral course of action worth supporting	7 Canada should get off the ICSC, help stop the communists with as much material support as it can spare

war through either direct attacks on Chinese sanctuaries or possible resort to nuclear weaponry. As Pearson prosaically phrased it, Canada was the ham in the super-power sandwich.[146] Canada's very existence depended upon the maintenance of nuclear peace between the super powers. Indochina threatened that peace by feeding the ambitions of Washington's adventurists. For the conservatives, the matter was more straightforward: the Americans had undertaken a thankless and costly sacrifice of which Canadians would be indirect beneficiaries. Any carping from the sidelines over methods would rightly anger the US government and a sizeable segment of American public opinion. Washington deserved assistance and praise, not meddling, quarrelsome scrutiny.

As in the 1950s, Canadian conservative support for US objectives in Asia was nevertheless qualified. Even the most enthusiastic systemist supporters of the American role stopped short of recommending rollback of the communist sphere of influence. The game to be played according to Canadian anti-communists was containment, not confrontation and counter-revolution.[147]

Thus both liberal-moderates and conservatives advocated a policy of no public criticism of the American intervention. So-called 'quite diplomacy' prevailed. While both liberal-moderates and conservatives recognized the significance of the China factor in the debate, neither doctrinal tendency espoused action on the issue which might seriously have threatened Canadian-American relations. One notable difference between these two marginalist camps concerned possible future peacekeeping duties. Given the thrust of their rhetoric after February 1966 on behalf of peace, the liberal-moderates had to support the notion of an eventual peacekeeping role for Canada. The conservative marginalists would have preferred that the government simply declare its support for the RVN/US side, dispatch a symbolically significant flow of material aid, then bow out of any future post-hostilities arrangements. The conservative element in Canada both in Parliament and within External Affairs was fed up with the frustration, financial costs, and politically ambiguous status of the peace interlocutor role. To many conservatives it suggested waffling indecision, a shirking of responsibility, and a failure to stand on principle when the going became difficult.

The vigour of such demands for a stand on anti-communist principle was undercut, however, by fears of World War III and by the belief that Canada should offer only very limited support to the 'allied' war effort. For example, following the bombing escalation of the summer of 1966 PC enthusiasm for the war fell away quickly. Thereafter they tended to argue only that Ottawa should drop its pretence of impartiality by casting off the ICSC role altogether and ceasing criticism of Washington's actions. Although never clearly articulated in the Commons, Parliamentary conservatives subscribed implicitly to the view of the senior departmental conservative who declared:

Our strategic interests were not in that part of the world. They were not in Indochina, but in NATO. And we were not a big power. We had limited resources. You know it's very much like a man coming to the door asking for charity saying if you pay me, that will be all. But you know there are many more who will come. So when this fellow points to your income and says, 'look, you can afford to pay more,' you can only respond by saying, 'I have my priorities. They are all sorted out. You take what I want to give – or lump it.' NATO was not relevant for Southeast Asia. Our strategic commitments have to be fixed. We cannot be flitting about all over the globe.[148]

Or as another departmental conservative phrased matters rather more bluntly: 'To talk in strategic terms you have to have a strategic viewpoint. And you have to put up or shut up. From our point of view it would have been very dangerous to start discussing strategic concerns. We did in Korea. Grand strategy has its price.[149]

Neither of these partial rationalizations for prudent avoidance of the delicate subject of strategic commitments was well founded. At a time when Canadian contributions to NATO were declining (and soon to be cut drastically following the defence review of 1968–9), the priorities argument fails to account for conservative restraint. So too does the Korean 'example' because Canada only participated given the exceptional and never-to-occur-again circumstance of a UN umbrella, not because of the compelling logic of American strategists. It is more reasonable to infer that Canadian conservatives did not subscribe to a truly firm commitment to containment in Asia – especially if that stance seemed likely to play into the hands of American pro-rollback hawks.

In short, the conservative doctrinal position in Canada was relatively weakly rooted. There was no truly extreme systemist variant. The Canadian marginalist debate may be compared to the American intra-governmental marginalist debate in this regard through the schematic representation provided in figure 6. Canadian conservatives never articulated policy positions comparable to those of American bureaucratic right-wingers. Rollback was no urgent priority for Canadian anti-communists. It is perhaps because of the absence of an extreme right wing in the Canadian political debate (even the systemists talked only of containment) that left-liberal pressure was able to produce as much movement in the government's position as it did. There

FIGURE 6
The relative positions of Canadian and American marginalist schools of thought

Canadian marginalists		
Left-liberals	Liberal-moderates	Conservatives

American marginalists		
	White House	
Pro-containment		Pro-'rollback'
State Department		CIA-covert
CIA-analysis section		operations
US Army-esp.		section
Green Berets		US Air Force
		US Navy
Senate Foreign		CINCPAC (Honolulu)
Relations Committee		
		Senate Armed
Europe-firsters		Services
geopolitically		Committee
pro-non-nuclear		Asia-firsters
'flexible response'		
		pro-nuclear
		adventurism

had never been a 'Pacific-first' doctrinal tradition in the Canadian strategic perspective. Canadians were Atlanticists all. This fact, together with the creeping strategic isolationism of both the Canadian political élite and middle class, produced a rapid back-pedalling by the liberal-moderate forces led by Pearson and Martin, as soon as the Opposition began to hint that it would soon call for a Canadian military commitment to the war in February 1966.[150] Perhaps fearing that the Liberals might attempt to call an election on the issue, the PCs soon reversed themselves and declared that they too did not favour the dispatch of Canadian troops.[151] That declaration assured the

FIGURE 7
The mid-1960s tendency shifts of key policy actors
Fundamental value commitment

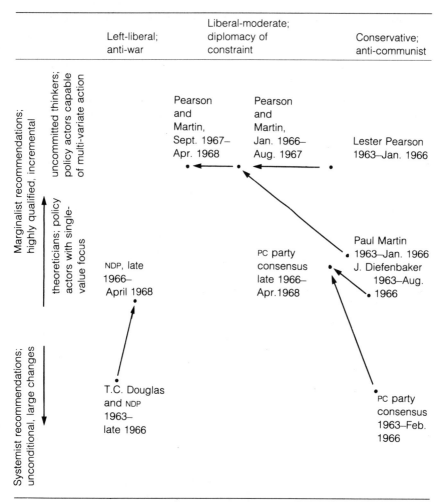

political feasibility of the further shift to the doctrinal left by Pearson and Martin in September 1967. Figure 7 schematically illustrates the tendency shift in the government's position, and the related shifts by the Progressive Conservatives and New Democrats in response to the new governmental moderation. Over the 1963–8 period all three parties showed decisive movement towards more marginalist postures vis-à-vis the war. And all three moved progressively towards the doctrinal centre.

Pearson quite correctly sensed that the bombing was alienating Canadian support for American policy, as was the lack of political credibility of successive governments in Saigon. As a prudent liberal-moderate, Pearson was worried about how far he could safely move government policy to the left without foreclosing all opportunities for diplomatic influence (and intelligence-gathering) in Washington. The movement upward and leftward by Paul Martin was probably dictated as much by personal political circumstance (his bid for Liberal party leadership was then going quite well)[152] as by international environmental factors. Both men were comfortable with the rhetoric of liberal-moderate doctrine. Neither wished to jeopardize Canadian-American relations. Martin was no longer able or eager to sustain a single-value theoretical focus on the war.[153] Especially in view of his prospective bid to move to the very apex of the Canadian political system, he had to demonstrate the sort of doctrinal flexibility characteristic of all the most senior policy-makers. Given the chronic ambiguity of decision-making environments and the flux of Canadian domestic politics, Martin was forced to abandon his previous conservative enthusiasm on Vietnam. All his policy statements after February 1966 would be uniformly conditional, qualified, and tentative. From early 1966 onward he was the very model of an 'uncommitted,'[154] liberal-moderate marginalist.

For Pearson and Martin, the 1963–8 period of Vietnam policy-making was cause for chronic frustration and anxiety. There was no easy solution to the war. It was unlikely that there would be early negotiations. The risk of serious escalation was ever-present. The careful distancing of Canada from the conflict which they fostered was a tactic aiming to minimize the country's maximum potential losses – a classically bureaucratic if not typically Canadian response to an insecure environment. The interlocutor-for-peace posture forestalled American demands for participation in the allied crusade, participation which could only be expensive in terms of Canadian lives and government support. It also guaranteed that External Affairs officials still had relatively open access to the ebb and flow of policy debate in Washington about the war. Had a bureaucratic threat to the nuclear peace materialized in the Pentagon, Pearson would still have heard of it, probably before it became presidentially legitimized. Canadian action would still have been possible to try to head it off. Domestically, Canadian Vietnam policy was a political success. The Liberal party consistently obtained favourable ratings for its foreign policy approach.[155] Just as in the nuclear weapons debate of 1962–3, Pearson divined the true mood of the electorate concerning a key foreign policy issue. Although Pearson was no doubt too weak on the issue of communist expansionism in Asia in the eyes of the few conservative systemists left in Canadian public life by the autumn of 1967, it was just as clear to a grateful majority of Canadians that he was not going to allow Canada to become a tool for America's most bellicose Pentagon planners. Eventually even the New Democrats were forced to acknowledge the practical wisdom and popular success of Pearson's unending series of compromises which they did by muting their criticism of the government line.

II

The 'new' national interest versus traditional liberal-moderate doctrine: the ICCS replay 1973

For the United States policy was very difficult. Once you are in, you can't just back out since millions would suffer. Big countries can't back out. They have a moral responsibility to maintain their commitments ... In the end Nixon and Kissinger wanted out. They felt they had been sucked in, in the first place. They wanted an end to the war as sincerely as Eisenhower wanted to end the Korean conflict in 1952. They were prepared to stop the assaults on the North, even to give recognition. The slogan 'Peace with Honour' was real. If there had been no Watergate then there would have been no collapse in 1975.

External Affairs conservative, 1976

PRELUDE TO RE-ENGAGEMENT

In April 1968 Pierre Trudeau became prime minister. Canadian-American relations loomed large on his agenda. If Vietnam was not seen as a major problem, it was certainly looked on as a potential hazard. Trudeau had an overwhelming mandate for charting new directions in policy, domestic and foreign, but he possessed no experience in the making of foreign policy. He came to power having repudiated the American bombing in Indochina as 'an error in basic psychology.'[1] But he was not on record in opposition to American war aims in Vietnam.

From the outset the new prime minister implicitly supported the theory of containment in Asia, but rejected what he perceived to be counterproductive modalities directed at this objective, such as air war against the DRVN. The new, allegedly more realistic perspective he brought to foreign policy found the Pearson-Martin approach to Vietnam to be reasonable in so far as it undercut domestic criticism and precluded costly military commitments in alliance with the United States, while respecting Canada's modest interests in Pacific Asia. Calculation of the national interest, narrowly construed, would be the hallmark of the first Trudeau ministry.

The general thrust of the new government, as enunciated by Secretary of State for External Affairs Mitchell Sharp, involved a somewhat greater distancing of Ottawa from the conflict compared to policy-making during the last two years of Pearson's leadership. Nationalism, not neutralism, was the conceptual thrust behind the new posture. Neither Trudeau nor Sharp declared themselves in favour of any particular scheme for negotiating an end to the war. Both pointedly ignored Pearson's final act in office: a declaration on American television that elections were an 'unrealistic way' to frame a peace settlement in Vietnam and that exploration of the coalition government option was the most probable route to success. In this same interview, Pearson said that although the original rationale for intervention was not in error, the US government had subsequently committed itself far too heavily to Indochina. The incoming government ignored this observation as well. Part of Pearson's interview was congenial to the government. Canada, said Pearson, would accept a future peacekeeping role only if there were prospects for successful execution of the task, if both sides invited Canada, and if the terms of reference met with Canadian approval.[2] These qualifications were soon endorsed by the government.[3] They were not new. In fact, Paul Martin had been stating such conditions publicly since February 1966.[4]

Ottawa officials in External Affairs undoubtedly approved the new Cabinet's propensity for distancing Canada from the conflict and for avoiding any a priori unconditional commitment to future peacekeeping operations. The consensus among External Affairs personnel was now if anything even more strongly disposed towards indirect support for the South Vietnamese/ American cause. Despite great distaste for US methods of warfare, as well as persistent fears of uncontrolled escalation, the balance of professional opinion still approved of American ends in Vietnam. The department's consensus for the 1968–72 period was based on the premise that although 'strategic considerations' had 'dictated' the extent of the American interventionary commitment to Indochina, it was fundamentally reasonable for the United States 'to provide a shield behind which necessary changes can take place, to buy time,' and thus forestall a destructive revolutionary transformation of all Southeast Asia.[5] The essentially conservative character of this particular premise produced a deep ambivalence within the department about possible future involvement in Indochina. The future 'peace' might very well be a disguised American withdrawal. Another source of ambivalence was the department's collective judgment that 'the shifting power balance' and the 'unresolved tensions' of the Pacific Asian region were likely to continue for some time to come as the United States redefined its role following the articulation of the Nixon Doctrine, and as the Chinese and Soviets adjusted their commitments correspondingly to create a new power equilibrium in the region.[6] Large change implied high risk. Caution was therefore doubly important.

The foreign policy review which Trudeau initiated in the spring of 1969 culminated in the issuing of *Foreign Policy for Canadians*, six pamphlets on the government's new approach. The position on Vietnam, while not developed in detail, was reasonably clear. Canada's status as a non-belligerent but non-neutral power interested primarily in the restoration of peace would continue unchanged. Strategic commitments to the Pacific Asian region were out of the question. As a concession to left-liberal sentiment within the department, the review declared that there would be 'rehabilitation aid' and 'a contribution to longer-term reconstruction efforts' for post-war Indochina. Participation in a new supervisory role would occur only if Canadians judged the arrangements to be 'acceptable,' 'workable,' and possessed of 'a clear mandate, adequate resources and the full co-operation of the parties.'[7] Certainly many in the department hoped to avoid the draft call for peace-keeping service then shaping up. Four months after the publication of *Foreign Policy for Canadians*, President Nixon issued his first plan for a cease-fire in place, a negotiated timetable for the withdrawal of all US forces, and a political settlement which would involve *all* parties to the conflict (ie, the National Liberation Front)[8]. This was the first time that American proposals had dropped the demand that all DRVN forces in the south be withdrawn concurrent to the American withdrawal.

The foreign policy review process in Canada between May 1968 and June 1970 may be viewed functionally as a valuable stalling device for the Trudeau government. Like royal commissions, it shelved many contentious decisions but still allowed concerned citizens and influential academics and clergy to partake in a great national 'debate,' thus promoting the belief that many people had taken part in the formulation of the government's new approach. Equally important, much public criticism was defused by its exposure to detailed bureaucratic 'counterattacks' elaborating the complex rationales for the existing set of policies. But ironically enough, for all the winds of change unleashed by Trudeau the net consequence of the review for Canadian Indochina policy was negligible. A cautious policy of restrained and 'balanced criticism' of the two sides to the conflict remained the effective policy consensus of the government no matter how intense was public pressure from left-liberal systemists for condemnation of American 'atrocities.'[9]

This somewhat paradoxical outcome (given Trudeau's reformist mandate) may have been due to sheer public exhaustion on the Vietnam issue, as well as to the prime minister's latent conservatism in areas of policy-making wherein he had little personal experience on which to draw. For the dedicated Canadian anti-war systemists, the US intervention remained a disgraceful, barbaric excercise in the most brutal forms of intimidation. Television coverage of the effects of search and destroy operations in the south, of the effects of the 'lavish' use of artillery and airborne firepower in both the north and the south, of the deterioration of morale among the American conscript forces (including the onset of 'fragging' of officers, racial violence, and drug abuse among the enlistees) had helped to convince many Canadians that this was a tragically misguided war. By 1971–3 most Canadians found the Vietnam problem to be a wearisome, depressing issue. Almost as much as their American neighbours, Canadians were fed up with the war, America's great 'mistake,' and wanted it ended.[10]

The foreign policy review helped to direct attention away from insoluble issues like Vietnam and the potentially divisive charges from the left-systemists of Canadian 'complicity' in alleged American war crimes. In the most widely read commentary on the foreign policy review, only three of seventeen commentators involved noted critically the absence of any systematic policy analysis of the Vietnam problem, and only one of the three felt the omission required any lengthy comment.[11] By opening up the foreign policy debate to include all of Canada's international commitments Trudeau, intentionally or not, succeeded in directing the critics' attention to topics and problems where consensus was still achievable.

Had there been no foreign policy/defence policy review, the My Lai controversy in 1969–70, the American–South Vietnamese 'incursion' into Cambodia in May 1970, the bombing of the north in the spring of 1972, and finally the Christmas bombing of Hanoi-Haiphong from 18 to 30 December 1972 might very well have led to extreme outbursts of anti-American sentiment that would have had highly damaging repercussions for Canadian–American relations for years to come. As it was, anti-American sentiment was definitely rising in Canada throughout the first Trudeau ministry's tenure of office, but it did not focus on the Vietnam war. Economic issues such as the unilateral Nixon tariff surcharge of 1971, US monetary policy generally, and the rapidly proliferating domination of the Canadian economy by American multinational corporations were instead the basic catalysts of this phenomenon.[12]

THE TRUDEAU-SHARP VERSION OF
LIBERAL-MODERATE DIPLOMACY

Foreign Policy for Canadians had explicitly criticized the rhetoric of liberal-moderate peacekeeping and peace-promoting policies. The document asserted that in the past – presumably under men such as Pearson and Holmes – Canadian policy had been too 'reactive.'[13] This approach was held to be inadequate. Influence abroad was not maximized. But the quasi-isolationist impact of the 'new' nationalism being offered as an alternative was counterproductive. The new approach which Trudeau and Sharp legitimized was premised upon a too optimistic reading of collaborative and co-operative trends in the international environment. In Vietnam policy-making, Trudeau, Sharp, and the disillusioned Indochina peacekeepers in External Affairs would soon learn that being 'reactive' was still the inevitable, though not necessarily desperate, lot of the middle-power state if it wished to channel, constrain, or modify the behaviour of the great powers, especially American behaviour.

The sequence of government actions on Indochina may be summarized briefly. In late 1968 the government reaffirmed Canadian support of an indefinite halt to the bombing of the DRVN.[14] This reaffirmation was made in language carefully phrased not to offend American authorities. Secretary of State for External Affairs Mitchell Sharp declared that henceforth the government would aim at 'balanced criticism' because Ottawa wanted both sides to 'contribute significantly to military de-escalation.'[15]

In November 1968 Trudeau indicated that the government would not begin to look at plans for future Indochina peacekeeping until and unless the conditions of such involvement were known to be acceptable to Ottawa.[16] The prime minister pointedly ignored John Diefenbaker's suggestion to revive the Ronning contact with Hanoi, and Postmaster General Eric Kierans's suggestion that Canada should withdraw from NATO so as to be able to provide a large peacekeeping force for Indochina when needed[17]. NDP criticism intensified over the course of the next year, but Progressive Conservative policy under Robert Stanfield became more liberal-moderate in character than the line taken by the government.[18]

In early 1969 Prince Norodom Sihanouk had complained to the Cambodian ICSC that DRVN forces were infiltrating and occupying the eastern provinces of Cambodia, especially Svay Rieng. At this time and throughout

1968, both the Indians and Poles refused to permit any attempt at ICSC investigation of the charges. By March 1969 Sihanouk ceased requesting ICSC action. By October 1969 he began asking the commission to leave. On 4 December 1969 he asked the ICSC to adjourn sine die by 31 December 1969. By 7 January 1970 all Canadians and ICSC personnel had left Cambodia as requested.[19] In mid-March 1968 the secret 'Menu' bombings of the Cambodian-Vietnamese border area began. Such bombing became regular in May 1969 and continued until May 1970 when the American–South Vietnamese 'incursion' into Cambodia commenced. From then on, the bombing of DRVN base camps was executed openly.[20]

In early 1970 most of the remaining Canadian personnel in Laos were withdrawn, allegedly for reasons of economy. In mid-1970, the Royal Laotian Government requested the ICSC for Laos to investigate the occupation of eastern Laos by DRVN troops. The vestigial Canadian delegation on the Laotian ICSC pressed for investigations. The Indians and Poles once more declined.[21] In February 1971 Ottawa again asked its commission colleagues to begin talks on conducting such investigations, but was turned down. In March they pressed for formal discussion of the problem and refused to consider an Indo-Polish proposal for an ICSC 'call for peace' in the area until the still outstanding Canadian proposal had been dealt with.[22] No action was taken.

From the government's point of view a passive policy was most appropriate. President Nixon and his then National Security Adviser Henry Kissinger were irrevocably committed to disengagement. They had shown themselves to be far more flexible on the China recognition question than previous Democratic administrations. Only six months into his first term in office it became Nixon's policy to recognize Beijing and exploit the benefits of the now openly violent Sino-Soviet rift.[23] By late 1970 the signs were unmistakable that the new American administration was going to try to take advantage of the grave mutual mistrust between the two communist giants of Eurasia. Unknown to the Canadians, the Soviets had already made behind-the-scene requests to the Americans for a commitment not to intervene in the event of Soviet military action against the PRC's nuclear installations.[24] Canadian recognition of the communist Chinese government on 13 October 1970 grew out of this rapidly shifting environment. So-called 'ping-pong diplomacy' began in April 1971. Kissinger visited Beijing in July 1971. Nixon followed him in October. In May 1972, while US bombs rained down on North Vietnam, Nixon and Kissinger were toasted in Moscow.

In the actual conduct of the war by the Americans there seemed less cause for anxiety in Ottawa with respect to ultimate American intentions. Prior to

1970 there had been genuine grounds for fears that Washington might adopt a 'winning' strategy which would lead to eventual American attacks on Chinese staging areas and logistical supply lines into North Vietnam. The last time when such fears were truly justified was May 1970, following Nixon's panicky reaction to Soviet testing of a multiple warhead on one of its ICBMs, the sudden appearance of Soviet pilots in Egyptian MiG aircraft, the near-simultaneous launching of an earth satellite by the PRC, and the coeval deterioration of political order within the United States exemplified by the massive increase in demonstrations and bombings on university campuses.[25] That potential crisis passed, following joint American–South Vietnamese actions to eliminate all DRVN/Viet Cong base camps in the Cambodian–Vietnamese border areas by the end of June 1970. Time was purchased for a militarily feasible disengagement of American troops from combat roles and their replacement by ARVN forces, a process known as 'Vietnamization.' By the spring of 1971 US troops in Vietnam were down to 300,000 from a peak of 543,000 in April 1969.[26] American deaths in combat fell from 9,414 in 1969 to 1,380 in 1971, and only 300 in 1972, while ARVN deaths rose from 21,833 in 1969 to over 40,000 in 1972.[27] The Nixon Doctrine (also known as the Guam Doctrine, enunciated 25 July 1969) was clearly being implemented with haste.

To the Canadian government these were welcome statistics suggesting the possibility of either an early negotiated withdrawal from the conflict by the United States, or else a reduction in the conflict's scale. However odious was the substitution of 'immaculate' air war for infantry footslogging by the Americans, the tactic promised less opposition at home for the hard-pressed Nixon team, a credible threat to prosecute the war on this basis indefinitely, and therefore a stronger incentive for the DRVN to abandon its wholly intransigent attitude towards a settlement of the war.

In Canada, the domestic political problem posed by Vietnam had diminished by 1971–2. Although some 5,000 demonstrators turned out for a violent anti-war rally at the US consulate in Toronto on 9 May 1970 (in which ninety-one protesters were arrested) the disorder which occurred there, and during the 'symbolic' invasion of Blaine, Washington, by other protesters, seems to have done much to discredit the legitimacy of anti-war protest in the eyes of Canada's own silent majority.[28]

By 1971–2 the New Democratic Party was recommending the effective termination of the ICSCs through unilateral Canadian withdrawal.[29] Left-liberals in Parliament saw ICSC membership as offering a politically convenient excuse for the government's alleged moral cowardice in not 'deploring' every act of bombing by the United States, or every apparent escalatory act.[30] The heated anti-war rhetoric became vitriolic and vituperative with publication of the Pentagon Papers. Even the Progressive Conservatives, now in the full flush of self-righteous liberal moderation, joined in the NDP's barrage of criticism on Liberal party policy. To New Democrats, the release of the Pentagon Papers proved that Canada had been 'an agent of the United States,'[31] that Ottawa has surrendered its posture of 'complete impartiality' and allowed itself to become 'a messenger boy for the disastrous policies of escalation,' and that Canada had shown 'subservience' to American war aims.[32] To the new-model PCs, the revelations showed that Canada's 'neutrality' (sic) had been a sham, that Ottawa had functioned as 'an errand boy bearing threats of an expanded war,' and that peace promotion was not at all the basis of Canadian policy under Pearson and Martin.[33] These comments were all made by spokesmen of the same party which only five years earlier had flirted with public advocacy of sending Canadian troops to Vietnam.

Secretary of State for External Affairs Sharp was not in top form in attempting to defend the Pearson–Martin record as 'interlocutors for peace.' To his government's continuing discomfort, he did not immediately repudiate PC references to Canada's supposed policy of 'neutrality' nor did he candidly admit the fact that implicit threats were carried to Hanoi. He lamely argued that the Poles had carried out a similar diplomatic function, and that the previous government had merely tried to promote a dialogue 'to try to end the war.'[34] Lack of understanding of both the public and classified record of events was fast becoming evident on both sides of the House of Commons, and such ignorance was compounding the difficulty of responding effectively to the rapidly changing parameters of the war and the American role in it. It was left to Trudeau to assert in a speech at Aurora, Ontario, on 22 June 1971 that Canada had never tried to be 'neutral,' but only impartial in its conduct on the ICSC.[35]

Throughout 1971–2, Canadian personnel were instructed to cease informal contacts with American officials and military staff in the south.[36] Ottawa made no serious effort to intercede in the dispute between the Indian government and the RVN in 1972 when the former officially recognized the Hanoi regime, leaving New Delhi's Saigon office at consular status only.[37] In late 1972, the ICSC's headquarters was transferred to Hanoi as a result of RVN exclusion of Indian personnel. This marked the final decline of the ICSC for Vietnam. The last official business of this now debt-ridden body was transacted on 13 March 1973 at the International Secretariat in Vientiane. A joint Indo-Polish statement declared that 'the Commission is happy to note that Peace is again returning to this war-torn Region and would like to wish Peace and Prosperity to the courageous people of Viet Nam and every success in their building of their country.'[38] Canadian delegate R.D. Jackson protested the sudden dissolution of the ICSC at DRVN urging, called for an audit, and condemned the long-moribund ICSC as a 'sad monument to poorly conceived and poorly employed international machinery.'[39]

In Ottawa, the prime minister and his secretary of state for external affairs tried throughout 1972 to exhibit a posture of benign but hopeful non-involvement towards the war. When President Nixon met with Trudeau in April 1972, the prime minister refrained from making any criticism of the renewed bombing of the north, claiming that the Canadian government's opposition to the bombing was on record and well known to Washington. Later, in Ottawa, Trudeau indicated that he fully believed Nixon's assertions of a commitment to a 'negotiated settlement in Vietnam' and a 'continued withdrawal of United States troops.' One week after Trudeau's comments, Sharp indicated once again the government's general willingness to co-operate in any viable peacekeeping or peace supervisory scheme, which United Nations Secretary General Kurt Waldheim might achieve 'either by the provision of observers or anything of this kind, if suitable terms can be worked out, or in any other way that might be useful.'[40] During the massive May 1972 offensive by DRVN forces which precipitated renewed American bombing over the North and the mining of Haiphong harbour, Trudeau declared that unilateral criticism of the US bombing was quite out of order because there were some twelve North Vietnamese divisions engaged in an invasion of the RVN at that very moment. The prime minister noted also that the violent American response did not necessarily imply the creation of any insuperable obstacle to a negotiated end to the war, and that Nixon's imminent Moscow trip might very well produce major progress towards ending the conflict. Sharp noted later that month that it was not the Western side that was blocking any reconvening of the Geneva Conference, it was the Soviet Union.[41] Officially, Ottawa had been retreating from its commitments in Southeast Asia; but it was also true that high government officials had indicated a continuing Canadian interest in seeing the war ended as soon as possible. Both Trudeau and Sharp had evinced more than a merely theoretical willingness to look at participation in any emergent peacekeeping arrangements.

From 1970 through 1972, the government spoke of specific conditions of future involvement, asserting that any commitment had to 'make a real contribution to peace,' that any such commitment would not be of indefinite duration, that the future International Commission had to have 'adequate resources for its work and immediate access to any part of the territory to be supervised,' and finally that any reports of the new IC had to go to a competent 'continuing political authority' (CPA) which would publish them 'as might any participating supervisory powers.'[42] While such conditions might have been seen by Canadian analysts as unambiguous signs of governmental reluctance to become reinvolved, Kissinger, Secretary of State Rogers, and the other members of the Nixon administration may be forgiven for assuming that the Canadians were willing to help implement the forthcoming 'peace agreement,' and were merely trying to do their utmost to strengthen the terms of reference of the new commission. If Ottawa was not exactly preaching for a call, it was certainly very far from making any categorical refusals to participate.

The complex Canadian position was in fact irrelevant. When Kissinger announced on 26 October 1972 that 'peace was at hand,' Ottawa could not realistically avoid duty in Indochina on a new International Commission. The Nixon administration had expended some 15,000 American lives and many billions of dollars to avoid an overt defeat in Vietnam. The agreement worked out with Hanoi was perceived to be of vital importance in Washington. Any Canadian actions which in any way interfered with or jeopardized the execution of the agreement, especially the return of American prisoners of war, would be remembered angrily for years to come. No Canadian government could risk such ill will merely to safeguard Canadian self-esteem. Moreover, it was in the Canadian interest that Washington disengage quickly. If many Canadians railed at becoming 'the American representative' on this new body, seeing in such a development the realization of all previous left-wing criticism of Canada's alleged satellite status, a solid majority in government understood that failure to assume this distasteful burden might jeopardize the execution of the agreement between Hanoi and Washington. This would leave the Americans with no other option but unilateral withdrawal (which would have been political suicide without a return of US prisoners), or still more violent escalation to force Hanoi to surrender (still a real option involving brutal conventional air assaults on the north and possibly the selective use of nuclear weapons).

As always there was no shortage of hypocrisy on both sides. Hanoi leaders still refused to acknowledge the existence in the south of some 140,000 DRVN regular troops. To do so would have meant opening the door to international pressure for reciprocal withdrawal of their forces as US forces were removed from the south. Not until 8 September 1972 did the North Vietnamese drop their dangerously unrealistic demands for the removal of President Nguyen Van Thieu from office prior to any projected military and political settlement, and the creation of a coalition government which would effectively deprive the southern government of control over the territory it had already won by force of arms.[43] Not until then did Hanoi agree to 'separate' the military and political aspects of the war, the necessary first step in Kissinger's long-term plan for effecting American withdrawal 'with honour.'[44]

On the American side there was much false talk of a genuine peace settlement emerging from the negotiations, despite the fact that the whole thrust of the American bargaining position aimed at avoiding political clauses threatening Thieu's retention of power in the south, something which guaranteed that peace could not be realized. The essential point of separating the political and military dimensions of the conflict was to obviate the necessity of forcing an unwanted political settlement on Thieu, an ally, in full public view. The ultimate 'peace agreement' was, as both sides understood from the outset, an agreement to de-escalate the violence by disengaging American ground forces from the war. The quid pro quo for US withdrawal from this aspect of the fighting was return of the American POWs, an accounting for MIAs (those missing in action), and a temporary face-saving armistice, which would permit the Americans to claim subsequently that they had stood firm by their South Vietnamese allies even as they were exiting from the battlefield. The American role in Indochina would thus be reduced to dimensions consistent with the Nixon Doctrine: the United States would 'furnish only the *matériel* and the military and economic assistance to those nations willing to accept the responsibility of supplying manpower to defend themselves,' with the additional provision that 'in case a major nuclear power engaged in aggression against one of [its] ... allies or friends ... [the United States] would respond with nuclear weapons.'[45]

The final agreement between Hanoi and Washington was a gamble on both sides,* just as the 'peace settlement' of 1954 had been. In 1973, Hanoi leaders hoped that the pressure for complete and irrevocable disengagement from Indochina would be increased dramatically by the return home of

---

* According to Gareth Porter, from May 1969 the American negotiating position had been based upon the idea of free elections which were to be administered by Thieu's government with only a nominal oversight by an international supervisory body. Such elections were to be for the presidency only, no constituent assembly. See *A Peace Denied* (Bloomington, London: Indiana University Press 1975) 83–6. According to Kissinger the American side had been offering to agree on some sort of joint electoral commission since 14 May 1969. The proposed commission was outlined, however, in 'a formula which represented only the thinnest pretense of a joint body and reduced the electoral commission to impotence.' The commission was to be charged with overseeing elections that would elect a government with proportional communist representation in Cabinet, not merely a president in a 'winner take all' format. Kissinger himself admits that these proposals were not serious, but were designed rather to give the US government 'a defensible position at home.' See *White House Years*, 1321–2.

America's conscript army, and that any intention on the part of the Nixon administration to stay involved indirectly (via economic and military assistance) or directly (via occasional B-52 air raids to repel conventional frontal assaults on the south as occurred in the spring of 1975) would be stymied by congressional doves and an increasingly isolationist public opinion.[46] The Americans hoped, to the contrary, that Kissinger's bargain had 'provided the only sound basis for America's staying *in* and continuing to play a responsible role in helping the non-Communist nations and neutrals as well as our Asian allies to defend their independence.'[47]

For the Canadian government, participation in the new International Commission was inevitable. Sketching out conditions for participation was a virtual guarantee of an 'invitation' from Washington. Who better to nominate, from their point of view, than a country that had shown consistent sympathy for the RVN cause, that understood the intransigent and duplicitous character of the northern regime, that had vast experience in truce supervisory operations in Indochina, and which was prepared to take a very hard-nosed attitude on peacekeeping modalities? Only a clear-cut refusal to serve in Vietnam articulated well in advance of October 1972 could have kept Canada out.

THE INTERNAL POLICY DEBATE ON PARTICIPATION, THE US 'INVITATION,' AND A QUALIFIED ACCEPTANCE

By 1972 fully one-third of External Affairs staff had seen duty in Indochina. Although many of these 'Indochina hands' were disillusioned with the ICSC and were preparing to manifest such disenchantment through recommending very stiff conditions to be met prior to future Canadian participation, the political environment was shifting rapidly, precluding prosecution of this line of action. The department's staff, moreover, had no broadly based consensus position about the forthcoming role on the International Commission of Control and Supervision (ICCS). According to one liberal-moderate's recollection of events during late 1972 and early 1973:

Many 'hawks [ie, conservatives] with much experience in Indochina said: 'Let's not be patsies again. We'll be smeared by the obloquy of association to an instrument that causes the fall of South Vietnam. And if the ICCS proves to be a fake, External won't have the guts to pull out later.' The 'doves' in this debate argued that the foremost consideration in Canadian policy should be to get the United States out of Vietnam and nothing Canada should do should obstruct that eventuality. They argued that Canada should push as hard as possible for the most effective structures of super-

vision and control that were politically possible – and even accept the fact, if necessary, that they will prove completely deficient and will necessitate eventual withdrawal by Canada.[48]

Vietnam still evoked major differences in political and tactical response.
External Affairs staff were now torn between their desire to cut loose entirely from the frustrating Indochina role and their equally strong desire to
expedite an American military withdrawal. Just as in 1954, the final decision
of the department to recommend involvement was reluctantly given and
couched in qualifications.

Many (but not all) conservatives in External Affairs disagreed with such
'optimism' vehemently. One of them, who had been so unfortunate as to
encounter a 'smirking,' condescending Richard Nixon while the former was
accredited to the ICSC in Vietnam, declared:

My advice from the beginning was not to accept. Don't go! In international affairs
you make a few decisions, or a decision, and there are a few screams from offended
parties. But they die down and people forget. Look at Soviet behaviour against
Czechoslovakia in 1968. And people will come to forget Vietnam too. An unpopular
decision by Canada, unpopular for the United States, was very possible to take.

This same conservative also observed:

For the ICCS to have worked, it would have had to backed by force. The threat of
renewed intervention ... [by punishing means] had to be real. Deterrence based on
force is the reality. The United Nations provides the moral sanction of world opinion, but more than moral sanction was needed in Vietnam. There had to be physical
threats. All we had [on the ICCS] was the authority to report to the parties.[49]

Such logic was internally consistent and from its own perspective quite
realistic, but it was not at all politically appealing for a government facing an
imminent election and needing to avoid charges of dereliction of duty.
Moreover the policy/attitudinal cleavages within External Affairs could only
have had the effect of convincing Trudeau and Sharp of the need to allow
domestic political considerations to determine the pattern of Canadian response.

The Canadian anti-war left could still achieve electoral gains on the Vietnam issue for the NDP. Caution was therefore appropriate. The liberal-moderate, pro-supervision approach still had the outstanding virtue of an innate
capacity for deflecting or defusing criticism from both the right and the left.

PC policy had also blessed the liberal-moderate line since 1968. Thus when Trudeau and Sharp received the first word on 25 October 1972 that a peace agreement was in the offing between the Americans and North Vietnamese and, further, that Canada was being considered for the new International Commission, they could not help but think of the possible impact on the election scheduled for 30 October. As soon as this word was received the government reiterated its previous conditions,[50] without indicating to the Americans what the ultimate decision might be. On 26 October an inter-departmental task force was established to study the participation question and to formulate recommendations. On the same day, Hanoi went public with its version of the negotiations, forcing Kissinger to make his 'peace is at hand' speech to the Washington press. In Washington, also, the US State Department's deputy assistant secretary of East Asian and Pacific affairs, William Sullivan, briefed Canadian officials on the progress of negotiations and provided a general outline of projected ICCS functions. A Canadian protocol on guidelines for future IC procedures and mandate given to the Americans several weeks prior to this meeting was ignored.[51] On 28 October the Department of National Defence announced that it was examining contingency plans for the dispatch of personnel to Indochina. Since 1969 National Defence had been engaged in 'constant planning' for the eventuality of such supervisory work.[52]

Such planning was disrupted, however, by the major setback suffered by the Liberal party on the evening of 30 October. The Liberals were reduced to minority government status, at best; moreover, it was not known whether they would form a government at all until closely contested seats were recounted. The NDP, although its popular vote only went from 17 per cent to 18 per cent, gained nine seats in the House of Commons and now held the parliamentary balance of power. Despite this unsettled political situation, decisions had to be made very quickly.

On 31 October the government repudiated as 'pure speculation' press reports that the Canadian, Hungarian, Polish, and Indonesian governments had all assented to a role. On 2 November Secretary of State for External Affairs Sharp restated the government's reservations, but then offered the services of Canada's existing nineteen-man contingent to the old ICSC for any preliminary duties necessary prior to the projected international conference. In this same statement Sharp reiterated the general qualification to acceptance: Canada would not agree to 'any long-term commitment that would result in a non-constructive role for us.'[53] Undoubtedly the government felt severely constrained concerning the options of unqualified acceptance or refusal because of the probability that they would be sharing power with the

New Democrats within a few weeks. Without a doubt they must also have been influenced by the many disillusioned conservatives within the DEA who counselled rejection, or at the very least, a highly conditional role acceptance. But given Richard Nixon's imminent electoral victory on 7 November (the polls showed him far ahead of George McGovern), Trudeau and Sharp were also cognizant of having to deal with a very unforgiving and ruthless administration in Washington bent on achieving a peace that was politically tolerable vis-à-vis America's super-power status and its global alliance commitments. The American economic initiatives of the summer of 1971 had demonstrated that the Nixon administration was not going to treat difficult allies cautiously. Intimidation and coercion were its stock-in-trade.

Liberal-moderates in External Affairs had always cautioned the government against overt political opposition to the American air war on instrumental grounds: 'Taking a stand would have accomplished nothing in terms of reorienting American policy for the better, while costing the country perhaps very much if a hostile American reaction resulted.'[54] Liberal-moderates articulated the problem in terms of anticipated American reaction at a number of levels. One of them declared subsequently:

One had to look very closely not just at Administration reactions but also at the reaction of Congress. The capacity of Congress to affect the economy through the extra-territoriality of U.S. corporations must be reckoned with. One must make policy in light of potential action, not the certain prospect of retaliation, which is a difficult thing to do.

Specifically with respect to the ICCS role, he added: 'The irrationalities of the whole process had to be weighed, as well as the complex political influences in U.S. domestic politics. At the Paris Conference our only allies for a strong Continuing Political Authority and supervisory contingent were the Chinese.'[55]

External Affairs liberal-moderates ultimately spoke to the dominant concerns of Cabinet, which were strongly influenced by the passionate determination of the Americans to disengage militarily from Indochina at the earliest possible date. There was undoubtedly a strong school of thought in both Cabinet and DEA that Canada should do what it could to help effect this disengagement. It was in Canada's perceived interest that US withdrawal should occur. Just as France had been bled white in the early 1950s, thus hurting indirectly Canada's perceived interests in a strong NATO, so in the late 1960s and early 1970s the massive overcommitment of the United States to Indochina was precluding effective American leadership in the North

Atlantic community, impeding the development of super-power détente and arms control, and thus indirectly frustrating the improvement of both global order and Canadian security.

Occasional consultation between Trudeau's personal foreign policy adviser Ivan Head and Henry Kissinger no doubt had produced caution at the highest levels in Ottawa.[56] Kissinger was determined to 'master events,' to preserve America's reputation as a reliable ally (the primary stake at issue for the US in his view),[57] and to create the conditions for a new and highly stable, global power balance. Creating an illusion of peace in Vietnam was part of this master plan for a new global order.[58] Cavilling from the wings, which drew attention to the fraudulent character of the 'settlement' and thus threw into jeopardy the hard-won, right-wing political support for disengagement from Vietnam in the United States (cf. the right's previous commitment to total military victory), might well have brought an irate and probably crushing response.

On 19 November 1972 Mitchell Sharp met with US Secretary of State William Rogers in New York and reiterated Canada's principal conditions. Rogers and Kissinger were naturally upset. The effort to reach agreement with Hanoi was bogging down and now the Canadians were becoming difficult. On 23 November Robert Stanfield declared his support for a Canadian role in Vietnam provided there were 'very clear terms of reference.' This was a notably softer position than that of the government. In November, Ottawa officials held consultations with members of the Polish Institute of International Affairs. The Poles were not eager to go either; they claimed to be impressed by Canadian rigour.[59] On 3 December Sharp reiterated his four conditions.

RICHARD NIXON'S TWELVE DAYS OF CHRISTMAS

Meanwhile in Vietnam the Americans were rapidly building up Thieu's forces in Operation Enhance Plus 'to have as high a base as possible for one-for-one replacement'[60] of weapons, a provision that was certain to be embodied in the final agreement. Despite this program, which made the RVN's Air Force the fourth largest in the world, and despite high-level assurances from Washington, Thieu was proving very difficult to persuade. Thieu rightly saw US disengagement not as a constructive rationalization of the US commitment towards a politically sustainable footing, but rather as a possible first step towards eventual abandonment.

In late November and early December newly elected President Nixon, according to Henry Kissinger, was not celebrating his victory but instead was in 'the darkest and perhaps most malevolent frame of mind of his Presidency.'[61] With the DRVN negotiating team still insisting that the release of US POWs had to be tied to the release of Viet Cong prisoners,* and that US troop withdrawal had to be matched by the withdrawal of all 'civilian technicians' (who would be needed to maintain Thieu's new weaponry, especially his air armada), an agreement seemed far away. Nixon was not going to compromise on these points of substance.

From 9 to 13 December Le Duc Tho stalled the talks, according to Kissinger, by reopening previously agreed-to formulations of various parts of the draft agreement. Evidently banking on Thieu's much publicized intransigence alienating the American public, and that a more 'dovish' returning Congress would virtually force Nixon to withdraw on Hanoi's terms, the North Vietnamese got ready for what they hoped would be Nixon's last-gasp assault.

On 31 October 1968 the bombing of the north had been halted indefinitely on the 'understanding' reached at Paris that there would be no shelling of cities in the south by the communist side and that the US would be allowed to make unarmed reconnaissance flights over DRVN territory. When such aircraft eventually attracted (or provoked) anti-aircraft fire, fighter-bomber air cover strikes were approved in 'protective reaction' sorties. In 1969, 285 air attack sorties were flown against DRVN targets. At that time, Laos bore the brunt of the air war as 144,323 sorties were sent to bomb the Laotian portion of the Ho Chi Minh trail. In 1970 American aircraft flew 1,113 sorties against DRVN targets, primarily against SAM (surface-to-air missile) sites moved ever closer to the Laotian border. In late 1971, secret air strikes were ordered against SAM and anti-aircraft gun sites, POL depots, and artillery concentrations by General John D. Lavelle. These illicit air strikes (147 were later identified) continued through the end of February 1972 when Lavelle was relieved of command. From his testimony in the course of subsequent congressional investigations, it is clear that the navy was also still authorizing strikes on the north through its by then traditional tactic of 'trolling' (as

* Revisionist critics such as Gareth Porter argue that it was the Americans who stalled the talks in November because they allegedly wished to complete Operation Enhance Plus and to convince Thieu of their strong commitment to his government so that he would not denounce the armistice. Kissinger's version seems more plausible, but resolution of this debate will require access to the classified record. According to Kissinger there were only some 30,000 civilian detainees held by the Saigon government, about 10,000 of them Viet Cong; see *White House Years* 1354. According to Andrew Brewin's sources there were several hundred thousand prisoners in the south. See *Debates*, 24 Jan. 1973, p 598.

Guenter Lewy defined it, 'sending an aircraft into an area as bait to provoke enemy fire, thus justifying retaliatory attacks').[62]

By early 1972 such activities were no longer manifestations of crypto-roll-back propensities within the American military, despite firm evidence that the highest levels of the Pentagon and possibly even the Secretary of Defense Melvin Laird had been pressing Lavelle to 'be more aggressive.'[63] Kissinger and Nixon now adhered to a new global strategy based on a concept of five-power equilibrium.[64] Rapprochement between the Americans and communist Chinese culminated in the summer of 1971. The emerging quasi-entente changed the nature of the American bureaucratic debate profoundly and perhaps irrevocably. China was now no longer a potential target, but rather a potential ally. The significance of this change cannot be overstated. For many hawkish supporters of unlimited air war against the north the very raison d'être of the Vietnam war was now evaporating. They now had to have far more limited objectives in sight vis-à-vis Indochina: the destruction of the DRVN's capacity to prosecute the war in the south, to defend itself, and to be able to receive supplies and weapons from its socialist allies. Everyone in Washington now played the containment game; it was merely a question of how brutally. For a time, possibly for good, the rollback policy current had dried up.

From 8 May to 22 October 1972 the DRVN's territory had been heavily bombed in the LINEBACKER I campaign. Television and laser-guided 'smart bombs' did tremendous damage to scores of military targets in the north with comparatively little collateral damage to civilians or non-military property. Improved electronic counter-measures reduced US aircraft losses dramatically. American bombers destroyed the port facilities at Haiphong and Cam Pha. Rail imports from the PRC were 'crippled.'[65] Thus, the threat to resume unlimited bombing was not to be taken lightly.

Following the breakdown of talks in Paris, Nixon ordered LINEBACKER II into operation on 17 December. Over the next twelve days, encompassing the entirety of the Christmas holiday period in North America and Europe, 729 B-52 sorties and 1,000 fighter bomber missions were flown that dropped some 20,370 tons of ordnance on the North. Bombing was concentrated most heavily on the Hanoi-Haiphong region, where B-52s bore the brunt of the campaign.[66] Over 1,000 SAMs were fired at American planes. Most of them fell back on the cities they were intended to protect. The northern authorities had evacuated the children and much of the adult population of the two cities and apparently claimed at most some 2,200 fatalities from the twelve-day assault. International reaction to the bombing was strongly negative. Charges of 'terror' and 'torture,' a reversion to barbarism, and 'Guernica tactics' were common. The governing Congress party in India, newly freed from the inhibitions of ICSC diplomacy, indulged itself by passing a resolution condemning the air attacks as 'the most horrible tragedy in man's recorded history' (sic) and as 'indiscriminate bombing of the civilian population in a senseless desire to impose the will of an outside power.' Swedish premier Olof Palme declared that this latest American crime against humanity was comparable to Nazi atrocities at Treblinka.*

The reaction in the North American press to DRVN propaganda was favourable to Hanoi's interests. Although the bombing was intense, it was not 'terror bombing' or anything approaching it. Nevertheless, many unhappy Canadians were quick to condemn the air attacks. The primate of the Anglican Church of Canada and the moderator of the United Church of Canada asked the prime minister to urge Nixon to stop the air war. They also appealed directly to Nixon. Walter Gordon condemned the bombing as 'truly barbarous.' Some western Canadian veterans sent their war medals to Governor General Roland Michener to protest continued Canadian support for the American war effort under the Defence Production Sharing relationship. On 21 December 1972 Trudeau told reporters: 'We have always felt the bombing was the wrong way to bring the war to an end.' He added that he thought a negotiated peace was still possible and that 'it would be wrong for us to ... put our nose into it and to try and make the negotiations any more difficult.'[67] After the campaign was ended Trudeau and his government would reverse themselves, undoubtedly with much ambivalence, and approve a resolution introduced by the secretary of state for external affairs which deplored the 'recent large-scale bombing in the Hanoi-Haiphong area,' noted 'the possibility that Canada would be called upon to play some new supervisory role following [the] cessation of hostilities,' requested 'all the parties' to 'refrain from acts of a warlike nature that could jeopardize the success of the present negotiations,' and specifically requested the US government not to resume bombing in the Hanoi-Haiphong area.[68] American official reaction was one of cold indifference. No formal reply was ever lodged, but the Canadian ambassador to Washington, Marcel Cadieux, an-

---

* On casualty figures see Porter, *A Peace Denied* 160. Lewy claims that DRVN officials estimated fatalities at between 1,300 and 1,600 shortly after the twelve-day assault ended. (*America in Vietnam* 413). He also notes that the Feb. 1945 raid on Dresden killed 35,000 people. Such actions more accurately justified the charge of 'terror bombing.' International reaction is in 'Nixon's Blitz ...' and 'Outrage and Relief,' *Time*, 8 Jan. 1973, pp 10, 14; also 'More Bombs than Ever,' *Time*, 1 Jan. 1973, pp 14–16.

other old Indochina hand, was pointedly snubbed by American officials for several months thereafter.

By 27–28 December North Vietnamese air defences had been destroyed, virtually all the SAMs had been expended, and 'American planes roamed the skies with impunity.'[69] Cost-free bombing was now a reality; this may have been a daunting factor in Hanoi's calculations. Following accommodating noises from Paris, Nixon sent a private ultimatum on 27 December to the North Vietnamese demanding a resumption of negotiations at the point reached in mid-November. Hanoi agreed on 28 December. The bombing ended the next day. Talks resumed on 1 January. On 2–4 January both the House and Senate Democratic caucuses voted to cut off money for Indochina military operations 'contingent only upon the safe withdrawal of American forces and the release of U.S. prisoners.'[70] Nevertheless, Hanoi agreed to Kissinger's demands in Paris, a development which as Kissinger noted was almost certainly 'a measure of the extremity in which Hanoi found itself that it felt that it could not wait for the almost certain aid cutoff.'[71] On 12 January White House spokesmen denied that the administration was looking at possible use of nuclear weapons in the event the Paris talks broke down. This denial (possibly a calculated ploy designed to raise doubts in the minds of Hanoi's militants) followed a statement by William Clements, Nixon's nominee for deputy secretary of defense, in which Clements refused to rule out recommending use of nuclear weapons during a Senate armed services committee hearing. Saigon official press welcomed the statement as clear evidence of a new willingness to cross the nuclear threshold.[72]

With the negotiations proceeding rapidly in Paris, President Nixon wrote to Nguyen Van Thieu personally on 5 January 1973, assuring him that in the event Hanoi violated the agreement, he would 'take swift and severe retaliatory action.'[73] By 9 January the heart of the agreement had been worked out in Paris. But the very basis of the new ICCS had been compromised; a principle of unanimity in reporting was written into the section pertaining to truce supervision. On 20 January Nixon sent an ultimatum to Thieu that the US was ready to go ahead without Thieu's concurrence if it had to. On 23 January Kissinger and Le Duc Tho initialled the agreement. On 27 January the formal signing took place.

Hanoi officials and their American revisionist supporters subsequently claimed that the 'battle of Hanoi' was a victory for the DRVN, that American negotiating intransigence (re the issue of a stipulated withdrawal of all DRVN troops from South Vietnam after the cease-fire) was broken by the loss of thirty-four B-52s (the US claimed that only fifteen were shot down of some

200 employed but this number apparently did not include planes put out of action which went down at sea).[74] However many planes were lost, this seems an utterly improbable construction of events. The DRVN was now wide open to air attack. Its harbour facilities had been closed by the renewed mining operations of the Americans. While it may be doubtful whether the partial or complete obliteration of a defenceless Hanoi and Haiphong would have won still better terms for Washington, as Alexander Haig and others have claimed (for it would have meant 'killing the hostage' in strategic parlance), it is clear that those twelve days of Christmas convinced the Hanoi leaders that they had very much to gain by agreeing to the bilateral 'gamble' offered by the Americans in November. The alternative risked provoking Nixon into genuine terror bombing of North Vietnam's civilian population and possibly some limited use of nuclear weapons.

The negative Canadian reaction to Nixon's bombing of Hanoi was conveyed to the US government on more than one occasion. The all-party resolution of 5 January merely added emphasis to an already established line of response. The Department of External Affairs had forwarded three protest notes over the bombing to Washington prior to 5 January. On 3 January 1973 the Prime Minister's Office had dispatched a note deploring the bombing to Nixon.[75]

In his speech explaining the government's introduction of the House of Commons resolution, Sharp reiterated the former's willingness to serve in a supervisory capacity but he stressed that any participation would be conditional on fulfilment of the government's conditions. Failure of the upcoming Paris Conference to create a viable 'continuing political authority' would be considered grounds for Canadian withdrawal after an initial sixty days of duty. Apparently alerted to American concessions on the unanimity in reporting question, Sharp indicated that the new IC would be regarded by Ottawa 'not as a diplomatic conference held under the normal rules of confidentiality but as an international forum where the proceedings are normally open to the public.' Furthermore, the Canadians 'would not regard the new commission's proceedings as confidential or privileged in any way unless there was in any particular instance a unanimous decision of all the members to the contrary.' Publicity, he said, would be given 'in any way we saw fit to ensure that our view of events and, if necessary, the difference between our view and that of others were publicly available.'[76]

By 5 January 1973 the 'invitation' to serve on the ICCS was more than a 'possibility'; it was a virtual certainty. The offer by Ottawa to lend the use of Canadian ICSC staff still in Vietnam to the incoming commission in a 'preliminary support' role may very well have been a last-minute gambit to avoid ICCS duty, as one commentator has suggested.[77] And it is equally clear that the elaborate statement of conditions was prompted by a desire to establish a priori grounds for eventual withdrawal if some sort of conditional acceptance was given and then events went awry. To say that such planning was 'devious,' or simply inappropriate vis-à-vis Canadian interests, is nonsensical. This highly qualified line of action was entirely reasonable in terms of the domestic political position with which Trudeau and Sharp had to deal, and still more so in light of the fact that the Canadian government was being asked to give a blanket consent to participate in a supervisory role that had not yet been fully defined – and would not be so defined until conclusion of the Paris Conference in early March. The *Globe and Mail* editorial of 11 January calling a role by Canada a 'rear-guard intervention to cover a U.S. withdrawal' may have been bluntly accurate, but prefacing the comment with the word 'futile' was surely an unwarranted and premature response. It was far too soon to say whether the commission role would be more farcical than functional; moreover, it was clear that Canada had a major interest in seeing the US end its direct involvement in Vietnam. Rejecting the ICCS role out of hand before it had even been fully defined would have been quite irresponsible. Laying the groundwork for eventual withdrawal was simply prudent self-interest.

In an analysis presented to the Commons' Standing Committee on External Affairs and National Defence on 15 March, John W. Holmes declared: 'I do not think in 1954 any more than in 1972 we really had any choice. A country which had the kind of reputation which we then had, and I think have now, and which talked a great deal about our responsibility to the international community and our willingness to do things which would help preserve the peace, I just do not think there was any other answer that we could have given.' Canada had 'special expertise' in Indochina, had 'the respect of the other party, the North Vietnamese,' and was recognized outside Canada (although not by Canadians) 'as not being a satellite of the United States.' Canadians had 'a certain decent pride in our reputation,' and moreover, 'there was also a perfectly justified belief that we could do a better job than most countries.' There was still a slim chance after all, said Holmes, that the 'better-drafted agreement' of 1973 might in fact produce an ultimate political settlement.[78]

Holmes firmly believed that it was important 'just to get the Americans out.' Canadian as well as American interests would be served by accomplishing this task. And finally, a rejection of a role would have caused 'very

346 In the interests of peace

serious displeasure in Washington' in 'an administration which ... is not disposed to take a very magnanimous attitude towards Canada anyway.'[79] Articulating an arbitrarily negative Canadian definition of the prospects for peace concerning a fluid and relatively unpredictable situation (an inevitable corollary to Canadian rejection) was not at all appropriate to the gravity of the Canadian stake in the attainment of peace in Indochina. As Holmes had noted earlier: 'Unlike the Americans, our besetting sin has been avoiding rather than exaggerating our international responsibilities. If we want to replace a Pax Americana with something more multi-lateral, we have to take on some unpleasant assignments ourselves – but only of course when we are sure that we are acting on behalf of the international community.'[80]

Holmes's logic was persuasive. Pre-emptive rejection would have been petulant, short-sighted, and only narrowly self-serving. Enlightened self-interest as well as the general doctrinal commitment to 'responsible internationalism' argued for conditional acceptance at a minimum. External Affairs' liberal-moderates understood this position clearly.

Fear of economic retaliation from the Nixon administration cannot be discounted either. In late 1972 and early 1973, impending trade and energy negotiations of great moment for Canada were under way. Neither Energy Minister Donald Macdonald nor Trade and Industry Minister Alastair Gillespie were willing to see these talks compromised because of differences over the truce supervisory role.[81]

By 24 January the die was cast. Sharp's conditional acceptance of 5 January was firmed up with a specific time qualification of sixty days for the duration of Canada's first period of service on the commission. Ottawa officials would in this time study all the provisions of the agreement and the still to be negotiated protocols and could then evaluate the prospective efficacy of the ICCS more effectively. Then a 'more formal decision' would be made about the issue of 'full' participation.[82]

Sharp's acceptance of the role on a tentative basis and his left-liberal offer to contribute to post-war 'reconstruction' in both Vietnams (by implication) were resoundingly applauded by NDP spokesperson Andrew Brewin. While PC external affairs critic Claude Wagner generally welcomed the decision, he hinted that the Opposition was prepared to make life difficult for the Liberals should the government fail 'to ensure that our participation be effective and sufficiently potent to guarantee some measure of success,' and to protect Canada's 'right as a nation to insist on firm and clearcut conditions to our participation.'[83]

On 27 January the Paris Agreement was signed and Sharp formally communicated Ottawa's provisional commitment to serve for the next sixty days (ie, until 27 March). The first group of the 290 Canadians who were to serve on the ICCS arrived in Saigon on 29 January.

The six weeks from the onset of the Christmas bombing until Sharp's statement to the Commons on 24 January was a time of intense ambivalence and self-doubt at all levels of the Canadian government. Ottawa was edging towards a role that virtually no one greeted with any enthusiasm. The projected number of ICCS personnel was certainly going to be too few to police South Vietnam's frontiers effectively. According to one military affairs analyst, the ICCS would have required between 80,000 and 100,000 troops to think seriously about a capability for enforcing the cease-fire and adequately policing the 700 miles of border which would have to be monitored for infiltration.[84] What could 1,160 truce supervisors hope to accomplish? Neither was there strong Asian representation on the commission, something which External officials and Sharp himself had long supported. With all of these internal reservations, not to mention the still distressing unanimity clause in the agreement, it was clear to Canadian decision-makers that there was a substantial body of opinion in the country which did not think Canada should dispatch a contingent at all.

Left-liberals in Cabinet, External Affairs, and the Commons wanted nothing to do with a commission which seemed indirectly supportive of American policy. Many conservatives were equally depressed at the thought of an ICCS role but not because of the bombing. Many Canadian conservatives saw in the Paris negotiations little more than elaborate preparations for a shabby sell-out of America's South Vietnamese allies. Most conservatives suspected that there would be neither peace nor honour once US troops had exited; moreover, they felt that an American disengagement was inevitable in any case, so why expend Canadian resources and possibly Canadian lives in an effort at masking American betrayal of those South Vietnamese still willing to resist communist tyranny? Let the Americans get someone else to do their dirty work. Nor were Ottawa's liberal-moderates immune to the growing atmosphere of distrust and scepticism concerning the prospects of peace and the real motivations inspiring American and North Vietnamese actions in concluding an 'armistice.' If the liberal-moderates were prepared to play whatever game of peace was offered at least part of the way to help secure an American exit, they were also very anxious to avoid entrapment in the self-perpetuating 'commission-as-symbol-of-peace'/'commission-as-last-communications-link' rationales which had justified the last desperately tedious ten years of duty on the ICSC.

THE ICCS IN ACTION

Michel Gauvin, a dedicated conservative, headed up the new Canadian delegation. He soon earned a reputation as an ardent defender of South Vietnamese interests, far too ardent for some observers. Gauvin brought a strongly anti-communist perspective to this task. He was more than 'unsympathetic to Communist points of view,'[85] especially when Vietnamese communists were involved. His experience of communist behaviour in 1955–6 had made him 'an anti-Communist zealot.'[86] Despite his partisan views, the new Canadian ambassador did his job effectively in terms of establishing the ICCS presence while he executed his duties as its first chairman. For his efforts Gauvin was lauded by the Canadian press. He was credited with showing 'strong leadership, great competence and consistent purpose,' for striving hard to remain impartial in face of Hungarian and Polish duplicity, for exhibiting 'relentless drive,' for running press briefings that were 'outspoken, dedicated and energetic,' and for being 'a Canadian Zorba the Greek' and 'the prime mover of the international supervisory machinery exhausting his men with sixteen hour-a-day seven-day weeks.'[87] Gauvin's invigorating personality and his obvious sincerity had much to do with such glowing reports, but so too did the fact that his generally anti-communist approach found favour with most Canadians, a fact which his critics have overlooked.[88]

One trio of specialists in the field of peacekeeping noted that the appointment of Gauvin was in fact a 'wise decision.'[89] The head of the Canadian delegation was determined to be as impartial as circumstance allowed (ie, given the degree of bias shown by the Poles and Hungarians) but just as the prime minister had noted in his 1971 Aurora speech he was not going to pretend to any sort of Canadian neutrality towards the struggle. The Canadian government, especially its conservative element, had been backing the principle of South Vietnamese self-determination since 1956. It was not going to jettison this commitment wholesale at this late date. A serious commitment to impartiality in truce supervisory work does not presuppose neutrality, as left-wing critics have argued. Gauvin made every effort to make the ICCS an active, effective *investigatory* body in line with Ottawa's policy but this was precisely what the communist side had always opposed. It was in communist interests that the ICCS be ineffectual so that it could not be used to generate adverse publicity or propaganda about the 140 to 150 thousand regular troops from the DRVN stationed in the south, nor take any action to slow their ongoing rotation and augmentation (which was quite illicit under the Paris Agreements). Thus from the very beginning of the

US-DRVN talks, Hanoi negotiators had wished to limit the new commission to less than 300 personnel, whereas initial American proposals had spoken of some 5,000 truce supervisory personnel patrolling clearly marked zones of control for the two sides.[90]

The actual record of the Canadian role on the ICCS may be dispensed with briefly. Little of consequence was accomplished by the commission, but this was not for lack of effort on the part of the Canadian contingent. The source of the commission's ineffectiveness lay in the very terms of the new armistice arrangements, a problem beyond the remedy of the member states of the ICCS. If the quality of the 1954 Geneva Cease-Fire Agreement and Final Declaration was marred by major omissions and intentional ambiguities, the Paris Agreements of 1973 were if anything more gravely flawed because they embodied absolutely irreconcilable contradictions. The Agreement on Ending the War and Restoring the Peace in Viet Nam that was signed on 27 January 1973 was in reality no more than an 'in-place' cease-fire agreement.[91] Despite the agreement's formal title there was, as in 1954, no effective substantive basis for a political settlement between the parties to the conflict. There was only a call for the establishment of a National Council of National Reconciliation and Concord to be composed of 'the two South Vietnamese parties,' operating 'on the principle of unanimity.' The council was to promote implementation of the armistice, to ensure 'democratic liberties,' to organize 'free and democratic general elections,' and to decide 'the procedures and modalities of any local elections.'

No sanctions were threatened should agreement not be reached. No mandatory timetable for political reconciliation was provided. No third parties obligated themselves unilaterally towards remedial action in the event of failure in the political talks between the Republic of Vietnam authorities and the delegates of the Provisional Revolutionary Government of the Republic of South Vietnam (PRG/RSVN). There was merely provision for a reconvening of the Paris Conference in the event of a 'joint request' by the American and DRVN governments or 'six or more' of the twelve signatories to the Declaration of the International Conference on Viet-Nam.[92] Such lacunae occurred despite the fact that there was little possibility that the bilateral South Vietnamese talks would have any constructive results given Saigon's refusal even to acknowledge formally the existence of the PRG, as was pointedly shown by the insistence of the RVN on extremely contrived signing procedures in which delegates of the two South Vietnamese parties never once signed the same document.

The most major internal contradiction of the agreement involved the simultaneous acknowledgment of the 'independence, sovereignty, unity, and territorial integrity of Vietnam as recognized by the 1954 Geneva Agreements' (ie, the indivisibility of North and South Vietnam) as well as the 'sacred, inalienable' right to 'self-determination' for the South Vietnamese people. Given the pro-partition policies of the incumbent regime in the south these provisions were, to say the least, paradoxical.

Militarily the United States was obligated in Chapter 2 of the Agreement to cease 'all its military activities' against the DRVN, to deactivate or destroy all its harbour mines in the north, to withdraw all its forces from South Vietnam (as well as its allies' forces) 'including technical military personnel and military personnel associated with the pacification program, armaments, munitions, and war materials,' and to dismantle 'all military bases in South Vietnam of the United States within sixty days.' In Nixon's greatest concession to Hanoi, this chapter failed to stipulate the withdrawal of some 150,000 DRVN troops from the south. But Article 7 did stipulate, as Kissinger has subsequently emphasized, that the 'two South Vietnamese parties shall not accept the introduction of troops, military advisers, and military personnel, including technical military personnel.' This provision was demanded by the Americans in the hope that it would cause the DRVN's expeditionary force to 'wither on the vine' provided the ICCS could ensure that there would be no further troop deployments to South Vietnam. Here was the source of Canada's allegedly too partisan approach to the peace agreement. Following the wording of Chapter 3 of the 1954 Cease-Fire Agreement, both South Vietnamese parties were allowed 'periodic replacement of armaments, munitions and war material which have been destroyed, damaged, worn out or used up after the cease-fire, on the basis of piece-for-piece of the same characteristics and properties.'

Under Chapter 3, American prisoners of war were to be returned within sixty days and assistance was to be given mutually in tracing those missing in action and repatriating their remains if necessary. In one of its major concessions to the American side the Vietnamese communists agreed that there would be negotiations between 'the two South Vietnamese parties' regarding captured Vietnamese civilian personnel in South Vietnam. No mandatory schedule was provided for release of such detainees, only a suggested period of ninety days for resolution of 'this question.' It was probably not coincidental that the initial period of service accepted by Ottawa precisely matched the length of the period designated for release of American prisoners.

Under Chapter 4, the Saigon government and the PRG were obliged to 'respect the cease-fire and maintain peace in South Vietnam,' to 'settle all matters of contention through negotiation,' to 'end hatred and enmity,' to prohibit 'reprisal and discrimination,' to form the tripartite National Council (the sole extremely vague reference to the projected role of a third political force in South Vietnam), and to sign the bilateral 'agreement on the international matters of South Vietnam as soon as possible and to do their utmost to accomplish this within ninety days after the cease-fire comes into effect.'

Chapter 5 called for the 'reunification' of Vietnam but stipulated the need for consent by the government of each zone. This was yet another massive contradiction, given the policies of the incumbent regime in Saigon. This same chapter stipulated respect for the demilitarized zone on each side of the 1954 'provisional' military demarcation line, but also the commencement of negotiations to restore 'civilian movement' across the DMZ. No date was mentioned for the achievement of this latter objective, nor were penalties stated for the failure of one or both parties to agree.

Chapter 6 outlined the characteristics and tasks of the Four-Party Joint Military Commission (FPJMC), which was to last for sixty days only, and the Two-Party Joint Military Commission (TPJMC), which had a virtually open-ended mandate. Both were charged inter alia with implementing the cease-fire, prisoner exchange, and withdrawal provisions of the agreement. In this same chapter the functions of the International Commission of Control and Supervision (ICCS) were also laid out. Like the FPJMC, the ICCS was to 'operate in accordance with the principle of consultations and unanimity.' It was also supposed to respect the 'sovereignty of South Vietnam' (still another overt contradiction of the call for the unity of all Vietnam in Article 11). Among its designated tasks the most important were: reporting to the four parties concerning the status of the cease-fire in South Vietnam, the progress of American troop withdrawals and base dismantling, and progress in prisoner exchanges; reporting to the two South Vietnamese parties concerning the status of the cease-fire after the end of the sixty-day period, respect for the prohibition against introduction of foreign troops, progress in solving the civilian detainee question, progress in negotiating a political settlement for South Vietnam (another anomaly since the South Vietnamese parties were doing the negotiating); and providing international supervision of the forthcoming general elections. Termination of the ICCS's activities was to be by 'the request of the government formed after the general elections in South Vietnam provided for in Article 9(b).' The bilateral Protocol pertaining to the ICCS was drawn up after the agreement and stipulated (no doubt in light of the already expressed Canadian reservations in this regard) that member states could withdraw on three months' notice to the four parties. The Canadian government never formally acknowledged this constraint.

The ICCS was also charged with mediating disagreements occurring in the TPJMC, investigating all violations within its mandate, and co-operating with the two JMCs 'when necessary' in 'deterring and detecting violations.' Failure of the ICCS delegations to reach unanimity would occasion the submission of 'different views' to the parties 'but these submissions would not be considered as reports of the Commission.' The member states were to ensure full representation at all times. Liaison officers from the parties were to be allowed to accompany investigations, provided no delay resulted. ICCS teams were to be allowed 'such movement for observation as is reasonably required for the proper exercise of its functions.' Teams were to receive 'all necessary assistance and co-operation from the parties concerned.' As one Canadian official commented, the wording of these provisions afforded 'loopholes big enough to drive a truck through.'[93] So too did the provision that ICCS personnel would be accorded diplomatic immunities and privileges only 'while carrying out their tasks.'[94]

In Chapter 7 of the agreement, the parties clearly obligated themselves to 'respect the neutrality of Cambodia and Laos,' to 'refrain from using the territory of Cambodia and the territory of Laos to encroach on the sovereignty and security of one another and of other countries,' and to 'totally withdraw from and refrain from reintroducing into these two countries troops, military advisers and military personnel, armaments, munitions and war material.' Kissinger clearly hoped that cessation of DRVN assistance to the Pathet Lao and Khmer Rouge forces would shortly lead to internal settlements in both countries, and that these provisions would provide an adequate legal and political basis for cessation of use of the Ho Chi Minh Trail by the DRVN troops. American hopes vis-à-vis Laos may have been justified. Concerning Cambodia they were not. The war between General Lon Nol's regime in Phnom Penh and the communist guerrillas worsened in the year after the cease-fire in Vietnam. The utter breakdown of Article 20's injunctions against continued North Vietnamese involvement in Laos and Cambodia was ultimately a major factor in the Canadian decision to pull out of the commission, according to Michel Gauvin.[95]

Chapter 8 of the agreement, what might be termed a quasi-reparations clause, called for an American contribution of unspecified size towards 'the postwar reconstruction of the Democratic Republic of Viet Nam and throughout Indochina.' In fact the provision was more a matter of bribery. According to subsequent revelations, Nixon and Kissinger apparently made a private 'pledge' of some $4.75 billion to the DRVN authorities. This was tacitly conditional on the achievement of a cease-fire in Cambodia, and also, in effect, on congressional concurrence in the scheme.[96]

President Thieu initially referred to the ICCS as 'useless and helpless,' while the PRG and DRVN leaders apparently did not hold out much hope that the armistice would inhibit RVN operations against communist-held zones in the south.[97] Vietnamese scepticism and Canadian apprehensions were fully justified by subsequent events. Thousands of armistice violations occurred within weeks. This period saw the so-called war of the flags in which the two sides tried to gain control of as much land as possible in anticipation of a possible demarcation of zones by the ICCS/TPJMC. Hundreds of complaints were forwarded to the ICCS. Of those received only a few score ever produced actual investigations, and of the investigations carried out hardly any at all led to commission reports.

The ICCS was hamstrung by the provisions of the Paris Agreements. It was also constrained by a collision of concepts among the member states. The Poles and Hungarians allegedly conceived of their role as mediatory and persuasive in character.[98] The Canadians under Gauvin's direction believed in maximizing the ICCS's investigatory field presence so as to optimize its capability for detection and deterrence of violations. Contrary to Canadian hopes (but probably not expectations), the Paris Conference from 26 February to 2 March did not create any effective 'continuing political authority' to oversee the activities of the ICCS and implementation of the agreements by the parties. As Robert Randle noted, the provision for possible reconvening of the Paris conference hardly constituted the 'definitive arrangements' in oversight and reporting of commission activity which had been suggested by the wording of Article 18(b) of the agreement.[99] The communist delegations did make one minor concession to Ottawa: copies of ICCS reports were permitted to be sent jointly or on an individual basis to UN Secretary General Kurt Waldheim.

In February, the unrelenting war of attrition failed to improve significantly in South Vietnam. The weaponry and munitions acquired under 'Enhance Plus' were now being put to use. In Cambodia there was no let-up in the fighting at all. General Lon Nol's forces in the capital had been surrounded by the 50,000 strong Khmer Rouge forces since December and now found that they could not move shipments of food, gasoline, or ammunition up the Mekong to Phnom Penh.[100] By early 1973 the government of Cambodia was a full-fledged client of American patronage, totally dependent upon American financial and military support.

On 7 February 1973 Prince Norodom Sihanouk and the Hanoi government issued a joint communiqué declaring that the struggle to liberate Cambodia would continue. But privately, Hanoi leaders were pressuring the exiled prince and Khmer Rouge (KR) leaders to enter into negotiations by cutting back severely on the supply of arms being provided to the KR forces.[101] On 9 February American air strikes against communist positions resumed. Aircraft of the US Seventh Air Force, formerly based in South Vietnam but now redeployed to Thailand, began attacking the Khmer Rouge in earnest.[102] With out-of-date maps, poor communications links to Phnom Phenh's forces, but apparent enthusiasm for their task, American pilots rained between 30,000 and 55,000 tons of bombs per month on Cambodia, slaughtering thousands of non-combatants in the process.[103]

By mid-February the lack of progress in implementing the cease-fire was embarrassingly obvious. In military action the Saigon authorities alleged that over 1,400 cease-fire violations had been committed by the communist side. The Two-Party Joint Military Commission (TPJMC) was not functioning and thus there had not even been a tentative beginning made at designating zones of influence of the parties. The ICCS was still not fully deployed at all its seven regional and twenty-six local centres.

On 7 February the Canadian government officially announced recognition of the DRVN. Because of North Vietnamese pressure to also extend recognition to the PRG, which Ottawa categorically refused, no legations were exchanged. As a cease-fire approached in Laos pursuant to a secret US-DRVN understanding of that January, the Canadians made clear their conviction that the terms of the Indochina armistice had to be tightened up. When approached to serve again on a reactivated ICSC for Laos, the government initially expressed a willingness to consider such a role provided that: the text of the 1973 armistice agreement conformed to the provisions of the 1962 international agreement on Laos; there was a 'reasonable chance' for the armistice to hold; all parties accepted the terms of any new agreement; and Canada would be reimbursed for the $840,000 still owed to it for previous service in Laos.[104] When the first qualification was not met, Ottawa thereby evaded acceptance of a role. In July, Canadian officials repeated this procedure of articulating strict reservations and then turning down a role when such conditions were not met vis-à-vis proposals for a revived ICSC in Cambodia.[105]

In Ottawa in mid-February the politics of the ICCS role were becoming more complex. Claude Wagner declared that 'the Government has been sucked into a situation with its frustrations and dangers and now it wants us to be a party to the decision.' NDP leader David Lewis made it clear that he thought abrupt withdrawal was in order should the fighting not cease very soon.[106]

Five days prior to the convening of the Paris Conference and shortly after a three-day visit to Hanoi by Kissinger,[107] the Pathet Lao and Souvanna

Phouma's Vientiane government concluded an armistice agreement in which the communist side won substantial concessions. The continuing illicit DRVN military presence in Laos (perhaps 50,000–60,000 troops) was not formally acknowledged in the cease-fire, but neither were there any subsequent official protests about continued B-52 strikes along the Laotian section of the Ho Chi Minh Trail.[108]

As the Paris Conference opened, news from South Vietnam was not encouraging. ICCS helicopters were being fired at with regularity and some attacks involved heat-seeking, shoulder-launched SA-7 'Grail' missiles.[109] Because of the DRVN's traditional antipathy to UN involvement in what they considered was a civil war and not an international conflict, the North Vietnamese opposed Canadian attempts at having Secretary General Kurt Waldheim chair the conference or become involved in oversight duties. In the course of Sharp's remarks, he reaffirmed that a new tentative withdrawal date of 30 April was now in effect, and that it would be resorted to if the problem of a viable continuing political authority was not resolved satisfactorily.[110] Said Sharp just prior to the end of the conference: 'It's not a bluff we are making or an ultimatum but a challenge to the international community ... Our goal is to participate in an effective commission.'[111]

At the conclusion of the conference, after the participants had written in a marginal role for the secretary general by making him an indirect recipient of ICCS reports, Sharp noted that 'an effort has undoubtedly been made to meet our requirements but does it go far enough and will it work?'[112] The secretary of state for external affairs signed the Paris declaration but accompanied his signature with an explicit verbal reservation of the right to withdraw on Canadian terms. Sharp, visibly upset before the press corps in Paris, lamented the 'disgraceful' treatment of Mr Waldheim by the DRVN and PRG delegates. His assistants from the Department of External Affairs criticized DRVN-American domination of the conference as well as the utter lack of American support for Canadian objectives in the conference.[113] In an unfortunate but probably revealing choice of words, Sharp also declared that the government's demanding stand at the conference demonstrated that Canadians were 'no longer Boy Scouts,' that Canada had 'come of age,' and that he was merely following a 'practical, down-to-earth' approach in the talks. 'We don't expect miracles.'[114]

March was a decisive month. On 5 March the Canadian Red Cross team which had been dispatched to Saigon to assist in prisoner exchanges left Vietnam. Major General Arthur Wrinch declared that it was 'pointless to stay' any longer because of communist obstruction. Charging a complete lack of assistance from 'the North Vietnamese and the Viet Cong' he added that he wanted to 'put on record who stopped us doing our job.'[115] In the Commons the Liberals faced continuing strong criticism from the Progressive Conservatives for agreeing to serve on the ICCS at all. In February Claude Wagner termed the role 'a poorly contrived and planned mission fraught with uncertainty and political difficulty,' criticized the government for failing to safeguard Canadian personnel via sound contingency plans for emergency removal from Vietnam, and lamented the lack of parliamentary consultation prior to governmental decisions. John Diefenbaker was unhappy with participation because the Paris Agreements seemed to him to be 'the Munich of 1973.'[116] But his opinions were no longer representative of his party's position on Vietnam at all. Gordon Fairweather, for example, joined with David Lewis in demanding UN input in the peace process and, more surprisingly, in seeking Canadian pressure on President Thieu to release all his prisoners of war.[117]

On 5 March Sharp informed the House about plans for a personal visit to Vietnam and after these remarks he told the press that Canada would withdraw if the ICCS was not allowed 'to operate more effectively than at present.'[118] Claude Wagner again criticized the government for concurring in the inadequate procedures adopted at Paris. He also refused to accept the government's invitation to send a PC representative with Sharp on his tour of Vietnam, saying that the proposed trip was nothing more than 'window-dressing.' The NDP agreed, however, and MP Douglas Rowland was designated to go.

Prior to Sharp's arrival in Vietnam, Commissioner Gauvin had been embroiled in a lengthy dispute with the Poles and Hungarians concerning SA-2 'Guideline' anti-aircraft missiles which had allegedly been installed at the former American air strip at Khe Sanh after the cease-fire. The Canadians pressed for an ICCS field investigation of RVN charges, but the communist half of the commission rejected any investigation, saying that there was no way to prove when the missiles had been installed, and that the aerial photos submitted by the RVN proved that the Saigon authorities had themselves violated the cease-fire. The evidence supporting these counter-charges was highly ambiguous.[119] After some weeks of wrangling, PRG/DRVN forces apparently removed the missiles. American Secretary of State William Rogers soon credited the Canadians for the removal. An External Affairs spokesperson then rejected Rogers's comment as 'unwarranted flattery,'[120] claiming that the whole affair demonstrated the weakness of the ICCS machinery. Of the controversy Gauvin later reported:

The Khe Sanh case ... marked something of a turning point. For the first time, we were unable to get agreement within the Commission to take any action whatsoever in connection with a complaint that unequivocally attracted the Agreement and necessitated an investigation. The arguments put forward by the Hung and Pol dels in refusing to agree to an investigation were specious and unconvincing, such as the argument that there were quote inadequate grounds unquote (aerial photos) to justify an investigation, and it was clearly a matter where they simply did not/not wish the investigation to take place ... Our regional teams have met with similar obstructive tactics on the part of the two dels.[121]

Other reports were apparently receiving similar biased treatment from the Poles and Hungarians.[122] Physical movement of ICCS teams was also now greatly hampered by recently imposed restrictions upon the use of helicopters following four shoot-down attempts during the last week of February.

On 13 March Sharp left Ottawa accompanied by Rowland and Créditiste MP Eudore Allard. By this time, according to RVN estimates, 12,590 communist troops and 2,597 government soldiers had been killed since 28 January. Infiltration allegations were now being made by the American government. In Tokyo on 15 March, Sharp received a 'strong' and 'forceful' plea from Japan's premier Kakuei Tanaka and the then foreign minister Masayoshi Ohira not to abandon the commission. On 16 March President Nixon implied that he was getting ready to bomb the DRVN once more and possibly Hanoi as well unless the attempted infiltration of some 300 tanks and 30,000 men ceased immediately. The same day Hanoi counter-charged that US warplanes had illegally overflown the DRVN.[123]

Upon his arrival in South Vietnam on 17 March, the secretary of state for external affairs was told by Gauvin and his senior military adviser, Major General Duncan McAlpine, that communist obstructionism was now very serious. Gauvin did not counsel withdrawal, however. External Affairs officials posted in Saigon informed the press entourage following Sharp that the Canadian government was being subjected to 'tremendous' diplomatic pressure. Said one senior diplomat: 'We are being told that if Canada pulls out the whole peace-keeping operation will collapse like a pack of cards.'[124]

In Hanoi on 18 March after a whirlwind visit to Vientiane, Sharp had lengthy conversations with Premier Pham Van Dong and Foreign Minister Nguyen Duy Trinh. Both expressed the wish that Ottawa not resign its role. Shortly thereafter External Affairs staff spoke for the first time of a possible extension of the Canadian role, but they also noted that any extensions beyond a one-time renewal would inevitably erode Canada's diplomatic credibility. NDP representative Rowland opined that after viewing the situation first-hand he would probably agree to 'almost any decision Sharp made.' Sharp noted that he would offer his recommendations to Cabinet as soon as he returned to Ottawa but added that he had not yet made up his mind.[125]

On 21 March Sharp appeared before the Commons Standing Committee on External Affairs and National Defence (SCEAND) to brief the assembled parliamentarians on the results of his trip. As in his previous appearance before the committee on 6 March when he had briefed SCEAND's members on the Paris Conference, the minister once more gave a factual and sombre presentation. In his earlier appearance he had talked of being 'pragmatic,' of being an 'agitator on behalf of the international community,'[126] and of trying 'to improve the [operation of the] agreement ... in the interests of world peace.'[127] His tone was clearly liberal-moderate. But by the end of March a new more self-interested spirit was evident in his rhetoric.

Sharp began by noting that his government 'was not greatly impressed' by arguments for staying on the ICCS which claimed that 'any international presence is better than no international presence' or that constructive action in the future might be possible even if it was not possible at present. The crux of the problem as he saw it and as he had explained to both the Hanoi and Saigon authorities was that 'the composition of the Commission rendered it virtually impossible for it ever to make a report that would be unfavourable to the Democratic Republic of Viet Nam or the Provisional Revolutionary Government side while, because of our desire to be objective, it is quite conceivable that we should find ourselves supporting a report detrimental to the RVN position.' Saigon understood this fact but still wanted Canada to remain because of Canadian effectiveness in bringing 'all points of view into the public domain.'[128] But the minister did not find this justification especially compelling either.

Participation in Laos on a reactivated ICSC was still a remote possibility, Sharp noted, but the decision depended upon a satisfactory conclusion to the drafting of the relevant protocol to the new Laotian cease-fire. Turning to North Vietnam, Sharp was clearly greatly troubled by Hanoi's blindered approach to the conflict.

Regarding the strife in South Vietnam, he noted that up to 15 March some 7,000 incidents (some on a scale involving 'divisional strength') had occurred after the armistice. Only thirty-one official requests for investigation had been lodged with the ICCS by the parties. Of the thirty-one requests only two had led to investigations and actual findings. But despite such a dreadful record, thousands of prisoners of war were now in the process of being released: 'Shortly the last United States forces in Viet Nam will have departed. The ICCS has had its role to play in these developments and if it did nothing else, this would have justified its existence."[129] Sharp's priorities were now crystal clear. He added that he did not want Canada to linger on in its role as an international nag for so long that the Canadian contingent would become nothing but a dismal 'bore.'[130] Sharp also noted that the ICCS had helped to make possible the bilateral political talks in Paris. He did not mention that the talks were going nowhere. He also declined to say precisely what he would be recommending to Cabinet, but it was obvious to all concerned that he now favoured withdrawal in the near future.

Most of the members of the Standing Committee were sympathetic to Sharp's problem. The minister's efforts to educate the opposition had succeeded to an extent, no doubt assisted by international publicity and the sensitivity of the subject now that Canadian lives were actually on the line. By the end of March there was a virtually unanimous consensus that ICCS decision-making should be a non-partisan process. The NDP caucus recommended giving ninety days notice on 28 March, but persisting in the 'open-mouth' tactics because 'they are the only tactics that have produced any results.' There was not the slightest hint in their position that they would withdraw support from the government should it follow a somewhat different course. It was firm policy in the NDP to do 'everything possible, everything reasonable, in an untenable situation to ensure that it was not our action which contributed to a lack of peace through the collapse of the ICCS.'[131]

Among the PCs, Douglas Roche was the most outspoken in favour of remaining on the commission indefinitely. Gordon Fairweather, Flora MacDonald, and Peter Reilly went on record to support this point of view – or at least to favour some form of extended commitment. Erik Nielsen on the other hand was a strong advocate of early withdrawal. The leader of the Opposition, Robert Stanfield, cognizant of the divergence of opinion within his party's ranks, declared that he had 'an open mind' on the problem.[132]

On the same day that Sharp appeared before the Standing Committee, American officials released a report indicating that infiltration of men and materials to South Vietnam had slowed significantly. There was a real possibility that infiltration was being limited 'to the forces and heavy equipment that presumably were en route to South Vietnam before January 27.'[133] It was also learned that day that the previous week President Thieu had reversed his stand on the irrelevance of the ICCS (no doubt directly because of the favourable impact of Gauvin's press briefings). He had told an assembly of his province chiefs and 'other key officials' that henceforth better implementation of the cease-fire was deemed in the national interest and that ICCS members were to be treated 'as honoured guests.'[134] Unfortunately his change of heart did not extend to include better treatment for PRG representatives, many of whom were being held as virtual captives at their quarters at Tan Son Nhut airfield.

These encouraging reports were countered, however, by the inability of Gauvin to obtain an investigation of a major battle occurring at Rach Bap, only twenty-two miles north of Saigon, because of PRG refusal to assure ICCS safety. Said Gauvin, as he called for an immediate halt to air and rocket strikes near ICCS team sites: 'We came here to observe peace, not a war.'[135]

At this juncture the government was confronted with a difficult decision. Sharp was determined to 'get out' if 'war breaks out again.' But of course a real peace had yet to 'break out.' Attempting to decide what level of hostilities warranted a definitive withdrawal was a terribly imprecise and uncertain exercise at best. In the circumstances, with truce violations the norm and not the exception, but with the great powers still hopeful that a political breakthrough might yet be negotiated in Paris, and with a unanimous chorus by other foreign governments exhorting Canada to tough it out, Sharp's liberal-moderate prudence triumphed over his conservative concern for Canadian credibility and lives. Sharp's apparent belief that there was still some objective basis for an eventual peace in Indochina arising from the mutual interest of the great powers in excluding each other from further intervention in the region[136] was probably the decisive factor in opting to 'walk the last mile' in the interests of peace. Sharp was also concerned about appearances: 'We do not want to act in such a way that people say, "oh, well, you know, Canadians did not like the way the game was being played so that they got out and took the ball and bat and went home." We do not want to create that impression either.'[137] Credibility cut in two directions: peacekeeping standards had to be maintained, but any exit had to be conducted prudently, precisely, and responsibly as well. In some respects the latter was the more difficult of the two tasks.

On 23 March the Polish and Hungarian delegations withdrew their personnel from two designated team sites following mortar attacks on adjacent areas by PRG forces. Ambassador Gauvin immediately protested the action, saying that it amounted to a violation of the agreement.[138] On the same day, the NDP caucus officially announced that it favoured early withdrawal from the ICCS.[139] At this time some 138 American prisoners of war still remained in the DRVN.

On 28 March Sharp informed the Commons of the Cabinet's decision (taken two days earlier) to accept service for a maximum of ninety more days. A further review would be taken at the end of May (then sixty days hence) to determine whether or not a withdrawal would be made at the end of June. Without 'definite improvement' in the truce by the end of May, Canada would leave.[140] To all but the naïvely optimistic, the Canadians were now set on a course for eventual withdrawal. The day after Sharp's announcement, the last American troops left Vietnam boarding aircraft (so-called 'freedom birds') at Da Nang and Saigon to the sound of tape-recorded band music. At almost the same time, the last sixty-seven American POWs were flown out of Hanoi's Gia Lam airport. General Frederick Weyand, the last commander of US forces in Vietnam, announced that the US 'mission ... to prevent an all-out attempt by an aggressor to impose its will through raw military force' had been 'accomplished.'[141] With departure of the American military the Four-Party JMC dissolved. This left the ICCS with no official body to report to because the RVN and PRG had thus far failed to establish the Two-Party JMC. RVN harassment of PRG representatives and shelling of PRG-designated rendezvous points continued unabated.[142]

On 3 April the Canadians and Indonesians found the PRG guilty of a 'calculated act of terrorism' in the bombing of a Buddhist pagoda after hearing convincing testimony of attempted intimidation directed against the chief monk. The Polish and Hungarians delegations refused to accept these findings. A second split report found Indo-Canadian agreement concerning a bridge-bombing incident; the communist delegations declared that the bridge had fallen down.[143]

On Saturday 7 April, Captain Charles Laviolette of Quebec City was killed when a clearly marked ICCS helicopter in which he was travelling was shot down by a PRG missile near Gio Linh. Two Hungarians, one Indonesian, two PRG liaison officers, and three US crewmen were also killed. At almost the same time, another JMC helicopter was shot down in the Mekong Delta while escorting an ICCS helicopter. PRG spokespeople claimed that Laviolette's helicopter was some fifteen miles off course. Both Sharp and Prime Minister Trudeau immediately declared that this was not sufficient grounds for a rapid pull-out of the Canadian contingent, but that they would examine the incident closely to determine whether early withdrawal might be justified.[144] Sharp's dedication to the cause of peace was not strengthened by the news that survivors of the helicopter attack (a second helicopter accompanying Laviolette's had been grounded) had been forced to sign statements that the destruction of the helicopter had been an 'accident.'[145]

Gauvin and Vernon Turner, his senior political adviser, immediately began to consider withdrawal of all Canadian personnel from PRG-controlled territory. More important, the Canadian commissioner drafted 'a considered statement' that was delivered to the commission on 13 April. The statement implied that DRVN troops were responsible for the downing of the two helicopters. The basis for this accusation apparently was American military intelligence reports that indicated that communist forces in the zone concerned had traditionally been North Vietnamese rather than locally recruited southerners. Said Gauvin:

We have strong reason to believe that in other parts of South Vietnam, as well as in the area where the helicopter incident took place, non-South Vietnamese troops are stationed in, or are infiltrating, South Vietnam for the purpose of supporting militarily one of the two parties in South Vietnam.

When we came here as members of the ICCS we had, and still have, every right to expect that the differences which exist between the two parties in South Vietnam will be resolved through peaceful means and through the process of free and democratic elections.

The self-determination of the people of South Vietnam is guaranteed by the agreement and it is evident that the self-determination of South Vietnam cannot be expressed if outsiders take sides in support of one South Vietnamese party against the other.

As journalist James Anderson noted, Gauvin's comments 'came very close to supporting the demands of the Saigon government which has tried to set ... withdrawal [of DRVN troops] as a condition for elections and a general political settlement.'[146] Gauvin came under increasingly bitter personal attack in ensuing weeks from Hanoi, the PRG, and the communist governments belonging to the ICCS. It was probably more than coincidental that the number of incidents of attempted helicopter shoot-downs, as well as mortaring of areas adjacent to ICCS team sites, rose steadily as Canadian efforts to make the ICCS effective became more demanding.

The 13 April statement involved a first tentative but unmistakable step in addressing the problem of continuing infiltration of North Vietnamese men and materials. Such movement was occurring, according to American technical reconnaissance, and if it was not halted soon by some effective scheme of border monitoring the already slender prospects for peace would vanish altogether. Gauvin's statement was less an example of bias than it was a challenge to the communist side to begin observing the important no-infiltration provision of the agreement. If Gauvin did show bias in referring to DRVN troops as 'outsiders,' it is hard to know how else one might describe North Vietnamese soldiers who had entered 'sovereign' South Vietnam illic-

itly after the cease-fire. The word 'foreign' was probably the best approxima-
tion of their status even if the agreement also spoke of the unity of all
Vietnam. The agreement had decreed that 'the South Vietnamese people's
right to self-determination' was 'sacred' and 'inalienable' and that only the
South Vietnamese people and the South Vietnamese parties would decide
the political future of South Vietnam 'through genuinely free and democratic general elections under international supervision.' How could one
plausibly argue that this objective could be accomplished with over 150,000
non-South Vietnamese troops on South Vietnamese territory? It was hardly
an abandonment of impartiality to point out a major and continuing violation by one of the parties, especially when it was done in such a restrained
way. Unmasking Hanoi's propaganda fiction that there were no DRVN
troops in the south was an unavoidable task that the ICCS had to confront at
some time if the armistice was ever going to be made to endure.

It may not have been coincidental that Gauvin's pressure upon the infiltration question, and by implication on the overall status of DRVN troops in
the south, occurred shortly before the Saigon authorities tabled their plan
for a political settlement of the war which stipulated inter alia: a restoration
of democratic freedoms on 27 May; simultaneous withdrawal of DRVN
troops and demobilization of an equal number of RVN troops; internationally supervised elections on 26 August for a constitution-drafting 'organism.'
Communist plans, on the other hand, involved no suggested dates but carefully stipulated that there would be no discussion of military issues until
after the release of all political prisoners and after the holding of elections.[147]

The prospects for a real peace faded quickly in mid-April. DRVN and PRG
forces built a series of new roads from North Vietnam to complement the
Ho Chi Minh Trail. Construction of a petroleum-oil-lubricants pipeline
progressed rapidly down into central South Vietnam. New highly accurate
130-millimetre artillery was introduced which out-ranged all artillery possessed by RVN forces.[148] Heavy B-52 bombing continued to prop up the
internally divided, coup-ridden, and wholly incompetent and corrupt regime
of Lon Nol, while heavy fighting broke out along the South Vietnamese–
Cambodian border between RVN forces and two North Vietnamese regi-
ments. According to US Senate estimates, almost 50 per cent of the population of Cambodia were now refugees. In Hanoi, DRVN air defence units were
taking delivery of more advanced SA-3 'Goa' anti-aircraft missiles with a
low-level interception capability that could double previous American loss
rates if bombing of Hanoi and Haiphong was resumed. Finally on 17 and 18
April, B-52s struck at targets in Laos for the first time since 22 February.

Hanoi responded by declaring that US bombing in Laos jeopardized 'implementation of the agreement as a whole' and posed 'a direct threat to peace in South Vietnam.'[149]

According to a White House spokesperson, 'diplomatic pressure' was at this time being applied to try to force more 'responsive' behaviour from the Hungarians and Poles.[150] In a State Department note to Budapest and Warsaw, the American government accused the communist delegations to the ICCS of being 'substantially less prepared to authorize or participate in impartial investigation ... than the spirit and the protocol of the Paris Agreement might call for.'[151] On 25 April a new Paris meeting between Kissinger and Le Duc Tho was announced for May or early June to discuss the manifold problems of the armistice.

Cambodia was at the heart of the deteriorative process. The intensity of the bombing in Cambodia by then exceeded the intensity of the 'Christmas bombing' of North Vietnam. During the last week of April, large quantities of napalm and cluster bombs were dropped by B52s, FB-111s, and F-4s on Khmer Rouge forces then attempting to advance on Phnom Penh. On 4 May Nixon warned Hanoi that it must pull its forces out of Laos and Cambodia or face a renewed war.[152] But Hanoi did not and could not control the Khmer Rouge, and here the path to peace was stymied.

Perhaps exhausted by the last eighteen months of the conflict, international opinion was relatively restrained at the continuing mass destruction being wrought by American aircraft in the defence of an unpopular and worthless regime. One of the few leaders who did speak out, Swedish Premier Olof Palme, once more alluded to Nazi terror tactics.[153] On this occasion the comparison was justified. Thousands of civilians were being slaughtered without mercy, all in a campaign intended only to protect Saigon's 'flank' from the mere possibility of new communist pressure. The very limited objective being sought by American officials was in no way proportionate to the violence inflicted upon the Cambodian people. The Khmer Rouge were not instruments of Hanoi (as the 1977–9 Khmer Rouge–Vietnamese war demonstrated). It is thus highly doubtful that they would ever have collaborated with Hanoi in attacking Saigon. Washington did not want to risk that possibility. By the spring of 1973 'credibility' was an issue in Cambodia as well. Here Kissinger and Nixon and especially their military advisers erred badly – one might fairly say criminally. Sihanouk's comment to American journalists seemed only too true: 'Your people cannot be moved by the killing of yellow people. The killing of Cambodians mean nothing to them. Watergate is more important to them and we put our hope in the Watergate affair.'[154]

While US aircraft were dismembering a sizeable chunk of Cambodia's population and turning the Khmer Rouge leaders towards a shell-shocked, revolutionary mania,[155] the Canadians in South Vietnam were eventually brought to admit that Captain Laviolette's helicopter was off course and that it had not been moved by PRG forces subsequent to the crash as some American officials had charged.[156] On 3 May Mitchell Sharp addressed the annual meeting of the Canadian Press and noted a generally deteriorating condition of the 'cease-fire' in Indochina: 'I don't think Canadians would mind if someone died in the interests of peace but we don't want Canadians dying for no good purpose.'[157] This statement followed yet another attempted shoot-down of clearly marked ICCS helicopters by PRG forces near the de-militarized zone in Quang Tri province. PRG officials claimed that their forces had merely been firing at American reconnaissance aircraft which had been attempting to use the ICCS flight corridor. Ambassador Gauvin rejected this explanation completely.[158] The Canadian delegation, while admitting that the 7 April incident was due in part to the helicopters' deviation from their flight plan, refused to agree to a report which fully exonerated the PRG-DRVN forces. Gauvin did his best to try to turn the controversy to good effect by having ICCS flight corridors widened from two and one-half to five miles. PRG officials refused, offering a three-mile 'compromise' instead. On 6 May yet another ICCS helicopter was attacked, this time in the Mekong Delta.

On 8 May Canadian officials revealed that an Indonesian-Canadian investigation of the stories of three prisoners held by RVN forces had demonstrated convincingly that personnel had been infiltrated into South Vietnam from the DRVN after the cease-fire. The Poles and Hungarians refused to partici-pate in the investigation or to permit the results of the investigation to go forward as commission reports.[159] For the rest of the month the commission sought unsuccessfully to have ICCS helicopter corridors widened. Towards the end of May, Gauvin fought to have discussions held on the Indo-Cana-dian report on illegal DRVN infiltration. The communist delegations after considerable stalling agreed to discuss the report (which to this point had been submitted only informally to the Two-Party JMC by the Canadians) but they never agreed to accept the bilateral investigation as a valid official report of the commission.[160] This was somewhat odd since they did not have any 'different views' on the substance of the investigation. Now beyond a shadow of a doubt it was clear that the Poles and Hungarians were following obstructionist tactics.

In sum, the months of April and May provided no basis for optimism that the armistice would truly take hold or that the defects in the supervisory machinery could be rectified by incremental tinkering with procedures and personalities. On 29 May the secretary of state for external affairs rose in the House of Commons to announce the Canadian withdrawal. Sharp began by declaring that 'we have served in more peacekeeping and peace observer roles than any other country and we remain ready to serve wherever we can be effective.' The government was withdrawing because there had been 'no significant change in the situation' towards a genuine cessation of hostilities. Sharp noted that he looked on the Paris Agreement as 'a good agreement that provides as sound and honourable a basis for peace as was negotiable.'[161] Had the parties and the other ICCS states not rejected 'the Canadian concept of the functioning of the International Commission,' Canada might have stayed on. They did not, and Canada was therefore obliged to leave in the interests of all concerned. In a press conference following this statement, Sharp noted that the Canadians had striven for impartiality and objectivity while the Poles and Hungarians thought it their duty merely 'to back the interests of North Vietnam and the Viet Cong.' To soften the possible negative effects of withdrawal, and to meet a telephone request from Kissinger on 25 May, Sharp declared that Canada would serve until 31 July to ease any problems the states of the Paris Conference might have in locating a suitable replacement for Canada. If elections were to be held, although Sharp thought this highly improbable, and if no replacement had yet been found, Ottawa would then 'consider sympathetically a request temporarily for this purpose [ie, electoral supervision], in the light of the circumstances then prevailing and our assessment of the chances for effective supervision.' All three opposition parties welcomed the decision and virtually all of them indicated that they thought that leaving would in no way harm Canada's traditional commitment to its international responsibilities.[162]

One hour before Sharp announced the departure, Henry Kissinger broke the news in Washington, committing a minor breach of diplomatic etiquette. Kissinger was not happy with the decision, 'especially at this time when Washington is negotiating with Hanoi on an agreement to implement the cease-fire more strictly.' However, he went on, 'Canada made this decision in the light of many considerations, including a strong domestic opposition to this course [ie, staying on in Vietnam]. You can say we regret it but understand it.'[163] In any case the American State Department immediately sounded out Mexico and Brazil as possible replacements. Eventually Iran would accept the role.

During June, Commissioner Gauvin attempted vainly to secure official 'report' status for the Indo-Canadian findings on infiltration. For the entire month, Gauvin refused to hold meetings unless the Poles and Hungarians agreed to accept his methods. They did not. But just prior to the end of Gauvin's second tenure of the office of commission chairman, the Canadian ambassador elected to send the findings to the Two-Party JMC with a covering letter from himself in his capacity as chairman. This line of action was made necessary when the Poles and Hungarians absolutely refused to accord the document official status. They categorically refused to accept Canadian arguments that the mandatory character of ICCS investigations superseded the requirement that unanimity be adhered to in official reports. The Canadian argument was technically supportable and plausible, but the communist delegations were determined, according to one press report, to keep the commission in 'a vaguer, broader' and nominally more ambitious role as mediator 'between the hostile sides,' 'a righter of past wrongs,' and 'an ultimate judge of the issues.'[164] Such rhetoric was really no more than the window-dressing for the attempted emasculation of commission investigatory powers. A competent ICCS was anathema to the communist side. Investigations might 'discover' DRVN troops.

Prior to the departure of the Canadian contingent in the first two weeks of August, the only other interest generated by Canadian involvement concerned the detention of Captain Ian Patten and Captain Fletcher Thomson by PRG forces for seventeen days from 30 June to 16 July. Patten and Thomson had been out attempting to exercise what the Canadian delegation had argued were twenty-four-hour-a-day diplomatic immunities for ICCS personnel. The PRG never accepted this interpretation of Article 10(f) of the ICCS Protocol and claimed the detention was justified given the lack of authorization to travel in the PRG zone. Canadian logic on behalf of commission mobility and effectiveness again failed to prevail. Thomson and Patten were released unharmed but after having been treated in an insulting, degrading, and thoroughly 'uncivilized' fashion. By the end of July there had been only ten unanimous ICCS reports – all of them citing violations by the RVN authorities. The PRG was 'never found guilty of even a minor infraction.'[165] There could be no more damning evidence of the complete lack of impartiality by the Poles and Hungarians than this. Despite this bizarre testament to Canadian objectivity, PRG authorities were nevertheless quick to condemn the Canadian record for extreme partiality. Prime Minister Trudeau's welcoming telegram to some of the first returning members of the ICCS contingent was far more accurate and appropriate: these Canadians, he said, had contributed 'an element of sanity to the ICCS.'[166]

On 14 August Iran officially accepted an ICCS role. Throughout 1973 and 1974 the ICCS continued to exist only on the basis of extraordinary subventions from the US government. With the departure of the Canadians, no

368 In the interests of peace

more investigatory activity was attempted. In 1973 and 1974 according to RVN data, some 27,000 troops, 5,400 South Vietnamese civilians, and 103,800 PRG-DRVN forces were killed. Nor would the Vietnamese people's trouble end in April 1975 when Hanoi's armoured divisions finally overran Saigon. War with the Khmer Rouge would cause thousands more deaths and would lead to a costly occupation of 'Democratic Kampuchea' (ie, Cambodia) that continues to this day. Costly too would be the border war with China in early 1979. For the Vietnamese people it seems there will be no early end to their generation of war, nor for their still more unfortunate neighbours in occupied Kampuchea.

CANADIAN POLICY THE SECOND TIME AROUND:
TENDENCY SHIFT AND TENDENCY EVOLUTION

According to one early and very capable post-mortem of the ICCS affair, Canadian policy-makers were not intrinsically interested in the problem of peace in Indochina in the winter of 1972–3. Their primary concern was placating the minimum demands of a potentially dangerous American administration. The search for a modus vivendi with the United States government was in essence why Canada joined the International Commission in the first place, and why it was not until May that the government was able to announce a Canadian withdrawal at the end of July."[167] Basically, Canadian decision-makers were animated by a deep concern for avoiding American hostility. This explanation of policy is a very reasonable, 'one-dimensional,' rational-actor interpretation of Canadian ICCS policy-making.[168]

The ICCS experience, of course, may also be viewed by examining the interplay of the three principal foreign policy tendencies of the political system. Table 3 provides a summary of the policy preferences of these tendencies on seven aspects of the Canadian ICCS involvement.

Left-liberal attitudes in 1972–3 were not surprising. They were generally consistent with previous stances by External Affairs left-wing elements and the views held by CCF-NDP parliamentarians. The major differences in opinion occur in the centre and right of the Canadian Vietnam policy debate.

Articulators of the liberal-moderate position retained their classic commitment to peace promotion, but they were now finding great difficulty in locating opportunities for effectively constraining any great power's behaviour. The Nixon-Kissinger era did not really lend itself to the benevolent moderation or interdiction of great-power machinations by concerned middle powers. In early 1973 Canadian liberal-moderates believed it to be vitally important that the US disengage from Indochina, rethink its security commitments in Asia, and learn to act sensibly, prudently, and efficiently as one of the managing directors of global order. To that end, Canadian liberal-moderates were prepared to risk some loss of prestige for Canada by agreeing to serve for a limited time in a supervisory role which might prove to be even more of a charade than the old ICSC role that had been necessitated in first instance by the need to mask the French withdrawal from Indochina in 1954–5.

Liberal-moderates were reluctantly prepared to play Henry Kissinger's game of disengagement despite its possible hypocritical falsity. Such artifice was apparently the only way of extricating the United States, given the alignment of political forces in the American politico-bureaucratic élite. The Republican party and the American right wing generally was still very much a force to be reckoned with both within the Congress and executive branch. The US right wing almost certainly would not tolerate an overt defeat in · Indochina. They might, however, accept a defeat of RVN forces following Vietnamization and a so-called 'decent interval' after American troop withdrawal.[169] Not coincidentally, this last proviso constituted the policy foundation of Kissinger's whole approach to 'peacemaking' in Indochina, both because he apparently believed deeply in the objective need to maintain strategic credibility and because he understood the minimum terms of disengagement demanded by the extreme Republicans.[170] Three factors seemed likely to cause potentially grave obstacles for the realization of the 'decent interval' scenario: Nixon's personal determination to salvage 'peace with honour'; the president's landslide electoral mandate to effect a tolerable outcome for so many years of pain and effort; and, finally, Nixon's passion for avoiding an appearance of weakness. To the liberal-moderate elements of the Canadian system, the Indochina crisis was still fraught with great risk, not least because American domestic opinion seemed to be on the verge of hysteria as a result of the highly irrational and irresponsible media treatment of the prisoner-of-war issue.

The chief anxiety in this situation for liberal-moderates arose from the commonly held belief that participation in truce supervisory charades demeaned the very concept of third-party peacekeeping and mediation. This dubious but politically influential argument was wielded by many high-minded purists of both right and left who merely wanted a plausible excuse for evading service. Nevertheless, the idea had to be taken seriously. If the ICCS did turn out to be merely a cloak masking American desertion of a small but incompetent ally, many feared that Ottawa's reputation as an effective

TABLE 3
Canadian Indochina policy tendencies 1968–73

Issue	Left-liberal; peace through respect for national self-determination and humanitarian concern	Liberal-moderate; peace through constraint of great-power behaviour where possible	Conservative; peace through containment, but also new commitment to simple maximization of welfare, power, prestige
	–o–o–o–o–o–		
1 Initial attitude towards an ICCS role	Willing to serve to help get the US out through effecting early release of POWs	Reluctant, fearing a sham peace; but willing to do what could be done to see the repatriation of the US POWs and an end to America's destructive involvement	Opposed acceptance fearing an American betrayal of a small ally; angry at past US incompetence and present duplicity
		–*–*–*–*–	
	–o–o–o–o–		
2 Prospects for a genuine political settlement	Sceptical but optimistic that the US would withdraw from the fighting for good once its troops were home	Plausible; belief in the mutual interest of the great powers in leaving the Indochinese to resolve the war on their own	Very poor; US will had weakened but the DRVN was as determined and aggressive as ever – witness the 1972 offensive
		–*–*–*–*–	
		–o–o–o–o–	
3 Operational concept of the ICCS	Mediatory, humanitarian, as well as investigatory; a necessary device for cloaking US departure; a possible tool for freeing RVN political prisoners	Cloaking device in the interim, but must meet stringent conditions thereafter or withdrawal ensues	Stringent conditions from the outset, a total rejection of the mediatory function; an uncompromising defence of legitimate RVN interests
			–*–*–*–

		-o-o-o-o-	
4 Risk of escalation to great-power confrontation or use of weapons of mass destruction	Still serious; the American involvement must be ended before the US government lurches into some catastrophe	The opportunities of detente must be seized; risk is lower than in 1950s or 1960s but is still considerable, especially if American minimum terms are not met　　-*-*-*-	Low because of US determination to jettison troublesome dependents, Nixon's willingness to resort to brutality, and America's overwhelming military power
	-o-o-o-o-		
5 Reaction to American air war tactics	Totally repugnant, barbaric	Inhumane and counterproductive; one of the major causes of America's political defeat　-*-*-*-	Counterproductive politically but the DRVN was guilty of overt aggression against the South Vietnamese people
6 Attitude to early withdrawal from the ICSC	The sooner the better after the American POWs are out	Favoured it in principle, but only under conditions that will not give rise to recriminations	Against withdrawal; better to 'fight to the finish' (within the law) on behalf of the RVN
7 Attitude to US 'restraint' in 1975	No direct adverse consequence foreseen; such 'restraint' was long overdue	The whole war was a tragedy with unforeseeable effects — especially the 'end game'	American 'credibility' badly damaged; US leadership now in doubt

-*-*-*- Government's effective operational consensus, 1973
-o-o-o-o- Government's effective operational consensus, spring 1968

peacekeeper might be severely diminished. Canada could be vulnerable to a new charge of 'complicity' in America's 'crime' of betraying a weak ally valiantly fighting communist aggression.

On the other hand, a failure to accept the new Indochina draft call would tend to undermine the obviously fragile political compromise between the Americans and the North Vietnamese, which despite the enormous lacunae in the armistice still had some theoretical potential for beginning the movement towards an eventual political settlement in the region. More important, evasion of the 'invitation' would tend to sour relations with the Nixon administration, which may have been counting on both Canadian expertise to provide the necessary organizational impetus for the commission as well as Canadian political determination to see that the ICCS operated fairly. The notion of an acceptance of limited duration also seemed doubly appealing because it promised to leave the option of withdrawal open while in no way threatening the emotionally charged prisoner-of-war issue.

Conservative opinion was deeply troubled by the issue of ICCS participation. Many thought a policy of determined non-involvement was essential. Nixon and Kissinger were 'after bigger game'; the South Vietnamese were about to become victims of the newly revised American global strategy. Ironically enough it was the conservatives who argued most strongly for non-involvement within the government. For these Canadian officials and politicians the most galling aspect of the Vietnam tragedy was the fact that 'the U.S. could have won if they had used all the means at their disposal.'[171]

Somewhat surprisingly, many of these same conservatives who had first argued strongly for rejection of the ICCS role subsequently argued that once accepted, the role should be played to the absolute limits of Canadian experience and political skill in an effort to apply the ambiguous provisions of the armistice in such a way that Saigon's *legitimate* interests would be protected as far as possible. Thus any attempt to debase the commission for communist purposes would be immediately obvious. These arguments formed part of the basis for an important policy compromise involving all three doctrinal tendencies at work in the Canadian foreign policy process.

In sum, the broad pattern of policy comprised a time-delimited acceptance of the supervisory role coupled with a literalist and defensibly partisan approach to the interpretation (but not the mechanical operation) of the provisions of the armistice. The initial decision to accept a role was essentially a collaboration of the policy-making centre with the left-liberal elements of the policy system. The 'price' which the liberal-moderate centre exacted in return for support on joining the commission was the prudent time limit and the list of further hedges against any indefinite participation on politically undesirable terms. Second, the style and methods of participation were the product of concessions by the centre to the policy-making right wing of the system. The liberal-moderates agreed that a perfectionist, investigatory, 'deterrence of violation' approach would be followed, not a mdeiatory, conciliatory style of operations. Liberal-moderate tactics, conservatively applied, would be beyond reproach – or so many centrists hoped.

Canadian Indochina involvement ended as it had begun with an internally complex set of perceptions and policy preferences animating the various elements of the policy process. As it had so often in the past, the liberal-moderate tendency was the predominant influence in shaping Canadian policy, but it must be appreciated that this was accomplished by selectively accommodating the policy preferences of each of the other two tendencies in the system.

It is reasonably certain that there was a modest tendency shift rightward in the effective operational consensus on Vietnam in the Canadian government over the years 1967–73. (See points 1–5 in table 3 and also figure 8.) From the left-liberal tinged liberal-moderate approach followed in the last months of the Pearson-Martin ministry, the Trudeau-Sharp team presided over the adoption of a new, more conservative slant to traditional liberal-moderate values and tactics. By 1973, Canada's Vietnam policy was truly a matter of 'liberal moderation conservatively applied.' But because this last tendency shift was not really appreciated or understood (unlike, for example, the more dramatic swings that had occurred in 1955–6 or 1966) by the public, one found government officials still proclaiming the essential continuity of Canadian foreign policy. The continuity was more imagined than real. The major changes in the international environment after 1969 – the accession to power of Nixon-Kissinger, the proclamation of the Nixon Doctrine, the Nixon economic shocks of 1971, the American openings to the PRC and the Soviet Union in 1971–2, and the realization at the highest levels of the Western world that there was an emerging resource crisis – had created a new and far more problematic world, one in which neo-conservatives might do very well. The conservative element in the system, partly because of its inherent sensitivity to nationalist questions, seems to have recognized the wider significance of these changes before the 'theoreticians' in either the liberal-moderate or left-liberal camps.

During the ICCS experience, the conservative element succeeded to a large degree in imposing its policies and definitions of situation on the decision-making process. Proof of that fact is shown most clearly in the surprisingly severe criticism of American policy voiced implicitly by Prime Minister Trudeau on 1 May 1975, as DRVN heavy armour rolled through the streets of

FIGURE 8
The final tendency shift 1969–73

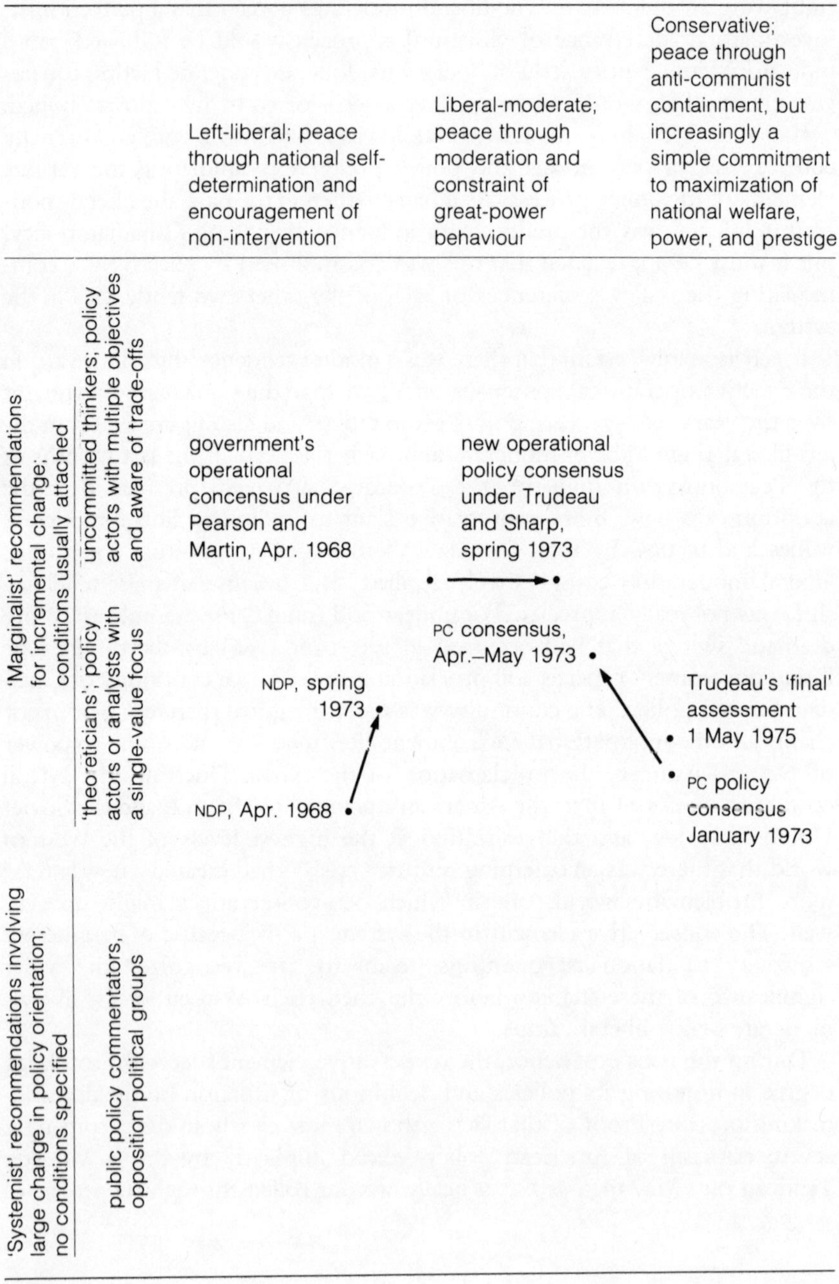

	Left-liberal; peace through national self-determination and encouragement of non-intervention	Liberal-moderate; peace through moderation and constraint of great-power behaviour	Conservative; peace through anti-communist containment, but increasingly a simple commitment to maximization of national welfare, power, and prestige

'Marginalist' recommendations for incremental change; conditions usually attached

uncommitted thinkers; policy actors with multiple objectives and aware of trade-offs

government's operational concensus under Pearson and Martin, Apr. 1968

new operational policy consensus under Trudeau and Sharp, spring 1973

PC consensus, Apr.–May 1973

'theoreticians'; policy actors or analysts with a single-value focus

NDP, spring 1973

Trudeau's 'final' assessment 1 May 1975

NDP, Apr. 1968

PC policy consensus January 1973

'Systemist' recommendations involving large change in policy orientation; no conditions specified

public policy commentators, opposition political groups

Saigon/Ho Chi Minh City. Said Trudeau while attending a Commonwealth Ministers' Conference in Jamaica:

The inevitable has happened. It's a very serious situation from the point of view of the United States and their whole interest in that part of the world. The leadership in Southeast Asia came to nought because of the inability of the president to get from Congress approval to carry out the policy he felt necessary. It will certainly cause concern for those who otherwise would have relied on the United States ... Cambodia, Laos, the whole area. *The president wasn't able to deliver what he wanted to deliver. It's very worrisome for those who might be looking around the world for where the power is. Will they look to the United States in the future or will they look elsewhere?*[172]

This comment reflected a very deep apprehension about the future of American power. Articulators of the conservative point of view within the government undoubtedly had a strong hand in the expression of such apprehension.

The prime minister's remarks were most probably directed at the failure of the Congress to keep liberal amounts of economic and military assistance flowing to Saigon, so that when 'the inevitable happened' there would be absolutely no question of where to allocate blame for the collapse of the RVN. Only a narrow circle of military analysts knew at this time that Saigon had more than enough equipment and supplies 'in the pipeline' to meet its immediate needs in repelling the DRVN invasion.[173] What the RVN lacked then was what it had always lacked: internal political cohesion, efficiency, and genuine popular support from the people it controlled. But the image remained of a congressionally imposed, financial noose strangling the RVN's ability to defend itself the only way it knew how, the so-called 'rich man's' war. Trudeau implicitly agreed with Kissinger's thesis that American credibility as a great-power guarantor was no trivial matter. It cut to the heart of the psychology of international political relationships.

By commenting on the waning of American credibility, Trudeau was articulating an essentially conservative concern. Liberal-moderate or left-liberal commentaries would have noticed something optimistic in the fact that the war was now finally over, and that American efforts could now be directed to more constructive endeavours. Mitchell Sharp played a number of policy tunes in counterpoint. Unlike Trudeau, his policy interventions were those of an 'uncommitted thinker' who was able to entertain multiple objectives simultaneously, and able to recognize and cope with trade-offs among them. The mark of the true uncommitted policy actor is a deep reluctance to take irrevocable positions. It was just such a capacity for incremental flexibility which Sharp evinced in his handling of the ICCS.

Sharp's economic background made him favour liberal-moderate political tactics instinctively. As a former minister of finance and a former senior executive with one of the largest corporate enterprises in the country, he understood that one was unlikely to get very far with policies which attacked American positions head on. The careful formulation of zones of mutual interest and the methods of quiet persuasion were far more likely to advance Canadian interests while strengthening the overall effectiveness of managing the Western world's system of political economy. Sharp had long since committed himself to the notion of the increasing economic interdependence of the Western world's economies. Not coincidentally, once he had left office, Sharp, along with Jean-Luc Pépin, would be one of the first Canadian public figures to become associated with David Rockefeller's Trilateral Commission.

Given this background, it was not surprising that as secretary of state for external affairs Sharp did his utmost to integrate and reconcile the objectives of the various political tendencies at work in the system. First he chose to join with the left-liberal element under the banner of 'help the US get out of Vietnam by assuring the prisoner-of-war release.' Then he agreed to the necessary compensating concession to conservative elements who wished to see the Canadian role, if it were to occur at all, executed in as forceful and kudos-winning a manner as possible. Precisely because he engineered this compromise, he was ultimately able to win the rarest of political accolades: effective approval of his policy across the parliamentary political spectrum.

Certainly tactical errors were made. Fixing the initial period of acceptance on a sixty-day basis, which coincided exactly with the scheduled period for the withdrawal of American forces and the return of their prisoners of war, was an avoidable mistake. An experimental period of three to six months would have been far less problematic. Second, the attempt to influence the shape of the settlement only through public declaration of conditions for participation was misguided. More effort should have been directed behind the scenes as well, working through the US government. If Trudeau and Sharp had already decided by late 1972 that some form of participation was inevitable, they might have tried to provide more input directly to Kissinger's negotiating team. Briefing State Department personnel on a lengthy technical memorandum by the External Affairs task force on the proper specifications for the new ICCS role was not appropriate in Richard Nixon's Washington if results were truly desired. To be sure there would have been a price for such input, had Nixon and Kissinger been amenable to it. But an increased share of responsibility for the wording of the armistice and associated protocols, something which Trudeau and Sharp had apparently strongly wished to avoid, was not necessarily something to be feared. Pure liberal-moderates would have taken such risks, and also would have given serious consideration to supplementing the commitment to investigatory excellence with independent efforts at diplomatic mediation between the Vietnamese parties, however improbable a political settlement might have seemed at the time. When confronted by the full array of environmental pressures, Trudeau and Sharp adhered to the liberal-moderate line out of political necessity, not personal doctrinal preference.

Retrospectively one must judge the Trudeau-Sharp response to the ICCS affair as a significant example of shrewd and successful crisis management. Participation in a costly farce of indefinite duration was avoided. Although unhappy with Canada's ultimate withdrawal, the Nixon administration was pleased by the vigorous sustained effort of the Canadian contingent to make the ICCS an effective supervisory body. Furthermore, no important American interests (viz., return of US prisoners of war) were damaged by the manner of Ottawa's exit. Finally, Canadian experience in Southeast Asia had not been withheld from this admittedly slender opportunity for peace in Vietnam. The Canadian conception of the requirements for supervisory work was thoroughly aired. Canada's international obligations in the situation were thus satisfactorily discharged. A difficult trial was handled with more than a little finesse.

12

Epilogue:
Canadian Vietnam decision-making
and the cybernetic paradigm

There is a natural argument that analytic procedures are more sophisticated, second-order processes which build upon more primitive cognitive operations. In some sense that must be true, for, as many have pointed out, full analysis of any complex problem is far beyond the capacity one can plausibly attribute to mental operations.

John Steinbruner[1]

After all, we tend to think of peace as something that lasts forever. Peace is in a sense a postponement of conflict. Personally I think it was quite well worthwhile having a United Nations force in the Middle East to get a relative peace for ten years.

John Holmes, 15 March 1973[2]

THE LIBERAL-MODERATE TENDENCY AND
CONSTRUCTIVE ADAPTATION IN THE NUCLEAR AGE

Over two decades of Canadian Vietnam decision-making there was a demonstrable oscillation in policy approach reflecting a pattern of adaptation to varying perceptions of threat in the environment. Figure 9 depicts the periods of liberal-moderate and conservative dominance in the Canadian approach to Indochina decision-making. The central fact to be observed is the sustained input of liberal-moderate articulators from the beginning to the very end of Canada's involvement in the problems of Southeast Asia. In both 1954 and 1973, but especially 1954 Canadian acceptance of a truce supervisory task was strongly motivated by a desire to reduce the threat to the nuclear peace. Continued prosecution of the Franco-American intervention in 1954 would have carried with it a very high probability of eventual resort to tactical nuclear warfare, and thus, in the liberal-moderate view, war with China and probably the Soviet Union. In 1973, failure to secure withdrawal of US troops from Vietnam on terms minimally acceptable to Nixon and Kissinger would certainly have risked unilateral resort to nuclear strikes which would probably have alienated Asian opinion from the West irrevocably and also have split the North Atlantic community badly on the morality of such methods. Periods of liberal-moderate ascendancy reflected the abiding Canadian concern for the establishment of a stable armistice in Vietnam and the easing of interventionary pressures in Washington, which repeatedly threatened to breach the nuclear peace. But it is also clear that the furthering of the Canadian objective of buttressing the nuclear peace was in constant tension with another systemic imperative of the Canadian policy process: preserving the fundamental harmony of Canadian-American relations.

The rise of conservative doctrinal axioms in Vietnam policy coincided with the periods of reduced threat to the nuclear peace. (See figure 9 for comments and figure 10 for a detailed schematic review of changes in US strategic doctrine.) Such periods of threat reduction permitted the incorporation of Canadian conservative objectives that had evolved naturally from systemically derived anti-communist policy tendencies in Ottawa. Conservative goal articulations became more and more frequent with the experience of the 14(d) affair, the perceptions of DRVN totalitarianism, and the growing departmental awareness of the DRVN's campaign of subversion in South Vietnam. Conservative objectives – emphasizing the commitment to containment so as to 'save' the southerners from the northerners – became an integral part of the operational consensus of the Canadian policy community between 1957 and 1965. But it is very instructive to note that such objectives could not be accommodated once the threat to the nuclear peace intensified as a result of pressures from the Pentagon and the extreme congressional right for a decisive US victory through resort to unlimited air war, and if need be tactical nuclear weaponry. American nuclear unilateralism was not at all acceptable to Pearson, Martin, or the Canadian policy community at large. The risk of uncontrolled escalation was too high. The ensuing strain in Canadian–American relations was seen by Canadian officials as the necessary price that had to be paid because of an unavoidable trade-off between promoting peace (ie, the nuclear peace) and promoting containment, given the unstable character of the American containment initiatives after 1967. It is certainly true that Pearson had made his April 1965 Temple speech as a 'political act,' that is, to indicate Canadian popular disquiet and unhappiness with US bombing. The tendency shift of February–March 1966 was, however, much more than a reflection of popular pressure on the government. It was the product of governmental perceptions of movement in US policy towards destabilizing and provocative methods in the campaign against Hanoi.

FIGURE 9
Phases of liberal-moderate ascendancy in Canadian Vietnam policy 1953–73

LM (with LL support)	LM-C fusion	C-LM fusion	LM	C-LM fusion	LM-C fusion
1953–mid-1955 avoiding SEATO and encouraging a French withdrawal from Indochina	1955–7 keeping the peace through holding the line	1957–65 sustaining the armistice through the promotion of an equilibrium of force	1966–68 pro-talks and bombing pauses – unilateral concessions by us	1969–72 'balanced criticism' and a desire to avoid supervisory duties	1973 acceptance of a supervisory role to facilitate American disengagement

LM – liberal-moderate
C – conservative
LL – left-liberal

Probable risk of American nuclear adventurism

1953–61: high
the era of the massive retaliation doctrine and proliferating counterforce tactical and strategic capabilities; a constant threat of 'asymmetrical' strategic response in the event of local breaches in the line of containment

1962–7: low
the Kennedy-Johnson era of graduated deterrence and 'flexible response' lowers the risk of escalation past the nuclear threshold

late 1967 to 1973: medium to high
steadily increasing resort to the twin tactics of air war and 'Vietnamization' (the military aspect of the Nixon doctrine); and increased willingness to threaten to use (and presumably to use) tactical nuclear weapons in Indochina and elsewhere; a repudiation of the high costs of a 'flexible response' approach

FIGURE 10
American strategic doctrine 1953–73

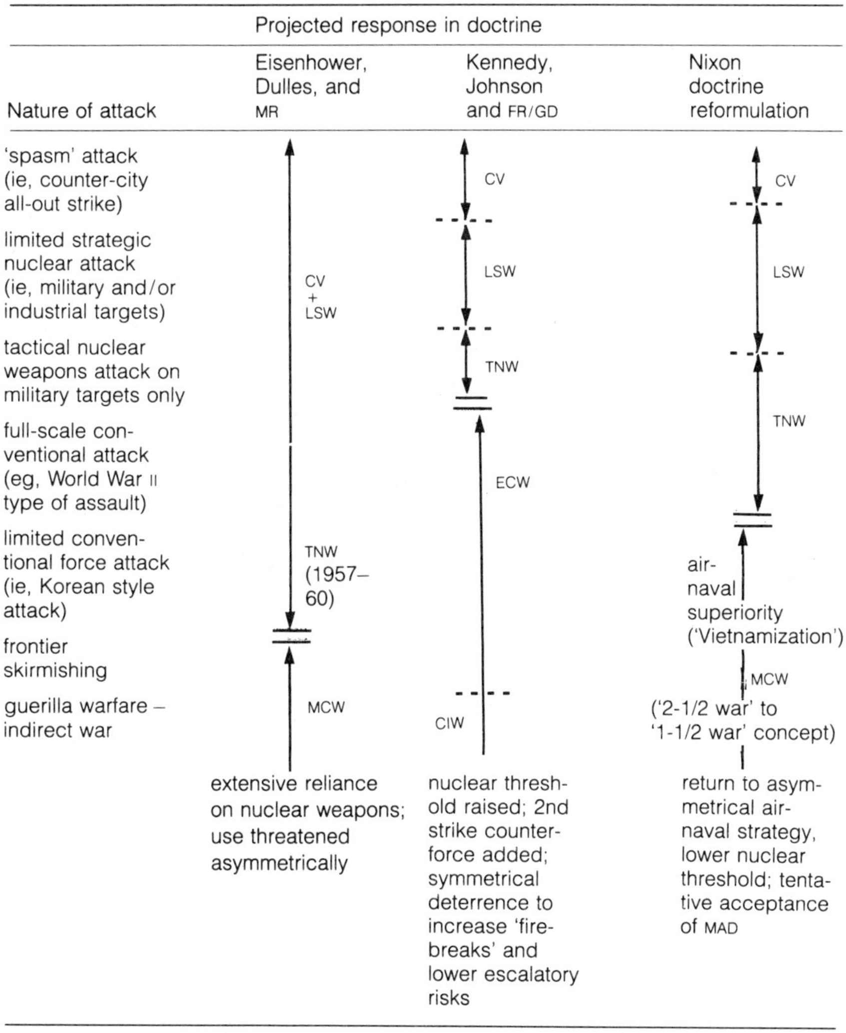

Nature of attack	Projected response in doctrine		
	Eisenhower, Dulles, and MR	Kennedy, Johnson and FR/GD	Nixon doctrine reformulation
'spasm' attack (ie, counter-city all-out strike)		CV	CV
limited strategic nuclear attack (ie, military and/or industrial targets)	CV + LSW	LSW	LSW
tactical nuclear weapons attack on military targets only		TNW	
full-scale conventional attack (eg, World War II type of assault)		ECW	TNW
limited conventional force attack (ie, Korean style attack)	TNW (1957–60)		air-naval superiority ('Vietnamization')
frontier skirmishing			
guerilla warfare – indirect war	MCW	CIW	MCW ('2-1/2 war' to '1-1/2 war' concept)
	extensive reliance on nuclear weapons; use threatened asymmetrically	nuclear threshold raised; 2nd strike counterforce added; symmetrical deterrence to increase 'firebreaks' and lower escalatory risks	return to asymmetrical airnaval strategy, lower nuclear threshold; tentative acceptance of MAD

The reassertion of a more conservatively tinged line occurred from 1969 to 1972 precisely because the risk of Sino-American confrontation had declined so dramatically with the Nixon-Kissinger opening to China and the realization among moderate American Republicans that China was a potential asset

LEGEND TO FIGURE 10

CV   — counter-value (ie, counter-city) strikes
=   — principal nuclear threshold
TNW   — tactical nuclear warfare (against battlefield formations)
LSW   — limited strategic nuclear warfare (counter-sanctuary assaults)
CIW   — counter-insurgency warfare
ECW   — extensive conventional warfare capability
MCW   — minimum conventional warfare capability
MR   — massive retaliation doctrine
FR/GD — flexible response/graduated deterrence doctrine
- - - — minor, or hypothetical, escalatory threshold
MAD   — mutual assured deterrence

in the global balance of power. This permitted a tentative retreat from Canadian interest in facilitating US disengagement and an increased emphasis on Canada's narrowly defined national interests. The particular manifestation of this conservatism was elaborately specified conditions upon future Canadian service with a new International Commission for Vietnam. But when the violence flared high in late 1972, especially during the Christmas bombing, the liberal-moderate line proved irresistible once more. Just as in 1954 the Ottawa policy community was confronted with a precariously won 'peace agreement.' And Canadian interest in American disengagement was even more compelling than Ottawa's interest in French disengagement in 1954. Under the neo-Dullesian tenets of the Nixon Doctrine, Vietnamization of the ground war and an unlimited commitment to the air war, the risk of crossing the nuclear threshold had climbed once more to an intolerable level. Conservative concerns, both for Canada's reputation as a responsible peacekeeper and for minimizing the direct costs of US involvement to Canada financially and administratively, led to an early Canadian departure from the ICCS. Nevertheless, the core liberal-moderate objectives were respected by the time-delimited supervisory role. America's retreat from Southeast Asia had been facilitated.

The most critical aspect of liberal-moderate tradition was its consistent desire to constrain US adventurism, and to contribute wherever possible to the limitation and de-escalation of violence in Vietnam and Indochina. A temporary peace was preferable to war. And, to use Norman Robertson's words from an earlier era, a Pax Americana was held to be better than no Pax at all.[3]

Canadian left-liberal systemist critics have indicted the Canadian foreign policy community for a record of alleged collaboration in American interventionary aims. The critics have misread the evidence and its implicit meaning, and in so doing have repeated the errors of other Cold War revisionists who have analysed Canadian responses to US policy.[4] Clearly there was some co-operation in, and sympathy for, US *containment* objectives in Indochina – but only so long as the American arms community did not seem likely to resort to a policy of nuclear unilateralism or anti-communist 'rollback.' There was, in fact, a partisan regard for South Vietnamese security interests, as expressed through the Canadian political and diplomatic initiatives in pursuing the Indo-Canadian entente in the ICSC between 1956 and 1962. But the left-liberal critics have here missed the fact that Canadian diplomacy, even in its most partisan phase, was unmistakably focused on buttressing a precarious armistice. The recommendations in 1961 to US officials to evade the ICSC's control procedures were made in an effort to shore up the crumbling armistice structure. Similarly, the transmission of threats to Hanoi in 1964–5 (however politely they were made) was also carried out in the hope that it would dissuade Hanoi from prosecuting the war against a determined superpower. Canadian policies were never 'neutral,' but the Canadian government was consistently disposed to impartial service if it could have been made practical. Circumstances decreed otherwise.

Finally, the Canadian policy community never subscribed to American strategic rationales for intervention. Beginning with Pearson, Canadians had consistently stressed the need to come to an accommodation with Chinese leaders and to respect their legitimate security needs and objectives. That attitude commenced during the Korean conflict and endured throughout the length of the Indochina violence. Ottawa gave most reluctant support to the SEATO concept and to the defence of 'free Vietnam' via US military assistance to Saigon, primarily because the Canadian officials rightly believed that the Americans were determined to follow through on their campaign of 'bastion-building' in Southeast Asia, and were beyond persuasion. It is not plausible to argue in light of Canadian refusals to make any meaningful material commitments to SEATO, or even to the South Vietnamese directly, that the Canadian policy community found the American domino logic particularly persuasive – despite the occasional echoes of this doctrine in Canadian policy debates. All three Canadian policy tendencies saw both French and American interventionary efforts as terrible misallocations of strategic assets in the global struggle for both peace and containment.

But having disagreed with US priorities and methods, Ottawa was not going to forsake its entrée to the corridors of power in Washington by publicly calling for unilateral US retreat from the Asian mainland. Credibility as a sympathetic ally of the United States had to be sustained. Maintenance of access to key US decision-makers was an independently important objective. In defence of Canadian policy it can accurately be said that Ottawa sought credibility in Washington, the better to dissuade American officials from resort to weapons of mass destruction. At each critical point when the policy consensus in Washington threatened to shift to decisive confrontations with China, Canadian policy advocated liberal-moderate restraint. The price for access to Washington decision-makers was substantial: a self-imposed prohibition on moral criticism of the US air war instrument as it was used. In the nuclear age such painful compromises are likely to become all too common. In every age 'bargaining with the devil' will take on new forms. And in every age, the results of such compromises will be ambiguous, and their lessons uncertain. In the case of Canadian diplomacy towards the Vietnam conflict, it may be said that Ottawa consistently helped to forestall 'the unthinkable.' Many left-liberal and conservative elements in the Canadian policy process have come to believe that the liberal-moderate diplomacy of constraint was an ineffectual strategy that carried intolerably high moral costs. They may be right. But the central fact remains that nuclear weapons were *not* used in the Indochina wars, although their use was a very real option for American leaders for almost two decades of interventionary planning.

The Canadian role in Indochina diplomacy and politics from 1954 to 1973 may have been particularly important in sustaining American nuclear self-restraint. In conjunction with Canada's European NATO allies, successive governments in Ottawa avoided the articulation of criticism which might only have driven the American arms community towards more radically unilateralist methods. There was always a risk that public repudiation by NATO of the US intervention would seriously degrade Washington's responsiveness toward 'world opinion' – one of the chief factors inhibiting resort to the tactical nuclear option. This is so because without doubt the most significant sector of world opinion for American decision-makers has always been the attitudes of the peoples of the North Atlantic community – and Japan. America allied is substantially less inclined to resort to provocative and unstable decisions than an America unconstrained by a decent respect for the opinions of mankind. The expression of fundamental differences in policy over Indochina might have called into question in American minds the value of the NATO alliance itself, and thereby encouraged the drift towards unconstrained and unpredictably escalatory methods of warfare in Vietnam. In stating this hypothetical and therefore unverifiable argument I am necessarily appealing to the speculatively plausible. But surely this is an admissible procedure. Concerning the most major questions of power and influence in the international system, the development of a capacity to speculate imaginatively, empathetically, and with balanced judgment – towards allies as well as adversaries – is an essential prerequisite for successful diplomacy in the nuclear age. And in the nuclear era, the cost of abandoning such skills and sensitivities to achieve the short-term maximization of national interests may not merely be 'high': it may be catastrophic. Awareness of this fact should guide Canadian foreign policy indefinitely.

THE CYBERNETIC CHARACTER OF CANADIAN POLICY

The oscillation in Canadian policy tendencies is strongly suggestive of an explanation that rejects 'analytic' or 'rational-actor' premises. Vietnam policy-making for Ottawa was not susceptible to any all-embracing rational scheme. Key policy variables were in a trade-off relationship (buttressing the nuclear peace versus the commitment to anti-communist containment). Large areas of policy were characterized by fundamental uncertainty (eg, the political and military stability of the Diem regime and its successors; the actual degree of influence in Washington wielded by America's air war-nuclear unilateralist zealots). The Canadian policy system, as a system, functioned cybernetically in that it 'tracked' several critical variables attentively – one of them, the state of the nuclear peace, very closely – and attempted to keep each within a tolerable range of values. Of the variables so tracked, the state of the nuclear peace was far and away the most important. Even when viewed cybernetically, Canadian policy-makers can be said to have worked diligently 'in the interests of peace.' The tendency shift of 1956 clearly helped improve the state of Canadian-American relations and satisfy the anti-communist containment imperative in Canadian policy. But this partial shift was exceptional and was permitted only by the fact that a temporary balance of force obtained in Vietnam in the late 1950s and was then followed by a temporary moderation in US strategic doctrine. This partial shift towards conservative objectives merely highlighted the essential dominance of the liberal-moderate tendency. The shift back to unconstrained liberal moderation in 1966 was effected again in an effort to shore up a deteriorating condition that threatened the nuclear peace of Asia and the world. From 1969 onward, emerging Sino-American détente permitted an easing of the commitment to liberal-moderate axioms. Clearly there was no attempt to impose an optimizing rational method to the flux of events and the changing character of environmental threats. Perceptive and constructive adaptation – but adaptation none the less – was the central characteristic of Canadian policy.

APPENDIX

The Geneva Cease-fire Agreement for Vietnam, and the Final Declaration of the Geneva Conference on Indochina

Agreement on the cessation of hostilities in Vietnam, signed at Geneva, July 20, 1954[1]

Chapter 1
Provisional Military Demarcation Line and Demilitarised Zone

ARTICLE I
A PROVISIONAL military demarcation line shall be fixed, on either side of which the forces of the two parties shall be regrouped after their withdrawal, the forces of the People's Army of Vietnam to the north of the line and the forces of the French Union to the south.

The provisional military demarcation line is fixed as shown on the map attached (see Map No. 1).[2]

It is also agreed that a demilitarised zone shall be established on either side of the demarcation line, to a width of not more than 5 kms from it, to act as a buffer zone and avoid any incidents which might result in the resumption of hostilities.

ARTICLE 2
The period within which the movement of all forces of either party into its regrouping zone on either side of the provisional military demarcation line shall be completed shall not exceed three hundred (300) days from the date of the present Agreement's entry into force.

---

1 *Further Documents Relating to the Discussion of Indochina at the Geneva Conference* (Misc. no. 20) [1954], cmnd 9239); (London: Her Majesty's Stationery Office 1954) 27
2 Not reproduced

ARTICLE 3

When the provisional military line coincides with a waterway, the waters of such waterway shall be open to civil navigation by both parties wherever one bank is controlled by one party and the other bank by the other party. The Joint Commission shall establish rules of navigation for the stretch of waterway in question. The merchant shipping and other civilian craft of each party shall have unrestricted access to the land under its military control.

ARTICLE 4

The provisional military demarcation line between the two final regrouping zones is extended into the territorial waters by a line perpendicular to the general line of the coast.

All coastal islands north of this boundary shall be evacuated by the armed forces of the French Union, and all islands south of it shall be evacuated by the forces of the People's Army of Viet Nam.

ARTICLE 5

To avoid any incidents which might result in the resumption of hostilities, all military forces, supplies and equipment shall be withdrawn from the demilitarised zone within twenty-five (25) days of the present Agreement's entry into force.

ARTICLE 6

No person, military or civilian, shall be permitted to cross the provisional military demarcation line unless specifically authorised to do so by the Joint Commission.

ARTICLE 7

No person, military or civilian, shall be permitted to enter the demilitarised zone except persons concerned with the conduct of civil administration and relief and persons specifically authorised to enter by the Joint Commission.

ARTICLE 8

Civil administration and relief in the demilitarised zone on either side of the provisional military demarcation line shall be the responsibility of the Commanders-in-Chief of the two parties in their respective zones. The number of persons, military or civilian, from each side who are permitted to enter the demilitarised zone for the conduct of civil administration and relief shall be determined by the respective Commanders, but in no case shall the total number authorised by either side exceed at any one time a figure to be determined by the Trung Gia Military Commission or by the Joint Commission. The number of civil police and the arms to be carried by them shall be determined by the Joint Commission. No one else shall carry arms unless specifically authorised to do so by the Joint Commission.

ARTICLE 9

Nothing contained in this chapter shall be construed as limiting the complete freedom of movement, into, out of or within the demilitarised zone, of the Joint Commission, its joint groups, the International Commission to be set up as indicated below, its inspection teams and any other persons, supplies or equipment specifically authorised to enter the demilitarised zone by the Joint Commission. Freedom of movement shall be permitted across the territory under the military control of either side over any road or waterway which has to be taken between points within the demilitarised zone when such points are not connected by roads or waterways lying completely within the demilitarised zone.

Chapter 2

Principles and procedures governing implementation of the present Agreement

ARTICLE 10

The Commanders of the Forces on each side, on the one side the Commander-in-Chief of the French Union forces in Indo-China and on the other side the Commander-in-Chief of the People's Army of Viet Nam, shall order and enforce the complete cessation of all hostilities in Viet Nam by all armed forces under their control, including all units and personnel of the ground, naval and air forces.

ARTICLE 11

In accordance with the principle of a simultaneous cease-fire throughout Indo-China, the cessation of hostilities shall be simultaneous throughout all parts of Viet Nam, in all areas of hostilities and for all the forces of the two parties.

Taking into account the time effectively required to transmit the cease-fire order down to the lowest echelons of the combatant forces on both sides, the two parties are agreed that the cease-fire shall take effect completely and simultaneously for the different sectors of the country as follows:

Northern Viet Nam at 8:00 a.m. (local time) on 27th July, 1954.

Central Viet Nam at 8:00 a.m. (local time) on 1st August, 1954.

Southern Viet Nam at 8:00 a.m. (local time) on 11th August, 1954.

It is agreed that Peking mean time shall be taken as local time.

From such time as the cease-fire becomes effective in Northern Viet Nam, both parties undertake not to engage in any large-scale offensive action in any part of the Indo-Chinese theatre of operations and not to commit the air forces based on Northern Viet Nam outside that sector. The two parties also undertake to inform each other of their plans for movement from one regrouping zone to another within twenty-five (25) days of the present Agreement's entry into force.

ARTICLE 12

All the operations and movements entailed in the cessation of hostilities and regrouping must proceed in a safe and orderly fashion:

(a) Within a certain number of days after the cease-fire Agreement shall have become effective, the number to be determined on the spot by the Trung Gia Military Commission, each party shall be responsible for removing and neutralising mines (including river and sea mines), booby traps, explosives and any other dangerous substances placed by it. In the event of its being impossible to complete the work of removal and neutralisation in time, the party concerned shall mark the spot by placing visible signs there. All demolitions, mine fields, wire entanglements and other hazards to the free movement of the personnel of the Joint Commission and its joint groups, known to be present after the withdrawal of the military forces, shall be reported to the Joint Commission by the Commanders of the opposing forces;

(b) From the time of the cease-fire until regrouping is completed on either side of the demarcation line:

(1) The forces of either party shall be provisionally withdrawn from the provisional assembly areas assigned to the other party.

(2) When one party's forces withdraw by a route (road, rail, waterway, sea route) which passes through the territory of the other party (see Article 24), the latter party's forces must provisionally withdraw three kilometres on each side of such route, but in such a manner as to avoid interfering with the movements of the civil population.

ARTICLE 13

From the time of the cease-fire until the completion of the movements from one regrouping zone into the other, civil and military transport aircraft shall follow air corridors between the provisional assembly areas assigned to the French Union forces north of the demarcation line on the one hand and the Laotian frontier and the regrouping zone assigned to the French Union forces on the other hand.

The position of the air corridors, their width, the safety route for single-engined military aircraft transferred to the south and the search and rescue procedure for aircraft in distress shall be determined on the spot by the Trung Gia Military Commission.

ARTICLE 14

Political and administrative measures in the two regrouping zones, on either side of the provisional military demarcation line:

(a) Pending the general elections which will bring about the unification of Viet Nam, the conduct of civil administration in each regrouping zone shall be in the hands of the party whose forces are to be regrouped there in virtue of the present Agreement.

(b) Any territory controlled by one party which is transferred to the other party by the regrouping plan shall continue to be administered by the former party until such date as all the troops who are to be transferred have completely left that territory so as to free the zone assigned to the party in question. From then on, such territory shall be regarded as transferred to the other party, who shall assume responsibility for it.

Steps shall be taken to ensure that there is no break in the transfer of responsibilities. For this purpose, adequate notice shall be given by the withdrawing party to the other party, which shall make the necessary arrangements, in particular by sending administrative and police detachments to prepare for the assumption of administrative responsibility. The length of such notice shall be determined by the Trung Gia Military Commission. The transfer shall be effected in successive stages for the various territorial sectors.

The transfer of the civil administration of Hanoi and Haiphong to the authorities of the Democratic Republic of Viet Nam shall be completed within the respective time-limits laid down in Article 15 for military movements.

(c) Each party undertakes to refrain from any reprisals or discrimination against persons or organizations on account of their activities during the hostilities and to guarantee their democratic liberties.

(d) From the date of entry into force of the present Agreement until the movement of troops is completed, any civilians residing in a district controlled by one party who wish to go and live in the zone assigned to the other party shall be permitted and helped to do so by the authorities in that district.

ARTICLE 15

The disengagement of the combatants, and the withdrawals and transfers of military forces, equipment and supplies shall take place in accordance with the following principles:

(a) The withdrawals and transfers of the military forces, equipment and supplies of the two parties shall be completed within three hundred (300) days, as laid down in Article 2 of the present Agreement;

(b) Within either territory successive withdrawals shall be made by sectors, portions of sectors or provinces. Transfers from one regrouping zone to another shall be made in successive monthly instalments proportionate to the number of troops to be transferred;

(c) The two parties shall undertake to carry out all troop withdrawals and transfers in accordance with the aims of the Agreement, shall permit no hostile act and shall take no step whatsoever which might hamper such withdrawals and transfers. They shall assist one another as far as this is possible;

(d) The two parties shall permit no destruction or sabotage of any public property and no injury to the life and property of the civil population. They shall permit no interference in local civil administration.

(e) The Joint Commission and the International Commission shall ensure that steps are taken to safeguard the forces in the course of withdrawal and transfer;

(f) The Trung Gia Military Commission, and later the Joint Commission, shall determine by common agreement the exact procedure for the disengagement of the combatants and for troop withdrawals and transfers, on the basis of the principles mentioned above and within the framework laid down below:

1. The disengagement of the combatants, including the concentration of the armed forces of all kinds and also each party's movements into the provisional assembly areas assigned to it and the other party's provisional withdrawal from it, shall be completed within a period not exceeding fifteen (15) days after the date when the cease-fire becomes effective.

The general delineation of the provisional assembly areas is set out in the maps[3] annexed to the present Agreement.

In order to avoid any incidents, no troops shall be stationed less than 1,500 metres from the lines delimiting the provisional assembly areas.

During the period until the transfers are concluded, all the coastal islands west of the following lines shall be included in the Haiphong perimeter:

meridian of the southern point of Kebao Island,

northern coast of Ile Rousse (excluding the island), extended as far as the meridian of Campha-Mines,

meridian of Campha-Mines.

2. The withdrawals and transfers shall be effected in the following order and within the following periods (from the date of the entry into force of the present Agreement):

Forces of the French Union

Hanoi perimeter	80 days
Haiduong perimeter	100 days
Haiphong perimeter	300 days

Forces of the People's Army of Viet Nam

Ham Tan and Xuyenmoc provisional assembly area	80 days
Central Viet Nam provisional assembly area – first instalment	80 days
Plaine des Joncs provisional assembly area	100 days
Central Viet Nam provisional assembly area – second instalment	100 days
Pointe Camau provisional assembly area	200 days
Central Viet Nam provisional assembly area – last instalment	300 days

3 Not reproduced

Chapter 3
Ban on the introduction of fresh troops, military personnel, arms and munitions.
Military bases

ARTICLE 16
With effect from the date of entry into force of the present Agreement, the introduction into Viet Nam of any troop reinforcements and additional military personnel is prohibited.

It is understood, however, that the rotation of units and groups of personnel, the arrival in Viet Nam of individual personnel on a temporary duty basis and the return to Viet Nam of the individual personnel after short periods of leave or temporary duty outside Viet Nam shall be permitted under the conditions laid down below.

(a) Rotation of units defined in paragraph (c) of this article and groups of personnel shall not be permitted for French Union troops stationed north of the provisional military demarcation line laid down in Article 1 of the present Agreement during the withdrawal period provided for in Article 2.

However, under the heading of individual personnel not more than fifty (50) men, including officers, shall during any one month be permitted to enter that part of the country north of the provisional military demarcation line on a temporary duty basis or to return there after short periods of leave or temporary duty outside Viet Nam.

(b) 'Rotation' is defined as the replacement of units or groups of personnel by other units of the same echelon or by personnel who are arriving in Viet Nam territory to do their overseas service there;

(c) The units rotated shall never be larger than a battalion – or the corresponding echelon for air and naval forces;

(d) Rotation shall be conducted on a man-for-man basis, provided, however, that in any one quarter neither party shall introduce more than fifteen thousand five hundred (15,500) members of its armed forces into Viet Nam under the rotation policy.

(e) Rotation units (defined in paragraph (c) of this article) and groups of personnel, and the individual personnel mentioned in this article, shall enter and leave Viet Nam only through the entry points enumerated in Article 20 below;

(f) Each party shall notify the Joint Commission and the International Commission at least two days in advance of any arrivals or departures of units, groups of personnel and individual personnel in or from Viet Nam. Reports on the arrivals or departures of units, groups of personnel and individual personnel in or from Viet Nam shall be submitted daily to the Joint Commission and the International Commission.

All the above-mentioned notifications and reports shall indicate the places and dates of arrival or departure and the number of persons arriving or departing;

(g) The International Commission through its Inspection Teams, shall supervise and inspect the rotation of units and groups of personnel and the arrival and departure of individual personnel as authorized above, at the points of entry enumerated in Article 20 below.

ARTICLE 17

(a) With effect from the date of entry into force of the present Agreement, the introduction into Viet Nam of any reinforcements in the form of all types of arms, munitions and other war material, such as combat aircraft, naval craft, pieces of ordnance, jet engines and jet weapons and armoured vehicles, is prohibited.

(b) It is understood, however, that war material, arms and munitions which have been destroyed, damaged, worn out or used up after the cessation of hostilities may be replaced on the basis of piece-for-piece of the same type and with similar characteristics. Such replacements of war material, arms and ammunitions shall not be permitted for French Union troops stationed north of the provisional military demarcation line laid down in Article 1 of the present Agreement, during the withdrawal period provided for in Article 2.

Naval craft may perform transport operations between the regrouping zones.

(c) The war material, arms and munitions for replacement purposes provided for in paragraph (b) of this article, shall be introduced into Viet Nam only through the points of entry enumerated in Article 20 below.

(d) Apart from the replacements permitted within the limits laid down in paragraph (b) of this article, the introduction of war material, arms and munitions of all types in the form of unassembled parts for subsequent assembly is prohibited.

(e) Each party shall notify the Joint Commission and the International Commission at least two days in advance of any arrivals or departures which may take place of war material, arms and munitions of all types.

In order to justify the requests for the introduction into Viet Nam of arms, munitions and other war material (as defined in paragraph (a) of this article) for replacement purposes, a report concerning each incoming shipment shall be submitted to the Joint Commission and the International Commission. Such reports shall indicate the use made of the items so replaced.

(f) The International Commission, through its Inspection Teams, shall supervise and inspect the replacements permitted in the circumstances laid down in this article, at the points of entry enumerated in Article 20 below.

ARTICLE 18

With effect from the date of entry into force of the present Agreement, the establishment of new military bases is prohibited throughout Viet Nam territory.

ARTICLE 19

With effect from the date of entry into force of the present Agreement, no military base under the control of a foreign state may be established in the regrouping zone of either party; the two parties shall ensure that the zones assigned to them do not adhere to any military alliance and are not used for the resumption of hostilities or to further an aggressive policy.

ARTICLE 20

The points of entry into Viet Nam for rotation personnel and replacements of material are fixed as follows:

Zones to the north of the provisional demarcation line: Laokay, Langson, Tien-Yen, Haiphong, Vinh, Dong-Hoi, Muong-Sen;

Zone to the south of the provisional military demarcation line: Tourane, Quinhon, Nhatrang, Bangoi, Saigon, Cap St Jacques, Tanchau.

Chapter 4

Prisoners of War and Civilian Internees

ARTICLE 21

The liberation and repatriation of all prisoners of war and civilian internees detained by each of the two parties at the coming into force of the present Agreement shall be carried out under the following conditions:

(a) All prisoners of war and civilian internees of Viet Nam, French and other nationalities captured since the beginning of hostilities in Viet Nam during military operations or in any other circumstances of war and in any part of the territory of Viet Nam shall be liberated within a period of thirty (30) days after the date when the cease-fire becomes effective in each theatre.

(b) The term 'civilian internees' is understood to mean all persons who, having in any way contributed to the political and armed struggle between the two parties, have been arrested for that reason and have been kept in detention by either party during the period of hostilities.

(c) All prisoners of war and civilian internees held by either party shall be surrendered to the appropriate authorities of the other party, who shall give them all possible assistance in proceeding to their country of origin, place of habitual residence or the zone of their choice.

Chapter 5
Miscellaneous

ARTICLE 22
The Commanders of the Forces of the two parties shall ensure that persons under their respective commands who violate any of the provisions of the present Agreement are suitably punished.

ARTICLE 23
In cases in which the place of burial is known and the existence of graves has been established, the Commander of the Forces of either party shall, within a specified period after the entry into force of the Armistice Agreement, permit the graves service personnel of the other party to enter the part of Viet Nam territory under their military control for the purpose of finding and removing the bodies of deceased military personnel of that party, including the bodies of deceased prisoners of war. The Joint Commission shall determine the procedures and the time limit for the performance of this task. The Commanders of the Forces of the two parties shall communicate to each other all information in their possession as to the place of burial of military personnel of the other party.

ARTICLE 24
The present Agreement shall apply to all the armed forces of either party. The armed forces of each party shall respect the demilitarized zone and the territory under the military control of the other party, and shall commit no act and undertake no operation against the other party and shall not engage in blockade of any kind in Viet Nam.

For the purposes of the present article, the word 'territory' includes territorial waters and air space.

ARTICLE 25
The Commanders of the Forces of the two parties shall afford full protection and all possible assistance and co-operation to the Joint Commission and its joint groups and to the International Commission and its Inspection Teams in the performance of the functions and tasks assigned to them by the present Agreement.

ARTICLE 26
The costs involved in the operation of the Joint Commission and joint groups and of

the International Commission and its Inspection Teams shall be shared equally between the two parties.

ARTICLE 27
The signatories of the present Agreement and their successors in their functions shall be responsible for ensuring the observance and enforcement of the terms and provisions thereof. The Commanders of the Forces of the two parties shall, within their respective commands, take all steps and make all arrangements necessary to ensure full compliance with all the provisions of the present Agreement by all elements and military personnel under their command.

The procedures laid down in the present Agreement shall, whenever necessary, be studied by the Commanders of the two parties and, if necessary, defined more specifically by the Joint Commission.

Chapter 6
Joint Commission and International Commission for Supervision and Control in Viet Nam

ARTICLE 28
Responsibility for the execution of the Agreement on the cessation of hostilities shall rest with the parties.

ARTICLE 29
An International Commission shall ensure the control and supervision of this execution.

ARTICLE 30
In order to facilitate, under the conditions shown below, the execution of provisions concerning joint actions by the two parties, a Joint Commission shall be set up in Viet Nam.

ARTICLE 31
The Joint Commission shall be composed of an equal number of representatives of the Commanders of the two parties.

ARTICLE 32
The Presidents of the delegations to the Joint Commission shall hold the rank of General.

The Joint Commission shall set up joint groups, the number of which shall be determined by mutual agreement between the parties. The joint groups shall be composed of an equal number of officers from both parties. Their location on the demarcation line between the regrouping zones shall be determined by the parties whilst taking into account the powers of the Joint Commission.

ARTICLE 33
The Joint Commission shall ensure the execution of the following provisions of the Agreement on the cessation of hostilities:

(a) A simultaneous and general cease-fire in Viet Nam for all regular and irregular armed forces of the two parties.

(b) A regroupment of the armed forces of the two parties.

(c) Observance of the demarcation lines between the regrouping zones and of demilitarised sectors.

Within the limits of its competence it shall help the parties to execute the said provisions, shall ensure liaison between them for the purpose of preparing and carrying out plans for the application of these provisions, and shall endeavour to solve such disputed questions as may arise between the parties in the course of executing these provisions.

ARTICLE 34
An International Commission shall be set up for the control and supervision over the application of the provisions of the agreement on the cessation of hostilities in Viet Nam. It shall be composed of representatives of the following states: Canada, India, and Poland.

It shall be presided over by the Representative of India.

ARTICLE 35
The International Commission shall set up fixed and mobile inspection teams, composed of an equal number of officers appointed by each of the above-mentioned states. The fixed teams shall be located at the following points: Laokay, Langson, Tien-Yen, Haiphong, Vinh, Dong-Hoi, Muong-Sen, Tourane, Quinhon, Nhatrang, Bangoi, Saigon, Cap St Jacques, Tanchau. These points of location may, at a later date, be altered at the request of the Joint Commission, or of one of the parties, or of the International Commission itself, by agreement between the International Commission and the command of the party concerned. The zones of action of the mobile teams shall be the regions bordering the land and sea frontiers of Viet Nam, the demarcation lines between the regrouping zones and the demilitarised zones. Within the limits of these zones they shall have the right to move freely and shall receive from the local civil and military authorities all facilities they may require for the fulfilment of their tasks (provision of personnel, placing at their disposal documents

needed for supervision, summoning witnesses necessary for holding enquiries, ensuring the security and freedom of movement of the inspection teams, &c. ...). They shall have at their disposal such modern means of transport, observation and communication as they may require. Beyond the zones of action as defined above, the mobile teams may, by agreement with the command of the party concerned, carry out other movements within the limits of the tasks given them by the present Agreement.

ARTICLE 36

The International Commission shall be responsible for supervising the proper execution by the parties of the provisions of the Agreement. For this purpose it shall fulfil the tasks of control, observation, inspection and investigation connected with the application of the provisions of the Agreement on the cessation of hostilities, and it shall in particular:

(a) Control the movement of the armed forces of the two parties, effected within the framework of the regroupment plan.

(b) Supervise the demarcation lines between the regrouping areas, and also the demilitarised zones.

(c) Control the operations of releasing prisoners of war and civilian internees.

(d) Supervise at ports and airfields as well as along all frontiers of Viet Nam the execution of the provisions of the agreement on the cessation of hostilities, regulating the introduction into the country of armed forces, military personnel and of all kinds of arms, munitions and war material.

ARTICLE 37

The International Commission shall, through the medium of the inspection teams mentioned above, and as soon as possible either on its own initiative, or at the request of the Joint Commission, or one of the parties, undertake the necessary investigations both documentary and on the ground.

ARTICLE 38

The inspection teams shall submit to the International Commission the results of their supervision, their investigations and their observations; furthermore they shall draw up such special reports as they may consider necessary or as may be requested from them by the Commission. In the case of a disagreement within the teams, the conclusions of each member shall be submitted to the Commission.

ARTICLE 39

If any one inspection team is unable to settle an incident or considers that there is a violation or a threat of a serious violation, the International Commission shall be informed; the latter shall study the reports and the conclusions of the inspection teams and shall inform the parties of the measures which should be taken for the settlement of the incident, ending of the violation or removal of the threat of violation.

ARTICLE 40

When the Joint Commission is unable to reach an agreement on the interpretation to be given to some provision or on the appraisal of a fact, the International Commission shall be informed of the disputed question. Its recommendations shall be sent directly to the parties and shall be notified to the Joint Commission.

ARTICLE 41

The recommendations of the International Commission shall be adopted by majority vote, subject to the provisions contained in Article 42. If the votes are divided, the chairman's vote shall be decisive.

The International Commission may formulate recommendations concerning amendments and additions which should be made to the provisions of the Agreement on the cessation of hostilities in Viet Nam, in order to ensure a more effective execution of that Agreement. These recommendations shall be adopted unanimously.

ARTICLE 42

When dealing with questions concerning violations, or threats of violations, which might lead to a resumption of hostilities, namely:

(a) Refusal by the armed forces of one party to effect the movements provided for in the regroupment plan;

(b) Violation by the armed forces of one of the parties of the regrouping zones, territorial waters, or air space of the other party; the decisions of the International Commission must be unanimous.

ARTICLE 43

If one of the parties refuses to put into effect a recommendation of the International Commission, the parties concerned or the Commission itself shall inform the members of the Geneva Conference.

If the International Commission does not reach unanimity in the cases provided for in Article 42, it shall submit a majority report and one or more minority reports to the members of the Conference.

The International Commission shall inform the members of the Conference in all cases where its activity is being hindered.

ARTICLE 44

The International Commission shall be set up at the time of the cessation of hostilities in Indo-China in order that it should be able to fulfil the tasks provided for in Article 36.

ARTICLE 45

The International Commission for Supervision and Control in Viet Nam shall act in close co-operation with the International Commissions for Supervision and Control in Cambodia and Laos.

The Secretaries-General of these three Commissions shall be responsible for co-ordinating their work and for relations between them.

ARTICLE 46

The International Commission for Supervision and Control in Viet Nam may, after consultation with the International Commissions for Supervision and Control in Cambodia and Laos having regard to the development of the situation in Cambodia and Laos, progressively reduce its activities. Such a decision must be adopted unanimously.

ARTICLE 47

All the provisions of the present Agreement, save the second sub-paragraph of Article 11, shall enter into force at 2400 hours (Geneva time) on 22nd July, 1954.

Done in Geneva at 2400 on the 20th of July, 1954, in French and Vietnamese, both texts being equally authentic.

For the Commander-in-Chief of the People's Army of Viet Nam:

TA-QUANG-BUU,
Vice-Minister of National Defence of the Democratic Republic of Viet Nam

For the Commander-in-Chief of the French Union Forces in Indochina:

DELTIEL,[4]
Brigadier-General

Final Declaration of the Geneva Conference on the Problem of Restoring Peace in Indo-China[5]

Geneva, July 21, 1954

1 The Conference takes note of the Agreements ending hostilities in Cambodia, Laos and Viet Nam and organising international control and the supervision of the execution of the provisions of these Agreements.

4 Spelling as in original. The annexes to the agreement are not reproduced.
5 Great Britain, Miscellaneous No. 20 (1954) (cmnd 9239) 9; *British and Foreign State Papers* 359 (1954)

2 The Conference expresses satisfaction at the ending of hostilities in Cambodia, Laos and Viet Nam; the Conference expresses its conviction that the execution of the provisions set out in the present declaration and in the Agreements on the cessation of hostilities will permit Cambodia, Laos and Viet Nam henceforth to play their part, in full independence and sovereignty, in the peaceful community of nations.

3 The Conference takes note of the declarations made by the Governments of Cambodia and of Laos of their intention to adopt measures permitting all citizens to take their place in the national community, in particular by participating in the next general elections, which, in conformity with the constitution of each of these countries, shall take place in the course of the year 1955, by secret ballot and in conditions of respect for fundamental freedoms.

4 The Conference takes note of the clauses in the Agreement on the cessation of hostilities in Viet Nam prohibiting the introduction into Viet Nam of foreign troops and military personnel as well as of all kinds of arms and munitions. The Conference also takes note of the declarations made by the Governments of Cambodia and Laos of their resolution not to request foreign aid, whether in war material, in personnel or in instructors except for the purpose of the effective defence of their territory and, in the case of Laos, to the extent defined by the agreements on the cessation of hostilities in Laos.

5 The Conference takes note of the clauses in the Agreement on the cessation of hostilities in Viet Nam to the effect that no military base under the control of a foreign state may be established in the regrouping zones of the two parties, the latter having the obligation to see that the zones allotted to them shall not constitute part of any military alliance and shall not be utilised for the resumption of hostilities or in the service of an aggressive policy. The Conference also takes note of the declarations of the Governments of Cambodia and Laos to the effect that they will not join in any agreement with other states if this agreement includes the obligation to participate in a military alliance not in conformity with the principles of the Charter of the United Nations or, in the case of Laos, with the principles of the Agreement on the cessation of hostilities in Laos or, so long as their security is not threatened, the obligation to establish bases on Cambodian or Laotian territory for the military forces of foreign Powers.

6 The Conference recognises that the essential purpose of the Agreement relating to Viet Nam is to settle military questions with a view to ending hostilities and that the military demarcation line is provisional and should not in any way be interpreted as constituting a political or territorial boundary. The Conference expresses its conviction that the execution of the provisions set out in the present declaration and in the Agreement on the cessation of hostilities creates the necessary basis for the achievement in the near future of a political settlement in Viet Nam.

7 The Conference declares that, so far as Viet Nam is concerned, the settlement of political problems, effected on the basis of respect for the principles of independence,

unity and territorial integrity, shall permit the Vietnamese people to enjoy the fundamental freedoms, guaranteed by democratic institutions established as a result of free
general elections by secret ballot. In order to ensure that sufficient progress in the
restoration of peace has been made, and that all the necessary conditions obtain for
free expression of the national will, general elections shall be held in July 1956, under
the supervision of an international commission composed of representatives of the
member states of the International Supervisory Commission, referred to in the
Agreement on the cessation of hostilities. Consultations will be held on this subject
between the competent representative authorities of the two zones from 20th July,
1955, onwards.

8 The provisions of the Agreement on the cessation of hostilities intended to ensure
the protection of individuals and of property must be most strictly applied and must,
in particular, allow everyone in Viet Nam to decide freely in which zone he wishes to
live.

9 The competent representative authorities of the Northern and Southern zones of
Viet Nam, as well as the authorities of Laos and Cambodia, must not permit any
individual or collective reprisals against persons who have collaborated in any way
with one of the parties during the war, or against members of such persons' families.

10 The Conference takes note of the declaration of the Government of the French
Republic to the effect that it is ready to withdraw its troops from the territory of
Cambodia, Laos and Viet Nam, at the request of the governments concerned and
within periods which shall be fixed by agreement between the parties except in the
cases where, by agreement between the two parties, a certain number of French
troops shall remain at specified points and for a specified time.

11 The Conference takes note of the declaration of the French Government to the
effect that for the settlement of all the problems connected with the re-establishment
and consolidation of peace in Cambodia, Laos and Viet Nam, the French Government will proceed from the principle of respect for the independence and sovereignty, unity and territorial integrity of Cambodia, Laos and Viet Nam.

12 In their relations with Cambodia, Laos and Viet Nam, each member of the Geneva Conference undertakes to respect the sovereignty, the independence, the unity
and the territorial integrity of the above-mentioned states, and to refrain from any
interference in their internal affairs.

13 The members of the Conference agree to consult one another on any question
which may be referred to them by the International Supervisory Commission, in
order to study such measures as may prove necessary to ensure that the Agreements
on the cessation of hostilities in Cambodia, Laos and Viet Nam are respected.

Notes

CHAPTER 1: CANADA IN VIETNAM: A THREE-DIMENSIONAL
APPROACH TOWARDS POLICY EXPLANATION

1 See James Eayrs, *In Defence of Canada*, v, *Indochina: The Roots of Complicity* (Toronto: University of Toronto Press 1983) and Charles Taylor, *Snow Job: Canada, the United States and Vietnam (1954 to 1973)* (Toronto: Anansi 1974) for the two major works written in this vein. Cited hereafter as Eayrs, *Indochina* and Taylor, *Snow Job*.

2 *The Logic of World Power* (New York: Random House/Pantheon 1974)

3 Leslie Gelb with Richard K. Betts, *The Irony of Vietnam: The System Worked* (Washington: Brookings 1979); see also Daniel Ellsberg, *Papers on the War*. (New York: Simon and Schuster 1972).

4 Both Eayrs's *Indochina* and Taylor's *Snow Job* suffer in this respect, as do Ramesh Thakur's two articles 'Peacekeeping and Foreign Policy: Canada, India and the International Commission in Vietnam, 1954–1965,' *British Journal of International Studies* VI (1980) 125–53; and 'India's Vietnam Policy, 1946–1979,' *Asian Survey* XIX (1979) 957–76. Thakur's normative assessments are considerably more dispassionate and balanced than those provided by Eayrs or Taylor.

5 See Daniel Ellsberg, 'Introduction: Call to Mutiny,' in E.P. Thompson and Dan Smith, eds, *Protest and Survive* (New York: Monthly Review Press 1981); cited hereafter as Ellsberg, 'Mutiny.'

6 *Ibid.* v–vi, xx–xxvi

7 *Ibid.* v, xxiii–xxiv. Dulles is on record denying such offers. See *Foreign Relations* of the United States, 1952–4, XII, Part 2 (Washington 1982), 1928. On US Army planning see Drew Middleton, 'Dien Bien Phu: A Footnote to Its Fall,' *New York Times*, 14 Feb. 1984.

8 Arnold Smith to author

9 See 'Memorandum Involving Conversation among Rusk, McNamara et al.,' in Gareth Porter, ed., *Vietnam: The Definitive Documentation of Human Decisions* (Stanfordville, NY: E.M. Coleman Enterprises 1979) II, 96–9.

10 Ellsberg, 'Mutiny,' vi, xxiv–xxv

11 *Ibid.* vi, xxv–xxvi. For details on the most egregious instance of nuclear adventurism by Nixon and Kissinger, pursuant to the so-called 'madman theory' of coercive diplomacy, see Seymour M. Hersh, *The Price of Power: Kissinger in the Nixon White House* (New York: Simon and Schuster 1983) 124–5.

12 *Ibid.* vii–viii. For a brilliant and incisive review of American strategic thinking and nuclear policy from a conservative point of view, see John Lewis Gaddis, *Strategies of Containment: A Critical Appraisal of Postwar American National Security Policy* (New York, Oxford: Oxford University Press 1982). Inter alia, Gaddis notes (p 149) that Eisenhower 'considered the idea of preventive war [ie, nuclear surprise attack] in the autumn of 1953. One year later he had discarded the idea, although others in his administration had not.

13 Ramesh Thakur, 'Change and Continuity in Canadian Foreign Policy,' *India Quarterly* XXXIII 4 (Oct.–Dec. 1977) 413

14 'Canada's Relations with Asia,' in Department of External Affairs, *Statements and Speeches*, no. 52/33, 5 Sept. 1952

15 See Peter C. Newman, *Renegade in Power: The Diefenbaker Years* (Toronto: McClelland and Stewart, Carleton Library 1973) 252.

16 Thakur, 'Change and Continuity' 404

17 The bulk of the primary research for this book was conducted in the course of preparation of my doctoral thesis, 'In the Interests of Peace: Perception and Response in the History of Canadian Foreign Policy Decision-Making Concerning the International Commission for Supervision and Control for Vietnam, 1954–65' (PHD thesis, University of Toronto, 1979). Some 40,000 pages of documents were examined: principally the verbatim minutes of the ICSC for Vietnam and the main decision file for Vietnam policy for the Department of External Affairs from July 1954 through Sept. 1959.

18 John Holmes, 'Canada and the Vietnam War,' in *War and Society in North America*, J.L. Granatstein and R.D. Cuff, eds (Toronto, Montreal, Vancouver: Thomas Nelson and Sons 1971) 189

19 *Ibid.*

20 Escott Reid, *Envoy to Nehru* (Toronto, Oxford, Delhi: Oxford University Press 1981) 69

21 Holmes, 'Canada and the Vietnam War' 189

22 For a perceptive review of the political and ethical proclivities of the Holmesian world-view see Denis Stairs's excellent introductory essay 'The Pedagogics of John W. Holmes,' in Kim Richard Nossal, ed., *An Acceptance of Paradox:*

Essays on Canadian Diplomacy in Honour of John W. Holmes (Toronto: Canadian Institute of International Affairs 1982).

23 See Holmes's 'Key issues in Canadian Foreign Policy,' in Donald Evans, ed., *Peace, Power and Protest* (Toronto: Ryerson Press 1967) 210. My thanks to Denis Stairs for drawing this passage to my attention.

24 Confidential interview material (hereafter CIM)

25 ICSC for Vietnam, *Minutes*, 770th Meeting, 13 Mar. 1973, pp 4–5; Dept of External Affairs files, 2-50052-A-12-40

26 For a solid introduction and overview of interest-group literature see Mildred A. Schwartz, 'The Group Basis of Politics,' in John H. Redekop, ed., *Approaches to Canadian Politics* (Scarborough, Ont.: Prentice-Hall 1978); also A. Paul Pross, ed., *Pressure Group Behaviour in Canadian Politics* (Toronto: McGraw-Hill Ryerson 1975).

27 See in particular Griffiths, 'A Tendency Analysis of Soviet Policy-Making,' in H. Gordon Skilling and Franklyn Griffiths, eds, *Interest Groups in Soviet Politics* (Princeton, NJ: Princeton University Press 1971); Robert A. Levine, *The Arms Debate* (Cambridge, MA: Harvard University Press 1963); and Schurmann, *Logic of World Power*.

28 Griffiths, 'Tendency Analysis' 336

29 *Ibid.*

30 *Ibid.* 339

31 For data on the DPS procurement, 1959–80, see Stephen Clarkson, *Canada and the Reagan Challenge* (Ottawa: Canadian Institute for Economic Policy 1982) 261.

32 For Canadian trade statistics concerning Indochina and all countries of Southeast Asia, 1953–73, see Ross, 'In the Interests of Peace' Appendix IV, pp 1055–61.

33 *Ibid.*

34 See Douglas A. Ross, 'Canadian Foreign Policy and the Pacific Rim: From National Security Anxiety to Creative Economic Co-operation?' in F.Q. Quo, ed., *The Politics of the Pacific Rim* (Vancouver: Simon Fraser University Publications 1983).

35 See Ernie Regehr, *Making a Killing: Canada's Arms Industry* (Toronto: McClelland and Stewart 1975).

36 Schurmann, *Logic of World Power* 38–9

37 For a helpful formulation of the notion of mental closure see Milton Rokeach and Frank Restle, 'A Fundamental Distinction between Open and Closed Systems,' in Milton Rokeach, ed., *The Open and Closed Mind* (New York: Basic Books 1960).

38 Griffiths, 'Tendency Analysis' 360

39 John Steinbruner, *The Cybernetic Theory of Decision* (Princeton, NJ: Princeton

University Press 1974); see in particular Chs 2 and 3 for elaboration of the points summarized.

40 The quotations are from Karl Deutsch, *Politics and Government: How People Decide Their Fate*, 2nd ed. (Boston: Houghton Mifflin 1974) 180.

41 See Charles E. Lindblom, *The Policy-Making Process*, 2nd ed. (Englewood Cliffs: Prentice-Hall 1980), Ch. 5; also David Braybrooke and Charles E. Lindblom, *A Strategy of Decision* (New York: Free Press 1963).

42 Graham T. Allison, 'Conceptual Models and the Cuban Missile Crisis,' *American Political Science Review* LXIII, 3 (Sept. 1969) 702

43 See Lindblom, *The Policy-Making Process* (1968) 24.

44 See Steinbruner, *Cybernetic Theory* Ch. 2.

45 Levine, *The Arms Race*

CHAPTER 2: INDOCHINA AND THE DIPLOMACY OF CONSTRAINT 1950–4

1 See W. Scott Thompson and Donaldson D. Frizzell, eds, *The Lessons of Vietnam* (New York: Crane Russak 1977) 22–3. See also Bernard B. Fall, *Street without Joy* (Harrisburg: Stackpole 1963) 367.

2 Roosevelt as quoted in *The Defense Department History of United States Decision-Making on Vietnam* (Pentagon Papers), Senator Gravel Edition, 4 vols (Boston: Beacon Press 1971) I 9–10; hereafter cited as *PP*.

3 On conditions in Vietnam in the early twentieth century see Donald C. Lancaster, *The Emancipation of French Indochina* (London: Oxford University Press 1961), Dennis J. Duncanson, *Government and Revolution in Vietnam* (New York, London: Oxford University Press 1968), and Bernard B. Fall, *The Two Viet-Nams: A Political and Military Analysis* (New York, London: Praeger 1963). For specialists, Fall's thesis at the University of Syracuse is useful, 'The Political Development of Vietnam: VJ Day to the Geneva Cease-Fire,' 3 vols. (Ann Arbor, MI: University Microfilms 1955). On the evolution of the communist-nationalist movement see the recent masterful study by Huynh Kim Khanh, *Vietnamese Communism, 1925–1945* (Ithaca, London: Cornell University Press 1982); also King C. Chen, *Vietnam and China, 1938–1954* (Princeton: Princeton University Press 1969). Another readable work that is highly sympathetic to the nationalist cause is James Pinckney Harrison's *The Endless War: Fifty Years of Struggle in Vietnam* (New York, London: Free Press 1982).

4 On British policy at this time see George Rosie, *The British in Vietnam: How the Twenty-Five Year War Began* (London: Panther 1970).

5 *PP*, I 49–50; see also Chen, *Vietnam and China* 154.

6 See Chen, *Vietnam and China* 99.

7 See Chester A. Bain, *Vietnam: The Roots of Conflict* (Englewood Cliffs, NJ: Prentice-Hall 1961) 110–12.

8 See Fall, 'Political Development,' II, 254.

9 George A. Nicolas, 'France and the Indo-China War,' *International Journal* VIII, 3 (summer 1955) 184. For detailed accounts of the war see Edward Doyle, Samuel Lipsman, Stephen Weiss, et al., *The Vietnam Experience*, I, *Passing the Torch* (Boston: Boston Publishing 1981), and Edgar O'Ballance, *The Indo-China War, 1945–1954: A Study in Guerrilla Warfare* (London: Faber & Faber 1964).

10 See C.A. Julien, 'From the French Empire to the French Union,' *International Affairs* (London) XXVI 4 (Oct. 1950) 487–502. On French political debate concerning Indochina see R.E.M. Irving, *The First Indochina War: French and American Policy, 1945–1954* (London: Croom Helm 1975).

11 See Fall, 'Political Development,' II, 318–20.

12 James Eayrs, *In Defence of Canada*, V, *Indochina: Roots of Complicity* (Toronto, Buffalo, London: University of Toronto Press 1983) 12–16; cited hereafter as Eayrs, *Indochina*.

13 *Ibid.*

14 See the definitive work on Indian policy towards Indochina in this period, D.R. SarDesai's *Indian Foreign Policy in Cambodia, Laos and Vietnam* (Berkeley and Los Angeles: University of California Press 1968) 12–16, 25.

15 *Ibid.* 25

16 *Ibid.* 27

17 *Ibid.* 17

18 See Pearson's statement to the House of Commons at Canada, House of Commons, *Debates*, 22 Feb. 1950, p 133; cited hereafter as *Debates*.

19 On the China recognition question see the discussion in John W. Holmes, *The Shaping of Peace: Canada and the Search for World Order, 1943–1957*, II (Toronto: University of Toronto Press 1983) 136–40.

20 Eayrs, *Indochina* 21–4

21 See excerpts from the relevant memorandum of Cabinet discussion on 4 Dec. 1950 in Eayrs, *Indochina* 28–9.

22 *Ibid.* 26

23 See Fall, *Two Viet-Nams* 219–23; also the analysis of the State of Vietnam's status under international law contained in Robert Randle, *Geneva, 1954* (Princeton, NJ: Princeton University Press 1969).

24 See the maps in George McT. Kahin and John W. Lewis, *The United States in Vietnam* (New York: Dell-Delta 1967) 34, also Fall, *Two Viet-Nams* 128, and finally *PP* I, 123.

25 See Janos Radvanyi, *Delusion and Reality: Gambits, Hoaxes and Diplomatic One-Upmanship in Vietnam* (South Bend, ID: Gateway 1978) 8–10.

26 See Fall, *Two Viet-Nams* 127 ff.; also Bernard B. Fall, *Hell in a Very Small Place* (Philadelphia and New York: J.B. Lippincott 1966).

27 See NSC Action no. 1074-a, 5 Apr. 1954 in *PP*, I, 466–70; also Chairman of the Joint Chiefs of Staff, Admiral Arthur Radford to Secretary of Defense Charles Wilson, 26 May 1954, *ibid.* 512–14; and 'Communist Reactions to Certain U.S. Courses of Action with Respect to Indochina,' 15 June 1954, *ibid.* 525–31. This last document envisaged full-scale tactical nuclear warfare against Chinese territory. See interpretive comments on these documents by John Lewis Gaddis, *Strategies of Containment* 169. On the growth of US Army opposition to tactical nuclear planning see Drew Middleton, 'Dien Bien Phu: A Footnote to Its Fall,' *New York Times*, 14 Feb. 1984. This article is based on information contained in Ronald H. Spector's *Advice and Support: The Early Years* (Washington: US Army Historical Office 1984).

28 Denis Stairs, *The Diplomacy of Constraint: Canada, the Korean War and the United States* (Toronto: University of Toronto Press 1974) 93: hereafter Stairs, *Diplomacy*

29 Department of External Affairs, *Statements and Speeches*, no. 50/50, as in Stairs, *Diplomacy* 131 (emphasis added); *Statements and Speeches*, cited hereafter as *S and S*

30 See John Kenneth Galbraith, 'The Strategic Mind,' *New York Review of Books*, 12 Oct. 1978, p 72.

31 Gaddis, *Strategies of Containment* 197

32 *Ibid.* 163

33 Schurmann, *Logic of World Power*, Part I

34 One of the best single summaries of this perspective as applied to communist China is to be found in *PP*, I 525–31, entitled 'Communist Reactions to Certain U.S. Courses of Action with Respect to Indochina,' dated 15 June 1954.

35 Gaddis, *Strategies of Containment* 155

36 For early examples of domino 'logic' see Omar Bradley, Chairman of the Joint Chiefs of Staff, to the Secretary of Defence, 10 Apr. 1950, in *PP*, I, 364; also National Security Council, Statement of Policy of 25 June 1952, in *ibid.*, esp. 385–6.

37 Townsend Hoopes, *The Devil and John Foster Dulles* (Boston, Toronto: Atlantic, Little Brown 1973) 208

38 See *PP*, I 100; also Chalmers M. Roberts, 'The Day We Didn't Go to War,' *The Reporter* XI (14 Sept. 1954) 31–5, which is reprinted in Marvin E. Gettleman and Susan Gettleman, eds, *Vietnam: History, Documents and Opinions*, rev. ed. (New York, Toronto: New American Library, Mentor 1970) 124–33.

39 See Holmes, *The Shaping of Peace*, I 210–22.

40 Arnold Smith to author, 1 Nov. 1979; Smith was present at the time the

American query was made. Apparently no other Canadians besides these three men were aware that this request had been made. Smith was then senior special assistant to the prime minister.

41 Hoopes, *The Devil and John Foster Dulles* 211–12

42 A. Smith to author, 1 Nov. 1979

43 Holmes, *The Shaping of Peace*, II, 35

44 See Dwight D. Eisenhower, *Mandate for Change: 1953–56* (London: Heinemann 1963) 453, n7.

45 See John Robinson Beal, *John Foster Dulles: A Biography* (New York: Harper and Bros 1957) 181–2; cited in George Quester, *Nuclear Diplomacy* (New York: Dunellen 1970) 196. According to Gaddis's evidence the threat was made and it became 'an article of faith' in Eisenhower's administration that the threat was decisive in establishing the July 1953 Korean armistice. See Gaddis, *Strategies of Containment* 169.

46 On Eisenhower's flirtation with the preventive war concept see Gaddis, *Strategies of Containment* 149n.

47 Holmes, *Shaping*, I, 221; see also Schurmann's description of the premises of 'nationalist' policy in *Logic of World Power* 83–91. On Pearson's views about keeping the use of the 'ultimate weapon' ultimate, see James Eayrs, *In Defence of Canada* (5 vols), IV, *Growing Up Allied* (Toronto, Buffalo, London: University of Toronto Press 1980) Documents 1, 3, 4, and 5, pp 369–82. See esp. Pearson's trenchant and prescient critique of the doctrine of massive retaliation.

48 Arnold Smith to author, 1 Nov. 1979

49 Stairs, *Diplomacy of Constraint* 93

50 Canada, House of Commons, Standing Committee on External Affairs, *Minutes of Proceedings and Evidence*, 18 Nov. 1949, p 24; hereafter SCEA, MPE.

51 See *Mike*, II, J.A. Munro and A.I. Inglis, eds (Scarborough: Signet, 1975) 202–4. Pearson's April 1950 comment is SCEA, MPE, n1, 20 Apr. 1950, p 11.

52 See Pearson's address, 'Our Changing World,' *S and S*, no. 52/3, 21 Jan. 1952.

53 See Pearson's comment in Holmes, *The Shaping of Peace*, II, 163.

54 See 'Memorandum by L.B. Pearson for the Prime Minister, "United States Defence Policy,"' 2 Feb. 1954, DEA files, 50115-P-40; as in Eayrs, *In Defence of Canada*, 381.

55 'Canada's Relations with Asia,' *S and S*, no. 53/33, 5 Sept. 1952 (emphasis added)

56 SCEA, MPE, 29 Apr. 1952, p 130

57 *Ibid.* 127

58 Schurmann, *Logic* 156–8

59 Quoted in Tang Tsou, *America's Failure in China, 1941–50* (Chicago and London: University of Chicago Press 1963) 537 n219

60 Eisenhower, *Mandate* 123

61 Schurmann, *Logic* 163. In April 1954 Pearson acknowledged hearing 'stories' of KMT raids. See SCEA, MPE, no. 1, 6 Apr. 1954, p 24.

62 *Ibid.* 163–74, 173. For corroborative evidence of CIA assistance to KMT raids on the Chinese coast as well as evidence of CIA activities in Laos, Tibet, and Vietnam, see Victor Marchetti and John D. Marks, *The CIA and the Cult of Intelligence* (New York: Dell 1975) esp. 46, 151–2, and 286.

63 Schurmann, *ibid.* 169–71

64 SCEA, MPE, 29 Apr. 1952, p. 131

65 *Ibid.* 116

66 *Ibid.* 131

67 On Japan's importance see Pearson's remarks at *ibid.* 115.

68 *Debates*, 12 Feb. 1953; quoted in B.S. Kierstead, *Canada in World Affairs, September 1951 to October 1953*, VII (Toronto: Oxford University Press/Canadian Institute for International Affairs 1956) 60

69 See Pearson's fears on the racial aspect of nuclear weapons use regarding Korea in *Mike*, II, 185–6.

70 Eisenhower, *Mandate* 18

71 Gaddis, *Strategies of Containment* 149

72 *Ibid.* 150, for Eisenhower's views. For Pearson's see Eayrs, *In Defence of Canada*, IV, *Growing Up Allied* 369.

73 See *PP*, I, 85–6.

74 'Don't Let Asia Split the West,' reprinted from *World*, Dec. 1953, in *S and S*, 53/50, p 5 (emphasis added). See also, *Debates*, 31 Jan. 1954, 3542–5.

75 See *Debates*, 29 Jan. 1954, 1622

76 *Ibid.*, 16 Nov. 1953, p 58

77 See *S and S*, no. 54/5, 29 Jan. 1954.

78 *PP*, I, p 89

79 *Ibid.* 87

80 *Ibid.* 90–3

81 See Townsend Hoopes, *The Devil and John Foster Dulles* (Boston, Toronto: Atlantic Little Brown 1973) 191–2.

82 See Eisenhower, *Mandate* 345.

83 Robert F. Randle, *Geneva, 1954* (Princeton, NJ: Princeton University Press 1969) 29; for more detail see Philippe Devillers and Jean Lacouture, *End of a War* (New York: Praeger 1969) 45–151. See also *PP*, I, 97–8.

84 *PP*, I, 97

85 See *Foreign Relations of the United States, 1952–1954*, XIII, *Indochina*, Part I (Washington: Government Printing Office 1982) 1274; cited hereafter as *FRUS, 1952–1954*, XIII, Part I.

86 See *PP*, I, 98 for excerpts from Dulles's speech 'The Threat of a Red Asia.' Full text may be found in Department of State, *Bulletin*, 12 Apr. 1954, pp 539–42.

87 *Debates*, 31 Mar. 1954, 3542–3
88 *FRUS, 1952–1954*, XIII, *Indochina*, Part I, p 1275 n1
89 *Ibid.*, 1277–8
90 *Debates*, 31 Mar. 1954, p 3544
91 *Ibid.*, 31 Mar. 1954, p 3546
92 *Ibid.*, 30 Mar. 1954, pp 3476–8
93 *Ibid.* 3499–3500
94 *Ibid.*, 25 Mar. 1954, pp 3358–9
95 *Ibid.*, 26 Mar. 1954, p 3375; also *ibid.*, 31 Mar. 1954, p 3457
96 *Ibid.* 3225–6
97 *Ibid.* 3225–30, 3374–5
98 See Chalmers Roberts, 'The Day We Didn't Go to War' supra n38.
99 *PP*, I, p 100. See also Hoopes, *Devil and Dulles* 211; and Eisenhower, *Mandate*, 347.
100 *PP*, I, p 203; also Hoopes, *Devil and Dulles* 218; and Anthony Eden, *Full Circle* (London: Cassel 1960) 93–4
101 See Eisenhower, *Mandate* 346–7.
102 SCEA, MPE, 6 Apr. 1954, pp 22–4
103 SCEA, MPE, 13 Apr. 1954, p 65
104 *Debates*, 26 Apr. 1954, pp 3374–5
105 During the prime minister's visit to India in February 1954 he explicitly broke with American policy on the desirability of non-recognition of the PRC. See Dale C. Thomson, *Louis St.-Laurent, Canadien* (Montreal: Cercle du Livre de France 1968) 366.
106 John Holmes to author, 1978
107 Eden, *Full Circle* 94
108 Escott Reid, *Envoy to Nehru* (Delhi, Toronto, Oxford: Oxford University Press 1981) 26
109 *Ibid.* 69

CHAPTER 3: THE DESCENT BEGINS: FROM GENEVA TO THE JUNGLES

1 See John W. Holmes, 'Geneva: 1954,' *International Journal* XXII, 3 (Summer 1967) 467.
2 Great Britain, Secretary of State for Foreign Affairs, *Documents Relating to the Discussion of Korea and Indochina at the Geneva Conference, April 27–June 15, 1954*, Cmd 9186 (London: Her Majesty's Stationery Office 1954) 7–8; cited hereafter as *Documents, April 27–June 15, 1954*
3 Schurmann, *Logic of World Power* 64. For further evidence of Dulles's bellicose proclivities in comparison with Eisenhower see *PP*, I, 129n. Dulles's

nephew, Allen's son, was permanently disabled by action in Korea. See Leonard Mosley, *Dulles: A Biography of Eleanor, Allen and John Foster Dulles and Their Family Network* (New York: Dial/James Wade 1978) 297–8.

4 *Documents, April 27–June 15, 1954* vi–vii
5 Stairs, *Diplomacy of Constraint* 290–1
6 *Documents, April 27–June 15, 1954* 80–2; also Chester Ronning, 'Statement at Geneva,' *S and S*, no. 54/32, 11 June 1954. For details of Canadian proposals see Stairs, *Diplomacy of Constraint* 291–2.
7 Stairs, *ibid.* 292; also Chester Ronning, *A Memoir of China in Revolution* (New York, Toronto: Pantheon 1974) 214–35
8 *Debates*, 28 May 1954, p 5190
9 *Ibid.* 5191
10 *Ibid.* 5192
11 *Ibid.*
12 *Ibid.* 5197
13 *Ibid.* 5194–5202
14 Chester Ronning to author, June 1976
15 Bidault's opening proposals are in *Documents, April 27–June 15, 1954* 111; Eden's call for a detailed armistice 'with provision for control and enforcement' *ibid.* 122–3; and Smith's remarks, *ibid.* 114–15.
16 See 'Secretary of State to the Department of State,' 24 Apr. 1954, in *Foreign Relations of the United States, 1952–1954* XVI (Washington: Government Printing Office 1981) 553; cited hereafter as *FRUS, 1952–1954*, XVI.
17 On Ridgway see Chalmers Roberts, 'The Day We Didn't Go to War' and Leslie H. Gelb with Richard K. Betts, *The Irony of Vietnam: The System Worked* (Washington: Brookings Institution 1979) 57; Smith held this view strongly according to Chester Ronning. See also Eisenhower's difference with Dulles over possible unilateral intervention in the event of overt Chinese involvement, *PP*, I, 129n.
18 Gelb, Betts, *ibid.* 60
19 *Ibid.*
20 *PP*, I, 106
21 Gelb, Betts, *Irony of Vietnam* 60
22 The reasons offered by Robert Randle, *Geneva, 1954* (Princeton, NJ: Princeton University Press 1969) 122
23 See the comment by Churchill, for example, quoted by Victor Bator in his *Vietnam, a Diplomatic Tragedy: Origins of U.S. Involvement* (London: Faber and Faber 1965), 205–6. Quoted also by Holmes at 'Geneva: 1954' 460.
24 'Memorandum of Conversation by the Secretary of State,' *FRUS, 1952–1954* XVI, 555

25 US National Intelligence Estimate of 15 June 1954, as in *PP*, I, 122
26 *PP*, I, 153
27 Eden, *FC* 132–3; see also *PP*, 144–5
28 The reasoning offered in *PP*, I, 168
29 *Ibid.* 167
30 *Ibid.*
31 See *Development of Strategic Air Command*, Office of the Historian, Head-quarters Strategic Air Command 1976; also Edgar Bottome, *The Balance of Terror* (Boston: Beacon 1971).
32 See *PP*, I, 144, where a naval blockade of China is discussed in retaliation for Chinese assistance to the Vietminh.
33 See Alice L. Hsieh's authoritative study of China's nuclear weapons debate, *Communist China's Strategy in the Nuclear Era* (Englewood Cliffs, NJ: Prentice-Hall 1962) 8; hereafter Hsieh, *China's Strategy*.
34 See Adam Ulam's comments in this regard in his *Expansion and Coexistence: Soviet Foreign Policy, 1917–73*, 2nd ed. (New York, Washington: Praeger 1974) 552–4.
35 *PP*, I, 171
36 See Chen, *Vietnam and China* 313 on Chinese diplomacy; also *PP*, I, 148–9.
37 *PP*, I, 123
38 See 'Appeal by the Vietnam Worker's Party Central Executive Committee,' 5 Aug. 1954 in Gareth Porter, ed., *Vietnam: The Definitive Documentation of Human Decisions*, 2 vols (Stanfordville, NY: Earl M. Coleman 1979) I, 663–6.
39 See Mosley, *Dulles: Family Network* 293–4.
40 *PP*, I, 155
41 For details on the last days of the conference see *PP*, I, 153–78; Randle, *Geneva, 1954*, ch. 18; and Philippe Devillers and Jean Lacouture, *End of a War* (New York: Praeger 1969).
42 See Eayrs, *Indochina* 42–3.
43 *Documents, April 27–June 15, 1954* 35
44 Eayrs, *Indochina* 43
45 D.R. SarDesai, *Indian Foreign Policy in Cambodia, Laos and Vietnam, 1947–64* (Berkeley and Los Angeles: University of California Press 1968) 46 n121; also 11–12, 15–17. Cited hereafter as SarDesai, *IFP*
46 Quoted by Krishnaprasad G. Bhansali in, 'India's Role in the Settlement of the Indochina Conflict, 1947–58,' PHD dissertation. Political Science, The American University (Ann Arbor, MI: University Microfilms 1962) 18; hereafter, Bhansali, 'India's Role'
47 *Economist* (London), 31 July 1954
48 SarDesai, IFP 51

49 *Further Documents Relating to the Discussion of Indochina at the Geneva Conference* (Misc. no. 20), Cmnd. 9239 (London: Great Britain Parliamentary Sessional Papers, XXXI, 1953–4) 5–9; reprinted in A.W. Cameron, ed., *Viet-Nam Crisis: A Documentary History*, I: 1940–56 (Ithaca and London: Cornell University Press 1971) 308–19. See also *FRUS, 1952–1954*, XVI, 1500–1.

50 The agreements are in *FRUS, 1952–1954*, XVI, 1521–39; also Marvin and Susan Gettleman *et al.*, eds, *Conflict in Indochina* (New York: Vintage 1970) 84–111.

51 For the transcript of the closing session of the conference see relevant portions of Randle, *Geneva, 1954*; Chen, *Vietnam and China*; and Cameron, *Viet-Nam Crisis* I.

52 Cameron, *ibid.* 284–5; see also Randle, *Geneva, 1954* 315; and Porter, *Vietnam Documentation*, I, 656–7.

53 See Further Documents 86; also Porter, *Vietnam Documentation*, I, 656.

54 Robert H. Hull and John C. Novogrod, *Law and Vietnam* (Dobbs Ferry, NY: Oceana Publications 1968) 56; cited hereafter as Hull and Novogrod, *LV*

55 *Ibid.*

56 For dates of recognition see Nguyen-Huu-Tru, *Quelques problèmes de succession d'états concernant le Viet-Nam* (Brussels: Emile Bruylant 1970) 67 n23.

57 The 1946 Franco-Vietnamese agreement was signed by Jean Sainteny for France, Ho Chi Minh for the Vietminh, and Vu Hong Kanh for the VNQDD (a right-wing nationalist party). Juridically, as Randle points out, the 'Republic of Vietnam' which the French recognized at this time was quite distinct from the proclaimed 'Democratic Republic of Vietnam.' This first RVN was not granted 'independence' except within the French Union – which meant no independence at all given the prevailing relationships within the French Union. See Robert F. Randle, *Geneva, 1954* 451–2 n17; also Ellen J. Hammer, *The Struggle for Indochina, 1950–55* (Stanford: Stanford University Press 1954) 82–4, 153.

58 Randle, *Geneva, 1954* 431

59 *Ibid.*, ch. 23

60 Nguyen-Huu-Tru, *Quelques problèmes* 127–8

61 See J.G. Castel, *International Law* (Toronto: Butterworth's 1976) 127.

62 O'Connell, *State Succession in Municipal Law and International Law* (Cambridge: Cambridge University Press 1967) II, 231. O'Connell has also commented elsewhere that the RVN was not legally obliged to hold the elections called for in the FD or Article 14 of the CFA. He also implicitly rejects communist bloc assertions that the Geneva Agreements were meant to lead ultimately to the unification of Vietnam. For all the rhetoric about unification in the FD, the inevitable consequences of regroupment, civilian population transfers, and absence of clearly stipulated electoral modalities in the FD could only

be partition. O'Connell declares approvingly of the study by Nguyen-Huu-Tru: 'The author concludes realistically that the effect of the Geneva Accords has been in practice to stabilize the respective territorial bases of North and South Vietnam and to fix their frontiers.' See D.P. O'Connell's review of *Quelques problèmes de succession d'états concernant le Viet-Nam* in *The British Yearbook of International Law (1971)* (London, New York, Toronto: Royal Institute of International Affairs–Oxford University Press 1973) 475–7.

63 See Charles S. Rhyne, *International Law* (Washington: CLB Publishers 1971) 34; also Castel, *International Law* 126–7.

64 See Rhyne, *ibid.* 262

65 Randle, *Geneva, 1954* 443–4 n13

66 *Ibid.* 413

67 French officials subsequently said that Article 7 of the FD pertaining to elections was no more than a 'declaration of intention.' See Nguyen-Huu-Tru, *Quelques problèmes* 131 n30.

68 Randle, *Geneva, 1954* 446–7

69 *Ibid.* 420–1, esp. 421 n25

70 For an elaboration of this alternative but quite inadequate line of argument see Quincy Wright, 'Legal Aspects of the Vietnam Situation,' in Richard A. Falk, ed., *The Vietnam War and International Law* (Princeton, NJ: Princeton University Press 1968) 271–91, esp. 277–81. The most important works examining legal aspects of the Geneva Agreements and the developing pattern of legal responsibility for the onset of the Second Indochina War are: Randle, *Geneva, 1954*, esp. chs 23–7; R.A. Falk, ed., *The Vietnam War and International Law*, esp. Parts II and III of vol. I; John Norton Moore, *Law and the Indo-China War* (Princeton, NJ; Princeton University Press 1972) esp. chs 7–9; R. Hull and J. Novogrod, *Law and Vietnam*. See also the brief drawn up by the Lawyers Committee on American Policy towards Vietnam as printed in the *New York Times*, 15 Jan. 1967, p E9, which was supported to varying degrees by, inter alia, Richard Falk, John Herz, Stanley Hoffmann, Hans Morgenthau, Richard J. Barnet, and Quincy Wright. Nguyen-Huu-Tru's monograph (see n56) is also worth close attention.

71 See Eayrs, *Indochina* 50.

72 *Globe and Mail*, 18 July 1954; *Ottawa Evening Journal*, 19 July 1954

73 *Montreal Star*, 22 and 24 July 1954; *Ottawa Evening Journal*, 23 July 1954. More critical views were contained in 'From Positions of Weakness,' *Canadian Forum* (June 1954), and Frank Underhill, 'After the Washington Conference,' *Canadian Forum* (Aug. 1954).

74 Fraser, 'Backstage in Ottawa,' *Maclean's*, 15 July 1954

75 Quoted in Christopher Dagg's unpublished, untitled manuscript on the Cana-

dian role in Indochina, p 14: hereafter Dagg, *MSS*. A copy of Dagg's *MSS* is available through the Canadian Institute of International Affairs (CIIA) for viewing – but only in Toronto. See also Eayrs, *Indochina* 56.

76 A recurrent theme in R.A. Spencer, *Canada in World Affairs, 1946–49* (Toronto: University of Toronto Press 1959)

77 Lt Gen. E.L.M. Burns had just been appointed UNTSO's chief of staff in Feb. 1954. See Donald C. Masters, *Canada in World Affairs*, VIII: 1953–5 (Toronto: University of Toronto Press/CIIA 1959) 175.

78 Canada, Department of External Affairs, 'Statement on Canadian Membership in the International Commissions for Vietnam, Laos, and Cambodia,' Press Release no. 43, 28 July 1954 (emphasis added); hereafter *DEA*, 'Canadian Membership.'

79 *Maclean's*, 15 Aug. 1954

80 See 'Memorandum of Conversation, by Paul J. Sturm' in *FRUS, 1952–1954*, XIII, Part II, 1874–6.

81 Eayrs, *Indochina* 51

82 On the problem posed by ICSC composition see Holmes, 'Geneva: 1954' 470.

CHAPTER 4: THE EMERGENCE OF THE REFUGEE DILEMMA:
AUGUST–NOVEMBER 1954

1 Confidential interview material (cited hereafter as *CIM*)

2 See Dooley, *The Night They Burned the Mountain* (New York: Signet 1960) 67–8; and *Deliver Us from Evil* (New York: Farrar, Straus and Cudahy 1956). Dooley was a former US Navy medical officer who resigned from the service in 1956 and subsequently established MEDICO, a medical relief organization in Laos.

3 *CIM*

4 *Ibid.*; but see also 'Eye-Witness,' 'Canadians in Indochina,' *External Affairs* VII, 2 (Feb. 1955). See also Eayrs, *Indochina* 59–60.

5 ICSC Vietnam, *Minutes*, 1st to 8th Meetings. See holdings in 51 vols in DEA files, 2-50052-A-12-40, for Aug 1954–May 1963. Cited hereafter as *Minutes*

6 *Minutes*, 9th Meeting, 24 Aug. 1954, p 5

7 *Ibid.*, 24th Meeting, 30 Aug. 1954, p 2

8 *Ibid.*, 15th Meeting, 31 Aug. 1954, p 2

9 *Ibid.*

10 *Ibid.*

11 *Ibid.* 3

12 *CIM*. See also Pearson to Lett in Eayrs, *Indochina* 193.

13 *Ibid.*

14 From 1948 to 1951 Desai was posted in London; from 1951 to 1953 he represented India in Sweden, Finland, and Denmark. In early 1954 he was India's acting high commissioner in London. After his duty in Vietnam he became commonwealth secretary in the Indian Ministry of External Affairs from 1955 to 1961, and foreign secretary from 1961 to 1963.

15 *Minutes*, 18th Meeting, 4 Sept. 1954, p 4

16 *Ibid.*, 19th Meeting, 6 Sept. 1954, p 1. See SarDesai, *Indian Foreign Policy* 54.

17 *Minutes*, 19th Meeting, 6 Sept. 1954, p 1

18 A.R. Menzies (letter of transmittal) to Lett, 'Letter of Instructions,' 27 Aug. 1954; DEA files 50052-A-40, vol. II. See also Eayrs, *Indochina*, 66–7.

19 Eayrs, *Indochina* 220

20 *PP*, I, 204. See NSC 5429/2 abstract.

21 See in this regard Mosley, *Dulles* 329.

22 *PP*, I, 212

23 For a complete text of the treaty and protocol see US Department of State, *Southeast Asia Treaty Organization*, Publication 6305 (Washington: US Government Printing Office 1956); also available in R.A. Falk, ed., *The Vietnam War and International Law*, I (Princeton, NJ: Princeton University Press 1968) 561–4, and M.E. Gettleman, ed., *Vietnam: History, Documents and Opinions* 121–3.

24 The Saigon Military Mission under Col. Edward G. Lansdale organized the planting of rumours in the north as early as June and July 1954. See *PP*, I, 573–83.

25 On the Christ-Mary rumour see Fall, *TVN*, 153–4. On the atomic attack fears see the comments of the Indian deputy secretary general in B.S.N. Murti, *Vietnam Divided* (New York: Asia Publishing House 1964) 83. Also *Minutes*, 61st Meeting, 13 Nov. 1954, pp 2–10

26 *PP*, I, 237–8; see also Kahin and Lewis, *The U.S. in Vietnam* 67, and Robert Scheer's contribution to Gettleman, ed., *Vietnam: History, Documents and Opinions* 268–86, but esp. p 274.

27 *CIM*. See also Eayrs, *Indochina* 208.

28 Figure from Kahin and Lewis, *The U.S. in Vietnam* 74. For more detail on US Navy activities in the refugee migration see Edwin Bickford Hooper, Dean C. Allard, and Oscar P. Fitzgerald, *The United States Navy and the Vietnam Conflict*, I: *The Setting of the Stage to 1959* (Washington: Naval History Division, Department of the Navy/US Government Publications Office 1976).

29 Secretary of State for Foreign Affairs, Government of the United Kingdom, *Fourth Interim Report of the International Commission for Supervision and Control in Vietnam*, 11 Apr. 1955 to 10 Aug. 1955, Command 9654 (London: Her Majesty's Stationery Office 1955) 30; hereafter *4th IR*

30 Kahin and Lewis, *The U.S. in Vietnam* 75

31 *4th IR* 30

32 R.P. Stebbins and the Research Staff of the Council on Foreign Relations, *The U.S. in World Affairs, 1954* (New York: Harper and Bros 1956) 285; also Kahin and Lewis, *The U.S. in Vietnam* 75 and Bernard Fall, *The Two Viet-Nams: A Political and Military Analysis* (New York: Praeger 1963) 154

33 Mieczyslaw Maneli, *War of the Vanquished* (New York and Evanston, etc.: Harper and Row 1971) 39–41; hereafter Maneli, *War*. According to Maneli, a former ICSC commissioner, a Polish ship, *Boleslaw Bierut*, was the first communist-bloc ship to arrive in the DRVN with desperately needed rice.

34 'Supervisory Commissions in Indo-China,' CBC radio interview text of 27 Sept. 1954, as in *External Affairs*, VI, 10, pp 299–302 (emphasis added)

35 Sherwood Lett, Diplomatic Papers, 1947–55: Vancouver City Archives, Add. MSS 361, 138–386, Finding Aid no. 84, vol. 4B, file no. 7. See also Eayrs, *Indochina* 62–3.

36 *Minutes*, 31st Meeting, 29 Sept. 1954, p 1

37 'Canadians in Indo-China' 39

38 *CIM*

39 Holmes to Macdonnell, *Holmes Papers*, 26 Aug. 1954

40 Dagg, *MSS*

41 These figures are an average of the numbers exchanged according to the two parties. In each case the numbers differed by a few hundred. See Secretary of State for Foreign Affairs, Government of Great Britain, *First and Second Interim Reports of the International Commission for Supervision and Control in Vietnam*, 11 Aug. 1954 to 10 Dec. 1954 and 11 Dec. 1954 to 10 Feb. 1955, Command 1961 (London: Her Majesty's Printing Office 1955) 18; hereafter *1st and 2nd IRs.*.

42 *Minutes*, 39th Meeting, 12 Oct. 1954, pp 3–4

43 *Ibid.* 6

44 *Minutes*, 41st Meeting, 14 Oct. 1954, p 4

45 *Ibid.* 6

46 *Minutes*, 42nd Meeting, 15 Oct. 1954, p 2

47 *CIM*

48 *Ibid.* (emphasis added)

49 *Ibid.*

50 *Ibid.*

51 *Minutes*, 51st Meeting, 31 Oct. 1954, pp 2–3

52 *Minutes*, 52nd Meeting, 1 Nov. 1954, pp 4–5

53 Maneli, *War* 28–9. Maneli claims this was the only instance of a Polish-Canadian majority overruling an Indian opinion.

54 *Minutes*, 54th Meeting, 4 Nov. 1954, pp 5–6 (emphasis added)

55 *Ibid.* 6, 7
56 See Maneli, *War of the Vanquished* 27, 31–2.
57 *Minutes*, 54th Meeting, 4 Nov. 1954, pp 8–9
58 *1st and 2nd IRs*, p 29
59 *CIM*
60 *CIM*
61 Fall, *TVN* 191–2
62 Holmes to Ronning, 19 Oct. 1954, *Holmes Papers*
63 See Document 59, innocuously entitled 'Communist Reactions to Certain U.S. Courses of Action with Respect to Indochina,' *PP*, I, 525–31.
64 See *PP*, I, 576.
65 *Ibid.* 577. Mansfield's public opinion as embodied in the *Report to the Senate Committee on Foreign Relations*, 6 Oct. 1955, was only slightly less pessimistic. For excerpts from the report see Bator, *Vietnam* 160–1.
66 *PP*, II, pp 577–8
67 Cameron, *Viet-Nam Crisis* 346–7
68 According to Fall's sources some American 'psywar' officials helped the Vietnamese under Diem to incite anti-French feeling in the south, acts that led directly to the murders of some French personnel. *TVN*, 256
69 See Fall, *TVN* 255–7 and Bator, *Vietnam* 161, who categorically deny conventional American arguments that Diem drove the French out during 1954–5.
70 Bator, *Vietnam* 164

CHAPTER 5: ... THE TERRIBLE THINGS THAT ARE BEING DONE

1 W.T. Delworth and Christopher Dagg, 'Canada and the Vietnam Refugee Crisis of 1954/55,' in T. Cohn, G.B. Hainsworth, and L. Kavic, eds, *Canada and Southeast Asia: Perspectives and Evolution of Public Policies* (Vancouver: Kaen Publishing, 1983). The author would like to thank G.B. Hainsworth for access to the article in manuscript form.
2 See Pearson's remarks to the North Atlantic Council in May 1955 quoted by Eayrs in *Indochina* 153.
3 Lett to SSEA, '14(d) – consultations,' no. 289, 9 June 1955: DEA files, 50052-A-40, vol. 13. See also Eayrs, *Indochina* 159.
4 *CIM*
5 Fall, *TVN*, 155–6. See also Jean Lacouture, *Vietnam: Between Two Truces* (New York: Vintage-Random House 1966) 48. Both of these works may have relied on inaccurate and apparently intentionally exaggerated figures provided by Hoang Van Chi.
6 See Edwin E. Moise, 'Land Reform and Land Reform Errors in North Vietnam,' *Pacific Affairs* XLIX, /1 (Spring 1976) 78; see also Noam Chomsky and

Edward S. Herman, *The Political Economy of Human Rights*, 2 vols, I (*The Washington Connection and Third World Fascism* (Montreal: Black Rose 1979) 343–4.

7 *Minutes*, 56th Meeting, 8 Nov. 1954, pp 7–13
8 *Minutes*, 57th Meeting, 8 Nov. 1954, p 3
9 *Ibid.* 10–11
10 *CIM*
11 B.S.N. Murti's account reflects the Indian perspective on 14(d) well, with all its blindered rationalization and internally contradictory arguments. Nevertheless, the book is worth reading closely. *Vietnam Divided: The Unfinished Struggle* (New York: Asia Publishing 1964) esp. 70–92
12 Eayrs, *Indochina*, 136–7
13 *Ibid.* 139
14 *Minutes*, 69th Meeting, 24 Nov. 1954, p 21
15 *Minutes*, 72nd Meeting, 29 Nov. 1954, pp 4–5
16 *Minutes*, 73rd Meeting, 30 Nov. 1954, pp 8–9
17 *Ibid.* 9
18 As quoted in Cameron, *Viet-Nam Crisis* 352
19 See Lett's comments on the porous frontiers in Eayrs, *Indochina* 133.
20 *Minutes*, 73rd Meeting, 30 Nov. 1954, pp 13–16
21 See Heath to State Dept, 17 Aug. 1954, *FRUS, 1952–1954*, XIII, Part II, 1951–2. Also see T. Dooley, *Deliver Us from Evil*.
22 *Minutes*, 76th Meeting, 3 Dec. 1954, pp 9–10
23 *Ibid.*; also see Appendix I of *Minutes*, 103rd Meeting, 14 Jan. 1955. The record in the *Minutes* contradicts Murti's account, which claims that 'in many cases food, medicines and transport' and 'in certain cases financial subsidies' were given to intending evacuees; *Vietnam Divided* 81. If true, these 'cases' were a tiny percentage of the refugees, and probably involved the dispatch of pro-DRVN agents to the south, as Saigon feared.
24 *Minutes*, 133rd Meeting, 9 Mar. 1955, pp 17–19
25 *CIM*. But see Appendix V, *Fourth Interim Report of the International Commission for Supervision and Control in Vietnam.* (11 Apr. 1955–10 Aug. 1955, 'Command 9654 (London: Her Majesty's Stationery Office 1955) 32: hereafter, *Fourth Interim Report*. And also *Minutes*, 101st Meeting, 11 Jan. 1955, pp 4–5; 102nd Meeting, 13 Jan. 1955, pp 6–8; 113th Meeting, 31 Jan. 1955, p 11; 131st Meting, 5 Mar. 1955, pp 5–6; 132nd Meeting, 8 Mar. 1955, pp 1–3.
26 See Eayrs, *Indochina* 138–9.
27 S.F. Rae to Ottawa, no. 183, 6 Apr. 1955: DEA files, 50052-A-40, vol. 10
28 J. Léger to L.B. Pearson, 'Refugees,' 23 Mar. 1955: DEA files, 50052-A-40, vol. 10
29 ICSC in Vietnam, *Fourth Interim Report* 10
30 See Lett's fears on this in Eayrs, *Indochina* 196.

31 *Minutes*, 79th Meeting, 9 Dec. 1954, pp 7–9
32 *Minutes*, 87th Meeting, 21 Dec. 1954, pp 4–8. See also Dagg *MSS* B26–8.
33 *Minutes*, 114th Meeting, 1 Feb. 1955, pp 25–6
34 *Ibid.*, Appendix 1, 1–5
35 The 'forced evacuation' controversy surfaces at *Minutes*, 127th Meeting, 24 February 1955, pp 2–4.
36 *Ibid.* 2
37 Marcel Cadieux to author, 24 Nov. 1976
38 *Fourth Interim Report* 32 (emphasis added). See also pp 11–12, which contain the unanimous corroboration of all figures in the Canadian material.
39 *Minutes*, 133rd Meeting, 9 Mar. 1955, pp 17–19
40 S. Lett to Ottawa, 'Future of the International Commission,' 7 Feb. 1955; DEA files, 50052-A-40, vol. 8. See also Eayrs, *Indochina* 147.
41 Lett to Ottawa, *ibid*.
42 Eayrs, *Indochina*, 149
43 *Minutes*, 135th Meeting, 12 Mar. 1955, pp 21–3
44 *Ibid.* 8–10
45 *Ibid.* 26–31
46 *Ibid.* 35
47 *Minutes*, 136th Meeting, 14 Mar. 1955, pp 9–12
48 *Minutes*, 137th Meeting, 15 Mar. 1955, p 5
49 Eayrs, *Indochina* 149–50
50 *Minutes*, 139th Meeting, 18 Mar. 1955, p 19
51 *Ibid.* 25–7
52 *Minutes*, 141st Meeting, 20 Mar. 1955, pp 16–20
53 For details on this turbulent period and additional information on the sects see Joseph Buttinger, *Vietnam: A Dragon Embattled* (New York: Praeger 1967) 878–89; Roy Jumper, 'Sects and Communism in South Vietnam,' *ORBIS* III, 1 (Apr. 1959); Bernard B. Fall, 'The Political-Religious Sects of Viet-Nam,' *Pacific Affairs* XXVIII, 3 (Sept. 1955), for detailed treatment of Diem's victory in the civil war; and finally, Fall's 'Indochina since Geneva,' *Pacific Affairs* XXVIII, 1 (Mar. 1955), for some contemporary reporting. Also relevant, B.S.N. Murti, *Vietnam Divided*, 125–44
54 *PP*, I, p 297
55 L.B. Pearson to Canadian Commissioner, Hanoi, 'Freedom of Movement,' no. 139, 7 Apr. 1955: DEA files, 50052-A-40, vol. 10
56 *Ibid.*
57 For the text of the Canadian minority note see Secretary of State for Foreign Affairs, Government of Great Britain, *Third Interim Report of the International Commission for Supervision and Control in Vietnam*, 11 Feb. to 10 Apr. 1955, Command 9499 (London: Her Majesty's Stationery Office 1955) 4: hereafter *3rd IR*

58 Harold C. Hinton, *China's Turbulent Quest* (Bloomington and London: Indiana University Press 1973) 67

59 André Fontaine, *History of the Cold War*, 2 vols (New York, Toronto: Random House-Pantheon 1969) 113; hereafter, Fontaine, *HCW*

60 See Donald C. Masters, *Canada in World Affairs, 1953–1955* (Toronto: University of Toronto Press/Canadian Institute of International Affairs 1959) 100

61 Hinton, *China's Quest*

62 Fontaine, *HCW*, II, 114

63 As quoted in Masters, *Canada in World Affairs* 102

64 Fontaine, *HCW*, II, 116

65 Masters, *Canada in World Affairs* 105–6

66 *Ibid.* 106–7

67 *Ibid.* 109

68 S. Lett to SSEA, 're Elections,' no. 156, 18 Mar. 1955: DEA files, 50052-A-40, vol. 10

69 *CIM*

70 *Debates*, 24 Mar. 1955, p 2339

71 *Ibid.*

72 *Ibid.* 2340

73 *Ibid.* 2342

74 *Ibid.* 2343

75 *Ibid.* 2344

76 *Ibid.* 2345

77 *Ibid.* 2346

78 D.M. Johnson, Office of the Canadian Permanent Representative to the UN, New York to Ottawa, 18 Mar. 1955: DEA files, 50052-A-40, vol. 9

79 See comments by Léger and his summary of the Johnson conversation at Eayrs, *Indochina*, 205–6.

80 For text of the dispatch see *Third Interim Report*, 4.

81 J. Léger to L.B. Pearson, 'Memorandum for the Minister, Discussion with Mr Robertson,' 18 Apr. 1955,: DEA files, 50052-A-40, vol. 11

82 See the summary of comments by John Holmes of 8 July 1955 in Eayrs, *Indochina* 159.

83 *Newsweek*, 18 Apr. 1955, p 18

84 *Debates*, 4 May 1955, p 3389 (emphasis added). Eayrs does not include the first sentence of this passage.

85 *Ibid.* (emphasis added)

86 See excerpts from Lett to Ottawa of 9 June 1955, and messages from External Affairs to Lett of 17 June and 12 July, in Eayrs, *Indochina* 158–61.

87 Eayrs, *ibid.* 161

425 Notes pp 141–53

88 *Fourth Interim Report* 19–24
89 Léon Mayrand, Vientiane, to Ottawa, 'Visit to Hanoi,' no. 22 , 17 Jan. 1955: DEA files, 50052-A-40, vol. 8
90 See portions of the Holmes memorandum in Eayrs, *Indochina* 164
91 Escott Reid, *Envoy to Nehru* (Delhi, Toronto, Oxford: Oxford University Press 1981) 83
92 *Ibid.*
93 *CIM*

CHAPTER 6: COPING WITH THE ELECTORAL DILEMMA 1955–6

1 SCEA, *MPE*, 24 Apr. 1956, p 108
2 *CIM*
3 See Philippe Devillers, 'The Struggle for the Unification of Vietnam,' *China Quarterly* 9 (Jan.–Mar. 1962) 9.
4 See, for example, Lett's statement on CBC of 27 September 1954 in *External Affairs* VI, 10 (Oct. 1954) 299–302.
5 On Nehru's concept of the 'zone of peace,' see Sar Desai, *IFP* 58. See also Sar Desai's updated interpretation of the sphere-of-influence calculations behind Indian policy towards Indochina in his 'India: A Balancer Power?' in S. Chawla, M. Gurtov, and A.G. Marsot, eds, *Southeast Asia under the New Balance of Power* (New York, Washington, London: Praeger 1974). Here Sar Desai notes that in 1954–61 the Indian government presented itself as 'a disinterested catalyst, peacemaker, mediator or negotiator'; however, 'a closer look at the classified Indian documentation of the period reveals an Indian awareness of a balance of power in Southeast Asia that would not allow a single power to dominate the region.' He concludes, therefore, that 'India's "tilting" in her crucial role during the period could have upset the balance; in that sense India acted as a balancer' (p 97).
6 An opinion to which many DRVN officials subscribed, Canadians thought. *CIM*
7 ICSC for Vietnam, *Minutes*, 171st Meeting, 10 May 1955, p 2 (emphasis added)
8 *Ibid.* 3 (emphasis added)
9 *Ibid.* 4 (emphasis added)
10 ICSC for Vietnam, *Minutes*, 175th Meeting, 17 May 1955, p 3
11 *Ibid.* 7 (emphasis added)
12 ICSC for Vietnam, *Minutes*, 176th Meeting, 18 May 1955, p 14
13 *CIM.* See also *FRUS 1952–1954*, XIII Part 2, p 2248, on French resistance.
14 The phrase is used by Jean Lacouture in *Vietnam: Between Two Truces* (New York: Vintage–Random House 1966).

15 See Giap to Lett in Eayrs, *Indochina* 168.

16 *CIM*

17 See Lett's comments on the presence of DRVN agents as the cause of 14(c) allegations in Eayrs, *Indochina* 166–7; on subversion generally, see *ibid.* 158, 175–6.

18 L.B. Pearson, Canada House, London, to Ottawa, 5 and 6 Feb. 1955: DEA files, 50052-A-40, vol. 8

19 Jules Léger to Mr Pillai, Indian Ministry for External Affairs, 7 Feb. 1955: DEA files, 50052-A-40; vol. 9

20 *CIM*

21 *Ibid.*

22 *Ibid.*

23 *Ibid.*

24 *Ibid.*

25 *Ibid.*

26 *Ibid.*

27 'Memorandum of interview with Menon at Norman Robertson's,' 12 Apr. 1955. Lett Working and Organizational Papers, 1955; Vancouver City Archives, Add. MSS 361, vol. 4B, file 9

28 *CIM*

29 *Ibid.*

30 *Ibid.* See also Escott Reid, *Envoy to Nehru* (Delhi, Toronto, Oxford: Oxford University Press 1981) 82–3.

31 *CIM*

32 ICSC for Vietnam, *Minutes*, 179th Meeting, 23 May 1955, p 30

33 *Ibid.* 32–3

34 *CIM*

35 *Ibid.*

36 *Ibid.*

37 *Ibid.*

38 See Eayrs, *Indochina* 158–9.

39 J.R. Maybee and A.R. Menzies to Lett, 17 June 1955: DEA files, 50052-A-40, vol. 13. See Eayrs, *Indochina*, 160 for direct excerpts. Eayrs attributes the document to Pearson, who may have approved the message.

40 Lett to Ottawa, 'Future of the International Commission – What Lies Ahead?'; DEA files, 50052-A-40, vol. 13. See Eayrs, *Indochina* 175–6 for verbatim excerpts.

41 Saul Rae to J. Holmes, 3 Mar. 1955, Holmes Papers

42 Holmes to George Glazebrook, Canadian Embassy, Washington, 7 July 1955, Holmes Papers

43 Holmes to Pearson, 'Memorandum for the Minister: Prospects in Indochina,' 11 July 1955, p 2 (emphasis added), Holmes Papers. Other excerpts are provided by Eayrs at *Indochina* 177.

44 Holmes to Pearson, 'Memorandum for the Minister: Prospects in Indochina,' 11 July 1955, p 3, Holmes Papers
45 *Ibid.* 5–7 (emphasis added)
46 *Ibid.* 8 (emphasis added)
47 *Ibid.* (emphasis added)
48 *Ibid.* 9 (emphasis added)
49 *Ibid.* 10
50 *Ibid.* 9
51 SarDesai, *IFP* 88
52 *CIM*
53 Exerpts from radio broadcast by Diem of 16 July 1955, contained in Republic of Vietnam, Ministry of Information, *The Problem of Reunification in Vietnam* (Saigon 1958) 30–1; as in SarDesai, *IFP* 89 (emphasis added). See also *PP*, 1, 329
54 SarDesai, *IFP* 95–7
55 *CIM*
56 *Ibid.*
57 *Ibid.*
58 *Ibid.*
59 *Ibid.*
60 *Ibid.*
61 *Ibid.*
62 *Ibid.*
63 *Ibid.*
64 'Memorandum of interview with Menon at Norman Robertson's,' 12 Apr. 1955. Lett Working and Organizational Papers, 1955; Vancouver City Archives, Add. MSS 361, vol. 4B, file 9
65 *CIM*
66 Holmes to Saul Rae, 10 Aug. 1955, Holmes Papers
67 Saul Rae, Hanoi, to Holmes, Ottawa, 15 Aug. 1955, Holmes Papers
68 Two brief notes concerning restriction of ICSC MT investigations and patrols in the south were made regarding narrowed access at Saigon airport and the increased time notice provisions demanded by Diem's government. See paras 35 and 45 of Secretary of State for Foreign Affairs, Government of Great Britain, *Fifth Interim Report of the International Commission for Supervision and Control in Vietnam, 11 August to 10 December 1955* (London: Her Majesty's Stationery Office 1956) Cmd 9706; hereafter, *5th IR.*
69 *CIM*
70 *Ibid.*
71 Holmes to Jules Léger, 2 Sept. 1955, Memorandum for the Under Secretary: Discussions with the State Department on Indochina, Holmes Papers (emphasis added).

72 Holmes in an off-the-record lecture to the Canadian Institute of International Affairs, 1956; Holmes Papers
73 *CIM*
74 *Ibid.*
75 On developments in Laos and Cambodia see Eayrs, *Indochina* 71–124.
76 *CIM*
77 *Ibid.*
78 The Indian aide-mémoire and Nutting's comments are in Allan W. Cameron, *Viet-Nam Crisis* 374–8. See also evidence of agreement with Canadian legal analysis by 'the legal adviser of the British Foreign Office' in Escott Reid, *Envoy to Nehru* 85.
79 *CIM*
80 *Ibid.*
81 *Ibid.*
82 *Ibid.*
83 *Ibid.*
84 *Ibid.*
85 *Ibid.*
86 *Ibid.*
87 See Johnson's remarks in Eayrs, *Indochina* 181.
88 Canada, Department of External Affairs, 'Canada-India Atomic Reactor Project,' *External Affairs* VIII, 5 (May 1956) 113–16
89 See Canada, Department of External Affairs, 'The Colombo Plan,' *External Affairs* VII, 11 (Nov. 1955) 283–7, but esp. 287.
90 *CIM*
91 SarDesai, *Indian Foreign Policy* 99
92 *CIM*
93 On the election, in which 75 per cent of the registered electors voted, Sihanouk's Sankum Riyastr Niyum (Popular Socialist Community) won 83 per cent of the votes cast and all 91 seats in the new National Assembly, see Great Britain, Secretary of State for Foreign Affairs, *Fourth Interim Report of the International Commission for Supervision and Control in Cambodia for the Period April 1 to September 30, 1955* (London: Her Majesty's Stationery Office 1956), Command 967, pp 8–18; hereafter, *4th IR – Cambodia*. On the Cambodia-US military aid agreement and the ensuing DRVN protest, see Great Britain, Secretary of State for Foreign Affairs, *Third Interim Report of the International Commission for Supervision and Control in Cambodia for the period April 1 to July 28, 1955* (London: Her Majesty's Stationery Office 1955), Cmd 9579: hereafter, *3rd IR – Cambodia*.
94 See Annexes I and II in Great Britain, Secretary of State for Foreign Affairs, *Fifth Interim Report of the International Commission for Supervision and Control*

in Cambodia for the period October 1, 1955 to December 31, 1956 (London: Her Majesty's Stationery Office 1957), Command 253, pp 6–15; hereafter, *5th IR – Cambodia*.

95 Eayrs, *Indochina* 272

96 *CIM*; also Eayrs, *ibid*.

97 *CIM*

98 On the public relations work done on Diem's behalf in the American press between 1955 and 1957, see R. Scheer, 'The Genesis of United States Support for Ngo Dinh Diem,' in Gettleman, ed., *Vietnam: History, Documents and Opinions* 285–6

99 J.W. Holmes, 'Canadian Objectives in Indochina,' 30 Nov. 1955: DEA files, 50052-A-40, vol. 19. Long passages from the document may be found in Eayrs, *Indochina* 252–5.

100 J. Léger to L.B. Pearson, 'The Next Move in Vietnam,' 23 Dec. 1955: DEA files, 50052-A-40, vol. 19

101 *Ibid*.

102 A.D.P. Heeney to Ottawa, 6 Jan. 1956: DEA files, 50052-A-40, vol. 19. See Eayrs, *Indochina* 256–7.

103 Heeney to Ottawa, *ibid*.

104 *Ibid*.

105 Holmes advocated the neutralist outcome in a letter to Saul Rae, 5 Dec. 1955, Holmes Papers.

106 Saul Rae to Holmes, 16 Jan. 1956, Holmes Papers

107 *CIM*

108 *Ibid*.

109 *Ibid*.

110 *Ibid*. See Léger's comment on Pentagon pressure on State made in late February 1956 in Eayrs, *Indochina* 229.

111 *CIM*. Public evidence of British opposition before PRCBRVN pressure is to be found in the British Foreign Office statement inserted into the ICSC's *4th IR*. After declaring 'considerable concern' over the failures of the parties in Vietnam, the statement asserted that the British had no 'special responsibilities' for improving the situation arising from status as a co-chairman power. See *4th IR* 2.

112 *CIM*. For French reaction to the request see Foreign Minister Christian Pineau's statement to the Council of the Republic on 23 February 1956, in A.W. Cameron, *Viet-Nam Crisis* 417–18.

113 See Great Britain, Parliament, Papers by Command, *Documents Relating to British Involvement in the Indochina Conflict, 1945–65* (London: Her Majesty's Stationery Office 1965) Cmd 2834, p 118, for the text of the Chinese letter to the British foreign secretary; hereafter, *Documents Relating*.

114 Pham Van Dong to the Geneva Co-Chairman, 14 Feb. 1956, in *Documents Relating* 117

115 *CIM.* Also Eayrs, *Indochina* 229

116 The Soviet message is in *Documents Relating* 118–20.

117 The British response is in *ibid.* 120.

118 *Ibid.* 120–3

119 Guy Beaudry was born in July 1913. He received a BA Hon. in Social Science and Political Economy at the University of Ottawa, 1934; served in the Canadian merchant marine, 1935–7; served with the Canadian Army in 1942 as second lieutenant; served with British intelligence in the UK, North Africa, Italy, and northwestern Europe; joined DEA in December 1946 and served in Santiago, Buenos Aires, and Ottawa prior to posting in Indochina.

120 Guy Beaudry, Saigon, to Holmes, 15 Dec. 1955, Holmes Papers

121 Comments appended to *ibid.*

122 *CIM*

123 *Ibid.*

124 *Ibid.*

125 Ottawa received the text of the declaration by Saigon, made public on 3 April 1956, on 31 March 1956. For the text of the declaration see *Documents Relating* 95–6.

126 See 'Washington Unhappy Over Snag ...' *New York Times,* 10 Feb. 1956.

127 *CIM*

128 *Ibid.;* also J. Holmes to David Johnson, Hanoi, 23 Mar. 1956 (emphasis added), Holmes Papers

129 Canada, Department of External Affairs, 'Canada-India Atomic Reactor Project,' *External Affairs* VIII, 5 (May 1956) 113

130 Fred A. Knelman, *Nuclear Energy: The Unforgiving Technology* (Edmonton: Hurtig 1976) 150

131 'Report of Discussions with Krishna Menon,' 29 Mar. 1956, Holmes Papers

132 ICSC for Vietnam, *Minutes,* 299th Meeting, 2 May 1956

133 Great Britain, Secretary of State for Foreign Affairs, *Vietnam and the Geneva Agreements: Documents Concerning the Discussions between Representatives of Her Majesty's Government and the Government of the Union of Soviet Socialist Republics held in London in April and May 1956, March 30-May 9, 1956* (London: Her Majesty's Stationery Office 1956), Cmd 9763, 10–11; as reprinted in Cameron, *Viet-Nam Crisis* 432–3 (emphasis added); hereafter, *Documents Concerning.*

134 *Documents Concerning* 11; per Cameron, *Viet-Nam Crisis* 434–5 (emphasis added)

135 *Documents Concerning* 12; per Cameron, *Viet-Nam Crisis* 435–6

136 Reprinted in Cameron, *Viet-Nam Crisis* 439

137 Eayrs, *Indochina* 222

138 See Holmes's comments in *ibid.* 177.

139 For evidence recently made available see the collision between Radford and the State Department at *FRUS, 1952–1954* XIII, Part II, 2433. For numerous doctrinal contrasts see Franz Schurmann, *The Logic of World Power* (New York: Random House/Pantheon 1974).

CHAPTER 7: PERCEPTIONS OF AGGRESSION 1954–6

1 See remarks by Joseph Buttinger quoted by Noam Chomsky and Edward S. Herman, *The Political Economy of Human Rights*, 2 vols, *The Washington Connection and Third World Fascism* (Montreal: Black Rose 1979) 302.

2 See, for example, Guenter Lewy, *America in Vietnam* (New York: Oxford University Press 1978) 454.

3 See 'Internal Study Document by Secretary of the Lao Dong Party Committee for the South, Le Duan: "The Path of Revolution in the South," November 1956,' in Gareth Porter, ed., *Vietnam: The Definitive Documentation of Human Decisions*, 2 vols, (Stanfordville, NY: E.M. Coleman 1979) II, 24–9.

4 *CIM*

5 *Ibid.*

6 See 'Ordinance No. 6 ...' II Jan. 1956 in G. Porter, *Vietnam Documentation*, II, 14–15.

7 See Marvin E. Gettleman, ed., *Vietnam: History, Documents and Opinions* 291–6 for the text of Law 10/59.

8 See the 12-volume edition of the Pentagon Papers, *U.S.-Vietnam Relations*, II, IV A5, Table 4, p 25.

9 According to King C. Chen, the Fifteenth Conference of the Central Committee of the Lao Dong party decided to authorize the formation of armed units in the south to attack Diem's regime in January 1959. See Chen's date as cited by Guenter Lewy, in *America in Vietnam* 16–7.

10 *Ibid.* 17. See also Pike, *Viet Cong* 78.

11 Lewy, *ibid.*

12 Daniel Gareth Porter, 'Imperialism and Social Structure in Twentieth Century Vietnam' (unpublished PH D thesis, Cornell University 1976) 250

13 Pham Van Thuyet, 'Government Finance and Economic Development in Viet-Nam with Special Reference to the Impact of US Aid' (unpublished PH D thesis, University of Pennsylvania 1967) 45, as cited by Porter, *ibid.*

14 Porter, *ibid.* 252

15 *Ibid.* 148–50

16 *Ibid.* 260

17 See Toye, *Laos*, chs 5 and 6; also Bernard B. Fall, *Anatomy of a Crisis: The Laotian Crisis of 1960–61* (Garden City, NY: Doubleday 1969) 84–5, III–12.

18 Porter, 'Imperialism and Social Structure' 338

19 On this point see Robert Scigliano, *South Vietnam: Nation under Stress* (Boston: Houghton Mifflin 1964) 53–62.

20 *CIM*; also Dave Richard Palmer, *Summons of the Trumpet* (San Rafael, CA: Presidio 1978) 11–12, for Tran Van Don's comment on initial SVN-RVN desires to set up a counter-insurgency oriented military which were overruled by American MAAG officers; and A. Dommen, *Conflict in Laos* 272, where it is noted that Magsaysay's death precluded the holding of a major conference on 'people's war' under SEATO auspices.

21 See Lett's comments on subversion in Eayrs, *Indochina* 166–7.

22 Lett to Ottawa, 4 May 1955: DEA files, 50052-A-40, vol. 12. See Eayrs, *Indochina* 228 for rather different comments on Endicott.

23 *CIM*

24 *Ibid.*

25 *Ibid.*

26 For background on communist fronts see Carlyle A. Thayer, 'Southern Vietnamese Revolutionary Organizations and the Vietnam Workers' Party: Continuity and Change, 1954–74,' in Joseph J. Zasloff and MacAlister Brown, eds, *Communism in Indochina* (Toronto, London: D.C. Heath-Lexington 1975) 34–7. For the text of the Front's program with its emphasis on realizing the terms of the Final Declaration, see Cameron, *Viet-Nam Crisis* 394–401.

27 *CIM*

28 *CIM*

29 ICSC for Vietnam, *Minutes*, 601st Meeting, 9 Feb. 1961, p 22.

30 *Ibid.*

31 ICSC for Vietnam, *Minutes*, 609th Meeting, 13 June 1961, p 23 (emphasis added)

32 ICSC for Vietnam, *Minutes*, 610th Meeting, 24 June 1961, p 2 (emphasis added)

33 Government of Great Britain, Secretary of State for Foreign Affairs, *Tenth Interim Report of the International Commission for Supervision and Control in Vietnam, February 1, 1959 to January 31, 1960* (London: Her Majesty's Stationery Office 1960) Cmd 1040, p 13, para. 24; hereafter, *10th IR*

34 Government of Great Britain, Secretary of State for Foreign Affairs, *Eleventh Interim Report of the International Commission for Supervision and Control in Vietnam, February 1, 1960 to February 28, 1961* (London: Her Majesty's Stationery Office 1961) Cmd 1551, p 13, para. 32; hereafter, *11th IR*

35 Government of Great Britain, *Special Report to the Co-Chairmen of the Geneva Conference on Indo-China*, (London: Her Majesty's Stationery Office 1962) Cmd 1755, p 7; hereafter, SR-1962

36 *CIM*. This vain expectation was frequently evidenced in American policy debates. See, for example, comments on Walter Robertson and Dean Rusk in Michael Leonard Nacht, 'Vietnam Policy: Some Theoretical Perspectives' (unpublished PH D dissertation, Columbia University 1973) esp. 85–124.

37 Saul Rae, New Delhi, to Holmes, Ottawa, 16 Jan. 1956, Holmes Papers (emphasis added)
38 *CIM*
39 *CIM*
40 Holmes to David Johnson, 23 Mar. 1956, Holmes Papers (emphasis added)
41 See, for example, ICSC for Vietnam, *Minutes*, 294th Meeting, 7 Apr. 1956.
42 *CIM*
43 *CIM*
44 *Ibid.*
45 Text of the British note to the Soviet Foreign Ministry of 9 Apr. 1956 is in Government of Great Britain, Secretary of State for Foreign Affairs, *Documents Relating to the British involvement in the Indo-China Conflict 1945–65* (London: Her Majesty's Stationery Office 1965) Cmd 2834, pp 124–5; hereafter, *Docs Rel.*
46 ICSC for Vietnam, *Minutes*, 316th Meeting, 21 July 1956, Item 3
47 ICSC for Vietnam, *Minutes*, 323rd Meeting, 6 August 1956, pp 2–13
48 J.R. Maybee (Holmes and Léger approving) to Canadian Delegation, Saigon, 'Reduction Team Personnel,' 23 Mar. 1956: DEA files, 50052-A-40, vol. 22
49 Léger to Pearson, 'Memorandum for the Minister,' 3 Aug. 1956: DEA files, 50052-A-40, vol. 28. Appended written comment. See also Eayrs, *Indochina* 279.
50 B. Williams, Hanoi, to Ottawa, 16 May 1956: DEA files, 50052-A-40, vol. 25
51 B. Williams, Hanoi to Ottawa, 'Future of the Commission,' 14 June 1956: DEA files, 50052-A-40, vol. 26
52 Eayrs, *Indochina* 68
53 Williams, 'Future of the Commission,' 14 June 1956

CHAPTER 8: THE PARTISAN COMMISSION IN OPERATION 1956–62

1 Eayrs, *Indochina* 206
2 *Ibid.* 222
3 R. Thakur, 'India's Vietnam Policy, 1946–79,' *Asian Survey* XIX, 10 (Oct. 1979) 961
4 R. Thakur, 'Peacekeeping and Foreign Policy: Canada and India and the International Commission in Vietnam, 1954–1965,' *British Journal of International Studies* VI (1980) 135
5 Data from the *Sixth* through *Eleventh Interim Reports* of the ICSC Vietnam, 11 Dec. 1955–28 Feb. 1961
6 Peter Bachrach and Morton S. Baratz, 'Decisions and Non-Decisions: An Analytical Framework,' *American Political Science Review* LVII (Sept. 1963) 632–42
7 *The Pentagon Papers* (New York Times edition 1971) 23

8 See Eayrs, *Indochina* 229–30.
9 See Williams to Ottawa in *ibid*. 231.
10 See Léger's comments to Pearson of 27 Feb. 1956 in *ibid*. 229.
11 ICSC for Vietnam, *Minutes*, 293rd Meeting, 6 Apr. 1956, pp 1–51
12 Eayrs, *Indochina* 232–3
13 J.R. Maybee (Pearson approving) to Robertson, London, 27 Feb. 1956: DEA files, 50052-A-40, vol. 21
14 Frank H. Golay, Ralph Anspach, M. Ruth Pfanner, and Eliezer B. Ayal, *Underdevelopment and Economic Nationalism in Southeast Asia* (Ithaca, London: Cornell University Press 1969) 402–3
15 *CIM*
16 ICSC for Vietnam, *Minutes*, 304th Meeting, 30 May 1956, p 23
17 *CIM*
18 See Government of Great Britain, Secretary of State for Foreign Affairs, *Sixth Interim Report of the International Commission for Supervision and Control in Vietnam, December 11, 1955 to July 31, 1956*, Cmd 31, p 25; cited hereafter as *6th IR*. Other *Interim Reports* in the same series will be similarly abbreviated.
19 *8th IR* 11
20 *7th IR* 17
21 *Ibid*.
22 ICSC for Vietnam, *Minutes*, 431st Meeting, 20 Sept. 1957, pp 12–13 (emphasis added)
23 See *7th IR* 17, *8th IR* 11, and *9th IR* 13.
24 ICSC for Vietnam, *Minutes*, 442nd Meeting, 8 Nov. 1957, p 9 (emphasis added)
25 ICSC for Vietnam, *Minutes*, 442nd Meeting, 8 Nov. 1957, p 16
26 *Ibid*. 19–20 (emphasis added)
27 ICSC for Vietnam, *Minutes*, 463rd Meeting, 21 Mar. 1958, pp 10–11 (emphasis added
28 ICSC for Vietnam, *Minutes*, 470th Meeting, 14 May 1958, pp 35–8
29 *9th IR* 15
30 SarDesai, *IFP* 107
31 *Ibid*. 108
32 *Ibid*. 111
33 ICSC for Vietnam, *Minutes*, 535th Meeting, 27 June 1959, pp 19, 23
34 ICSC for Vietnam, *Minutes*, 551st Meeting, 17 Nov. 1959, pp 67–70
35 See *9th IR* 13 and *10th IR* 18–19.
36 *11th IR* 17
37 *Ibid*.
38 ICSC for Vietnam, *Minutes*, 571st Meeting, 8 Apr. 1960, pp 10–12 (emphasis added)

39 *Ibid*. 28 (emphasis added)
40 ICSC for Vietnam, *Minutes*, 572nd Meeting, 13 Apr. 1960, pp 7–8
41 See *11th IR* 18.
42 *Ibid*. 26
43 *Ibid*. 25
44 ICSC for Vietnam, *Minutes*, 614th Meeting, 26 July 1961
45 Eayrs, *Indochina* 166–7
46 *Ibid*. 175–6
47 *Ibid*. 172
48 *CIM*
49 Thakur, 'Peacekeeping and Foreign Policy' 133–4
50 See Martin's enthusiastic comments in Eayrs, *Indochina* 125.
51 SarDesai, *IFP* 107–8
52 *CIM*
53 *Ibid*.
54 Quoted in 'Mr. Nehru Visits Ottawa,' *External Affairs* IX, 1 (Jan. 1957) 19
55 *CIM*
56 See note from H.M. Embassy, Moscow, to the Soviet Foreign Ministry, 25 July 1957, in *Docs Rel*. 129. Concerning DRVN repression, Buttinger gives a figure of 10–15 thousand killed and 100–150 thousand imprisoned or deported. See *Dragon Embattled*, II 913–16. Bernard Fall's estimate of those killed, imprisoned, or deported as a result of land reform and peasant revolts is considerably higher. See Fall, *TVN* 188–90, for details of how the 'Hundred Flowers' dissenters were suppressed. But recent evidence indicates that even Buttinger's lower figures may be too high. Edwin E. Moise's careful review of the evidence, much of it manufactured by the Saigon regime's Ministry of Information or its Central Psychological War Service, suggests that only some 5,000 were executed in the course of land reform. See Edwin E. Moise, 'Land Reform and Land Reform Errors in North Vietnam,' *Pacific Affairs* (Spring 1976); also Chomsky and Herman, *The Political Economy of Human Rights*, 2 vols: I 341–5.
57 *CIM*
58 ICSC for Vietnam, *Minutes*, 358th Meeting, 2 Nov. 1956, pp 1–3. Here Parthasarathi postponed the Legal Committee's report for further evaluation.
59 See Williams's statement in *ibid*. 38.
60 For text, see ICSC for Vietnam, *Minutes*, 362nd Meeting, 3 Dec. 1956, Appendix A.
61 ICSC for Vietnam, *6th Informal Meeting: Summary of Decisions*, 11 Dec. 1957
62 For example, see the frustrations of the Canadians in the exchanges contained in ICSC for Vietnam, *Minutes*, 434th Meeting, 8 Oct. 1957, pp 20–2.

63 *CIM*

64 See 'Letter from Pham Van Dong to Ngo Dinh Diem, 7 March 1958,' in Porter, *Vietnam: Definitive Documentation*, II, 35.

65 Buttinger, *Dragon Embattled*, II, 977

66 P.G. Honey per *ibid.*

67 Bernard Fall, *Two Viet-Nams*, 2nd rev. ed (New York, Washington, London: Praeger 1967) 272

68 Buttinger, *Dragon* II, 983

69 This is one of the basic theses of Douglas Pike's *Viet Cong* (Cambridge, MA: MIT Press 1968). See especially chs 3 and 4. Though Philippe Devillers, for one, dissents from the NLF-as-cause-of-insurgency thesis. See his 'The Struggle for the Unification of Vietnam,' *China Quarterly*, IX (Jan.-Mar. 1962).

70 See Sidney Smith's statement to the committee of 6 Dec. 1957, which demonstrated a complete acceptance of DEA's operational consensus on Indochina policy by the new secretary of state for external affairs. Canada, House of Commons, Standing Committee on External Affairs, *Minutes of Proceedings and Evidence*, no. 3, 6 Dec. 1957, p 97; hereafter, SCEA, *MPE*.

71 Canada, House of Commons, *Debates*, 26 Nov. 1957, p 1517

72 Canada, House of Commons, *Debates*, 25 July 1958, p 2701 (emphasis added)

73 ICSC for Vietnam, *Minutes*, 500th Meeting, 8 Jan. 1959, pp 25–7; also *Minutes*, 506th Meeting, 21 Jan. 1959, p 19

74 ICSC for Vietnam, *Minutes*, 515th Meeting, 14 Mar. 1959, pp 3–4; *Minutes*, 517th Meeting 3 Apr. 1959, pp 31–3. See Jean Lacouture, *Between Two Truces* 29 for a brief but quite incomplete account of the affair. Chomsky and Herman in *The Political Economy of Human Rights*, I, 301, uncritically accept Lacouture's unproven charge that there was a massacre at Phu Loi. Erichsen-Brown's initial defence of the RVN occurs in ICSC for Vietnam, *Minutes*, 507th Meeting, 14 Feb. 1959, p 8.

75 J.P. Erichsen-Brown, Saigon to John Holmes, Ottawa, 20 Mar. 1959, Holmes Papers

76 Holmes to Erichsen-Brown, 17 Apr. 1959, Holmes Papers

77 *Ibid.* (emphasis added)

78 Between 1955 and 1962 the industrial labour force in the RVN expanded by only 8,000 through the construction of fewer than a dozen plants. By 1962 the RVN's rice production had surpassed the pre-war production volume, but since the RVN's population was 50 per cent greater than in 1938, this was hardly an achievement. By 1965 the DRVN had over 1,200 plants operating, many of very large scale, probably half of them built before 1961. Only a small proportion of this new industrial base was built through foreign aid. See Buttinger, *Dragon Embattled*, II, 966.

79 See *6th IR* 12–13.
80 For the text of Law 10/59 see Gettleman, *Vietnam: History, Documents and Opinions* 291–6.
81 ICSC for Vietnam, *Minutes*, 537th Meeting, 23 July 1959, pp 10–14 (emphasis added)
82 *Ibid.* 122
83 ICSC for Vietnam, *Minutes*, 552nd Meeting, 24 Nov. 1959, p 24
84 ICSC for Vietnam, *Minutes*, 574th Meeting, 25 Apr. 1960, p 8
85 *Ibid.* 18–20
86 *Ibid.* 22
87 ICSC for Vietnam, *Minutes*, 581st Meeting, 24 June 1960, pp 24–5
88 John G. Diefenbaker, *One Canada: The Years of Achievement, 1957–62* (Toronto: Macmillan 1976) 183. Diefenbaker alleges US pressure on Ottawa to obtain more favourable results in Laos.
89 See 'Telegram from Nolting to Rusk, June 21, 1961,' in Porter, ed., *Vietnam: Definitive Documentation*, II 110–12, esp. III para. 3B.
90 ICSC for Vietnam, *Minutes*, 601st Meeting, 9 Feb. 1961, pp 25–6 (emphasis added)
91 ICSC for Vietnam, *Minutes*, 602nd Meeting, 21 Feb. 1961
92 See 'Memorandum of Conversation Involving Rusk, McNamara, the Joint Chiefs of Staff and Other Officials, April 29, 1961' in *U.S.-Vietnam Relations*, Book II, pp 62–6; reprinted in Porter, ed., *Vietnam: Definitive Documentation*, II, 96–9.
93 See comments on Lansdale in *Pentagon Papers* (Gravel) II 37–41, 43–4; esp. his advocacy of the 'liberal of North Vietnam,' and 'unqualified support for Diem.'
94 *Ibid.* 43–4
95 See 'Memorandum of Conversation' as at Porter, ed., *Vietnam: Definitive Documentation* 96–9.
96 'Telegram from Rusk to Various Embassies,' in *ibid.* 102–4, esp. 103
97 'Telegram from Nolting to Rusk, June 21, 1961,' in *ibid.* 110–12
98 'Telegram from Nolting to Rusk, October 5, 1961,' in *ibid.* 127–8
99 ICSC for Vietnam, *Minutes*, 609th Meeting, 13 June 1961, p 21
100 *Ibid.* 26–7
101 See, for example, ICSC for Vietnam, *Minutes*, 614th Meeting, 26 July 1961; also *Minutes*, 615th Meeting, 26 July 1961, pp 2–24.
102 ICSC for Vietnam, *Minutes*, 652nd Meeting, 2 June 1962, p 5
103 *Ibid.* 5–6
104 Government of Great Britain, Secretary of State for Foreign Affairs, *International Commission for Supervision and Control in Vietnam: Special Report to*

the Co-Chairmen of the Geneva Conference on Indo-China, 13 February 1965,
(London: Her Majesty's Stationery Office 1965), Cmd 2609, pp 12 (para. 3),
and 14–15 (para. 8); hereafter, *IC-SR 1965*
105 ICSC for Vietnam, *Minutes*, 571st Meeting, 8 Apr. 1960, pp 12–13
106 *Ibid.* 28
107 *Ibid.* 11–12
108 *Ibid.* 12–13
109 ICSC for Vietnam, *Minutes*, 572nd Meeting, 13 Apr. 1960, pp 7–8

CHAPTER 9: CONSTRAINING LYNDON JOHNSON 1963–6

1 See Charles Taylor, *Snow Job*, esp. ch. 5; also essays by Clarkson and Steele in
Stephen G. Clarkson *et al.*, *An Independent Foreign Policy for Canada?*
(Toronto: McClelland and Stewart 1968).
2 For Pearson's informal but still careful comments on American Vietnam policy see John A. Munro and Alex I. Inglis, eds, *Mike: The Memoirs of the Rt
Hon. Lester B. Pearson 1957–68*, III (Scarborough, Ontario: Signet/New American Library 1976) 146–58.
3 Marcel Cadieux, *The Canadian Diplomat: An Essay in Definition* (Toronto:
University of Toronto Press, Canadian Institute of International Affairs 1963)
23; and John W. Holmes, *The Shaping of Peace: Canada and the Search for
World Order* 2 vols (Toronto, Buffalo, London: University of Toronto Press
1982) II, 15
4 *Mike*, III, 147
5 *Ibid.* (an excerpt from his Temple University address)
6 Canada, House of Commons, *Debates*, 24 May 1967, pp 529–30
7 Transcript of Prime Minister Pearson's address at Temple University in
accepting their second World Peace Award, Philadelphia, 2 Apr. 1965, p 6;
clipping files of the Canadian Institute of International Affairs Library,
Toronto
8 *Ibid.* 7–8
9 *Ibid.* 9–10 (emphasis added). The phase 'I would not dare' is missing from
the Munro-Inglis version of this portion of the speech. See *Mike*, III, 148.
10 *Ibid.* 11
11 *Ibid.* 8–9
12 Charles Ritchie, 'The Day LBJ Confronted LBP,' *Maclean's*, Jan. 1974
13 See *Mike*, III, 150–1. Kissinger's comment may be found at *White House Years*
(Boston: Little Brown 1979) 43–4.
14 *Mike*, III, 149
15 *Ibid.* 151

16 *Ibid.*
17 Peter Stursberg, *Lester Pearson and the American Dilemma* (Toronto, New York: Doubleday 1980) 223
18 *CIM*: Reid's comment may be found in Stursberg, *Lester Pearson and the American Dilemma* 216.
19 Taylor, *Snow Job* 38–9
20 Stursberg, *Lester Pearson and the American Dilemma* 223–4
21 See Geoffrey Pearson's comment at *ibid.* 217–18.
22 *Ibid.* 216
23 *Ibid.* 218–19
24 Franz Schurmann, *Logic of World Power* 433; also 391–8 for more detail
25 See Joseph Alsop, *New York Times Magazine*, 11 Mar. 1973, p 31; quoted by Schurmann, at *ibid.* 508.
26 *CIM*
27 See Admiral Ulysses S.G. Sharp, US Navy (retired), *Strategy for Defeat: Vietnam in Retrospect* (London, San Rafael, California: Presidio Press 1978) 70–2.
28 *Ibid.* 77
29 *CIM*
30 Schurmann, *Logic* 486, 488
31 *PP*, III 100
32 *Ibid.* 101; see also Sharp, *Strategy* 72–4.
33 Sharp, *ibid.* 73
34 McGeorge Bundy listed this point explicitly as a justification for the half-measure of reprisals. See *PP*, III, 314.
35 Sharp, *Strategy* chs 6–8
36 Schurmann, *Logic* 112; for General LeMay's views in detail see his *America Is in Danger* with Dale O. Smith (New York: Funk and Wagnalls 1968). See also 'Memorandum of Conversation ...' as at Porter, ed., *Vietnam: Definitive Documentation* 96–9.
37 *Aviation Week and Space Technology*, 6 Apr. 1964; as quoted in Schurmann, *Logic* 474. See also Schurmann 480, 484.
38 Schurmann, *Logic* 477
39 See William Shawcross, *Sideshow: Kissinger, Nixon and the Destruction of Cambodia* (New York: Simon and Schuster 1979) esp. chs 18 and 19.
40 *Mike*, III 153–4 (emphasis added)
41 *Ibid.* 154
42 *United States–Vietnam Relations 1945–67*, VI. C.I. Settlement of the Conflict, History of Contacts, Negotiations 1965–1966; as in *Canadian Forum* (Sept. 1973) 10
43 Taylor, *Snow Job* 51

44 On Johnson's insecurities and his compulsive need to be respected and appreciated see Doris Kearns, *Lyndon Johnson and the American Dream* (New York: New American Library/Signet 1977).

45 For a more politically orthodox but less insightful treatment (cf. Schurmann) of the policy vacillations in Washington at this time see Leslie H. Gelb with Richard K. Betts, *The Irony of Vietnam: The System Worked* (Washington: Brookings Institution 1979) 116–24. Gelb was one of Admiral Sharp's principal adversaries in the Office of the Secretary of Defense during the war. Yet another account worth examining is William R. Simons, 'The Vietnam Intervention, 1964–65,' in Alexander L. George, *et al.*, *The Limits of Coercive Diplomacy* (Boston: Little Brown 1971).

46 John Holmes to author, 27 Mar. 1975

47 *CIM*

48 *Ibid.*

49 *Ibid.*

50 Canada, House of Commons, Standing Committee on External Affairs, Minutes of Proceedings and Evidence, no. 1, 10 June 1965, pp 8–9; hereafter cited as SCEA, *MPE.*

51 *Ibid.* 10

52 *Ibid.* 11

53 *Ibid.*

54 *Ibid.*

55 *CIM*

56 SCEA, *MPE*, no. 1, 10 June 1965, pp 15–16

57 *Ibid.* 17–21

58 *CIM*

59 *Debates*, 8 Mar. 1962, p 1605

60 SCEA, *MPE*, no. 1, 10 June 1965, pp 13–14. For NDP attacks on Canadian government support of America's 'illegal and unwise war' in Vietnam, on American 'brinkmanship of the worst kind,' on US client regimes in Asia ('sawdust Caesars who are perpetuating dictatorships without the consent of their subjects'), and on other perceived failures in government policy see *Debates*, 16 Apr. 1964, p 2594; 28 June 1964, p 4752; 5 Aug. 1964, p 6418; 16 Feb. 1965, p 11373.

61 *Debates*, 8 Mar. 1962, p 1604

62 *Ibid.* 1604–5

63 Taylor, *Snow Job* 55–7; Stursberg, *Lester Pearson and the American Dilemma* 255

64 Stursberg, *ibid.* 259

65 18 June 1964, STATE 115 TO AMEMBASSY (TS/EXDIS), SENT JULY 11, 1964, EMBTEL 74, as at *Canadian Forum* (Sept. 1973) 13, para. 16

66 See Mendenhall to U. Alexis Johnson, 1 June 1964, 'Outline of Subjects for Mr Seaborn,' at *ibid.* 12

67 18 June 1964, STATE 115 TO AMEMBASSY at *ibid.* 12

68 *Ibid.* 13, para. 7

69 *Ibid.* 13, para. 8

70 *Ibid.* 13, para. 16

71 *Ibid.* 13, para. 10

72 See 'Remarks of Prime Minister Pham Van Dong to J.B. Seaborn, Hanoi, June 18, 1964,' *ibid.* 15.

73 *Ibid.*

74 See Gareth Porter, *A Peace Denied: The United States, Vietnam and the Paris Agreement* (Bloomington and London: Indiana University Press 1975), 19. Porter's sources include an interview with Tran Van Dinh, one of Diem's diplomats in 1963. He cites as well Mieczyslaw Maneli, 'Vietnam '63 and Now,' *New York Times*, 27 Jan. 1975. See also Porter, ed., *Vietnam: The Definitive Documentation of Human Decision*, 2 vols (Stanfordville, NY: E.M. Coleman Enterprises 1979) II, document 95, p 183. Kissinger confirms this interpretation of events in *White House Years* 231.

75 See SNIE 53-2-64: 'The Situation in South Vietnam,' 1 Oct. 1964, in Porter, *Vietnam Documentation* 322–6.

76 18 June 1964, STATE 115 TO AMEMBASSY in *Canadian Forum* (Sept. 1973) 13, para. 14

77 Stursberg, *Lester Pearson and the American Dilemma* 259

78 Seaborn to Maclear as in the CBC presentation of 29 Oct. 1980, part of Michael Maclear's documentary series, 'The Ten Thousand Day War'

79 17 August 1964, REPORT OF CONVERSATION WITH PRIME MINISTER PHAM VAN DONG – Hanoi, 13 Aug. 1964, in *Canadian Forum*, Sept. 1973, p 16, para. 8

80 See 'Staff Memorandum by the Senate Foreign Relations Committee Staff on the Gulf of Tonkin Incidents,' Jan. 1968 (extracts), as in Porter, *Vietnam Documentation* 486–94. Also relevant is 'Memorandum by William Bundy, September 8, 1964,' which authorized the resumption of De Soto patrols in mid-September but 'beyond the 12-mile limit ... and clearly dissociated from 34A maritime operations.' See Porter, *Vietnam Documentation*, II, 318–9.

81 The Canadians did have access to the totally different DRVN version of the Tonkin Gulf incident via Ha Van Lau's presentation to the ICSC of 13 August 1964. Col. Lau alleged that at 23.40 hours of 30 July US Navy ships shelled two offshore islands from inside DRVN coastal limits. On 1 August T-28 aircraft coming from Laos allegedly bombed a village and border post in Vietnam. On 2 August US Navy AD-6 and more T-28 aircraft hit the post again. On 3 August the 'Turner Joy' intruded 'brazenly' while four small craft hit the coast with

machine-gun fire while under cover of the destroyers. Ambassador Seaborn subsequently expressed Canadian doubts concerning this description citing the US version of events. See ICSC for Vietnam, *Minutes*, 668th Meeting, 13 Aug. 1964, pp 2–6; also *Minutes*, 669th Meeting, 17 Aug. 1964, p 14. The DRVN authorities had little credibility, however, in Canadian eyes given their past record of intentional deception of the international commission.

82 7 Mar. 1965, AMEMBASSY SAIGON 2880 TO SECSTATE WASH DE DC (S/EXDIS), as in *Canadian Forum* (Sept. 1973) 18

83 *CIM*. One liberal-moderate interviewee indicated explicitly that it was 'very reasonable' to assume that important information was passed on to Hanoi leaders.

CHAPTER 10: LIBERAL MODERATION REASSERTED 1966–8

1 20 Mar. 1966, Memorandum of Conversation Subject: Ronning Visit: Hanoi, *United States – Vietnam Relations* VI, C. 1, 'Ronning Missions – March and June 1966,' documents section, p 14; cited hereafter as 'Ronning Missions.' The author gratefully acknowledges the assistance of Charles Taylor in obtaining these documents.

2 See John Holmes's argument in this regard to the House of Commons's Standing Committee on External Affairs and National Defence, Minutes of Proceedings and Evidence, No. 5, 15 Mar. 1973, p 5: 9. For an incisive, detailed treatment of the collision of two concepts of right see Ralph K. White, *Nobody Wanted War: Misperception in Vietnam and Other Wars* (Garden City, NY: Doubleday/Anchor 1970) esp. Part II.

3 For the text of the four points and comments see Gareth Porter, *A Peace Denied* 27. For Kissinger's effective rebuttal see *White House Years* 269–71.

4 See ICSC for Vietnam, *Minutes*, 668th Meeting, 13 Aug. 1964, pp 13–21; 669th Meeting, 17 Aug. 1964, pp 17–23; and 670th Meeting, 18 Aug. 1964, pp 2–13. In a manner indicating great frustration, ambassador M.A. Rahman refused to engage in a debate over the status of the Final Declaration.

5 *CIM*

6 Chester Ronning, *A Memoir of China in Revolution* (New York, Toronto: Pantheon 1974) 250

7 Stursberg, *Lester Pearson and the American Dilemma* 269–71

8 *Ibid.* 270

9 Ronning to author, June 1976

10 *Ibid.*

11 *Ibid.*

12 Ronning, 'Nanking: 1950,' *International Journal* XXII, 3 (Summer 1967) 455–6 (emphasis added)

13 See, for example, House of Commons, Debates, 28 Oct. 1966, p 9236.
14 *CIM*; also Ronning to author
15 Gelb and Betts, *Irony of Vietnam* 126–32
16 *Ibid.* 130–3
17 See *ibid.* 145. Also *Pentagon Papers* (Gravel) II, 369–80; and Robert Shaplen, *The Road from War* (New York, Evanston: Harper and Row 1970) 48–82.
18 David Kraslow and Stuart H. Loory, *The Secret Search for Peace in Vietnam* (New York: Vintage Books 1968), provides detailed information. Taylor in *Snow Job* doubts US motives.
19 DRVN intransigence and Hungarian and Soviet diplomatic duplicity are noted in Janos Radvanyi, *Delusion and Reality: Gambits, Hoaxes and One-Upmanship in Vietnam* (South Bend, ID.: Gateway 1978).
20 Stursberg, *Lester Pearson and the American Dilemma* 276
21 See Lyndon Baines Johnson, *The Vantage Point: Perspectives of the Presidency 1963–1969* (New York: Popular Library 1971) 250.
22 'Arranging the Second Trip: Canada in the Middle,' 'The Ronning Missions,' summary, p 2
23 Pearson quoted from the 1 May speech which was given outside the House at *Debates*, 4 July 1966, p 7123.
24 'The June Visit: No Movement by Either Side,' 'The Ronning Missions,' summary, p 3
25 *Pentagon Papers* (Gravel) IV 5.
26 Stursberg, *Lester Pearson and the American Dilemma* 272
27 Ronning, *Memoir* 266; Stursberg, *ibid.* 267–8
28 Ronning, *ibid.* 267
29 *Ibid.* 268–9
30 'Embassy Ottawa to SECSTATE 981 (SECRET-EXDIS), 31 Jan. 1966,' 'The Ronning Missions,' documents p 3
31 *Ibid.*, summary p 2
32 *Debates*, 4 July 1966, p 7123 (emphasis added)
33 *Ibid.*, 28 Oct. 1966, p 9236. See also *ibid.*, 3 Feb. 1967, p 12, 769; and 10 Feb. 1967, p 13,070; 6 Feb. 1967, pp 12,679–80. Also relevant is Martin to SCEA, MPE, no. 7, 26 Oct. 1967, p 146.
34 Stursberg, *Lester Pearson and the American Dilemma* 280. See also 'The Ronning Missions,' summary p 4.
35 Taylor, *Snow Job* 105–6
36 'Memorandum to the Government of Canada,' 'The Ronning Missions,' documents p 17 (emphasis added)
37 'May 24, 1966 SAIGON TT External 42 Immed DE DELHI,' *ibid.* 22–3
38 Taylor, *Snow Job* 107

39 The text of the Four Points may also be found at SCEA, *MPE*, no. 1, 4 April 1966, pp 41–2.

40 'Saigon 5379 to Secretary of State,' 'The Ronning Missions,' documents, p 25. Taylor omits mention of the Moore-Lau conversations on the NLF altogether.

41 Taylor, *Snow Job* 109

42 Stursberg, *Lester Pearson and the American Dilemma* 280

43 For a detailed exploration of the possible role of the unconscious in policy-making see John D. Steinbruner, *The Cybernetic Theory of Decision* (Princeton, NJ: Princeton University Press 1974) esp. chs 4, 5.

44 The 1 May speech to the World Veterans Federation was read for Pearson by Roger Teillet. See excerpt at *Debates*, 4 July 1966, p 7123.

45 SCEA, *MPE*, no. 1, 4 Apr. 1966, p 21

46 *Ibid.* 22

47 *Ibid.* 29

48 *Debates*, 8 July 1966, p 7426

49 *Ibid.* 7427

50 *CIM* But see also Ronning *Memoir* 149–84

51 John Holmes, 'Alliances in Trouble,' *Canadian Forum* (Aug. 1963) 8–9. Holmes left External Affairs in 1960 and was soon working for the Canadian Institute for International Affairs.

52 Stursberg, *Lester Pearson and the American Dilemma* 273–4

53 *Ibid.* 272–3

54 See comments by both William Bundy and George Ignatieff at *ibid.* 283–5.

55 House of Commons, Standing Committee on External Affairs and National Defence, Minutes of Proceedings and Evidence, no. 23, 21 Apr. 1970, p 23: 17; hereafter SCEAND, *MPE*.

56 S. Clarkson, ed., *An Independent Foreign Policy for Canada?* (Toronto: McClelland and Stewart 1968) is the most comprehensive attack on 'quiet diplomacy.' Lewis Hertzman *et al.*, *Alliances and Illusions: Canada and the NATO-NORAD Question* (Edmonton: Hurtig 1969) provides in some respects a more interesting and varied set of criticisms of the political assumptions made by supporters of the liberal-moderate approach. Hertzman and John Warnock criticize the centre from the left, Dalton Camp and Thomas Hockin from the right. See also Ian Lumsden, ed., *Close the 49th Parallel, etc.: The Americanization of Canada* (Toronto: University of Toronto Press 1970), and John Warnock, *Partner to Behemoth: The Military Policy of a Satellite Canada* (Toronto: New Press 1970), and in a more abstract vein at the other end of the political spectrum George Grant, *Technology and Empire* (Toronto: Anansi 1969.)

57 SCEA, *MPE*, 28 Apr. 1966 p 87

58 *Debates*, 4 Feb. 1966 p 758 (emphasis added)

59 See Martin at SCEA, *MPE*, no. 10, 11 Apr. 1967, p 328; also *Debates*, 13 Feb. 1967, p 12,963.
60 *Debates*, 24 Feb. 1966, p 1707
61 *Ibid.*, 1 Feb. 1967, p 12523
62 See Martin's comments and statistics on aid to the RVN at SCEA, *MPE*, no. 10, 11 Apr. 1967, p 317; also *ibid.*, no. 8, 3 Nov. 1967, pp 180–1; and *ibid.*, no. 9, 9 Nov. 1967, pp 198, 214–15.
63 SCEA, *MPE*, no. 3, 28 Apr. 1966, p 82; also, *ibid.*, no. 11, 13 Apr. 1967, p 342
64 *Debates*, 26 Jan. 1967, p 12, 260. The Quakers did run into difficulties, however, in 1967 when Canadian customs officials insisted that Quaker medical shipments sent to Canada for trans-shipment to the DRVN have American export permits. Goods were turned back when the permits were not provided.
65 SCEA, *MPE*, no. 11, 13 Apr. 1967, p 356
66 *Ibid.*, no. 10, 11 Apr. 1967, p 305
67 *Ibid.* 306
68 *Ibid.*
69 See Gordon Churchill's remarks at SCEA, *MPE*, no. 6, 4 July 1967, p 122.
70 T.C. Douglas to the Commons; see *Debates*, 8 July 1966, p 7428.
71 See Drury at *ibid.*, 5 Oct. 1966, p 8329.
72 *Ibid.*, 1 Feb. 1967, p 12,520
73 *Ibid.*, 14 Mar. 1966, p 2983
74 *Ibid.*, 29 Aug. 1966, p 7765
75 *Ibid.*, 5 Oct. 1966, p 8329
76 *Ibid.*, 18 Jan. 1967, p 11,945
77 *Ibid.*, 7 Feb. 1967, p 12,755
78 *Ibid.*
79 *Ibid.*, 13 Feb. 1967, p 12,966
80 *Ibid.* 12,967
81 *Ibid.* 13,988
82 *Ibid.* 12,922, 12,991
83 *Ibid.* 12,922
84 *Ibid.*
85 *Ibid.* 12,995
86 Rt Hon. L.B. Pearson, 'Canada, the United States and Vietnam,' Department of External Affairs, Information Division, *Statements and Speeches*, no 67/8, 10 Mar. 1967. The speech is reprinted in J.L. Granatstein, ed., *Canadian Foreign Policy since 1945* (Toronto: Copp Clark 1969) 135–7.
87 See Martin to the Standing Committee on External Affairs; SCEA, *MPE*, no. 11, 13 Apr. 1967, p 369
88 *Ibid.*

89 From 1959 to 1980 Canadian industry exported some $4.9 billion in commodities to the United States. For recent comments regarding the economic and technological significance of the DPS Agreements, see the testimony pursuant to NORAD renewal discussions at SCEAND, *MPE*, 25 Nov. 1980, pp 25:29–25:48

90 See Douglas' comment at *Debates*, 13 Feb. 1967, p 12,991.

91 According to Canadian Institute of Public Opinion data, 44 per cent of Canadians approved of American handling of the war in July 1965, while 33 per cent disapproved. Among those with university education 51 per cent approved, and only 25 per cent disapproved (CIPO release 24 July 1965). By May 1966 after one year of 'sustained reprisals' bombing of the DRVN only 35 per cent approved while 34 per cent disapproved of American handling of the war (CIPO release 21 May 1966). Still more telling is the fact that the number of Canadians advocating American continuation of the war dropped from 66 per cent to 45 per cent between June 1965 and June 1966, while the percentage advocating withdrawal 'within the next few months' rose from 20 to 35 (CIPO release 29 June 1966). By November 1967 after further escalation of the air war over the DRVN the number of those favouring withdrawal, 41 per cent, was almost twice as high as those favouring escalation, 23 per cent, while those favouring the present 'present level of fighting' declined from 18 per cent in the fall of 1966 to 16 per cent by Nov. 1967. Those who had no opinion declined from 24 to 20 per cent in the same period. In Quebec 52 per cent of respondents favoured withdrawal (CIPO release 4 Nov. 1967).

92 A bombing pause chronology is provided at Johnson, *The Vantage Point* 578. For Canadian statements of regret see: Martin's comments noting Canadian advocacy of bombing pauses at 'appropriate' times, *Debates*, 28 May 1965, p 1778; Martin's reply to Diefenbaker at *ibid.* 4 Feb. 1966, p 758; Martin noting the government's belief in the advantages of a prolonged cessation of bombing; and finally, Pearson's reply to T.C. Douglas at *ibid.*, 30 June 1966, p 7081.

93 *Ibid.*, 1 Feb. 1966, p 1516

94 See Pearson to the Commons at *ibid.*, 29 June 1966, pp 7017–18.

95 See Martin to SCEA, *MPE*, no. 10, 11 Apr. 1967, p 322

96 *Debates*, 8 July 1966, p 7424

97 *Ibid.*

98 *Canadian News Facts 1967* (Toronto) 6

99 The first issue of *Canadian Dimension* featured 'The Crisis in South Vietnam' (see 25 Aug. 1963, pp 7–9). Coverage thereafter was regular. See 'Ending the War' (Mar.-Apr. 1965) 3–5; 'What Every Canadian Should Know about Vietnam' (May-June 1965) 3–7; John Warnock, 'Canadian Policy in Vietnam: "Ready Aye Ready"' (May-June 1965) 19–20; 'What Every Canadian Should Know about Vietnam – Part II' (July-August 1965) 3–5; 'The Ugly Canadian'

(July-Aug. 1965) 10–11; Eman Thor, 'Open End: China, USSR, Vietnam' (July-Aug. 1965) 24; and the entire issue July-Aug. 1966, esp. 'An Open Letter to Lester B. Pearson,' by Cy Gonick

Relevant articles in *Canadian Forum*, not all of them negative towards government policy, include: Charles Hanly, 'The Toronto Teach-In' (Sept. 1965) 130–1; Paul Fox, 'The Teach-In: Education or Propaganda? (1),' and R.J. Madden, 'Education or Propaganda (2)' (Nov. 1965) 172–4; contributions by A. Rotstein, M.H. Watkins, D. Ward, M. Pilisuk, A. Pape, and R.C. Pratt in Nov. 1965; A. Rotstein, 'Pearson's Choice' (July 1966) 76; M.M. Thompson, 'Quaker Medical Aid to Vietnam' (Nov. 1966) 169–70; S. Clarkson and A. Rotstein, 'China Teach-in: The Ivory Microphone' (July 1966) 176–9.

100 A detailed record of Hord's activities and his influence on attitudes within the United Church may be found at the Church archives in Emmanuel College, Victoria College, University of Toronto.

101 From Hord's 'The Christian Conscience and War in Vietnam,' a statement to Warren Gerrard of the *Globe and Mail* of 7 Aug. 1965. The text may be found in File 305, Board of Evangelism and Social Service, United Church Archives, Emmanuel College, Victoria University, Toronto. Victoria College (one and the same institution as Victoria University) was Lester Pearson's alma mater.

102 Rev. and Dr H.G. Forster, Welland, Ont., to Hord 7 Aug. 1965, in File 305, *ibid.*

103 'Larry,' Trinity Church, Simcoe, Ontario, to Hord, n.d., File 306, *ibid.*

104 Rev. Bruce Underhill, Hamilton, to Hord, 22 Feb. 1966, File 306, *ibid.*

105 File 305, *ibid.*

106 J.R. Hord to United Church Ministers in the Pastorate, 5 Feb. 1966, File 306, *ibid.*

107 Hord to J.W. Norman, Clerk of Session, St Luke's United Church, Islington, Ont., File 309, *ibid.*

108 A November 1968 survey indicated that 32 per cent of Canadians had sympathy for American 'draft-dodgers,' 47 per cent had no sympathy, while 21 per cent characterized their views as 'qualified' or 'undecided.' Among those with university education 33 per cent had sympathy, 53 per cent no sympathy, and only 14 per cent declared themselves to be qualified or undecided (CIPO data released 23 Nov. 1968).

109 *Debates*, 8 July 1966, pp 7428–31

110 See speeches by Andrew Brewin and Colin Cameron of the NDP and by the atypically anti-war PC MP Terry Nugent at *ibid.*, 11 July 1966, pp 7474–86. For detailed statistical information concerning the evidence of the conflict about which they were protesting see Guenter Lewy, *America in Vietnam* (New

York: Oxford University Press 1978) esp. chs 2, 3, 7, and 9. Also relevant is
Jonathan Schell, *The Village of Ben Suc* (New York: Knopf 1967).

111 *Debates*, 17 Nov. 1966, p 9997
112 *Ibid.*, 24 Nov. 1966, p 10,927–8
113 *Ibid.*, 11 Jan. 1967, p 11,666
114 SCEA, *MPE*, no. 10, 11 Apr. 1967, p 306
115 *Ibid.*
116 *Debates*, 13 Feb. 1967, pp 12,965–6
117 SCEA, *MPE*, no. 10, 11 Apr. 1967, pp 312–13
118 *Ibid.* 314
119 *Ibid.*, no. 11, 13 Apr. 1967, p 369
120 See Denis Smith, *Gentle Patriot: A Political Biography of Walter Gordon* (Edmonton: Hurtig 1973) 323.
121 *Ibid.* 401, no. 75; see also Walter L. Gordon, *A Political Memoir* (Toronto: McClelland and Stewart 1977) 281. For Steele's views see his contribution to Clarkson, *An Independent Foreign Policy for Canada?*; and *Rationale for War in Vietnam* (Willowdale, Ont.: The Conference on Canada's Role in Vietnam, n.d.) with an introduction by Kenneth McNaught, Department of History, University of Toronto.
122 Gordon, *ibid.* 281–2
123 *Ibid.* 283
124 *Ibid.* 284
125 See excerpts from editorials at *ibid.* 283–4. Gordon states that he received over 1,200 letters concerning the speech, 97 per cent in his favour.
126 Smith, *Patriot* 325
127 *Ibid.*
128 *Debates*, 24 May 1967, pp 529–30
129 *Ibid.* 531 (emphasis added)
130 *Ibid.*, 12 Feb. 1968, p 6608
131 See Pearson, *Mike*, III, 151, 153, and esp. p 155 concerning Johnson's comments to Pearson and Martin on resisting the 'superhawks' in the spring and summer of 1967.
132 See Martin's reference in this regard at *Debates*, 8 Feb. 1966, p 928.
133 According to Geoffrey Pearson, Johnson flew in to Harrington Lake for a three-hour visit and spent three-quarters of the time arguing over Vietnam in a rather irrational fashion. See Stursberg, *Lester Pearson and the American Dilemma*, 286; and Pearson's more guarded comments in this regard in *Mike*, III, 155–8.
134 See Admiral Sharp's account of the immediate and 'constructive' effect of the hearings on Johnson's bombing policy at *Strategy for Defeat* 187–98, esp. p 194.

135 *Pentagon Papers* (Gravel), IV, pp 13, 195
136 *CIM*; see also *Debates*, 29 Sept. 1967, p 2646; and SCEA, *MPE* no. 7, 26 Oct. 1967, p 134
137 As quoted in 'Canada Says Bombing Should Stop,' *Canadian News Facts 1967* (Toronto) 147
138 As quoted in 'Canadian Peace Plan Rejected,' *ibid.* 62
139 *CIM*
140 Pearson, *Mike*, III, 158
141 *Ibid.* 156 (emphasis added)
142 *Ibid.* 158 (emphasis added)
143 United States, Department of Defense, *United States–Vietnam Relations, 1945–1967*, IV, c. 7b, p 98; as quoted by Sharp, *Strategy for Defeat* 196–7
144 *US-Vietnam*, IV, c. 7b, p 101; as in Sharp, *ibid.* 198
145 *Pentagon Papers* (Gravel) IV, 168
146 Quoted by George Ignatieff, 'Canadian Foreign Policy in an Interdependent World,' *Spectrum* I, 4 (Toronto: Canadian Imperial Bank of Commerce 1981) 3
147 Diefenbaker and W.B. Nesbitt were vigorous proponents of the Munich analogy and the domino theory in 1965 for the PC party; see *Debates*, 2 Apr. 1965, p 13,093 and 28 May 1965, p 1,785. Gordon Churchill recommended that the government massively increase economic and medical assistance to the RVN/US/Commonwealth side, send military observers to study techniques of war, increase the Canadian contribution to NATO so as to free US troops for action in Southeast Asia; *Debates*, 3 Feb. 1966, pp 666–79. Fred Bigg actually said he was ready to go to Vietnam 'as a free Canadian citizen ready to fight for the things he believes in and ready to pay the price'; *ibid.*, 8 Feb. 1966, p 894. Bigg took an atypically extreme anti-communist position among the PC caucus members. After the onset of the POL strikes in July 1966, PC ardour in supporting the US cause waned dramatically. Only 'systemists' like Bigg or Robert Thompson of the Social Credit party continued to argue forcefully on behalf of US government actions. See *ibid.*, 11 July 1966, pp 7468–73; and *ibid.*, 12 Oct. 1967, pp 3036–40.
148 *CIM*
149 *Ibid.*
150 See Heath Macquarrie at *Debates*, 3 Feb. 1966, p 691; Gordon Churchill at *ibid.* 668, 679; John McIntosh at *ibid.*, 4 Feb. 1966, p 859.
151 See Churchill at *ibid.*, 8 Feb. 1966, p 923; and more emphatically at *ibid.*, 11 Feb. 1966, p 1073.
152 According to CIPO data Martin was the front-runner in the race to succeed Pearson as leader of the Liberal party in 1966–7.
153 See John Steinbruner, *Cybernetic Theory of Decision* 133–5.

154 *Ibid.* 128–31

155 See, for example, CIPO release of 15 Apr. 1967 in which respondents characterized Liberal foreign policy as 'sound' three times more frequently than PC
foreign policy, and eight times more frequently than NDP foreign policy.

CHAPTER 11: THE 'NEW' NATIONAL INTEREST VERSUS
TRADITIONAL LIBERAL-MODERATE DOCTRINE: THE ICCS REPLAY 1973

1 *Canadian News Facts 1968* 50. The best summary of Trudeau's foreign policy
proclivities at this time is to be found in Bruce Thordarson, *Trudeau and Foreign Policy: A Study in Decision-Making* (Toronto: Oxford University Press
1972).

2 Pearson to 'Face the Nation,' 21 Apr. 1968. Pearson resigned on 20 April but
the interview was videotaped on 19 April. See *Canadian News Facts 1968* 60.

3 See Trudeau at *Debates*, 1 Nov. 1968, p 2293.

4 See, for example, Martin to the House of Commons at *Debates*, 4 Feb. 1966,
p 758; Martin on the hedges to Canadian willingness 'to cooperate fully in the
constitution of a new supervisory force,' *ibid.* 13 Feb. 1967, p 12,965; Martin to
the Standing Committee on External Affairs advocating a new Canadian role
'within the limits of our capacity,' in SCEA, *MPE*, no. 10, 11 Apr. 1967, p 307;
and Martin's detailed list of qualifications on future participation in SCEA,
MPE, no. 10, 11 Apr. 1967, p 325.

5 Canada, Secretary of State for External Affairs, *Pacific: Foreign Policy for
Canadians* (Ottawa: Information Canada 1970) 6. The first draft of this part
of the foreign policy review was written by a long-time departmental liberal-
moderate, Arthur R. Menzies. *CIM*

6 *Pacific* 8

7 *Ibid.* 20, 24

8 See Richard Nixon, *The Memoirs of Richard Nixon*, 2 vols (New York: Warner
1978) I, 580.

9 For examples of NDP pressure for government criticism of American actions
see comments by T.C. Douglas at *Debates*, 1 May 1970, pp 6502–37; A. Brewin
and L. Nystrom, *ibid.*, 4 May 1970, pp 6517–18.

10 Some 51 per cent of Canadians felt that American intervention in Indochina
was a 'mistake' by February 1972; only 27 per cent did not. Some 59 per cent
of those with university education felt it was a mistake. See CIPO release of 5
Feb. 1972.

11 See Andrew Brewin et al., 'Foreign Policy for Canadians: Comments on the
White Paper,' *Behind the Headlines*, vol. 29, nos 7–8, Aug. 1970; esp. p 13 for
the comments on the Pacific sector paper by Gilles Lalande.

12 For example, see CIPO release of 5 Apr. 1972.
13 *Foreign Policy for Canadians* (General) (Ottawa 1970) 8
14 Sharp to the Commons; see *Debates*, 12 Sept. 1968, p 274.
15 *Ibid.*, 24 Sept. 1968, p 386
16 *Ibid.*, 1 Nov. 1968, p 2293; also *ibid.*, 4 Nov. 1968, p 2364
17 See *Ibid.*, 12 Nov. 1968, p 2632; also *ibid.*, 25 Nov. 1969, p 3129.
18 See David Lewis, *ibid.*, 25 Nov. 1969, p 1203; 1 Dec. 1969, p 1849; 1 May 1970, pp 6488–91. Gordon Fairweather's comments are in *ibid.*, 1 Dec. 1969, pp 1848–9; Stanfield's in *ibid.*, 1 May 1970, pp 6460, 6491–3.
19 See *ibid.*, 1 May 1970, p 6494.
20 See Kissinger, *White House Years* (Boston, Toronto: Little Brown 1979) 247–9; also William Shawcross, *Sideshow: Kissinger, Nixon and the Destruction of Cambodia* (New York: Simon and Schuster 1979) 93–5.
21 See Sharp to the Commons at *Debates*, 8 Feb. 1971, p 3137. See also David Van Praagh, 'Canada and Southeast Asia,' in Peyton V. Lyon and Tareq Y. Ismael, eds. *Canada and the Third World* (Toronto: Macmillan/Maclean-Hunter 1976) 313.
22 See *Debates*, 12 Feb. 1971, p 3326; *ibid.*, 4 Mar. 1971, p 3946; also *ibid.*, 17 Mar. 1971, p 4347.
23 Kissinger, *White House Years* 179. Kissinger was already on record favouring a negotiated end to the war on tolerable political grounds. See his 'The Viet Nam Negotiations,' *Foreign Affairs* XLVII, 2 (Jan. 1969) 211–34, for a truly remarkable analysis which foreshadowed all his actions in office.
24 *White House Years* 183–4, 188; also John Newhouse, *Cold Dawn: The Story of SALT* (New York, Chicago, San Francisco: Holt Rinehart Winston 1973) 164–5
25 Schurmann, *Logic of World Power* 550–6; also Nixon, *Memoirs*, 1, 581–3.
26 See Frank Snepp, *Decent Interval* (New York: Random House 1977) 21.
27 Combat death figures at Shawcross, *Sideshow* 172. ARVN figures are said to be less reliable.
28 See 'Canadians Protest U.S. War,' *Canadian News Facts 1970* 449–53; also MP George Muir's reference to events in Blaine being caused by 'a large group of hoodlums, queers and just plain fools,' in *Debates*, 11 May 1970, p 6793.
29 See Andrew Brewin in *Debates*, 8 Feb. 1971, p 3137.
30 *Ibid.*, 4 May 1970, p 6517
31 *Ibid.*, 15 June 1971, p 6706; 16 June 1971, p 6806
32 *Ibid.*, 15 June 1971, p 6706
33 *Ibid.*, 16 June 1971, p 6806
34 *Ibid.*, 16 June 1971, p 6770
35 *Canadian News Facts 1971* 661
36 Van Praagh, 'Canada and Southeast Asia' 313

37 See *International Canada*, 13 Oct. 1972, 190–1

38 ICSC for Vietnam, *Minutes*, 770th Meeting, 13 Mar. 1973, p 4

39 *Ibid.* 45. By this time some $10 million was owed to Canada for expenses incurred in ICSC duties. See James Anderson, 'What the Old ICC Taught Canada,' *Globe and Mail*, 13 Mar. 1973, p 7.

40 *Debates*, 17 Apr. 1972, pp 1347–8; 26 Apr. 1972, p 1649

41 *Ibid.*, 9 May 1972, pp 2084–5; 15 May 1972, p 2250

42 See the Hon. Mitchell Sharp, Secretary of State for External Affairs, *Viet-Nam: Canada's Approach to Participation in the International Commission of Control and Supervision October 25, 1972–March 27, 1973* (Ottawa: Information Canada 1973) 1. Hereafter cited as Sharp, *Viet-Nam*. These principles were apparently formally approved by Cabinet in early 1971; see Kim Richard Nossal, 'Canada and the International Commission of Control and Supervision' (unpublished MA dissertation, University of Toronto 1974) 13–15 (hereafter cited as Nossal, 'Canada and the ICCS'). The 1970 list of qualifications may be compared with Trudeau's statement two years earlier that 'Canada will do all it can to play a role in re-establishing peace in that area.' See *Globe and Mail*, 14 May 1968.

43 Kissinger, *White House Years* 1344–5

44 Kissinger's first elaboration of the separation concept may be found in his 'Viet-Nam Negotiations' 231–2.

45 Nixon, *Memoirs*, I 487–8

46 On the DRVN leadership's approach at this time see Porter, *A Peace Denied* 115.

47 Nixon, *Memoirs*, I, 488 (emphasis in original)

48 CIM

49 CIM

50 Sharp, *Viet-Nam* 4

51 Nossal, 'Canada and the ICCS' 18–19. Marcel Cadieux, Canadian ambassador to Washington, met with William Rogers on 26 October 1972. Other officials took Sullivan's briefing. See Taylor, *Snow Job* 145–7.

52 On the contingency plans see *Globe and Mail*, 28 Oct. 1972. On the planning record see Brigadier Bell to Bentley at Lorne William Bentley, 'Canada and Vietnam: Open Mouth Diplomacy, 1972–73' (unpublished MA thesis, University of Western Ontario 1973) 23. See also Taylor, *Snow Job* 149, re the alleged enthusiasm at DND.

53 Canada, Department of External Affairs, communique no. 78, 2 Nov. 1972; as at Nossal, 'Canada and the ICCS' 20–1

54 *Ibid.*

55 *Ibid.*

56 See Taylor, *Snow Job* 145; also Nossal, 'Canada and the ICCS' 25–8.

57 This argument is at the core of Kissinger's 'The Viet Nam Negotiations,' and is a constant theme in *White House Years*.

58 Tad Szulc, *The Illusion of Peace: Foreign Policy in the Nixon Years* (New York: Viking 1978); cited hereafter as Szulc, *Illusion of Peace*

59 Nossal, 'Canada and the ICCS' 28–33

60 Kissinger, *White House Years* 1366

61 *Ibid.* 1419

62 Lewy, *America in Vietnam* 406–8

63 *Ibid.* 409

64 See Schurmann on the strategic rationale behind this shift at *Logic of World Power* 543–5.

65 Lewy, *America in Vietnam* 411. See also 'New Arms, More Bombs,' and 'Why U.S. Bombing Is More Accurate Now,' *Time*, 5 June 1972, pp 31–3.

66 Kissinger, *White House Years* 1448

67 See 'Public Protests U.S. Vietnam Bombing,' in *Canadian News Facts 1972* 939.

68 *Debates*, 5 Jan. 1973, p 29

69 Lewy, *America in Vietnam* 412

70 Kissinger, *White House Years* 1461

71 *Ibid.*

72 See the UPI story, 'U.S. Rules Out Use of Nuclear Weapons in North Viet Nam,' *Toronto Star*, 13 Jan. 1973, p 10. Nixon had previously executed a similarly ambiguous manoeuver (if indeed it was a calculated ploy also) when he made a half-hearted denial of any intention to bomb the DRVN's dike system, an act which could have caused from 1 to 2 million deaths had it been carried out. See Nixon's apparently purposefully ambiguous comments at Szulc, *The Illusion of Peace* 548.

73 *New York Times*, 1 May 1975, p 16; also see 'Letters Say Nixon Promised to Fight,' *Toronto Star*, 1 May 1975.

74 Gareth Porter, *A Peace Denied* 161–2. See also Michael Maclear, *The Ten Thousand Day War, Vietnam: 1945–1975* (Toronto, New York, London, Sydney: Methuen 1981) 309–11.

75 *Globe and Mail*, 9 Jan. 1973; as at Nossal, 'Canada and the ICCS' 34–5

76 *Debates*, 5 Jan. 1973, pp 30–1

77 Taylor, *Snow Job* 157–8. By late 1972 when this offer was made there were probably only some twenty Canadians serving in Indochina from the Canadian Forces. See SCEAND, *MPE*, no. 3, 3 Mar. 1975, Appendix 'C,' p 3:26.

78 SCEAND, *MPE*, no. 5, 15 Mar. 1973, p 5:7.

79 *Ibid.* 5:8, 5:10, 5:14

80 See 'Former Diplomat Says Canada Has a Duty to Supervise Truce,' *Toronto Star*, 24 Jan. 1973, p 10.

81 See 'Is Canada the U.S. Patsy in Vietnam?' *Globe and Mail*, 17 Apr. 1973, p 7. See also the editorial comment that the US government was using trade talks resumption to pressure Ottawa into agreeing to an ICCS role at 'No U.S. Pres-

sure?' *Montreal Star*, 19 Dec. 1972. David Van Praagh notes without citing any source that President Nixon telephoned Trudeau just prior to the qualified acceptance of 24 January and a second time just prior to the official declaration of Canadian intent to withdraw. See his 'Canada and Southeast Asia' 331.

82 *Debates*, 24 Jan. 1973, p 596

83 *Ibid.* 597

84 See John Gellner, 'Would Canada Help Police a Cease-Fire?' *Globe and Mail*, 27 Oct. 1972.

85 For such negative assessments of the ICCS role see: 'Policing Viet Nam: A Thankless Task,' *Toronto Star*, 3 Nov. 1972; James Eayrs, 'Canada Must Tell U.S. We're Staying Out of Viet-Nam,' *Toronto Star*, 6 Dec. 1972; Peter Desbarats, 'Viet Nam Policeman: A Job We Don't Want,' *Toronto Star*, 18 Jan. 1973, p 8; 'The Second Time Around,' *Time*, 29 Jan. 1973. For more details on intra-departmental reservations about participation see Jack Cahill, 'Viet Nam Peace-keeping: Ottawa Fears Involvement Means Just Another "Farce",' *Toronto Star*, 15 Jan. 1973, p 9.

86 Porter, *A Peace Denied* 221. Taylor accuses Gauvin of unjustifiable arrogance and impatience in *Snow Job* 159. Van Praagh was not happy with Gauvin's general deportment either, especially his habit of wearing a cap with the word 'BOSS' emblazoned on it. See 'Canada and Southeast Asia' 320.

87 James Anderson, 'Canada Out, ICCS Heads into Limbo,' *Globe and Mail*, 1 Aug. 1973; Stephen Scott, 'Canadians Shed Their Neutralist Views ...' *Toronto Star*, 21 July 1973; Mark Gayn, 'Canada's the Loser ...' *Toronto Star*, 21 July 1973; James Anderson, 'Canada's ICCS Head Leaves Saigon Post,' *Globe and Mail* 20 July 1973; 'Michel Gauvin: An Unquiet Canadian in Saigon,' *Time*, 9 Apr. 1973

88 See, for example, the CIPO poll of 7 April 1973 in which 53 per cent of the sample approved of the ICCS role and 39 per cent disapproved. Among the university-educated the ratio in favour was 71 to 25. Although the question did not specifically ask for assessment of Canadian performance to that point presumably any dissatisfaction would have shown up indirectly.

89 Indar J. Rikhye, Michael Harbottle, Bjorn Egge, *The Thin Blue Line* (New Haven, London: Yale University Press 1974) 199

90 See Cahill, 'Viet Nam Peacekeeping ..."Farce,"' *Toronto Star*, 15 Jan. 1973, p 9 on the DRVN estimate of numbers required for ICCS duty. On the initial figure proposed by the US side see Szulc, *The Illusion of Peace* 657. Both figures are confirmed at 'Nixon's Blitz Leads Back to the Table,' *Time*, 8 Jan. 1973, p 11.

91 Text of the Agreement and Protocols as in Porter, *A Peace Denied* 319–49

92 See 'Declaration of the International Conference on Viet Nam,' Article 7(b), emphasis added.

93 John Best, 'Vietnam Affair: Ottawa Gets a Lesson in How the U.S. Doesn't Listen,' *Globe and Mail*, 24 July 1973

94 ICCS Protocol, Art. 12. For evidence of violation of this provision through gross mistreatment of Capt. Ian Patten and Capt. Fletcher Thomson during 17 days of imprisonment by PRG forces see 'Freed Canadians Say Viet Cong Treated Them as U.S. Spies,' and 'We Were Bound ... with a Noose around Our Necks,' *Toronto Star*, 16 July 1973, pp 1, 9; also James Anderson, 'Marched with Arms Tied, Nooses round Necks ...' *Globe and Mail*, 16 July 1973 p 1.

95 See 'Neutrality Violations Led to Pullout: Gauvin,' *Globe and Mail*, 30 May 1973, for the Canadian commissioner's comments at his farewell press conference in Saigon.

96 See Tom Wicker, who provides a figure of $3.5 billion in 'The Dark Shadow of Secret Diplomacy,' *Montreal Star*, 9 May 1977. Tad Szulc mentions a figure of $4.75 billion in *The Illusion of Peace* 669, as does Frank Snepp, a former senior CIA official in Saigon, in his *Decent Interval* (New York: Random House 1977) 51.

97 Porter, *A Peace Denied* 219

98 See 'Hungary Attacks Canada "Inaction"' *Globe and Mail*, 30 July 1973.

99 Robert Randle, 'Peace in Vietnam and Laos, 1954, 1962, 1973,' *ORBIS* XVIII, 2 (Summer 1974) 875

100 T.W. Lippmann, 'Cambodia: Bad Omens Are Everywhere,' *Toronto Star*, 13 Jan. 1973

101 Shawcross, *Sideshow*, 164; see also 'Ex-Cambodia Ruler Vows to Fight On,' *Toronto Star*, 22 Jan. 1973. An excellent short summary of the deterioration in DRVN–Khmer Rouge relations in the 1973–6 period may be found at Keesing's *Contemporary Archives*, 27 Oct. 1978, pp 29, 269–70.

102 Shawcross, *Sideshow* 281

103 *Ibid.*, 265–72

104 See 'Canada Agrees to Help Observe Truce in Laos, Cambodia,' *Toronto Star*, 14 Feb. 1973. According to Arthur Andrew, Director General of the Bureau of Asian and Pacific Affairs, Canada was owed some $2 million for services on the ICSC for Vietnam. SCEAND, *MPE*, no. 1, 1 Mar. 1973, p 1:15.

105 See 'Cambodian ICC Urged to Reconvene,' *Ottawa Journal*, 21 July 1973.

106 See 'Shaky Start in Vietnam,' *Time*, 12 Feb. 1973.

107 For the text of the bilateral communiqué issued at the end of the Kissinger visit see Porter, *A Peace Denied* 346.

108 See Szulc, *Illusion of Peace* 677; also 'Laos PM Gives in, Communists Dictate Terms of Cease Fire,' *Toronto Star*, 22 Feb. 1973.

109 'Canadians Are Being Shot at in Helicopters in Viet Nam,' *Toronto Star*, 26 Feb. 1973; also Michel Gauvin to External Affairs, Ottawa, 'ICCS: Progress Report for SSEA Visit: Part II,' 26 Mar. 1976 as at Sharp, *Viet-Nam* 46. Gauvin notes three separate attempts at helicopter shoot-downs. In 'ICCS

Helicopters in Vietnam Grounded ...' *Globe and Mail*, 1 Mar. 1973, James Anderson notes four incidents in four days. Use of the SA-7 was noted at Jack Cahill, 'Our Young Diplomats on the Viet Nam Force Keep Cool under Fire,' *Toronto Star*, 3 Mar. 1973, p 22.

110 See 'Communists Reject Canadian Proposals to Guarantee Peace,' and William Frye, ''12 Nations Seek the Formula for a Lasting Viet Peace,' *Toronto Star*, 26 Feb. 1973.

111 Leo Ryan, 'Hopes Dim for Plan Proposed by Sharp,' *Globe and Mail*, 1 Mar. 1973

112 See 'Canada Will Sign Peace Pact – With Reservations,' *Toronto Star*, 1 Mar. 1973.

113 Leo Ryan, 'Sharp Disappointed but Signs Statement on Vietnam Policy,' *Globe and Mail*, 2 Mar. 1973; and 'Midnight Deals,' *Time*, 12 Mar. 1973, p 13. When back in Ottawa, Sharp declared that he had obtained 'a fair amount of support including that of the Americans, the British and others.' SCEAND, *MPE*, no. 3, 6 Mar. 1973, p 3:15.

114 Don Stevenson, 'Sharp Openly Proud of Canada's Role at Viet Truce Talks,' *Toronto Star*, 3 Mar. 1973; also 'Midnight Deals,' *Time*, 12 Mar. 1973, p 13

115 'Canadian Red Cross Team Cites Frustration, Leaves,' *Globe and Mail*, 5 Mar. 1973

116 *Debates*, 1 Feb. 1973, pp 866–71. Shortly after Wagner's criticism of lack of contingency plans the destroyer *Terra Nova* left for Southeast Asian waters to provide an emergency withdrawal option.

117 See Fairweather at *ibid.* 877; Lewis at *ibid.* 871. Amnesty International estimated that there were some 200,000 political prisoners in the RVN. After his trip to Vietnam MP Douglas Rowland estimated that there were no more than 60,000, and that earlier reports had been 'grossly exaggerated.' Senator Cameron gave a figure of 20,000. No basis for these estimates was given. 'Prisoner Count Disputed,' *Toronto Star*, 19 Mar. 1973

118 Jack Cahill, 'We Should Get Out If Viet Nam Peace Not Working: Sharp,' *Toronto Star*, 6 Mar. 1973, p 10

119 See 'A Mind-Spinning Dilemma,' *Time*, 19 Mar. 1973, p 11. Article 2(b)(1) of the Protocol on the Cease-Fire in South Viet-Nam and the Joint Military Commission prohibited 'armed patrols into area controlled by opposing armed forces and flights by bomber and fighter aircraft of all types, except for unarmed flights for proficiency training and maintenance.' It is doubtful that this wording explicitly forbade unarmed aerial reconnaissance. But of course it was highly unlikely that the RVN aircraft conducting the reconnaissance were unarmed.

120 See 'Viet Compliments are a Cover-up,' *Toronto Star*, 12 Mar. 1973. The flat-

tery came just days after Nixon invoked 'executive privilege' in an attempt to have John Dean barred from testifying before the Ervin Select Committee on Presidential Campaign Activities.

121 Sharp, *Viet-Nam* 34
122 See comments on the Sa Huynh report at James Anderson, 'Canadians See Khe Sanh Stalemate as Watershed for ICCS,' *Globe and Mail*, 12 Mar. 1973.
123 'U.S. Pullout Is Near, but Little Hope Seen for Truce in Vietnam,' *Globe and Mail*, 14 Mar. 1973, p 10; Jack Cahill, 'Japanese Plead with Canada to Stay on Viet Peace Team,' *Toronto Star*, 15 Mar. 1973; 'Stop Shipping Arms or Face Retaliation Nixon Warns Hanoi,' *Globe and Mail*, 16 Mar. 1973, p 10; also R. Evans and R. Novak, 'Nixon May Decide to Bomb Hanoi Again,' *Toronto Star*, 16 Mar. 1973; and '300 Tanks Brought from North in or Near South Vietnam: U.S.,' *Globe and Mail*, 17 Mar. 1973
124 Jack Cahill, 'Canadians Blame Poles, Hungarians for Truce Failures,' *Toronto Star*, 17 Mar. 1973
125 Jack Cahill, 'Hanoi Says Peace Role is up to Canadian Public,' *Toronto Star*, 19 Mar. 1973; James Anderson 'Sharp May Be Leaning Toward Extending ICCS Vietnam Role,' *Globe and Mail*, 19 Mar. 1973, p 1
126 SCEAND, *MPE*, no. 3, 6 Mar. 1973, p 3:11
127 *Ibid.* 3:17
128 SCEAND, *MPE*, no. 7, 21 Mar. 1973, p 7:6
129 *Ibid.* 7:9
130 *Ibid.* 7:16
131 *Ibid.* 7:14–15
132 William Johnson, 'Opposition MPs Still Undecided as Vote Nears on Role in ICCS,' *Globe and Mail*, 21 Mar. 1973, p 2
133 'U.S. Reports Dwindling Hanoi Infiltration into South,' *Globe and Mail*, 21 Mar. 1973, p 11
134 'Field Teams of ICCS Begin Truce-Breaking "Observations",' *Globe and Mail*, 21 Mar. 1973, p 11
135 '2,000 Saigon Troops Backed by Tanks Move on Viet Cong,' *Toronto Star*, 21 Mar. 1973, p 1
136 *Ibid.* 7:32
137 *Ibid.* 7:27
138 'Poles and Hungarians Desert Canadians at Viet Truce Outpost,' *Toronto Star*, 24 Mar. 1973
139 William Johnson, 'Canada Should Quit Vietnam Role, NDP Decides in Policy Caucus,' *Globe and Mail*, 22 Mar. 1973
140 See Michael Lavoie, 'Fighting Must Stop or We'll Quit Viet in 90 Days: Sharp,' *Toronto Star*, 28 Mar. 1973, p 1

141 'Last U.S. Troops Leave Viet,' *Toronto Star*, 29 Mar. 1973

142 James Anderson, 'Truce Team in Limbo as U.S. Presence in Vietnam Ends,' *Globe and Mail*, 30 Mar. 1973, p 10

143 James Anderson, 'ICCS Observers Split ...,' *Globe and Mail*, 3 Apr. 1973

144 James Anderson, 'Canadian Is Killed in Downed Copter,' *Globe and Mail*, 9 Apr. 1973, p 1; and 'Future of Entire Truce Effort Is Now in Doubt, Sharp Says,' *Toronto Star*, 9 Apr. 1973, p 4

145 Michael Lavoie, 'Canadians Forced to Admit "Accident" in Copter Attack,' *Toronto Star*, 9 Apr. 1973, p 1

146 Quotation is in James Anderson, 'Gauvin Allusions to Hanoi Troops Touch Communists on Sore Spot,' *Globe and Mail*, 27 Apr. 1973. See also James Anderson, 'Reds Infiltrated into South, ICCS Finds,' *Globe and Mail*, 17 May 1973

147 See 'South Vietnam, Viet Cong Put Forward Rival Plans for Future of the Country,' *Globe and Mail*, 26 Apr. 1973, p 10; also 'Gauvin Brands Charges of Bias as False and Unfounded,' *Globe and Mail*, 26 Apr. 1973, p 10

148 R. Evans and R. Novak, 'Hanoi Makes Ready a Major Offensive,' *Toronto Star*, 7 Apr. 1973

149 'U.S. Resumes Bombing Raids over Laos,' *Globe and Mail*, 17 Apr. 1973; and Murray Marder, 'Hanoi Warns of "Explosion of War",' *Toronto Star*, 18 Apr. 1973.

150 Marder, *ibid.*

151 'Washington Complains to Poland and Hungary,' *Globe and Mail*, 19 Apr. 1973, p 11

152 Murray Marder, 'Kissinger Will Face Formidable Task Trying to Salvage Cease-Fire,' *Toronto Star*, 26 Apr. 1973; 'Pinpoint U.S. Raids Forces Communists to Flee Phnom Penh,' *Toronto Star*, 27 Apr. 1973; 'Pullout or Face War, Nixon Warns Hanoi,' *Globe and Mail*, 4 May 1973

153 'Sweden Assails U.S. as a "War Machine" that Hits Small States,' *Toronto Star*, 2 May 1973

154 See 'Cambodia's Sihanouk: "I Am Very Angry,"' *Time*, 21 May 1973, p 38; also H.D.S. Greenway, 'Cambodia: U.S. Kills 700 Civilians a Week,' *Toronto Star*, 9 May 1973, p 29. The figure of 700 deaths per week was said to be a low estimate.

155 On this point see Noam Chomsky and Edward S. Herman, *The Political Economy of Human Rights*, 2 vols II: *After the Cataclysm, Post-war Indochina and the Reconstruction of Imperial Ideology* (Montreal: Black Rose 1979) ch. 6.

156 'Inspecting Canadian Doubts Copter Wreck Moved by Viet Cong,' *Toronto Star*, 27 Apr. 1973

157 'Our Viet Role in Doubt After Attack, Sharps Says,' *Toronto Star*, 3 May 1973

158 See 'Two ICCS Helicopters Are Fired on in Air Corridor,' *Globe and Mail*, 3
May 1973; 'Gauvin Criticizes Viet Cong Version of Shooting Incident,' *ibid.*,
4 May 1973. Gareth Porter cites poorly substantiated PRG claims that RVN
forces had on two occasions used helicopters with ICCS markings for reconnaissance. Even if true this hardly justifies the multiple attacks on those ICCS
helicopters that were proceeding with PRG approval on designated routes at
specified times. Of the many attacks on ICCS helicopters only the flight resulting in Capt. Laviolette's death was demonstrated to be well off course. See
Porter, *A Peace Denied* 222n.

159 James Anderson, in 'Infiltrated into South Vietnam after the Cease-Fire Was
Signed, Communist Prisoners Say,' *Globe and Mail*, 8 May 1973, p 11

160 'Communists Give in to Canadian Demands,' *Toronto Star*, 28 May 1973

161 *Debates*, 29 May 1973, pp 4194–5

162 *Ibid.*

163 See Ross H. Munro, 'Kissinger Understands but Regrets,' and William Johnson, 'Canada to Withdraw ... *Globe and Mail*, 30 May 1973, p 1. See the CIPO
press release of 15 Aug. 1973.

164 James Anderson, 'Viet Cong Make Overtures to Gauvin on Deadlocked
ICCS,' *Globe and Mail*, 29 June 1973; Anderson, 'Canada Ends Deadlock ...,'
Globe and Mail, 2 July 1973; and Anderson, 'The Narrowing Path that Canada
Walked in Vietnam,' *Globe and Mail*, 1 June 1973, p 10. This last article was an
exceptionally perceptive synthesis of trends in the diplomacy and politics of
the ICCS.

165 See 'U.S. Forced Canada to Quit Truce Role Viet Cong Contend,' *Toronto
Star*, 1 Aug. 1973, p A30. See also Porter, *A Peace Denied* 231. Porter confirms
the ten to zero 'score' of convictions but then buries the fact in tendentious
circumlocution. Unfortunately his ardent revisionism interferes with sound
scholarship on more than a few occasions, marring an otherwise valuable
work.

166 Quote is in 'Setting the Limits,' *Time*, 13 Aug. 1973, p 10

167 Nossal, 'Canada and the ICCS' 100

168 Taylor's *Snow Job* shares this analytical conclusion, for example, but adds the
normative judgment that such concern for the wishes of an ethically repugnant government was a serious error and, worse, a manifestation of moral
cowardice.

169 See Snepp, *Decent Interval* 50–1; and Szulc, *Illusion of Peace* 629.

170 On Kissinger's view see in addition to his own works John G. Stoessinger,
Henry Kissinger: The Anguish of Power (New York: Norton 1976) and Jonathan Schell, *The Time of Illusion* (New York: Knopf 1976) 335–87 for detailed
analysis of Kissinger's political and strategic predilections. Schell's presenta-

tion is an especially useful short summary of Kissinger's views on deterrence and their effect upon his approach to Vietnam.

171 *CIM*

172 See 'U.S. Credibility Now in Doubt,' *Toronto Star*, 1 May 1975, p 1 (emphasis added). Surprisingly, one analyst saw this response as far too mild and argued that Trudeau should have condemned DRVN 'aggression' outright. See David Van Praagh, 'Canada and Southeast Asia' 322.

173 See Snepp, *Decent Interval* 238.

CHAPTER 12: EPILOGUE: CANADIAN VIETNAM DECISION-MAKING AND THE CYBERNETIC PARADIGM

1 John Steinbruner, *The Cybernetic Theory of Decision* 329
2 See Holmes's remarks at SCEAND, *MPE*, no. 5, 15 Mar. 1973, p 5:17.
3 As quoted in John W. Holmes, *The Shaping of Peace*, II, 29
4 For an analysis of some earlier revisionist errors, see Don Page and Don Munton, 'Canadian Images of the Cold War 1946–47,' *International Journal*, XXXII, 3 (Summer 1977) 577–604.

Index

American harmony 156; and the demise of because of RVN collapse 252; and elections as a litmus test of co-operation 150; possible effect of nuclear aid on 178; and effect on left-liberal tendency 21; and joint action on exit procedures in north 127; and joint approval of the doubling in size of MAAG 231; and joint condemnation of the DRVN 212; and joint rejection of the DRVN's right to appeal to the co-chairmen 229; and nuclear anxieties at the root of 136; and its success in postponing warfare 253. See also Canada; India

Indochina: decision-making about as a policy of the lesser evil 8; negotiations concerning 68, 72, 75, 76; and NATO 53; Pearson's concern over 61

'interlocutor for peace' role 278–9

International Commission for Control and Supervision in Vietnam (ICCS, 1973): Canadian distrust of a role on 347; composition of 337, 347; communist obstruction of 365; conditions for Canadian participation 325, 332–3; inability to convict the PRG-SVN side 367; inevitability of Canadian involvement with 333, 335; investigatory preference for shown by Canada 348; and liberal-moderate tactical enthusiasm 24; and PRG attacks on helicopters 361, 365, 459 n158; and the principle of unanimity 349, 351; public attitudes in Canada concerning 454 n88; and the replacement of Canada 366; role acceptance in and fear of American 'retaliation' 346. See also Gauvin, M.; Kis-

singer, H.; Nixon, R.M.; Sharp, M.; Trudeau, P.

International Commission for Supervision and Control in Cambodia (ICSC, Cambodia) 154, 179, 329

International Commission for Supervision and Control in Vietnam (ICSC, Vietnam 1954–73) 7, 24, 88, 94, 95, 114, 168, 223, 236, 345; and assistance to the RVN through inaction 223; and the balancer mechanism 252; and Canadian role acceptance 87; and collusion over TERM 226; and criticism of the DRVN on civilian freedom of movement 114; and decline into passivity after 1965 23; as a deterrent to military aggression 148, 168, 220; and elections as a litmus test of Indo-Canadian co-operation 150; functional inadequacy of for policing subversion 208; lack of French and British support for 135; last session of 331; and Indo-Canadian harmony 92; as an instructive case-study 27; and the New Delhi Conference 107; new terms of reference for 184; obstruction of by DRVN 86; and the precluding of Canadian military involvement in Vietnam 294, 298; prisoner exchanges by 107; as revealing pure doctrinal assumptions in DEA 28; and special MTS 130; symbolic value of 148, 181; and the 'thin fabric of peace' 156; and its value in postponing war 25. See also Canadian Delegation ICSC Vietnam; Indian Delegation ICSC Vietnam; Polish Delegation ICSC Vietnam

International Court of Justice 84

intervention, morality of 4